Speech Recognition
Invited Papers Presented
at the 1974 IEEE Symposium

Speech Recognition

Invited Papers Presented at the 1974 IEEE Symposium

Edited by

D. Raj Reddy

Department of Computer Science
Carnegie-Mellon University
Pittsburgh, Pennsylvania

ACADEMIC PRESS

New York San Francisco London 1975

A Subsidiary of Harcourt Brace Jovanovich, Publishers

ACADEMIC PRESS, INC.
111 Fifth Avenue, New York, New York 10003

United Kingdom Edition published by
ACADEMIC PRESS, INC. (LONDON) LTD.
24/28 Oval Road, London NW1

IEEE Symposium on Speech Recongition, Carnegie
-Mellon University, 1974.
Speech recognition.

Bibliography: p.
Includes index.
1.   Automatic speech recognition—Congresses.
I.   Reddy, Dabbala Rajagopal, (date)
TK7882.S65I18   1974a   621.3819'598   75-30648
ISBN 0-12-584550-2

Contents

Preface

The IEEE Symposium on Speech Recognition was held at Carnegie-Mellon University, Pittsburgh, Pennsylvania, April 15-19, 1974.

The purpose of the symposium was to bring together scientists active in speech recognition research for an in-depth review of the state of the art and presentation of new results in the field. The symposium attracted over 130 researchers, including many from overseas, representing several scientific disciplines: acoustic-phonetics, linguistics, artificial intelligence, and computer architecture. This volume contains the texts of the invited talks presented at the symposium.

The papers appear in the order in which they were presented at the symposium and are grouped together under five topics: systems, parameter and feature extraction, acoustic-phonetics, syntax and semantics, and systems organization. Within each group a tutorial review of the area is followed by papers that deal with specific subtopics. Together they represent an exciting collection of viewpoints from leading researchers within the speech recognition and understanding community.

This volume was produced on Carnegie-Mellon University's XCRIBL computer typesetting system. Manuscripts were typed using a computer editing system and the resulting files were used to produce camera-ready copy of the papers on a Xerox Graphic Printer. Much of the credit for the specific layout of this book goes to Richard Suslick.

Many people helped to make the symposium a success. I wish to thank the Symposium Committee consisting of Jim Baker, Janet Baker, Bruno Beek, Lee Erman, Tom Martin, Paul Mermelstein, and Charles Teacher. Special thanks go to Lee Erman who edited the volume on contributed papers presented at the symposium[1] and also helped with the editing of this volume. We would also like to thank Beverly Howell for her patient and careful layout of much of the manuscript, Lucy Erman for technical editing of these papers, and Paul Stockhausen, Bunny Kostkas, Paul Newberry, Ruth Ann Seilhamer, and other members of the Computer Science Department for attending to many of the details which made the Symposium a success.

---

[1]The volume of contributed papers is available from IEEE—Catalog No.: 74CH0879-9AE.

vii

KEY-NOTE ADDRESS

Gunnar Fant
Royal Institute of Technology
Department of Speech Communications
Speech Transmissions Laboratory
S-100 44 Stockholm 70/Sweden

I have been asked to convey some personal impressions of the development of speech recognition. Our meeting has already been going on for three days so my key-note talk in part reflects the spirit of the meeting as it already has developed.

What is the key? Is it a gloomy minor to go with the funeral march of automatic speech recognition or is a triumphant major to mark the final success of the art? Indeed both pessimism and optimism belong to the picture, but let's not be extreme. As a lead I would like to state that the many interesting papers given here covering a broad area of activities and the enthusiasm of the participants add support to my opinion that we are experiencing a fruitful development. So let the budding spring with promises for the future set the key. What can we hope for and will the general problem of speech recognition remain the daydream of our scientific life?

To the more pessimistic views belongs undoubtedly that of John Pierce[†] expressed in the most debated Letter to the Editor of the Journal of the Acoustical Society of America ever published. Pierce expressed a clear warning against objectives which will remain fictional and out of our reach as long as we do not understand the problems we are set to cope with and with a special address to short-term projects run by "mad scientists" or naive untrustworthy engineers. If I were to expand further on this critical theme I might describe the whole field of speech research as a huge ant stack, where we the workers are a myriad of ants running around without knowing the key to the architecture of the stack, relying on everybody else to do his share. There might be something to this but if the result is a good stack so what? The goal was reached anyhow. Here is the opportunity for a critic to reply "What goal? You speech recognizers and other people

---

[†]Pierce, J.R., "Whither speech recognition," J. Acoust. Soc. Am., 46, pp. 1049-1051 (1969).

of this field are just building yourself a big ant stack to feed and work
and breed in to live happily there for continued work forever, and we
do not even have a guarantee that your work will come to practical
use. And who is going to pay for it?"

I recall the early days of vocoder development in this country,
when it was said by frustrated funders that speech research is like a
huge pit. You can throw any amount of money into it and nothing will
come out in return. Will the story be the same with speech
recognition? Undoubtedly Pierce's challenge seriously affected the
respectability of speech recognition at Bell Laboratories and brought
about some restrictions in the funding elsewhere but there followed a
period of upswing through the ARPA projects in this country and a
similar endeavor in Japan. In other countries the funding has remained
more stable or has been moderately increased.

Perhaps this is the place to turn over the case to the defense.
After all, vocoders eventually have come into use. Maybe it is the
funders of the research who are to blame for not understanding that
speech recognition is not a matter of development as much as of
research, and if you really want to give science a chance, it needs
money and time, money again and your faith in continued support. Even
a period of five years is too short and will provide but a part of the
knowledge needed for a successful system's development and
marketing. Surely speech recognition of today has already a market
although an extremely small one, and this market should be expanded in
competition with other means of communication and data handling. But
if we withdraw the support for the work on increasing our fundamental
knowledge of speech recognition, we will withdraw the basis for
further development and those, who are wise enough to continue their
work, will take the lead.

Here the critic may question the technical advantages of speech
recognition systems, even if they were to be realized, to stand up in
accordance with scientific expectations. Perhaps the most crucial point
is that speech is the most natural channel of human communication and
that we will prefer it for convenience especially when the hands are
occupied and in many cases out of sheer laziness. People will prefer
speaking to pressing buttons. The more simple word command systems
now being exploited will be even more useful, if the speaker can utter
the words within a command group without pauses between words. A
special area of interest is in aids for the deaf intended to provide a
channel for signaling some discrete phonetic elements extracted from
connected speech to be sensed through touch or vision and as a
supplement to lip reading. We have a project of this type in
Stockholm.

I shall turn to a discussion of some of the pertinent problems we run into when organizing and maintaining work on speech recognition. Automatic recognition of today shows strong signs of renewal, with a stronger influx from linguistics and phonetics and other sciences, than ever before. Difficulties in coordinating so many disciplines are apparent. We have, for instance, the spin-off or, rather, spin-away effect. An interesting problem in computer technology, in signal analysis, in phonetics or in human perception absorbs all the creative power of the man, who was supposed to be the key man of the project. In this way several scientists have received a launch in their carrier to the long term benefit of the field, but what happens with the project? At least someone has to see to the complete system. Here enters a second difficulty in executing proper control functions. In order to allow experiments with the entire system you have to put up with solutions to parts that you know or should know are unsatisfactory. The risk is that you never reach good insight in the real limitations or that the system lacks flexibility to adapt to new sources of insight. There is a real need for strategy evaluation and flexibility of operation. An abundance of computational power is not sufficient guarantee for success.

Are we still in an active stage of progress or have we already capitalized on the more obvious lines of approach? Several groups have gone ahead and developed syntactical and semantic analysis schemes. This is a most interesting development from the applied linguistics point of view and is needed for the realization of task-oriented applications, but people have perhaps been a bit too eager to exploit these domains while neglecting the primary phonetic element recognition. In spite of the current utilization of LPC techniques and other advanced methods of formant tracking I feel that there is much to gain in speech data sampling and acoustic-phonetic processing. We need more advanced models of speech production to describe the variability of phonetic element realizations with context. As judged from the conference papers there is quite an interest in phonological rules that describe the pronunciation. However, the lower level variability that we usually are not aware of relating to coarticulation and reduction and the whole interplay between prosody and segmental structures in connected speech is only recently beginning to develop from fundamental concepts such as proposed by Ohman and by Lindblom. Speech analysis directed to the needs of synthesis-by-rules can be made equally useful for speech recognition. However, the needs are even more demanding for recognition work and we need much more data from high speed cineradiographic studies to back up production models.

The perceptual end is equally important. Significant pieces of information are often overlooked or lost against a background of more irrelevant and varying data. As a rule the collection of data to be used as evidence for decisions concerning phonemes and features is at the same time redundant and devoid of some of the useful information. Once we learn to evaluate the perceptual importance of speech pattern aspects we can really optimize sampling procedures in speech recognition and apply just as much data as we can afford to with respect to the required system performance. Simple discriminations require low data rates only. I recall the first attempt I made to demonstrate the principles of speech recognition in public. It was at a meeting of the Swedish Academy of Engineering Sciences twenty-five years ago. A light bulb on a control panel was to light up each time the vowel [a] occurred in connected speech. An optimal a-filter was designed but it soon became clear that the system performed almost equally well on the basis of an intensity threshold alone.

Speech recognition workers may be excused for shortcomings in optimizing their sampling and phonetic element recognition units. As yet there has not been published any reasonably complete acoustic-phonetic study of any language. The data we need is scattered and incomplete. Perhaps it will be the workers in speech recognition and speech synthesis-by-rule that will lead the way to a more profound insight in human speech communication. In support of such a development we can refer to trends already exposed at this meeting. You have the technical resources and the manpower. In order to compete successfully you will have to go to more and more sophisticated studies, and more money will have to be delegated to basic research to secure a proper insight. In return this development will have a most stimulating effect on linguistics, phonetics, psychology, physiology and other supporting sciences. The general trend of an increased interest in the study of human functions supports this optimistic view.

Speech recognition work is sure to continue for ages yet, and new generations will eagerly take up the challenge. In the present underdeveloped stage we run the risk of becoming the victims of shortsighted economical objects of those who fund our work but also of our own temptation to sell our projects on short time basis. In this respect Pierce was right. But a better understanding will surely develop.

To those of you who want to secure documentation of some recent proceedings from work on speech production and speech perception I could mention the proceedings of the Symposium on

Auditory Analysis and Perception of Speech which was held in Leningrad in August 1973[†] and the Speech Communication Seminar to be held in Stockholm August 1974[††].

In summary I feel that speech recognition has a dubious past, a forceful present, and a hopeful future. In addition to advanced computer technology and a continued growth of speech language and hearing research to be integrated in our work, we need something like the diligence of the ants, the persistance of the mad scientist, plenty of time and enthusiasm of the kind exposed at this meeting to keep us on the right path. My congratulations to IEEE and to Raj Reddy and his staff of organizers for a fine meeting.

[†]Part I of the Leningrad symposium to be published by Acustica, part II by Academic Press, London.

[††]The proceedings of the SCS-74 to be published by Almqvist & Wiksell International and John Wiley.

Part One

Systems

A TUTORIAL ON SPEECH UNDERSTANDING SYSTEMS[†]

Allen Newell
Carnegie-Mellon University
Pittsburgh, Pennsylvania 15213

The purpose of this paper is to provide a tutorial on speech understanding systems. As the introductory paper in the book, it is truly to serve the function of an overview. The rest of the chapters in this book will take up specific content issues. The set of papers delivered at the IEEE Symposium on Speech Recognition (Erman, 1974) provides additional technical background which will be used as a source of illustration[††].

My intent is to give you a feeling for the underlying structure of the field -- for what seems to me invariant, hence should command your continual attention as you deal with the specifics of systems and of the facts about speakers, speech and the environment of conversation. Speech understanding signifies a particular current research endeavor, and I will start by locating it in scientific context. Then we turn to an examination of the basic structure of the task of speech understanding: first the notion of understanding; then why the task is difficult; then what representations are available; and finally the important processing mechanisms. This section is really the heart of the paper. However, additional insight can be gained into the fundamental structure of the field by looking at two aspects; we devote a section to each. One is our relatively good ability to specify the systems we wish to achieve. This gives to the entire research endeavor a clarity not usually attainable in scientific affairs. The other is the issue of performance analysis. Our endeavor is focussed

---

[†]I would like to thank Raj Reddy for comments on an early draft of this paper. This work was supported by the Advanced Research Projects Agency of the Office of the Secretary of Defense (Contract F44620-73-C-0074) and is monitored by the Air Force Office of Scientific Research.

[††]Many of these papers or expansions of them have appeared in a special issue of the IEEE Transactions on Acoustics, Speech, and Signal Processing, February 1975.

strongly on total complex systems, whose behavior is difficult to analyze. Hence, not only are the techniques of analysis important, they also affect how we view speech understanding systems. In the concluding section I note two general tensions that characterize our endeavor, hopefully in a creative way. I end, as all good system views should, with reflections on the payoff structure.

SPEECH UNDERSTANDING AS A RESEARCH ENDEAVOR

THE HISTORY OF THE TERM.

A good place to start is with the genesis of the term "speech understanding", for this will reveal enough history to make clear the nature of the scientific endeavor.

There is an extensive history of work in speech recognition. I say this glibly, for it is a common statement. This means only that work in the mechanical recognition of speech goes back enough years so that most newcomers to the field do not recall it personally. In exponentially expanding fields, where always the majority of investigators who have ever worked in the field are currently active, anything slightly over the historical horizon is ancient and classical, and satisfies the accolade of an "extensive history".

To be more accurate, then, work on speech recognition goes back to the fifties. For instance, a paper by Fry and Denes (1956) describes a system for recognizing a few isolated words. But that is about the beginning, for they cite no predecessors. Indeed, one has only to go back another few years to the book by Potter, Kopp and Kopp on <u>Visible Speech</u> (1947) to be at the very threshold of the application of electronic instrumentation to speech. Telephony goes back much further, but only since the sound spectrograph may we date the present era.

Three flavors characterized the early work in speech recognition. First, it focussed on the acoustic signal and how it appeared to encode the phones of speech. Second, it forced a technological transformation of a field. That the papers of this book were originally given at an IEEE symposium, rather than at a linguistics conference, is testimony to this. One does not find the term "acoustic-phonetics" before this time. Third, there was a strong awareness that the problems of recognition required attention to other aspects of the situation than just the pure speech signal, namely to the linguistic and semantic context.

Since this last point is especially germane to our topic, let me supply a couple of quotations. The first is by Flanagan and was used in the ARPA Study Group Report (Newell, et al,1971) to make the same point:

> Automatic speech recognition -- as the human accomplishes it -- will probably be possible only through the proper analysis and application of grammatical, contextual, and semantic constraints. This approach also presumes an acoustic analysis which preserves the same information that the human transducer (i.e., the ear) does. It is clear, too, that for a given accuracy of recognition, a trade can be made between the necessary linguistic constraints, and complexity of vocabulary, and the number of speakers (Flanagan, 1965, p. 163).

This was in the mid-sixties, well after the early days. But we can go back to the very early paper of Fry and Denes, noted above, and find essentially the same sentiment:

> Primary recognition alone is not sufficient to accomplish this [recognition] in a mechanical recognizer, any more than it is sufficient for the human brain. Linguistic knowledge must be added to primary recognition and to be completely successful the machine would have to "know" as much about the language as a human brain does. Such a machine is impracticable ... (Fry & Denes, 1956, p. 207).

The task of recognition has proved difficult. At least this is true in terms of the modest efforts devoted to it. For one must recognize that the "extensive" history quoted above is still small in terms of man-years, instrumentation, and successive generations of scientists. Be that as it may, the myth grew that it was a problem whose time had not yet come. I do not use "myth" as a pejorative term, but only to indicate a belief of a social group -- here the speech researchers -- founded on an intuitive assessment of a situation. The actual work showed that particular investigations had made limited progress and had not gone far toward solving the full problem. The myth found a common and characteristic expression:

> The ten-digits counter example: It is difficult enough to get a system to recognize the ten digits in isolation, even when specialized for a single speaker.

A quote is perhaps worthwhile. This is from a letter to the JASA by John Pierce (1969) commenting (negatively) on the prospects and scientific motivation of the speech recognition field.

It is hard to gauge the success of an attempt at speech recognition even when statistics are given. In general, it appears that recognition around 95% correct can be achieved for clearly pronounced, isolated words from a chosen small vocabulary (the digits, for instance) spoken by a few chosen talkers. Better results have been attained for one talker. Performance has gone down drastically as the vocabulary was expanded, and appreciably as the number and variety of talkers were increased. It is not easy to see a practical, economically sound application for speech recognition with this capability. (Pierce, 1969, p. 1050)

In any event, work on speech recognition fell off in the sixties, as the difficulties came to be appreciated and as other topics became attractive, notably, speech synthesis (Flanagan, Coker, Rabiner, Schafer & Umeda, 1970).

In the spring of 1970 a feeling permeated the community of Artificial Intelligence laboratories supported by ARPA[†] that speech recognition was again ripe for tackling, given the progress made in other parts of artificial intelligence and in some direct work on isolated word recognition (e.g., Bobrow & Klatt, 1968; Gold, 1966; Vicens, 1969)[††]. A study group was formed from within the ARPA community to look critically at the problem. The result, issued early in 1971, was the report entitled "Speech Understanding Systems" (Newell, et al, 1971).

[†]The Advanced Research Projects Agency of the U.S. Department of Defense, which has had a broadly based research effort in computer science since the early sixties.

[††]This work reveals the mythic character of the "ten-digits" case; prior to when the Pierce letter was written, one of these systems (Vicens, 1969) could recognize with about 90 percent accuracy 50 words for 10 speakers or 500 words for a single speaker (with specialization). Such efforts do not gainsay that the attitudes in Pierce's letter accurately reflect opinions widely held in the field at the time, derived from the envelope of work in the field.

The term "speech understanding systems" (hereafter SUS) was coined in that report to characterize a concern with the total system, as opposed to just a concern with the speech signal. It acknowledged, as in the Flanagan quotation above, that awareness of the requirement for context had always existed, but it viewed the earlier research as writing promissory notes. It took it that the time had arrived for payment.

THE DOGMA OF SPEECH UNDERSTANDING RESEARCH.

The Study Group report, and the subsequent research program that developed from it, has led to what we can call the dogma of speech understanding research. As exhibited in Figure 1, it consists of three propositions. Let us be clear that dogmas are not all bad, just as myths are not. Dogmas are heuristics. They energize groups to attend to selected aspects of reality and on occasion to perform heroic feats. They always crumble eventually, and by then usually with good riddance. But they can be useful, as are (I believe) the dogmas of speech understanding research.

1. The performance criterion is understanding the message, not recognizing phonemes, words or sentences.
2. All sources of knowledge must be used.
3. There is not enough information in the speech signal alone to determine the message.

Figure 1. The Dogmas of Speech Understanding Research

The first dogma is simply an enunciation of the basic system principle that system behavior counts, not component behavior. What it says in real (as opposed to philosophical) terms is that the final performance criterion is a source of negative noise. There are many sequences of sentences that map into (i.e., determine) a single final performance. This is exactly analogous to the fact that, working up from the bottom with an errorful signal, many sequences of phones map into a single word, and that many sequences of words map into a single sentence. These converging mappings permit leeway in the recognition at the lower level. The important question is how much freedom is contained in this final mapping. If much, it is an important principle; if little, it is mostly rhetoric. The blatant fact is that no one knows, for no one has taken the trouble to measure it for various tasks -- not even for the tasks that are being actively pursued in the current SUS efforts. My conjecture is that it is not worth very much. There are a few things, e.g., the irrelevance of the unstressed (hence confusable) determiners "a" and "the", but not many. But we will have to wait and see.

The second dogma is the really important one -- the one that guides behavior in strong ways. It lets people put more effort into the structure of the system than into particular speech analyses, because the task of putting all the sources of knowledge together is central, not peripheral. It lets people get upset because a source of knowledge is not being properly exploited -- prosodics, or discourse, or whatever. It is a thoroughly operational principle which is the cornerstone of the SUS effort. It will have served its purpose (and hence need discarding) only when it becomes an excuse for not plowing component aspects deeply enough.

The third and final dogma is a quite plausible principle. Fry and Denes in the quote above essentially subscribed to it. Take an adaptive view of human behavior, in which people will not pump more specificity into the speech signal than is necessary for the receivers. Thus, if normal human receivers typically use certain context, speakers will degrade the input until that context is required. Ergo, the principle. I must confess, however, that this third principle seems primarily a line of defense for the second one. If <u>Three</u> holds, then <u>Two</u> is certainly safe. If <u>Three</u> is false, then it is always possible that some brilliant and/or hardworking scientist-engineer will discover the invariants in the signal and <u>presto</u>! the entire SUS endeavor is beside the point -- though speech recognition itself gains immensely. Although a "systems" man much of my life, I must confess partiality to a basic principle that states that at heart the solution to all systems problems is the development of an appropriate component. So I will not be surprised if some morning . . .

THE BASIC STRUCTURE OF THE TASK

The task of speech understanding is simply a big <u>transduction</u>. The input is a representation of the speech and the output is a representation of the understanding.

In this section we will try to lay bare the nature of this transduction. First, we must be sure we understand the input/output specifications of the task -- what it means to take speech in, what it means to ship understanding out. Next we must ask why this transduction is difficult. Many transductions are easy; speech-to-understanding is difficult. However, the nature of that difficulty is reasonably clear. Inexorably we are led from contemplation of the problem to a general view of the basic structure of a speech understanding system (SUS). After describing this abstractly, we can attend in more detail to two fundamental aspects of it. One is the nature of the representations we can use to carry out the transduction, what purposes they serve and what options exist. The other is the mechanisms that process these representations, converting knowledge about the encoding of speech into an act of transduction.

DEFINING THE INPUT (SPEECH) AND OUTPUT (UNDERSTANDING)

We all understand clearly what constitutes a representation of the speech input. Starting with the pressure waves in the air produced by the articulatory apparatus, we can develop various near isomorphs: the movement of a diaphragm or crystal; a time-varying electric signal; a sequence of discrete amplitude measurements taken to a high enough accuracy (e.g., 12 bits) and at a high enough rate (e.g., 20,000 samples/sec) to capture all the relevant variation.

On the representation of understanding to be output the consensus is not so clear. It is common, in fact, to fret about the meaning of meaning, counting up the multiple ways in which this term is used and, by implication, raising doubts that we know what we are talking about, scientifically speaking[†].

But the issue is not really so mysterious, at least for us. In Figure 2 I present a brief definition of the representation of meaning. We need to posit an information processing system of some kind. Meaning (equivalently, understanding) does not exist in the abstract but only relative to some system. Then the representation of understanding in the system is simply the representation from which action is derived. This representation must sometimes be extended to include additional representations that are used by the system to store information for its own later use in deriving action. This definition is not, of course, completely operational, since it is not given a priori how a system encodes its knowledge for action. However, in practice for digital systems, where we can examine the internal structure of the program, and where all state (of appreciable duration) is statisized in a uniform way (as bits), there is little difficulty determining from what representation action is derived.

This definition of understanding is almost banal. That will be true of much that this tutorial contains. Its banality, however, does not keep it from being essentially correct.

We have at present no universal representation of meaning.

[†]A recent reader in semantics (Steinberg & Jakobovits, 1971) provides a fine sampling of the variety of approaches to meaning.

Given an information processing system:

The representation of understanding is the
representation from which action is derived

extended to include representations in which
knowledge is stored by the system from which to
derive later action (if different).

Figure 2. The Representation of Understanding

This is often seen to stem from our lack of knowledge of what
representations humans use for understanding. The definition of Figure
2 argues that this is not the key issue -- that even when we finally
succeed in developing a clear picture of the representations humans
use (and in fact we are not without progress on this), we will still not
have such a universal representation. The representation will remain
relative to the information processing system. Even for humans it is
likely that the representations will differ from person to person (and
from domain to domain within a person), since these representations
have been built up from an idiosyncratic learning history. When we
finally get down to biological bedrock -- to where all humans have the
same representation because of their common genetic ancestry -- we
will likely find that we have lost all specific representational character
except a capacity to hold variety. A similar situation obtains in
computers. The representation of understanding must be, at some
level, just the representation of bit arrays, since that is digital
technology's way of holding all state. But at this level, we have lost
the answer to our question of what is the representation of meaning.
    All of the representations in our transduction -- the input
speech signal, any intermediate ones, as well as the final one that is
so-labeled -- are representations of the meaning of the utterance, in
the sense that they hold the information that the utterance provides
about action. They simply do not hold this information in a way that the
action can be obtained directly. It is necessary to add the qualifier,
since the whole point of the speech understanding transduction is to
apply a process to convert the information into a form where the action
consequences can be derived.
    There is nothing inherent in a representation per se that
determines whether or not action can be derived from it. The
complexity of the task situation relative to the way information is coded
in the representation is the critical factor. In a world of great silences

punctuated by loud whistles that signal danger (as in approaching artillery shells), one can devise processes that derive action directly from the speech signal. Normally, the world is abundantly more complex.

WHY IS RECOGNITION DIFFICULT?

What is the difficulty in this transduction? It is often said that the message is contaminated with noise. That is not quite the whole story, for the message is also intricately encoded.

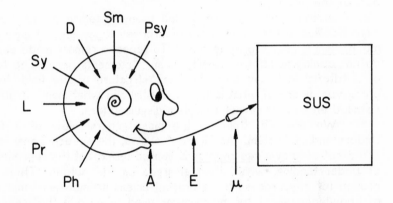

Figure 3. The many mechanisms that affect the message

Let us expand this view. As shown in Figure 3, on its trip to the hearer, the representation of the intended communication is affected by many distinct mechanisms.[†] Working backwards from the final received signal, there is the microphone, the ambient noise of the environment, the speaker's articulatory apparatus, the phonemic system, the prosodic system, the lexicon, the syntax, the rules of discourse, the semantics, the psychology of the speaker, and so on. The spiral in the figure is to emphasize that the list of mechanisms is both conventional and incomplete, being best known at the external end

---

[†]By the term mechanism I mean a determinate physical process. I will use the term frequently throughout the paper. The term is naturally extended to a process that has random components and, more importantly, to an abstract process that could in principle be realized by a physical process, for example, by a computer program.

and most uncertain as we spiral in on the speaker's intentions. Furthermore, we understand some of these aspects not as mechanisms but by some resulting representation (e.g., syntax or the phonemic system).

Some of these mechanisms we think of as adding noise to the utterance, others as being stages in the encoding, others as adding redundancy. But which is which makes little difference. They all add variety and structure to the signal in accordance with their own inner natures. And they all have to be peeled away in order to obtain finally a representation of the understanding of the message. They are all part of the problem.

In the light of Figure 3, and taking encoding broadly, a banal assertion lies at the heart of our enterprise: Knowledge of an encoding mechanism is required to decode it. To repeat a remark made earlier: I do not apologize for the banality of my statements here. The function of a tutorial is to lay bare the basic structure of the field, to make ourselves aware of what is truly essential and what many of our more detailed endeavors reveal, though in disguised form.

We are led, then, to the most general view of a Speech Understanding System. As Figure 4 shows, the speech signal is input, and a set of knowledge sources is applied to extract the representation of understanding, which then emerges as the output. There is no reason for any process to be present unless it embodies some source of knowledge about the mechanisms used to encode the message or add noise to it, or about the nature of the message itself.

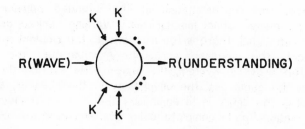

Figure 4. Speech Understanding System: General view 1

A convenient way to think of the knowledge embodied in a process is to imagine yourself about to write a program to accomplish what the process does. For instance, imagine analysing a string of words to produce the tree showing the parse. Then, assuming you know all about the programming language and the representation of the data, ask what you have to know in order to write the program. That is the knowledge embodied in the process. When you examine the program after it is written, you will find that knowledge distributed in various ways -- in tables and other data structures inside the program and in the routines themselves. These are tactical issues so to speak, and alternative programs might have been written which organized the processing differently. But they would have required the same knowledge (in our example, the grammatical regularities) in order for the program to produce the required parse.

Knowledge itself then is to be taken as analogous to a competence (using that term essentially as it is used in modern linguistics). To say of a system that it knows X is to make an abstract statement, without commitment to how that knowledge is embodied. Thus, we must distinguish in our figure the implementing mechanisms from the knowledge itself; Figure 5 gives the modified structure.

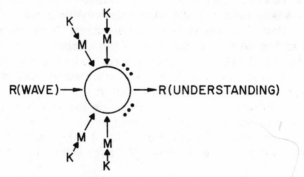

Figure 5. Speech Understanding System: General view 2

Now consider the role of the representation. It holds the knowledge of the message as received. Further, the mechanisms, M_i, must be so constructed that they work in terms of the representation available. This is one way, for example, that the mechanisms differ from the knowledges they embody. The knowledge is seen as being independent of any particular representation. In so far as the mechanisms, M_i, work at different times, there must be internal representations that hold the partially accumulated results of processing, so that further processing can occur. The mechanisms, then, will work on some particular representation, so that we can modify the general picture yet again, as shown in Figure 6.

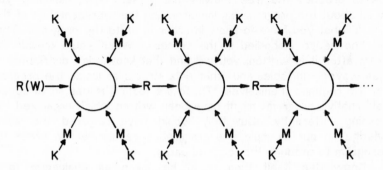

Figure 6. Speech Understanding System: General view 3

Viewing a SUS in the form of Figure 6 makes certain questions seem the imperative ones to answer. What knowledge is actually incorporated in the SUS? How is that knowledge distributed among the individual sources? What is the redundancy among the sources, so that processing reflecting the same knowledge is performed in several places? That the knowledge sources stem from quite disparate aspects of the world guarantees a certain independence. But that we must take the sources much as they are given to us in the scientific literature implies that we don't fully understand how much mutual knowledge is involved. The complement of the question of redundancy is that of where the gaps are. Where do the sources of knowledge not cover the variations in the message (at whatever level)? Such gaps represent ultimate ambiguities which it is beyond a particular SUS to resolve without the addition of knowledge orthogonal to that already available.

What is the efficiency of conversion of knowledge in a source into changing the representation of the message? By efficiency I mean to cover at least two distinct things. The first is the usual one in which any mechanism is located in a time-memory-hardware space, so that one can inquire whether alternative mechanisms exist that are uniformly better, or trade off the dimensions in preferable ways. The second type of efficiency is whether all the implications of the knowledge (as abstractly stated, say) are realized in the particular mechanism, i.e., in the actual algorithm programmed. Thus, one might have available a body of phonological rules, say, but implement the mechanism so that they were applied only in special circumstances, e.g., within words but not between words. Asking about this kind of efficiency implies a way of characterizing knowledge other than just pointing at a mechanism (the program) and saying that it does what it does.

How much of the total action is attributable to each source of knowledge? Collectively they must engage in a total transduction that uses the incoming message to select from the space of all understandings (i.e., messages in the final understanding-representation) the one that was intended by the speaker. Each knowledge source must contribute something to that selection. The mutual knowledge among sources, to the extent it exists, complicates matters, but only nominally.

Normally, in a computation made up of a web of operations that feed on each other -- outputs of some to inputs of others -- one does not fruitfully ask about the contribution of each operation to the whole. But the role of each bit of knowledge in the speech transduction is much more akin to adding another constraint to a total set to finally eliminate all ambiguity. For each collection of knowledge sources there is a final message set: the less knowledge, the larger the final set (i.e., the more ambiguous). This is unlike the case of assigning contributions in a web of operations, where in general the removal of an operation changes the result from sense to nonsense.

The view of a SUS in Figure 6 is only a view. It brings certain questions to the fore and provides a perspective from which to examine existing SUSs. Lurking behind it one senses a basis of an actual calculational scheme for analysing SUSs. But the development of that scheme is well beyond a tutorial -- or my current understanding.

REPRESENTATIONS

Given that some representation must be used, what governs which ones and how many? There seem to be two quite distinct general principles, giving rise to two distinct classes of representations:

Knowledge-source driven representations
The first principle might be stated:
Knowledge knows its own representation.
Thus, if we ask what is known about a particular aspect of the problem -- about microphone noise, about syntactic encoding, etc. -- the answer we get is always in some representation. At the moment of dealing with a new problem such as speech understanding, we do not get the option of specifying the representation of this knowledge. It is

determined by scientific history. Since contact must be made between the signal and the knowledge, we must adopt a representation of the signal that will jibe with the representation of knowledge.

The mechanisms involved in the production of the signal, as indicated in Figure 3, are by and large independent, and so the knowledge about them is by and large independently represented. Therefore we tend to recapitulate the external mechanisms in the internal representations. This leads to the feature, so familiar in speech understanding systems, of a sequence of representational levels.

Figure 7 gives a conventional list of these sources of knowledge. They parallel Figure 3, though some of the romanticism has been removed. There is no exact agreement on them and need not be. They are all familiar in the main and nothing will be served by describing each in cursory fashion. Basic description and references to each level can be found in the Speech Report (Newell et al, 1971); advanced treatment can be obtained through the papers of this book.

It is noteworthy that there are a number of empty spots -- so empty in fact that we do not even have good names for them. We certainly don't know much about what constraint they offer or about how much they are used by humans in normal discourse. They are hardly dealt with in the conference at which these papers of this book were presented. A paper by Deutsch (1974) on discourse is perhaps an exception -- but its preliminary character makes the point as well.

However, we have no genuine cause for complaint. The array of knowledge sources dealt with at this conference exceed that at any prior conference on speech recognition, a fact directly attributable to the force of the speech-understanding dogma. When a repeat conference is held a few years from now, the range will be much broader still.

As asserted above, there are two available approaches to the representation of sources of knowledge. We have been describing the one that stems from a direct analysis of the knowledge as it exists in the scientific environment. A diametrically opposite choice is available: to use a general mathematical representation of the output desired in terms of the inputs available. Its principle might be stated:

Only the form matters.

This is not a single unified approach, but contains a wide diversity of methods which differ considerably in their tractability and efficacy. Included in this approach are linear discriminant analyses, Markov models, orthogonal function expansions, and general pattern recognition schemes. The approach is of more universal applicability than just in

COMMUNICATION SYSTEM NOISE
ENVIRONMENTAL NOISE
ACOUSTICS
PHONETICS
PHONEMICS
PROSODICS
LEXICON
SYNTAX
DISCOURSE - STYLE, LOGIC, HISTORY, PERCEPTUAL
              & MOTOR ACCESS
SEMANTICS (DOMAIN)
TASK STRUCTURE
USER - STYLE, STATE, INTENTIONS, KNOWLEDGE,
             PROCESSING LIMITS
HISTORY

Figure 7. Sources of Knowledge

speech recognition, for at the heart of the approach is independence of the detailed structure of a particular subject matter. Factor analysis and analysis of variance are examples of the approach, though as far as I know, they have no exemplification yet in speech recognition work. For lack of a better name I will refer to this entire collection of schemes as that of generalized input-output functions.

Let me illustrate this approach by means of its most common exemplar in speech recognition. One general form of the logic of recognition is the following. An abstract space, $\mathbf{X}$, of utterances is posited. Each point, X, is determined by N numbers $(X_1, X_2, \ldots X_n)$. Actual utterances, as emitted by a speaker, can be mapped into this space by a transformation on the speech signal: $T(S) \Rightarrow (X_1, X_2, \ldots X_n)$. Understandings are identified by a set of particular points in the space, U(1), U(2), ... U(K). To identify an incoming utterance with a point U(k) is to decide that the incoming utterance conveys the understanding associated with U(k). The space permits a metric D(X,Y) so that a point X in the space can be nearer to one point Y than to another point Z. Thus, a general principle of recognition can be adopted, usually called the Nearest Neighbor Principle, in which the incoming utterance is identified with that meaning-point it is nearest to. Formally:

$$U[X] = \text{Minimizer[over k]} (D(X,U(k)))$$

Given a transformation, T, which defines the numbers X_i and a metric, D, we have a complete recognition system. All that remains in this approach is (1) evaluation of the computational requirements (i.e., costs) and (2) evaluation of the accuracy of recognition (i.e., performance).

Such schemes can work for suitable T, D and choice of utterance class. An almost classically simple system, reported at the Conference (Danforth, Rogosa & Suppes, 1974), can serve to illustrate our relatively abstract characterization. The utterances are isolated words, which are all taken as lasting a fixed time (.5 sec.). T maps the speech signal into 300 numbers composed of the amplitudes and frequencies for three frequency bands each 10 ms. D is taken to be a weighted Euclidian distance, the weights running inversely to the measured variance of the components (thus introducing a slightly adaptive distance measure). The U's correspond to 14 words (the digits and a few commands), being the vectors composed from a weighted average of a series of spoken examplars.

The simplicity of the Danforth scheme is not inherent in the notion of nearest-neighbor recognition. A system by Itakara (1974), reported at the same Conference, illustrates a more sophisticated application. T is formed by autocorrelation coefficients; the U's are the LPC coefficients (of some 200 names), and D is formed from a likelihood ratio, where the time scale of the input signal X is dilated and compressed in being put into correspondence with a U vector, so as to optimize the fit. (The original should be consulted for details.)

An assertion was made earlier that the only way to decode a signal was by knowledge of the mechanisms that encoded it. This was the philosophic cornerstone that leads to the array of knowledge sources in Figure 7. What has become of the proposition here? There seems to be no trace of the knowledge sources; only the most general features of the speech signal encoding are utilized: that frequencies are information rich (in Danforth) and the more sophisticated version of this (in Itakura) represented by the LPC, which responds to resonances.

The proposition is alive and well, it turns out. Each generalized input-output function scheme is a family of functions, which involves a set of free parameters that determine the particular representation. In the neigberest neighbor scheme these are the location of the ideal understanding points (the U's). These parameters are determined by a process of data-fitting to instances of speech that are known exemplars of the produced utterance. The Danforth scheme uses an iterative linear adjustment on a sequence of exemplars; the Itakura scheme uses an algorithm derived from maximum likelihood on a single exemplar.

The parameters thus soak up the knowledge in the exemplar

about the nature of the encoding, storing it in a composite form that, by design, is directly related to use in the recognition algorithm. That we, the scientists, cannot make much sense of the knowledge so extracted is of no account. The algorithm can, and it is the algorithm, not the system's designers, that must do the recognition and needs the knowledge.[†]

Though generalized input-output functions have a direct analog of the knowledge sources, there is an interesting difference beyond the surface (though important) one of the knowledge being pre-digested for use in the specific recognition algorithm. They use only a small amount of data of a quite casual (though relevant) kind. The single utterance per understanding point in Itakura's scheme, for instance, is to be contrasted with the dozens of scientific papers which supposedly should go into the development of a source of knowledge -- e.g., of phonological rules, or of the phonetic alphabet itself. Is the single utterance so rich? Or, alternatively, is the scientific process so indirect and obtuse that its yield is only a fraction of what the direct utterance is? I cannot answer this question in a tutorial paper -- but I can surely ask it.

Let me summarize. We have two broad classes of representations available to us in constructing SUSs. One is responsive to getting into the system all of the knowledge available about speech. The other is responsive to constructing a single uniform algorithm. In practice one can find mixed cases, e.g., a system fundamentally constructed around knowledge sources, but with the attempt to characterize the lexicon by bigram letter frequencies. Nevertheless, they are in conflict philosophically. For instance, the generalized input-output functions pose a challenge to knowledge-based SUSs to justify all the extra complexity and inhomogeniety that they seem to require.

MECHANISMS FOR CONVERTING KNOWLEDGE TO ACTION.

Let us turn now from a consideration of the representations to the processing mechanisms. These mechanisms, according to Figure 6, convert the knowledge into action. Their action is to transform the

---

[†]A side note is perhaps permissible, since this is an important point. A system can have and use knowledge without its designers having or being able to use that knowledge. This point is missed by all those who assert that programs do only what they are "told" to do (by their designers). They do, of course, do only what they are told to do, but by their designers plus their environment, taken throughout their history. Even as you and I.

speech-as-represented to a more decoded form. It might seem that nothing could be said about such mechanisms. Each knowledge source leads to its own algorithms and that is that. In some sense this is true. For example, the semantic knowledge source in HEARSAY-I (Reddy, Erman, Fennell & Neely, 1973) is a chess program. It constructs lists of legal moves ordered by preference, hence by presumptive probability, of occurrence in the utterance; the ordering is used to evaluate hypothesized words. This mechanism, from a speech-understanding viewpoint, does not lead beyond itself.

But if one looks more broadly, characteristic implementation problems arise that reflect pervasive features of the speech understanding task environment. Their detailed study is a necessity. Let's consider some examples. I list them in Figure 8, just to bring them together for your attention.

Representation of partial knowledge for future use
Searching in combinatorial spaces
Transformation from generative to analytic representations
Time-domain vs. frequency domain
Ideal type vs. error-transformed representation
Flexible control vs. attention focussing
Multiple idiosyncratic knowledge sources

Figure 8. Problems of Converting Knowledge to Action

REPRESENTATION OF PARTIAL KNOWLEDGE FOR FUTURE USE
Inherent in the approach of multiple sources of knowledge is that each contributes something to an ongoing decoding process. That something is of course an imperfect resolution. Of necessity the resulting representation must hold a partial state of knowledge until it can be further specified at some later stage.

Again, this description sounds banal. Yet its consequences are so pervasive that I will cast them into a principle:

Principle:
The ability of a SUS is limited by the representational devices it has for holding partial knowledge.

The mechanics of this are worth exhibiting in the abstract. Mechanism M, working on representation R of the utterance, concludes that some situation, (X or Y), holds, where X and Y are two specific features of the utterance representable in R (e.g., two phones at some point in time, two words, two formant positions). The issue is whether R can also represent the disjunction of X and Y, that is, has an expression equivalent to (X or Y). If not, then a decision must be made to represent one or the other. In either case, information has been lost by fitting to the Procrustean bed of the representation.

The solution might seem simple: just include expressions of the type (X or Y). Consider it done. Then comes a mechanism, M', which produces (.3X, .7Y), i.e., X with probability .3 and Y with probability .7. Now the representational capabilities of disjunctives are not rich enough. We can encode (X or Y) at least, but cannot retain the differential weighting. Simple, you say: we should have known that probabilities are required. But do not make the mistake of believing that all uncertainty is just a question of probabilities. For in fact our expression of p=.3 already is an instance of taking the true state of uncertainty (expressed, possibly, by saying that p is somewhere around .3 but not likely below .1 or above .35) and crunching it into the bed of two simple numbers that add to 1. In truth, the complexities of expressing uncertainty elaborate endlessly, to the full range of conditional expressions, not only on the concrete items (the Xs and Ys) but on the other uncertainties.

Two things prevent a solution to this problem. The first is conceptual. We do not necessarily have available in our conceptual inventory the appropriate concepts of uncertainty. We can do nothing about this in the short run for a project such as the speech understanding systems. Probability theory, pervasive and developed as it is, still does not seem to provide us all the representations we need. Often when, in a computation of uncertain worth, we produce a list of possible results ordered by their plausibility, neither could we have computed probabilities (even conceptually) nor do we feel that the simple ordering exhausts our knowledge.

The second difficulty, and the more pressing one, is that each additional step in adequacy in representation of uncertainty requires an increase in the complexity of the representation. Replace every symbol in a representation by a list of alternatives, or a list with associated weights, or with ranges of weights, etc. Each requires more space, more processing, more complexity in the algorithms.

We know little about such computational matters. Instead, we have a series of case examples, as each SUS design incorporates a specific (and in many ways unprincipled) collection of uncertainty concepts. Sustained scientific study of this issue is required for success in constructing speech understanding systems.

SEARCHING IN COMBINATORIAL SPACES

Combinatorial search spaces are the ultimate brute-force representation of partial knowledge. Whenever the representation fails to be able to express the partial knowledge attained by a problem solver (in our case a mechanism M in our SUS), progress can still be made by degrading the information to alternative representable components, and considering these one by one through time in an over-instantiated state of knowledge. By the recursive occurrence of these acts of instantiation (i.e., of trial moves) the full flower of exponential growth occurs.[†]

Thus, combinatorial search processes will occur in every SUS of any complexity. They do in each of the ones represented at the conference. Exceptions occur only for some generalized input-output systems which are designed to obtain only the information they can represent.

We are in moderately good shape in the study of combinatorial search, since it has been at the focus of artificial intelligence research since its beginnings. We understand its ubiquity. We understand the classes of mechanisms that bring it under control. We understand the kinds of processing organizations (push-down stacks and the like) to realize such searches in otherwise diverse environments. We understand a modest amount about how to realize complex control strategies. Thus, except to bring these processes to the attention of the uninitiated, there is no need to emphasize their study. Rather, one can give references (Nilsson, 1971; Bobrow & Raphael, 1974).

TRANSFORMATION FROM GENERATIVE TO ANALYTIC REPRESENTATION

As noted earlier, we are at the mercy of scientific and technical history in working with sources of knowledge. They come dressed as they are, not as we might wish them to be. Much knowledge is in so-

---

[†]Again, a side note is worthwhile. The nature of all problem solving is disjunctive -- of trying alternatives to reach a goal. Behind that disjunction is the phenomena we have just been discussing: that a problem solver's next step leads to an advance in partial knowledge about the problem that he cannot capture in the representational means available to him, hence must stipulate to be one or another more certain alternatives that he can represent. A device with complete capabilities for representing partial knowledge would problem solve in a linear fashion, never adding anything to the expanding current knowledge state that would have to be retracted later.

called generative form, whereas one wishes it were in so-called analytic form. Let me define these two terms. It requires that we have some object, Y, which can be viewed as being produced by some process, P, acting on some input, X; thus, $P(X) \Rightarrow Y$.

A generative law is one that, given X (or aspects of X) determines Y (or aspects of Y).

An analytic law is one that, given Y (or aspects of Y) determines X (or aspects of X).

Thus a generative law mimics P; an analytic law is its inverse. Though inverses, these two forms of knowledge do not divide up the world. It is possible to have knowledge that is neither generative nor analytic, but simply descriptive of the object. "That the amplitude of a signal is always less than a certain value" is an example.

Given our model of Figure 3 in which the received utterance has been formed (i.e., produced) by a series of encoding transformations, it seems only natural that much speech knowledge is generative. In particular, much of our knowledge about the lower levels of speech derives from the study of the articulatory apparatus. Since speech is produced, it is only natural that its regularities reflect the idiosyncracies of the producing mechanism. So it does, and we have a whole science devoted to unravelling a most peculiar set of physical phenomena. On purely a priori esthetic grounds, it would seem that no one should have to care about details of co-articulation, acoustic consequences of the fine structure of the glottis, etc. I realize this tramples on the some of the intellectual children of reader-parents. But my tutorial role enjoins me to describe the important characteristics of the endeavor as clearly as I can. That speech science is in some essential way an accidental science, seems to me important in setting our expectations about what can be achieved and with what mix of theory and experiment.

But the generative character of our sources of knowledge has more accidental and conventional elements than may seem apparent. First, the human equally recognizes his speech as he produces it. Thus, there are mechanisms that are as finely tuned to the analysis of the utterance as to its generation. It is an accident of the accessibility of the production apparatus and the (so far) almost complete inaccessibility of the recognition apparatus that knowledge shows up in generative form. Reverse the situation and our formulations would be strongly analytic.

In general, where the available physical system is inaccessible, we get swings between analytic and generative representation that are molded by scientific fashion and creative accident. For example, the emphasis on generative laws at the syntactic level is not inherent. It was analytic before Chomsky (with structural linguistics), the arguments for its current generative form are mostly philosophic, and one can confidently predict it will become analytic again under the right stimulus (e.g., models of performative sentence comprehension).

In all events, much knowledge is generative and it should be clear that recognition desires that knowledge be expressed analytically, so that the final totally encoded utterance can be peeled back layer by layer to reveal the original input from which it came -- understanding.

There is of course a general way of adapting generative knowledge to recognition. In artificial intelligence it goes by the name of generate and test. Within the speech world it tends to be called analysis by synthesis. This method has application at all levels of representation. The original analysis by synthesis model put forward by Halle and Stevens (1962) (and casually at that, as a specification of mechanism) was aimed at a particular level. A representation of the utterance at the parametric level was created and used to test the hearer's hypothesis of the analysis of the incoming utterance. But wherever one takes some information from the utterance (at any level), uses that to hypothesis a more complete form and then match against the more detailed utterance, one is engaged in a form of analysis-by-synthesis or, as I would prefer to label it, of generate-and-test.

The difficulty with generate-and-test is that it can be, and often is, immensely expensive. The basic objection raised to the Halle-Stevens analysis-by-synthesis proposal is that either it is impossibly expensive or that all the important part is hidden in the black box they called Preliminary Analysis.

Thus an imperative topic for investigation is the general task of inverting generative laws to obtain analytic ones. This is not a single task, of course, for it depends strongly on the structure of the generative laws. For grammars, where interest has always centered on parsing, the issues are well in hand. We can see this, not only in the large number of successful parsing systems, but in the rapidity with which SUS parsing systems developed techniques for parsing from arbitrary starting locations. The entire technology of parsing systems grew up in a world (error-free text) where left-to-right scanning could be assumed. Simple BNF grammars were modified in short order (Neely, 1973) and more adequate systems have followed promptly (Bates, 1974; Miller, 1973).

Consideration of the ingredients for success in the case of

grammars makes it apparent that the first and most important step is constructing formal systems for the rules themselves. These are invariably baroque when first invented, so that a period of iteration and purification is always required. But only with an abstract rule system in hand can the issue of inversion be properly tackled. Then, almost always, one can be assured of some progress. Fears are often raised that the inversions are not possible because of a lack of uniqueness. But this is always the case in any complex production system. Such ambiguity is inherent in the knowledge source and it infects attempts at using either generative or analytic laws. The relative advantages of analytic formulations remain. They are akin to the gain from compiling over interpreting (to draw the simile from computer science) or to the gain from analytical over numerical solutions of equations (to draw the simile from mathematics). One performs once and for all (in the act of analytic conversion) the derivation of the implications of given features in the utterance for the decoded signal. In generative forms this is derived again and again in each specific case.

To repeat the central point: The issue of the conversion of generative knowledge into analytic knowledge is a fundamental issue in speech understanding systems. We need to develop a generalized understanding of how to go about it. It will recur for many of our knowledge sources. The first step is to formalize the knowledge as a generative system. This is why the current efforts to develop systems of phonological rules are so important; it is the first new area that the work in SUS has tackled. Other ones need to follow, e.g., the co-articulation rules at the acoustic-phonetic level.

SIGNAL PROCESSING

Two features dominate the initial speech input data: its wave nature and its volume.

We have long recognized that the basic nature of wave phenomena leads to useful analyses in terms of frequency. Here, as opposed to talking about the future, we have a long history of specialized investigations leading to an entire domain of technique: Fourier series and transforms, the FFT, etc. I need not belabor this, nor does my opinion add weight necessary to continuing attention to this area.

An interesting change has taken place in the two years since the SUS research program began. At the beginning, orientation remained focussed on straight frequency representation, as had been true since the fifties. But since then, linear predictive analysis has risen to become a major signal processing technique (see the review

by Markel, Gray & Wakita, 1973). By now it is used in most of the
SUSs. It provides a more direct means to assess the strengths of the
primary resonances (i.e., the formants) that characterize the speech
wave. The speed with which this technique was picked up and
exploited shows what can happen in an area that has already been the
subject of intensive scientific attention.

   This area provides an example of what it means to investigate a
class of mechanisms. It may seem to many readers unclear when I
say: Investigate encodings of partial knowledge! Investigate heuristic
search! ... and so on through the list of Figure 8. I mean: Do to
them what has been done in the past to the domain of frequency and
resonant cavity analysis. Characterize the problem; formalize it;
develop algorithms; discover the essential ingredients of these
algorithms; worry about computational problems, about complexity (to
use a computer science phrase); design specialized computer
structures. My list of mechanisms in Figure 8 is much larger than what
is classically considered worth exploring in speech research. This
measures the conceptual benefits to be gained by finally trying to pay
the promissory note and broaden our sights to the entire speech
understanding problem.

   The wave nature of speech dictates the form its primary
analysis must take. Equally important in its impact is the volume of data
to be processed. The input signal consists of some 240,000 bits/sec
(12 bits x 20,000 samples/sec), which is sustained for a few seconds.
The understanding signal hiding within this, on the other hand, is not
much over 10 bits/sec and most often is much less. Thus, the
characteristic feature of the transduction is that of data reduction. In
fact, it might have been thought that this feature of speech, which is
so striking, should have formed the core of the earlier discussion of
why the transduction is difficult. But, except for one aspect discussed
below, the difficulty lies in the complexity of the encoding, not simply in
the fact that the signal must be extracted from a large volume of
irrelevant variation. It is no problem to throw information away if the
irrelevant is easily factored from the relevant.

   The one important aspect is the sheer magnitude of the data
and its rate relative to the speed and memory of the processing
devices available. Until recently this has indeed been a problem, taking
normally available digital computers as the standard. One was forced
to use analog techniques at the front end, with their inevitable rigidity
and limitations.[†] As long as the speech data rate presses the limits of

---

[†]Whoever still believes that analog devices provide a form of flexibility

available digital devices, the data rate problem remains a primary determinant of difficulty.

However, the back of the problem has been essential broken by now for speech, though the solution will still take another year or two to fully spread. The first step -- the development of the Fast Fourier Transform -- occurred some time ago. The second step is the increase in speed and capacity of digital technology, coupled with the development of specialized microprocessors, which bring the computations down to manageable size while providing the flexibility that comes with programming. The sign of this is in the recent commercial availability of such processors at modest cost (e.g., see Knudsen, 1974).

MATCHING

Matching algorithms are another central concern of speech understanding systems. By the term matching I wish to specify much more than that two representations of the same thing are compared with an attempt to measure or score their similarity. Rather, one of the objects is a form or ideal-type which can be subjected to various transformations in order to increase the correspondence between it and another representation.[†] A prototypical example, though not from speech, is that $(X + 5)$ matches $(3 + 5)$ because 3 can be substituted for the variable X. Notice how this differs from the comparison operation in the Nearest-neighbor scheme discussed earlier. There, the two points, X and U, are fully given and $D(X,U)$ simply measures their similarity. "$(X + 5)$" is no closer to "$(3 + 5)$" than to "$(X + 7)$" viewed simply as patterns, yet it matches one and not the other.

For speech, matching arises at the lexical level almost uniformly, but it also arises at the phonological level and at the semantic level. It will also arise at the parametric level if anyone seriously tries to implement the Halle-Stevens scheme of analysis-by-synthesis. It will arise ubiquitously wherever certain minimal conditions on our knowledge are satisfied. Moreover, it is one of the most powerful methods of processing known, and lies at the heart of a great many algorithms in diverse fields.

---

still to be cherished in signal processing should contemplate well the rapid assimilation of LPC techniques and inquire whether this would have happened if our front-ends relied on analog processing.

[†]Most generally, transformations can be applied to both sides.

Let us understand its anatomy a little better. In the formulation used earlier, at some point there was an input X subject to a transforming process P yielding an output utterance Y, which is what we have in hand (represented in R). We wish to recover X. In the matching situation typical in speech our knowledge of P is expressed by a set of possible transformations $\{T_i\}$ on X. A sequence of T's applied to X yields a possible Y. Hence if a candidate X is really the one that produced Y, then there must exist a sequence of T's that verify it. If no such sequence can be found, then the candidate X can be eliminated as the underlying message.

To give an example, take X to be a sequence of phonetic symbols representing a word in a lexicon, with Y to be a segmented and labeled string in the same phonetic alphabet as generated from the spoken utterance. Then the T's are a set of rules for deleting, substituting and inserting phonetic symbols in the lexicon string X as a function of the local phonetic context. The T's may be rule-like operations or they may be stored variations, reflecting, say speaker variation due to dialect. This example can be seen in several of the systems described in the Conference (e.g., the Degarbler of CASPERS, Klovstad & Mondshein, 1974).

I deliberately express the problem in a general form in order to make three points. First, the task of matching in its underlying structure is an instance of general combinatorial search. One is forced to consider all sequences of T's and to engage in a backtrack search (or some of its alternatives such as best-next). Indeed the match task is viewed in several efforts as essentially a sequential decoding task. Second, what makes matching special -- what make it look different from general heuristic search -- is a set of special properties on the T's that permit strong inference, namely that a specific T_i (or small set) must be used at a given place in order for the match to work. This is what happens when the two objects, X and Y are put into correspondence and the structure of Y selects directly the transformation T necessary to make X agree with Y at a given point.

Third, the set of T's that characterize speech differ considerably from the T's that characterize the matching with which we are most familiar, namely the matching of forms involving only substitution for variables. But the essential features of a match are still present. Thus, again we have currently a wide collection of specific matching algorithms, often formulated in quite disparate terms (e.g., as string matches or, sequential decoding). These vary not only in the algorithm but in the formulation of the allowable transformations, in what information is kept to keep the final agreement score and so on.

To repeat my theme: It seems to me that much can be done in laying bare the structure of the matching tasks that occur in SUSs and in discovering the appropriate algorithms and showing their computational properties.

FLEXIBLE CONTROL AND ATTENTION FOCUSING

A pervasive problem is the control of a complex of separate mechanisms. Which M's shall be applied to which parts of the utterance and in what order? The limited total computational capacity of the system and the varying yield of application of knowledge all make this an important issue.

Typically the problem has been met with a rigidly fixed scheme of application. The literature is full of flowcharts representing the designer's a priori decision of what shall be applied when. These are often accompanied by a view that <u>the</u> correct scheme has been found.

A moments consideration shows that such a fixed decision on control represents one of two situations. First, it may reflect a logical data dependence, in which M_2, which requires data of form X, can only be executed after M_1 which produces the data in that form. These situations reflect a valid necessity in the executive structure of the system. Second, it may involve a genuine decrease in the problem solving options available to the system. The problem is often that the designers could not conceive the organization in a more flexible and variable form. We are up against a genuine cognitive difficulty here, in which we humans create designs by imagining frameworks and then fleshing out the details. Whatever is written down becomes fixed: everything cannot be variable; something must be written down first or the system will never get specified; and what does get written down first conditions strongly all that follows. Once a basic structure is fixed it is extremely difficult to make it variable, since it invalidates all the content built upon it. The upshot is that only slowly do we create flexible control structures.

It is easy to preach flexibility. However, with each increase in variability comes a concomitant requirement for selection -- for <u>binding</u> that variability at some moment. Two problems occur here. For one, we do not have a thorough understanding of flexible control mechanisms. We are not totally in the dark. Recent work both in artificial intelligence (Bobrow and Raphael, 1973) and operating systems (Lorin, 1972) have provided some tools and some understanding. In the existing SUSs just being put together one finds this issue being addressed directly (Lesser, Fennell, Erman & Reddy, 1974; Rovner, Nash-Webber & Woods, 1974). However, a close persual of these schemes reveals that variability is still kept under varying degrees of close control.

The second problem is that all acts of selection require processing so that as the amount of freedom increases, the price paid for that freedom also increases. We do not fully understand the trade-offs, and we will not understand them until we have built systems which have an excess of flexibility whose cost we can assess.

MULTIPLE IDIOSYNCRATIC KNOWLEDGE SOURCES

I seem unable to express the last type of mechanism with any precision. As we accept the notion of a large collection of knowledge sources, each in its own terms, the total system not only begins to grow but becomes extremely heterogeneous. Heterogeneous is, I'm afraid, a euphemism for the more descriptive computer term, kludge.

We need to understand how to build graceful and controllable large systems of highly diverse elements. We must be careful in assessing this problem, because at some level all systems become homogeneous and simple. Technology demands it. At some level, all programs are simply a large bit array. What could be simpler? If one is working in LISP, to pick another level, all program are lists. Again, what could be simpler? In Hearsay-II they are all independent cooperating processes with identical functions of generation, testing, and self-evocation. Such levels of uniformity are necessary. Such levels of uniformity are in part a solution to the problem of how to organize large systems. However, to my eye, the levels that have been developed to date do not seem sufficient yet to tame the complexity.

Moreover, diversity must occur at some stage. To have knowledge (i.e., information) is to have variability, and therefore to have lots of knowledge is to have lots of variability. The content of an encyclopedia is indeed a conceptual kludge. Therefore, there must be some limits to how much the complexity can be tamed.

Still, it seems certain that we have not yet found the highest levels of uniformity that will be necessary to permit incorporation of large diverse knowledge sources in a single intercommunicating system.

CONCLUSION

There are several types of mechanisms that are characteristic of SUSs. I have listed in figure 8 those that seem most important to me, though it surely is an imperfect list. My purpose in the iteration is to emphasize that we need intensive development of each class of mechanism. I hope it is clear that each has an underlying structure that will yield to such study.

SYSTEM SPECIFICATION

The goal of research in speech understanding systems is the construction of an operational system. This serves, of course, deeper scientific goals of understanding the nature of speech and of understanding. But in the usual exegesis of science, these deeper goals of understanding also serve other goals of usefulness to society and our fellow man -- goals well epitomized by the construction of a SUS and the technology flowing therefrom. We need not adjudicate here between scientific and engineering goals. In the speech understanding field they are inextricably and circularly intertwined.

At the center of this task of goal-setting is our ability to specify SUSs: to describe, both in advance and after the fact, what sort of system we have and what its capabilities are. Our ability to do this, and do it well, is not only of value to us; it becomes a characteristic of our scientific endeavor, stamping it with a particular clarity of goals, and with the capacity to tell success from failure. Such clarity has its negative aspects; that is not to be argued here. From a tutorial point of view, this characteristic of our field is surely of note.

THE ORIGINAL 19 DIMENSIONS

The initial Speech Understanding Systems Study Group Report (Newell et. al., 1971) contained an attempt to specify SUSs in detail. In my own estimation, it is one of its remarkable features. Let me recap it briefly. A series of 19 dimensions were developed that covered the task environment, system structure, and performance. Each dimension was characterterized by a set of choices and also, where appropriate, by the problem represented by that dimension. Figure 9 gives a brief summary. A particular SUS could be specified by giving the values on these 19 dimensions.

Extensive use was made of this specification vector in the report. It was used to argue that there was no such thing as the speech understanding system, but an entire space of them, differing in capability and in task environment. The aspirations initially presented to the Study Group as a charge were recast as such a vector, as was each of several systems described in the report as examples of possible SUSs. Most important, the final recommendations were given primarily by another vector. These have continued to provide the goals of the SUSG effort. In sum, the ability to specify SUSs gave the report a high level of coherence.[†]

[†]I must be a little circumspect about my evaluation, being one of the authors. Nevertheless, I stand by the judgment.

QUESTION	PROBLEM
What sort of speech	Continuous speech
How many speakers	Multiple speaker
What sort of speaker	Dialect
What sort of auditory environment	Environmental noise
What sort of communication system	Transducer
How much training of the system	Tuneability
How much training of the users	User training
How large and free a vocabulary	Vocabulary
What sort of language	Syntactic support
What task is to be performed	Semantic support
What is known about user psychology	User model
How sophisticated a dialogue	Interaction
What kinds of errors can be tolerated	Reliability
When must the interpretation be available	Real time
How much processing is available	
How large a memory is available	
How sophisticated an organization	Systems organization
What should be the cost	Cost
When should the system be operational	

Figure 9. Study Report Criteria

Looked at coolly, these dimensions are crude and have only imperfect measures associated with them. Withal, they present a tight enough picture so one can make a number of assertions. For instance, consider the vector that forms the five-year goals of the ARPA SUS effort. We can say of these:

(1) They are definitely in advance of the art at the time they were laid down, and in specific ways.
(2) We will know when a system has been built that has satisfied these specifications.
(3) Currently (the April 74 IEEE conference) measurable progress has been made (e.g., continuous speech for a few speakers is being recognized) which is still measurably short of the posited goals (e.g., in vocabulary size).

Furthermore, as researchers we can orient ourselves to these dimensions, determining where to put our effort. All of this can only be done roughly and with a margin of error, but still well enough to work.

How To Specify SUSs

The vector of the initial Report is just the starting point for addressing the issues of specification of SUSs. They will continue to play a continuing strong role in the development of the field. We need to attend to the completeness of the dimensions, to how they are defined and to how they are measured. As throughout this paper, though we cannot delve far into any matters of substance, we can highlight the issues.

The dimensions fall into four separate categories, according to what aspect they specify: knowledge sources, system structure, performance, and time scale. Two of these -- the time scale of the research and the specification of final performance criteria -- need no further elaboration. We need to discuss primarily the system structure and the knowledge sources.

Specifying System Structure

The specification of system structure is divided into four components in the original vector: speed (in Mips, millions of instructions per second); primary memory (in megabits); systems organization (in a conglomerate of discrete choices); and cost (in dollars per second of speech). Such a set of four numbers is both more and less than what is actually required to specify the relevant structure of the system.

It is more than is required because trade-offs are possible among the various structural components. Within a given technology era one can trade bits of memory for speed of processing. Even organization can be traded. The greater the speed and memory available, the simpler the organizational scheme required. Conversely, doing with less hardware permits more resources into programming the software system. Thus, the relevant structure variable is total system cost.

In reality, the trade-offs are not perfect. Both in the array of devices offered by the hardware technology and in the possible algorithms and organizations conceptually available, there are gaps. Beyond a certain point, additional memory doesn't help. Certain minimum Mips are required to perform any of the algorithms known. And so on. Thus, the technological state (interacting with the underlying nature of the task) dictates that the dollars be spent in a specific way.

Breaking the single cost figure into components -- Mips, Megabits and organization in the report -- is a way of expressing that required pattern -- the inhomogeneities of the trade-off space. But then it seems that less is given than needed. We need to specify the secondary storage requirements and the real-time requirements. As the use of specialized microprocessor architectures becomes standard for the signal processing, then signal processing Mips becomes distinguishable from the Mips need for the remainder of the system. We also need to ask whether we can split cleanly the specifications of the final performing system from the development system, or whether the types of graphics access and debugging and system-implementation tools are not so essential that they should be included.

SPECIFYING KNOWLEDGE SOURCES

The main category of dimensions specify the nature of the task environment in which the SUS will work. They do this by giving specifications for each encoding mechanism. In terms of our general picture of knowledge sources, there should be a uniform way of treating these specifications. Our concern with all encoding mechanisms is in some sense identical. How much variability does the encoding mechanism introduce? What sources of knowledge do we have for decoding them? How expensive is the application of these knowledge sources? And so on.

Only a certain set of things can be done about an encoding mechanism -- any encoding mechanism -- with respect to a prospective SUS. These options are generated by how encoding mechanisms and their sources of knowledge enter into the structure of a SUS. They constitute the primary terms on which a specification must be written.

Figure 10 lists these options. I have associated an abbreviation with each one, which will be used below. The first possibility (N) is to accept the normal values of the encoding mechanism. For instance, accept whatever dialects people who participate in the task happen to have. The second possibility (E) is to eliminate the encoding mechanism entirely. This is not possible with dialect; it is possible with respect to environmental noise. The third and fourth option, eliminating bad values of the mechanism (-B), or specifying a particular good value (=G), are two sides of the same coin, though not equivalent in how easy they are to apply to a particular mechanism. One could eliminate foreign accents, on the one hand, or insist on only isolated words, on the other.

The last three options specify the knowledge source, rather than the properties of the encoding mechanism itself. One can restrict the value to where one happens to have knowledge (K). An example is male speakers, since much of the existing scientific knowledge about speech has been developed with male subjects. Alternatively, one can

```
N   ACCEPT NORMAL VALUES
E   ELIMINATE
-B  ELIMINATE BAD VALUES
=G  SPECIFY TO GOOD VALUES
K   SPECIFY TO A KNOWLEDGE SOURCES WE HAVE
DK  SPECIFY KNOWLEDGE SOURCE SHOULD BE DEVELOPED
RK  REQUIRE RUN-TIME ACQUISITION OF KNOWLEDGE
```

Figure 10. What to Do About An Encoding Mechanism?

accept the impact of an encoding mechanism, but insist that success of the SUS depends on developing an adequate source of knowledge (DK). An example is phonological rules, where little control is available over their evocation, but it is felt that the context dependent variability they introduce must be responded to. Finally, one can accept the variability from a mechanism for the population of tasks or speakers as a whole, but require run-time acquisition of the knowledge for the individual speaker or task (RK). A typical example is acquisition of the individual speaker's formant frequencies for vowels.

Why spin out all these options? Because one wants to develop a uniform approach to specifying a system. Different options are often simply alternative ways of responding to a single underlying state of knowledge about an encoding mechanism. How to constrain a mechanism may be purely tactical. And some response should be developed to all of the encoding mechanisms.

We can look at the specifications of the Speech Report in terms of these options and the entire set of knowledge sources (equivalently, here, the encoding mechanisms). Figure 11 shows the result. A small pair, such as (#5 E) opposite Communication System, indicates that the 5th criteria of the report (see Figure 9) is a choice of option E (of Figure 10). Our concern is not with the details of this. Rather, we wish to emphasize the ways in which the specifications need improvement. The gaps, such as for Prosodics and Discourse, call for being specified. A rationale is required for why particular options are suitable for particular dimensions, rather than equivalent options. The collection of options all focussed on a single knowledge source (Acoustics) indicates that the sources of knowledge should be expanded. There seems to be no rational reason why the specification should not consist of a single option for each knowledge source involved.

I cannot even begin here an adequate treatment of how the dimensions should be measured, especially those for the knowledge

Communication system					#5 E
Environmental noise					#4 E
Acoustics	#1 N	#2 N	#3 K	#6 RK	#7 N
Phonetics				#2 N	#1 N
Phonemics				#3 K	DK
Prosodics					
Lexicon					#8 -B
Syntax				#9 =G	DK
Discourse					
Semantics (domain)					#10 =G
Task structure				#10 =G	(SAME AS SEMANTICS)
User					#11 I
History					

Figure 11. Sources of Knowledge

sources. But let me simply emphasize its importance with an example. Vocabulary size is not only easy to quantify (i.e., number of words), but seems to be an important task specification. Now, the main effect of vocabulary is the probability of confusability between words. This is governed not by the total vocabulary size (i.e., the stated measure) but by the number of words that are too close to each other in some sense. This is not an academic distinction. As vocabulary size grows words tend to become polysyllabic and thus the total space occupied by N words grows with N, and no one knows currently how much the density also grows. We would do well to substitute a density measure for a size measure of vocabulary, though it will take some substantial empirical work before this can be done.

PERFORMANCE ANALYSIS

Speech understanding systems are substantial complexes of hardware and software. In size they currently run about 100,000 instructions and have real time constraints in addition to being large programs, a matter of some importance in gauging system complexity (Wolverton, 1974). This momentary size is a bit adventitious. The current systems are first generation SUSs (counting Hearsay-I, rather than Hearsay-II). Thus, they are smaller than they will be later, since an immense amount of code will be added as they increase in sophistication and completeness. But they are also larger than they will be later, since iteration of design in the interests of efficiency always provides substantial factors in space and speed. At a guess, I would place their size at about 300,000 instructions at the end of

1976 (the predicated end of the five year initial program), with shrinkage back to 100,000 in a pure performance program at some later time. These estimates are based not on detailed consideration of the code, but on general feelings about software systems and their development.

Such a system is not, actually, of overwhelming size, compared to the art (e.g., the NASA complex used for monitoring space flights). It had better not be, since the ultimate role of a SUS is to allow communication between a user and a task program, and this latter should dominate the computational demands. Still an SUS is good sized and on a par with other complex artificial intelligence programs currently under development and exploration.

Programs of this size and complexity require substantial attention to the analysis of their performance. So far, only extremely modest efforts have been devoted to it. You will not find any papers, in either this volume or in the companion proceedings, devoted to the problem at the system level.† This is in part natural. The SUSs of the ARPA program have just come into being and they are hardly stable enough to rate much performance analysis.

I wish I could be sanguine -- that attention to performance analysis will follow automatically with maturity. But inattention to this matter has been a failing of research with AI programs from the start. The difficulties are clear. The programs, being complex, are always inadequate and incomplete. Direct perception into the program's structure leads its creators always to improvements that are eminently worthwhile. At the margin, it always seems a better decision to press on than to stop and analyze. Nor is the AI field strongly vocal on the necessity for analysis. Some of the most highly regarded efforts in AI (e.g., Winograd's thesis, 1971) are completely silent on the need for critical analysis of the programs structure against actual performance data. Finally, the complexity of the programs mitigate against analysis directly, since there seems to be too many aspects to look at and it is so expensive per look.

The reasons are persuasive. As a builder of AI programs, I feel their force at first hand. Still, I would like to press for devoting much attention to the analyses of the structure and performance of SUSs.

This paper is a tutorial, I assert, and not an attempt to influence the field directly. Therefore I will cleanse the editorial remark just

---

†There are some papers on evaluation of various components (O'Malley & Cole, 1974; Goldberg, Reddy & Suslick, 1974), which are most welcome.

made by tutorializing it. There are a number of approaches to the study of the performance of complex systems and I consider it part of a basic view of this field to understand these approaches. They owe their development to other fields, sometimes to parts of computer science but often to more distant sciences. Thus, their exposure is indeed tutorial in nature. Taken collectively they also express a view of SUSs that is valuable in understanding the field's structure.

Figure 12 lists eight distinct approaches to performance analysis, just for handy reference. Each is worth a few remarks.

BENCHMARKS
O-R MODELS OF SYSTEMS
ANALYSIS OF ALGORITHMS
NULL MODELS
OPTIMAL MODELS
ABLATION STUDIES
ANALYSIS OF VARIANCE
CAUSALITY ANALYSIS

Figure 12. Performance Analysis Types

BENCHMARKS
The simplest scheme of performance analysis, used throughout computer science, is the development of a set of benchmark problems. Performance on these problems is taken as a indicator of success. The benchmark set is constructed with some care to assure an appropriate mix of computational demands, so that performance on the set can be taken as indicative of performance on the entire space of problems.

Benchmarks already form the core of current ideas on performance analysis in SUSs. In part, this is because the speech input data is complex and expensive to prepare, since it must be carefully processed by hand to provide a reliable definition of the correct output. Thus typically a fixed collection of benchmark utterances is obtained and used for long periods.

Long experience with benchmarks in the evaluation of computers and programming languages (where it is the standard technique) shows that they are an exceedingly rough and unreliable tool. The difficulty is mostly the variability in the task space, so that no small set of points seems to safely characterize total performance. The same concern exists for speech, where a benchmark set will only contain a small set of the total difficulties. This is especially true for systems organized as multiple knowledge sources, where separate difficulties are to be solved by the application of distinct items of knowledge. Success on one difficulty (say one included in a benchmark problem set) says nothing about behavior on another difficulty.

OPERATIONS RESEARCH MODELS

There is a specialty within computer science called <u>Performance Analysis</u>, which thus has prima facie relevance to the task at hand. It is concerned with the construction of operations research style models that approximate the behavior of complex total computer structures. Typical concerns are with the expected throughput of a multiprocessor, the access behavior of a rotating drum system, the response time of a time sharing system. Such systems are too complex to be modeled in detail (though sometimes small segments of their detailed behavior can be simulated), and the models used are gross approximations that balance mathematical tractability against degree of fidelity, often with substantial success.

The essential ingredients for such models are two: (1) a fundamental repetitiveness (with variation, of course) in the operation that contributes to the stochastic emergence of order within complexity; (2) a body of stochastic theory that makes modeling a reasonable endeavor, rather than an exercise in prime mathematical creativity. In the computer science performance analysis specialty, the first ingredient can be seen in the systems selected for analysis. For example, the response time in a time sharing system of multiple users makes a large sequence of essentially similar requests for service. The second ingredient is provided essentially by queueing theory, which has now reached a rather well developed state.

There has been no serious modeling of SUSs in such fashion, again, for the good reasons stated above. Therefore the question is whether the ingredients exist, so that one might expect work in this vein to pay off. Certainly the repetition exists, for the SUSs are dominated by the statistics of the same mechanisms being applied over and over again under slightly different contextual conditions. A segmentation algorithm, a phone lexicon in terms of features, a word-level lexicon, etc., all are definers of an ensemble of algorithmic occurrences which are the always the same, though always different.

As to the mathematical theory, the situation is less clear -- though in part because the mathematical demands are not fully clear. The natural source is information theory, which deals with the probabilities of error of various encoding and decoding rules under conditions of noise. What could be more relevant? However, it may not be quite up to the mark as it stands. The essential difficulty can be seen in two paradigmatic problems: (1) given a confusion matrix and a decoding scheme, find the expected error; (2) given a confusion matrix and a decoding scheme, find the resulting confusion matrix. Information theory has tackled the first problem with a vengeance; it has hardly touched the second. SUSs, with their multiple levels of representations, through which errorful representations transist (confusion matrix to confusion matrix) are much more easily modeled by the second problem.

By pointing to a difficulty I wish to indicate a possibility. Much is to be gained by the construction of global stochastic models of our SUSs, and they seem to be strongly amenable to the technique.

ANALYSIS OF ALGORITHMS

Another thriving specialty in computer science has become known as the Analysis of Algorithms. It is concerned with the detailed structure of the algorithms used to accomplish a given task. Typical concerns are algorithms for sorting or for finding the median (they are closely connected it turns out). Typically the results are given by a formula expressing the time and/or space required as a function of parameters characterizing the task environment.

Such analyses can be performed only in relatively simple cases. It is unrealistic to think of applying such techniques to a SUS as a whole. However, there are various subparts of the speech understanding task that might be amenable. In particular, the matching process and the heuristic search process, discussed in an earlier section, are likely candidates.

NULL MODELS

An important technique in assessing the performance of systems is the null model. The term, for those not familiar with it, comes from the social sciences, where it is taken in analogy to the null hypothesis of statistical testing, especially as employed in psychology. The null model typically tries to answer the question: How well would an unsophisticated model do? Knowing this, one has some notion of whether a seriously proposed model is really doing any better.

For instance, in economic forecasting a difference equation might be proposed to predict the future as a function of past values:
$$Y(t+1) = A*Y(t) + B*Y(t-1)$$
How well does it do against the null model that "tomorrow is like today", i.e., $Y(t+1) = Y(t)$. It is surprising how often the answer turns out depressingly, even when the model makes significant predictions taken by itself.

In a fit of smugness one is tempted to define the null model for speech as a pure guess about the potential meanings of an utterance taken in ignorance of any information about the utterance itself. That is, the null model is the a priori guess, given the static semantics. For most tasks the probability of being correct is so slight that any genuine program comes on looking significant.

However, the game of null models is not to select one you know you can beat -- that is setting up a straw man. The game is to find a null model that is simple (yea, simple minded) yet effective. Such a one poses the appropriate challenge to why added complexity is necessary.

The right place to look for null models is within the class of generalized input-output functions. These offer uniform schemes which depend only upon locally obtained information or (at most) carefully gathered statistics obtained by a uniform method. The nearest-neighbor type of scheme illustrated earlier provides at the moment only limited possibilities for becoming an appropriate null model, since there are no simple extensions to continuous speech. They depend on an essentially fixed utterance length. Ways would have to be found to eliminate that restriction while avoiding complex segmentation schemes (which would move them back toward full scale systems).

A much more attractive null model is found in systems like DRAGON (Baker, 1974), reported at the IEEE Conference. This is a generalized input-output function, but its underlying representation is a Markov process. The representational levels are retained, each being formed as a sequence of states, each state being a sequence of states of the Markov process one level lower in the hierarchy: semantics to sentences to words to syllables to phones, etc. Each sequence (at whatever level) is generated by a Markov process. Two things can then be done. First, the probabilities of the Markov process can be estimated from utterance data, thus providing a way of soaking up knowledge about speech (much as the empirically determined coordinates of the U's did in the nearest-neighbor scheme). Then, a Bayesean formulation can be used to build a dynamic programming algorithm to provide the optimal estimate of the actual sequence of states that occurred given an utterance.

Null models are particularly effective roads to research action, and substantial effort should go into their cultivation. In several areas of science good null models have been developed, always with beneficial effect as far as I can see. Just to quote from AI research, we have recently come to understand that a so-called "technology" chess program (Gillogly, 1972)[†] can perform reasonable chess in 1970 technology (1260 point rating). Performance will grow as technology improves, though estimates of the gain in chess-rating-points per Mips do not yet exist. But already it puts an interesting floor under the development of sophisticated chess programs.

OPTIMAL MODELS

Null models provide a lower bound for performance, challenging the significance of complex procedures. Optimal models provide an upper bound on performance, limiting attempts to improve systems where it cannot have good effect and revealing places where there seems to be lots of room for exploitation.

Optimal models characterize certain parts of operations research, such as game theory, and parts of psychology, such as signal detection theory. An example I recall from the early days of linear programming was the use of the Transportation Model of LP to show that the amount of oil shipped (and transhipped) by tanker among world ports was already within 5% of the theoretical optimum, thus not leaving much scope for the application of formal methods.

Superficially, what seems to be required is a good mathematical theory. Closer to the mark is the need for a simple abstract situation which can serve as the model to be optimized. A completely specific system cannot be optimized -- it is what it is. Optimizations requires the envelopment of the given system in an ensemble of systems, so that alternatives can be imagined which might be better (ultimately, optimal) according to some valuation. But the actual freedoms of real systems, here real SUSs, are much too complex. Thus, the program structure must be schematized so that a space of systems of relatively simple structure can be used to address questions of optimal performance.

There are no existing models for SUSs that have been shown to have the right properties. However, this is exactly what the Knowledge-source analysis leads to, and it is a promising lead that needs to be investigated. The knowledge available in the sources puts an upper bound on the amount of constraint available. The actual mechanisms (the Ms) can only lower the effectiveness of a system, failing to covert some knowledge into action. It should be possible to build a knowledge-source model that permits estimation of the upper bound performance in terms of the total knowledge available.

[†]This is a perfect example of a null model: only brute force search is allowed on an evaluation function of only material -- though with as much search as technology permits.

Ablation Studies

A common and important technique for studying systems is to remove various components and study the performance of the diminished system. Ablation techniques are much used where the total system is available but uncertainty exists about the relation of anatomy (i.e., visible structure) to functioning, for example, in studies of whole organisms. The situation in SUSs approximates this condition more than one might initially be prepared to admit. Although each piece of mechanism has been added by an act of deliberate rational design, little feeling is available for the contribution of the parts to the whole. Direct analysis of the algorithm, as described earlier, is not possible. Consequently, ablation of parts of the program to see how well the surviving mutilated system performs is a good tactic of performance analysis.

Programmed systems have a tendency to be all-or-none -- failing completely at the least error. This is at least the standard mythology of programming, in which bugs cause a program to do nothing reasonable, and certainly not to degrade gracefully. However, the organization of SUSs suggested by the Knowledge-sources model does permit ablation as a useful technique, since the mechanisms associated with knowledge sources can be freely added and deleted. The Hearsay-I organization (Reddy, Erman, Fennell & Neely, 1973) does closely approximate this and ablation has been used there from the start. Performance figures have been quoted for various combinations of modules (usually Acoustics, Acoustic+Syntax, and Acoustic+Syntax+Semantics). However, this is still a relatively crude form of ablation, and one that is roughly available in most SUSs today (partly because they all cause a sharp separation between the "lower" acoustic part of the system and the "higher" syntactic-semantic part, which permits a natural ablation). Hearsay-II (Lesser, Fennell, Erman & Reddy, 1974) provides a much more radical experiment in decomposition of a SUS into multiple separate knowledge sources. Ablation studies here should actually provide a genuinely interesting experiment in this form of performance analysis.

Analysis of Variance Models

A technique that has seen almost no use with computer systems is that of analysis of variance. It is much used elsewhere in science and technology, of course, to provide a simplified model of a total system. To pick the classic example, one wishes to understand the yield of a given crop. Preliminary experience and analysis yield a number of candidates for what might affect the yield: the type of fertilizer (F), the drainage (D), and the weeding performed (W), say. Each of these factors can be restricted to a finite set of alternatives (usually called levels), e.g., two types of fertilizer or none at all; four rows of the crop that lay with the drainage pattern of the field; and to-weed or not-to-weed. Then a generalized input-output model is constructed:

$$[Y] = [F] + [D] + [W] + [FD] + [FW] + [DW] + [FDW]$$

This symbolic formula states that the yield, Y, can be written as a sum of contributions that arise from the levels of each of the factors, F, D and W. There is a contribution from each taken separately, from each of the combinations taken two at a time, and from each taken three at a time. Implicit in the model is that nothing will be assigned to a higher interaction term if it can be assigned to a lower term. For example, the maximum effects are assigned to the factors taken in isolation, say Fi and Dj, and an effect is assigned to their interaction [Fi Dj] only if Yij deviates from Fi+Dj.

A moments consideration will show that the model just expressed is an arithmetic tautology -- that an arbitrary function of the levels can be so expressed if all of the interaction terms are included. The importance of the model is that real situations invariably have large low-order effects so that the higher order interactions can be treated as noise. For example, the actual model that might fit data that comes from raising the crop in the field could be:

$$[Y] = [F] + [D] + [W] + [WF] + Error$$

There is an effect of each treatment taken separately, but only one interaction worth noting, that between weeding and fertilizing (for example, there might have been no effect of weeding if one did not fertilize, but if one did then weeding increased the yield significantly). Now the model asserts something worth knowing about.

Why this excursion into yet another generalized input-output model? Because a crop-yield on a field is not so different as one might think from the recognition-yield by a SUS. Note, by the way, that the Analysis of Variance model is not a performance model in the way that the Nearest-neighbor or Markov model is. In the latter two cases, one can actually construct a performing system. With analysis of variance one can only describe abstractly the relation of some inputs to some outputs; it is thus useful for analysis only.

As noted, such models are hardly used at all in computer science to analyze the performance of complex programs. However, the potential can be seen in a classic paper by Yntema and Torgersen (1961) in which they successfully modeled the evaluation function of human airplane controllers bringing planes into land (as a function of distance to airport, amount of fuel, weather, etc.) Though the humans were undoubtedly engaged in complex reasoning of some sort, their behavior could be closely approximated by simple additive effects of the main factors with hardly any interaction.

Though not yet completed, I can mention an effort underway to construct an analysis of variance model to describe a chess program (Gillogly, 1974).[†] The collection of heuristics used in the program have been taken as the factors, the levels being whether they are on or off. (In some ways it becomes a complex ablation study). A designed set of experiments has been run, which permits finding out how the heuristics interact either to enhance each other synergistically or to cancel each other out. This also permits assessing the size of the effect of these heuristics against characterizations of the task environment. We hope this study will reveal what can be gained by applying analysis of variance techniques to a complex program. The results should be directly applicable to SUSs.

CAUSALITY ANALYSIS

I have saved the most common form of performance analysis to last. This is to take a single run, with a sequence of partial results to track the computation, and to make a reasoned assessment of what contributed to forming the result. This is what we all do when debugging a system. Doing this over and over is what provides the sense of familiarity with a system and how it achieves its performance. It provides the consequent conviction that we know exactly what should be done to improve its performance or to increase its generality.

I have given this the name of causality analysis, but only because it has no real name of its own already. I am aware of no formalizations of this technique that have been carried out on large systems in a deliberate way, so we can see what is really involved and whether it can be developed into a consistent valuable tool of objective performance analysis. It is a technique that deserves deliberate study.

SUMMARY

We have now covered a large number of techniques of performance analysis. They are not all of proven worth with SUSs, though they all have their uses elsewhere. They form a rich tool kit from which to work in developing a serious and continuing effort to analyze the performance of the SUSs that we are beginning to construct.

[†]In fact, the program is TECH, the technology program mentioned earlier and the one used in the Hearsay-I.

SUMMARY AND CONCLUSION

In this tutorial on speech understanding systems I have tried to give a picture of the basic structure of the field. The picture is certainly not the one that a speech scientist would give, at least not the mythical speech scientist of my imagination. His picture, I believe, would put much more emphasis on the content of those sources of knowledge that are unique to speech. He would take the primary emphasis to be conveying an up-to-date view of the articulatory mechanisms, the phonetic system, etc. Flanagan's admirable book (1965) compressed to 30 pages is my image of such a tutorial.

On the contrary, I have given a picture as it appears to someone in artificial intelligence. I have tried to exhibit the underlying structural features of the domain that will persist and dominate our efforts. Let me pass the features in review:

(1) The dogmas of speech understanding research (see Figure 1), which commits the present efforts to the attempt to integrate all available sources of knowledge in the service of understanding speech.

(2) The source of difficulty (see Figure 3), which is the number and complexity of the mechanisms that join in creating the received speech wave. They range from noise, to encoding to situational redundancy; and from psychological to linguistic to phonetic to acoustic.

(3) The fundamental organization of a SUS (see Figure 6), which consists of a collection of decoding mechanisms, each embodying a distinct source of knowledge.

(4) The alternative organization for a SUS, which creates a parametric family of generalized input-output functions to be instantiated by samples of immediate speech data to hold the knowledge about speech in a form totally assimilated to the mathematical family.

(5) The methods of converting knowledge into action (see Figure 8), which represent classes of algorithms that must be studied and developed if we are to succeed in reaching technically adequate SUSs.

(6) The ability to specify SUSs (see Figure 9), which lends to our endeavor a precision that we should cherish, though it causes us considerable exposure.

(7) The requirement for performance analysis (see Figure 12), which is a primary item on the agenda of the area as the field matures and becomes populated with many complex SUSs.

It may have seemed in this view that I am treating all sources of knowledge as equal before the bar of performance. Properly normalized, of course, that is true. Each is important as it offers constraint to the recognition task, and acquires special importance as the constraint it provides is not providable from other sources. But some sources give much more action than others. And some sources are universally present in all speech environments, thus giving action all the time. Thus, such sources of knowledge are much to be cultivated and much to be analyzed.

By smoothing out the knowledge sources under a uniform label, I have not denied that one must develop the knowledge in terms of its own content and structure. My level of abstraction was not meant to imply a content-free approach to recognition. There are content-free methods, as we have seen, but they are just one tool in the total kit. My own predilections are for constructing systems that make maximal use of all the knowledge science can muster. My suspicions, however, are that, in the long run, content-free algorithms will be developed that win the cost-benefit contest for practical tasks. These latter, however, will not emerge without massive scientific exploration of the domain, such as we are now beginning to carry out.

It is important to realize that all naturally occurring complex tasks requiring intelligence have this same characteristic of requiring a diverse set of knowledge sources, each in their own terms. The problem of vision, of designing a complex system, of planning an expedition, of playing chess, of constructing a theory, of tracking down a thief -- each of these has the same basic structure. This includes by the way the ability of generalized input-output methods to soak up some part of the knowledge and to perform moderately well. Amid this unity of structure, it remains the case -- as is true for speech -- that the knowledge sources cannot be dealt with abstractly. Knowledge about syntax is different from knowledge about co-articulation. Thus, all work in artificial intelligence comes fundamentally to the detailed exploration of specific knowledge sources, each in its own terms. Speech is no exception. But neither is anything else.

Two Creative Tensions

Our field is characterized by two creative tensions. First, it is interdisciplinary. No field is inherently interdisciplinary, of course. If enough people work long enough on speech understanding systems, it will develop into a homogeneous scientific and technical endeavor. But at the moment it is interdisciplinary. Speech science, computer science, linguistics, signal processing, artificial intelligence and psychology constitute its main components. It is hard to trim the list. You might think psychology should not be included. But that only shows how slow is the creep of progress into all the relevant knowledge sources.

The second creative tension is between general mechanisms and knowledge-specific mechanisms. We have seen it emerge in the discussions above. But it is more wide spread. Besides the generalized input-output models versus multiple specific-knowledge-source models, there is tension between general semantic models and task-specific models, between using just the right parametric representation and believing one can extract the information from any sufficiently rich representation, and between an emphasis on the general systems organization of a SUS and on the content of the knowledge sources.

These two tensions, though they sometimes appear correlated when a specific concern comes up (e.g., systems organization is the computer scientist's own special worry), are in fact relatively orthogonal. In all events, they both contribute strongly to the dynamic pace of the attempts to build speech understanding systems, including a sensation that important aspects of the problem are being neglected. This sensation exists fairly broadly, though the assertion of what is being neglected changes diametrically with the position of the scientist along the two dimensions.

THE SCIENTIFIC PAYOFF

What would be gained scientifically if we could indeed construct a successful SUS? I think of five major advances.

First, we would have taken a crucial step in understanding human speech recognition. There is, of course, a standing myth (and here I use the term almost pejoratively) that the creation of an artifact to do X shows nothing about how man might do X. There is no necessary connection; that is manifest. There is no necessary connection between any theory and the real world. But that mistakes where progress is made. A necessary ingredient in discovering how man understands speech is to have a space of possible speech understanding systems within which the one corresponding to man can be located. Artificial SUSs provide a major step in obtaining that space, of getting a ballpark within which man can be found. The first SUSs created will not provide the space; they will be more like isolated points. But the character of the ARPA speech effort, in encouraging the creation of several SUSs simultaneously already will produce some of the diversity necessary to span a usefully wide space.

Second, we will have developed a complete formalization of the influences of the speech signal, e.g., co-articulation effects, phonology, discourse, etc. Unlike the usual scientific course, which rarely yens after completeness, the SUSs must deal with vast amounts of speech, hence with variability that ultimately touches all the odd encoding phenomena.

There is a good possibility that this result will be cut short. Success of some generalized input-output technique could dampen efforts to explore and understand all the encoding mechanisms. In the light of such a success, it will be argued that all one really was after was a practical SUS. Once that has been achieved (or is in sight) by some special techiques, then nothing further is to be obtained by research. That would be a sad thing; and I retain my hope that the short-cutting uniform techniques lie far enough in the future to permit the more fundamental scientific results to emerge.

Third, we will have provided AI with its first real example of a multiple knowledge-source system. I commented above that the SUS problem was not much different from that of many other AI tasks. But that does not imply that AI has yet produced many examples of such systems; it has not yet produced any system which is really heterogeneous in its knowledge sources. There are other systems, especially the vision-robot projects, which are also en route toward such a capability -- and for the very same reasons that SUSs are moving in this direction. But we have yet to learn really how to do it, and the work in SUS has a good chance of making a fundamental contribution to AI by being the first such system.

I would like to hope for a theoretical breakthough with a firm analysis in terms of sources of knowledge, as we have sketched it out in this paper. I somehow doubt that we will get it. Progress can proceed well without it, and the press of the five year goals will preclude it. However, it would be a major contribution to AI all by itself.

Fourth, we will finally have laid to rest one more myth: that men recognizes speech easily whereas machines have a great difficulty in doing this. This mythic assertion is often coupled with the clause that machines accomplish symbolic reasoning easily. The assertion is based on a completely inappropriate comparison: the difficulty that human designers seem to be having in creating a SUS, compared with the performance of a fully designed and operational black box where we have no appreciation of how much processing or of what kinds are going on to accomplish the recognition. Given an artificial SUS of whatever complexity algorithmically, but packaged in a small (say one-foot cube) box operating at one-tenth real time (because of technology) and inaccessible to the casual observer, people will remark how easily the machine seems to recognize. Only we designers will realize how much huffing and puffing the electrons do.

Fifth, the work on SUSs will re-instrument the field of acoustics and speech research, just as the advent of electronics did a decade ago and the minicomputer did again a few years ago. The net result should be a great increase, not only in the Mips that can be brought to bear per data point delivered, so to speak, but in the level of context that can be folded into the research and the amount of empirical data that can be processed. The basic cause of this re-instrumentation is, of course, the advance of computer technology. The SUS efforts are simply the vehicle that shapes this to the particular scientific endeavor and makes the agencies who fund such research finally aware of what is appropriate in the way of instrumention for scientific progress. But, in truth, this has been exactly the nature of the other two instrumention revolutions in the field. Neither in the case of electronics nor of the mini did speech science do other than ride the crest of a more basic technological wave, shaping it to its own needs.

THE PRACTICAL PAYOFF

The effort on speech understanding systems is not purely a scientific endeavor, viewed from any of the participating sciences. What good things would happen to society, then, if we succeed in obtaining practical speech recognition?

I am afraid my biases show here. Clearly the first order event is that we could speak to computers. There is actually no more precise nor more contentful way of stating the matter. In all of the myriad ways in which we need to communicate with computers on various tasks we could use speech in addition to all the other communicative interfaces we have developed.

Indeed, all the more specialized applications that one can think of are all just special cases. To tie to the computer is to tie to the main stream of advancing technology and so to assure that the range of applications grows without ultimate limit, constrained only by local cost/benefit analyses. So it has happened with basic computing capacity; so with the introduction of minicomputers; so it is happening with graphics; and with computer networks. So it will happen with speech understanding, if we obtain the basic technological goals.

I am aware that there are some objections to this view, objections that assert that speech is unnecessary as an input, because existing modes of communication are deemed either optimal or proper. Pierce's letter can again stand us in good stead:

It seems dubious, anyway, whether Turing's interesting game is sufficient justification for spending much money on speech recognition. When we look further for reasons, we encounter that of communication with computers.

In this general form, the reason is as specious as insisting that an automobile should respond to gee, haw, giddap, whoa, and slaps or tugs of the reins. We communicate with children by words, coos, embraces, and slaps. We communicate with people by these means and by nods, winks, and smiles. It is not clear that we should resort to the same means with computers. In fact, we do very well with keyboards, cards, tapes, and cathode-ray tubes. (Pierce, 1969, p. 1049)

As I seek to understand the basic structure of the computer field, I find such reasoning hard to understand.[†] Speech is man's preferred mode of communication for many things. It is the only unplanned channel of any capacity for his issuing communications to the environment. To keep the channel to computers closed to speech, is to cast computers into a very special role -- a role that is hard to characterize with any precision, but must somehow be a device to be used only deliberately and in constrained ways. To permit speech with computers is to open them up to a wider participation in human affairs, a participation that cannot be characterized any more clearly than can the uses of language.

Some readers may find in these final paragraphs a possible overtone of technology for technology's sake. I would like to scotch that. The reader may take such a conclusion out; I deliberately did not put such a conclusion in. All technology is means; all therefore serves different ends -- ends not foreseeable at creation-time. Even more, some modern technologies, of which the computer is the epitome but hardly the sole example, evolve into new types of means which cannot be foreseen. Thus, there is an inevitable loss of control in launching technologies and the greater the freedom and power in the technology, the smaller the control retained. No case can be made for developing technology willy-nilly and, especially, for developing it in the face of counter-indications about its ultimate costs to society. The technology of speech understanding does not seem to me to have such negative consequences associated with it. The potential for being utilized in

---

[†]Hard to understand from a rational viewpoint; it is easy enough to understand both psychologically and sociologically.

socially undesirable ways exists for speech understanding systems, as certainly as it does for all technology. The ability to control its uses or predict them is just about nil, being part of computer technology at large. But its development seems to me primarily to expand society's options for dealing with it problems.

We thus come to the end of the tutorial. I hope it has given the reader a feeling for the form of the effort to construct speech understanding systems. For the content, to clothe that form in substance, I recommend the rest of the papers of this book and the papers delivered at the IEEE Symposium.

REFERENCES

Baker, J. K. (1974), "The DRAGON System -- An overview," in L. Erman (ed.) Contributed Papers, IEEE Symposium on Speech Recognition, pp. 22-26.

Bates, M. (1974), "The use of syntax in a speech understanding system," in L. Erman (ed.) Contributed Papers, IEEE Symposium on Speech Recognition, pp. 226-233.

Bobrow, D. G. & D. Klatt (1968), "A limited speech recognition system," Proc. AFIPS Fall Joint Computer Conference, Vol. 33, pp. 305-318.

Bobrow, D. G., & Raphael, B., (1974), "New programming languages for AI research," Computer Surveys. Vol. 6, no. 3, pp. 153-174.

Danforth, D. G., D. R. Rogosa & P. Suppes, (1974), "Speaking of learning models," in L. Erman (ed.) Contributed Papers, IEEE Symposium on Speech Recognition, pp. 57-61.

Deutch, B., (1974), "The structure of task oriented dialogs," in L. Erman (ed.) Contributed Papers, IEEE Symposium on Speech Recognition, pp. 250-254.

Erman, L. (ed.) (1974), Contributed Papers, Proceedings of the IEEE Symposium on Speech Recognition, IEEE Catalog no. 74CH0878-9AE, N.Y. 10017

Flanagan, J. L. (1965), Speech Analysis, Synthesis and Perception, Academic Press.

Flanagan, J. L., C. H. Coker, L. R. Rabiner, R. W. Schafer, & N. Umeda (1970), "Synthetic voices for computers," IEEE Spectrum, Vol. 7, pp. 22-45.

Fry, D. B. & P. Denes (1956), "Experiments in mechanical speech recognition," in C. Cherry (ed.) Information Theory: Third London Symposium, Butterworth, London, pp. 206-212.

Gillogly, J. J., (1974), PhD. Thesis (in progress), Computer Science Department, Carnegie-Mellon University.

Gillogly, J. J. (1972), "The TECHNOLOGY Chess Program," Artificial Intelligence, Vol. 3, pp. 145-163.

Gold, B. (1966) Word-recognition Computer Program, Tech Report 452, Research Lab for Electronics, MIT.

Goldberg, H. G., D. R. Reddy, & R. L. Suslick (1974), "Parameter-independent Machine Segmentation and Labeling," in L. Erman (ed.) Contributed Papers, IEEE Symposium on Speech Recognition, pp. 106-110.

Halle, M. & Stevens, K. (1962), "Speech recognition: A model and a program for research," IRE Trans PGIT, IT-8, pp. 155-159.

Itakura, F. (1974), "Minimum prediction residual principle applied to speech recognition," in L. Erman (ed.) Contributed Papers, IEEE Symposium in Speech Recognition, pp. 101-105.

Klovstad, J. W. & L. F. Mondshein (1974), "The CASPERS linguistic analysis system," in L. Erman (ed.) Contributed Papers, IEEE Symposium on Speech Recognition, pp. 234-240.

Knudsen, M. (1974), "Real-time linear-predictive coding of speech on the SPS-41 microprogrammed triple processor system," in L. Erman (ed.) Contributed Papers, IEEE Symposium on Speech Recognition, pp. 274-277.

Lesser, V. R., R. D. Fennell, L. D. Erman & R. Reddy (1974), "Organization of the Hearsay-II speech understanding system," in L. Erman (ed.) Contributed Papers, IEEE Symposium on Speech Recognition, pp. 11-21.

Lorin, H. (1972), Parallelism in Hardware and Software: Real and Apparent Concurrency, Prentice-Hall.

Markel, J. D., A. H. Gray & H. Wakita (1973), "Linear prediction of speech -- theory and practice," SCRL Monograph No-10, Speech Communication Research Laboratory, Santa Barbara.

Miller, P. (1973), "A Locally Organized Parser for Spoken Input," Technical Report 503, Lincoln Laboratory, Cambridge, Mass.

Neely, R. B. (1973), "On the use of syntax and semantics in a speech understanding system," PhD. Thesis, Stanford University, Stanford, California.

Newell, A., J. Barnett, J. W. Forgie, C. Green, D. Klatt, J. C. R. Licklider, J. Munson, D. R. Reddy & W. A. Woods (1971), Speech Understanding Systems: Final Report of a Study Group, Reprinted by North-Holland/American Elsevier, 1973.

Nilsson, N. (1971), Problem Solving Methods in Artificial Intelligence, McGraw-Hill.

O'Malley, M. H., & A. Cole (1974), "Testing Phonological Rules," in L. Erman (ed.) Contributed Papers, IEEE Symposium on Speech Recognition, pp. 193-196.

Pierce, J. R. (1969), "Whither speech recognition," JASA Vol. 46, pp. 1049-1051.

Potter, R. K., G. A. Kopp & H. G. Kopp (1947), Visible Speech, Van Nostrand.

Reddy, D. R., L. D. Erman, R. D. Fennell & R. B. Neely (1973), "The HEARSAY speech understanding system," Proc. Third International Joint Conference on Artificial Intelligence, pp. 185-193.

Rovner, P., B. Nash-Webber & W. A. Woods (1974), "Control concepts in a speech understanding system," in L. Erman (ed.) Contributed Papers, IEEE Symposium on Speech Recognition, pp. 267-272.

Steinberg. D. D. & L. A. Jakobovits (1971), Semantics, Cambridge University Press.

Vicens, P. (1969), "Aspects of speech recognition by computer," PhD. Thesis, Computer Science Department, Stanford University.

Winograd, T. (1971), "Procedures as a representation for data in a computer program for understanding natural language," PhD. Thesis, AI Lab - MIT, Cambridge Mass.

Wolverton, T. (1974), "The cost of developing large-scale software," IEEE Trans. on Computers, C23, pp. 615-636.

Yntema, D. B. & W. S. Torgerson (1961), "Man-computer cooperation in decisions requiring common sense," IEEE Trans on Man-machine Systems, MMS-2, pp. 20-26.

APPLICATIONS OF LIMITED VOCABULARY RECOGNITION SYSTEMS

Thomas B. Martin
Threshold Technology Inc.
Cinnaminson, New Jersey 08077

A. INTRODUCTION

The purpose of this paper is to consider what has been achieved in practical applications of automatic speech recognition (ASR). The discussion will be narrowed to the consideration of what recognition accuracies can be achieved with limited vocabulary ASR systems, and of what practical value are such machines. The emphasis will be placed on the current status, rather than predictions for the future. Such predictions tend to be outdated at the moment of publication in a dynamic field such as automatic speech recognition. It is hoped that this discussion will provide a baseline of insight upon which future developments can be referenced. As everyone working in this field realizes, it is always difficult to determine at any particular point in time the exact capability that exists, either in research or in practical machine implementation.

B. TYPES OF ASR SYSTEMS

For the purposes of this presentation, all automatic speech recognition systems will be considered as belonging to one of two categories; continuous (or connected) speech systems or isolated (or discrete) speech systems. The differences between these two types of systems can become obscure and overlapping when attempting to classify a particular approach to ASR as either discrete or continuous. This paper will be limited to the characteristics of isolated speech systems. Only those systems will be discussed that require a short pause before and after utterances that are to be recognized as entities.

The minimum duration of the pause that separates independent utterances is on the order of 100 ms. Anything shorter can become confused with the closure of stop consonants that can produce stop gaps approaching 100 ms in duration. In actuality a stop gap can approach any length that is selected. For example, the word "rapid" can be spoken with a relatively long silence interval after "ra-". For a cooperative speaker, however, a 100 ms minimum separation between words is a reasonable compromise value.

The speaking rate that can be achieved with isolated speech recognition systems is naturally much less than for connected speech. Speaking rates over 300 words per minute can be achieved quite easily for short intervals of connected speech. The upper bound for an isolated word speaking rate has been measured informally for trained speakers reading digits in random order.[†] A rate of 120-125 digits per minute was achieved with the best speakers. Each of the digits was classified correctly by a machine capable of recognizing isolated utterances. Measuring these rates is not possible without some objective measure that the words are not connected. The human ear is not a good judge of whether a brief pause actually exists between rapidly spoken words.

Another factor that should be mentioned concerns the duration of the utterances to be classified. A limited vocabulary system could be hypothesized in which each of the utterances in the limited vocabulary was of considerable duration. However, in keeping with the intentions of this review, the limited vocabulary systems described accept isolated words and short phrases up to several seconds in duration.

C. ADAPTATION

One of the major obstacles to progress in the field of ASR is the variation in speech between individuals. Such differences have made the search for the "universal" speech recognizer a formidable task. A practical bypass of the problem can be achieved by adapting a recognition system to the characteristics of the user. Since inter-speaker differences are far greater than intra-speaker differences, an order of magnitude of complexity can be eliminated by automatic speaker adaptation. It is for this reason that the first ASR systems to be used in practical applications have all employed speaker adaptation. No universal systems have been developed up to now that can perform for most users with an accuracy sufficient to be useful in an operating system.

D. OPERATIONAL CONSIDERATIONS FOR LIMITED VOCABULARY APPLICATIONS

1. NOISE BACKGROUND

Let us now consider some of the practical aspects of a limited vocabulary speech recognition system intended for operational use.

[†]Tests conducted by author.

One of the first to be considered is interfering acoustical signals and noise background. If a system is to be used with a high quality wide-ranging microphone, it will naturally pick up other sounds from within the immediate vicinity of the individual attempting to use the speech recognition system. There are two such solutions to this problem. The first solution is to remove the interfering sounds by placing the individual in an acoustically-shielded environment. Should this be possible, noise backgrounds can be reduced generally to the point where they are non-interfering. However, the restrictions resulting from an acoustic enclosure are such that the mobility of the individual is reduced and can possibly eliminate any ability to perform any other functions. Many applications which are economically justifiable for a speech recognition system involve an individual who will do more than one function at a time. The purpose of the speech recognition system is to add to his capabilities or remove some of the overload on his manual or visual operations. Usually this type of an individual cannot be placed in a restrictive enclosure.

The second method of removing interfering sounds is to eliminate the noise at the microphone itself. Close-talking, noise-cancelling microphones and contact microphones will both achieve a degree of noise cancellation. The contact microphone, however, does not pick up many of the attributes of the unvoiced frictional sounds. It is, therefore, a device which can be used only with a very limited capability speech recognizer. The contact microphone can also produce erroneous signals that are a result of body movement. Therefore, a close-talking, boom-mounted, noise-cancelling microphone worn on a lightweight headband is the optimum compromise between obtaining high quality speech and reducing noise backgrounds.

2. BREATH NOISE

Once it is determined that a close-talking, noise cancelling microphone is to be used for a speech recognizer, a very critical factor must be considered in the system. This factor relates to extraneous signals caused by breath noise. A highly-trained speech researcher working in a laboratory will be able to pronounce distinct utterances to an automatic speech recognizer. Unconsciously he will control his breathing such that when he is producing the speech signal it is crisp and well-pronounced. He can be lulled into a sense of false achievement until the first time an untrained speaker, having little or no interest in his work, speaks into the system with very poor results. A similar result will occur for an individual who is doing no physical movement whatsoever. This individual can achieve very high recognition accuracies on a particular system. However, once he begins to move around and perform other functions, recognition can deteriorate. The most likely cause for lower recognition accuracy in both cases is breathing noise. A strong tendency exists to exhale at the end of isolated words and to inhale at the beginning. Inhaling produces no significant direct air blast on the close-talking microphone, whereas exhaling can produce signal levels in a microphone comparable to speech levels. In a limited vocabulary, isolated word recognition system, the breath noise can be a serious problem.

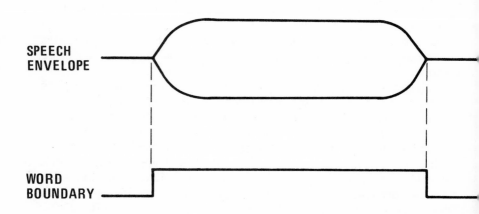

SPEECH
ENVELOPE

WORD
BOUNDARY

Shown in Figure 1 is a well-pronounced, isolated utterance and a logically derived word boundary signal. Regardless of the method used for determining the word boundary it is very important that the actual beginning and ending of the word are determined. Accurate word boundary determination is the single most critical factor in an isolated word or phrase recognition system. Gross inaccuracies in word boundary detection can occur because of breath noise as shown in Figure 2. The detrimental effects caused by the incorrect word boundary indication because of breath noise can be somewhat overcome by backing-up a constant amount from a tentative initial word boundary indication. This is not a total solution, however, since many times the duration of the breath noise is longer than the speech signal and is of comparable magnitude. Furthermore, the spectrum of the

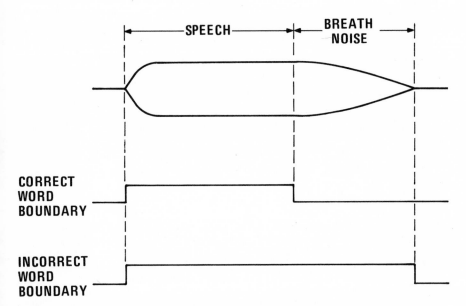

Figure 2. Speech and Breathing

speech signal overlaps the spectrum where significant speech information occurs. In order to achieve recognition accuracies in a practical operational system equivalent to or superior to those rates obtainable with keying, it is necessary to separate speech from breath noise, regardless of the duration and magnitude of the breath noise. This can be achieved only by utilizing pattern recognition processing which discriminates between speech sounds (voice or unvoiced) and the frictional breath noises. The back-up duration will then be of a variable duration, depending on the duration of the breath noise.

3. Word Boundary

It has already been mentioned in the discussion on breath noise that a variable back-up duration was desirable from an initially derived word boundary signal. If a variable back-up is not used, a fixed duration back-up can be of some value. An initial word boundary signal can be derived from a combination of amplitude of the speech signal overall or amplitude within predetermined spectral bands. This word boundary signal must not, however, be responsive to brief intervocalic pauses caused by the stop consonants and affricatives. Figure 3 illustrates this point for the word "sixteen". The initial word boundary extends beyond the end of the word by an amount somewhat greater

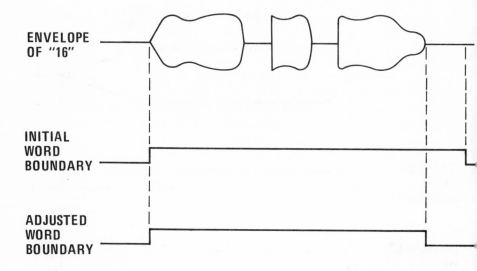

ENVELOPE
OF "16"

INITIAL
WORD
BOUNDARY

ADJUSTED
WORD
BOUNDARY

Figure 3. Internal Stop Consonant Pauses Within a Word

than the duration of the short pauses from the internal stop consonants. In this case an adjustment to the actual word boundary can be made by a fixed duration back-up. The fixed duration back-up will more accurately locate the end of the word, although the best results are obtained with variable back-up.

4. Operator-Originated Babble

It is inevitable that an operator using an automatic speech recognition system will wish to communicate with his supervisor or other individuals within his area. Regardless of the ease with which an ON/OFF switch can be utilized by an operator, he will occasionally forget to turn the microphone off and will begin to carry on a conversation with another individual. Since the operator will rarely use the words that are in the limited vocabulary the speech recognition system should generally reject the ordinary conversation. It is important in practical applications that a reject capability exists so that inadvertent conversation, sneezes, coughs, throat clearings, etc. do not produce spurious recognition decisions. Both audible and visual alerts can be supplied to the operator indicating that he is talking into a live microphone. This will minimize the number of inadvertent entries that are made into a speech recognition system. Another safeguard to prevent inadvertent message entry to the speech recognition system is to format the data entry sequence as much as possible so that after a block of data has been entered, a verification word is required before the entry is considered to be valid by the speech recognition system.

5. Aids to Operator

It is possible to utilize some of the unique features of ASR to assist the user in performing a particular function. The following discussion is a partial list of such features:

a. Multiple-Task Capability

ASR systems are unique in their ability to obtain data or commands from a user whose hands are already occupied in other functions. The only alternative in this situation is to have the data recorded by tape or a listener, or to require the manual process to be interrupted for the purpose of data collection.

b. Operator Mobility

By the use of a wireless transceiver an operator can have complete freedom of movement and still communicate with an ASR system.

c. Vocabulary Flexibility

An adaptive ASR system is trained for the speech characteristics of the user. Generally this is achieved by providing 5-10 repetitions of each word in the vocabulary as a set of reference data with which to compare future utterances. This reference data is usually stored for future use so that retraining need not be required each time an individual uses an ASR system. Because of the adaptive feature, a user is free to choose any word for a particular function. For example, the word chosen to verify the accuracy of a block of data that has been spoken and displayed to a user could be "GO" or "OK". The adaptive feature also makes it possible for limited vocabulary ASR systems to operate for any language.

d. Operator Interaction

When ASR systems are employed in data entry systems, all the advantages of source data entry are incurred. Only a single individual is responsible for the accuracy of the data being entered since no intermediate operators are required. It is also possible to interact directly with the operator when spoken entries indicate the need for special instructions. This interaction occurs in real-time and is, therefore, a very useful feature in applications with a requirement for real-time processing. Real time feedback, either visual or aural, can guide the operator through a complete process and can allow for error correction by control words such as "erase".

E. ECONOMICS OF ASR

The final factor that will determine if ASR systems achieve widespread application is an economic one. Assuming that ASR systems can achieve acceptable recognition accuracies for limited vocabularies, we are then left solely with a determination of whether an ASR system offers cost savings. Direct cost savings can result from either increased productivity or labor savings. Indirect savings can result from elimination of training (since relatively unskilled personnel can use ASR systems) and of subsequent keying operations which usually follow data capture. In considering the fact that ASR systems fall into this category of source data entry systems, some interesting statistics should be cited. In the data entry field for every dollar spent in keying operations (keypunch, key-to-disc, key-to-tape) another three to four times this amount is spent in data capture.[†]

With respect to the direct cost savings it is apparent that anything performed by an ASR system can be achieved by a human listener and a keyboard. In this regard the ASR system competes directly with the cost of a human listener. A critical threshold occurs when the cost of an ASR system equals that of a human used for data capture. When ASR systems cost less than the equivalent functions performed by humans, a strong cost justification results for ASR systems. Indeed, this is the classical justification for virtually all recent trends toward automation. It is not surprising, therefore, that the very first practical applications of ASR occurred in the early '70's in industries with 2 or 3 shift operations. The ASR system can perform quite adequately 24 hours a day, thereby increasing the cost justification for these applications. The present trend is such that ASR systems will fall below the annual costs of a human operator on a single shift basis in early 1975. This will broaden the applications potential substantially.

F. PROCESSING FUNCTIONS IN ASR SYSTEMS

In an isolated-word speech recognition system, the individual words are spoken with a short pause between each word. Consequently, the words can be segmented prior to decision and classification processes. The fact that the word is segmented by pauses before a decision is required permits a wide variety of decision techniques to be applied. Knowledge of word boundaries implies that high recognition accuracies for the limited vocabulary can be obtained with any of several methods. Complex logical processing is avoided by

---

[†]Phillip H. Dorn, "Whither Data Entry", Datamation, p. 41, March 1973.

choosing a vocabulary of dissimilar words whenever possible. If words other than the limited vocabulary are spoken into the system, either rejects or sporadic recognition outputs may result. Such responses may be minimized, however, by requiring that the input utterance possess a minimum number of properties which are common to one of the vocabulary words.

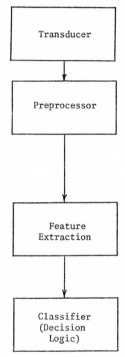

Figure 4   Speech Recognition Processes

Four processing functions are common to most automatic speech recognition systems. These functions as shown in Figure 4 consist of a microphone transducer, a preprocessor, a feature extractor and a final decision-level classifier. Early attempts at automatic speech recognition either deleted entirely the feature extraction process or utilized a simplified form of template matching. Experience with template matching soon led to the realization of its limitations. Slight variations of the individual speech samples of a particular word would result in gross misclassifications. This limitation resulted in the impractical requirement for a large memory containing a pattern and all its prototypes. These systems were generally quite sensitive to less than ideal speech and deteriorated rapidly with respect to poor articulation, noise background, emotional stress, coughs, or other extraneous acoustic events.

Considerable mathematical formalism has been developed for various automatic speech recognition processes. However, no general theory exists which can preselect the information-bearing portions of the speech signal. Therefore, the design of the feature extractor is heuristic and must use ad hoc strategy. Only actual experimental data can determine the value of a particular feature set. It is this particular dilemma which has resulted in the recent increased emphasis given feature extraction research.

It is possible to form many transformations of the speech signal which would enhance certain properties and make them more easily detectable in an automatic speech-recognition system. However, speech is neither periodic nor aperiodic, but must be considered as a quasi-periodic signal so that analytical techniques that are developed must reflect temporal features of significance as well as spectral features. Maintaining this dual viewpoint throughout the analysis requires a modification of classical time-domain and frequency-domain analytical techniques. To retain both of these characteristics in a frequency analysis, a method which produces a short-duration spectrum is essential.

Frequency-domain representation of the speech signal is particularly advantageous since (1) it is known that the human auditory system performs a crude frequency analysis at the periphery of auditory sensation and (2) because it has been shown, by acoustical analysis of the vocalization system, that an exact description of the speech sounds can be obtained with a natural frequency concept model of speech production.

Spectrum analysis can be achieved either by direct analog circuitry or through the use of the Fast Fourier Transform (FFT) and a high-speed digital computer. In both these methods, equivalent problems occur. The FFT produces a discrete spectrum which, with a sufficiently high sampling rate, approaches that of the continuous Fourier Transform. Many different types of data windows have been utilized in the FFT. The choice of the window is similar to the choice of the filter response in the analog spectrum analyzer. A "picket-fence" effect can occur both in the FFT and the analog spectrum analyzer representing the contributions of the individual filters in the analog analyzer or the separate coefficients of the various terms in the FFT calculation. The point to be made here is that spectrum analysis is only the first step in the feature extraction process. Considerable additional processing is required in order to achieve the detection and recognition of the information-bearing elements (significant features) of the speech signal which has been transformed to accentuate these elements in the spectrum analysis process.

The final processing level after the recognition of the elemental speech features is the decision logic. For isolated words, it is possible to examine the feature sequences produced and to determine the closest match to a set of stored samples previously obtained for a given talker (or talkers). The decision involving the closest match is made at the end of the word and can be achieved with relatively simple processing techniques.

G. RECOGNITION ACCURACY

A representative indication of recognition accuracies that can be obtained with limited vocabulary ASR systems is available from test data obtained in early 1974. It should be stated that only those results are quoted that have been obtained from systems with which the author is associated. No attempt has been made to poll workers in the field about their results. However, the results quoted are all for systems developed for practical operational requirements. The recognition accuracies quoted have either been witnessed or verified by independent parties. At the time of this writing in mid-1974, significant improvements have been made in recognition accuracy from that of early 1974. It is expected that general progress in ASR will be reflected in exceptionally high recognition accuracies in limited vocabulary systems.

1. High Quality Tests

The simplest test of performance for a limited vocabulary ASR system is to test performance for the digits 0-9. Recognition accuracy is defined as the number of correct responses divided by the total number of words spoken, i.e.,

$$\text{Per cent recognition accuracy} = \frac{100 \text{X Correct responses}}{\text{Correct responses} + \text{Incorrect responses} + \text{Reject responses}}$$

The test results for the digits are shown in Figure 5.[†] Each of the

---

[†]T. B. Martin, E. F. Grunza, "Voice Control Demonstration System", Final Contract Report, Contract No. F33615-73-C-1075, Wright-Patterson Air Force Base, Ohio, June, 1974.

speakers used in the tests trained the system on 10 repetitions of each digit. The training data was obtained one week prior to the test for 5 speakers, and immediately prior to the test for 5 other speakers. The digits were spoken in quasi-random order, and each speaker was tested for 240 digits (24 occurrences of each digit). The average recognition accuracy of 99.79% was obtained for a noise background typical of a normal office.

Speaker No.	No. of Test Utterances	No of Incorrect Responses	No of Reject Responses	% Recognition Accuracy
1	240	0	0	100
2	240	0	0	100
3	240	0	0	100
4	240	0	0	100
5	240	0	0	100
6	240	0	0	100
7	240	0	0	100
8	240	1	0	99.58
9	240	0	1	99.58
10	240	2	1	98.75
	2400		Ave.	99.79%

Figure 5. Digit Recognition Results.

A comparison of the results that can be achieved with other vocabulary groups was also measured. In the appendix is a list of eleven groups of words containing 12 words in each group. The vocabulary represents words used in various aircraft operations and contains words much longer than the digits. The grouping is a functional one and does not reflect any attempt to eliminate phonetically similar words. Each of the speakers used for the digit tests was tested on one of the vocabulary groups. One of the speakers was tested on two sets to make up the total test of eleven vocabulary groups. The results of these tests are shown in Figure 6. An overall recognition average score of 99.32% was obtained for these tests.

Vocabulary Group	Speaker No.	No. of Test Utterances	No. of Incorrect Responses	No. of Reject Responses	% Recog. Accuracy
S1	1	120	0	0	100
S2	2	120	1	1	98.33
S3	3	120	0	0	100
S4	3	120	0	1	99.17
S5	4	120	0	0	100
S6	5	120	2	0	98.33
S7	6	120	0	1	99.17
S8	7	120	1	0	99.17
S9	8	120	1	0	99.17
S10	9	120	0	1	99.17
S11	10	120	0	0	100
		----			-----
		1320		Ave.	99.32%

Figure 6. Non-Digit Recognition Results.

2. HIGH BACKGROUND NOISE TESTS

A series of performance tests were conducted with a system operating in a high noise background of 85-90 dB. The 34 word vocabulary for these tests consisted of the digits 1 through 34. The normal pronunciations used in counting were utilized, e.g., 21 was pronounced as a single word "twentyone"; rather than the two separate words "two" - "one". The results from these tests are shown in Figure 7. The overall recognition accuracy of 98.5% was obtained using 12 speakers, 6 of whom had less than one hour of experience with the ASR system.

H. TYPICAL APPLICATIONS

Some of the areas in which ASR systems have applications are

1. Automated Material Handling

2. Quality Control Inspection

3. Inventory Taking and Control

4. Direct Communication with Computers

5. Machine Control

TEST CONDITIONS

VOCABULARY: 34 WORDS (1 THROUGH 34)

NO. OF SPEAKERS: 12 TOTAL

                                                - 6 EXPERIENCED
                                                - 6 LESS THAN 1 HOUR EXPERIENCE

NOISE LEVEL: 85-90 dB OF MACHINE NOISE

SPEAKING RATE: 20-30 WORDS/MIN.

TEST RESULTS

NO. OF TEST UTTERANCE= 9,149

NO. OF CORRECT RESPONSES   = 9,012

NO. OF REJECTS & INCORRECT RESPONSES   = 137

% RECOGNITION ACCURACY   = 98.5%

Figure 7. Results for 34 Word Vocabulary.
In High Noise Background

One of the characteristics common to most applications of ASR is that the operator's hands and/or eyes are already busy with other functions. The first ASR systems to be used by industry in these various applications were installed in the early '70's. The results obtained from these initial operating systems indicate that a factory worker with minimal training can use an ASR system quite successfully. Recognition accuracies obtained were equal to or superior to keying accuracies obtained from the same personnel. Original training data for a speaker has been found to be stable over many months, thereby eliminating the need for frequent retraining and updating of the reference data.

As of this writing well over 10,000,000 words have been

spoken into operational ASR systems with which the author is familiar. This type of statistical base has pointed out many previously unsuspected aspects of the human factors of ASR systems. Extreme care must be given to designing ASR systems to operate in a manner most acceptable to the user.

I. CONCLUSIONS

The significant conclusion that can be drawn from the above discussion is that, for the first time, limited vocabulary ASR systems have moved from the laboratory to successful applications in industry. Future developments in both new applications and increased capability ASR systems can be expected to follow.

ACKNOWLEDGEMENT

The author would like to acknowledge that portions of the test results presented were sponsored by AF Avionics Laboratory, Wright-Patterson AFB, Ohio.

APPENDIX I. VOCABULARY SUBSETS FOR NON-DIGIT RECOGNITION.

S1	S2
COMMUNICATIONS	OFF
IFF	INTERCOM
STORES	UHF
FAILURE MONITOR	VHF
PEN AIDS	DATA LINK
ENERGY MANAGEMENT	VOICE
FLR	SECURE
HEADING	CLEAR
MASTER MODE	VOLUME
NAVIGATION	CHANNEL
INERTIAL MEASUREMENT	FREQUENCY
ILS	FIRE CONTROL

S3	S4
OFF	RADAR
NORMAL	IR
EMERGENCY	RHEW
MODE	LASER
ONE	TV
TWO	RDI

THREE – A
C
ACCEPT COORDINATES
ALIGN
MANUAL
AUTOMATIC

VISUAL
SINGLE
RIPPLE
SALVO
MANUAL STEP
JETTISON

S5

FOOT
SECONDS
NOSE
TAIL
SAFE
BOTH
BALLISTIC
GUIDED
RETARDED
QUANTITY
SELECT
REPEAT

S6

MANUAL READY TEST
PRE FLIGHT TEST
FIRE CONTROL
NAVIGATION
B DA
PEN AIDS
STORES
COMMUNICATIONS
IFF
ENERGY MANAGEMENT
DISPLAYS
LANDING GEAR

S7

FUEL SYSTEM
ENVIRONMENT CONTROL
LIGHTS
ESCAPE CAPSULE
ELECTRICAL SYSTEM
HYDRAULIC SYSTEM
LASER SPOT
LASER RANGE
LOW LEVEL TV
FLIR
WEAPON INERTIAL NAVIGATION
AUTOMATIC

S8

HF JAMMER
MF JAMMER
LF JAMMER
IR JAMMER
CHAFF
FLARES
LOCATE
DESTROY
EVADE
ENTER
ERASE
TERMINATE

S9

Min Time Climb
Min Fuel Climb
Min Time Dive
Terrain Follow
Min IFC Altitude
Altitude Command
Clear Plane
Doppler Inert
Inert
Doppler Air Mass
Air Mass
Erase

S10

Beacon
Groun Map Shaped
Air Ground Ranging
Ground Map Pencil
Terrain Avoidance
T.V.
Off
Terrain Following
Skip
Automatic
Tacan
Manual

S11

Terrain Following
Landing
Visual
Offset
Radar Bomb
Nav Bomb
Ground Allign
Normal
Inertial
Magnetic Slave
Grid
Off

S12

Zero
One
Two
Three
Four
Five
Six
Seven
Eight
Niner
Erase
Terminate

AUTOMATIC SPEECH RECOGNITION: OLD AND NEW IDEAS

Peter•B. Denes
Bell Laboratories
600 Moutain Avenue
Murray Hill, New Jersey 07974

ABSTRACT

A review of the literature indicates that automatic speech recognition of 20 to 50 words spoken in isolation by one or more cooperative speakers is now possible with above 90% recognition rates: a number of different methods for acoustic analysis and decision logic - when competently performed by state of the art techniques - appear to be equally effective.

It may well be that the phonetic contrasts of a suitably chosen small set of words are an important factor in making these high success rates possible. However, when dealing with a larger number of words or with connected speech, the phonetic contrasts are no longer sufficient and the acoustic ambiguities of the speech wave can be resolved only by applying articulatory, linguistic, and semantic information.

Two quite separate directions are emerging in automatic speech recognition research. One direction will concentrate on recognizers restricted to a small vocabulary. It will explore ways of maintaining under real-life, in-the-field conditions the high recognition rates already being obtained in the laboratory. The finding of practical applications where such recognizers can be used effectively is an important part of this work.

The second direction will - hand in hand with research on the human speech process - explore operational methods for applying higher level information to decoding the acoustic ambiguities encountered when recognizing larger vocabularies and continuous speech.

HISTORICAL NOTES

The first papers on automatic speech recognition were published just over 22 years ago (Dreyfus-Graf, 1950; Davis et al., 1952; Fry and Denes, 1953). Typically, these devices could achieve high recognition scores for a dictionary of about ten words. The words had to be spoken in isolation and by a single speaker whose voice the machine was adjusted to; considerably lower scores were obtained when the voice of several speakers was used. Many further attempts followed which aimed at successful recognition of a larger variety of words, spoken either in isolation or in context, and by more than just one speaker. The earlier devices used analog circuits to perform the necessary acoustic analysis and decision logic; from about 1960 onwards, computers were used to an increasing extent. By now, well over one hundred papers have appeared in the literature describing various experiments on such devices.

This extensive research has, over the years, brought about noticeable improvements in the performance of automatic speech recognizers. Devices that offer over 90% recognition for about twenty to fifty words spoken in isolation are now a possibility. Such devices might cope successfully with the voice of not just one but of several speakers, or they may be adjusted for a single speaker and readjust themselves to a new speaker, rapidly and automatically.

The experiments on automatic recognition usually dealt with words which were spoken in a reasonably careful, though not artificially slow, manner and under laboratory conditions. There is however little information about how speech produced under various more every-day conditions might affect recognition scores. For example, ambient noise and room reverberation might make a difference; there are also many noises, like heavy breathing, that are difficult to separate from the speech waves even though they occur fairly commonly in every-day, as opposed to laboratory, conditions. Also, ambient sounds are known to affect speaking habits: for example, in a noisy room speakers often shout without even being aware of it. The effect of such and similar factors has yet to be explored.

It is perhaps more significant that - despite claims to the contrary - there is little prospect that simple refinements of these present techniques will lead to devices which would recognize a substantially larger variety of words or deal with continuous speech. This might seem disappointing, but then past recognition techniques were concerned with only the acoustic characteristics of speech and largely ignored the many ways in which these acoustic properties are affected by conditions at other levels of the speech process. Yet the considerable advances that have been made during the same period of time in the understanding of the speech process (Liberman et al., 1967) leave little doubt that the acoustic properties of speech sounds are indeed strongly influenced by articulatory, linguistic, and semantic processes which are an essential part of our speech activity. The reason why these "higher" level activities have not been taken into account so far is probably only partly the deep-seated - and quite mistaken - feeling that "acoustic invariants" do exist, that is, acoustic features that uniquely define the phonemic, syllabic or word units of speech. Another, more practical, reason for why speech recognizers of the past have dealt largely on the acoustic level, might be that implementing the effect of those higher level influences is a truly difficult task and not enough is yet known about either how they operate or how to implement their influence. However, recently there have been clear indications that considerable research effort is being devoted to apply such higher level information to decoding the acoustic signals (Newell et al. 1971). This seems an appropriate point in time therefore to review past work and see how it can help in the new work ahead.

PAST METHODS OF ANALYSIS AND RECOGNITION

In reviewing this work, there is no need for discussing individually each recognition scheme tried in the past, because several excellent reviews of this kind already exist (Lindgren, 1965; Hyde, 1972), as well as extensive lists of references (Pierce, 1969; Martin, 1970). Instead, what follows is intended as a more general view, looking at what acoustic characteristics were - and were not - utilized by recognition devices and how these characteristics were analyzed; what decision logic was employed to obtain recognition; what recognition scores were obtained and what these scores reveal - or do not reveal - about the effectiveness of the various recognition schemes they claim to evaluate.

Automatic speech recognition research started in an era when it was firmly believed that the information necessary for recognition was embedded in the shape of the spectral envelope of the speech wave. Spectral analysis was probably adopted because at that time it was instrumentally the most convenient and historically the most appropriate: filter banks were readily available and the channel vocoder as well as the Speech Spectrograph were just becoming well known in the speech research community. In subsequent years, automatic recognition research benefited greatly from advances in bandwidth compression technology as used for speech transmission.

As a result of these advances - although spectral analysis continued to be used for recognition purposes - a great variety of other methods, some using time domain and others frequency domain analysis have also been tried. They included, among others, numerous techniques for spectral analysis and for formant extraction, autocorrelation techniques, zero-crossing density counts, and linear prediction analysis. The advantages and disadvantages of these various approaches are reasonably well understood (Flanagan 1972). Usually a choice of methods is available for analyzing a particular parameter of the acoustic speech signal. For example, several of the time and frequency domain analyses provide the same kind of information, although some might be preferable when hardware implementation is required and others might be selected when computers are used. Again, zero-crossing counts are sometimes easy to implement, but the result is no more - and no less - than an estimate of the principal spectral component or formant in a particular frequency band. Spectral envelopes can be obscured by the harmonic structure of the signal, but again methods are available for overcoming this difficulty. Formant extraction methods, some using time domain and others fequency domain techniques, have emerged which are considerably better than earlier methods such as spectral peak picking.

The various analysis techniques also differ in the extent to which they take into account known properties of the speech production mechanism. A bank of filters that analyzes the input signal in terms of energy distributions across the spectrum would deal equally with any acoustic signal: better results might perhaps be obtained by matching the analysis technique to the properties of the signal source. In the case of speech, one obvious way of doing this is by searching directly for the resonances of the vocal tract. Formant tracking using analysis-by-synthesis techniques - as opposed to picking spectral peaks - and the now so-popular linear prediction approach are examples of this: they both include a resonance model of the vocal tract and their analysis is performed by reference to this model.

This point of view is important also one stage futher, in the recognition process itself, when the analysis results are used by the discrimination logic. Here again, reference patterns of purely acoustic characteristics can be accumulated for each of the utterances to be recognized; highly sophisticated statistical discrimination techniques are then available for finding which of these reference patterns provides the best match for the pattern of acoustic cues derived from the utterance to be recognized. The alternative approach is "feature extraction." Here the acoustic characteristics of the signal are first interpreted according to "features" which are known to have perceptual or linguistic significance - for example, nasalization, front/back articulation, or stress. The recognition process is then performed by comparing the presence or absence of such features in the reference utterances and in the utterance to be recognized.

There can be no doubt though that feature extraction is considerably more promising for future improvement because the features can take into account known properties of human perception. The system can therefore selectively concentrate on those aspects of the input that are known to help in human recognition.

SEGMENTATION

A feature extraction approach is also more appropriate for segmentation - identifying the boundaries of specific articulatory or linguistic constituents of speech. Successful segmentation of course will have to utilize not only the steady-state features discussed so far but also the prosodic and grammatical cues which will be mentioned later. Such segmentation is indispensible for extending significantly the repertoire of words to be recognized and for achieving recognition of continuous speech.

Segmentation could also be important for certain phoneme identification procedures: consonantal identification might well be most effective when concentrated at "manner" of articulation boundaries (Keller 1971).

THE USE OF PROSODIC FEATURES

The acoustic analysis techniques discussed so far were all concerned with detecting quasi-steady-state features: in the traditional view, this is where the essential information needed for recognition is embedded. By contrast, very little, if any attention has been given to the possibility of relevant information being carried by the fundamental frequency or by the duration of the speech signal. This is likely to change in the future, particularly because of the increased interest in applying grammatical or even semantic criteria to the recognition process. The prosodic features may well provide important cues for applying such higher level inputs. For example, fundamental frequency may well be useful for identifying syllabic boundaries, stress, or even phonemic identity.

Duration cues in particular have not only been ignored, but some recognition devices even use elaborate time normalization to eliminate durational variations. In some cases of course, time normalization can certainly be of help. At the same time, at least two instances come immediately to mind where time normalization might actually mislead. First, in faster speech, articulatory targets are less likely to be reached than in slower speech: when the faster speech is time-stretched, the target values reached will still have different values from those obtained for slower speech, and might lead to the indentification of the wrong phoneme. The second example is concerned with duration changes in both vowel and final consonant of a syllable, as a function of "voicing" or not "voicing" the final consonant. These duration changes are often a stronger guide to the voiced or unvoiced nature of the final consonant than the presence or absence of vocal cord vibration (Denes, 1955). Time normalization, especially some non-linear methods, will eliminate such durational distinctions.

RELATIVE MERITS OF PAST RECOGNITION SYSTEMS

Comparison of the recognition scores recorded in the literature does not give as much information as one would like to have for assessing the relative advantages of the different recognition techniques. Almost all published scores refer to the performance of an entire system: only rarely are scores given for the individual components of the devices under investigation. It is therefore usually difficult to track the improvement due to a single element of the entire device.

Another difficulty in making meaningful comparisons is that, for each system described, the scores are given for a single, fixed set of words: there is little indication how quickly the scores obtained would change if the vocabulary of input words were to be increased or decreased.

Yet another difficulty in making meaningful comparisons is that the phonetic contrasts in the words chosen for the ensemble to be recognized will certainly affect the scores obtained. The phonetics of the speech material used for testing the various devices described in the literature vary sufficiently that it is doubtful whether it is the differences in recognition techniques or the differences in the phonetics of the words that were responsible for the different scores. This is compounded further by language to language phonetic differences and by the inevitable variations in subjects' speaking habits from one research project to another.

The overwhelming impression given by the mass of available literature is that present techniques can offer 90% scores or better for recognizing twenty to fifty words spoken in isolation, regardless of which of a number of techniques has been employed. Frequency or time domain techniques, formant tracking or linear prediction, pattern matching or feature extraction, when performed competently in the light of our current knowledge of speech signal analysis, will produce very similar results. In other words, in recent years acoustic signal analysis techniques have advanced sufficiently that a competent expert can select and implement a suitable method for extracting from the speech wave whatever of its characteristics he considers necessary for the automatic recognition task. Furthermore, there is no strong indication that greater accuracy or refinement in measuring the formants or other acoustic characteristics of the speech wave would lead to more successful recognition. The fact that human listeners have no difficulty in understanding the speech of a great variety of speakers who, after all, are unlikely to adjust their tongue and lips to exactly the same positions when pronouncing the same words, also indicates that considerable precision of acoustic analysis is not required.

THE USE OF CONTEXT FOR AUTOMATIC RECOGNITION

It might well be that a set of up to 50 or so words, reasonably chosen from the point of view of their phonetic structure, has sufficient phonetic/acoustic contrast to obtain successful recognition using well-chosen state-of-the-art methods of analysis and of discrimination. Once the vocabulary to be recognized exceeds such a limited number, or when connected speech is to be recognized, experience indicates that the acoustic ambiguities increase greatly. Recognition of such material - if possible at all - will require that linguistic/semantic influences, as well as the constraints arising from the physiological and anatomical structure of the vocal organs themselves, have to be taken into consideration.

A good example of the ambiguity of acoustic cues and of the extent to which human listeners use linguistic information in speech perception is given by what often happens during a conversation over a noisy telephone line. General conversation is relatively effortless; however, if an unfamiliar proper name is mentioned, it often has to be spelled before it is understood. The acoustic cues are equally ambiguous throughout the conversation. Yet contextual cues make conversation possible and may even convince the listener that he hears the acoustic cues of each word clearly and unambiguously. In actual fact the listener is relying on contextual cues for satisfactory perception: these contextual cues are weaker for proper names and these words therefore become unintelligible. Most automatic recognition devices of the past utilize acoustic cues only and they are therefore at a strong disadvantage compared with the human listener.

The intricate processing that is involved in human speech

recognition and that must be understood for designing automatic recognizers is well demonstrated by the difficulty that even experts have in reading speech spectrograms. Although the information presented by the spectrograms is in many ways similar to that used to control the output of a channel vocoder. The acoustically presented information from the vocoder is intelligible, while visual scanning of spectrograms is not. The problem of reading spectrograms also led to one of the most refreshingly novel speech recognition experiments of recent years (Klatt and Stevens 1972). This experiment studied the methods employed and the progress achieved by two speech experts who were set the task of reading the spectrograms of a number of spoken sentences. The lessons learnt from such and similar experiments should provide valuable information about the methods and strategies to be programmed into automatic recognizers.

DIRECTIONS OF FUTURE RECOGNITION RESEARCH

It appears therefore that the automatic speech recognition research of the next few years will advance in two, separate, directions: one direction will be concerned with the recognition of a limited vocabulary of words spoken in isolation; the other, with the recognition of larger vocabularies and probably with connected speech to some more limited extent.

As far as work on limited vocabulary recognizers is concerned, considerable further research is needed to make these devices cope with the real-life conditions of ambient noise, reverberation, and changing speaking habits. However, the main objective of this research must be to find the right practical application for such devices. Not only must the device prove that it can perform its recognition task successfully, but it must be shown that applications really exist where such devices can be employed economically and effectively. It must be remembered that push-buttons and photoelectric readers of labels are formidable and versatile competitors of voice input for controlling machinery and computers. They are real competitors because they can handle quantities of data quickly and reliably. It is up to automatic recognition research to show that voice input offers an attractive alternative.

The other direction of research aims to recognize a significantly wider range of words. These aims require almost a fresh start, because it appears that phonetic contrasts are no longer sufficient to distinguish the words by acoustic processing alone. Articulatory information will have to be applied to acoustic analysis, steady-state and prosodic cues must be utilized for segmentation, and the recognition procedure must be chanelled differently according to grammatic and semantic expectations.

Progress is likely to be very slow, partly because the entire system will now consist of so many separate components that must interact, and partly because so many of its parts are as yet largely unexplored. Some problems that will arise once such sophisticated systems are implemented can be guessed from what happened decades ago when application of linguistic information to automatic recognition was first tried (Fry and Denes, 1958). Linguistic information often helped, but occasionally also led to erroneous decisions. These errors were cumulative: an algorithm is therefore needed that from time to time assesses the recognition success, and re-starts the process when errors occur. An associated problem that immediately arises is -- how far to go back in the chain of decisions in such cases.

The articulatory mechanism is being studied extensively as part of on-going speech research: the results of this work will certainly be applied to improving automatic recognition devices. The formulation of operational methods for applying linguistic and semantic rules is a new area for speech research and its exploration is only just being started.

However difficult, these questions must be investigated - even if only on a limited scale at first - if progress is to be made with this type of automatic recognition.

It seems that both directions of research are now being pursued vigorously and the next few years should produce much interesting new knowledge about automatic recognition and also about human speech recognition on which all automatic recognition research must ultimately be based.

REFERENCES

Davis, K. H., R. Biddulph, S. Balashek, "Automatic recognition of spoken digits," J. Acoust. Soc. Am., Vol. 24, pp. 637-642, 1952.

Denes, P. B., "Effect of duration on the perception of voicing," J. Acoust. Soc. Am., Vol. 27, pp. 761-764, 1955.

Dreyfus-Graf, J., "Sonograph and sound mechanics," J. Acoust. Soc. Am., Vol. 22, pp. 731-739, 1950.

Flanagan, J. L., Speech Analysis, Synthesis, and Perception, Springer, New York, 1972.

Fry, D. B. and P. B. Denes, "Mechanical Speech Recognition," Communication Theory, London, Butterworth, pp. 426-432, 1953.

Fry, D. B. and P. B. Denes, "The solution of some fundamental problems in mechanical speech recognition," Language and Speech, Vol. 1, pp. 35-58, 1958.

Hyde, S. R., "Automatic speech recognition: a critical survey of the literature," Human Communication: A Unified View, E. E. David and P. B. Denes (eds), pp. 399-438, McGraw-Hill, New York, 1972.

von Keller, T. G., "On-line recognition system for spoken digits," J. Acoust. Soc. Am., Vol. 49, pp. 1288-1296, 1971.

Klatt, D. H. and K. N. Stevens, "Sentence recognition from visual examination of spectrograms and machine-aided lexical searching," 1972 Conference on Speech Communication and Processing, pp. 315-318, Inst. of Electr. and Electronic Engrs., New York, 1972.

Liberman, A. M., F. S. Cooper, D. P. Shankweiler, M. Studdert-Kennedy, "Perception of the speech code," Psychological Review, Vol. 74, pp. 431-461, 1967.

Lindgren, N., "Machine recognition of human language," IEEE Spectrum, Vol. 2, pp. 114-136, 1965.

Martin, T. B. Acoustic recognition of a limited vocabulary in continuous speech, University Microfilms, Ann Arbor, Mich., 1970.

Newell, A., (Chairman), Speech Understanding Systems: Final Report of a Study Group, Carnegie-Mellon University, Pittsburgh, 1971.

Pierce, J. R., "Whither speech recognition?," J. Acoust. Soc. Am., Vol. 46, pp. 1044-1051, 1969.

PHILOSOPHIES OF SPEECH RECOGNITION

E. P. Neuburg
National Security Agency
Fort Meade, Maryland 20755

In the few years that computers have been used to process speech there have appeared a number of papers describing the machine speech-recognition situation and suggesting lines of research that could lead to automatic speech recognition, e.g., Halle & Stevens (1962), Hyde (1968), Hill (1972) and Otten (1971). In this paper I would like to suggest that what accounts for most of the progress in automatic speech recognition, especially of continuous speech, is the enormous increase in compute power available to the speech researcher, rather than new discoveries about the speech signal. Similarly, many of the differences in emphasis between recognition research projects are attributable to differences in capacity and friendliness of local computer systems. If, as seems likely, advances in computers and systems are going to continue to make increased power available to the speech researcher, perhaps it behooves us, in planning research, to give more thought to how computers are being and should be used, than we presently do.

When one looks over the continuous speech recognition (CSR) situation, one has the impression that there was a stagnation in research until a couple of years ago, and one is led to ask why there was such a stagnation, and why there has been such a tremendous spurt of activity lately. One is also struck by the variety of philosophies and constraints underlying the projects currently under way, and it is natural to ask what constraints seem to be realistic and useful, why philosophies differ, and what methods seem to be most promising.

There is a popular belief in the speech community that research on recognition of connected speech went into limbo when John Pierce of Bell Labs wrote (Pierce, 1969) a letter in which he hinted that continuous speech recognition was a much harder problem than isolated word recognition; it is believed that this letter caused many researchers, especially those at Bell, to drop work on the subject, and that this accounts for the long stagnation. There is another popular belief that it was the fact that Defense Advanced Research Projects

Agency (ARPA) suddenly started putting many millions of dollars a year into speech understanding research that spurred the current interest in the problem.

These beliefs don't seem to jibe with the facts. By the time Pierce wrote his letter it had become clear to the speech community that isolated-word recognition was possible and even commercially exploitable. There had been any number of quite successful isolated word recognizers built, starting as far back as 1958 at University College (Denes, 1959). By May of 1970 a group from RCA was confident enough to strike out on their own and set up a new company (Threshold Technology Inc.) to market small-vocabulary word recognizers for use in industrial situations. But all of those who were working in this field and looking into the feasibility of applying their methods to continuous speech were convinced that many problems, such as contextual and stress transformations, and semantic and other ambiguities, made the continuous problem an order of magnitude more difficult than the isolated word problem. Thus long before the letter appeared the researchers who had looked at the problem already recognized Pierce's point. A few continuous-speech recognition projects were in progress, but by and large the speech recognition field was waiting for a significant occurrence that would allow more than the sort of marginal, nibbling-away advances that were taking place.

Now, why is it that a field that seemed to be in the doldrums in 1970 is the subject of so much research in 1974? It is true that the ARPA Speech Understanding Research project is putting a large amount of money into CSR and therefore attracting people to the field, but to say that this money caused the push is to put the cart before the horse, because at the same time ARPA was setting up the SUR project other organizations were getting into the continuous speech game. For example IBM launched a very ambitious CSR effort, planning to put some ten years, at 15 people per year, into an attempt to produce first-draft copy from spoken input. Sperry-Univac, too, started a sizeable CSR project, and so did several others. These efforts did not stem from or depend on the ARPA effort, but were parallel to it; in the case of IBM a part of their motivation may even be that they felt they could do better than the ARPA project.

Thus we must look beyond ARPA money to find the cause of all this interest. A naive conjecture might be that some advance in our knowledge of speech made a new attack seem feasible. Unfortunately, there is not a single speech parameter being extracted today that was not known about and being machine extracted ten years ago. The methods may be faster and more accurate, but there are no new facts or theories about speech. In fact the new ideas such as application of phonological rules or prosodics have arisen since or because of the start of the big push.

Is it possible that the building of a corpus of speech data was responsible? Again the answer is definitely no. One of the acute lacks felt by the ARPA system builders was a set of marked phonemic data on which to develop and test ideas. There was, it is true, a set of recently extracted data in the form of acoustic-phonetic rules or measurements on such things as phoneme duration, mostly developed by people working in speech synthesis. This was an advance that probably had some influence in pushing the community toward CSR research; however no large corpus of phonemically marked data is available even today.

An advance that perhaps did cause some impetus was the partial success of the artificial-intelligence people in devising such things as grammars and parsers for typed-input task-doing situations. Not being at ease in the subject of AI, I will not dwell on this topic, but it seems fairly clear, especially in view of the Newell report, (Newell et al., 1971) that some sort of signal was generated by the AI people to indicate that they thought they were ready to tackle the garbled input to be expected from a speech front end. Even here, the basis for their confidence seems to lie in advances made in the computer area.

Another possible factor was the recent advances in digital data processing techniques, examples being the FFT, digital filtering, off-axis Fourier transforms, and linear predictive coding, or LPC, which has enjoyed tremendous popularity lately.[†] These digital techniques, which of course are computer-based, have been of enormous benefit to the CSR effort; they seem to have played a large but not major part in the decision, if it can be called that, to start the effort. It is not clear that those responsible for CSR projects were aware of the potential of the new digital techniques, or perhaps even of their existence.

I would like to interject one comment here on the LPC calculation and subsequent derivation of spectrum, formants, and other parameters. I am among those who were dazzled by the great power afforded by LPC; however, a bit of reflection on the reasons for its widespread use has convinced me that the reason so many of us do the LPC-FFT in preference to other spectrum calculations is not its

---

[†]LPC is not exactly new, being a rediscovery of Wiener filtering, (Wiener, 1949) and even Wiener doesn't have priority since the idea was around in 1795 (Prony, 1795).

accuracy, or even its speed (which cannot be denied), but the fact that some of the hard decisions about spectral characteristics of the signal are taken out of our hands by the mechanical application of an LPC algorithm. It happens that LPC yields a smooth spectrum with well-defined peaks that are easy to find; the decision as to where the formants are may not be better or even as good as that made by a clever algorithm after a Fourier transform, but it is certainly easy to make. The real power of LPC lies in the fact that it throws away enough information that the speech researcher can get on with the job.

The developments and non-developments mentioned above do not seem to have been dominant in fostering CSR research. In fact the circumstance that seems to have made the whole thing possible has nothing to do with speech or even AI -- it was the availability (or promise) of friendly systems on large computers. Perhaps one can argue that speech or AI work had had some influence on hardware and software architecture; however such people as computational linguists seem to accept what tools they are given rather than trying to influence their development. It is true that Lincoln's Fast Digital Processor (the prizewinner for unimaginitive appellation) and other new very fast machines were developed in response to demands of speech researchers, among others; however they are not yet in wide use in CSR research, and certainly did not influence the decision to go ahead. It is also true that there were, and still are, a number of specially configured speech processing computer facilities, but it is only recently that computer systems have arisen that could handle not just (digitized) speech, but the whole hierarchical recognition process. And it is not the mere amount of calculation possible that makes computers so useful in CSR research. It is the fact that with a friendly system the speech or AI researcher can monitor the processes he is carrying out, and thereby get to understand and improve them. The new interactive computer systems bring the speech researcher right to the computer console, where he can manipulate the speech signal using whatever processes he feels are linguistically or phonetically appropriate. Real advances can be made by those who can observe on-line what effect a change in some process makes. Perhaps right now speech recognition is an art rather than a science; the artist doesn't want to wait for a compilation of results, he needs to be able to see now what he is doing.

The second impression mentioned at the beginning of this paper has to do with our posture today and with the differences among CSR efforts. It would be tedious and pointless to go into detail about what kinds of process take place in every module of every system, or how, for every decision made by a system builder, that decision affects the form of the recognizer. Further, analysis of the contribution from various parts of the recognition system and comparison of processes in modules are still in such a crude state that quantitative evaluation of techniques is difficult and unreliable. Thus the rest of this paper will simply be comments on a few places in the CSR operation where either 1) there seem to be important differences among systems, or 2) some or all CSR efforts appear weak, or 3) significant advances have taken place in CSR. As I have indicated earlier I will have to confine most of my remarks to the speech end of the process. This being the case, many of my remarks will apply equally to the recognition of isolated words, short phrases, and key words in running text, as well as to the general CSR problem.

The first problem to be dealt with in any CSR system is the speaker. Some projects seem to be setting up to deal with one or two speakers, some with several speakers. The consensus seems to be that a recognition system should have some sort of speaker normalization procedure and/or training of the machine for each speaker; the several-speaker requirement is, of course, spelled out in the ARPA specifications. My own feeling on this subject is that the consensus is wrong. We are trying to learn, at this stage, which processes will contribute to recognition and which will not, and I think, having to worry about speaker normalization makes harder a task that is already hard enough. If someone can build a continuous speech recognizer that works for just one speaker and satisfies, for example, all the other specs in the Newell report, he has made a major and useful breakthrough. This being the case, we should not waste time and energy on that part of the problem. It is not clear that extension of a working system to several speakers would be easy; there are some algorithms that are much harder to apply or less effective on some voices than on others. For example taking short-term spectra (that is, within a pitch period) is much more practical for males than for females, and impossible for children. However extension to several speakers should be trivial compared to the other problems that will have to be solved on the way to a working system.

Next in the process, and another point at which I seem to be at odds with most of the research community, is the input channel. The consensus here is that we should allow ourselves noise-free, distortion-free, high-bandwidth input to the system. Actually, the problems of overcoming noise and working with, say, telephone quality speech may be integral to the recognition process, especially if it is to have any applicability. Whereas having to deal with several speakers does little for our understanding of the problem, having to deal with noise, phase distortion, and limited bandwidth may actually help us find how the information is carried in speech. Further, there is some evidence that some of these are not difficult problems; commercial isolated-word recognizers are working today in 80dB ambient noise. Differential delay such as is found on telephone lines is not great enough to cause problems in parameter extraction algorithms like LPC, and the bandwidth limitation should affect only things like the fine categorization of fricatives from high-frequency spectral information; there are plenty of other clues to the identity of these sounds, as one can easily show by experiments with telephone speech.

In most recognition systems, after digitization rough segmentation is done, then through various decision processes generally involving spectral characteristics of 10-to-30ms slices, segmentation is improved and segments are labeled. The idea seems to be to produce a stream of elements having to do with the vocal gestures actually used by the speaker. A curious difference among projects arises here. Some installations have fast processors, and they extract and make available all parameters in every time slice. Other projects find parameter extraction painful, and think up clever schemes to do extraction of certain parameters only where necessary. Thus the decision as to what strategy will yield the best string of labeled segments may be based not on our knowledge of speech or vocal tract characteristics, but on compute power. A typical example of this situation is calculation of spectra, perhaps for finding formants. Some installations find this cheap, and routinely form spectra every 10ms, pick peaks, and track formants. Some even take two spectra, with long and short windows. Others find it expensive, and do it only at a few key places within segments already determined to be, say, vowels. It is not entirely clear which of the two situations leads to better end product, but the system having great compute power and extracting all parameters continuously should eventually do best; other researchers will think harder about what constraints are imposed by the nature of speech, but those with ability to compute and store will have a great deal more data at their disposal and will be willing to do more experimentation. In fact the magnitude of the semantics-syntax-lexicon driven speech-recognition problem is probably such that one should have as a research tool a computer setup considerably better than most of those being used now (typically a PDP-10 plus peripherals).

An example of a research area in which great compute power seems to be needed is the matching problem. By this is meant the following: at some stage every recognition scheme comes to a point at which some part of a stream of elements derived from the acoustic waveform is inspected to see if it contains a string, such as would be expected, if a word or syllable or other linguistic item were present. This must of course be done on some probabilistic basis, since no two acoustic manifestations of a linguistic entity are ever precisely identical. Thus some scoring scheme must be evolved to express the goodness of match between what is there and what is expected. So far, with few exceptions, the scoring schemes used can be charitably characterized as unsophisticated. Furthermore, it does not seem to have occurred to anybody to investigate the mathematical structure of the space in which matching takes place, or to find out what is meant by distance in such a space. Both these topics, the structure of the space of, say, phonemes, and the related search for a meaningful distance between linguistic (predicted) and acoustic (derived) elements, pose problems for which one wants a large data base and a large computer.

Another aspect of the system on which there is a wide divergence of opinion and technique is the question of how far up from the bottom to go before matching and scoring. That is, how much feature extraction and element identification should one do before matching with what the top end hypothesizes, and conversely how much synthesis or generative rule application should be carried out on top-end hypotheses. The answers range all the way from matching unnormalized frequency-domain patterns representing about half a phoneme, to matching long chains of extracted features representing syllables or even words. It would seem best if one could have a hierarchical system in which matching can be done at any of several levels; frequency domain, feature, phoneme, syllable, etc. One would match at the highest possible level as long as matches are good, dropping down toward the acoustic level only when the higher-level matching process gets in trouble. Incidentally, one suspects that humans operate in this way; perhaps the difference between so-called language-bound and stimulus-bound people is in the level at which they like to do their processing or matching. So far this sort of multi-level processing is being done in CSR only in the most rudimentary way.

Given a string of labeled elements and a scheme for scoring an element against a linguistic unit hypothesized by the top end, one must produce some kind of total score for a complete utterance. In this area, although much research is yet to be done, there have already arisen genuinely different philosophies of procedure. The differences arise from the fact that that one simply cannot score all possible strings of words at all places in the acoustic signal or even at all places in the segmented and labeled stream. One way of getting around this problem is to use some sort of additive score for a match at every point, and also for semantic and syntactic goodness at every point, and then use some form of dynamic programming or hill-climbing technique to find that string of linguistic units whose overall score is maximum given the string of acoustic-phonetic elements. Another approach is to choose places in the acoustic stream where decisions look easy to make, decide forever what linguistic events took place there, proceed to other parts of the stream and do the same, and continue until the chain of segments is consumed. Between these extremes are algorithms involving various forms and amounts of backtracking to develop and score candidate streams of linguistic elements. It is again not clear what technique is going to be most fruitful; I would conjecture, however, that whereas humans probably use a scheme close to the second one, the deterministic or islands-of-reliability technique, machine processes will do better using a maximum-likelihood technique. For if sophisiticated models and scoring schemes can be found, the probabilistic technique should evaluate all paths tried by any backtracking scheme, and thus be at least as powerful as backtracking. The added cost of a probabilistic scheme lies in the necessity for using information from the future to influence a present decision. That is, input must be stored and decisions delayed; but this mode of operation is natural for computers, while it is available to humans only in a very general sense.

The subject of prosodics is one that does not cause great differences in professed philosophy, but does cause differences in practice. All research groups vow an intention to use prosodics in their systems; however, very few are actually trying to do so. (In fact, there are a few who feel that it will not be necessary to use prosodics in view of the many other clues contained in speech.) The relative neglect of this source of information is most unfortunate. Prosodics would seem to be enormously important (certainly important to humans) and if we try to work on degraded speech, which we surely will sooner or later, prosodics will be indispensable. Such tasks as finding key words or word boundaries or even finding areas to start analysis on may depend heavily in CSR on prosodic information.

Before closing I would like to comment on a few of the places where speech recognition research has produced new information about speech. Certainly one such area is phonological rules. It is a little early to be commenting on this area, because it is at this moment in a state of rapid change, but some very good work has already been done as a direct result of the needs of CSR, and we have come a long way from the point where the number of published phonological rules could be counted on the fingers of one hand. We may even be on the threshold of evolving some theories of phonological change. To a lesser extent, acoustic-phonetic (more properly phonetic-acoustic) rules have been modified and sharpened; the improvements are not yet codified, but within the various CSR projects there are in use many improvements over the rules developed mostly by and for speech synthesis. Some definite progress has also been made in finding ways of normalizing across speakers. Before the CSR projects started, about the best scheme in use was that proposed by Gerstman (Gerstman, 1968). Here again the ideas are not yet in the literature, but individual projects are using quite sophisticated schemes. There are, of course, many advances in parameter extraction, digital processing, matching and decoding, perhaps even computer science, which are very important in CSR but do not particularly add to our knowledge of speech. All these, I am sure, will be brought out in later papers.

Regarded as systems to deal with very limited vocabulary, syntax and semantics, CSR efforts are beginning to yield results. Sentence recognition on the order of 10 to 40% is occurring, in times varying from 100 to 10000 times real time. I wish I could say that CSR research has also begun to give us a deeper understanding of how linguistic information is encoded into speech, but that doesn't seem to be so. It now looks as if CSR will soon achieve modest success, in that an expensive computer process will be able to understand connected human speech in highly special circumstances; the success will be due much more to advances outside the speech field, and to the careful selection and tuning of algorithms made possible by large and interactive computer systems, than to any discoveries about speech itself.

This last thought, if true, can be viewed in an optimistic light. For if we have come this far toward CSR with what many regard as a pathetically inadequate understanding of the speech-encoding process, the advances we can expect in our knowledge of speech should make genuine, useful, applied continuous-speech recognition a reality within the next 10 years.

REFERENCES

Atal, B. and Hanauer, "S., Speech Analysis and Synthesis by Linear Prediction of the Speech Wave." J. Acoust. Soc. Amer., Vol. 50, pp. 637-655 (1971).

Barnett, J., "A Vocal Data Management System." IEEE Trans. Audio Electroacoust., Vol. AU-21, (1973).

Bobrow, D. G., Hartley, A. K., and Klatt, D. H. "A Limited Speech Recognition System (II)." Bolt Beranek and Newman, Inc., Report No. 1819, Cambridge, Mass., (1969).

Broad, D. J., "Formants in Automatic Speech Recognition." Int. J. Man-Machine Studies, Vol. 4, pp. 411-424 (1972).

De Mori, R., "A Descriptive Technique for Automatic Speech Recognition." IEEE Trans. Audio Electroacoust., Vol. AU-21, No. 2 (1973).

De Mori, R., Gilli, L., and Meo, A. R., "A Flexible Real-Time Recognizer of Spoken Words for Man-Machine Communication." Int. J. Man-Machine Studies, Vol. 2, pp. 317-326 (1970).

Denes, P., "The Design and Operation of the Mechanical Speech Recognizer at University College, London." J. Brit. Inst. Radio Eng., Vol. 19, pp. 219-234 (1959).

Denes, P. and Mathews, M. V., "Spoken Digit Recognition Using Time Frequency Pattern Matching." J. Acoust. Soc. Amer., Vol. 32, pp. 1450-1455 (1960).

Dixon, N. R. and Tappert, C. C., "Derivation of Phonetic Representation by Combining Steady-State and Transemic Classification in Automatic Recognition of Continuous Speech." In Proc. Int. Conf. Speech Commun. Processing, pp. 319-321 (1972).

Fano, R., "A Heuristic Discussion of Probabilistic Decoding." IEEE Trans. Inform. Theory, Vol. IT-9, pp. 64-74 (1963).

Fant, C. G. M., "Automatic Recognition and Speech Research." Speech Transmission Lab., Royal Inst. Tech., Stockholm. STL/QPSR 1/1970, pp. 16-31 (1970).

Forgie, J. W. and Forgie, C. D., "Results Obtained from a Vowel Recognition Computer Program." J. Acoust. Soc. Amer., Vol. 31, pp. 1480-1489 (1959).

Fry, D. B., "Theoretical Aspects of Mechanical Speech Recognition." J. Brit. Inst. Radio Eng., Vol. 19, pp. 211-218 (1959).

Fry, D. B. and Denes, P. B., "The Solution of Some Fundamental Problems in Mechanical Speech Recognition." Lang. Speech, Vol. 1, pp. 35-38 (1958).

Gerstman, L. J., "Classification of Self-Normalized Vowels." IEEE. Trans. Audio Electroacoust., Vol. AU-16, pp. 78-80 (1968).

Halle, M. and Stevens, K., "Speech Recognition: A Model and a Program for Research." IRE Trans. Inform. Theory, Vol. IT-8, pp. 155-159 (1962).

Harris, K. S., "Cues for the Discrimination of English Fricatives in Spoken Syllables." Lang. Speech, Vol. 1, Part 1, pp. 1-6 (1958).

Hill, D. R., "An Abbreviated Guide to Planning for Speech Interaction with Machines: the State of the Art." Int. Jour. of Man-Machine Studies, Vol. 4, pp. 383-410 (1972).

Hill, D. R., "Man-Machine Interaction Using Speech." In Advances in Computers, Vol. 11, pp. 165-230. M. Yovits, Ed. Academic Press, N.Y. (1971).

House, A. S., Hughes, G. W., and Li, K-P., "Research on Word Spotting." Purdue Research Foundation, Purdue Univ., West Lafayette, Ind. Contract F19(628)-69-C-0276. Final Report, March 1972.

Hughes, G. W., "The Recognition of Speech by Machine." MIT Research Lab. Electron., Cambridge, Mass. Tech. Rep. 395 (1961).

Hughes, G. W., and Hemdal, J. F., "Speech Analysis." Purdue Research Foundation, Lafayette, Ind., Tech. Rept. TR-EE65-9 (1965).

Hyde, S. R., "Automatic Speech Recognition Literature Survey and Discussion." Res. Dept. Rept. No. 45, Post Office Res. Dept., Dollis Hill, London (1968).

Ichikawa, A., Nakano, Y., and Nakata, K., "Evaluation of Various Parameter Sets in Spoken Digits Recognition." IEEE Trans. Audio Electroacoust., Vol. AU-21 (1973).

Itahashi, S., Makino, S., and Kido, K., "Discrete-Word Recognition Using a Word Dictionary and Phonological Rules." IEEE Trans. Audio Electroacoust, Vol. AU-21 (1973).

Klatt, D. H. and Stevens, K. N., "On the Automatic Recognition of Continuous Speech: Implications from a Spectrogram-Reading Experiment." IEEE Trans. Audio Electracoust. Vol. AU-21 (1973).

Lea, W. A., "An Approach to Syntactic Recognition Without Phonemes." IEEE Trans. Audio Electroacoust., Vol. AU-21 (1973).

Lea, W. A., Medress, M. F., and Skinner, T. E., "Prosodic Aids to Speech Recognition," Tech. Reports PX 7940 and PX 10232, Univac Corp., St. Paul, Minn. (Oct. 1972 and April, 1973).

Li, K-P., Hughes, G. W., and Snow, T. B., "Segment Classification in Continuous Speech." IEEE Trans. Audio Electroacoust., Vol. AU-21 (1973).

Lindgren, N., "Machine Recognition of Human Language; Part 1: Automatic Speech Recognition." IEEE Spectrum Vol. 2, No. 3, pp. 114-136 (1965).

Makhoul, J. I., and Wolf, J. J., "Linear Predition and the Spectral Analysis of Speech." Bolt Beranek and Newman, Inc. Tech. Report No. 2304 (Aug. 1972).

Markel, J. D., "Formant Trajectory Estimation from a Linear Least Squares Inverse Filter Formulation." Speech Commun. Res. Lab., Santa Barbara, Cal. SCRL Monograph No. 7 (Oct., 1971).

Markel, J. D., "Digital Inverse Filtering - A New Tool for Formant Trajectory Estimation." IEEE Trans. Audio Electroacoust, Vol. AU-20, pp. 129-137 (1972).

Markel, J. D., "Application of a Digital Inverse Filter for Automatic Formant and FO Analysis." IEEE Trans. Audio Electroacoust., Vol. AU-21 (1973).

Medress, M., "A Procedure for the Machine Recognition of Speech." In Proc. Int. Conf. Speech Commun. Processing, pp. 113-116 (1972).

Neely, R. B. and Reddy, D. R., "Speech Recognition in the Presence of Noise." In Proc. 7th Int. Congr. Acoust., Vol. 3, pp. 177-180 (1971).

Nelson, A. L., Herscher, M. B., Martin, T. B., and Falter, J. W., "Acoustic Recognition by Analog Feature-Abstraction Techniques." In Models for the Perception of Speech and Visual Form, W. Wathen-Dunn, ed., MIT Press, Cambridge, Mass. (1967).

Newell, A. et al., "Speech-Understanding Systems: Final Report of a Study Group." Carnegie-Mellon Univ., Pittsburgh, Pa. (May 1971).

Niederjohn, R. J. and Thomas, I. B., "Computer Recognition of the Continuant Phonemes in Connected English Speech." IEEE Trans. Audio Electroacoust., Vol. AU-21 (1973).

O'Malley, M. H., Kloker, D. R., and Dara-Abrams, B., "Recovering Parentheses from Spoken Algebraic Expressions." IEEE Trans. Audio Electroacoust., Vol. AU-21 (1973).

Olson, H. F., and Belar, H., "Phonetic Typewriter III." J. Acoustical Soc. Amer. Vol. 33, pp. 1610-1615 (1961).

Otten, K., "Approaches to the Machine Recognition of Conversational Speech." In Advances in Computers, Vol. 11, pp. 127-163. M. Yovits, ed., Academic Press, N.Y. (1971).

Paxton, W. H., and Robinson, A. E., "A Parser for a Speech Understanding System." In Proc. International Joint Conf. on Artificial Intelligence (Aug., 1973).

Pierce, J. R., "Men, Machines, and Languages." IEEE Spectrum, Vol. 5, No. 7, pp. 44-49 (1968).

Pierce, J. R., "Whither Speech Recognition." J. Acoust. Soc. Amer., Vol. 46, p. 1049 (1969).

Prony, R., "Essai Experimental Et Analytique Sur Les Lois De Dilatabilite Des Fluides Elastiques Et Sur Celles De La Force Expansive De La Vapeur De L'Eau Et De La Vapeur De L'Alcool, A Differentes Temperatures." J. De L'Ecole Polytech. (Paris), Vol. 1, No. 2, pp. 24-76 (1795).

Reddy, D. R., "Computer Recognition of Connected Speech." J. Acoust.Soc. Amer. Vol. 42, pp. 329-347 (1967).

Reddy, D. R., and Robinson, A. E., "Phoneme-to-Grapheme Translation of English." IEEE Trans. Audio Electroacous., Vol. AU-16, pp. 240-246 (1968).

Reddy, D. R. and Vicens, P. J., "A Procedure for the Segmentation of Connected Speech." J. Audio Eng. Soc. Vol. 16, pp. 404-411 (1968).

Sakai, T. and Doshita, S., "The Automatic Speech Recogntion System for Conversational Sound." IEEE Trans. Electron. Comput., Vol. EC-12, pp. 835-846 (1963).

Scarr, R. W. A., "Zero-Crossings as a Means of Obtaining Spectral Information in Speech Analysis." IEEE Trans. Audio Electroacoust., Vol. AU-16, pp. 247-255 (1968).

Scarr, R. W. A., "Normalization and Adaptation of Speech Data for Automatic Speech Recognition." Int. J. Man-Machine Studies, Vol. 2, pp. 41-59 (1970).

Sebestyen, G., "Automatic Recognition of Spoken Numerals." J. Acoust. Soc. Amer., Vol. 32, p. 1516 (1960).

Stevens, K. N., "Toward A Model for Speech Recognition." J. Acoust. Soc. Amer., Vol. 32, pp. 47-55 (1960).

Tappert, C. C., Dixon, N. R., Rabinowitz, A. S., and Chapman, W. D., "Automatic Recognition of Continuous Speech Utilizing Dynamic Segmentation, Dual Classification, Sequential Decoding, and Error Recovery." Rome Air Development Center, Griffiss Air Force Base, Rome, N.Y. Tech. Rep. RADC-TR-71-146 (1971).

Tappert, C. C., Dixon, N. R., and Rabinowitz, A. S., "Application of Sequential Decoding for Converting Phonetic to Graphemic Representation in Automatic Recognition of Continuous Speech." IEEE Trans. Audio Electroacoust, Vol. AU-21 (1973).

Walker, D. E., "Automated Language Processing." In Annual Review of Information Science and Technology, Carlos A Cuadra, ed., American Soc. for Information Science, Washington, D.C. (1973).

Walker, D. E., "Speech Understanding Research." Annual Technical Report, Contract DAHC04-72-C-009, SRI Project 1526, Artificial Intelligence Center, Stanford Research Institute, Menlo Park, Cal. (1973).

Wiener, N., Extrapolation, Interpolation, and Smoothing of Time Series. M.I.T. Press, Cambridge, Mass. (1949).

Part Two

Parameter and Feature Extraction

PARAMETRIC REPRESENTATIONS OF SPEECH

Ronald W. Schafer
Lawrence R. Rabiner
Bell Laboratories
Murray Hill, New Jersey 07974

ABSTRACT

This paper presents several digital signal processing methods for representing speech. Included among the representations are simple waveform coding methods; time domain techniques; frequency domain representations; nonlinear or homomorphic methods; and finally linear predictive coding techniques. The advantages and disadvantages of each of these representations for various speech processing applications are discussed. By way of illustration, several examples of practical applications of each of the representations are given throughout the paper.

1. INTRODUCTION

The notion of a representation of a speech signal is central to almost every area of speech communication research. Often the form of representation of the speech signal is not singled out for special attention or concern but yet it is implicit in the formulation of the problem or in the design of the system. A good example of this situation is the telephone system, where speech is, in fact, represented by fluctuations in electrical current for purposes of long distance transmission. In other situations, however, we often must pay strict attention to the choice and method of implementation of the representation of the speech signal. This is true, for example, in such diverse areas as speech transmission, computer storage of speech and computer voice response, speech synthesis, speech aids for the handicapped, speaker verification and identification, and speech recognition. In all of these areas, digital representations, i.e., representations as sequences of numbers, are becoming increasingly dominant. There are two basic reasons for this. First, through the use of small general purpose digital computers, speech researchers have been able to apply a wide variety of digital signal processing techniques to speech communication problems. These techniques cover a range of complexity and sophistication that is impossible to match with analog methods. Second, the recent and predicted future developments in integrated circuit technology make it possible to realize digital speech processing schemes economically as hardware devices having the same sophistication and flexibility as a computer program implementation.

It is our purpose in this paper to survey the important and most useful methods for obtaining digital representations of speech signals. This is a formidable task since the number and variety of such methods is great. Thus, we must begin by disclaiming any pretentions to completeness; we shall only try to point out the methods that in our view are the most useful in the technical and research areas of speech communication and in particular those that are most widely applied in speech recognition.

The organization of this paper is as follows. First, we briefly review the speech production process and show how it can be modeled with a simple digital representation. We then discuss a class of waveform coding methods for representing speech. Included in this class are linear PCM, delta modulation, differential PCM, adaptive delta modulation, and finally adaptive differential PCM. It is shown at the end of this section that if an adaptive predictor is incorporated in these models, the waveform coding technique becomes quite similar to the linear predictive coding method to be discussed in a later section.

The next section discusses various time domain representations of speech. Included in this section are the concepts of zero crossing analysis, autocorrelation functions, "peak-to-peak" type estimations, and the use of "energy" functions. The following section discusses frequency domain representations of speech for which the concept of short-time spectrum analysis is dominant. Several examples of systems based on short-time spectrum analysis will be given in this section.

The last two sections discuss the increasingly important topics of homomorphic analysis, and linear prediction of speech. In the section on homomorphic representation of speech the concept of the cepstrum and its application to the problems of pitch detection, spectral envelope estimation, and formant analysis are discussed. In the final section on linear prediction analysis we discuss the two basic methods, explain their similarities and differences, and discuss the basic representations which are derivable from them including the spectrum, cepstrum, autocorrelation function, and the vocal tract area function.

2. DIGITAL MODEL FOR PRODUCTION OF THE SPEECH SIGNAL [1-3]

A schematic diagram of the human vocal apparatus is shown in Fig. 1. The vocal tract is an acoustic tube that is terminated at one end by the vocal cords and at the other end by the lips. An ancillary tube, the nasal tract, can be connected or disconnected by the movement of the velum. The shape of the vocal tract is determined by the position of the lips, jaw, tongue, and velum.

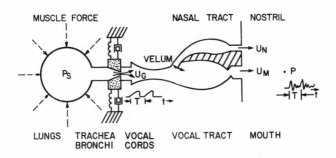

Fig. 1 Schematic diagram of mechanism of speech production. (After Flanagan, et al. [2])

Sound is generated in this system in three ways. Voiced sounds are produced by exciting the vocal tract with quasi-periodic pulses of air pressure caused by vibration of the vocal cords. Fricative sounds are produced by forming a constriction somewhere in the vocal tract, forcing air through the constriction, thereby creating turbulence that produces a source of noise to excite the vocal tract. Plosive sounds are created by completely closing off the vocal tract, building up pressure, and then quickly releasing it. All these sources create a wide band excitation of the vocal tract which acts as a linear time-varying filter which imposes its transmission properties on the frequency spectra of the sources. The vocal tract is characterized by its natural frequencies (or formants) that correspond to resonances in the sound transmission characteristics of the vocal tract.

A typical speech waveform is shown in Fig. 2. This plot illustrates some of the basic properties of the speech signal. We see,

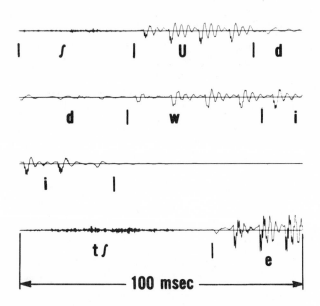

Fig. 2   An illustration of a speech waveform.

for example, that although the properties of the waveform change with time it is reasonable to view the speech waveform as being composed of segments during which the signal properties remain rather constant. Such segments are demarked in Fig. 2 below the waveform. These sample segments have the appearance either of a low level random unvoiced signal (as in ʃ or tʃ in Fig. 2) or of a high level quasi-periodic voiced signal (as in U or w or i) with each period displaying the exponentially decaying response properties of an acoustic transmission system. We note that the dynamic range of the waveform is large; that is, the peak amplitude of a voiced segment is much larger than the peak amplitude of an unvoiced segment.

Because the sound sources and vocal tract shape are relatively independent, a reasonable approximation is to model them separately, as shown in Fig. 3. In this digital model, samples of the speech waveform are assumed to be the output of a time-varying digital filter that approximates the transmission properties of the vocal tract. Since, as is clear from Fig. 2, the vocal tract changes shape rather slowly in continuous speech, and likewise its sound transmission properties, it is reasonable to assume that the digital filter in Fig. 3 has fixed characteristics over a time interval of on the order of 10 ms. Thus the digital filter may be characterized in each such interval by an impulse response or a set of coefficients for a recursive (IIR) digital filter. For voiced speech, the digital filter is excited by an impulse train generator that creates a quasi-periodic impulse train in which the spacing between impulses corresponds to the fundamental period of the glottal excitation.[†] For unvoiced speech, the filter is excited by a uniform random number generator that produces flat spectrum noise. In both cases, an amplitude control regulates the intensity of the input to the digital filter.

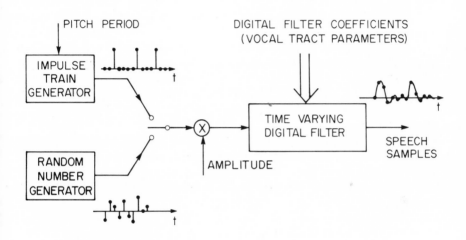

Fig. 3 Digital processing model for production of speech signals.

This model serves as the basis for obtaining a wide variety of representations of speech signals. These representations range in complexity from simply samples of the speech waveform taken periodically in time to estimates of the parameters of the model in Fig. 3. The choice of the digital representation is governed by three major considerations: complexity, information (bit) rate, and flexibility. By complexity we mean the amount of processing required to obtain the chosen representation. In many cases complexity is a measure of cost of implementation of the system in hardware. A simple representation can generally be implemented more economically than a complex

---

[†]It is assumed that the effects of the glottal pulse shape are included in the digital filer.

representation. Thus complexity is often the overriding consideration in some transmission applications where low terminal cost is crucial. Information rate or bit rate is a measure of the redundancy in the speech signal which has been removed by the processing. A low bit rate means that the parametric representation of the speech signal can be transmitted over a low capacity channel, or stored efficiently in digital memory. Finally flexibility refers to the ease with which the speech can be manipulated or altered for applications other than transmission -- e.g., voice response, recognition, etc. In general, greater complexity is the price paid to lower the bit rate and increase the flexibility. Generally, however, tradeoffs can be made between these three factors. In transmission and voice response applications the quality and intelligibility of the reconstituted speech are also prime considerations. Most of the techniques we will discuss are capable of producing good quality, highly intelligible speech, although some of the techniques are primarily analysis methods, limited to applications where the speech signal need not be reconstructed.

In the remainder of this paper we will discuss a number of digital representations that span the range of possibilities in each of the above areas of concern. We shall begin with the simplest, least efficient and least flexible representations of speech and progress to more complex ones which have the greatest flexibility and lowest bit rate.

3. DIGITAL WAVEFORM CODING

Perhaps the simplest digital representations of speech are those which are concerned with representation of the speech waveform. Such schemes as pulse code modulation (PCM), delta modulation (DM), and differential pulse code modulation (DPCM) are all based on the mathematical theorem which says that any bandlimited signal can be exactly reconstructed from samples taken periodically in time. We begin with a discussion of the simplest waveform coding technique -- pulse code modulation (PCM).

3.1 PCM

In applying the sampling theorem to a digital representation of speech there are two main concerns. These are depicted in Fig. 4. If the signal bandwidth is W Hertz, then the sampling period must be $T \leq 1/(2W)$. Since the samples $x(nT)$ of the signal generally take on a continuous range of values, they must be quantized for transmission or digital storage. If we represent the samples as B-bit binary words, (and assume sampling at just twice the signal bandwidth), then the bit rate is 2BW bits/sec. The value of W required for speech signals depends on the ultimate use of the samples. We know from measurements and theoretical studies that speech sounds such as fricatives have rather wide bandwidths (on the order of 10kHz). On the other hand much of the information required for speech intelligibility is contained in the variation of the first three formant frequencies of voiced speech and these are typically below 3 kHz. Thus, a sampling rate between 6 kHz and 20 kHz is generally used. Note that no matter what the sampling rate is, the speech signal must be suitably lowpass filtered prior to the sampling process to eliminate undesired high frequencies of the speech and high frequency noise.

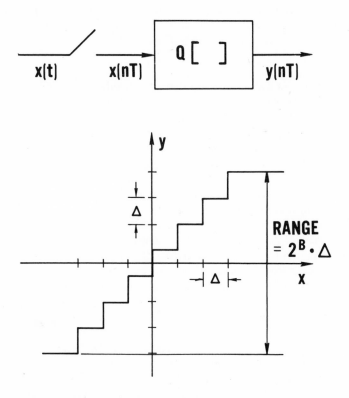

Fig. 4 Sampling and quantizing of an analog signal.

The choice of the number of bits per sample, B, is also dependent upon the intended use of the samples. If our purpose is transmission or computer storage followed by conversion back to an analog signal, we are only concerned that the resulting analog signal be acceptable perceptually. Also, the sampling process just described is generally the first step in any digital speech analysis technique. Since errors incurred in the sampling process will propagate to more refined digital representations, we are often justified in a very generous allotment of bits and sampling rate if the sampled speech wave is to undergo further processing. However it should be noted that the amount of processing required to implement most systems is proportional to sampling rate. Thus we should try to keep the sampling rate as small as possible, consistent with other objectives.

One objective measure of the fidelity of the PCM representation is the ratio of the signal power to the quantization noise power. If we define the quantization noise in Fig. 4 as

$$e(nT) = x(nT) - Q[x(nT)]$$

then it can be shown [4,7] that about 11 bits are required in order that the signal-to-noise ratio be 60 dB. (This is often referred to as "toll quality.") It is easily shown that the addition of one bit changes the signal-to-noise ratio by 6 dB.

The above discussion can be summarized by stating that an adequate PCM representation for most purposes requires from 66,000 bits/sec (11 bits X 6 kHz) to 220,000 bits/sec (11 bits X 20 kHz). This is a very significant consideration in transmission or storage for processing on a computer.

Since we generally have little flexibility in lowering the sampling rate, as this is governed by other considerations, the main hope for lowering the overall bit rate is in reducing the number of bits/sample. The key to such reductions lies in considering one of the basic properties of the speech signal: namely, that speech has a wide dynamic range. We see from Fig. 4 that if B is fixed, then the step size Δ must be chosen to so that $2^{B} \cdot \Delta$ spans the maximum peak-to-peak range of the signal. Thus the quantizer step size is determined by the amplitude of the voiced segments of speech whereas good representation of unvoiced segments requires a much smaller step size.

One solution to this problem is to use a nonlinear quantizer characteristic which distributes the quantization levels more densely for lower amplitudes than for high amplitudes. Based on empirical determinations of the amplitude distribution of speech signals, a logarithmic quantizer characteristic has been found to be nearly optimum [9]. Using a logarithmic quantizer, 7 bits/sample are sufficient to obtain toll quality. An alternative approach is the use of a time varying step size [5-7], i.e., an adaptive quantizer. When the signal is low level, a small step size is used, and when the signal amplitude is large, an appropriate large step size is used. The adjustment of the step size may be done by logical operations on the sequence of samples arising from the adaptive quantization process [5-7].

3.2 DIFFERENTIAL QUANTIZATION

Further reductions in bit rate for waveform quantization methods can be obtained by considering more of the detailed properties of the speech signal. Specifically, it is clear from Fig. 2 that there is a great deal of redundancy in the speech signal. Removal of some of this redundancy can yield a concomitant reduction in bit rate, at the expense of increased complexity in the signal processing algorithms. Figure 5 depicts a general differential quantization scheme. The scheme is based on the fact that even for sampling at just the Nyquist rate ($T=1/(2W)$), the correlation between successive samples is quite high and, as the sampling rate increases, the sample-to-sample correlation increases, approaching unity for very high sampling rates.

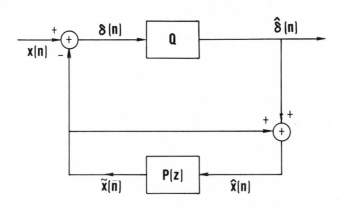

Fig. 5 General differential quantization scheme.

In the system of Fig. 5, let us assume that $\tilde{x}(n)$ is an estimate of the value of the speech sample $x(n)$. Then, if the estimate is good, the variance of the difference $\delta(n)=x(n)-\tilde{x}(n)$ should be smaller than the variance of $x(n)$ so that $\delta(n)$ can be more accurately represented by a fixed number of bits than the speech samples $x(n)$. The quantized difference signal $\hat{\delta}(n)$ when added to $\tilde{x}(n)$ produces a reconstructed signal $\hat{x}(n)$ which differs from $x(n)$ by only the quantization error of the difference signal, i.e.,

$$e(n) = \delta(n) - \hat{\delta}(n)$$
$$= x(n) - \hat{x}(n).$$

Due to the redundancy in the speech signal, it seems plausible that a given sample could be predicted as a linear combination of previous samples. In fact even the simplest linear combination may suffice, i.e., a constant times the previous sample. Therefore if the quantization error is small, $\hat{x}(n)$ will be a good approximation to $x(n)$ and

$$\tilde{x}(n) = a\hat{x}(n-1) \quad (a \sim 1), \tag{1}$$

will be a good estimate of $x(n)$. The z-transform of Eq. (1) is

$$\tilde{X}(z) = az^{-1}\hat{X}(z)$$

Thus the predictor is characterized by the polynomial

$$P(z) = \frac{\tilde{X}(z)}{\hat{X}(z)} = az^{-1}. \tag{2}$$

A more general predictor polynomial is of the form

$$P(z) = \sum_{k=1}^{p} a_k z^{-k} \tag{3}$$

The reader may recognize the similarity to linear prediction analysis when the predictor of Eq. 3 is used.

In using differential quantization we are free to choose the sampling rate, the quantizer and the predictor so as to reduce the bit rate. If the sampling rate is much higher than the Nyquist rate, the correlation between adjacent samples is very close to one and it is possible to use a 1-bit quantizer to obtain a good approximation to the input samples. This case, illustrated in Fig. 6a, is called delta modulation

(DM). In Fig. 6a we have illustrated how $x(n)$, $\tilde{x}(n)$ and $\hat{x}(n)$ vary with time. (We have shown the case where a=1.) The quantized difference signal has the form

$$\delta(n) = \Delta \cdot c(n)$$

where

$$c(n) = +1 \quad \text{if } \delta(n) \geq 0$$
$$= -1 \quad \text{if } \delta(n) < 0.$$

and Δ is the fixed step size. Figure 6a shows the two types of errors that are inherent in differential quantization schemes. On the left of the figure, the slope of the waveform is greater than the maximum rate of increase of the staircase approximation; that is, for this choice of sampling period, Δ is too small to follow rapid changes in the waveform. This is called slope overload. On the right side of the figure, we see that in slowly varying parts of the waveform there is a tendency to oscillate up and down about the waveform. This is called granular distortion. In such regions we would like to have a smaller step size to reduce the magnitude of the 'granular distortion.

One solution to this dilemma is to let the step size vary so that Δ becomes large during slope overload and small during granular distortion. This can be done by searching for patterns in the code word sequence $c(n)$. For example a run of +1's or -1's means slope overload, while an alternating pattern means granularity. A simple logic for varying the step size is [7]

$$\Delta(n) = P\Delta(n-1), \quad \text{if } c(n) = c(n-1)$$
$$= Q\Delta(n-1), \quad \text{if } c(n) \neq c(n-1).$$

The quantized difference signal is now

$$\hat{\delta}(n) = \Delta(n) \cdot c(n).$$

An optimum choice of the parameters is

$$P = 1.5 \quad Q = 1/P.$$

This scheme is illustrated by Fig. 6b. (Here, for simplicity we have assumed P=2 and a=1.) It can be seen that this adaptive delta modulator (ADM) is able to follow rapid increases in slope and also it is

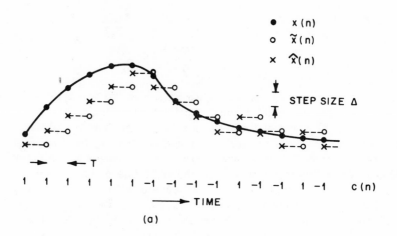

(a)

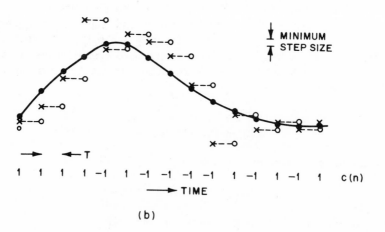

(b)

Fig. 6. Illustration of delta modulation for (a) fixed step size, or (b)adaptive step size.

able to use a smaller step size in regions of granularity. In practice, limits are placed on the step size variation so that $\Delta_{min} \leq \Delta(n) \leq \Delta_{max}$. This prevents the step size from becoming unreasonably large and from being driven to zero when the input to the differential quantizer is zero.

If we use a multibit quantizer in Fig. 5, then a lower sampling rate can be used. This case is called differential PCM (DPCM). If the sampling rate is the Nyquist rate, then we can use two bits less in the quantizer than required for straight PCM for the same signal-to-noise ratio [8]. Furthermore, we can adapt the quantizer step size to obtain further improvements. Schemes similar to the ADM system just described have been implemented for multi-bit quantizers. These are called adaptive DPCM (ADPCM) systems [5].

Such a representation has been used for storage of speech at 24kbits/sec for a computer voice response system [10,11]. An interesting result of this work is the observation that the adaptive quantizing provides a simple means of finding the beginning and end of a speech utterance. This is a problem that arises in many situations, including speech recognition.

The algorithm for isolating speech from silence is based on the fact that when no input is present the step size shrinks to its minimum value. Thus the multibit code words c(n) vary back and forth between the smallest negative and positive quantizer levels. On the other hand, when speech is present, the adaptation strategy attempts to insure that all the quantizer levels are used an equal percentage of time, regardless of the level of the speech signal. Thus unvoiced and voiced speech segments are treated much the same by the quantizer. This process is illustrated in Fig. 7. Figure 7a shows the code word sequence for the beginning of the word /three/. Note the low level variation prior to the beginning marker. Figure 7b shows the "energy" of the code word sequence measured over a 101 sample window.[†] This code word energy is low for silence but rises rapidly and remains constant through the low level fricative /th/ and the remaining voiced portion. Thus, a very simple threshold measurement serves to reliably locate the beginning and end of a speech segment [10]. Figure 7c shows the decoded speech waveform corresponding to the code word sequence of Fig. 7a. The beginning of the word is much more clearly evident in Fig. 7b than in Fig. 7c.

This is an example of the importance of matching the representation of the speech signal to the intended processing. By

---

[†]See section 4.2 for the definition of energy.

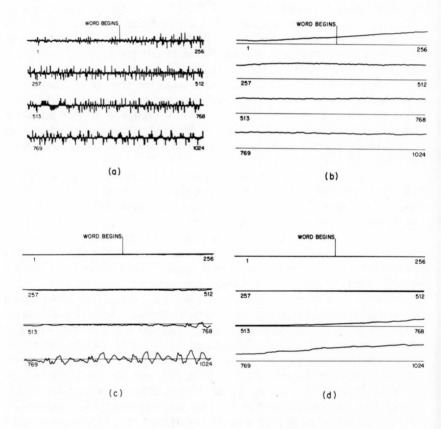

Fig. 7. Illustration of speech location (a) ADPCM code word sequence (b) "Energy" of code word sequence (c) Decoded speech waveform (d) Energy of the speech waveform.

using an ADPCM representation the task of finding the beginning and end of an utterance becomes very easy. However, ADPCM as we have described it clearly does not lead to simple solutions to other problems such as formant estimation. The differential quantization scheme even provides a good solution to this problem if we adapt the predictor polynomial P(z). This will be discussed at length in the section on linear predictive coding.

4. TIME DOMAIN ANALYSIS METHODS

There are a variety of speech processing methods that are based upon simple measurements on the time waveform. If digital processing is to be used, then, time domain methods usually operate on samples of the speech signal, i.e., a PCM representation. (The end-point algorithm just discussed is a time-domain scheme operating on ADPCM samples.) There are a wide variety of measurements which are used in various analysis schemes including: peak type measurements, energy, zero-crossing rate, and the autocorrelation function. In this section we discuss several time domain methods which use these measurements to estimate parameters of the model of Section 2.

4.1 SIMPLE PEAK MEASUREMENTS

Perhaps the simplest measurements which are easily made on the speech waveform are peak type measurements. Figure 8 shows a section of lowpass filtered speech (0-600 Hz) and indicates a set of peak type measurements which can be made on the waveform to aid in estimating the pitch period. Measurements m_1, m_2 and m_3 are made at each positive peak, and m_4, m_5 and m_6 are corresponding measurements for negative peaks. Measurement m_1 is an absolute positive peak measurement; m_2 is a peak-to-valley measurement; and m_3 is a peak-to-previous-peak measurement; m_4, m_5, and m_6 are corresponding measurements for negative peaks. If any measurement is negative (e.g., a positive peak is smaller than the previous positive peak) it is set to zero. Figure 9 illustrates how these measurements can be applied to two simple cases - a pure sinewave, and a sum of a strong second harmonic and a weak fundamental. For the pure sinewave measurements m_1, m_2, m_4 and m_5 indicate the period exactly whereas measurements m_3 and m_6 fail to indicate the period. For the combination of sinusoids measurements m_1, m_2, m_4 and m_5 tend to indicate half the period, whereas m_3 and m_6 indicate the true period. Considering each of these measurements as a rather simple pitch detector, a fairly simple technique can be used to combine the decisions of these six elementary pitch detectors to give one good

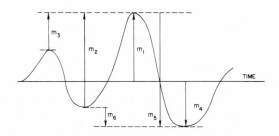

Fig. 8 Peak measurements for pitch detection.

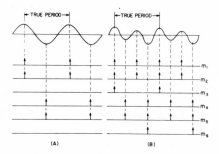

Fig. 9 Peak measurements on simple periodic waveforms.

overall decision as to the pitch period. Figure 10 shows a block diagram of a practical pitch detector based on these simple peak type measurements and parallel processing notions [12,13]. This pitch detector has been used in a variety of speech analysis, synthesis, and speaker verification applications.

4.2 ENERGY MEASUREMENTS

One of the most basic of speech measurements is the concept of energy. The energy in a discrete-time real signal x(n) is defined as

$$E = \sum_{n=-\infty}^{\infty} x^2(n) \tag{4}$$

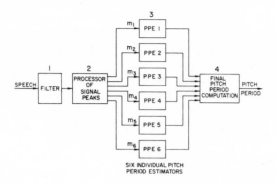

Fig. 10 Pitch detector using parallel processing.

and can be related to the Fourier transform of the signal, $X(e^{j\omega})$ by the Parseval relation

$$E = \sum_{n=-\infty}^{\infty} x^2(n) = \frac{1}{2\pi} \int_{-\pi}^{\pi} |X(e^{j\omega})|^2 d\omega \qquad (5)$$

For a non-stationary signal, such as speech, we must consider energy defined over reasonably short segments (on the order of 10 msec). For such cases a reasonable definition of energy is

$$E(n) = \sum_{m=0}^{N-1} [w(m)\, x(n-m)]^2 \qquad (6)$$

where $w(m)$ is a weighting sequence or window which selects a segment of $x(n)$, and N is the number of samples in the window. For the simple case of $w(m)=1$, for all m, $E(n)$ is the sum of the squares of the N most recent values of $x(n)$. This definition of energy was used, for example, in computing the energy curves of Figures 7b and 7d.

The difficulties with attaching physical meaning to the concept of energy for a non-stationary signal such as speech are apparent from Eq. 6. The first difficulty involves the choice of window. The purpose of the window is to attach lower weight to speech samples which occurred further back in time, thus w(m) generally tends to 0 monotonically as m gets bigger. When one wants to apply equal weight to the entire interval, a rectangular window is used. The second difficulty involves choice of measurement interval N. If N is too small, E(n) of Eq. 6 will fluctuate very rapidly depending on exact details of the waveform. If N is too large, E(n) will have very little variation, and will not reflect the changing properties of the speech signal. Suitable practical choices of N are on the order of 100-200 for a 10kHz sampling rate; that is, 10-20 msec. of signal is used in the measurement.

The major significance of E(n) is that it provides a good measure for separating voiced speech segments from unvoiced speech segments. E(n) for unvoiced segments is much smaller than for voiced segments. Furthermore the smaller the value of N, the less smearing there is in locating the exact instant at which unvoiced speech becomes voiced and vice versa. Also, for very high quality speech, the energy can be used to separate unvoiced speech from silence.

One difficulty with energy measurements as in Eq. 6 is that they are very sensitive to large signal levels (in that they enter the computation as a square), thereby emphasizing large sample-to-sample variations in E(n). One relatively simple way of alleviating this problem is to use as a measure of energy, the function

$$\hat{E}(n) = \sum_{m=0}^{N-1} |w(m) \, x(n-m)| \qquad (7)$$

where the sum of absolute values is computed instead of the sum of squares.

As a further refinement, the energy is often computed at the output of a bandpass filter, rather than directly on the speech samples themselves. In this manner one can use foreknowledge of the properties of speech sounds to determine the character of the speech based on the energy in certain frequency bands. Reddy has made extensive use of these ideas in his speech recognition work [14]. Another major application of the energy function is as an aid in isolating the beginning and end of an utterance. Figure 11 shows the energy function for the word six for a 10 msec rectangular window. It is easy to see the low energy fricative regions at the beginning and end of six, and the stop gap region during the /k/ for which the energy is almost zero.

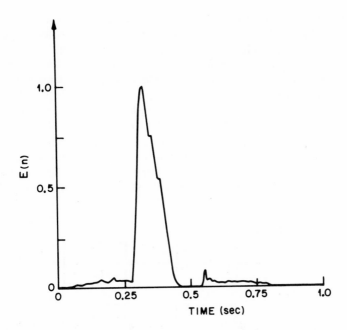

Fig. 11 Normalized energy for the word /six/.

4.3 ZERO CROSSING MEASUREMENTS

Another very simple time domain analysis method is based on zero crossing measurements. In the context of a digital implementation, a zero crossing can be said to occur between sampling instants n and n-1 if

$$sign[x(n)] \neq sign[x(n-1)]. \tag{8}$$

This measurement is trivial to implement and is often used as a gross estimate of the properties of a speech signal. Its use is motivated by the observation that if the signal is a sinusoid of frequence f_0, then the average number (over a short segment) of zero crossings is

$$n_z = 2f_0 \quad \text{crossings/sec.}$$

Whereas this is true for a sinusoid, the interpretation of zero crossing measurements for speech is much less precise owing to the broad frequency spectrum of most speech sounds. However, often very crude estimates of spectrum properties may suffice.

For example, it is well known that the energy of voiced speech tends to be concentrated below 3 kHz, whereas the energy of fricatives generally is concentrated above 3 kHz. Thus, zero crossing measurements (along with energy information) are often used in making a decision about whether a particular segment of speech is voiced or unvoiced. If the zero crossing rate is high, the implication is unvoiced; if the zero crossing rate is low, the segment is most likely to be voiced. Zero crossing measurements, coupled with a pitch detection scheme, provide a useful approach to estimation of excitation parameters [34].

The use of zero crossings has been suggested for estimating formant frequencies. A typical scheme of this sort is depicted in Fig. 12.

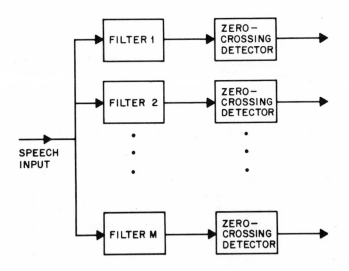

Fig. 12 Zero crossing measurements for a bank of bandpass filters.

The frequency band $0 \leq \omega \leq \pi$, is split up into several channels and zero crossing measurements are made on each output. The passbands of the filters are chosen so as to select individual speech formant frequencies. This approach is not completely successful because of the overlap among the ranges of the formant frequencies. For example if F_1, F_2 and F_3 denote the first three formant frequencies then typical ranges are [34]

$$200 \leq F_1 \leq 900$$
$$550 \leq F_2 \leq 2700$$
$$1100 \leq F_3 \leq 2950.$$

However, in some cases zero crossings have been successfully used as representations of the speech signal. [14]

In implementing zero crossing measurements digitally, there are a number of important considerations. Although the basic algorithm requires only a comparison of signs of two successive samples, special care must be taken in the sampling process. First, noise, d.c. offset and 60 cycle hum have disastrous effects on zero crossing measurements. Thus for zero crossing measurements a bandpass filter rather than a lowpass filter may be necessary prior to sampling to avoid the above difficulties. Second, the sampling period T determines the time resolution of the zero crossing measurements. Fine resolution requires a high sampling rate. Third, once the speech has been filtered into the desired frequency bands, very crude quantization (1-bit in fact) is all that is necessary to preserve the zero crossing information. Fourth, if multiple bands are to be used, the filtering can be done with analog filters prior to sampling. If the signal is sampled first then the digital filtering required to split up the frequency band will greatly increase the computational complexity of the zero crossing measurement.

4.2 SHORT-TIME AUTOCORRELATION ANALYSIS

The autocorrelation function of a discrete-time signal x(n) is defined as

$$\phi(m) = \lim_{N \to \infty} \frac{1}{2N+1} \sum_{n=-N}^{N} x(n)x(n+m). \tag{9}$$

The autocorrelation function is useful for displaying structure in any waveform, speech being no exception. For example, if the signal is periodic with period P, i.e., x(n+P)=x(n) for all n, then it is easily shown that

$$\phi(m) = \phi(m+P). \tag{10}$$

Thus, periodicity in the autocorrelation function indicates periodicity in the signal. Also, if the autocorrelation function is sharply peaked around m=0 and falls off rapidly to zero as m increases, this indicates a lack of predictable structure in the signal.

As we have observed, speech is not a stationary signal. However, the properties of the speech signal remain fixed over relatively long time intervals. This leads to the notion of short-time analysis techniques that operate on short segments of the speech signal. For example, we can define the short-time autocorrelation function as

$$\phi_i(m) = \frac{1}{N}\sum_{n=0}^{N'-1} x(n+i)\,x(n+i+m) \quad 0 \leq m \leq M_0 - 1 \tag{11}$$

We can interpret Eq. (11) as the autocorrelation of a segment of the speech signal of length N samples beginning at sample i. If N'=N, then data from outside the segment i≤n≤N+i-1 is used in the computation. If N'=N-M$_0$, then only data from that interval is required. In this case, the segment is often weighted by a "window" function that smoothly tapers the ends of the segment to zero. In using the autocorrelation function to detect periodicity in speech, either choice is satisfactory; however, we shall see in Sec. 7 that a similar distinction is important in analysis methods based on linear prediction. In either case, the direct computation of $\phi_i(m)$ for 0≤m≤M$_0$-1 requires computational effort proportional to M$_0$·N. This can be a significant overhead factor.

Short-time analysis methods typically are applied to estimate parameters of the speech model discussed in Sec. 2. The normal assumption is that although a sampling rate ranging from 6 kHz to 20 kHz may be necessary to preserve the essential features of the speech signal in a PCM representation, much lower sampling rates suffice for the slowly varying parameters of the model (50 to 100 Hz is typical). Suppose for example that the sampling rate of the speech signal is 10 kHz and the short time autocorrelation is to be computed 100 times/sec. The estimate of the autocorrelation is generally based upon a 20 to 40 msec segment of the speech signal. (For estimates of periodicity, the window must be long enough to encompass at least two periods of the speech signal.) Thus, for a 10 kHz sampling rate 200≤N≤400, and the autocorrelation estimates must be computed by moving in increments of 100 samples.

In using the short-time autocorrelation function for pitch period estimation, it is desirable that the correlation function be sharply peaked so that a strong peak will stand out at multiples of P, the period. The correlation function of speech is not sharply peaked because there is a great deal of predictable structure in each period of the speech waveform. Sondhi has given several methods of sharpening the peaks in the autocorrelation function. One of these, called center clipping, is illustrated in Fig. 13. The nonlinear operation of clipping out the middle of the speech waveform is very effective in reducing the sample-to-sample correlation of the signal. This is illustrated in Fig. 14 which shows a succession of autocorrelation functions each estimated from 30 msec segments of speech which are selected at intervals of 15 msec (66 2/3 Hz sampling rate).

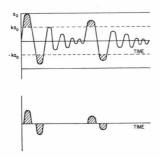

Fig. 13 Illustration of the process of center clipping.

From a set of correlation functions of this type it is possible to estimate the pitch period simply by locating the strong peak that is in evidence during voiced intervals. Sondhi gives a decision algorithm that formalizes this process. This scheme has been found to perform very well in situations where the speech is voiced but the wave shape is almost sinusoidal or when the fundamental frequency is missing [15].

5. SHORT-TIME SPECTRUM ANALYSIS
Short-time spectrum analysis has been one of the most important speech processing techniques for many years. The fundamental assumption underlying this and any other short-time analysis method is that over a long time interval speech is nonstationary, but that over a sufficiently short-time interval it can be

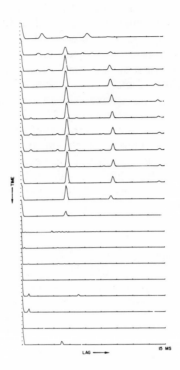

Fig. 14 Sequence of autocorrelation functions obtained
by center clipping.

considered stationary. Thus, the Fourier transform of a short segment
of speech should give a good spectral representation of the speech
during that time interval. Measurement of the short-time spectrum is
the basic operation in the channel vocoder [18,19,26] the phase
vocoder [17], spectrogram displays [21,23], and some speech
recognition systems [20]. Two methods are commonly used for
implementing short-time Fourier analysis. The first uses a bank of
bandpass filters;† the second uses a fast Fourier transform (FFT)

---

†This method was originally used with analog filters and it can be
implemented with even greater precision and flexibility with digital
filters.

algorithm.†† When implemented on a computer the FFT method is generally computationally superior to the filter bank model.

5.1 FILTER BANKS FOR SHORT-TIME SPECTRUM ANALYSIS

Figure 15 shows a simple way of implementing a short-time spectrum analyzer using a bank of bandpass filters. If the filter passbands are chosen to cover the speech band, then, roughly speaking, the outputs can be thought of as a Fourier representation of the input speech signal. If the filters are carefully designed, the sum of all the filter outputs will be a good approximation to the original speech signal [24]. This is the basis for communication systems such as the channel vocoder and the phase vocoder.

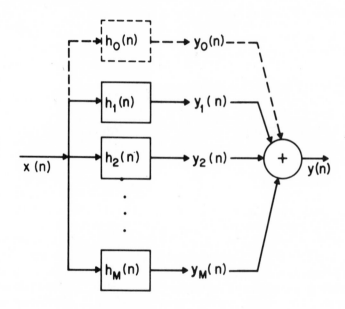

Fig. 15 A bank of bandpass filters.

---

††This method is fundamentally digital and has no analog counterpart.

Based on some fundamental ideas of spectrum analysis the discrete short-time spectrum of x(n) is defined as

$$X_i(\omega) = \sum_{n=-\infty}^{i} x(n)\, h(i-n)\, e^{-j\omega n} \qquad (12a)$$

$$= |X_i(\omega)|\, e^{j\theta_i(\omega)} \qquad (12b)$$

$$= a_i(\omega) - j b_i(\omega) \qquad (12c)$$

Equation 12 can be interpreted in a number of ways. As shown in Fig. 16, one interpretation is that $X_i(\omega)$ is the Fourier transform of a sequence x(n) that is weighted by a "window" h(i-n).

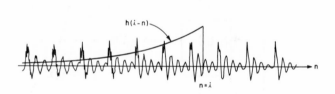

Fig. 16 Illustration of computation of the short-time Fourier transform.

Thus the short-time Fourier transform is a function of both frequency ω, and time, i. A second interpretation follows if we assume that h(n) is the impulse response of a lowpass digital filter. Further, assume that we wish to evaluate the short-time transform at frequency ω. Then $X_n(\omega)$ is seen to be the output of the lowpass filter with input $x(n)e^{-j\omega n}$. This is depicted in Fig. 17a. To avoid complex arithmetic, the system of Fig. 17a is generally implemented as shown in Fig. 17b where the output parameters are $a_n(\omega)$ and $b_n(\omega)$, the real and imaginary parts of the spectrum. The bandwidth of the lowpass filter determines the frequency resolution. Typically, this bandwidth is on the order of 50 Hz. Thus the spectrum signals can be sampled at a much lower rate ($\sim$100 Hz) than the speech signal itself.

Using digital filters, it has been shown [25] that the short-time

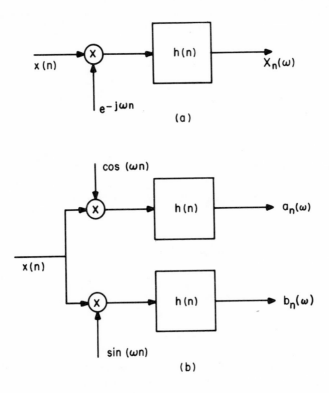

Fig. 17 Short-time Fourier analysis for one channel
centered at ω.

Fourier transform can be a very good representation of the speech
signal in the sense that the output obtained by summing appropriately
modulated bandpass channels can be made indistinguishable from the
input. This requires a bit rate on the order of the bit rate required for
comparable PCM representation. However, the resulting representation
of the speech signal permits greater flexibility in the sense that the
spectral parameters $a_n(\omega)$ and $b_n(\omega)$ provide information about the
parameters of the speech model in a convenient and useful form. For
example the time and frequency dimensions of a speech signal can be
independently manipulated through simple manipulations of the spectral
parameters [17].

5.2 USE OF THE FFT FOR SHORT-TIME SPECTRUM ANALYSIS

The fast Fourier transform (FFT) is a set of highly efficient algorithms for evaluating the discrete Fourier Transform (DFT) expressions

$$F(k) = \sum_{n=0}^{M-1} f(n) e^{-j\frac{2\pi}{M}kn} \quad k = 0,1,\ldots, M-1. \tag{14a}$$

$$f(n) = \frac{1}{M}\sum_{k=0}^{M-1} F(k) e^{j\frac{2\pi}{M}kn} \quad n = 0,1,\ldots, M-1. \tag{14b}$$

For using these expressions, it is convenient to define the short-time transform as

$$X_i(\omega) = \sum_{n=0}^{N-1} x_i(n) w(n) e^{-j\omega n} \tag{15a}$$

where

$$x_i(n) = x(n+i) \quad n = 0,1,\ldots, N-1$$
$$i = 0,L,2L,\ldots \tag{15b}$$

As in the case of the short-time autocorrelation function, we interpret Eq. 15a as the Fourier transform of a segment of speech N samples long (weighted by a window w(n)) beginning at sample i. The frequency resolution of the spectrum measurement is inversely proportional to the window length N. This is illustrated in Fig. 18. Figure 18a shows the short-time transform and Fig. 18b shows the corresponding windowed segment of speech data. A Hamming window [16] of length 50 msec was used. (N=500 samples at a 10 kHz sampling rate.) Note that the individual harmonics of the pitch period are resolved in the short-time transform. Figures 19a and 19b show the short-time transform and the windowed speech for N=50 samples. (The speech segment is the first 50 samples of the segment shown in Fig. 18b.) In this case the frequency resolution is much less than in Fig. 18. We note that the spectrum of Fig. 18 could be considered comparable to a narrow band spectrogram measurement while Fig. 19 is comparable to a wide band spectrogram analysis. In the first case both the pitch information and vocal tract transfer function information is present while in the latter case only the general shape of the vocal tract response is preserved.

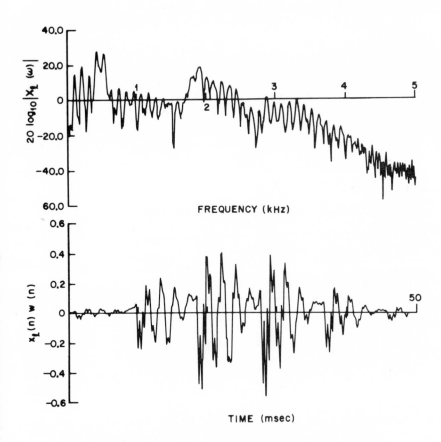

Fig. 18 (a) Log magnitude of the short-time transform;
(b) Corresponding windowed speech segment (N=500).

An FFT algorithm can be used to compute Eq. 15 at equally spaced frequencies $\omega_k = (k2\pi)/M$ for $k=0,1,...,M-1$. If $M \geq N$, then the sequence $x_i(n)w(n)$ must be augmented with $M-N$ zero valued samples to form a sequence of length M. In this case we can compute

$$X_i(\frac{2\pi}{M}k) = \sum_{n=0}^{N-1} x_i(n)w(n) e^{-j\frac{2\pi}{M}kn} \qquad k = 0,1,..., M-1.$$

using an FFT algorithm.

On the other hand if $M<N$, we can take advantage of the periodicity of the complex exponential $e^{-j2\pi kn/m}$ to express Eq. 15a as

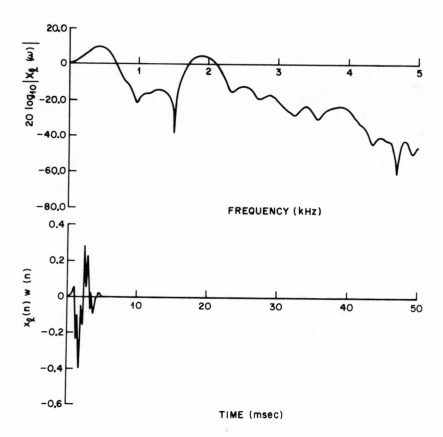

Fig. 19 (a) Log magnitude of the short-time transform; (b) Corresponding windowed speech segment (N=50).

$$X_i(\tfrac{2\pi}{M}k) = \sum_{n=0}^{M-1} g(n)\, e^{-j\frac{2\pi}{M}kn} \qquad k = 0,1,...,M-1, \qquad (17a)$$

where

$$g(n) = \sum_{r=0}^{[N/M]} x_i(n+r)w(n+r) \qquad (17b)$$

and [N/M] means the largest integer in N/M. This latter feature of FFT spectrum analysis is useful whenever one wishes to only evaluate the transform at intervals of $2\pi/M$ but at the same time wishes to obtain the better frequency resolution corresponding to a window of length N. Using the above approach, it is also possible to use the FFT to compute the outputs of a uniformly spaced bank of filters as required in a phase vocoder analyzer [24].

An important consequence of the definition of the short-time spectrum in Eq. 15 is that $|X_i(\omega)|^2/N$ is the Fourier transform of the short-time autocorrelation function

$$R_i(m) = \frac{1}{N} \sum_{n=0}^{N-1-m} x_i(n)w(n)x_i(n+m)w(n+m) \tag{18}$$

That is,

$$R_i(m) = \frac{1}{2\pi}\int_{-\pi}^{\pi} \frac{|X_i(\omega)|^2}{N} e^{j\omega m}d\omega. \tag{19}$$

Furthermore, it can be shown that if $X_i(2\pi k/M)$ is computed with $M \geq 2N$, then $R_i(m)$ is the inverse discrete Fourier transform of $|X_i(2\pi k/M)|^2/N$ i.e.,

$$R_i(m) = \frac{1}{M} \sum_{k=0}^{M-1} \frac{|X_i(\frac{2\pi}{M}k)|^2}{N} e^{j\frac{2\pi}{M}km} \quad 0 \leq m \leq N-1. \tag{20}$$

If we suppose that $R_i(m)$ is required for $0 \leq m \leq M_0-1$, where M_0 is a large number, as in pitch detection, it may be most efficient to first compute the short-time transform using Eq. 15, and then compute the autocorrelation function using Eq. 20.

5.3 Use of the Short-Time Spectrum for Pitch Detection

We have suggested that the short-time spectrum might serve as an intermediate step in the computation of the short time autocorrelation functions used in a pitch detection algorithm. However, we have also seen in Fig. 18a that pitch information is also contained in a narrow-band, short-time spectrum in the form of peaks at multiples of the fundamental frequency. This fact suggests a number of techniques for estimating the fundamental frequency directly from the short-time spectrum [22,27]. One of the most promising of these methods was the short-time harmonic product spectrum which is defined as

$$P_i(\omega) = \prod_{r=1}^{K} |X_i(r\omega)|^2 \tag{21}$$

Taking the logarithm of $P_i(\omega)$ we obtain

$$\hat{P}_i(\omega) = \sum_{r=1}^{K} \log|X_i(r\omega)|^2 \tag{22}$$

$P_i(\omega)$ is seen to be the sum of K replicas of the log of the short-time spectrum. The motivation behind using $P_i(\omega)$ for pitch detection is simply that for voiced speech, compressing the frequency scale by integer factors should cause harmonics of the fundamental to coincide at the fundamental frequency, thus causing a large peak at the fundamental frequency. The expectation is that the peaks in the frequency compressed log spectra should add coherently while all other portions of the log spectra should add incoherently. This technique was found to be particularly well suited for pitch detection on noisy speech [22,27].

An example of the use of this technique is shown in Fig. 20. Figures 20a and b show a sequence of short-time log harmonic product spectra and harmonic product spectra respectively for a section of voiced speech. A value of K=5 was used in this computation and the short-time spectra were computed every 10 msec using a 40 msec Hamming data window (N=400) and the spectrum was computed using Eq. 15 with M=2048. Figures 20c and d were computed under exactly the same conditions except noise was added to the speech signal prior to the computation. The signal-to-noise ratio was 0 db. It is clear from this figure that a peak picking algorithm for pitch detection can be structured around the harmonic product spectrum and that this algorithm should perform well even under noisy conditions. Noll [22] in fact finds this method superior to the cepstrum (see Sec. 6) in its noise resistance.

5.4 COMPUTER–GENERATED SPECTRUM DISPLAYS

The basic analysis techniques of this section have been used to generate spectrographic displays that are similar to, but in many cases more elaborate and flexible than, conventional spectrograms [21,23]. As we have pointed out, there is great flexibility in window length and shape or equivalently frequency resolution. Also, the spectrum can be shaped in a manner to enhance it for display, and it is possible to precisely correlate the speech waveform with the spectrographic display.

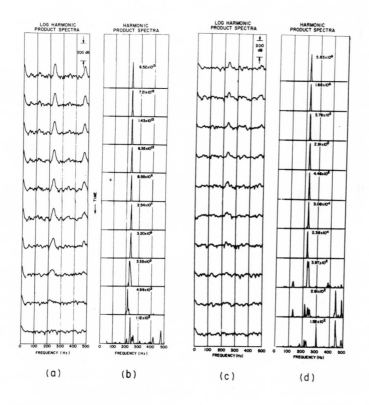

Fig. 20 Log harmonic product spectra and harmonic product spectra for noise free (a) and (b) and 0 dB S/N (c) and (d) [After Noll, [22]].

Such schemes have been implemented in a variety of ways but most of them use Eq. 15 to compute a set of short-time spectra at equally spaced time intervals. This set of spectra can be thought of as samples of the two dimensional function $X_i(\omega)$ which can be plotted as a frequency-time-intensity plot on an oscilloscope or television monitor. Using such techniques it has been possible to produce on-line spectrogram displays that are equal in quality to conventional spectrograms and far surpass them in flexibility and innovation.

6. HOMOMORPHIC SPEECH PROCESSING

Homomorphic filtering is a class of nonlinear signal processing techniques that is based on a generalization of the principle of superposition that defines linear systems. Such techniques have been applied in separating signals that have been combined by multiplication and convolution [31]. The application of these techniques to speech processing is again based on the assumption that although speech production is a time varying process, on a short-time basis it can be viewed as the convolution of an excitation function (either random noise or a quasi-periodic pulse train) with the vocal tract impulse response. Thus, methods for separating the components of a convolution are useful for speech analysis.

6.1 FUNDAMENTALS

A homomorphic system for speech analysis is shown in Fig. 21a. We assume that the signal at A is the discrete convolution discussed above. Then the short-time Fourier transform (computed using the FFT method of the previous section) at B is the product of the Fourier transforms of the excitation and the vocal tract impulse response. Taking the logarithm of the magnitude of the Fourier transform, we obtain at C the sum of the logarithms of the transforms of the excitation and vocal tract impulse response. Since the inverse discrete Fourier transform (IDFT) is a linear operation, the result at D (called the cepstrum of the input at A) is an additive combination of the cepstra of the excitation and vocal tract components. Thus, the effect of the operations DFT, log magnitude, and IDFT is to transform convolution into addition. The value of this transformation can be seen from Fig. 21b, which depicts the results of such an analysis for voiced speech. The curve labeled A is the input speech segment that has been multiplied by a data window. The rapidly varying curve labeled C is the log magnitude of the short-time transform. It consists of a slowly varying component due to the vocal tract transmission, and a rapidly varying periodic component due to the periodic excitation. The slowly varying

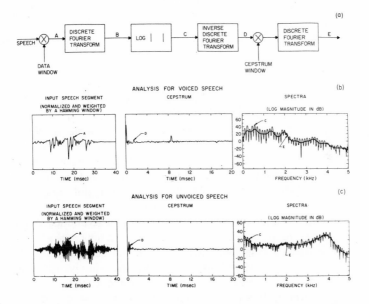

Fig. 21 Homomorphic processing of speech (a) basic operations(b) analysis for voiced speech (c) analysis for unvoiced speech.

part of the log magnitude produces the low-time part of the cepstrum (D), and the rapidly varying periodic component of the log magnitude manifests itself in the strong peak at a time equal to the period of the input speech segment. If we assume that the vocal tract transfer function in Fig. 3 is of the form

$$H(z) = \frac{A}{1 - \sum_{k=1}^{p} a_k z^{-k}} = A \prod_{k=1}^{p} \frac{1}{1 - z_k z^{-1}} \tag{23}$$

then the cepstrum of the vocal tract component of the convolution can be shown [30] to be

$$\hat{h}(n) = 0 \qquad n < 0$$
$$= \log A \qquad n = 0$$
$$= \sum_{k=1}^{p} (\frac{z_k^n}{n}) \qquad n > 0. \qquad (24)$$

If we assume that the excitation component is a periodic train of impulses, then it can be shown [30] that the cepstrum of the excitation component will also be a train of impulses with the same spacing as the input impulse train. This is clearly reflected in the cepstrum for voiced speech in Fig. 21b. The important point is that the cepstrum consists of an additive combination in which (due to the 1/n fall-off) the vocal tract and excitation components essentially do not overlap. The situation for unvoiced speech, shown in Fig. 21c, is much the same with the exception that the random nature of the excitation component of the input speech segment (A) causes a rapidly varying random component in the log magnitude (C). Thus in the cepstrum (D), the low time components correspond as before to the slowly varying vocal tract transfer function; however, since the rapid variations of the log magnitude are not, in this case, periodic, there is no strong peak as for the voiced speech segment. Thus the cepstrum serves as an excellent basis for estimating fundamental period of voiced speech and for determining whether a particular speech segment is voiced or unvoiced [29].

The vocal tract transfer function (spectrum envelope) can be obtained by removing the rapidly varying components of the log magnitude by linear filtering. This can be achieved by multiplying the cepstrum by a "cepstrum window" that only passes the short-time components. The results for voiced and unvoiced speech are labeled E in Figs. 21b and c, respectively.

6.2 ESTIMATION OF FORMANT FREQUENCIES AND PITCH PERIOD

The results depicted in Fig. 21 suggest algorithms for estimating basic speech parameters such as pitch period and formant frequencies. Specifically, voiced/unvoiced classification of the excitation is indicated by the presence or absence of a strong peak in the cepstrum [29]. The presence of a strong peak for voiced speech is dependent upon there being many harmonics present in the spectrum. In cases where this is not true such as voiced stops, zero crossing measurements are helpful in distinguishing voiced from unvoiced speech [34]. If a strong peak is present, its location is a good indicator of the pitch period. It should also be noted that the logarithm of the short-time spectrum is also required in implementation of the harmonic product spectrum. Thus, in using the cepstrum for pitch detection, we can also compute the harmonic product spectrum with little additional effort, thereby giving two semi-independent estimates of pitch.

The smoothed spectrum retains peaks at the vocal tract resonances or formant frequencies. One approach to estimating the formants is to search the smooth spectra for peaks and then decide which peaks correspond to formants [34]. Another approach uses iterative methods to adjust the parameters of a model similar to Eq. (23) until a good match to the smooth spectrum is obtained [33].

An illustration of the use of homomorphic processing is given in Fig. 22. On the left are shown a sequence of cepstra computed at 20 msec intervals. The strong peak indicates that the speech is voiced during the entire interval. On the right are successive short-time spectra and homomorphically smoothed short-time spectra. The lines connecting the peaks of the smooth spectra show the formant frequencies automatically estimated from the spectrum peaks. The peak picking approach is relatively simple except when two formants merge as in the 3rd and 4th frames from the top and the last 4 frames from the bottom. In this case it is useful to evaluate the vocal tract transfer function on a contour which passes closer to the poles thereby sharpening the resonances [34].

Speech can be synthesized from formant and pitch data by using the estimated parameters to vary the parameters of the model of Fig. 3. With efficient coding of the parameters, speech is thus represented by about 1000 bits/sec [2]. In addition to this high efficiency, the formant representation offers great flexibility in manipulating basic speech parameters. Also, since so much of the speech model is built into the representation we would expect that parameters of this type would be a very useful representation of speech for other purposes such as speech recognition and speaker verification.

6.3 THE CEPSTRUM AS A REPRESENTATION OF SPEECH

The low-time samples of the cepstrum contain mostly information about the vocal tract transfer function. Thus one representation of speech involves estimation of excitation parameters from the cepstrum and the use of the low-time cepstral values to represent the vocal tract response. This approach was used in an analysis/synthesis system called a homomorphic vocoder.

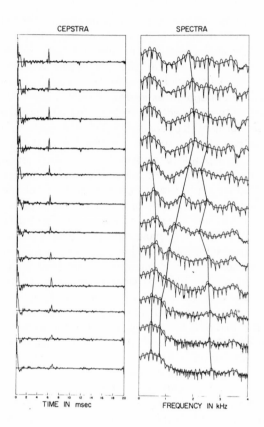

CEPSTRA   SPECTRA

TIME IN msec   FREQUENCY IN kHz

Fig. 22 Cepstra and spectra for a section of voiced speech.

Using this technique, speech can be represented quite well at 7200 bits/s [32]. Although this representation may be somewhat less flexible than the formant representation, it does offer the possibility of independently manipulating the frequency scale, time scale, and pitch. Also, this approach has been the basis for a speaker recognition scheme [28].

7. LINEAR PREDICTIVE ANALYSIS

One of the most powerful of speech analysis techniques is the method of linear predictive analysis. This method is rapidly becoming the predominant method for estimating basic speech parameters, e.g., pitch and formants, spectra, and vocal tract area functions. The importance of this method lies in its ability to provide extremely accurate estimates of the speech parameters, and in its speed of computation. In this section we present a formulation of linear predictive analysis and discuss some of the issues which are involved in using it in practical speech applications.

The basic idea behind linear predictive coding (LPC) is that a sample of speech can be approximated as a linear combination of the past p speech samples. By minimizing the squared difference between the actual speech samples and the linearly predicted ones, one can determine the predictor coefficients, i.e., the weighting coefficients of the linear combination. The basic philosophy of this scheme is reminiscent of and, in fact, related to the waveform quantization methods discussed in Section III. [35] There we suggested that a linear predictor could be applied in a differential quantization scheme to reduce the bit rate of the digital representation of the speech waveform. In this case, as in linear predictive analysis, the predictor coefficients must be adapted (i.e., updated regularly) to match the time-varying properties of the speech signal.

7.1 FUNDAMENTAL PRINCIPLES

The use of linear predictive analysis is suggested by the digital model of Sec. II. Assume that samples of the speech signal are produced by the model of Fig. 3, where over a short time interval the linear system has the transfer function

$$H(z) = \frac{A}{1 - \sum_{k=1}^{p} a_k z^{-k}}. \tag{25}$$

For voiced speech, the system is excited by an impulse train and for unvoiced speech it is excited by random white noise as depicted in Fig. 23. Linear prediction analysis is based on the observation that for such a system the speech samples x(n) are related to the excitation $\delta(n)$ by the difference equation

$$x(n) = \sum_{k=1}^{p} a_k x(n-k) + \delta(n) \tag{26}$$

Suppose that we process the speech signal with a linear predictor, i.e.,

$$\tilde{x}(n) = \sum_{k=1}^{p} \alpha_k x(n-k).$$

Then the predictor error is defined as

$$\epsilon(n) = x(n) - \tilde{x}(n) = x(n) - \sum_{k=1}^{p} \alpha_k x(n-k) \qquad (27)$$

It can be seen by comparing Eqs. 26 and 27 that if $\alpha_k = a_k$, and if the speech signal really does obey the model of Eq. 26, then $\epsilon(n) = \delta(n)$. Therefore, between the excitation impulses of voiced speech, the prediction error should be very small if the predictor coefficients, α_k, are equal to the parameters, a_k, of the vocal tract transfer function.

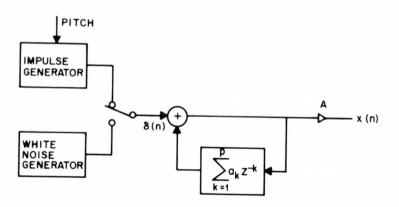

Fig. 23 Digital model for speech production.

Thus the predictor polynomial

$$P(z) = 1 - \sum_{k=1}^{p} \alpha_k z^{-k}$$

is a good approximation to the denominator of the vocal tract transfer function.

One approach for obtaining the predictor coefficients is based on minimizing the average squared prediction error over a short segment of the speech waveform. That is, we search for the values of α_k that minimize

$$E_i = \sum_{n=0}^{N-1} (x_i(n) - \tilde{x}_i(n))^2$$

$$= \sum_{n=0}^{N-1} (x_i(n) - \sum_{k=1}^{p} \alpha_k x_i(n-k))^2 \tag{28}$$

where $x_i(n)$ is a segment of speech that has been selected in the vicinity of sample i, i.e.,

$$x_i(n) = x(n+i).$$

There are two basic ways of choosing $x_i(n)$ each leading to procedures that are somewhat different in the details of their implementation and the results that are obtained. Leaving $x_i(n)$ unspecified for now, we can find the values of α_k that minimize E_i in Eq. 28 by setting $\partial E_i/\partial \alpha_k=0$, i=1,2,...,p, thus obtaining the equations

$$\sum_{n=0}^{N-1} x_i(n-j)x_i(n) = \sum_{k=1}^{p} \alpha_k \sum_{n=0}^{N-1} x_i(n-j)x_i(n-k) \tag{29}$$

$$1 \le j \le p.$$

If we define

$$\phi_i(j,k) = \sum_{n=0}^{N-1} x_i(n-j)x_i(n-k) \tag{30}$$

then Eq. 29 can be written more compactly as

$$\sum_{k=1}^{p} \alpha_k \phi_i(j,k) = \phi_i(j,0) \quad j = 1,2,..., p. \tag{31}$$

This set of p equations in p unknowns can be solved for the unknown predictor coefficients that minimize the average squared prediction error for the segment $x_i(n)$. To do this, the quantities $\phi_i(j,k)$ must be computed for $1 \le j \le p$ and $1 \le k \le p$. The details of this computation depend upon how $x_i(n)$ is defined.

By a simple substitution of variables, Eq. 30 can be written as

$$\phi_i(j,k) = \sum_{n=-j}^{N-1-j} x_i(n)x_i(n+j-k)$$

$$= \sum_{n=-k}^{N-1-k} x_i(n)x_i(n+k-j) \qquad (32)$$

Clearly, $\phi_i(j,k)=\phi_i(k,j)$. We observe from Eq. 32 that values of $x_i(n)$ are required outside the interval $0\leq n\leq N-1$. If we choose to supply the values outside this interval we note that we then require

$$x_i(n) = x(n+i) \qquad -p \leq n \leq N-2 \qquad (33)$$

to evaluate $\phi_i(j,k)$. This method and its attendant details was proposed by Atal [36] and has come to be called the <u>covariance</u> method because of the similarity of the matrix of values $\phi_i(j,k)$ to a covariance matrix [39].

    If we choose not to supply values of the signal outside the interval $0\leq n\leq N-1$, then we must resort to using a finite duration window $w(n)$ to reduce the end effects thereby obtaining,

$$x_i(n) = x(n+i)w(n) \qquad 0 \leq n \leq N-1$$
$$= 0 \qquad \text{otherwise.}$$

Using this definition of $x_i(n)$, Eq. 32 becomes

$$\phi_i(j,k) = \sum_{n=0}^{N-1-(j-k)} x_i(n)x_i(n+j-k).$$

$$= \sum_{n=0}^{N-1-(k-j)} x_i(n)x_i(n+k-j)$$

$$= r_i(j-k) = r_i(k-j) \qquad (34)$$

In this case Eq. 32 becomes

$$\sum_{k=1}^{p} \alpha_k r_i(|j-k|) = r_i(j) \qquad j = 1,2,...,p. \qquad (35)$$

From Eqs. 34 and 18 it is clear that

$$r_i(n) = NR_i(n)$$

i.e., $r_i(n)$ is equal (to within a constant multiplier) to the short-time autocorrelation function, which in turn is related to the short-time Fourier transform $X_i(\omega)$. Thus the method based on Eq. 35 is called the autocorrelation method. Methods of this type have been proposed by Itakura [38] (the maximum likelihood method) and Markel [41-43] (the inverse filter formulation).

The basic difference between the covariance method and the autocorrelation method is the necessity to use a window for the autocorrelation method. For the covariance method the section length is increased by augmenting p samples to enable the first p samples of the section ($x_i(n), 0 \leq n \leq p-1$) to be predicted from speech samples outside the section. Thus an equal number of samples go into the computation of $\phi(j,k)$ for all indices j and k, and no window is required. For the autocorrelation method one is trying to predict the first p samples from speech samples outside the section. Since these samples are arbitrarily zero, a fairly large error results. To reduce the error a window is applied which smoothly tapers the signal to zero at the ends of the window.

At this point, it is worth noting the mathematical and physical interpretation of using windows in the autocorrelation method. The process of multiplication of a signal by a window is equivalent to a circular convolution of the frequency response of the window with the speech spectrum. Thus a smearing occurs in the speech spectrum. The extent of this smearing depends on the section length N and the actual window used. However, it is clear that with the autocorrelation method, parameters such as formant bandwidths may not be accurately estimated. In many practical applications this is of little or no consequence; however, for vocoder applications this may be worth keeping in mind.

7.2 DETAILS OF IMPLEMENTATION

Both Eq. 31 or Eq. 35 are a set of p equations in p unknowns that can be expressed in matrix form as

$$\Phi \cdot \underline{a} = \underline{\Psi}. \tag{36}$$

These equations may be solved for the predictor coefficients using any general procedure for solving linear equations. However, if computational efficiency is important, as it usually is, some special properties of the matrix Φ can be exploited to reduce computation. In the case of Eq. 31 (the covariance method) Φ is symmetric and positive definite. Utilization of this fact leads to an efficient procedure for solving for the vector of predictor coefficients that is based on matrix factorization. This method is called the square root method, or the Cholesky decomposition [37].

Similarly for the autocorrelation method the matrix Φ is symmetric and positive definite and also has the property that the elements along any diagonal are equal. Such a matrix is called a Toeplitz matrix and in this case an even more efficient method for solving the equations can be found [43]. This method is called the Levinson method.

Since computational efficiency is an important consideration in any practical speech analysis scheme it is worthwhile comparing these two methods of linear prediction in this sense. The square root method for solving the covariance method formulation requires on the order of p^3 operations (multiplications) whereas the Levinson method for solving the autocorrelation formulation requires on the order of p^2 operations. Thus the autocorrelation formulation is inherently faster computationally than the covariance formulation. In particular for p=14, Makhoul and Wolf [39] note a ratio in computation time of 3.2 to 1 in favor of the autocorrelation method. However, this savings in computation is not significant when viewed in the total framework of the method for two reasons. First, the time required to compute the matrix of correlations is significantly greater than the time to solve the matrix equation. For example, for N = 150, Makhoul and Wolf [39] note that it takes ten times longer to compute the matrix than to solve the matrix equations using the autocorrelation method. Thus the savings in computation of the Levinson method becomes must less significant. As a second consideration the value of N required for both methods is not the same. For the autocorrelation method (for 10 kHz sampling) a value of N in the range 150 to 300 is generally required. For the covariance method a much smaller value of N can be used if care is taken to begin the section after a pitch pulse. In fact, Atal reports using values of N on the order of 30 with good results [36]. Thus there are many factors which determine computational efficiency, not the least of which is the intended application.

Another difference between the two methods concerns the roots of the predictor polynomial which are the poles of the digital filter that accounts for the vocal tract transmission properties. For stability of this system, the roots must be inside the unit circle of the z-plane.

This is not guaranteed by the covariance method [36]; however, given sufficient computational accuracy the autocorrelation method guarantees stability [39,43].

Another consideration in using these two methods is the numerical stability of the matrix inversion. Wilkinson [44] has shown that the square-root method is very stable numerically; no such statement has been made for the Levinson method. Markel [43] has pointed out that when implemented with finite precision arithmetic, the Levinson method requires careful scaling, and it is beneficial if the speech spectrum has been equalized by a simple first order network.

Until now we have dealt with considerations which can be easily quantified and for which definitive statements can be made. When one becomes seriously interested in using linear predictive methods, several other considerations are involved. These include the necessity for spectrum equalization prior to analysis, the effects of the analog prefilter prior to A/D conversion, the effects of finite word length on the analysis, the desirability of various structures for implementing the system, and finally the ease of building the various alternatives in digital hardware. Markel [43] has provided some excellent insights into several of these issues but most of them are as yet unresolved.

7.3 APPLICATIONS

Once the predictor coefficients have been obtained, they can be used in various ways to represent the properties of the speech signal.

7.3(A) SPECTRUM ESTIMATION

If the predictor polynomial is assumed to represent the denominator of the vocal tract transfer function we can obtain the frequency response of the vocal tract (for a particular segment of the speech signal) as

$$H(e^{j\omega T}) = \frac{A}{1 - \sum_{k=1}^{p} \alpha_k e^{-j\omega kt}} \qquad (37)$$

An example is shown in Fig. 24, where the spectrum obtained using Eq. (37) (with the predictor coefficients estimated by the autocorrelation method) is compared to that obtained by cepstrum smoothing for the same segment of speech. The formant frequencies are clearly in evidence in both plots, however Fig. 24b has fewer extraneous peaks. This is because p was chosen so that at most 6 (p=12) resonance peaks could occur. To determine the appropriate value of p for a given

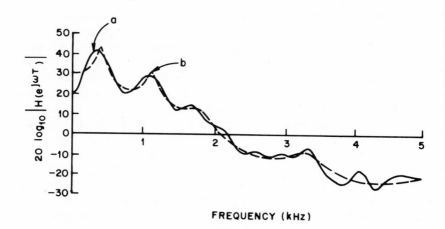

Fig. 24. Comparison of speech spectra obtained by cepstrum smoothing(a) and linear prediction (b).

sampling rate, a good rule of thumb is to allow one pair of poles to account for radiation and glottal effects, and one pair of poles for each formant frequency expected in the frequency range $0 \leq \omega \leq \pi$. Thus, for a 10 kHz sampling rate we expect not more than 5 formant frequencies so p=12 should give a good representation of the spectrum. For unvoiced speech it has been shown that a reasonably small prediction error can be obtained with p on the order of 12. [36,43]

Another point to notice is that the spectrum peaks in Fig. 24a are much broader than the peaks in Fig. 24b. This is an inherent property of the homomorphic method since the spectrum of Fig. 24a was obtained by smoothing the short-time spectrum.

7.3(B) FORMANT FREQUENCY ESTIMATION

Smooth spectra such as Fig. 24b have been used in a peak picking algorithm to estimate formant frequencies in much the same manner as spectra such as Fig. 24a were used.

If p is chosen as discussed above, it can be assumed that the roots of the predictor polynomial will in general correspond to the formant frequencies. These roots can be obtained by factoring the predictor polynomial. An example is shown in Fig. 25. It is clear by comparing the plot of Fig. 25b to the spectrogram that the roots of the predictor polynomial are generally very good estimates of the formant frequencies. As with all formant analysis problems the difficulty in the problem lies in giving a particular formant label to a pole. Several reliable algorithms exist for doing this job [34,41].

7.3(c) PITCH DETECTION

We recall that if we use the predictor coefficients as in our original formulation, then the prediction error

$$\epsilon(n) = x(n) - \sum_{k=1}^{p} \alpha_k x(n-k)$$

should appear very much like the excitation function $\delta(n)$ in Fig. 23. Thus, it might be expected that the prediction error signal might be useful as a starting point for determining properties of the excitation, i.e., pitch period and voiced/unvoiced decision. Several procedures of this type have been suggested [40,42].

7.3(D) OTHER APPLICATIONS

In addition to the above applications, the basic linear prediction coefficients can be transformed directly into a number of other representations of the speech signal. For example, recurrence formulas have been derived for computing the cepstrum and the autocorrelation function [36,39,43]. Also recurrence formulas have been obtained for deriving the area function of a lossless nonuniform acoustic transmission line [36,43]. Finally, the predictor coefficients and excitation information can be used in the model of Fig. 23 to reconstruct a speech waveform [36]. In this case it is necessary to estimate the constant A in Eq. 25 as well as the parameters of the predictor polynomial. This can be done as part of the computation of the predictor coefficients [43] but in most cases A is simply chosen to match the energy of the synthetic speech to the energy of the original speech [36].

7.4 DISCUSSION

The underlying structure of linear prediction analysis assumes that over short sections of speech one can accurately predict the current speech sample from the preceding p samples. Although a wide variety of different formulations of this problem have arisen, the inherent similarities between methods are much larger than the

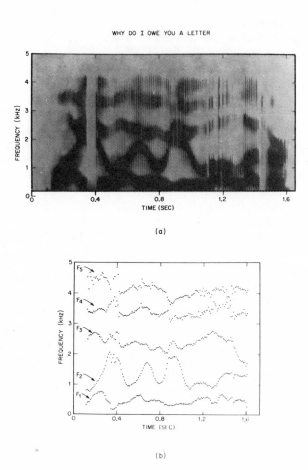

Fig. 25 (a) Spectrogram and (b) roots of predictor polynomial (after Atal[36]).

supposed differences. To make all the decisions as to which particular method to use, which section duration, etc., one must pay strict attention to the ultimate application of the method. Thus for most speech recognition applications, for example, the differences between formulations are not significant. For other more stringent applications, such as analysis/synthesis, systems, the differences may indeed be quite significant and may mean the difference between an acceptable and a non-acceptable system.

8. SUMMARY

In this paper we have discussed a wide variety of digital signal processing methods for representing speech signals. These methods have varied in complexity, information rate, and flexibility from simple waveform coding schemes to analysis schemes such as homomorphic filtering and linear prediction analysis which are directed toward the estimation of the parameters of a detailed model of speech production. We have focused our attention almost exclusively on analysis techniques that are of wide applicability. The results of most of these techniques can be applied in a variety of speech processing applications including speech recognition, speech synthesis, and speaker verification.

REFERENCES

General
1.   G. Fant, Acoustic Theory of Speech Production, Mouton, The Hague, 1970.
2.   J. L. Flanagan, C. H. Coker, L. R. Rabiner, R. W. Schafer, and N. Umeda, "Synthetic Voices for Computers," IEEE Spectrum, Vol. 7, No. 10, October 1970, pp. 22-45.
3.   J. L. Flanagan, Speech Analysis, Synthesis and Perception, 2nd edition, Springer-Verlag, New York, 1972.

Waveform Coding
4.   H. S. Black, Modulation Theory, D. Van Nostrand Co., Inc., Princeton, N.J., 1953.
5.   P. Cummiskey, N. S. Jayant, and J. L. Flanagan, "Adaptive Quantization in Differential PCM Coding of Speech," Bell Syst. Tech. J., Vol. 52, Sept. 1973, pp. 1105-1118.
6.   N. S. Jayant, "Adaptive Delta Modulation with a One-bit Memory," Bell Syst. Tech. J., Vol. 49, March 1970, pp. 321-342.
7.   N. S. Jayant, "Digital Coding of Speech Waveforms," Proc. IEEE., Vol. 62, No. 5, May 1974, pp. 611-632.

8. R. A. McDonald, "Signal-to-Noise and Idle Channel Performance of DPCM Systems -- Particular Application to Voice Signals," Bell Syst. Tech. J., Vol. 45, Sept. 1966, pp. 1123-1151.
9. J. Max, "Quantizing for Minimum Distortion," IRE Trans. Information Theory, Vol. IT-6, March 1960, pp. 7-12.
10. L. H. Rosenthal, R. W. Schafer, and L. R. Rabiner, "An Algorithm for Locating the Beginning and End of an Utterance Using ADPCM Coded Speech," Bell Syst. Tech. J. Vol. 53, No. 6, July-August 1974, pp. 1127-1135.
11. L. H. Rosenthal, L. R. Rabiner, R. W. Schafer, P. Cummiskey, and J. L. Flanagan, "A Multiline Computer Voice Response system Utilizing ADPCM Coded Speech," IEEE Trans. Acoustics, Speech, and Signal Processing Vol. ASSP. 22, No. 5, Oct. 1974, pp. 339-352.

Time-Domain Methods
12. B. Gold, "Note on Buzz-Hiss Detection," J. Acoust. Soc. Amer., Vol. 36, 1964, pp. 1659-1661.
13. B. Gold and L. R. Rabiner, "Parallel Processing Techniques for Estimating Pitch periods of Speech in the Time Domain," J. Acoust. Soc. Amer., Vol. 46, No. 2, August 1969, pp. 442-449.
14. D. R. Reddy, "Computer Recognition of Connected Speech," J. Acoust. Soc. Amer, Vol. 42, No. 2, August 1967, pp. 329-347.
15. M. M. Sondhi, "New Methods of Pitch Detection," IEEE Trans. Audio and Electroacoust., Vol. AU-16, No. 2, June 1968, pp. 262-266.

Short-Time Spectrum Analysis
16. R. B. Blackman and J. W. Tukey, "The Measurment of Power Spectra," Dover Publications, Inc., New York, 1959.
17. J. L. Flanagan and R. M. Golden, "Phase Vocoder," Bell Syst. Tech. J., Vol. 45, Nov. 1966.
18. B. Gold and C. M. Rader, "Systems for Compressing the Bandwidth of Speech," IEEE Trans. Audio and Electroacoust., Vol. AU-15, No. 3, Sept. 1967, pp. 131-135.
19. B. Gold and C. M. Rader, "The Channel Vocoder," IEEE Trans. Audio and Electroacoust., Vol. AU-15, No. 4, December 1967, pp. 148-160.
20. T. Martin, "Acoustic Recognition of a Limited Vocabulary in Continuous Speech," Ph.D. Thesis, Univ. of Pennsylvania, 1970. (Available from Univ. Microfilms, Ann Arbor, Mich.)

21.   P. Mermelstein, "Computer Generated Spectrogram Displays for On-Line Speech Research," IEEE Trans. Audio and Electroacoust. Vol. AU-19, March 1971, pp. 44-47.

22.   A. M. Noll, "Pitch Determination of Human Speech by the Harmonic Product Spectrum, The Harmonic Sum Spectrum, and a Maximum Likelihood Estimate," in Computer Processing in Communications Proceedings, New York, N.Y., April 8, 9, 10, 1969, Jerome Fox, ed., Polytechnic Press, New York, pp. 779-797.

23.   A. V. Oppenheim, "Speech Spectrograms Using the Fast Fourier Transform," IEEE Spectrum, August 1970, pp. 57-62.

24.   R. W. Schafer and L. R. Rabiner, "Design of Digital Filter Banks for Speech Analysis," Bell System Tech. J., Vol. 50, No. 10, Dec. 1971, pp. 3097-3115.

25.   R. W. Schafer and L. R. Rabiner, "Design and Simulation of a Speech Analysis-Synthesis System Based on Short-Time Fourier Analysis," IEEE Trans. Audio and Electroacoustics, Vol. AU-21, No. 3, June 1973, pp. 165-174.

26.   M. R. Schroeder, "Vocoders: Analysis and Synthesis of Speech," Proc. IEEE, Vol. 54, 1966, pp. 720-734.

27.   M. R. Schroeder, "Period Histogram and Product Spectrum: New Methods for Fundamental-Frequency Measurement," J. Acoust. Soc. Amer., Vol. 43, No. 4, April 1968, pp. 829-834.

Homomorphic Speech Analysis
28.   J. E. Luck, "Automatic Speaker Verification Using Cepstral Measurements," J. Acoust. Soc. Amer., Vol. 46, No. 4, October 1969, pp. 1026-1032.

29.   A. M. Noll, "Cepstrum Pitch Determination," J. Acoust, Soc. Am., Vol. 41, Feb. 1967, pp. 293-309.

30.   A. V. Oppenheim and R. W. Schafer, "Homomorphic Analysis of Speech," IEEE Trans. Audio and Electroacoustics, Vol. AU-16, No. 2, June 1968, pp. 221-226.

31.   A. V. Oppenheim, R. W. Schafer, and T. G. Stockham, Jr., "Nonlinear Filtering of Multiplied and Convolved Signals," Proc. IEEE,, Vol. 56, No. 8, August 1968, pp. 1264-1291.

32.   A. V. Oppenheim, "A Speech Analysis-Synthesis System Based on Homomorphic Filtering," J. Acoust. Soc. Amer., Vol. 45, Feb. 1969, pp. 458-465.

33.   J. Olive, "Automatic Formant Tracking in a Newton-Raphson Technique," J. Acoust. Soc. Amer., Vol. 50, Part 2, August 1971, pp. 661-670.

34.   R. W. Schafer and L. R. Rabiner, "System for Automatic Formant Analysis of Voiced Speech," J. Acoust. Soc. Amer., Vol. 47, No. 2, Feb. 1970, pp. 634-648.

Linear Prediction Analysis
35.   B. S. Atal and M. R. Schroeder, "Adaptive Predictive Coding of Speech Signals," Bell Syst. Tech. J., Vol. 49, 1970, pp. 1973-1986.
36.   B. S. Atal and S. L. Hanauer, "Speech Analysis and Synthesis by Linear Prediction of the Speech Wave," J. Acoust. Soc. Amer., Vol. 50, Part 2, August 1971, pp. 637-655.
37.   D. K. Faddeev and V. N. Faddeeva, Computational Methods of Linear Algebra, W. H. Freeman and Co., San Francisco, 1963.
38.   F. Itakura and S. Saito, "An Analysis-Synthesis Telephony System Based on Maximum Likelihood Method," Electronics and Commun. in Japan, Vol. 53, A, 1970, pp. 36-43.
39.   J. I. Makhoul and J. J. Wolf, "Linear Prediction and the Spectral Analysis of Speech," Bolt Beranek and Newman Inc., 50 Moulton St., Boston, Mass., BBN Report No. 2304, August 31, 1972.
40.   J. N. Maksym, "Real-time Pitch Extraction by Adaptive Prediction of the Speech Waveform," IEEE Trans. Audio and Electroacoustics, Vol. AU-21, No. 3, June 1973, pp. 149-153.
41.   J. D. Markel, "Digital Inverse Filtering--A New Tool for Formant Trajectory Estimation," IEEE Trans. Audio and Electroacoustics, Vol. AU-20, June 1972, pp. 129-137.
42.   J. D. Markel, "The Sift Algorithm for Fundamental Frequency Estimation," IEEE Trans. on Audio and Electroacoustics, Vol. AU-20, No. 5, Dec. 1972, pp. 367-377.
43.   J. D. Markel, A. H. Gray, Jr., and H. Wakita, "Linear Prediction of Speech-Theory and Practice," Speech Communications Research Laboratory, Inc., Santa Barbara, Calif., SCRL Monograph No. 10, Sept. 1973.
44.   J. H. Wilkinson, Rounding Errors in Algebraic Processes, Prentice-Hall, Inc., Englewood Cliffs, New Jersey, 1963.

ROUNDING ERRORS IN FIXED POINT ARITHMETIC

W. Morven Gentleman
Department of Applied Analysis & Computer Science
University of Waterloo
Waterloo, Ontario, Canada

ARITHMETIC

Numbers are generally represented in computers in one or two fixed wordlengths, and an immediate question is where is the binary point? For hardware reasons, it is attractive to put the binary point in the same place in all words, and moreover, to put it either at the right of all the bits in a word or at the right of the leading bit (which then becomes, in effect, a sign bit). The difference between these two is not essential and for convenience of presentation we will henceforth assume the latter.

A number representation like this is called "fixed point arithmetic". As a consequence of our choice of the binary point position, all representable numbers lie in the interval $[-1, +1]$, and if the wordlength is $t + 1$ bits, the gap between representable numbers is 2^{-t}. Addition and subtraction clearly can be performed without rounding error. Multiplication or division may, however, produce an erroneous result in that the true result may not be exactly expressable as a representable number – which is also true, of course, for arbitrary input numbers. In each of these cases the computed result should nevertheless be expressable as a perturbation in the true result of at most one bit in the last place, i.e. an absolute error of at most 2^{-t}.

Although the facts just presented have often been used to derive error analyses of fixed point computations, there is one crucial observation missing. It is a very unusual computation for which, when expressed in the natural way, the final result and all intermediate results are bounded in magnitude above by unity and below by something large enough that the inter number gap of 2^{-t} still permits acceptable accuracy. Thus computations cannot be done in the most natural way but must be scaled. Obviously the scaling will be by some power of two so that it is just shifting. It is the bits lost in this shifting which are the primary rounding errors in many computations. Even if no actual shifts are used during the course of a computation, the requirement that the input be scaled down enough to guarantee that no shifts will be needed, can produce a loss of accuracy relative to possible inputs that far exceeds any additional errors introduced in the computation.

How can the scaling be chosen? It is possible to build hardware which optimally scales each individual number so that it has no leading zero bits, and records the scale factor used in a separate field associated with that word. This is, of course, just the number representation called "floating point arithmetic". (The name comes from the alternate but equivalent interpretation that the binary point is not in the same position in all words, and that the extra field indicates where it is.)

Alternatively, we can sometimes show, particularly for matrix computations such as the fast Fourier transform, that the scaling of individual elements of an array does not matter much: all that really matters is the scaling of the array as a whole, and in particular its largest element. This leads to the use of a single scaling factor for the entire array. Such a number representation is called "block floating point". Typically, little overhead is incurred even in software in choosing a scaling factor optimal for the particular array obtained at each stage of a computation

By contrast, in fixed point computation, the scaling factors must be chosen by a priori analysis, and hence are apt to be unduly conservative, or they must be chosen by software at run time, which being expensive, is likely to be done infrequently, and hence also is apt to be conservative.

ERROR ANALYSIS

Many algorithms which appear to be quite satisfactory if performed with exact arithmetic are not satisfactory when performed with finite precision. In order to understand which algorithms are numerically unstable (i.e., unduly sensitive to perturbations like rounding errors) and which aspects of the problem induce this sensitivity, numerical analysts have, over the past twenty years, developed powerful techniques for the error analysis of algorithms. One of these is the use of norms to measure the magnitude of perturbations. Another is the concept of backward error analysis: characterizing errors by the amount the given problem would have to be changed in order to produce the computed result as the exact result for the modified problem. But perhaps most important was the discovery that floating point computation can be described as a small, bounded, relative error in the exact results of an operation whose operands are particular machine represented numbers, and that this description was amenable to analysis to derive error bounds.

Using these tools, we have been able to establish confidence in certain methods whose accuracy had been questioned (eg., the solution of simultaneous equations by Gaussian elimination with complete pivoting [9], or the modified Gram Schmidt algorithm for solving linear least squares problems [1] -- in both cases it having been possible to establish that the answers obtained are the exact solution to problems differing from the given ones only in the last few bits of the input data). We have been able to demonstrate why certain methods fail and when they should be avoided (eg., the classical Gram Schmidt algorithm for orthogonalizing vectors which does not completely remove from new vectors the components in the directions of vectors already produced and hence causes trouble if the original vectors are too close together, or Goertzel's method for computing Fourier coefficients -- for low frequencies the recurrence values for the error can grow much faster than the recurrence values for the signal are growing [2]). We have even been able to discover unexpected aspects of the behaviour of error (eg., that naive iterative improvement of the solutions to linear least squares problems doesn't work, because the dominant term in the error is associated with the square of the condition number of the matrix times the ratio of the norm of the residual vector to the norm of the solution vector, which naive iterative improvement does not change [5]).

Unfortunately, what we have not been able to develop are tools to answer the much more difficult questions, which often arise in engineering, of realistic error estimates. With bounds, there is always a danger of over-bounding. The original error analysis for the fast Fourier transform correctly predicted that the ratio of rms error to rms signal would grow linearly with the number of stages in the transform, but the constant in the bound was about 6 to 10 times larger than what is observed. More recently it has been shown that this bound can be reduced to 2n by doing the analysis differently [3] -- whereas for the past 15 years it has been thought that the effective perturbation induced in a matrix by computing the QR decomposition by Givens transformations could be as big as n^2. Regrettably, another problem with bounds is that the magnitude of the errors actually observed in practice can depend strongly on seemingly trivial details of the implementation of the algorithm or the arithmetic hardware -- details which will probably vary from implementation to implementation.

As an example (due to M. G. Cox) of how seemingly trivial differences can matter, consider the floating point computation of the image y of a point x in the interval (a,b) under the linear transformation that maps that interval into (-1, 1). Three ways to compute y are

I $Y = 2x/(B-A) - (A+B)/(B-A)$

II $Y = (x-(A+B)/2)/((B-A)/2)$

III $Y = ((x-A) + (x-B))/(B-A)$.

There seems little to among these, except one might suspect II is better than I. By analysis or experiment one can verify that II is slightly better than I, but III can be significantly better than either I or II, since they each involve an error of magnitude (a+b)/(b-a) times roundoff error, which III does not.

The mathematical manipulations required to produce error bounds of floating point computations are still sufficiently difficult that analyses have not yet been obtained for many computations of interest. Attempting error estimates, rather than bounds, increases the difficulty enormously. (The fast Fourier transform analysis by Kaneko and Liu [7] is perhaps the only derivation of satisfactory error estimates for a complicated computation). Working with fixed point, rather than floating point, increases the difficulty enormously too, largely because of the lack of any convenient way to incorporate scaling into the analysis (corresponding, of course, to the difficulties of providing appropriate scaling in the programs to be analyzed).

From time to time, attempts have been made to use statistical assumptions to derive error estimates directly. For example, in digital signal processing, roundoff error is sometimes treated as white noise injected at certain points in the processing circuit. Although acceptable for simple enough fixed point computations, such analyses are frequently unsuccessful at predicting observed roundoff errors in complicated algorithms for two reasons: they treat the errors as independent random variables, which can be a very bad assumption, and they cannot easily handle data dependent scaling shifts.

PRACTICAL ADVICE

    Given that there is a need to do computations in fixed point, and to answer certain types of questions (eg., which algorithm should be used and how should it be programmed; how many bits need be used for the arithmetic of some special purpose machine) and given that, as discussed above, our error analysis techniques have been primarily successful at examing stability of floating point computations, what can be done today?

    For some simple algorithms, such as linear digital filters [6] or block floating point fast Fourier transforms [8], it is possible to completely analyze the computation and obtain both error estimates and bounds which is fortunate, given the importance of these computations.

More generally, we cannot expect to be able to do the fixed point error analysis, but it may be possible to do the floating point error analysis. If an error estimate can be obtained, or if through simulation it can be determined how much of an overestimate the error bound is, this floating point error analysis can be used as an indication of what a fixed point computation might hope to achieve with optimal scaling. We can then separately examine how much additional is lost by not having optimal scaling.

In some cases, not even the floating point analysis can be obtained. One can often, however, conjecture what form an error estimate might have, and through simulation conduct experiments to test this conjecture and incidentally obtain the parameter values for the form.

Finally, one might hope that when none of these are possible, one could at least extrapolate from the analyses that are available to be able to program an algorithm in a way not likely to be excessively inaccurate. Use of orthogonal transformations when possible, for example, controls both scale change and rounding error. Performing computations in an order that minimizes the number of transformations made to a single data item (tree-like summation, for instance, where pairs of numbers are added, then pairs of sums of pairs, etc.) often controls linear error growth. One conclusion about hardware that we might draw is that if even a limited exponent range floating point arithmetic could be built that was competative in speed and cost with fixed point, when used in connection with conventional scaling techniques to reduce the exponent range required to that available, the gain in accuracy due to optimal scaling would more than offset the loss of a few bits to the exponent.

REFERENCES

1. Bjorck, A. "Solving Linear Least Squares Problems by Gram Schmidt Orthogonalization", BIT, Vol. 7, 1967, pp. 1-21.
2. Gentleman, W. M., "An Error Analysis of Goertzel's (Watt's) Method for Computing Fourier Coefficients", Computer Journal, Vol. 12, No. 2, (May 1969) pp. 160-165.
3. Gentleman, W. M., "Error Analysis of QR Decomposition by Givens Transformation", to appear in Linear Algebra and its Applications.
4. Gold, B., and Rader, C. M., Digital Processing of Signals, McGraw-Hill, New York, 1969.

5.   Golub, G. H., and Wilkinson, J. H., "Note on the Iterative Refinement of Least Squares Solution", Num. Math. Vol. 9, 1966, pp. 139–148.

6.   IEEE Transactions on Audio and Electroacoustics AU–20, No. 4 October 1972 (Issue based on Arden House Digital Signal Processing Conference of January 1972).

7.   Kaneko, T., and Liu, B., "Accumulation of Roundoff Error in Fast Fourier Transforms", JACM, Vol. 17, No. 4, (October 1970) pp. 637–654.

8.   Welch, P. D., "A Fixed Point fast Fourier transform error analysis", IEEE Transaction on Audio and Electroacoustics, Vol. AU–17, No. 2 (June 1969) pp. 151–157.

9.   Wilkinson, J. H. Rounding Errors in Algebraic Processes, Prentice Hall, Englewood Cliffs, N. J., 1963.

10.   Wilkinson, J. H. The Algebraic Eigenvalue Problem, Oxford University Press, London, 1965.

GENERAL SPEECH MODELS AND LINEAR ESTIMATION THEORY[†]

Martin Morf[††]
Thomas Kailath
B. Dickinson[†††]
Dept. of Electrical Engineering
Stanford University
Stanford, California 94305

ABSTRACT
We discuss how some new procedures developed in linear system theory and least-squares estimation can be used to determine a poles and zeros linear filter model for speech waveforms. This is a potentially more accurate model for speech and appears to be computable with only a small additional effort beyond that required for the currently popular all-pole models.

I. INTRODUCTION

Recently some techniques of linear estimation theory have been applied to the problems of analysis and synthesis of speech. Encouraging results have been reported by many authors, and the so called linear predictive encoding (LPC) of speech for data compression seems to be a natural way of eliminating the two major components of redundancy in speech signals, the quasi-periodicity of the waveform and the non-uniformity of the short-term power spectrum. In addition, the linear predictive models, which are linear recursive digital filters, can sometimes be made to correspond to actual physical models of the

---

[†]This work was supported by the Air Force Office of Scientific Research, AF Systems Command, under Contract AF 44-620-69-C-0101 and partially by the Joint Services Electronics Program under Contract N-00014-67-A-0112-0044.

[††]Hasler Foundation Fellow

[†††]Currently at Dept. of Electrical Engineering, Princeton University, Princeton, N.J. 08540.

vocal tract and hence offer certain other possibilities in the study of speech. Since a detailed discussion of these aspects is outside our scope, we refer here only to the works of Atal, Atal and Schroeder, Atal and Hanauer, Wakita, Markel, Itakura, Itakura and Saito, Markel and Gray, and others as well. - Several references are quoted in the bibliography.

Our purpose in this paper will be to point out some recently developed algorithms for linear estimation that are closely related to the LPC (autocorrelation) algorithms used in recent speech work. The new algorithms are of interest, because they can deal with more general signal models (having poles and zeros) and can also handle the types of non-stationarity that may arise in speech models. Furthermore, the computational burden of these new algorithms is of the same order of magnitude as that of the algorithms currently used in linear predictive encoding (LPC). Moreover, as in LPC, our algorithms can be implemented by recursive digital-filter structures, so that standard hardware realizations can be used. Finally, we shall show that these algorithms offer some insight into the important problem of finding methods that enable one to work directly on the observed signal without first computing covariance or autocorrelation functions.

The justification for these claims will be developed in the succeeding sections. However we must stress that the above comments are admittedly tentative since our own experience with speech models is very limited. The main purpose of this exposition is that more knowledgeable workers might find some new possibilities with the new algorithms that we shall describe.

We begin by reviewing the speech model currently used in LPC, which is an all-pole recursive filter. While this model has been quite successfully used, we point out in Section II that a more general poles-and-zeros model may take better account of certain speech characteristics. In Sections III & IV we describe some algorithms for computing such general models. The computational effort required for these algorithms is not substantially greater than that for the standard LPC algorithms.

We actually have a two-step procedure for determination of the general speech model from estimates of the covariance sequence. The first step is to determine a finite representation of the covariance sequence, and this can be done by using what is known in linear system theory as a minimal realization algorithm. The one we use is a version of the Berlekamp-Massey procedure. Given the covariance representation, Section IV describes an efficient new algorithm, using Chandrasekhar-type equations, for calculation of a particular (innovations) model of the speech process.

In Section V we give an alternative interpretation of the above procedure in terms of ARMA (autoregressive-moving average) rather than state-space equations. This is useful because it suggests some possibilities for on-line modeling procedures, avoiding explicit preliminary estimation of the covariance. Finally in Appendix I, we recast our solution in terms of determining the impulse response of an all-pole (autoregressive) model, and show that it reduces to the usual Levinson algorithm for this problem in the purely stationary (Toeplitz matrix) case.

II. A GENERAL SPEECH MODEL

The linear predictive coding of sampled speech signals is depicted in Figure 1. In this scheme, one models a voiced sound over a period of roughly 10 msec by extracting a pitch frequency and fitting an all-pole (autoregressive) filter to the short-term auto-correlation function of the speech waveform. Unvoiced sounds are modeled as "white noise" exciting a recursive filter. Generally, the pitch excitation waveform is taken to be a series of periodic pulses at the measured pitch period.

Now, it seems to us that the lack of "zeros" in all-pole recursive filters is a notable drawback to accurate modeling. Although zeros have been determined to be far less effective than the poles of the model, their importance in sounds that have a strong nasalized component is much greater. For such sounds, zeros arise from the interaction of signals arriving via the nose and the mouth. Modeling of such sounds by all-pole recursive filters will require many additional delays. Furthermore, assuming that the vocal track really has an underlying rational (poles and zeros) model, the fitted parameters may have somewhat more physical significance since they can probably be estimated more consistently (see [CR]).

We next observe that an important reason for the wide use of all-pole filters in linear predictive data compression schemes is the availability of fast computational procedures for obtaining recursive (autoregressive) models from autocorrelation function data. However, these fast schemes are based on the assumption that the speech signal is statistically stationary, apart from the periodic excitation function (the pitch). It seems to us that this stationarity assumption is somewhat tenuous over intervals as short as 5-10 msec and that a more reasonable assumption might be that while the process is not stationary, the underlying model is time invariant (i.e., has constant parameters) over the period of interest, which might actually be much longer than 5 - 10 msec. For example, it could be the duration of a phoneme.

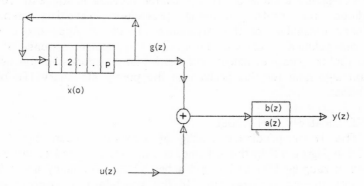

x(0)   one pitch period (initial condition) of the
g(z)   sampled glottal waveform (z-transformed),
u(z)   white excitation noise (z-transformed),
b(z)   numerator polynomial (containing the zeros) and
a(z)   denominator polynomial (containing the poles) of the
       linear model producing
y(z)   the sampled (z-transformed) speech.

Figure 1. The Finite-Dimensional Linear Space Model

Another potentially useful consequence of replacing the stationarity assumption by that of a constant model is that we would have the possibility of also lumping the periodic pitch waveform into the model. This will enable us to work over longer time intervals, with consequent advantages for statistical estimation. The pitch can be incorporated by using a circulating shift register of length equal to the pitch period, driven by a single pulse or some other appropriate sequence. Although the order of this model might be large, the actual number of nonzero parameters can be much less.

Here we wish to note that all the above factors motivate us to postulate that the speech waveform y(.) over an appropriate interval can be regarded as being generated by driving a general constant-parameter finite-dimensional linear system with a combination of partially deterministic (only initial conditions are random) and white noise (purely random) excitations.

Such systems have of course been the object of study in linear system theory for several decades, but their interaction with random processes has been especially intensively explored in the last decade under the heading of linear estimation theory. It has become clear that the estimation problem is essentially just a particular stochastic modeling problem, to wit, finding a representation of the observed process as the output of a causal and causally invertible linear system driven by white noise. The significance of this (essentially unique) representation has been known for some time, but it is only comparatively recently that efficient recursive methods for obtaining it have been studied.

   To be more specific, it will be necessary to introduce some notation. We shall begin by summarizing the standard ways of describing finite-dimensional linear systems (FDLS).
A FDLS with

$$\text{input} \quad = \quad u(0) , \ u(1) , \ u(2) , \ \ldots$$
$$\text{output} \quad = \quad y(0) , \ y(1) , \ y(2) , \ \ldots$$

can be described by an ARMA (autoregressive-moving average) model,

$$y(i) + a(1)y(i-1) + \ldots + a(n)y(i-n) = w(i) ,$$
$$w(i) = b(0)u(i) + \ldots + b(m)u(i-m) , \ i \geq 0 , \ n > m \geq 0$$

with the values $\{ y(-1) , \ldots , y(-n) \}$ and $\{ u(-1) , \ldots , u(-m) \}$ as initial conditions. It will be convenient to introduce the z-transform

$$y(z) = y(0) + y(1) \ z^{-1} + \ldots .$$

Then the z-transform of the above difference equation is

$$a(z)y(z) = b(z)u(z) + \{ \text{ terms involving the initial conditions } \}$$

where

$$a(z) = z^n + a(1)z^{n-1} + \ldots + a(n)$$

$$b(z) = b(0)z^n + b(1)z^{n-1} + \ldots + b(m)z^{n-m}$$

The transfer function is the ratio of $y(z)$ and $u(z)$ with zero initial conditions,

$$H(z) \quad = \quad b(z)/a(z)$$

Finally we could also use a state-space description, with initial condition $x(0)$,

$$x(i+1) = \Phi \, x(i) + \Gamma \, u(i+1),$$

$$y(i) = H \, x(i) , \ i \geq 0$$

The matrices $\{ H, \Phi, \Gamma \}$ can be chosen in many ways provided

$$H \, (zI - \Phi)^{-1} z \, \Gamma = H(z) = b(z)/a(z)$$

A particular way, which is often convenient, is the so-called "observer canonical form" in which

$$\Phi = \begin{vmatrix} -a(1) & 1 & & & \\ -a(2) & 0 & 1 & & \\ \cdot & & \cdot & \cdot & \cdot \\ \cdot & & & & \cdot \\ \cdot & & & & \cdot & 1 \\ -a(n) & & & & 0 \end{vmatrix}, \quad \Gamma = \begin{vmatrix} b(0) \\ b(1) \\ \cdot \\ \cdot \\ b(m) \\ 0 \end{vmatrix}$$

$$H = [\, 1 \quad 0 \; 0 \, . \, . \, 0 \,]$$

When the input $\{\, u(.) \,\}$ is a random white-noise sequence,

$$E\, u(i) = 0\,, \quad E\, u(i)u(j) = Q\, \delta_{i\,j}$$

the initial value $x(0)$ is usually taken as a random variable with

$$E\, x(0) = 0, \quad E\, x(0)x(0)^T = \Pi(0)\,, \quad E\, u(i)x(0)^T = 0$$

The state-space model gives us a convenient way of computing the covariance function of the output process y. Some simple calculation gives

$$R_y(i,j) \;=\; \begin{cases} M\, \Phi^{i-j}\, N(j)\,, & i \geq j \\ N(i)^T (\Phi^T)^{j-i} M^T\,, & i \leq j \end{cases}$$

where the row matrix M and the time-variant column matrix N(i) can be taken as

$$M = H, \quad N(i) = \Pi(i)\, H^T$$

and the state-variance matrix obeys the recursion

$$\Pi(i+1) \;=\; \Phi\, \Pi(i)\, \Phi^T + \Gamma\, Q\, \Gamma^T\,, \quad \Pi(0) = \Pi_0$$

We observe that even though the underlying model $\{\, H, \Phi,$ grk-G>, $Q \,\}$ or $\{\, a(z), b(z), Q \,\}$ is time-invariant, the output process $\{\, y(i)\, c\}$ is not stationary in general. However if Φ is a stability matrix, that is, if the magnitude of all eigenvalues of Φ are less than one then as $i \to \infty$, $\Pi(i+1) \to [\Pi]$ where $[\Pi]$ is the positive definite solution of the so-called Lyapunov equation:

$$[\Pi] = \Phi[\Pi]\Phi^T + \Gamma Q \Gamma^T.$$

The covariance now reduces to a function only of $|i-j|$

$$R_y(i,j) = M \Phi^{|i-j|} N$$

where N is now the constant matrix $[\Pi]$ H^T.

The nonstationarity is of course due to the "transients" caused by the initial condition and the above merely states the transients eventually die out and the process becomes stationary. This "steady-state" condition is immediately achieved if the initial variance is $\Pi(0) = [\Pi]$, but this may not always be a good assumption in the speech problem.

In the stationary case, we can also take the z-transforms to get the power-spectral density

$$S_y(z) = M (zI-\Phi)^{-1} zN + N^T(I-z\Phi)^{-T} M^T,$$

Which can also be written in terms of the transfer function and the ARMA model as

$$S_y(z) = H(z)H(z^{-1}) = b(z)Qb(z^{-1})/a(z)a(z^{-1}).$$

THE MODELING PROBLEM:

One part of the speech problem can be described as follows: we observe $\{ y(i) \}$ and estimate $R_y(i,j)$, and from this attempt to reconstruct a finite-dimensional model. In linear predictive coding it is assumed that $\{ y(i) \}$ is stationary and purely autoregressive (i.e., that $b(z)z^{-n}$ = a constant). We note here that the LPC algorithm is not usually described in this stochastic language, but via certain deterministic minimization problems -- see, e.g. [MW]. However, embedding the LPC approach in a stochastic framework brings out its connections with much related work and makes possible further insights and developments, as shown, for example, by the present paper. In our stochastic point of view all statistical averages are initially to be regarded as ensemble averages; however, in the final implementation, such averages will generally have to be replaced by time averages (see [DR]).

In this paper, we shall show how the LPC assumptions can be relaxed to include "transient" nonstationarity and to permit models with zeros. However, we should first note the important fact that it is not possible to uniquely identify { a(z), b(z) } or { H, Φ, Γ, Q, Π(0) } from knowledge of the R_y (i,j). In the stationary case, we can identify the products $a(z)a(z^{-1})$ and $b(z)Qb(z^{-1})$. Now a(z) can be fixed uniquely by the (stability) requirement that its roots lie within the unit circle, but there is no such constraint on b(z). We can obtain a <u>unique</u> model by insisting that all the roots of b(z) also lie within the unit circle. This means that the transfer function b(z)/a(z) will be both causal and causally invertible, a requirement that can be extended to the nonstationary case as well. As we shall see presently, we pay a certain price for restricting ourselves to such models, but we believe that the advantages outweigh these costs.

Therefore we shall say that our modeling problem is to find a causal and causally invertible finite dimensional linear system, that when driven by white noise and suitable initial conditions yields an output with a specified covariance, R_y (i,j). We assume that this R_y (i,j) comes from a FDLS (H, Φ, Γ) with dimension n. We do not assume that { H, Φ, Γ, n } are known. One solution to this problem involves the following three steps:

1) determination of the { R_y(i,j) } from a record of { y(i) }
2) factorization of R_y(i,j) into the triple { H, Φ, N(i) }
3) determination of the IR from knowledge of { H, Φ, N(i) }.

There are several statistical procedures for estimating R_y(i,j), especially when it is stationary (i.e., a function only of |i-j|), and we shall not go into these here (see [JW], [Brg], [Ca]). The fact that we can obtain only estimates of the { R_y(i,j) } and not their actual values has to be kept in mind and brought into a final evaluation. However the main aim of this survey paper is to describe some methods for carrying out steps 2) and 3). Therefore we shall assume here that we are given the true R_y(i,j). An efficient method for step 2) will be covered in the next section, while several different methods for step 3) will be discussed in Sections IV and V.

III. DETERMINING THE COVARIANCE TRIPLE

The problem of finding { H, Φ, N(i) } so that the covariance R_y(i,j) can be written

$$R_y(i,j) = \begin{cases} H\,\Phi^{i-j}\,N(j), & i \geq j \\ N(i)^T (\Phi^T)^{j-i}\,H^T, & i \leq j \end{cases}$$

will be shown to be equivalent to the by-now much studied minimal realization (MR) problem of linear system theory [KFA], [Si1]. In the standard MR problem, one seeks to find a triple { C,A,B } so that

$$C \, A^i B = T(i), \quad i \geq 0$$

where { T(i) } is a given set of numbers (usually characterizing the impulse response of a linear system). To relate the two problems we merely have to note that for every j we can write

$$R_y(i+j,j) = H \, \Phi^i N(j), \quad i \geq 0$$

and then we can identify a triple by

$$H = C \, , \quad \Phi = A \, , \quad N(j) = B(j)$$

and use the standard MR procedure.

If the process is stationary, we clearly only need to carry out the above procedure for a single value of j , e.g., j = 0 [RK]. We shall see in the next section that there are certain fast algorithms for determining the IR that require only the value N(0) (rather than the whole sequence { N(j) }) whether or not the process y is stationary.

Actually there are also fast algorithms for minimal realization. The first algorithms, associated with the names of Ho and Kalman [HK], Silverman [Si2], and Youla and Tissi [YT], required $O(n^3)$ operations to compute the triple { C, A, B }, n being the dimension of the state - vector of the realization. In a new approach to the minimal realization problem, Rissanen [Ri2] developed a recursive algorithm to find nested solutions for increasing lengths of the sequence. It turned out that a similar but more efficient algorithm requiring storage and operations of order n per iteration, was developed in a coding theory context by Berlekamp several years earlier [Be]; then Massey [Ma] applied this algorithm to the realization of finite-state linear systems. More recently, we have shown [DMK] how such algorithms may be naturally extended to realization of matrix sequences, but this refinement is not needed in speech coding, except perhaps in some approaches to the pitch problem.

The Berlekamp-Massey algorithm works by finding a sequence of monic polynomials { $a_k(z)$ } of least degree such that $a_k(z)$ is the denominator of a rational function whose expansion in z^{-1} has its first k terms equal to the first k terms of a given sequence . In our case, we take the covariance sequence { $R_y(0,i)$ }. Let its z-transform be

$$r_0(z) = R_y(0,0) + R_y(0,1)z^{-1} + R_y(0,2)z^{-2} + \dots$$

and its rational approximation

$$r_0(z) = c_{0k}(z)/a_k(z) + \Delta(k)z^{-k} + \Delta(k+1)z^{-k-1} + \dots$$

where $\{ \Delta(.) \}$ is a sequence of residuals.

This is the so-called Pade' approximation problem. Then a triple can be found by writing down the matrices for any state-space realization of this rational approximation, e.g. the observer realization mentioned in Section II.

To present the algorithm, we let $\alpha(z)$ be an auxiliary polynomial. Then the algorithm proceeds as follows, where only changes in the variables are indicated.

0.   We initialize with $k = N$, the index of the first non-zero $\{ r(i) \}$ by setting $a_n(z) = z^n$ and $\alpha(z) = 1$.
1. $\Delta \leftarrow r(N)$
2.   Compute $q(k)$ as the coefficient of $z^{-(k+1-d(k))}$ in the product $r(z)$ $a_k(z)$, where $d(k)$ is the degree of $a_k(z)$.
3.   If $a(k) = 0$, $k \leftarrow k + 1$ and go to 2   (no change)
4.   If $k > 2\,d(k)$ go to 7
5. $a_{k+1} \leftarrow a_k - z^{k-d(k)}\, \alpha\, q(k) / \Delta$ (minor change)
6. $k \leftarrow k + 1$ and go to 2
7.   a) $a_{k+1} \leftarrow z^{k-d(k)}a_k - \alpha\, q(k) / \Delta$
       b) $\alpha \leftarrow a_k$
       c) $\Delta \leftarrow q(k)$, $d(k+1) \leftarrow k - d(k)$ (major change)
8. $k \leftarrow k + 1$ and go to 2

Since we have assumed that there is an underlying rational model of order n, the algorithm will give $q(k) = 0$ for all $k > 2n$, thus also identifying n. We shall in the sequel assume that the true n has been found by this procedure and shall not enter here into the numerical question of when the algorithm has terminated.

From $a_n(z)$ and $c_n(z) = r(z)\, a_n(z)$, we can find $\{ H, \Phi, N(0) \}$ by for example using the observer canonical form discussed in Section II.

IV. DETERMINING THE INNOVATIONS REPRESENTATION

Given a process $\{ y(i), i \geq 0 \}$ with the covariance

$$R_y(i,j) = H \Phi^{i-j} N(j) \quad , \quad i \geq j$$

it can be shown that a causal and causally invertible model for $\{ y(i), 0 \leq i \leq N \}$ can be written [GK1]

$$\xi(i+1) = \Phi \xi(i) + K(i)R^\epsilon(i)^{-1} \epsilon(i) , \quad \xi(0) = 0$$

$$Y(i) = H \xi(i) + \epsilon(i), \quad i \geq 0$$

where $\{ \epsilon(i) \}$ is a white - noise sequence with $E \epsilon(i) \epsilon(j)^T = R^\epsilon(i) \delta_{ij}$ and the $\{ K(i), R^\epsilon(i) \}$ are deterministic sequences that can be calculated in several ways.

    A general method, which holds even for time variant H and Φ, is [GK1] via the solution of a matrix Riccati difference equation for an auxiliary $n \times n$ matrix Σ:

$$K(i) = \Phi (N(i) - \Sigma(i) H^T) ,$$

$$R^\epsilon(i) = H N(i) - H \Sigma(i) H^T = N(i)^T H^T - H \Sigma(i) H^T$$

with $\Sigma (i)$ obeying the nonlinear recursion

$$\Sigma(i+1) = \Phi \Sigma(i)\Phi^T + K(i)R^\epsilon(i)^{-1}K(i)^T , \quad \Sigma(0) = 0$$

This model is time-variant, but it is causal and causally invertible which is a useful property for many applications, e.g. in predicting the $\{ y(i) \}$ sequence. Such models also have certain "minimal variance" properties ([GK2], [Fa]) and can be regarded as the "projection" upon the observable $\{y(i)\}$ space of any other (not necessarily causally invertible) model generating $\{ y(i) \}$ with the specified covariance. In this case, $\hat{x} (i+1) = E x(i+1) | [y(i), \ldots, y(0)]$ the linear least squares estimate of the state $x(i+1)$ of the model, given observations up to time i. This property may be useful in certain adaptive identification schemes.

    Note also that if Φ is a stability matrix, then

as $i \to \infty$, $\Sigma(i) \to [\Sigma]$, a constant matrix,

and we have a time-invariant model. This model may of course be used as a satisfactory approximation over a sufficiently large time interval.

To obtain the IR by the above method requires knowledge of the entire { N(i) } sequence and also $O(n^3)$ operations to solve the Riccati equation. We now describe a scheme that can exploit the assumed constancy of H and Φ. This scheme, which only needs knowledge of N(0) and only requires $O(n^2)$ operations, can be specified by the equations [MSK]

$$K(i+1) \;=\; K(i) + \Phi Y(i)M(i)Y(i)^T H^T \;,\quad K(0) \;=\; \Phi N(0)$$

$$R^\epsilon(i+1) \;=\; R^\epsilon(i) + HY(i)M(i)Y(i)^T H^T, \quad R^\epsilon(0) \;=\; HN(0)$$

where Y(i) and M(i) are $n \times \alpha$ and $\alpha \times \alpha$ matrices found via the recursions

$$Y(i+1) \;=\; (\, \Phi - K(i)\, R^\epsilon(i)^{-1} H\,)\; Y(i)$$

$$M(i+1) = M(i) + M(i)\, Y(i)^T H^T R^\epsilon(i)^{-1} H\, Y(i)\, M(i)$$

and Y(0), M(0) and α are generally found by a certain auxiliary calculation (see below). In the special (stationary) case where

$$N(i) = N \;\;,\quad \text{a constant} \;,$$

we have

$$\alpha = 1, \;\; Y(0) \;=\; \Phi\, N(0), \quad M(i) = -R^\epsilon(i)^{-1} \;,\;\; i \geq 0$$

so that the n x n matrix Riccati equation is replaced by vector equations. This can be a substantial computational saving, though we have not as yet developed experience with the best way of implementing this algorithm [MSK]. Recently certain square-root algorithms have been developed that seem to have even more computational advantages [MK].

For time-variant N(i), the number α and the initial conditions are determined as follows. Let

$$y[i,j] = [y(i), y(i+1), \ldots, y(j)]^T ,$$

$$R_y[i,j] = E \, y[i,j] \, y[i,j]^T ,$$

and

$$\bar{\mathcal{O}} = [(\Phi^T)^{n-1} H^T, \ldots, \phi^T H^T, H^T]^T .$$

Then form

$$D = \bar{\mathcal{O}}^{-1} [R_y[1,n] - R_y[0,n-1]] \bar{\mathcal{O}}^{-T} - \Phi \, N(0) \, R^\epsilon(0)^{-1} N(0)^T \Phi^T$$

and factor it as

$$D = [Y][M][Y]^T$$

$$[M] = \begin{bmatrix} M+ & 0 \\ 0 & M- \end{bmatrix}$$

where M+>0 , M-<0 , [M] is $\alpha \times \alpha$ and α is the rank of D. Then the initial conditions for Y(.) and M(.) can be taken as

$$Y(0) = [Y] \quad \text{and} \quad M(0) = [M]$$

More details can be found in [MSK], [Mo], [S] and [SKM], where in particular, the use of canonical forms to make Y(0) and M(0) easy to evaluate is also discussed. The connections of these algorithms to the fitting of autoregressive models by Levinson's algorithm and to the fitting of moving average models by Cholesky factorization are also discussed in these references and, more briefly, in Appendix I of this paper.

V. ALTERNATIVE APPROACH VIA ARMA MODELS

In Sections III and IV, the calculations were carried out in terms of general state-space representations. It will be useful to reconsider those arguments in terms of ARMA models (or equivalently in terms of certain <u>canonical</u> state-space models [Mo]).

In Section III our aim was to find a triple $\{ H, \Phi, N(i) \}$ to match $R(i,j)$, $i \geq j$, (the subscript y has been dropped for convenience). Actually, however, we first found polynomials $c_0(z)$ and $a(z)$ such that

$$r_0(z) = R(0,0) + R(0,1)z^{-1} + R(0,2)z^{-2} + ...$$

$$= c_0(z)/a(z)$$

where

$$a(z) = z^n + a(1)z^{n-1} + ... + a(n)$$

We could also have worked with the sequence $\{ R(j,i),$ fixed $j \}$ obtaining

$$r_j(z) = R(j,0) + R(j,1)z^{-1} + R(j,2)z^{-2} + ...$$

$$= c_j(z)/a(z) ,$$

where

$$c_j(z) = c_j(0)z^n + c_j(1)z^{n-1} + .. + c_j(m)z^{n-m}$$

The denominator polynomial $a(z)$ is independent of j because of our assumption of an underlying constant-parameter model of order n. The equations

$$r_j(z) a(z) = c_j(z) , \quad j = 0,1,...,t , \quad t \geq n$$

can be written as a single matrix equation

$$R_+ A^T = C^T .$$

The matrix R_+ has entries

$$R_+(j,1) = \begin{cases} 0 , & j < i \\ R(j,j)/2, & j = i \\ R(j,i), & j > i \end{cases}$$

R_+ is actually the lower-triangular part of the covariance matrix

$$E\, y[t,0]\, y[t,0]^T \;=\; R[t] \;=\; \begin{bmatrix} R(t,t) & \cdots & R(t,0) \\ \cdot & & \cdot \\ \cdot & & \cdot \\ \cdot & & \cdot \\ R(0,t) & \cdots & R(0,0) \end{bmatrix}$$

The matrices A and C are

$$A \;=\; \begin{bmatrix} 1 & & & \\ -a(1) & 1 & & 0 \\ \cdot & \cdot & \cdot & \\ -a(n) & \cdot & 1 & \\ 0 & \cdot & -a(1) & 1 \end{bmatrix}$$

$$C \;=\; \begin{bmatrix} c_i(0) & & & \\ \cdot & c.(0) & & 0 \\ c.(0) & \cdot & c.(0) & \\ 0 & c_j(n) & \cdot & c_j(0) \\ 0 & 0 & c_0(n) & \cdot & c_0(n) \end{bmatrix}$$

Now observe that
$$\begin{aligned} A^T\, R[t]\, A \;&=\; A^T R_+ A \,+\, A^T R_- A \\ &=\; A^T C \,+\, C^T A \\ &=\; \text{a } \underline{\text{banded matrix}} \text{ with all zeros} \end{aligned}$$
above and below at least the
n-th off-diagonal.

If we define

$$y[t]^T \;=\; [\, y(t), \ldots, y(0)\,]$$

then the vector

$$w[\,t\,]^T = y[\,t\,]^T A$$

is seen to be a process with covariance

$$R_w[t] = E\,w[t]\,w[t]^T = A^T C + C^T A = A^T R[t]\,A$$

Thus by prefiltering y(.) by A we reduce it to a finitely - correlated process w(.). Moreover, since a(0) = 1 ≠ 0 , A is invertible and w(.) and y(.) can be causally determined from the other. The process w(.) can be called a generalized innovations process. We can relate w(.) to a white innovations process (.) by

$$w\,[t]^T = v[t]^T K[t], \quad R_w[t] = K[t]^T K[t]$$

The determination of K[t] can be made by using the so-called Cholesky factorization of the banded nonnegative definite matrix $R_w[t]$ [WR]. However in our problem $R_w[.]$ has a special structure because of our assumption of an underlying constant-parameter model. This enables us to use a fast-Cholesky algorithm [Mo]. For the special case of Toeplitz matrices, a fast Cholesky algorithm was independently obtained in [Ri1]. Actually there are several methods for Cholesky factorization -- we can successively calculate rows of the factors or the columns, or various hybrids [GGMS].

Here, by noting that the Cholesky factor K[t] is just the innovations representation (IR) for the process w(.), we can obtain the Cholesky factors column-by-column by using the Chandrasekhar-type equations. Thus let the lower-triangular part of $R_w[t]$ be denoted $R_{w+}[t]$, where

$$R_{w+}[t] = [\,N_{wt},\,...,\,N_{w0}\,]^T$$

and the row N_{wj}^T is given as

$$N_{wj} = [\,0,...,\,0,N_w(j)^T,\,0,...,\,0]^T \ ,$$

where

$$N_w(j)^T = [R(j,j+n),...,R(j,j+1), R(j,j)/2]$$

With this notation we have for each j and $i \geq j$,

$$R_w(j,i) = [H_w \Phi_w^{i-j} N_w(j)]^T$$

where

$$H_w = [0 ... 0 \quad 0 \quad 1 \quad]$$

$$\Phi_w = \begin{vmatrix} 0 ... 0 & 0 & 0 \\ & & 0 \\ I_{n-1} & : \\ & & 0 \end{vmatrix}$$

Now in Section IV, we noted that the IR for a process whose covariance had this form was given by a state model with the appropriate initial conditions. The impulse response of the IR is, for each i and $j \geq i$

$$\{ H_w \Phi_w^{j-i} K_w(i)R^\epsilon(i)^{-T/2} \} ,$$

where $K_w(i)$, the Kalman gain, is defined in Section IV. With this identification it is easy to see that $K_w(i)$ appears (normalized by $R^\epsilon(i)^{-T2}$) as the non-zero portion of column i of the upper-triangular Cholesky factor $K[t]^T$. The fact that $R_w[t]$ is banded of course means that $K[t]$ is also banded so that we have to calculate only a fixed finite number, $m \leq n$, of non-zero entries in each column. It can be verified that the recursions for the columns of $K[t]^T$ coincide with those directly obtained in [Mo]; also once we know recursions for the columns it is not hard to determine recursions for the rows and for other hybrid procedures.

It is interesting to note that the Kalman gain of the overall IR is related to $K_w(.)$ by the simple formula

$$K(i) = K_w(i) - a[n,1]$$

where $a[n,1] = [a(n), . . . , a(1)]^T$. This is discussed further in [MKS2].

We should note that if R_w is computed by the formulas $A^T R[t] A$ or as $A^T C + C^T A$, then we would need $O(n^2)$ operations for each $j = 0$, $1, \ldots, t$. Therefore the procedure described in this section will, as it stands, be less efficient then the method of Section IV, where we obtained a triple $\{H, \Phi, N(0)\}$ from $\{ a(z), c_0 (z) \}$ and directly applied the Chandrasekhar equations. However, there does exist a way of finding $K[t]$ from A and C without explicitly forming $R_w[t]$ and this method will be computationally equivalent to that of Section IV. We shall not go into this method here because our aim is only to motivate the possibility of the "prefiltering plus fast Cholesky factorization" route to the final answer. It seems that the steps in this route lend themselves more easily to the development of on-line procedures, in which the estimation of $R_y(i,j)$ is combined with the prefiltering and fast Cholesky calculations [Mo].

VI. CONCLUSIONS

In this paper we have presented some algorithms for fitting rational models to the (perfectly known) covariance function of a process known to arise from a finite dimensional, constant linear system. The numerical problems encountered when real data is used to estimate the covariance of course need further study. The ultimate test of any method will certainly depend on the objective of the speech modeling exercise, be it data compression or linguistic analysis. However we believe that the freedom to include zeros in the model and to account for nonstationarity gives our algorithms some potential advantages that seem worthy of further exploration.

While particular applications may not need the flexibility of a full rational model, we have shown that our statistical approach provides the insight for extending the class of covariances to which simpler algorithms may be adapted (see Appendix 1). Further results concerning on-line procedures for modeling directly from the observed data, and concerning the pitch extraction problem can be obtained through this approach. These are the object of continuing research.

APPENDIX 1

GENERALIZATIONS OF THE LEVINSON ALGORITHM

The matrix notation of Section V. can be used to develop the relationship between the estimation algorithms presented in this paper and the Levinson algorithm. We shall show that what we have is a "generalized" Levinson algorithm for a class of non-Toeplitz matrices, which includes the matrix of the "covariance method". This generalized algorithm has the same order of number of computations as the usual Levinson algorithm.

Recall our matrix notation:

$$\text{observations} \quad y[i,j] \;=\; [\, y(i),..., y(j) \,]^{T}$$

$$\text{innovations} \quad \epsilon[i,j] \;=\; [\, \epsilon(i),..., \epsilon(j) \,]^{T}$$

$$R_{y}[t] \;=\; E\, y[t,0]\, y[t,0]^{T}$$

$$=\; \begin{bmatrix} R(t,t) & .... & R(t,0) \\ . & & . \\ . & & . \\ . & & . \\ R(0,t) & .... & R(0,0) \end{bmatrix}$$

The Innovations Representation (IR) can of course be determined from the factorization

$$R_{y} \;=\; R_{y\epsilon}^{T}\, R_{\epsilon}^{-1}\, R_{y\epsilon}$$

where

$$R_{y\epsilon}^{T} \;=\; E\, y[t,0]\, \epsilon[t,0]^{T} \quad \text{and}$$

$$R_{\epsilon} \;=\; E\, \epsilon[t,0]\epsilon[t,0]^{T} \;=\; \text{diag}(\, R^{\epsilon}(i)\,).$$

Notice that $R_{y\epsilon}^{T}$ is upper-triangular because of the causality of the IR. This is true whether or not we have a finite order model for $y[i,j]$. But if we assume the existence of a finite - order model, we can use the results of Section IV, to write down the impulse response of the IR as

$$R_{y_\epsilon}(j+1,i+1) = H \Phi^{j-i} K(i+1)$$
$$= H \Phi^{j-i} K(i) - H\Phi^{j-i} \Phi \, Y(i) \, M(i) \, Y(i)^T H^T$$
$$= R_{y_\epsilon}(j,i) - C(j+1,i) \, M(i) \, C(i+1,i)^T \quad,$$

where
$C(j,i) \triangleq H \Phi^{j-i} Y(i)$. Using the recursion for $Y(i)$, we get

$$C(j+1,i+1) = C(j+1,i) - R_{y_\epsilon}(j-1,i)R^\epsilon(i)^{-1}C(i+1,i)$$

These recursions define a "fast" algorithm for the columns of the Cholesky-type factor $R_{y\epsilon}{}^T$.

From this recursion we can now derive Levinson type algorithms for this class of processes. Let us first rewrite the factorization equation for R_y as

$$R_{y_\epsilon}^T = R_y[t][R_{y_\epsilon}^{-1}R_\epsilon] = R_y[t] A \, , \quad \text{say}$$

where it is easily verified that $A \triangleq [R_{y\epsilon}^{-1} R_\epsilon]$ has the lower-triangular form

$$A = \begin{vmatrix} 1 & & & \\ -a(1,t) & 1 & & 0 \\ . & . & & \\ . & . & & 1 \\ -a(t,t) & . & & -a(1,1) & 1 \end{vmatrix}$$

The columns of A define the coefficients of the impulse response of the prediction-error filter for estimating $y(i+1)$ given $y[0,i]$, $i = 0, \ldots, t-1$. The Levinson algorithm gives a recursion for these columns in the special case of $R_y[t]$ being Toeplitz. In our more general case, we see that the the previously derived recursions for the columns of $R_{y\epsilon}{}^T$ clearly induce a recursion for the columns of A. Since $R_{y\epsilon}{}^T$ is upper-triangular, comparing the first columns of both sides of the equation, we get

$$R_y[t] \begin{vmatrix} 1 \\ -a_t[1,t] \end{vmatrix} = \begin{vmatrix} R^\epsilon(t) \\ 0 \end{vmatrix}$$

which is precisely the linear equation to be solved for the prediction error filter gains $-a_t[1,t]$ and the prediction error covariance $R^\epsilon(t)$ given the covariance matrix. When the process y is stationary, then R_y is a Toeplitz matrix and we get the standard Levinson (LPC) equation for $-a_t$ [1,t]

$$a(j+1,i+1) = a(j-1,i) - b(j+1,i) M(i) C(i+1,i)^T$$

$$b(j+1,i+1) = b(j,i) - a(j,i)R^\epsilon(i)^{-1}C(i+1,i)$$

where we used the fact that (cf. Section IV.)

$$C(i+1,i) = H\Phi Y(i) = [R(i+1,i),..., R(i+1,0)] b_i[i,0]$$

and the equations for $R^\epsilon(i)$ and M(i) are the same as before. If we calculate the initial conditions as in Section IV, they are, as we know, somewhat more complicated than in the stationary case. For the computation of the prediction parameters a_i [1,i], as we are now considering, we can get a simplification. For the derivation via Chandrasekhar equations, we need the factorization

$$\mathcal{O} \delta\Pi \mathcal{O}^T - \mathcal{O} \Phi N R(0,0)^{-1}N^T\Phi^T\mathcal{O}^T = C[t,0]M(0) C[t,0]^T$$

Now note that

$$\mathcal{O} \delta\Pi \mathcal{O}^T = \delta R_y[t] = R_y[t,1] - R_y[t-1,0],$$

and that we will often automatically (or easily) have a factorization of the usually low rank $\delta R_y[t]$ as $\delta R_y [t] = Y[t,0] D Y[t,0]^T$, where the number of columns in Y[t,0] is equal to the rank of $\delta R_y[t]$. Then C[t,0], M(0) and b_o [t,0] can be expressed as follows,

$$C[t,0] = [Y[t,0],[R(0,t),...,R(0,0)]^T],$$

$$M(0) = \begin{vmatrix} D & 0 \\ 0 & -R(0,0)^{-1} \end{vmatrix}$$

For the initial condition of b_o [t,0] we can choose

$$b_0[t,0] = [q[t,0], [0,..., 0,1]^T], \quad R_y[t] q[t,0] = Y[t,0].$$

We note here that the structure of R_y [t] is only Toeplitz in the stationary case (then q[t,0] = 0 = Y[t,0]). In general it is of the form:

$$R_y[t] = T[t] Q[t] T[t]^T + \mathcal{O}[t] \Pi(0) \mathcal{O}[t]^T$$

where T[t] is a triangular Toeplitz matrix, Q[t] is a diagonal matrix, and $\mathcal{O}$[t] is the Observability matrix (see section IV) whose rank is equal to n , a constant -- usually much less than t. This structure includes the matrix obtained in Atal's "covariance method"; the details of the application to this particular case can be found in [MKD]. The matrix in the "covariance method" is a sum of products of Toeplitz matrices, which fact yields a certain shift invariance (see also [SKM]) of solution vectors so that these equations were said to have a "shift low rank updating" property in [Mo].

RELATIONS TO LINEAR PREDICTIVE ENCODING

Applying our vector notation, we consider the derivation of the usual LPC equations for the vector a[1,n] of the coefficients of the denominator polynomial of the all-pole filter. We choose these coefficients in order to minimize the sum of the squared prediction errors. Denoting the error vector as e[.], we have

$$e[i,0] = y[i,0] - Y[i] a[1,n].$$

This equation represents the convolution of the observation sequence with the filter gains by a Toeplitz matrix equation involving the i+1 by n matrix Y[i] whose j,k-th elements equals y(i-k) for $i \geq j > k \geq 0$ and zero for $k \geq j \geq 0$. The sum of squares of the prediction errors is then given by

$$e[i,0]^T e[i,0] = y[i,0]^T y[i,0] - 2y[i,0] Y[i] a[1,n] + a[1,n]^T Y[i]^T Y[i] a[1,n]$$

This error measure can be minimized by setting the gradient with respect to the filter gains equal to zero to obtain

$$Y[i]^T (y[i,0] - Y[i] a[1,n]) = 0$$

which gives as the solution to these so-called normal equations

$$a[1,n] = [Y[i]^T Y[i]]^{-1} Y[i]^T y[i,0]$$

The matrix to be inverted in this procedure is often called the covariance matrix [MW] and this method of computing the filter gains a[.] is the "covariance method".

An alternative analysis method is obtained by "windowing" the observed process and exploiting the resulting Toeplitz structure of the matrix which must be inverted to obtain a[1,n]. A computationally efficient solution for this case was obtained by Levinson and was reprinted as an appendix to Wiener's monograph on linear prediction [Wie]. This algorithm has been used extensively in applications because the stability properties of the resulting filter can be analyzed quite easily. Levinson's algorithm is often called the "autocorrelation method", and it also has some interesting connections with polynomials which are orthogonal on the unit circle. These algorithms can be obtained from many other considerations, among them being Markel's inverse filter formulation [MG], maximum entropy spectral estimation [Brg], and other frequency domain spectral approximation schemes [MW]. We wish to emphasize that the common approaches most frequently treat the linear prediction problem as a deterministic least squares problem. Our approach, on the other hand, has been to start with the structural properties of a certain class of stochastic processes, in particular a covariance function of a special type, and to keep separate the statistical problem of estimating the covariance function. Once the structure of the problem is laid bare, the question of actual data processing schemes can be addressed. It may be possible, for example, to combine maximum likelihood estimation techniques with the algorithms of this paper, to obtain methods which work directly on the data (see [Mo]).

REFERENCES

[AH]   Atal, B. S., and S. L. Hanauer, "Speech Analysis and Synthesis by Linear Prediction of the Speech Wave, " J. Acoust. Soc. Amer., vol. 5, 1971, pp. 637-655.

[AS]   Atal, B. S., and M. R. Schroeder, "Adaptive Predictive Coding of Speech Signals, " BSTJ, 1970, pp. 1973-1986.

[At1]   Atal, B. S., "Determination of the Vocal Tract Shape Directly from the Speech Wave, " J. Acoust. Soc. Amer., V47(A), 1970, p. 64.

[At2]   Atal, B. S., "Sound Transmission in the Vocal Tract with Applications to Speech Analysis and Synthesis, "International Congress on Acoustics, " Budapest, 1971.

[Be]   Berlekamp, E. R., Algebraic Coding Theory, McGraw-Hill, New York, 1968.

[Brg] Burg, J. P., "Maximum Entropy Spectral Analysis, " presented at the 37-th Ann. Meeting of Soc. Explor. Geophys., Oklahoma City, Oklahoma, 1967.

[Ca] Capon, J., "High-resolution frequency-wavenumber spectrum analysis, " Proc. IEEE, Aug. 1969, pp. 1408-1418.

[CR] Caines, P. E., and J. Rissanen, "Maximum Likelihood Estimation of Parameters in Multivariate Gaussian Stochastic Processes, " IEEE Transaction on Information Theory, Vol. IT-20, pp. 102-104. January 1974.

[DMK] Dickinson, B., M. Morf and T. Kailath, "A Minimal Realization Algorithm for Matrix Sequences, " IEEE Transactions on Automatic Control, Vol. AC-19, 1974, pp. 31-38.

[DR] Davenport, Jr. W. B., and W. L. Root, An Introduction to the Theory of Random Signals and Noise, McGraw - Hill, New York, 1958.

[Fa] Faurre, P., "Realisations Markoviennes de Processus Stationnaires, " IRIA, France, Res. Rept. No. 13, March 1973.

[GGMS] Gill, P. E., G. H. Golub, W. Murray, and M. A. Saunders, "Methods for Modifying Matrix Factorizations, " Stanford Univ. Computer Science Rept. STAN-CS-72-322, 1972.

[GK1] Gevers, M., and T. Kailath, "An Innovations Approach to Least-Squares Estimation, Part VI, " IEEE Trans. Automat. Contr. Vol. AC-18, 1973, pp. 588-600.

[GK2] Gevers, M., and T. Kailath, "The Discrete-Time Stochastic Realization Problem: Minimum Variance Property of the Innovations Representation, " Proc. 1973 IEEE Conf. on Decision and Control, San Diego, 1973, pp. 168-171.

[HK] Ho, B. L., and R. E. Kalman, "Effective Construction of Linear State - Variable Models from Input - Output Functions, " Regelungstechnik, Vol. 14, 1966, pp. 545-548.

[IS] Itakura, F., and S. Saito, "Analysis Synthesis Telephony Based on the Maximum Likelihood Method, " Rept. 6th Intl. Congress on Acoustics, Y. Kohashi, ed., Tokyo, 1968, pp. C-5-5.

[It] Itakura, F., "Extraction of Feature Parameters of Speech by Statistical Methods, " Proc. 8th Symp. on Speech Information Processing, REIC Tohoku Univ., Sendai, Japan, pp. II-5-1 to II-5-12, February 1971.

[JW] Jenkins, G. M., and D. G. Watts, Spectral Analysis and its Applications, Holden-Day, San Francisco, 1969.

[KFA] Kalman, R. E., P. L. Falb and M. A. Arbib, Topics in Mathematical System Theory, McGraw-Hill, New York, 1969.

[Ma] Massey, J. L., "Shift-Register Synthesis and BCH Decoding, " IEEE Trans. on Inform. Theory, Vol. IT-15, 1969, pp. 122-127.

[Mak]   Maksym, J. N., "Real Time Pitch Extraction by Adaptive Prediction of the Speech Waveform, " IEEE Transaction on Audio Electroacoust., Vol. AU-21, 1973, pp. 149-154.

[MG]   Markel, J. D., and A. H. Gray, Jr., "Autocorrelation as Applied to Speech Analysis, " IEEE Trans. Audio Electroacoust., Vol. AU-21, 1973, pp. 69-76.

[MK]   Morf, M., and T. Kailath, "Square-Root Algorithms for Least-Squares Estimation and Control, " Proc. 8th Princeton Symp. on Information and System Sci., March 1974. Also see IEEE Trans. Automat. Contr. August 1975.

[MKD]   Morf, M., T. Kailath, and B. Dickinson, "Notes on a Fast Algorithm for solving Atal's Normal Equations, " to appear.

[Mo]   Morf, M., "Fast Algorithms for Multivariable Systems, " Ph.D. dissertation, Stanford University, Stanford, California, 1974.

[MSK]   Morf, M., G. S. Sidhu and T. Kailath, "Some New Algorithms for Recursive Estimation in Const., Lin., Discrete-Time Systems, " IEEE Trans. Automat. Contr. August 1974.

[MSK2] Morf, M., B. W. Dicinson, and T. Kailath, "Canonical Matrix Fraction and State-Space Descriptions for Deterministic and Stochastic Linear Systems, " IEEE Trans. Automat. Control, December 1974.

[MW]   Makhoul, J. I., and J. J. Wolf, "Linear Prediction and the Spectral Analysis of Speech, " Bolt Beranek and Newman Inc., Rept. No. 234, San Francisco, 1972.

[RK]   Rissanen, J., and T. Kailath, "Partial Realization of Random Systems, " Automatica, Vol. 8, June 1972, pp. 389-396.

[Ri1]   Rissanen, J., "Algorithms for Triangular Decomposition of Block Hankel and Toeplitz Matrices with Applications to Factoring Positive Matrix Polynomials," Math. of Computation, Vol. 27, no. 121, January 1973.

[Ri2]   Rissanen, J., "Recursive Identification of Linear Systems, SIAM J. Control, Vol. 9, 1971, pp. 420-430.

[S]   Sidhu, G. S., Ph.D. dissertation, Stanford University, Stanford, California, 1974.

[Si1]   Silverman, L., "Realization of Linear Dynamical Systems, " IEEE Trans. Automat. Contr., Vol. AC-16, 1971, pp. 554-567.

[Si2]   Silverman, L., "Representation and Realization of Time-Variable Linear Systems, " Dept. of Elect. Engrg., Columbia Univ., Tech. Report 94, 1966.

[SKM]   Sidhu, G. S., T. Kailath and M. Morf, "Development of Fast Algorithms via Innovations Decompositions, " Proc. of the Hawii Intl. Conf. on Inf. and System Sciences, Honolulu, Hawaii, pp. 192-195, Jan. 1974.

[Wa]   Wakita, H., "Estimation of the Vocal Tract Shape by Optimal Inverse Filtering and Acoustic/Articulatory Conversion Methods, " Monograph No. 9, Speech Communications Res. Lab. Inc., Santa Barbara, Calif., July 1972.

[Wie]   Wiener N., Time Series, M.I.T. Press, Massachusetts Institute of Technology, Cambridge, Massachusetts, 1949.

[WR]   Wilkinson, J., and C. Reinsch, Handbook for Automatic Computation, Vol. II, Linear Algebra, Springer-Verlag, New York, 1971.

[YT]   Youla, D. C. and P. Tissi, "N-Port Synthesis via Reactance Extraction Part I, " IEEE Int. Convention Record, Vol. 14, pt. 7, 1966, pp. 183-205.

LINEAR PREDICTION IN AUTOMATIC SPEECH RECOGNITION

John Makhoul
Bolt Beranek and Newman Inc.
50 Moulton Street
Cambridge, Massachusetts 02138

ABSTRACT

This paper describes the recent applications of linear prediction to automatic speech recognition. Linear prediction is presented both as a spectral smoothing and a spectral modeling technique in which the signal spectrum is modeled by an all-pole spectrum. The method allows for the modeling of selected portions of a spectrum, for arbitrary spectral shaping in the frequency domain, and for the modeling of continuous as well as discrete spectra (such as filter bank spectra). Linear prediction is then compared to traditional analysis-by-synthesis techniques for spectral modeling.

Different parametric representations of the all-pole spectrum are introduced and compared for the purpose of speech recognition. These include the predictor coefficients, autocorrelation, spectrum, cepstrum, and reflection coefficients. The log area ratios are then proposed as a possibly optimal representation if a simple distance measure is used in the classification. A different approach to classification is also presented, where the distance measure is given in terms of a log likelihood ratio.

Recently developed parameters based on linear prediction for the purpose of feature extraction are given. These include formants, two-pole model parameters, spectral spread (a measure of the spectral dynamic range), and the first predictor and autocorrelation coefficients. An energy-independent spectral derivative is also proposed.

1. INTRODUCTION

One of the principal tools in the automatic recognition of speech has been the use of the short-time power spectrum. The spectrum has been used in different ways to achieve the desired recognition. Spectral "template matching," where a new spectrum is classified (i.e., recognized) by matching it against a stored set of templates, has been a very simple, widely used and often effective method of recognition. Other recognition systems have attempted to extract salient features of the spectrum and then compare those features against stored values. Examples of such features include formants (resonances of the vocal tract), antiformants, regions of maximum energy concentration, regions of maximum spectral slope, spectral dynamic range, etc. The choice of which type or types of analysis to employ in a particular recognition system is often a function of ease of implementation, cost, speed, accuracy of recognition, scope of the recognition problem, and also knowledge of the acoustics of speech and speech production.

1.1 SPECTRAL SMOOTHING AND MODELING

Whatever the type of recognition system desired and in whatever manner the spectrum is used, it is always desirable to deal with a "smooth" spectrum. Smoothness is clearly a relative matter, and the degree of smoothness is dependent on the particular application, as we shall see later on. However for many applications, a smooth spectrum is one that approximates the transfer function of the vocal tract. Such a spectrum might include the general characteristics due to the glottal excitation and radiation, but would not include any effects due to periodicity of the excitation.

There are many methods available to obtain smooth short-time spectra. Below we list the most prominent ones.

1. Filter bank spectrum -- Here, the smoothing is performed by time averaging, partly due to the filter bandwidths, but mostly due to an integrator following the rectifier at the output of each filter.

2. Spectrum of a single pitch period -- For low pitched voices this spectrum is a rather accurate representation of the transfer function of the vocal tract plus the effects of the glottal waveform and radiation.

3. Autocorrelation smoothing -- This is applied by low-pass filtering the spectrum, usually computed by a fast Fourier transform (FFT). The filtering is normally performed by windowing the autocorrelation function,

which is the Fourier transform of the spectrum. This
method is popular in the statistics literature.

4. Cepstral smoothing -- This type of smoothing is the
   same as autocorrelation smoothing, except that the
   filtering is performed on the logarithm of the spectrum
   (log spectrum). The windowing here is applied to the
   cepstrum, the Fourier transform of the log spectrum.
   This method is popular in speech analysis because, for
   low pitched voices, it does a good job of eliminating
   the effects due to periodicity.

5. Spectral modeling -- Here the smoothing is
   accomplished a priori by assuming a model for the
   spectrum, usually in terms of poles and zeros. The
   values for the parameters of the model are obtained
   by minimizing some error criterion between the
   original and model spectra. Analysis-by-synthesis and
   linear prediction are examples of spectral modeling
   methods, as we shall see below.

Of the first four types of smoothing given above, none offers
any basic advantage over the others, whether for spectral template
matching or feature extraction. Henceforth, I shall refer collectively to
these types of smoothing as plain spectral smoothing. In comparing
plain spectral smoothing with spectral modeling, on the other hand,
there is one encompassing basic difference: spectral modeling is
parametric while plain spectral smoothing is not. What I mean by
"parametric" here is that the spectrum is completely representable by
a relatively small set of parameters, e.g., poles and zeros. In plain
spectral smoothing, the spectrum is specifiable only in terms of specific
spectral values at some set of frequencies. Here the representation is
made more complete by computing more spectral values (or adding
more filters to a filter bank), while in spectral modeling a complete
representation is given by the parameter values alone.

This basic difference between spectral modeling and plain
smoothing has implications in the way the spectrum is used in speech
recognition. If spectral template matching is desired, and the smoothed
spectrum is to be used as the basis for the match, then spectral
modeling offers no real advantage over plain spectral smoothing.
However, as we shall see in Section 3, because of the parametric
representation in spectral modeling, one can perform template matching
without actually computing the spectrum.

For the purposes of feature extraction, it is clear that a

parametric model representation offers a richer variety of possibilities by allowing the flexibility of applying various mathematical operations on the model. However, even if we assume that features are to be extracted only from the spectrum, then spectral modeling still has an advantage over plain spectral smoothing -- a model spectrum is inherently smoother than one obtained by plain smoothing. The number of possible peaks and valleys in a model spectrum is well known in advance and is controllable by prior specification of the model; there are no peaks and valleys other than those predictable from the model. In smoothed spectra, there are major peaks and valleys as well as "kinks" in the spectrum, which are quite unpredictable. These kinks can play havoc with any peak picking scheme to identify formants, for example, or points of maximum slope. The "spectral noise" that is present in smoothed spectra is simply nonexistent in model spectra. Therefore, for the extraction of features, it should be easier to work with a model spectrum than with one obtained by plain smoothing. However, in terms of accuracy, the matter is not so clear. If the assumed model is accurate, then features obtained from the resulting spectrum should be quite accurate relative to results obtained from smoothed spectra. If the model is not a good representation of the spectrum, then results could be worse than for smoothed spectra, depending on the application. As an example, assume we are given an all-pole model with an appropriate number of poles. Such a model normally gives accurate results for formant values of nonnasalized vowels. However, if our objective is to determine nasal zeros, then the all-pole model can give very inaccurate results. In that case, one might get better estimates of the zeros from a smoothed spectrum. In general, however, it is simpler to deal with model spectra (provided the computations are not excessive), and their use is recommended for speech recognition purposes. One must simply be careful in interpreting the results produced by the model.

1.2 METHODS FOR SPECTRAL MODELING

Until recently, the only significant spectral modeling method used in speech analysis has been analysis-by-synthesis (AbS), which was introduced at M.I.T. and Bell Laboratories in 1961. At M.I.T. the method was used on filter-bank spectra to extract the pole pattern of vowels [1,2] and pole-zero patterns of nasals [3]. At Bell Laboratories, AbS was applied to the computed spectrum of a single pitch period to extract the formants of the vocal tract as well as the zeros of the glottal spectrum [4]. In AbS, a speech spectrum is fitted by a model spectrum that is specified in terms of poles and zeros. The fit is optimized through the minimization of an error criterion that is defined to be the average of the squared (or absolute value) difference between the original and model log spectra. The solution can be obtained iteratively by the Newton-Raphson method [5]. The term "analysis-by-synthesis" came about originally [1] as a result of the fact that during each iteration, a model spectrum was actually "synthesized" (computed) and compared with the given spectrum. Had the solution to the minimization problem been noniterative, the term AbS would probably not have been applied to this type of spectral modeling.

During the last few years, the method of linear prediction (LP) was introduced to speech analysis. The two basic formulations of LP, the stationary or autocorrelation method and the nonstationary or covariance method, can be traced back partly to the works of Yule [6] and Prony [7], respectively. Linear prediction has been known by different names and used in different fields during the last forty years. The autocorrelation method was first introduced to speech analysis by Itakura [8] in Japan. He actually used a maximum likelihood formulation to design an analysis-synthesis system. The method was also seen as a statistical method for the parametric estimation of the speech short-time spectrum and for formant extraction [9]. Markel [10] reinterpreted the method in the time domain in terms of inverse filtering. Atal's work in predictive coding [11] led to the development of what has come to be known as the covariance method of linear prediction [12,13]. This method was seen by Atal basically as a time domain analysis. The speech community in the U.S. was exposed to the works of Atal and Markel, but was generally unaware of Itakura's work. As a result, linear prediction became popular as a time domain type of analysis. An air of confusion resulted because of a lack of understanding of the fundamental differences between Atal's and Markel's methods. This confusion was cleared through the publication of a comprehensive report by the author [13] showing that both methods were special cases of a more general formulation of all-pole modeling of nonstationary two-dimensional spectra. Linear prediction was seen as a correlation type of analysis which can be approached either from the time or frequency domain. (The terms "autocorrelation" and "covariance" were given to refer to the type of matrix of coefficients that was used in the solution for the model parameters.) A brief analysis of time and frequency domain interpretations of the autocorrelation and covariance methods is given below. The reader is referred to a recent tutorial review paper [40] for the details. A paper by Schafer and Rabiner [14] in this volume gives the time domain derivations for the two methods.

Although the autocorrelation method can be approached from the time domain, its properties are best understood in the frequency domain. It is difficult, for example, to explain the necessity for time windowing unless one appeals to the spectrum. In fact, the problem of linear prediction in this case becomes the problem of modeling the short-time spectrum by an all-pole model spectrum. This is very convenient since now we can capitalize on our large body of experience in working with short-time spectra. For example, it becomes clear that applying the autocorrelation method to a portion of the signal that is much smaller than a pitch period is unwise. It is important to realize this if one wants good estimates of the formants. For best results, one should use either a rectangular window over exact multiples of the pitch period (often a tricky and sensitive procedure), or a smooth window (such as Hamming or Hanning) over a time period equal to about two pitch periods or more. The latter method is the one most widely used in speech analysis.

Unlike the autocorrelation method, the workings of the covariance method are best explained in the time domain. It is very difficult to explain the fact that windowing is totally unnecessary by appealing to the frequency domain; the explanation is much more natural in the time domain. Because of the absence of windowing, one is free to choose the length of data to be analyzed. For example, if one is interested in getting formant data by examining the portion of a pitch period that corresponds to the closed glottis condition, then the covariance method should be used. For data lengths greater than a pitch period, the covariance method gives results similar to the autocorrelation method.

The author is unaware of any concrete results from analyses performed on portions of pitch periods using linear prediction. All speech recognition systems to date, to the author's knowledge, have used data lengths greater than a pitch period. Since under the latter condition the two methods of linear prediction give similar results, we shall concentrate in this paper on only one of the methods, namely, the autocorrelation method, because it makes it much simpler to discuss the spectral modeling of linear prediction and compare it to analysis-by-synthesis. The comparisons will be brief; more details are given elsewhere [9, 13, 15-17].

2. SPECTRAL MODELING BY LINEAR PREDICTION

2.1 COMPUTATION OF MODEL PARAMETERS

Let us assume that we are given a power spectrum $P(\omega)$ that is defined over the unit circle in the z plane. In this manner, we can view $P(\omega)$ as the spectrum of some sampled signal $s(n)$, irrespective of how the spectrum was actually obtained. We desire to model $P(\omega)$ in some optimal manner by an all-pole model spectrum $\hat{P}(\omega)$.

Let us assume that the model spectrum corresponds to a transfer function $H(z)$ given by

$$H(z) = \frac{G}{A(z)} = \frac{G}{1 + \sum\limits_{k=1}^{p} a_k z^{-k}} \quad , \tag{1}$$

where

$$A(z) = 1 + \sum_{k=1}^{p} a_k z^{-k} \tag{2}$$

will be called the inverse filter, p is the number of poles in the model spectrum, and G is a gain factor. The model spectrum $\hat{P}(\omega)$ is then given by

$$\hat{P}(\omega) = |H(e^{j\omega})|^2 = \frac{G^2}{|A(e^{j\omega})|^2} \tag{3}$$

$$= \frac{G^2}{\left|1 + \sum\limits_{k=1}^{p} a_k e^{-jk\omega}\right|^2}$$

Given a spectrum $P(\omega)$ and a number of poles p, we must determine the model parameters $\{a_k, 1 \le k \le p\}$ and G. The parameters are obtained as a result of the minimization of some spectral error measure between the two spectra $P(\omega)$ and $\hat{P}(\omega)$. We define the following error measure E:

$$E = \frac{G^2}{2\pi} \int_{-\pi}^{\pi} \frac{P(\omega)}{\hat{P}(\omega)} d\omega \tag{4}$$

$$= \frac{1}{2\pi} \int_{-\pi}^{\pi} P(\omega) |A(e^{j\omega})|^2 d\omega \quad . \tag{5}$$

From (5), E can be interpreted as the total energy of the residual signal obtained by passing the (hypothetical) signal s(n) through the inverse filter A(z). Note also from (5) that E is defined to be independent of G, which is determined from energy considerations.

The parameters a_k are determined by minimizing E in (5) with respect to each of the parameters. This is accomplished by setting $\partial E/\partial a_i = 0$, $1 \leq i \leq p$. The result can be shown to be [13]

$$\sum_{k=1}^{p} a_k R_{|i-k|} = -R_i \ , \ 1 \leq i \leq p \ , \tag{6}$$

where

$$R_i = \frac{1}{2\pi} \int_{-\pi}^{\pi} P(\omega) \cos(i\omega) \, d\omega \tag{7}$$

is the autocorrelation function corresponding to the signal spectrum $P(\omega)$. Equation (6) is a set of p linear equations in p unknowns which can be solved for the parameters a_k of the all-pole model spectrum. Several computationally efficient methods to solve (6) have been proposed in the last thirty years. The most efficient method is a recursive solution that seems to have appeared first in a paper by Durbin [18]. The same solution has appeared in numerous papers since then (see, for example, [19-21, 40]).

The minimum error is obtained by substituting (6) and (7) in (4). The result can be shown to be [13]

$$E_p = R_0 + \sum_{k=1}^{p} a_k R_k \ , \tag{8}$$

where the dependence of the minimum error on p is shown explicitly. Of interest also is the normalized error V_p which is the ratio of the minimum error to the energy in the signal spectrum, i.e.,

$$V_p = E_p/R_0 \ . \tag{9}$$

The gain factor G in (3) is obtained by conserving the total energy between the signal and model spectra. The gain can be shown to satisfy [13,15]

$$G^2 = E_p = R_0 V_p = R_0 + \sum_{k=1}^{p} a_k R_k \ . \tag{10}$$

Therefore, G^2 is equal to the minimum error E_p.

Equations (6), (7) and (10) completely specify the model spectrum $\hat{P}(\omega)$. Given a spectrum $P(\omega)$ and a desired number of poles p, the parameters of $\hat{P}(\omega)$ are obtained by first computing the autocorrelation coefficients R_i, $0 \le i \le p$, using (7). The coefficients a_k are then computed from (6) and the gain G from (10).

Equivalently, if the speech signal itself is given, it is not necessary to compute $P(\omega)$ first. Instead, the autocorrelation coefficients R_i can be computed from the signal directly:

$$R_i = \sum_{n=-\infty}^{\infty} s_n \, s_{n+i} \quad , \quad 0 \le i \le p \ . \tag{11}$$

It is clear that (11) can be evaluated only if the signal is of finite duration, which is ordinarily attained by multiplying the signal by a finite window. (See [13] for an analytical study of windowing of speech signals.)

The spectral modeling method described above is equivalent to the autocorrelation (stationary) method of linear prediction, where the coefficients a_k are the predictor coefficients. Therefore, we can call this method the linear predictive (LP) spectral modeling method. The model spectrum $\hat{P}(\omega)$ in (4) is also known as the LP spectrum.

The manner in which the model spectrum $\hat{P}(\omega)$ approximates $P(\omega)$ is largely reflected in the relation between the corresponding autocorrelation functions. In particular, it can be shown that [15]

$$\hat{R}_i = R_i \ , \ 0 \le i \le p \ , \tag{12}$$

where

$$\hat{R}_i = \frac{1}{2\pi} \int_{-\pi}^{\pi} \hat{P}(\omega) \cos(i\omega) \, d\omega \tag{13}$$

is the autocorrelation function corresponding to the model spectrum. Since $P(\omega)$ and $\hat{P}(\omega)$ are the Fourier transforms of R_i and $\hat{R}_i$, respectively, it follows that increasing the value of p increases the range over which R_i and $\hat{R}_i$ are equal, resulting in a better fit of $\hat{P}(\omega)$ to $P(\omega)$. In the limit, as $p \to \infty$, $\hat{R}_i$ becomes identical to R_i for all i, and hence the two spectra become identical:

$$\hat{P}(\omega) = P(\omega) \ , \ \text{as } p \to \infty \ . \tag{14}$$

Another property of the model spectrum $\hat{P}(\omega)$ is that it has zero slope at angles of 0 and π.

2.2 Selective Linear Prediction

Above we have assumed that the model spectrum spans the same frequency range as the signal spectrum. Suppose that we wish to model the spectrum $P(\omega)$ only in the region $\omega_a \leq \omega \leq \omega_b$ by an all-pole spectrum given by (3). Call the signal spectrum in that region $P'(\omega)$. In order to compute the parameters of the model spectrum $\hat{P}(\omega)$, we simply map the given region onto the unit circle in the z plane such that ω_a corresponds to an angle of zero, and ω_b corresponds to π, and then follow the procedure outlined earlier with $P'(\omega)$ replacing $P(\omega)$ in (7). Selective linear prediction has had applications in speech recognition as well as speech compression [16]. Below I describe the manner in which selective linear prediction is used in the current speech understanding system at Bolt Beranek and Newman (BBN) [22].

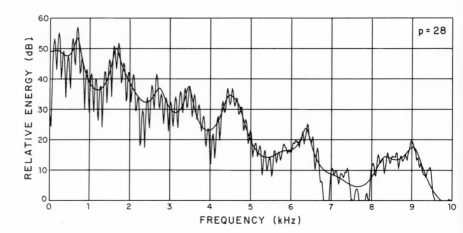

Figure 1A. A 28-pole spectral fit ot an FFT-computed signal spectrum.

Figure 1A shows a spectrum computed from a speech signal sampled at 20 kHz. In order to model the spectral envelope for the whole frequency range from 0-10 kHz, one would probably use between 24 to 28 poles for the all-pole model spectrum. A 28-pole fit is shown in Fig. 1A. For speech recognition applications, however, the main region of interest is the 0-5 kHz region. The spectrum in the 5-10 kHz region is of interest mainly for the recognition of the presence of frication, in which case the energy in that region might be sufficient.

We also know that in linear prediction the spectral matching process performs uniformly over the whole frequency range (see Section 2.4), which might not be desirable in cases where the all-pole assumption is less applicable for frequencies greater than 5 kHz. Therefore, instead of modeling the whole spectrum, we use selective linear prediction to model the lower 5 kHz by a lower order all-pole spectrum. A 14-pole fit is shown in Fig. 1B. In this manner, not only have we reduced our computations for the poles, but we are also in the advantageous position of having to interpret 14 instead of 28 poles. The total energy in the 5–10 kHz region can be easily computed directly from the spectrum and used for the detection of fricatives if desired.

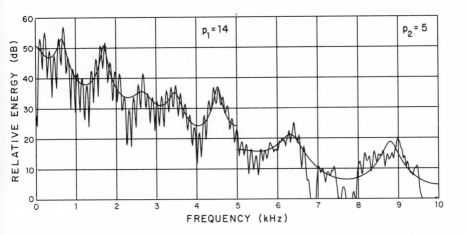

Figure 1B. Application of selective linear prediction to the same signal spectrum as in Figure 1A, with a 14-pole fit to the 0–5 khz region and a 5-pole fit to the 5–10 kHz region.

If instead of simply finding the energy in the 5–10 kHz region, one is interested in modeling that region by another lower order all-pole spectrum, then, following the same procedure as before, one obtains the desired model spectrum. A 5-pole spectral fit to the 5–10 kHz region is shown in Fig. 1B. The fact that the two spectral fits do not meet at 5 kHz is a direct consequence of this method of matching.

Now, the same type of analysis discussed above could be done in the time domain, but consider what one would have to do. First, the

20 kHz sampled signal must be sharply filtered at 5 khz. Second, and very importantly, the signal must be down-sampled to 10 kHz by discarding every other sample. Third, a 14-pole LP analysis is performed on the resulting signal. And fourth, in order to obtain the energy in the 5-10 kHz region, one subtracts the energy in the 10 kHz signal from the energy in the original 20 kHz signal. (It is even more complicated if one wants to perform an LP analysis on the 5-10 khz region in the time domain.)

Not only is the time domain analysis more involved and costly, it is also very inflexible. Consider the problem of having to carry out the same procedure to match the spectrum in the 0-3.5 kHz region instead of 0-5 kHz. In that case, it would be necessary to perform the time-domain down-sampling from 20 kHz to 7 kHz: a rather difficult task. The elegance of the method of selective linear prediction lies in the fact that the two problems of sharp filtering and down sampling are completely solved by working in the frequency domain.

From the above discussion it becomes evident that it would have been highly unlikely for the method of selective linear prediction to have emerged had linear prediction been thought about mainly in the time domain.

An important point, which should be clear by now, is that since we assume the availability of the signal spectrum $P(\omega)$, any desired frequency shaping or filtering can be performed directly on the signal spectrum before linear predictive modeling is applied.

2.3 MODELING DISCRETE SPECTRA

Thus far we have assumed that the spectrum $P(\omega)$ is a continuous function of frequency. More often, however, the spectrum is known at only a finite number of frequencies. For example, an FFT-derived spectrum has values at equally spaced frequency points. On the other hand, filter bank spectra usually have values at frequencies that are not necessarily equally spaced. For these discrete cases, the error measure E in (4) is defined as a summation instead of an integral. The analysis remains the same except that the autocorrelation coefficients R_i in (6) are now computed from

$$R_i = \frac{1}{N} \sum_{n=0}^{N-1} P(\omega_n) \cos(i\omega_n) , \qquad (15)$$

where N is the total number of spectral points on the unit circle. Note that the frequencies ω_n need not be equally spaced. Below we demonstrate the application of linear prediction modeling for filter bank and harmonic spectra.

Figure 2A shows a typical 14-pole spectral fit to a vowel spectrum that was obtained from a time signal by an FFT. Figure 2B shows a similar fit to a line spectrum that is typical of filter bank spectra. What we have actually done here is to simulate a filter bank where the filters are linearly spaced up to 1.6 kHz and logarithmically spaced thereafter. Note that the all-pole spectrum for the simulated filter bank is remarkably similar to the one in the top figure, even though the number of spectral points is much smaller.

The dashed curve in Fig. 3A is a 14-pole spectrum. If one applied LP analysis to this spectrum, the all-pole model for $p=14$ would be identical to the dashed spectrum. The situation is not so favorable for discrete spectra. Let us assume that the dashed spectrum corresponds to the transfer function of a 14-pole filter. If this filter is excited by a periodic train of impulses (unit samples) with fundamental frequency F_0, the spectrum of the output signal will be a discrete line spectrum with spectral values only at the harmonics (multiples of F_0). The line spectrum for $F_0=312$ Hz is shown in Fig. 3A. Note that the dashed spectrum is an envelope of the harmonic spectrum. The result of applying a 14-pole LP analysis to the harmonic spectrum is shown as the solid curve in Fig. 3A. The discrepancy between the two all-pole spectra is obvious. In general, the types of discrepancies that can occur between the model and original spectra include merging or splitting of pole peaks, and increasing or decreasing of pole frequencies and bandwidths. Pole movements are generally in the direction of the nearest harmonic. As the fundamental frequency decreases, these discrepancies decrease, as shown in Fig. 3B for $F_0=156$ Hz. The problems existent with higher fundamentals make linear prediction less accurate for the analysis of high pitched voices.

2.4 Linear Prediction vs. Analysis-by-Synthesis

For any modeling procedure, it is important to recognize its strengths and weaknesses in order to fully utilize its capabilities. Here we shall discuss the modeling properties of LP analysis and compare it to the well known method of AbS.

The basic difference between LP and AbS is in the definition of the error measure between the signal and model spectra. Equation (4) gives the definition of the error measure in LP. For AbS, the error

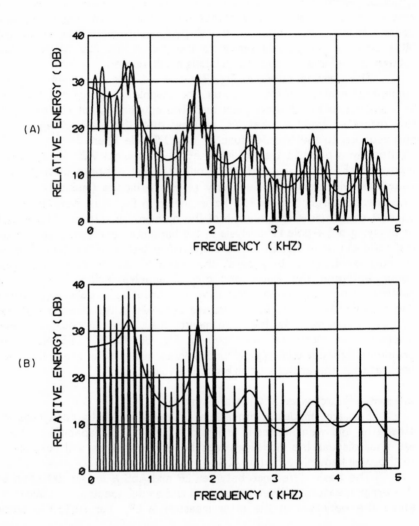

Figure 2. Application of LP modeling to a filter blank vowel spectrum. (A) A 14-pole fit to the original spectrum. (B) A 14-pole fit to the simulated filter bank spectrum.

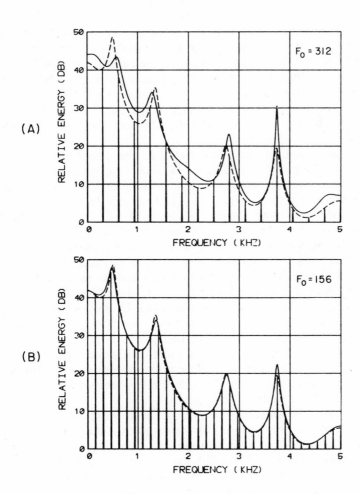

Figure 3. LP modeling of harmonic spectra. Dashed curve: 14-pole filter spectrum. Vertical lines: Corresponding harmonic spectrum for (A) $F_o=312$ Hz, and (B) $F_o=156$ Hz. Solid curve: A 14-pole fit to the discrete harmonic spectrum.

measure is given (in our notation) by

$$E' = \frac{1}{2\pi} \int_{-\pi}^{\pi} [\log P(\omega) - \log \hat{P}(\omega)]^2 \, d\omega$$

$$= \frac{1}{2\pi} \int_{-\pi}^{\pi} [\log \frac{P(\omega)}{\hat{P}(\omega)}]^2 \, d\omega \; . \tag{16}$$

The two methods have two properties in common: (a) The spectral modeling can be done selectively to any portion of the spectrum, and (b) both error criteria are functions of the ratio of the signal and model spectra, and therefore the matching process should perform uniformly over the frequency range of interest, irrespective of the shaping of the spectral envelope. These desirable properties have been known to apply to AbS for some time, and we see here that they also apply to LP analysis.

One point of departure between the two methods is in the amount of computation necessary to obtain the model parameters. If the model spectrum contains zeros (with or without poles) then the minimization of E in (4) and E' in (16) both lead to nonlinear equations that must be solved iteratively. However, if the model spectrum consists of poles only, as in (3), then LP offers a distinct advantage. We have seen above that for this special (but important) case, the LP parameters are the solution to a set of linear equations (6). In AbS one would still need to perform the nontrivial task of an iterative solution. Another special case of interest for the analysis of glottal pulses is the all-zero case. For this case, a suboptimal LP inverse solution can be obtained by performing LP modeling on the inverse spectrum. However, one must take care to smooth the spectrum first [16]. LP analysis offers another minor computational advantage. If the time signal is available, then the autocorrelation coefficients for the solution of (6) can be obtained directly from the time domain without the need to compute the spectrum first.

Although computational efficiency is of great concern, it must be weighed against the accuracy of the results and the price one is willing to pay to get the needed accuracy. We shall now discuss the differences between LP and AbS modeling in the manner in which they affect the quality of match between the model and signal spectra. The quality of match is determined (for our purposes) by how well the model spectrum approximates the envelope of the signal spectrum. This matter is completely determined by the definitions of error given in (4) and (16).

We note from (4) that values of $P(\omega)$ that are greater than the corresponding values in $\hat{P}(\omega)$ will contribute to the total error in a more substantial manner than points where $P(\omega)$ is much smaller than $\hat{P}(\omega)$. This means that, after the minimization of error, we expect a better fit of $\hat{P}(\omega)$ to $P(\omega)$ where $P(\omega)>\hat{P}(\omega)$ than where $P(\omega)<\hat{P}(\omega)$. For example, if $P(\omega)$ is the power spectrum of a quasi-periodic signal (such as in Fig. 2A), then the error measure (4) insures that the match of $\hat{P}(\omega)$ to $P(\omega)$ is far superior at the harmonics where the energy is greater, than between the harmonics where there is very little energy. Therefore, we conclude that the LP error measure in (4) results in a model spectrum that is a good estimate of the envelope of the signal spectrum. The situation is not as favorable for AbS. From the error measure in (16) we note that contributions to the total error are equally significant whether $P(\omega)<\hat{P}(\omega)$ or $P(\omega)>\hat{P}(\omega)$. This means that energy at the harmonics and the lack of energy between harmonics contribute equally to the total error. This, of course, will not lead to a good spectral envelope. In general, if the variations of the signal spectrum about the desired spectral envelope are large, then it is expected that LP analysis would give better results than AbS.

The situation is reversed if the signal spectrum is smooth relative to the desired envelope spectrum. First, we point out that if the signal spectrum is a continuous all-pole spectrum, then both methods will yield a model spectrum (with the same number of poles) that is identical to the signal spectrum. However, if the signal spectrum is discrete, then even though its envelope is exactly an all-pole spectrum, we know from above (see Fig. 3) that LP modeling will result in a different all-pole spectrum, with relatively large discrepancies for high fundamentals. For this case, AbS always gives the desired all-pole model, provided the number of harmonics in the spectrum is greater than the number of poles. Also, for modeling of filter bank spectra, such as in Fig. 2A, AbS is expected to give better results. There is independent evidence [21] that AbS gives a better quality match than LP if the signal spectrum is smooth relative to the desired spectral envelope. However, for many applications the differences in match quality may not warrant the extra computational cost associated with AbS.

Because of certain misinterpretations, it has been concluded by some that in LP modeling, the formants are matched better than the spectral envelope valleys in between. LP analysis should perform, on the average, equally well at formant peaks as well as the valleys between the formants. A detailed discussion of this matter is given in [16].

3. PARAMETRIC REPRESENTATIONS OF MODEL SPECTRUM

As mentioned in Section 1.1, one of the advantages of spectral modeling is that it is parametric. For the purposes of speech recognition, one can consider parameterization as a process of redundancy removal, where all spectral information is reduced to a small set of parameters. The parameters could then be treated as features that are matched against stored templates for recognition. Additional advantages include savings on computer storage and computations.

The LP model spectrum can be parametrically specified in many ways. Below we shall enumerate some of the possible parametric representations and discuss their possible utility for speech recognition. A discussion on the usefulness of the different representations in speech compression has been given elsewhere [21].

3.1 ALTERNATE PARAMETER REPRESENTATIONS

The LP all-pole model has a transfer function $H(z)$ given by (1). $H(z)$ can be rewritten as

$$H(z) = \frac{G}{A(z)} = \sum_{k=0}^{\infty} h_k z^{-k} , \qquad (17)$$

where h_k is the impulse response of the filter $H(z)$, and $A(z)$ is the inverse filter already defined in (2). Given below is a list of possible sets of parameters that characterize uniquely the linear prediction filter $H(z)$:

1.(a) Impulse response of the inverse filter $A(z)$, i.e. predictor coefficients a_k, $1 \leq k \leq p$.

(b) Impulse response of the all-pole model h_k, $0 \leq k \leq p$, which is easily obtained from (17) and (2) by long division. Note that the first $p+1$ coefficients uniquely specify the filter.

2.(a) Autocorrelation coefficients of a_k,

$$b_i = \sum_{k=0}^{p-|i|} a_k a_{k+|i|} , a_0 = 1, 0 \leq i \leq p . \qquad (18)$$

(b) Autocorrelation coefficients of h_k,

$$\hat{R}_i = \sum_{k=0}^{\infty} h_k h_{k+|i|} , 0 \leq i \leq p . \qquad (19)$$

Note that $\hat{R}_i$ is also given by (13), and that $\hat{R}_i = R_i$, $0 \leq i \leq p$.

3. Spectral coefficients of $A(z)$, Q_i, $0 \leq i \leq p$, (or equivalently spectral coefficients of $H(z)$, G^2/Q_i)

$$Q_i = b_0 + 2 \sum_{j=1}^{p} b_j \cos \frac{2\pi i j}{2p+1} \quad , \ 0 \leq i \leq p \ , \tag{20}$$

where b_j are as defined in (18). In words, $\{Q_i\}$ is obtained from $\{b_j\}$ by a discrete Fourier transform. It is interesting to note here that only p+1 values of the spectrum are necessary to uniquely characterize the whole spectrum.

4.   Cepstral coefficients of $A(z)$, c_n, $1 \leq n \leq p$, (or equivalently cepstral coefficients of $H(z)$, $-c_n$)

$$c_n = \frac{1}{2\pi} \int_{-\pi}^{\pi} \log A(e^{j\omega}) \, e^{jn\omega} \, d\omega \ . \tag{21}$$

Since $A(z)$ is minimum phase (i.e., all its zeros are inside the unit circle), (21) reduces to [23]

$$c_n = a_n - \sum_{m=1}^{n-1} \frac{m}{n} c_m a_{n-m} \quad , \ 1 \leq n \leq p \ . \tag{22}$$

Equation (22) is an iterative method for the computation of the cepstral coefficients directly from the predictor coefficients. The cepstrum can also be computed from the log spectrum.

5.   Reflection coefficients k_i, $1 \leq i \leq p$, or simple transformation thereof, e.g., area ratios. These coefficients occur naturally in the analysis of a lossless acoustic tube with transfer function $H(z)$ and with a discretely varying area function [12,24,25]. If the acoustic tube consists of elements with areas A_i, $1 \leq i \leq p$, then the reflection coefficient at the boundary between elements i and i+1 is given by

$$k_i = \frac{A_i - A_{i+1}}{A_i + A_{i+1}} \tag{23}$$

From (23) one obtains the area ratios

$$\frac{A_i}{A_{i+1}} = \frac{1+k_i}{1-k_i} \quad , A_{p+1} = 1 \ , \ 1 \leq i \leq p \ . \tag{24}$$

The reflection coefficients k_i (equal to the negative of the partial correlation coefficients [19]) are usually obtained as a byproduct of the recursive solution of (6). However, they can also be computed directly from the predictor coefficients as follows:

$$k_i = a_i^{(i)} \ , \tag{25}$$

$$a_j^{(i-1)} = \frac{a_j^{(i)} - a_i^{(i)} a_{i-j}^{(i)}}{1 - k_i^2} \quad , \ 1 \leq j \leq i-1 \ ,$$

where the index i takes values $p, p-1, \ldots, 1$ in that order. Initially, $a_j^{(p)} = a_j$, $1 \leq j \leq p$.

6. Poles of $H(z)$ (or equivalently zeros of $A(z)$).

Some of the above sets of parameters have $p+1$ coefficients while others have only p coefficients. However, for the latter sets the signal energy (or gain G) needs to be specified as well, thus keeping the total number of parameters as $p+1$ for all the cases. It should be mentioned here that the predictor coefficients can be recovered from any of the various sets of parameters listed above. The details are given elsewhere [21].

3.2 APPLICATIONS TO SPEECH RECOGNITION

One obvious manner in which to utilize the aforementioned sets of parameters in speech recognition is to store for each sound the corresponding parameter values, and then use some distance measure to classify a new set of parameter values. If we assume that the distance measure to be used is of a type similar to Euclidean distance measures, then this template matching process is possible for all parameter sets given in Section 3.1 except for the poles of the model. The reason is simple: the poles are not naturally ordered. For example, the predictor coefficients are naturally ordered because if the values for a_1 and a_2 are interchanged, then the filter $H(z)$ is changed. If the values of two poles are interchanged, on the other hand, the filter remains the same. A natural ordering is important for template matching since one is usually interested in comparing different values of the same parameter. Therefore, in order to be able to use the poles in a template matching system, they must be artificially ordered. Traditionally, poles have been ordered in terms of vocal tract resonances or formants. This is the familiar problem of formant extraction, which is discussed in Section 4.1.

Excluding the poles, there are five types of parameters given in Section 3.1, namely, impulse response, autocorrelation, spectrum, cepstrum, and reflection coefficients. These functions have been defined for the all-pole filter $H(z)$ as well as the inverse filter $A(z)$. The (log) spectrum, cepstrum and reflection coefficients for both filters are respectively identical for the purposes of template matching. Although the impulse responses and autocorrelation coefficients are different for the two filters, template matching experience gained from the representation of one filter would also apply approximately to the other filter.

All five types of parameters have been used in some template matching speech recognition task. The most popular parameter type is, of course, the spectrum. In fact, matches of the log spectrum are usually taken as a standard against which other measures are compared. However, the number of spectral points used for the comparison is usually much larger than that suggested in (20). It is not clear how drastically recognition results would be affected if one were to use only p+1 spectral points of a LP spectrum. The search by researchers for parameters other than the spectrum for the purpose of recognition is predicated partially on the assumption that a relatively large number of spectral points is needed for pattern matching. The search is always for parameters that perform well using a smaller number of parameter values and smaller amount of computation.

To the author's knowledge there has been only one study which compares the five types of parameter representations in a speech recognition task. This was a study by Ichikawa et al. [26] in Japan, using a digit speech recognition system as a base for the study. The result of the study was that the spectrum, cepstrum and reflection coefficients consistently gave better results than the predictor coefficients and the autocorrelation of the signal. Of the latter two, the predictor coefficients gave the worst results. The study was not conclusive about the relative merits of the best three parameter types. Of interest here also is a study by Makhoul and Viswanathan [21] on the relative merits of the five parameter types as possible transmission parameters in a speech compression system. The results of the quantization study were that there was a definite dichotomy between the spectrum, cepstrum and reflection coefficients on the one hand, with good quantization properties, and the predictor coefficients and autocorrelation on the other hand, with consistently poor quantization properties. Of the latter two, the predictor coefficients were worse. The results of this study mirror exactly the results of the study by Ichikawa et al. The reason for this is that both studies depend on similar distance measures.

Another spoken digit recognition system [27] has also been attempted using the predictor coefficients, with less than promising results. Fujisaki and Sato [28] used the familiar F-ratio as a "separability" measure in the evaluation of the performance of parameters in a classification system where linear discriminant functions are used. They found that the predictor coefficients perform worse than the first three formants in the recognition of vowels.

The cepstrum has been used in a few speech recognition studies [29,30] with generally optimistic results. The major aim of these studies was again to find a parameter that produces good recognition results using only a few parameter values instead of a whole spectrum.

3.3 Log Area Ratios: An "Optimal" Parameter Set

The reflection coefficients have some very desirable properties for pattern matching. For example, it has been shown that the reflection coefficients can be obtained as a result of the orthogonalization of the basis vectors for the predictor coefficients [31]. The fact that the reflection coefficients are representations in an orthogonal system of coordinates makes those coefficients very desirable in a pattern matching task. Another useful property is that the values of the reflection coefficient k_i, i<p, do not change as p is varied. These properties, as well as computational advantages, led Ichikawa et al. [26] to search for optimal methods of using the reflection coefficients to obtain good results. The methods they suggested, although they led to improved results, seemed to be somewhat forced. Here we present a different approach which is simple and should lead to good recognition results.

The reason for the less than optimal results obtained initially by Ichikawa et al. using the reflection coefficients lies, in the author's opinion, in the spectral sensitivity properties of the reflection coefficients. Spectral sensitivity is defined as the relative change in the LP spectrum with respect to a change in the parameter of interest. In the study made by Makhoul and Viswanathan [21] over several sentences spoken by different male and female speakers, plots of the spectral sensitivity versus k_i have the following properties in common:

    (i)   Each sensitivity curve versus k_i has the same general shape, irrespective of the index i and irrespective of the values of the other coefficients k_n, n≠i, at which the sensitivity is computed.

    (ii)   Each sensitivity curve is U-shaped. It is even-symmetric about $k_i=0$, and has large values when the magnitude of k_i is close to 1 and small values when the magnitude of k_i is close to zero.

For many speech sounds the first few reflection coefficients can have magnitudes close to 1, and therefore small changes in these coefficients can cause large spectral deviations. A simple distance measure for the reflection coefficients does not take into account these facts. One possibility is to weight each coefficient by its relative spectral sensitivity. Another possibility is to develop another parameter that is related to the reflection coefficient by a nonlinear transformation in such a manner that the new parameter will have a spectral sensitivity behavior that is flat. Using the latter approach,

Makhoul and Viswanathan [21] have shown that an approximately optimal transformation is given by

$$g = \log \frac{1+k}{1-k} \ . \tag{26}$$

It is clear from (24) that the new parameter g is the logarithm of the area ratio corresponding to the reflection coefficient k. The parameter g is known as the log area ratio. The log area ratio has all the desirable properties of the reflection coefficients with the added advantage of a flat spectral sensitivity behavior. This means that equal changes in the log area ratios result in approximately equal changes in the LP spectrum, which makes a simple distance measure an effective one for speech recognition tasks. Our conclusion is that the log area ratios should produce speech recognition results similar to those in which the spectrum is used in a pattern matching system.

3.4 AN ALTERNATE DISTANCE MEASURE

Thus far we have assumed that a simple distance measure (e.g., Euclidean) is to be used in the pattern matching. The approach, therefore, was to develop a parameter type that would produce results that are comparable to spectral results but that would require fewer parameters. The log area ratios were seen as possibly optimal for that purpose.

Given that our real aim is to produce the same good recognition results with less computation, another totally different approach suggests itself. The idea here is to develop a very different type of distance measure altogether. One such measure has been used recently by Itakura [32] in a 200 word speech recognition system. Given a reference set of predictor parameters $\{a'_k\}$ and another set of parameters $\{a_k\}$ that correspond to the matching signal with autocorrelations $\{R_i\}$, the distance measure between the two sets of parameters is given by [32]

$$d = \log \frac{\sum\limits_{i=-p}^{p} b'_i \, R_i}{\sum\limits_{i=-p}^{p} b_i \, R_i} \ , \tag{27}$$

where $\{b_i\}$ and $\{b'_i\}$ are obtained from $\{a_k\}$ and $\{a'_k\}$ by using (18). Using Parseval's theorem with (5) we see that the denominator in (27) is equal to the energy of the residual signal that results from passing the signal through the inverse filter A(z). The numerator is then the energy residual of passing the signal through the filter A'(z) corresponding to $\{a'_k\}$. Note that the denominator in (27) is also equal to the minimum error E_p given by (8). From (3), (5), (10), (12), it can be shown that the distance measure in (27) is equal to

$$d = \log \left[\frac{1}{2\pi} \int_{-\pi}^{\pi} \frac{|A'(e^{j\omega})|^2}{|A(e^{j\omega})|^2} \, d\omega \right] . \tag{28}$$

Thus, d is a also measure of the spectral difference between the two filters $A(z)$ and $A'(z)$. This measure is similar to that in (4) and, therefore, has the same properties. Note that $d \geq 0$, where the equality is true only if $A'(z) = A(z)$.

The motivation behind using (27) as a distance measure is that the decision procedure using this distance measure is equivalent to the likelihood ratio test [32], which is optimal in the maximum likelihood sense. However, (27) is optimal under the assumption that the predictor coefficients have a joint Gaussian probability distribution, which may or may not be true for speech signals. Generally, the likelihood ratio test with a Gaussian assumption is considered to be quite adequate even though the actual distributions may not be exactly Gaussian.

4. FEATURE EXTRACTION

In the previous section we assumed that the recognition decisions are based on distance measures between LP representations of the signal and corresponding reference patterns. This method of recognition based on pattern matching can be very useful in a limited vocabulary, isolated word speech recognition system. The system must usually be trained on all the words for each speaker. The extension of this method to more ambitious systems, such as speech recognition systems for continuous sentences, is by no means straightforward. A popular approach is to extract certain features that capture different aspects of the speech signal, and then perform the recognition based on these features. Such features often take the form of a new set of parameters that is extracted from the signal. In this section we shall give LP-related parameters that have been used recently in speech recognition systems.

4.1 FORMANT EXTRACTION

Many speech recognition systems have based their recognition schemes to a large degree on the identification of the vocal tract resonances (or formants) from the short-time spectrum. The identification of antiresonances (or antiformants) does not seem to be as crucial for recognition, and hence has not been pursued as vigorously by researchers. The problem of associating spectral peaks with specific formants is usually referred to as formant extraction. This problem has attracted the attention of many researchers in the last twenty-five years [24]. Formant extraction from linear prediction poles is only the most recent and promising method.

There are two main considerations in using linear prediction for the purpose of formant extraction: (a) The adequacy of the all-pole model for representing speech spectra, and (b) the determination of an optimal value for p, the number poles. These issues have been discussed in detail elsewhere [13,15]. For purposes of speech recognition, the all-pole model is adequate for many speech sounds. The adequacy of the model usually comes into question for the analysis of sounds that are known to have zeros as well as poles, such as nasals, fricatives and nasalized vowels. If the all-pole model is deemed to be adequate for a particular sound, then the optimal number of poles is usually taken to be equal to twice the number of expected formants in the spectral bandwidth under analysis, plus a few poles to take care of the general spectral slope due to the glottal spectrum. For example, for a 10 kHz sampled signal, a value of p=14 is typical.

Assuming that the all-pole model is adequate and that the number of poles is optimal, how are the formants extracted from the LP model? One method is to choose the formants from the poles of the transfer function H(z) in (1). These poles can be found by first computing the roots of the polynomial A(z) in (2). Some or none of the roots may be real and the rest are complex conjugate pairs. Conversion of the poles to the s plane can be achieved by setting each root $z_k = e^{s_k T}$, where $s_k = \sigma_k + j\omega_k$ is the corresponding pole in the s plane, and T is the sampling interval. If the root $z = z_{kr} + jz_{ki}$, then:

$$\omega_k = \frac{1}{T} \arctan \frac{z_{ki}}{z_{kr}} \quad , \tag{29}$$

$$\sigma_k = \frac{1}{2T} \log(z_{kr}^2 + z_{ki}^2) \quad , \tag{30}$$

where z_{kr} and z_{ki} are the real and imaginary parts of z_k, respectively. The formants can then be chosen from the complex poles as those with a high ratio between the frequency and bandwidth. In addition one can use already known frequency ranges for the formants to help in identifying them.

The main disadvantage of the method above is the vast amount of computation needed to solve for the roots of the polynomial. A much simpler method of formant extraction is to perform peak picking of the LP spectrum $\hat{P}(\omega)$ in (3) [9,10,12]. This method works well for more than 80 percent of the cases. Difficulties arise when two formants are so close to each other that they show up on the spectrum as a single wide peak. Most of these situations can be remedied by computing the spectrum inside the unit circle (closer to the poles) in order to enhance the formant peaks. This is easily done by multiplying the predictor coefficients a_k by a rising exponential before computing the spectrum [13,15]:

$$\hat{P}(\sigma,\omega) = \frac{G^2}{\left| 1 + \sum_{k=1}^{p} (a_k e^{-k\sigma T}) e^{-jk\omega T} \right|^2} \tag{31}$$

Values of $\tilde{\sigma}=_a-2\pi \times 75$ seem to work quite well. This method has been used recently in a complete formant tracking scheme [33].

4.2 LOWER ORDER MODELS

In speech recognition, it is often desirable to make a gross characterization of the spectrum of a particular sound. This is useful for the purposes of segmentation as well as the general classification of the different sounds. Previously, gross spectral characterizations have been obtained by computing parameters that depended on the energy contained in different regions of the spectrum. Other methods have employed measurements of zero crossing rates and zero crossing distances. Using linear prediction, it is possible to make a gross characterization of the spectrum by employing lower order models. An eight-pole model (10 kHz bandwidth) is used at System Development Corporation for the isolation and classification of fricatives and plosives [34]. A two-pole model (5 kHz bandwidth) [35] is currently being used in the BBN speech understanding system for segmentation and general classification [22]. The two-pole model is also employed by Itakura [32] in an isolated word speech recognition system to normalize for the gross spectral distribution of the utterance. Recently, a speaker independent digit recognition system has been designed by Sambur and Rabiner [36], based on the two-pole model. Because of the emerging importance of the two-pole model in speech recognition, we shall give a brief presentation of it below. A more detailed analysis is given elsewhere [35].

TWO-POLE MODEL

The transfer function of the two-pole model is given by

$$H(z) = \frac{G}{1 + a_1 z^{-1} + a_2 z^{-2}} \cdot \tag{32}$$

The coefficients a_1 and a_2 are computed from (6) which is now a set of two equations in two unknowns that can be easily solved. The autocorrelation coefficients R_0, R_1 and R_2 are the ones needed for the solution. The gain G is then computed from (10). The poles of H(z) in (32) are the roots of a second degree polynomial, which are easy to compute. Therefore, the specification of the parameters and poles of the two-pole model is simple and requires little computation.

The possible positions for the two poles of H(z) form four distinct cases. Figure 4 shows the four possible prototype amplitude responses for the two-pole model. The first case is that of the complex conjugate pair. The amplitude response is completely specified by the frequency and bandwidth of one pole. For real poles, there are three cases: The poles can be either both positive, both negative, or one positive and one negative. A positive real pole corresponds to a pole at zero frequency and indicates energy concentration at low frequencies. A negative real pole indicates energy concentration at high frequencies. All four prototype cases shown in Fig. 4 actually occur when modeling speech spectra.

For speech recognition applications, the two-pole model could be represented by the frequencies and bandwidths of the two poles. This type of representation is reasonable for complex conjugate poles since there is only one frequency and one bandwidth to interpret. The frequency indicates the position of the main region of energy concentration, and the bandwidth indicates the spread of energy in that region. However, in the case of real poles, we have to deal with two possibly distinct frequencies and two bandwidths. The frequencies are always either zero or equal to half the sampling frequency, and are easily interpretable. On the other hand, interpretation of two distinct bandwidths is far from straightforward, especially when the two frequencies are identical.

We have found that the bandwidth information can be represented in a more helpful manner in terms of the dynamic range of the two-pole spectrum and the direction or sign of its "slope". We define the spectral dynamic range D to be the difference in decibels between the highest and lowest amplitude points on the two-pole spectrum, or

$$D = 10 \log_{10} d \; , \tag{33}$$

where

$$d = \frac{[\hat{P}(\omega)]_{max}}{[\hat{P}(\omega)]_{min}} \tag{34}$$

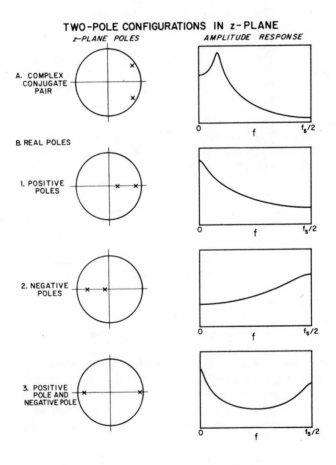

Figure 4. The four possible configurations of the two-pole model and representative spectra.

The dynamic range can be obtained analytically for the two-pole spectrum [35]. Figure 5 shows the results of a two-pole analysis for a typical utterance. The analysis was performed at 10 ms intervals over 20 ms Hamming-windowed segments of the 10 kHz sampled signal. (Note that the scale of the frequency plot is linear from 0 to 500 Hz, then logarithmic to 5000 Hz.)

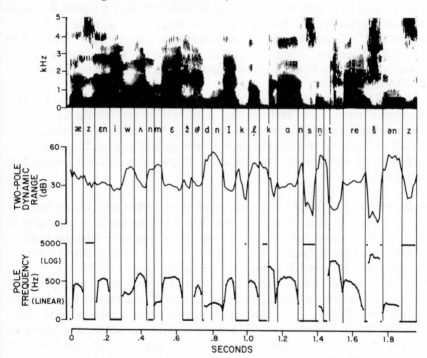

Figure 5. Two-pole frequency and spectral dynamic range at 10 msec intervals in the utterance "Has anyone measured nickel concentrations..."

Many segment boundaries, particularly those where a change of manner of articulation takes place, are clearly marked by abrupt or rapid changes in the two-pole frequencies. Many sonorant sequence transitions exhibit a rapid change in the two-pole frequency, which tends to follow the first formant if it is dominant, or lies between the first and second formants if they are close enough to each other.

The position of the two-pole frequency can be a good differentiator between sonorant and nonsonorant sounds. For example, any occurrence of a pole at 5000 Hz indicates strident frication, as do conjugate poles above about 1000 Hz.

The two-pole dynamic range is quite high during nasals, because of the dominance of the low first formant. This is quite a reliable indication. Conversely the dynamic range is usually quite low during unvoiced fricatives. The measure is not quite as reliable during voiced fricatives. A positive two-pole slope is, of course, a strong indication of strident frication.

The gross characterizations of speech spectra given by the two-pole model are certainly not sufficient in and of themselves to segment and roughly label continuous speech. However, together with other obvious measurements such as energy and voicing, they can form a powerful combination for the initial stages of a speech recognition system.

4.3 SPECTRAL SPREAD: AN ALTERNATIVE MEASURE TO THE SPECTRAL DYNAMIC RANGE

The spectral dynamic range D is a rather intuitive measure of one aspect of spectral shape. Its usefulness in speech analysis is quite encompassing. In Section 4.2 we have seen how the spectral dynamic range might be used in a speech recognition system. Although for the two-pole model the dynamic range can be evaluated analytically in terms of the two poles, in general it is difficult to compute the dynamic range analytically. One must first evaluate the spectrum and then search for the maximum and minimum values to obtain the dynamic range. Below we propose an alternative measure to the spectral dynamic range that is easy to compute for an all-pole spectrum.

The dynamic range is basically a measure of the "spread" of the spectrum. A more common measure of the spread of a collection of data is the variance. However, computing the variance of a spectrum about its mean is no more efficient than computing the dynamic range. Another measure of data spread that has been used occasionally is the ratio of the geometric mean to the arithmetic mean of the data. We shall see that this measure is easy to compute for an all-pole spectrum.

It has been shown [13,15] that the ratio of the geometric mean to the arithmetic mean for the all-pole spectrum $\hat{P}(\omega)$ is equal to the normalized error V_p given by (9). Thus,

$$V_p = \frac{\exp\left[\frac{1}{2\pi}\int_{-\pi}^{\pi} \log \hat{P}(\omega)\, d\omega\right]}{\frac{1}{2\pi}\int_{-\pi}^{\pi} \hat{P}(\omega)\, d\omega} \tag{35}$$

Equation (35) is also equal to

$$V_p = \frac{e^{\hat{c}_0}}{R_0}\ , \tag{36}$$

where $\hat{c}_0$ is the zeroth coefficient (quefrency) of the cepstrum. Therefore, the normalized error, which is easily computable from (8-9), is equal to the normalized zero quefrency of the cepstrum, which is also equal to the ratio of the geometric mean to the arithmetic mean of the spectrum. The spectral properties of V_p have been explored in detail by Makhoul and Wolf [13]. Other properties have been given recently by Gray and Markel [37].

In order to render V_p in a form that can be compared to the spectral dynamic range, we shall define the spectral spread S as follows:

$$S = -10 \log_{10} V_p\ , \tag{37}$$

where S is measured in decibels. Since V_p is always in the range $0 < V_p \leq 1$ for a positive definite spectrum, the spectral spread in (37) is then always nonnegative. The relation between the spread S and the dynamic range D is shown in Fig. 6, where 200 values of S versus D are plotted for the two seconds of continuous speech shown in Fig. 5. The spread generally increases with an increase in the dynamic range. The solid curve in Fig. 6 is an absolute upper bound on the spectral spread for each value of the dynamic range. The curve is a plot of the following relation [13]

$$S_m = -10 \log_{10}[\gamma e^{(1-\gamma)}]\ , \tag{38}$$

where

$$\gamma = \frac{\log d}{d-1}\ , \tag{39}$$

and d is given by (34).

The spectral spread is currently being used in the speech

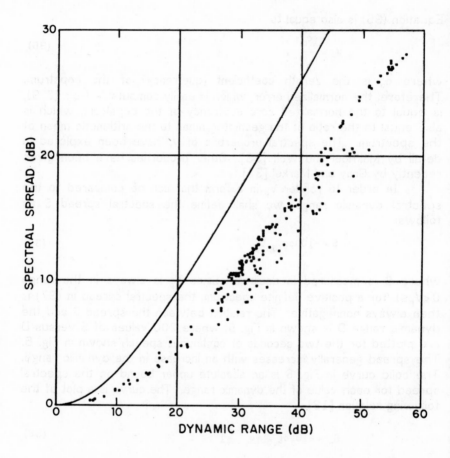

Figure 6. Spectral spread versus two-pole spectral dynamic range for the 200 data points in the utterance in Figure 5. The solid curve is a plot of S_m in equation (38), which is the absolute upper bound on the spectral spread.

recognition system at BBN [22] for segmentation and in the extraction of features such as voicing, nasality, and stridency.

4.4 OTHER LP-RELATED PARAMETERS

(i) R_1 AND A_1

Two parameters that are useful in comparing the spectral energy at low frequencies with the energy at high frequencies, are the first autocorrelation coefficient R_1 and the first cepstral coefficient c_1. R_1 is simply the average of a cosine weighted spectrum, and c_1 is the average of a cosine weighted log spectrum. If the cepstrum is given by (21), then we see from (22) that $c_1 = a_1$. Therefore, the first predictor coefficient can be used instead of c_1.

(ii) An Energy-Independent Spectral Derivative

In addition to energy peaks in the spectrum (represented by formants), it has been the experience of some researchers [38] that the spectral regions of increasing and decreasing energy (positive and negative slopes) are also important for the machine recognition of speech. This suggests the use of a spectral derivative with respect to frequency. A frequency spectral derivative $SD(\omega)$ for the all-pole log spectrum $\hat{P}(\omega)$ can be obtained from

$$SD(\omega) = \frac{\partial[\log \hat{P}(\omega)]}{\partial \omega} , \qquad (40)$$

which can be shown to be equal to

$$SD(\omega) = \frac{2 \sum_{k=1}^{p} k\, b_k \sin(k\omega)}{b_0 + 2 \sum_{k=1}^{p} b_k \cos(k\omega)} , \qquad (41)$$

where b_k is defined by (18). The denominator in (41) is just equal to $|A(e^{jw})|^2$, which can be computed as the real part of the FFT of the sequence $b_0, 2b_1, 2b_2, ..., 2b_p$. The numerator can be computed as twice the imaginary part of the FFT of the sequence $0, b_1, 2b_2, ..., pb_p$.

$SD(\omega)$ is independent of the energy in the spectrum. Its extrema correspond to regions of maximal spectral slope. Its negative going zero crossings correspond to formant peaks; hence, formant information remains essentially intact. (Note that $SD(\omega)$ is always zero at $\omega=0$ and at half the sampling frequency.)

In conjunction with the definition of a frequency spectral derivative $SD(\omega)$, one can also define a time spectral derivative as

$$SD(\omega,t) = SD_t(\omega) - SD_{t-1}(\omega) \qquad (42)$$

where the subscripts t and t-1 refer to consecutive time indices at which the frequency derivatives are computed. From (42) it is then reasonable to define a single parameter that represents the average spectral change from one frame to the next as

$$\overline{SD}(t) = \frac{1}{2\pi} \int_{-\pi}^{\pi} |SD(\omega,t)| \, d\omega \quad . \tag{43}$$

In practice, the integral in (43) is approximated by a summation. SD(t) is now a single parameter spectral derivative that is independent of the energy of the signal.

The proposed time-frequency spectral derivative $SD(\omega,t)$ in (42) is congruous with the notion of the "quadrapole" of Stevens [39], which is hypothesized to play a role in property detection in the perception of speech.

5. CONCLUSIONS

In this paper we presented current applications of linear prediction to automatic speech recognition. All the applications are based on a parametric representation of the short-time spectrum by an all-pole model. Linear prediction was presented as a spectral smoothing as well as a spectral modeling method. As a spectral smoothing method, it was compared with autocorrelation smoothing, cepstral smoothing, and with filter bank spectra. As a spectral modeling method, linear prediction was compared with traditional analysis-by-synthesis. It was found that linear prediction offers computational advantages as well as better modeling properties for spectra that have large fluctuations around the spectral envelope. For relatively smooth spectra and for filter bank spectra, analysis-by-synthesis is judged to give better results.

Many speech recognition systems base their recognition on pattern matching of the short-time spectrum with reference spectra, using a simple distance measure (such as the Euclidean distance). For this purpose, different parametric representations of the all-pole model spectrum were reviewed and compared with respect to their performance in pattern classification tasks. The parameters include the predictor coefficients, autocorrelation, spectrum, cepstrum, and reflection coefficients. The predictor and autocorrelation coefficients are consistently worse than the other three parameters, with the predictor coefficients being the worst. The log area ratios were introduced as a possibly optimal representation that would yield results similar to spectral matching. Another different approach to classification, introduced by Itakura, is to use a log likelihood ratio as a distance measure. It would be interesting to compare the last two methods in a speech classification experiment.

Other recognition systems base their recognition on parameters that capture different aspects of the signal spectrum. Several such parameters were presented. Perhaps the most widely used parameters in this respect are the formants. The extraction of formants from the all-pole model was reviewed. Lower order all-pole models are useful in giving gross representations of the spectrum. The two-pole model was seen to have applications in speech recognition for the purposes of segmentation and feature extraction, and for normalization for speakers. The spectral spread, a parameter derived from the linear prediction normalized error, was suggested as an alternative measure to the spectral dynamic range, which is also useful for segmentation and feature extraction. The first predictor and autocorrelation coefficients are useful parameters for comparing spectral energy at low frequencies with that at high frequencies. Finally, an energy-independent spectral derivative with respect to time and frequency was proposed. The measure is congruous with recent theories on perceptual property detectors. However, the extent of its usefulness in an automatic speech recognition system has yet to be explored.

ACKNOWLEDGMENTS

The author wishes to thank J. Wolf, R. Viswanathan, and C. Cook for their helpful comments. This work was supported by the Information Processing Techniques Branch of the Advanced Research Projects Agency.

REFERENCES

[1]   Bell, C. G., H. Fujisaki, J. M. Heinz, K. N. Stevens, and A. S. House, "Reduction of Speech Spectra by Analysis-by-Synthesis Techniques," J. Acoust. Soc. Am., vol. 33, No. 12, pp. 1725-1736, Dec. 1961.

[2]   Paul, A. P., A. S. House, and K. N. Stevens, "Automatic Reduction of Vowel Spectra: An Analysis-by-Synthesis Method and its Evaluation," J. Acoust. Soc. Am., Vol. 36, No. 2, pp. 303-308, Feb. 1964.

[3]   Fujimura, O., "Analysis of Nasal Consonants," J. Acoust. Soc. Am., Vol. 34, No. 12, pp. 1865-1875, Dec. 1962.

[4]   Mathews, M. V., J. E. Miller, and E. E. David, "Pitch Synchronous Analysis of Voiced Sounds," J. Acoust. Soc. Am., Vol. 33, pp. 179-186, 1961.

[5]   Olive, J. P., "Automatic Formant Tracking by a Newton-Raphson Technique," J. Acoust. Soc. Am., Vol. 50, pp. 661-670, 1971.

[6]   Yule, G. U., "On a Method of Investigating Periodicities in Disturbed Series, with Special Reference to Wolfer's Sunspot Numbers," Phil. Trans., Vol. A226, pp. 267, 1927.

[7]   See Hildebrand, F. B., Introduction to Numerical Analysis, McGraw-Hill, New York, p. 378, 1956.

[8]   Itakura, F. and S. Saito, "Analysis Synthesis Telephony based on the Maximum Likelihood Method," Paper C-5-5, Proc. of the 6th International Congress on Acoustics, Tokyo, Japan, Aug. pp. 21-28, 1968.

[9]   Itakura, F., and S. Saito, "A Statistical Method for Estimation of Speech Spectral Density and Formant Frequencies," Electronics and Comm. in Japan, Vol. 53-A, No. 1, pp. 36-43, 1970.

[10]   Markel, J. D., "Digital Inverse Filtering - A New Tool for Formant Trajectory Estimation," IEEE Trans. Audio Electroacoustics, AU-20, No. 2, pp. 129-137, June 1972.

[11]   Atal B . S. and M. R. Schroeder, "Predictive Coding of Speech Signals," Paper C-5-4, Proc. of the 6th International Congress on Acoustics, Tokyo, Japan, Aug. pp. 21-28, 1968.

[12]   Atal, B. S. and S. L. Hanauer, "Speech Analysis and Synthesis by Linear Prediction of the Speech Wave," J. Acoust. Soc. Am., Vol. 50, pp. 637-655, Aug. 1971.

[13]   Makhoul, J. I. and J. J. Wolf, "Linear Prediction and the Spectral Analysis of Speech." AD-749066, BBN Report No. 2304, Bolt Beranek and Newman Inc., Cambridge, Mass., August 1972.

[14]   Schafer, R. W. and L. R. Rabiner, "Parametric Representations of Speech," in this volume.

[15]   Makhoul, J., "Spectral Analysis of Speech by Linear Prediction," IEEE Trans. Audio and Electroacoustics, Vol. AU-21, pp. 140-148, June 1973.

[16]   Makhoul, J., "Selective Linear Prediction and Analysis-by-Synthesis in Speech Analysis," BBN Report No. 2578, Bolt Beranek and Newman Inc., Cambridge, Mass., April 1974. (Submitted for publication in IEEE Trans. Acoustics Speech and Signal Processing.)

[17]   Makhoul, J., "Linear Prediction vs. Analysis-by-Synthesis," Proc. Speech Communication Seminar, Stockholm, Sweden, Aug. pp. 1-3, 1974.

[18]   Durbin, J., "The Fitting of Time Series Models," Rev. Inst. Int. Stat., Vol. 28, No. 3, pp. 233-243, 1960.

[19] Itakura, F. and S. Saito, "Digital Filtering Techniques for Speech Analysis and Synthesis," Paper 25-C-1, Proc. 7th Int. Congress on Acoustics, Budapest, 1971.

[20] Markel, J. D. and A. H. Gray, Jr., "On Autocorrelation Equations with Application to Speech Analysis," IEEE Trans. Audio Electroacoust., Vol. AU-21, No. 2, pp. 69-79, April 1973.

[21] Makhoul, J. and R. Viswanathan, "Quantization Properties of Transmission Parameters in Linear Predictive Systems," BBN Report No. 2800, Bolt Beranek and Newman Inc., Cambridge, Mass., April 1974. (Submitted for publication in IEEE Trans. Acoustics, Speech and Signal Processing.)

[22] Schwartz, R. and J. Makhoul, "Where the Phonemes Are: Dealing with Ambiguity in Acoustic-Phonetic Recognition," Proc. IEEE Symp. Speech Recognition, Carnegie-Mellon University, Pittsburgh, Pa., 85-88, April 15-19, 1974. Also in IEEE Trans. Acoustics, Speech and Signal Processing, ASSP-23, 50-53, Feb. 1975.

[23] Gold, B. and C. M. Rader, Digital Processing of Signals, McGraw-Hill, New York, 1969.

[24] Flanagan, J. L., Speech Analysis Synthesis and Perception, Academic Press Inc., New York, Second Edition, 1972.

[25] Wakita, H., "Direct Estimation of the Vocal Tract Shape by Inverse Filtering of Acoustic Speech Waveforms," IEEE Trans. Audio and Electroacoustics, Vol. AU-21, pp. 417-427, Oct. 1973.

[26] Ichikawa, A., Y. Nakano and K. Nakata, "Evaluation of Various Parameter Sets in Spoken Digits Recognition," IEEE Trans. Audio and Electroacoustics, Vol. AU-21, No. 3, pp. 202-209, June 1973.

[27] Kohda, M., et al, "Spoken Digit Mechanical Recognition," Trans. IECE of Japan, p. 55-D, 3, 1972 (in Japanese).

[28] Fujisaki, H. and Y. Sato, "Evaluation and Comparison of Features in Speech Recognition," Ann. Rep. of Eng. Res. Inst., Fac. Eng., Univ. of Tokyo, Vol. 32, pp. 213-218, 1973.

[29] Strasbourger, E., "The Role of the Cepstrum in Speech Recognition," Proc. 1972 Conf. Speech Communication and Processing, Newton, Mass., pp. 299-302, April 24-26, 1972.

[30] Purves, R. B., "An Automatic Method for Computer Recognition of Continuous Speech," Ph.D. dissertation, Dept. Physics and Astronomy, Brigham Young Univ., Provo, Utah, April 1973.

[31] Matsui, E., T. Nakajima, T. Suzuki and H. Omura, "An Adaptive Method for Speech Analysis Based on Kalman Filtering Theory," Bull Electrotech. Lab., Vol. 36, No. 3, 1972 (In Japanese).

[32] Itakura, F., "Minimum Prediction Residual Principle Applied to Speech Recognition," Proc. IEEE Symp. Speech Recognition, Carnegie-Mellon University, Pittsburgh, Pa., pp. 101-105, April 15-19, 1974. Also in IEEE Trans. Acoustics, Speech and Signal Processing, ASSP-23, pp. 67-72, Feb. 1975.

[33] McCandless, S. S., "An Algorithm for Automatic Formant Extraction Using Linear Prediction Spectra," IEEE Trans. Acoustics Speech and Signal Processing, Vol. ASSP-22, No. 2, pp. 135-141, April 1974.

[34] Molho, L., "Automatic Recognition of Fricatives and Plosives in Continuous Speech," Proc. IEEE Symp. Speech Recognition, Carnegie-Mellon University, Pittsburgh, Pa., pp. 68-73, April 15-19, 1974.

[35] Makhoul, J. and J. Wolf, "The Use of a Two-Pole Linear Prediction Model in Speech Recognition," BBN Report No. 2537, Bolt Beranek and Newman Inc., Cambridge, Mass., Sept. 1973.

[36] Sambur, M. R., and L. R. Rabiner, "A Speaker-Independent Digit-Recognition System," Bell Syst. Tech. J., Vol. 54, pp. 81-102, Jan. 1975.

[37] Gray, A. H. and J. D. Markel, "A Spectral-Flatness Measure for Studying the Autocorrelation Method of Linear Prediction of Speech Analysis," IEEE Trans. Acoustics, Speech and Signal Processing, Vol. ASSP-22, No. 3, pp. 207-217, June 1974.

[38] Martin, T. B., A. L. Nelson and H. J. Zadell, "Speech Recognition by Feature Abstraction Techniques," Report AFAL-TR-65-317, AD-476317, December 1965.

[39] Steven, K. N., "The Potential Role of Property Detectors in the Perception of Consonants," Proc. Symp. on Auditory Analysis and Perception, Leningrad, U.S.S.R., Aug. 1973.

[40] Makhoul, J., "Linear Prediction: A Tutorial Review," IEEE Proc., Special Issue on Digital Signal Processing, Vol. 63, April 1975.

LINEAR PREDICTION OF SPEECH -- RECENT ADVANCES WITH APPLICATIONS TO SPEECH ANALYSIS

Bishnu S. Atal
Bell Laboratories
Murray Hill, New Jersey, 07974

INTRODUCTION

In recent years, the techniques of linear prediction have proved to be very useful in providing an efficient representation of speech for a variety of speech analysis and synthesis applications [1-11]. As is well known, the linear prediction model idealizes the human speech production process in several respects [7-9]. In applications, such as speech coding, it has been possible to test the accuracy of the linear prediction technique by listening to the synthesized speech. What can be said about the reliablity of these techniques for obtaining accurate information about the spectrum and the formants of the speech signal? It is important to know of any errors produced by the different approximations implicit in the method. In this paper, we investigate the influence of two important assumptions underlying the linear prediction method, namely, that the spectrum of the excitation is white and that there are no zeros in the spectrum. Let us now discuss both of these problems in detail.

INFLUENCE OF VOICE PERIODICITY

In the linear prediction method, we represent the vocal tract as a discrete linear time-invariant filter with p poles. The linear prediction method is exact provided the all-pole filter is excited by a single impulse. For voiced speech, however, the excitation is nearly periodic. Does the periodic nature of the excitation effect the predictor coefficients and the formant information derived from them? There are two conditions under which the linear prediction method provides a correct solution for periodic excitations: (1) The prediction error is minimized over an interval in which either the excitation is absent or the signal is exactly predictable by linear prediction. (2) The impulse response of the all-pole filter dies to zero at least p samples before the start of the next period. Usually, it is difficult to meet these conditions. A periodic excitation of the all-pole filter is thus likely to introduce errors in the linear prediction analysis.

We have investigated the magnitude of such errors by analyzing synthetic speech of known characteristics. As a first step, synthetic speech consisting of a single formant was generated on the computer for several different pitch frequencies. The excitation function for the synthetic signal was a periodic sequence of impulses with the period varying between 2 and 20 msec. The formant frequency was variable between 200 and 700 Hz. The bandwidth of the formant was kept fixed at 50 Hz. These choices of formant frequencies and bandwidth were selected since the errors due to voice periodicity are likely to be most important for low-frequency formants with small damping. Except for the periodic nature of the excitation, the synthetic signal met the requirements of the all-pole model exactly. The predictor coefficients were determined by minimizing the mean-squared error over one complete period of the signal. No window was used on the signal. The formant frequency and the bandwidth were then determined by computing the roots of the predictor polynomial [7]. The results comparing the computed formant frequency with the actual one used in the synthesis are shown in Figure 1 for three different pitch frequencies of 100, 200, and 400 Hz, respectively. Note, the estimated formant frequency is in error, which varies with the frequency of the formant; the error is zero if the formant frequency is located at a harmonic or exactly half-way between two adjacent harmonics. For other locations, the estimated formant frequency is pulled towards the nearest harmonic frequency. Thus, the error varies periodically with the formant frequency. The maximum error is 11 Hz at a pitch of 100 Hz, 30 Hz at a pitch of 200 Hz, and 67 Hz at a pitch of 400 Hz. The reported j.n.d. (just noticeable difference) for the formant frequency is about 3 to 5 % [12]. These formant errors are likely to be perceptually important only for high-pitched voices and even then only in the first formant region. The results for the formant bandwidth are shown in Figure 2. The bandwidth errors are considerably larger; maximum errors at the three pitch frequencies are 25, 92, and 250 Hz, respectively. Although the j.n.d. for the formant bandwidths are not known accurately, the bandwidth errors at the pitch frequencies of 200 and 400 Hz may be perceptible. Of course, the errors reported here are maximum errors for the worst possible location of the formant frequency in relation to the harmonics. In real speech, these errors will vary considerably depending upon the values of the formant frequency, its bandwidth, and the pitch.

Similar results were also obtained for synthetic signals consisting of two or more formants. A typical result comparing the spectral envelopes obtained for two pitch frequencies is shown in Figure 3.

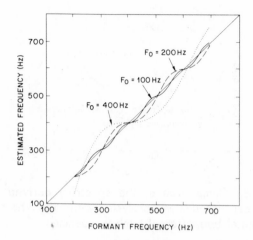

Figure 1. Comparison of the estimated formant frequency with the actual frequency used in the synthesis for three different pitch frequencies.

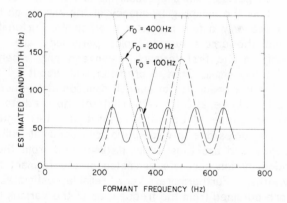

Figure 2. Plots showing the dependence of the estimated formant bandwidth on the formant frequency and the pitch.

The solid curve is for a pitch of 100 Hz while the dashed curve is for for a pitch of 200 Hz. The harmonic spectrum used in the synthesis is shown by the symbol '+' at 100 Hz intervals. The spectrum at the pitch frequency of 100 Hz is very close to the correct spectrum.

The above results suggest that the errors in the linear prediction analysis introduced by the voice periodicity are not serious

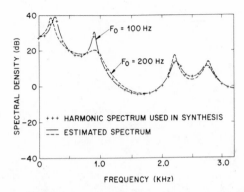

Figure 3. Comparison of the spectrum derived from the linear prediction analysis with the harmonic spectrum at two different pitch frequencies.

except for speech of some females and children. These errors are caused by the large prediction error at the beginning of a pitch period. The simplest solution is to increase the memory of the predictor by at least one pitch period. As a practical matter, this is not a desirable procedure unless the sampling frequency of the signal can be reduced so as to require only a few predictor coefficients. Fortunately, this is possible since the errors due to voice periodicity are perceptually significant only in the first formant region and only when the pitch period is relatively small. Thus, a predictor with about 14 coefficients is sufficient for the prediction of speech samples at frequencies below 1 kHz and pitch above 200 Hz. The roots of the predictor polynomial include now poles due to both the formant structure and the voice periodicity. The poles due to voice periodicity occur at multiples of the pitch frequency and are thus easily distinguished from the formants. This method provides accurate estimates of the formant frequencies and bandwidths. Furthermore, very reliable estimates of pitch frequency are obtained from the frequencies of the various harmonics.

LINEAR PREDICTION WITH SPECTRAL ZEROS
        Let us now turn to the problem of spectral zeros. The all-pole model of the vocal tract is quite accurate for vowels and other vowel-like sounds. This model, however, provides only an approximate representation of the speech signal if there are zeros in addition to the poles in the transfer function of the vocal tract as is the case for nasal consonants and nasalized vowels or if the source of excitation is not at the glottis but is in the interior of the vocal tract. The zeros can also be introduced by the transmission characteristics of the environment

where the recordings are made or by the low-pass filter used in analog-to-digital conversion. Finally, a model with both poles and zeros could provide a more accurate representation of the glottal pulse characteristics.

A spectral zero, unless it is cancelled by a closely-located pole, produces two separate effects in the spectrum, namely, a dip in the spectrum in the neighborhood of the frequency of the zero and an asymptotic 12-dB/octave rise in the spectrum beyond this frequency. In principle, the spectral properties of a zero can be approximated with arbitrary precision by additional poles in the all-pole model. Such an approximation, however, is likely to be inefficient except for the highly-damped zeros. In general, we find that the 12-dB/octave rise in the spectrum can be approximated satisfactorily by additional poles. However, significant errors are often introduced in the frequency region in the vicinity of the zero. Two examples, typical of the all-pole approximation of spectrum with a complex zero at 800 Hz, are shown in Figures 4 and 5. Note, that the all-pole approximation is not only inaccurate at the zero but also produces a shift in one of the formant frequencies. In Figure 5, two closely located formants with a zero in between appear as a single formant in the all-pole approximation.

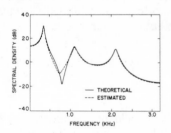

Figure 4. An example of the all-pole approximation of spectrum consisting of 10 poles and 2 zeros. The solid curve is the theoretical spectrum based on both the poles and the zeros. The dashed curve is the spectrum derived from the linear prediction analysis with 12 poles.

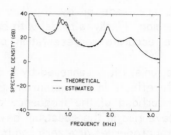

Figure 5. Another example of an all-pole approximation
of the spectrum.

Recently, a number of methods of estimating spectra in terms of
pole-zero models have been proposed [13-17]. It is possible that any
one of these methods will be suitable for estimating the poles and
zeros of the speech spectra. Let us see if we can take account of
zeros by linear prediction. There is no basic difficulty in including the
zeros in the linear prediction analysis. In linear prediction based on the
all-pole model (with p poles), every speech sample is predicted as a
linear combination of the previous p samples of the signal. Let us
assume now that there are q zeros in the transfer function in addition
to p poles. For a discrete linear filter with p poles and q zeros, the
n-th sample s(n) of its output is expressed as

$$s(n) = \sum_{k=1}^{p} a(k)\, s(n-k) + \sum_{k=0}^{q} b(k)\, e(n-k) \; , \tag{1}$$

where e(n) is the n-th sample of the excitation, the coefficients a(k)
represent the contribution of the poles, and the coefficients b(k)
represent the additional contribution of the q zeros. The predicted
value of the n-th speech sample is then given by

$$\hat{s}(n) = \sum_{k=1}^{p} a(k)\, s(n-k) + \sum_{k=1}^{q} b(k)\, \{s(n-k) - \hat{s}(n-k)\} \,. \tag{2}$$

Thus, in the presence of zeros, the predicted value of a speech sample
is represented as a sum of the linear combination of both the past p
speech samples and past q prediction-error samples or, alternatively,
the past q predicted samples. For comparison, in the all-pole model,
the predicted value is equal to the linear combination of only the past p

speech samples. As before, the unknown coefficients of Eq. 2 are found by minimizing the mean-squared prediction error over the appropriate analysis interval.

It is to be noted that that we now end up with p+q simultaneous nonlinear equations which must be solved by an iterative process. However, advantage can be taken of the fact that the coefficients a(k), representing the poles, can be estimated without any knowledge of the coefficients b(k) representing the zeros [13,14]. Thus, we need to solve only q nonlinear equations; the coefficients a(k) are determined by solving p linear equations similar to ones used in the all-pole case. Specifically, we skip first q normal equations and solve the next p equations.

The independent estimation of poles and zeros works reasonably well provided there is no appreciable interaction between the two. Without any noise, there was no error in the estimated spectrum -- as it should be. An example of a spectrum estimated by the above procedure in presence of noise is shown in Figure 6. The speech signal was synthesized with 10 poles and 2 zeros and noise was added to the signal by quantizing the speech samples at 10 bits per sample. The quantizing noise was found to have little adverse influence on the results. Two examples of the estimated spectra obtained from synthetic speech quantized at 7 bits per sample are illustrated in Figures. 7 and 8. Note, there is no shift in the formant frequency; the error is mostly in the bandwidth of the zero. It is, of course, not necessary to estimate poles and zeros independently of each other. Both poles and zeros can be estimated in one step by solving p+q nonlinear equations obtained by minimizing the mean-squared prediction error. Substantial savings in computational effort for the iterative solution of the nonlinear equations are achieved by using an initial estimate of the prediction error on the right side of Eq. 2 from an all-pole model.

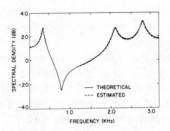

Figure 6. Comparison of the spectrum obtained from the linear prediction analysis using both poles and zeros with the actual spectrum used in the synthesis. The spectrum consisted of 10 poles and 2 zeros. Synthetic speech was quantized at 10 bits per sample.

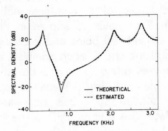

Figure 7. An example comparing the estimated spectrum with the actual spectrum used in the synthesis for synthetic speech quantized at 7 bits per sample.

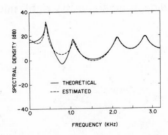

Figure 8. Another example of the spectrum estimated by the linear prediction analysis to include zeros for synthetic speech quantized at 7 bits per sample.

REFERENCES
[1]   B. S. Atal and M. R. Schroeder, "Predictive coding of speech signals," Proc. 1967 Conf. on Communication and Processing, pp. 360-361, November 1967.
[2]   B. S. Atal and M. R. Schroeder, "Predictive coding of speech signals," 1968 Wescon Technical Papers, Paper 8/2.
[3]   B. S. Atal and M. R. Schroeder, "Predictive coding of speech signals," Reports of the 6th International Congress on Acoustics, Tokyo, Vol. II, Paper C-5-4, 1968.
[4]   F. Itakura and S. Saito, "Analysis synthesis telephony based on the maximum likelihood method," Reports of the 6th International Congress on Acoustics, Tokyo, Vol. II, Paper C-5-5, 1968.
[5]   B. S. Atal, "Speech analysis and synthesis by linear prediction," J. Acoust. Soc. Amer. Vol. 47, 65(A), 1970.
[6]   B. S. Atal and M. R. Schroeder, "Adaptive predictive coding of speech signals," Bell Sys. Tech. Jour. Vol. 49, pp. 1973-1986, 1970.
[7]   B. S. Atal and S. L. Hanauer, "Speech analysis and synthesis by linear prediction," J. Acoust. Soc. Amer. Vol. 50, pp. 637-655, 1971.
[8]   J. I. Makhoul and J. J. Wolf, "Spectral analysis of speech by linear prediction," IEEE Trans. Audio Electroacoustics, Vol. AU-21, pp. 140-148, 1973.
[9]   J. D. Markel, A. H. Gray, Jr., and H. Wakita, "Linear prediction of speech - theory and practice," Monograph No. 10, Speech Communications Research Laboratory, Santa Barbara, California, 1973.
[10]   B. S. Atal, "Effectiveness of linear prediction characteristics of the speech wave for automatic speaker identification and verification," J. Acoust. Soc. Amer. Vol. 55, pp. 1304-1312, June 1974.
[11]   S. S. McCandless, "An algorithm for automatic formant extraction using linear prediction spectra," IEEE Trans. Acoustics, Speech, and Signal Process. Vol. ASSP-22, pp. 135-141, April 1974.
[12]   J. L. Flanagan, Speech Analysis Synthesis and Perception, New York: Springer-Verlag, 1972. p. 281.
[13]   T. S. Hsia and D. A. Landgrebe,"On a method of estimating power spectra," IEEE Trans. Instr. and Measurement, Vol. IM-16, pp. 255-257, 1967.
[14]   E. J. Hannan, "The estimation of mixed moving average autoregressive systems," Biometrika, Vol. 56, pp. 579-93, 1969.

[15] S. A. Tretter and K. Steiglitz, "Power spectrum identification in terms of rational models," IEEE Trans. Automatic Control, Vol. AC-12, pp. 185-188, 1967.

[16] H. Akaike, "Maximum likelihood identification of gaussian autoregressive moving average models," Biometrika, Vol. 60, pp. 255-265, 1973.

[17] E. C. Whitman, "The spectral analysis of discrete time series in terms of linear regressive models," Technical Report No. AD 710 390, U. S. Naval Ordnance Lab., White Oak, Silver Springs, Maryland, June 1970.

AN OPTIMAL LINEAR PREDICTION SYNTHESIZER STRUCTURE FOR ARRAY PROCESSOR IMPLEMENTATION

John D. Markel
Augustine H. Gray, Jr.[†]
Speech Communications Research Laboratory, Inc.
Santa Barbara, California 93109

I. INTRODUCTION

Itakura and Saito in 1971 demonstrated that synthesizer filters could be directly implemented from the k-parameters (reflection coefficients or PARCOR-parameters) from linear prediction analysis [1].

Since that time, the authors have made a number of extensions to the basic results. In particular: 1) the one-multiplier form has been generalized to allow for optimal sign parameter choice [2], 2) a new filter structure (referred to as the normalized form) has been developed [3], and 3) a complete theory of the roundoff noise characteristics of these orthogonal polynomial filter structures has been developed [4,5]. We have demonstrated that the normalized form is an optimal filter structure in the sense that 1) its roundoff noise characteristics are vastly superior to other structures including standard forms such as the direct and parallel form, and 2) it is the only filter we are aware of that can be proven stable under the important condition of time varying coefficients.

Here we shall focus upon several additional properties of the normalized form filter as they relate to array processor implementation. It is shown that this structure is precisely implementable as a series of complex multiplies. A new coding scheme based upon the inverse sine function is then discussed.

II. DEVELOPMENT OF THE NORMALIZED STRUCTURE

The lattice form introduced by Itakura and Saito is defined by the recursion equations[††]

[†]Also at Department of Electrical Engineering and Computer Science, University of California, Santa Barbara, California 93106

[††]Capital letters will be used to denote z-transform variables.

$$A_m = A_{m+1} - k_m \, B_m \tag{1a}$$

$$zB_{m+1} = k_m \, A_m + B_m , \tag{1b}$$

for m=0,1, . . . ,M-1 with boundary conditions $zB_0 = A_0 = 1$. A digital filter structure with input X and output X/A_M is defined by multiplying the above equations by X/A_M with the result

$$\frac{A_m X}{A_M} = \frac{A_{m+1} X}{A_M} - k_m \, \frac{B_m X}{A_M} \tag{2a}$$

$$\frac{zB_{m+1} X}{A_M} = k_m \, \frac{A_m X}{A_M} + \frac{B_m X}{A_M} \tag{2b}$$

Defining the inverse z-transforms as

$$x_m^+(n) \leftrightarrow \frac{A_m X}{A_M} \tag{3a}$$

and

$$x_m^-(n+1) \leftrightarrow \frac{zB_m X}{A_M} , \tag{3b}$$

allows the computational equation for the filter to be defined as

$$x_m^+(n) = x_{m+1}^+(n) - k_m \, x_m^-(n) \tag{4a}$$

$$x_m^-(n+1) = k_m \, x_m^+(n) + x_m^-(n) , \tag{4b}$$

with termination conditions $x_0^-(n+1)=x_0^+(n)$, and input $x(n)=x_M^+(n)$. Each of the node values of the filer is defined by (3). Assuming a unit sample input (X=1), the filter node energies or norm squared values can be computed as [2]

$$\left\| \frac{A_m X}{A_M} \right\|^2 = \left\| \frac{B_m X}{A_M} \right\|^2 = \alpha_m \tag{5}$$

where

$$\alpha_{m+1} = \alpha_m (1 - k_m^2) \tag{6}$$

for m=M-1,M-2, . . . ,0 with $\alpha_M = 1$.

Defining new variables

$$A_m' = A_m / \sqrt{\alpha_m} \tag{7a}$$

and

$$B'_m = B_m / \sqrt{\alpha_m} \, , \tag{7b}$$

so that $A'_M = A_M$, unity norm squared values are obtained, i.e.,

$$\left\| \frac{A'_m X}{A_M} \right\|^2 = \left\| \frac{B'_m X}{A_M} \right\|^2 = 1 . \tag{8}$$

A ladder structure can be defined from the lattice structure by substituting (2a) into (2b) with the result

$$\frac{A_m X}{A_M} = \frac{A_{m+1} X}{A_M} - k_m \frac{B_m X}{A_M} \tag{9a}$$

$$\frac{z B_{m+1} X}{A_M} = k_m \frac{A_m X}{A_M} + (1 - k_m^2) \frac{B_m X}{A_M} \tag{9b}$$

Now by substituting (6) and (7) into (9), a new unity norm or normalized ladder filter structure is obtained as

$$\frac{A'_m X}{A_M} = \sqrt{1 - k_m^2} \frac{A'_{m+1} X}{A_M} - k_m \frac{B'_m X}{A_M} \tag{10a}$$

$$\frac{z B'_{m+1} X}{A_M} = k_m \frac{A'_m X}{A_M} + \sqrt{1 - k_m^2} \frac{B'_m X}{A_M} \tag{10b}$$

with $z B'_0 = A'_0$ The unnormalized filter output is obtained as

$$Y = X / A_M = X A_0 / A_M \tag{11}$$

$$= \left[\frac{X A'_0}{A_M} \right] \alpha_0$$

$$= \left[\frac{X A'_0}{A_M} \right] \prod_{m=0}^{M-1} [1 - k_m^2]^{1/2}$$

This new structure has been demonstrated to have vastly superior finite word length properties when compared to the lattice form [4]. Shown in Figure 1 is a representative synthesizer filter spectrum of voiced speech along with the k-parameters used in its generation. The average noise level of the normalized form implementation (due to multiplicative roundoff effects in the filter) was measured as 25.4 dB below that of the lattice form when implemented with 16-bit two's complement arithmetic.

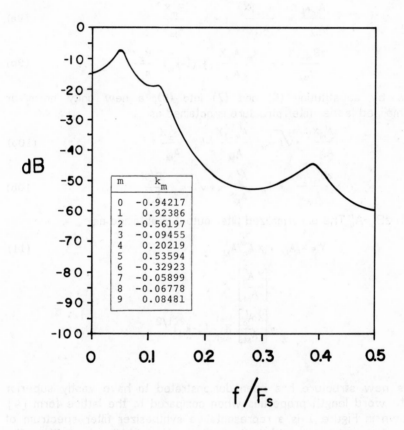

Figure 1. A representative voiced spectrum with listing of k-parameters.

III. IMPLEMENTATION IN AN ARRAY PROCESSOR

Even with the superior roundoff noise characteristics, the normalized structure is expensive to implement in a general-purpose computer. Four multiplies and two adds are required per section with M total sections. In addition, computation of $1-k_n^2$ m=0,1,...,M and an output gain term (11) is necessary.

It is a fortuitous result that each section defined by (10) can be precisely obtained from a single-complex multiply.

First, by noting that $|k_n|<1$ for a stable filter, a change of variables results in

$$k_m = \sin \theta \qquad (12a)$$

and thus,

$$\sqrt{1-k_m^2} = \cos \theta . \qquad (12b)$$

Next, by applying (3) to (10) and then dropping the primes, it can be rewritten as

$$x_m^+(n) = \cos \theta_m \, x_{m+1}^+(n) - \sin \theta_m \, x_m^-(n) \qquad (13a)$$

$$x_{m+1}^-(n+1) = \sin\theta_m \, x_{m+1}^+(n) + \cos \theta_m \, x_m^-(n) \qquad (13b)$$

This filter structure is shown in Figure 2. The input is $x(n)=x_n^+(n)$, the termination is $x_0^-(n+1)=x_0^+(n)$, and the final output is

$$y(n) = (\prod_{m=0}^{M-1} \cos \theta_m) \, x_0^+(n) . \qquad (14)$$

Now define the complex numbers

$$x = x_{m+1}^+ (n) + j \, x_m^-(n) \qquad (15)$$

as the filter section inputs, and

$$f = \cos \theta_m + j \sin \theta_m \qquad (16)$$

as the complex exponential filter coefficients. The complex product

$$y = xf, \qquad (17)$$

then results in precisely the filter section outputs as

$$y = x_m^+(n) + j \, x_{m+1}^- (n+1) . \qquad (18)$$

Since the complex multiply operation is an elementary operation in array processors such as the Signal Processing Systems Inc. SPS-41, each section can be computed in a single instruction. In the SPS-41, this computation requires 1 μsec. Furthermore, if a transformation from k_n to the angle θ_n is performed, the complex coefficient $f=\cos\theta_n+j \sin\theta_n$

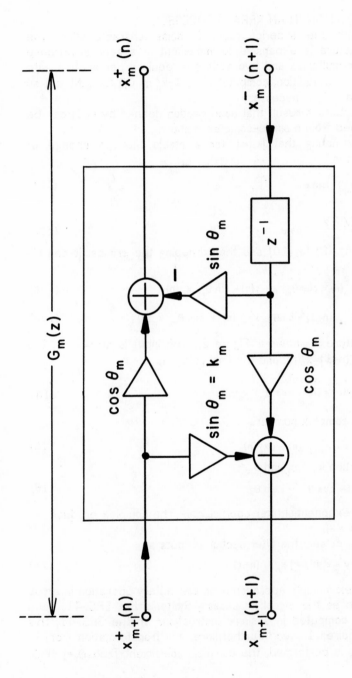

Figure 2. A section of the normalized form structure implemented for an array processor.

can be directly obtained since complex exponential tables are hardwired into the unit.

It is interesting to note that with an array processor, the normalized form can actually be implemented more efficiently than the lattice form which has half the number of multiplies per section, since to compute (4b), $x_n^*(n)$ of (4a) must first be computed.

IV. CODING AND DECODING CONSIDERATIONS

After the k-parameters have been computed from the analysis process, it is necessary to quantize them or a transformation of them into a limited number of levels for vocoder applications. Direct quantization of the k-parameters is easiest to perform but somewhat inferior to more complex coding and quantizing schemes.

For an array processor implementation of the normalized form, it is important that the decoded parameters (that were coded and quantized) be easily transformable into indices for a complex exponential or trigonometric table which will have uniformly spaced values around one quadrant of the unit circle. A coding scheme that will allow the above is inverse sine coding, i.e., if

$$\sin \theta_m = k_m,$$ (19)

then linear quantization of the theta parameter θ_n from

$$\theta_m = \sin^{-1}(k_m)$$ (20)

by definition, results in uniformly spaced theta values (and thus table index values). Surprisingly, we find that the inverse sine coding curve should be superior to the linear coding due to the fact that it affords more resolution for the more sensitive k-parameter region near unity magnitude, without seriously degrading the less sensitive k-parameter regions.

If it is desired to code and quantize $\sin^{-1}(k_n)$ to a total of β_n bits, a numerical evaluation for the inverse sign is necessary with an accuracy of at least β_n bits. Since $\beta_n \leq 8$ and $|k_n| \leq .98$ are very reasonable assumptions for all m, fairly simple polynomial evaluation algorithms should be possible. Possibly the best procedure would be to find an equiripple polynomial approximation to $\sin^{-1}(k_n)$ over the range $0 \leq k_n \leq .98$.

Assume an 8-bit (including sign) trigonometric table in the receiver having $2^7 = 128$ entries for the first quadrant -- the angular spacing would then be

$$\theta(n) = \frac{2\pi n}{512} \quad n = 0,1,...,127.$$ (21)

The table output would then be $\exp[j\theta(n)]$. For a maximum k-parameter $k_n=.98$, $\theta'_n=[[(256)\ (1.37047)/\pi+.5]]=112$. Therefore an inefficiency factor exists in the inverse sine coding since $128-112=16$ levels out of 128 are never used. The table elements extracted in the decoding process are shown in Table 1. It is seen from the table that as fewer bits are used, the relative number of unused levels decreases from .125 for 8-bit coding to .0625 for 5-bit coding and zero for 4-bit or less coding. If k_n is coded to 5 bits, for example, a maximum value of $k_n=.98$ results in $\theta'_n=[[13.94+.5]]=14$ as the integer transmission value. At the receiver, $|\theta'_n|$ is scaled up by $8-5=3$ bits to obtain the index $14\cdot8=122$. In general for $\beta\leq8$-bit coding, $|\theta'_n|$ at the receiver is scaled up by $8-\beta$ bits for the trig table index.

Coding Bits	Table Index Values Possible indices corr. to $0\leq k\leq.98$	indices for $.98<k<1$	Unused indices
8	0,1,2,...,112	113,114,...,127	16
7	0,2,4,...,112	114,116,...,127	7
6	0,4,8,...,112	116,120,124	3
5	0,8,16,...,112	120	1
4	0,16,32,...,112	–	0

Table 1
Trig. table indices used and not used as a function
of the number of bits used in coding.

Since $\cos\theta_n=[1-k_n^2]^{1/2}$ the real part of the trig table output is always positive. If θ_n is negative, the imaginary part of the trig table output is negated, since $\sin(-\theta_n)=-k_n$. This is the only condition for which an output of the trig table must be modified.

One final interesting property of inverse sine coding should be noted. For sampling frequencies below 10 kHz the k-parameter values excluding k_0 and k_1 can be restricted to $|k|<.7$ without perceived degradation in the synthesis. Thus by performing inverse sine coding, a factor of two (or exactly one bit) is gained as compared to the 0.51 bit savings from linearly quantizing k to $|k|\leq.7$.

The SPS-41 has a $2^7=64$-point cosine and sine table with equally spaced theta values. Thus up to (and including) 8-bit (7 bits plus sign) transmitted coefficients can be decoded. For a maximum 8-bit coding, the integer

$$I = \frac{2^7\theta}{(\pi/4)} = \frac{2^9\theta}{\pi} \tag{22}$$

will satisfy $I=\{0,1,\ldots,63\}$

for $0 \leq \theta < \pi/8$ since $|k| < .7$. Thus 8-bit coding (2^7 positive levels) only uses 2^6 of the total levels for $|k| < .7$. To minimize quantization error, rounding is used to define coding table dividing points. The k-parameter to index parameter table is computed by

$$KT(I) = \sin \left[\frac{\pi(I+1/2)}{2^\beta} \right] \qquad I = 0,1,...,2^\beta - 1 \qquad (23)$$

Given that a 2^7-point complex exponential table is available in the array processor, the table index I_R is computed from the transmitted index I as

$$I_R = I \, 2^{8-\beta} . \qquad (24)$$

The array processor table is defined by $\sin(2\pi I_R/512)$ and $\cos(2\pi I_R/512)$ where $I_R = 0,1,...,127$. The coding table and decoding k-parameters for $\beta = 4$ are shown in Table 2. As an example, if $.882 < k < .957$, then I=6 would be the coded index. The decoded k-parameter would be obtained from the table entry index $2^4 \cdot 6 = 96$ or 0.924.

I	KT(I)	$I_R = 2^{7-\beta}I$	$k = \sin\theta$
0	.098	0	0
1	.290	16	.195
2	.471	32	.382
3	.634	48	.555
4	.773	64	.707
5	.882	80	.832
6	.957	96	.924
7	.995	112	.981

Table 2
Coding and decoding tables examples.

REFERENCES

1.   F. Itakura and S. Saito, "Digital Filtering Techniques for Speech Analysis and Synthesis," 7th Int. Congr. Acoust., paper 25C-1, Budapest, 1971.

2.   A. H. Gray, Jr. and J. D. Markel, "Digital Lattice and Ladder Filter Synthesis," IEEE Trans. Audio Electroacoust., Vol. AU-21, No. 6, pp. 491-500, December 1973.

3.   A. H. Gray, Jr. and J. D. Markel, "A Normalized Digital Filter Structure," IEEE Trans. Acoust., Speech, and Sig. Process., June 1975. to be published.

4.   J. D. Markel and A. H. Gray, Jr., "Roundoff Noise Characteristics of a Class of Orthogonal Polynomial Structures", IEEE Trans. Acoust., Speech, and Sig., Process.

5.   J. D. Markel and A. H. Gray, Jr., "Fixed-Point Implementation Algorithms for a Class of Orthogonal Polynomial Filter Structures," IEEE Trans. Acoust., Speech, and Signal Process., To be published.

Part Three

Acoustic-Phonetics

Concepts for Acoustic Phonetic Recognition

David J. Broad
June E. Shoup
Speech Communications Research Laboratory, Inc.
800 A Miramonte Drive
Santa Barbara, California 93109

ABSTRACT
This paper discusses the acoustic phonetic
transformation in automatic speech recognition. The acoustic
parameters measured from the speech wave which serve as
the input to the transformation are selected for their close
connection to articulatory phonetics, and include the formant
parameters, the fundamental frequency, the energies in broad
contiguous frequency bands, autocorrelation and zero-crossing
measures, a measure for burst detection, and the rms energy.
The most fundamental concepts for the transformation are (1)
the interpretation of the continuously varying acoustic
parameters as a sequence of discrete units that can be
related to higher level linguistic structures and (2) the
characterization of the relation of phonetic equivalence
between segments. The first problem requires a definition of
the phone, or phonetic segment, which covers all the cases of
non-simultaneity of parameter changes, overlap between
characteristics of adjacent phones, and minimal differences
between adjacent phones that are phonetically similar or
phonetically equivalent. The second problem requires an
operational definition for phonetic equivalence, and different
definitions lead to different statistical distributions of the
sounds in acoustic space. Construction of the distributions is
complicated by speaker and context effects. Knowledge of
the distributions leads to recognition criteria and to theoretical
standards for evaluating recognition performance. Although
these distributions are not well known at present, their
determination by current signal processing techniques should
be an attractive prospect.

INTRODUCTION

This paper is concerned with the phonetic interpretation of acoustic speech data as a stage of automatic speech recognition. One can consider speech recognition to involve several stages of analysis and interpretation, as shown schematically in Figure 1. The bi-directional arrows indicate that information flow in both directions may be desirable. The input to the system is the acoustic speech wave; this is recorded and various measurements are done on it to produce estimates of its acoustic parameters; these are interpreted as a phonetic and prosodic array which is used to form a quasi-phonemic and prosodemic array. This is finally an input to syntactic and semantic analysis to give the final desired output, which may be an orthographic representation of the original speech, or which may be something entirely different, such as the execution of a verbal command by a machine.

It is the third stage of this schematic that is the topic of this paper: the conversion between physical measurements on the speech wave and phonetic units that can be passed on to higher levels of linguistic processing. The importance and difficulty of a phonetic level of processing for speech recognition have been discussed elsewhere [2,3], but we may summarize the main assertions here:

A phonetic stage is necessary because the allophonic variations within phonemes make direct recognition of phonemes impractical except in very limited cases of speech recognition. The same holds for syllable or word recognition. It also seems futile to expect higher levels of processing to overcome poor phonetic processing.

Indeed, phonetic recognition presents a major and non-trivial intellectual challenge that must be thought about and investigated with some care and perseverance. The present paper will by no means present the information needed to implement phonetic recognition because the needed information does not yet exist. One of our tasks will be to outline what the information might look like and how it might be organized if it did exist and to show how some of the extant studies from acoustic phonetics and from the allied areas of physiological phonetics and the theory of speech production illuminate the problem. Before discussing that, however, we should review some introductory concepts of acoustic phonetics.

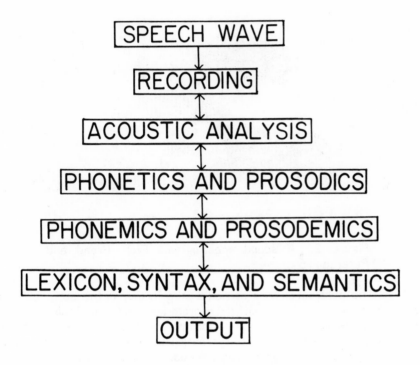

Figure 1.   Schematic diagram of the levels of processing in automatic speech recognition.

THE FORMALIZED SPECTROGRAM
It was the introduction of sound spectrography in the mid-1940's [16,27] that virtually created the field of acoustic phonetics as we know it today. The sound spectrograph produces an analog visual display of spectral energy as a function of time, as shown in Figure 2. The horizontal axis represents time and the vertical axis represents frequency, while the darkness of the marking indicates the concentration of spectral energy. From the very beginning, visual features have been abstracted from the sound spectrogram as

elements of acoustic phonetic description. These features have
included: the formant (or locus or hub), the voice bar, gap, spike, and
noise or turbulence. These concepts will be discussed later in more
detail.

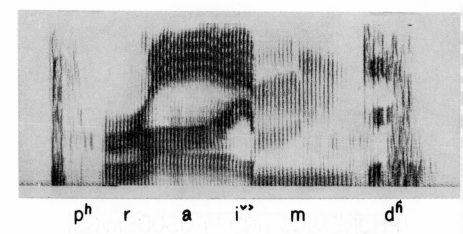

Figure 2. A sound spectrogram. From Broad and
Peterson [5].

The abstraction was carried a step further in the early 1950's
by scientists at the Haskins Laboratories [6,7] in their speech
perception work based on the pattern playback, which is a device for
converting spectrographic displays back into sound. It was here that
the stylized spectrogram was developed. As shown in Figure 3, the
stylized spectrogram is created by hand painting a spectrogram-like
display on transparent plastic. The stylization consists of the deliberate
representation of the abstract features mentioned above as simplified
stereotyped patterns. The formants become smooth bands, the noise
is given as a mottled area, and so forth. This step, then, accomplished
the transformation from spectrographic display to spectrographic
representation. This abstraction and representation permitted
systematic and reproducible construction of stimuli for speech
perception experiments. The significant point in the present context is
that although there is visual resemblance between sound spectrograms
and stylized spectrograms, the stylized spectrogram embodies a level
of abstraction and formalism that can only be read into the sound
spectrogram. It represents some complicated decisions on which
features of the spectrogram are the most important.

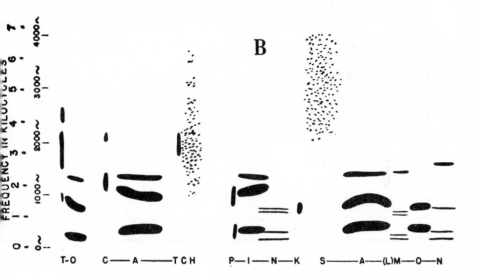

Figure 3.   A stylized spectrogram.   From   Cooper, Delattre, Liberman,and Borst [6].

More recently digital analysis has largely replaced analog analysis and digital spectrographic displays have been implemented [21]. As useful as such displays are, however, the real power of digital analysis is <u>not</u> the improved acquisition of spectrographic displays. Rather, it is in the ability to carry further the abstraction that was started with descriptions of sound spectrograms and continued with the construction of stylized spectrograms. With the digital extraction of acoustic parameters, we now have what might be called, for the sake of analogy, the <u>formalized</u> spectrogram. The formalized spectrogram is rather abstract, in that it is really an array of numbers that can be stored away and operated upon in any of a number of ways. The formalized spectrogram array consists of a sequence of time frames spaced, say, at 10 ms intervals, each of which is a vector of features and parameters. Some of these parameters, notably the formant frequencies, preserve features abstracted from even before the earliest days of sound spectrography.

The formalized spectrogram can be converted to a visual form resembling a sound spectrogram, as shown in Figure 4. Such a display might be useful as a visual heuristic. The display, however, is not the formalized spectrogram itself. Also, it should be noted that a formalized spectrogram is not just a digitized sound spectrogram either, because it already contains the results of considerable interpretation.

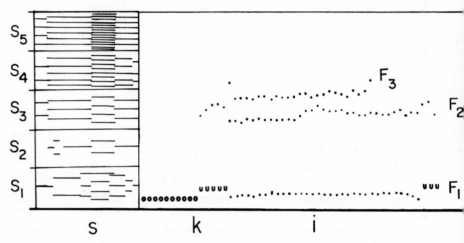

Figure 4. Visual display from a formalized spectrogram. S_i and F_i as in Table I. U=undefined lower formant; 0=rms energy below threshold for S_i or F_i measurement.

PARAMETRIC REPRESENTATION

One proposal for the parameter vector of a formalized spectrogram is shown in Table I.

The formants are the natural resonance modes of the vocal tract; that is, they correspond to the complex conjugate pole pairs of the Laplace transform of the vocal tract acoustic impulse response. A formant has a frequency of oscillation F_i and a time constant or, alternatively, a bandwidth B_i. The formant also has an amplitude A_i which has been shown by Fant [8] to be largely redundant if the formant frequency and bandwidth are known. The formant amplitude is not totally redundant, however, and is included here for the sake of completeness. The fundamental frequency F_0 is the same as the frequency of oscillation of the true vocal folds. Note that the formant frequencies have no necessary harmonic relation to the fundamental. Further parameters of interest include the energies in broad contiguous frequency bands -- which may be logarithmically spaced at third- or half-octave intervals or uniformly spaced at some interval such as 1000 Hz. When reliable measurements of the formant parameters can

Parameter Symbol	Range of Subscript	Parameter Definition
F_i	$i = 1,2,3,4$	Formant frequency
B_i	$i = 1,2,3,4$	Formant bandwidth
A_i	$i = 1,2,3,4$	Formant amplitude
F_o	–	Fundamental frequency
S_i	$i = 1,2,...,10$	Energy in contiguous broad bands
R	–	Autocorrelation measure for voicing detection
Z_c	–	Number of zero crossings
P	–	Measure of the extreme value vs. the local rms
E	–	The rms energy of the frame

Table I. The parameters proposed for the formalized spectrogram.

be made, the spectral energies are largely redundant; however, there are many cases, especially during voiceless sounds produced by turbulence noise, when the formants are not measurable, or perhaps not useful, and more accessible parameters such as spectral energy are needed. Four single parameters complete the proposed list: (1) an autocorrelation measure R for voicing detection. This can be derived by various techniques [18]. (2) The number of zero crossings Z_c. This can also be helpful for voicing detection, or for turbulence noise detection. It is therefore somewhat redundant. (3) A measure P of an extreme value of the wave relative to the local rms value. This is proposed as a possibility for locating bursts in the speech wave. These result from the releases of stop consonants. (4) The rms energy E of the frame. This parameter is simple, but can be very useful, for example, for the detection of silence and gaps.

There are certainly other possible choices for a parameter array, but we propose this one both for the sake of concreteness in illustration and because we believe it represents the most intelligent choice we are able to offer at this writing.

These parameters can be used to describe most of what we know about the acoustic speech wave and its relation to phonetic units.

The advantage of the formalized spectrogram generated digitally and stored in digital form as a sequence of parameter vectors is that it can be further operated upon by algorithms based upon this level of abstraction. These manipulations include the calculation of derived parameters such as formant slopes, or eigenvector values from the spectral bands, and such logical operations as the checking of thresholds and statistical computations. This step opens the possibility for a higher level of formal description in acoustic phonetic studies.

RELATION TO PHYSIOLOGY OF SPEECH PRODUCTION

The set of parameters just described have been shown to have close relationships with the physiology of speech production. Speech is produced in the human vocal mechanism by a coordinated control of the breath stream to generate sounds and by a very flexible control of the shapes of the air spaces within the vocal tract to filter the generated sounds in various ways. The relationship between the acoustic and the physiological domains is important because the phonetic concepts that are basic to the phonological description of speech are primarily defined in the physiological domain, the domain of articulatory phonetics. When we say that [b], for example, is a voiced bilabial plosive, we are giving a physiological definition to the sound. The physiological domain is essential to our understanding of speech, and it is this consideration that leads to the selection of acoustic parameters that have close connections to the physiological processes.

SPEECH WAVE TYPES

The most obvious connection between the physiological and acoustic processes is the one between the various speech wave types and the different kinds of acoustic sources in the speech mechanism. The speech wave types are designations for the basic categories of waveforms that can be observed in speech. The reason that such different kinds of waveforms appear at all is that various types of sound generators in the vocal mechanism are responsible for the production of the acoustic speech wave; these include:

(1) The laryngeal voice source, in which the quasi-periodic modulation of the breath stream by the vibrations of the true vocal folds produces the buzzing sound we call voicing;

(2) Noise sources, from turbulence in the breath stream resulting from flow through a constriction or past an obstruction; and

(3) Burst or transient sources which result from the release of a pressure built up against a closure in the vocal tract.

These types of sources turn on and turn off at various times in the speech stream and lead to the production of different characteristic waveforms as Figure 5 illustrates. The waveform is that of the word ski.

The initial part of the waveform is the sibilant [s]; it has a quasi-random speech wave type. The noise results from turbulent air flow as the breath stream is directed past the lower incisors.

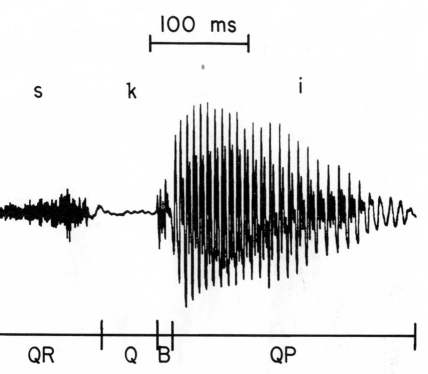

Figure 5. Acoustic waveform for an utterance of the
word ski. QR = quasi-random, Q = quiescent, B = burst,
QP = quasi-periodic.

The final part of the waveform is the vowel [i]; the regular
repetitive character of the waveform is obvious; it results from the
excitation of the laryngeal voice source and it has a quasi-periodic
speech wave type.

The short interval marked in the center of the word represents
the release of the plosive [k]; this interval of the waveform has a burst
speech wave type, which results from excitation by an acoustic
transient source. Note the small amplitude relative to the following
vowel.

Preceding the burst is an interval of approximately zero
amplitude. This is an example of the quiescent waveform; it occurs
when none of the sound sources in the vocal tract are active. As
trivial as it may appear, it is important to detect the occurrence of
quiescence in speech. When there is appreciable background noise,
even this wave type may be difficult to detect.

Figure 6 shows the waveform of the voiced sibilant [z]. In this case, both the laryngeal voice source and a turbulence noise source are active to produce a waveform that is predominantly regular and repetitive, but which has some random noise superimposed on it. Thus a compound quasi-periodic and quasi-random wave type results. As discussed by Halle and Stevens [13], the noise is amplitude-modulated as the rate of air flow changes periodically with vocal fold vibration. The noise is most intense when the vocal folds are open and disappears when they are closed.

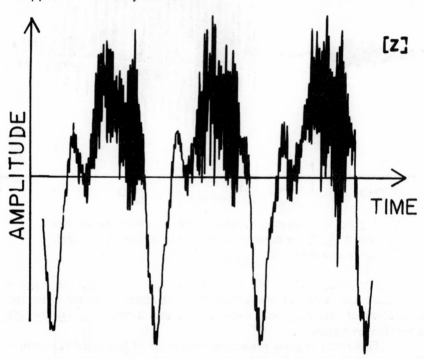

Figure 6. Acoustic waveform of the voiced sibilant [z].
From Broad and Peterson [5].

There are a few more wave types that could be shown here, but these examples illustrate the main ones that are important.

A review of the many methods for discriminating the speech wave types would be a useful contribution, but it will not be attempted here.

The detection of the speech wave types has been used in speech recognition systems for two purposes:

(1) The detection of a speech wave type feeds into a decision on what further type of acoustic analysis may be required. For example, the detection of a quasi-periodic interval may imply the subsequent measurement of a fundamental frequency and of the first few formant frequencies. The detection of quiescence may imply that no further measurements should be made on the frame.

(2) The detection of the speech wave type assists with some actual phonetic decisions, e.g.,

   a) A gap whose duration is within a certain range is likely to be associated with a voiceless stop [12].

   b) A burst is assumed to be associated with the release of some kind of stop.

   c) Unless the system is expected to handle whispered speech as an allowable input, an interval of quasi-random noise is to be associated with a fricative or sibilant or with plosive aspiration noise.

   d) Quasi-periodic waveforms are associated with voiced sounds, such as most vowels, sonorants, and nasals as well as voiced fricatives and sibilants.

It may well be asked where the speech wave types show up in our formalized spectrogram, which does not include wave type as a parameter. Actually, the wave type is to be derived from the parameters and could be appended to the parameter vector as a derived parameter. The wave type is also implicit in the formalized spectrogram because, as just mentioned, the wave type is used to decide whether or not certain parameters are to be measured. Thus the parameters of the formalized spectrogram are considered to be ordered in the sense that certain ones are measured before others, if at all.

The relation of the speech wave types and the parameters are shown in Table II, which is adapted from Peterson and Shoup [24]. The speech wave types are listed in the left-hand column while the acoustical parameters are listed in the top row. The symbol in each cell indicates whether, for the given wave type, the parameter is to be always, contingently, or never derived from the wave type.

FORMANTS

Somewhat less obvious than the relation between the speech wave types and the acoustic sources in the vocal tract is the relation between the resonance characteristics of the speech wave and the shape of the vocal tract. In 1948 Joos [15] and Potter and Peterson

Parameters

Wave Types	F_i	B_i	A_i	F_0	S_i	R	Z_c	P	E
Quiescent	N	N	N	N	N	N	N	N	A
Burst	C	C	C	N	A	A	A	A	A
Quasi-random	C	C	C	C	A	A	A	A	A
Quasi-periodic	A	A	A	A	C	A	A	A	A

Table II. The relation between the speech wave types and the measurement of acoustic speech parameters. A = the parameter is always to be measured for the given speech wave type; C = the parameter is to be contingently measured; N = the parameter is never to be measured.

[26] noted the relationship of acoustical charts of the formant frequencies to the vowel diagrams based on articulation. Figure 7 shows an example of such a diagram. The coordinate axes are the frequencies of the first two formants as measured from the acoustic speech wave; they are oriented so that, in terms of articulatory description, high vowels are at the top of the chart, low vowels are at the bottom, front vowels are toward the left, and back vowels are toward the right. The terms "high," "low," "front," and "back" refer to the size and location of the narrowest constriction between the tongue and the pharynx or between the tongue and the roof of the mouth.

Fant [9] subsequently demonstrated that the formant frequencies could be calculated from given vocal tract shapes, and several years later the studies by Schroeder [28], by Mermelstein [19], and by Heinz [14] showed that the inverse operation of deducing tract shapes from the formant frequencies was also possible within certain restrictions. More recent work [1,30] suggests that the combination of formant frequency and formant bandwidth information can give fairly reasonable estimates of vocal tract shapes. These results are very important for understanding the behavior of the acoustic speech wave in terms of underlying articulatory processes, although this possibility has not yet been exploited very extensively.

This concludes the introduction of the most elementary acoustic phonetic concepts. Briefly, these concepts include:
(1) the basic speech parameters as elements of an array which is thought of as a frame of a formalized spectrogram;
(2) the speech wave types that result from the activity of different types of sound sources; and

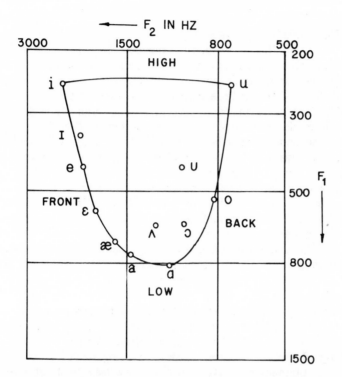

Figure 7. Frequency of the second formant plotted against the frequency of the first formant for a set of vowel sounds to illustrate the relationship to articulatory formations. The vowels are single tokens produced by a male speaker.

(3)   the relationships between the acoustical properties of speech and the physiological mechanisms of speech production that underly the basic concepts of physiological phonetics.

More extensive discussions of these and related topics are given by Broad and Peterson [5], Fant [10], and Flanagan [11]. Up to this point, then, we have specified the kinds of information that we expect the acoustic analyzer to provide as input to the acoustic-phonetic transformation and we have discussed why this particular information is considered to be important. We have so far said little about the actual acoustic phonetic transformation itself, and we now turn to a consideration of the more basic and difficult aspects of this transformation.

BASIC CONCEPTS

Some of the very basic concepts that we use in speech recognition are very difficult to define. Most importantly, the concept of the phone, or phonetic segment, is difficult to work out rigorously, and also, even if the criteria for the occurrence of phonetic segments are defined, it still remains to say when one segment is phonetically equivalent to another one. These two problems, the characterization of the phone and the specification of the phonetic equivalence between phones, are the two central problems of general phonetics and, in particular, of acoustic phonetics.

For example, consider the vowel [i]. Different people can say the vowel [i] under different circumstances, and we may talk confidently as if there is such a thing as the vowel [i]. Otherwise it would be impossible to even give this verbal example. And yet the processes by which we define it as an [i] are rather complicated, and very seldom performed in an explicit way.

DEFINING THE PHONE

The first basic concept in acoustic phonetics is the conversion of the continuous acoustic speech waveform into some kind of discrete unit which can be related to linguistic structures. When two people are talking to each other, they seem to be using some kind of unit, such as phones, phonemes, or syllables; or they may think of speech as consisting of streams of words. In any case, the speech stream is conceived as a sequence of discrete units, even though these discrete units are coded through a system of continuous physical processes. The articulators and the control of the breath stream change continuously to produce a correspondingly continuous stream of sound, the properties of which are always shifting so that in the physical domain the discrete units do not stand out from each other like the proverbial beads on a string. Rather, successive sounds are observed to merge into each other. One of the basic problems for phoneticians to contend with, then, is the specification of the conditions under which these varying physical properties are coded or decoded as discrete units. This problem is obviously very closely related to the segmentation problem. The segmentation problem is therefore more than the problem of building a device which detects the occurrence of segments which are in some sense "really there." It is also the problem of specifying what we mean by the segment in the first place, and it is only when we have solved that problem that we can even tell whether some segmentation procedure is doing its job or not. It is easy to imagine a given segmenter performing a certain way, but it is very difficult to evaluate that performance: Is it the device or the concept of the segment that accounts for the so-called "errors"?

Why should the conversion from continuous functions to discrete segments be complicated? It is obvious that the varying parameters of the speech wave have many landmarks such as discontinuities, minima and maxima, inflection points, and points of maximum change. These are certainly to be used to define and detect phones acoustically; indeed, there can be so many such landmarks that it is quickly seen that the problem is often one of selection: Which landmark at which time is the crucial one to pay attention to?

The problem is complicated by the fact that the acoustic speech parameters are not synchronized with one another. For example, in a two-segment word such as see, transcribed phonetically as [si], one can segment according to the end of turbulence noise from the [s] or according to the onset of voicing in the [i]; these two events are seldom simultaneous and there is more often than not a brief interval during which both voicing and friction exist. Indeed, a single 10 ms frame may resemble a [z] in character, but we would not wish to recognize the utterance as [s] followed by [z] followed by [i] on this basis. The reasons for this are not just the difficulties of associating such a sequence with the phonemic sequence /si/ and thence through the lexicon with the word see; they involve some deep considerations of the nature of the phonetic segment.

To illustrate how physiological phonetics can guide our thinking about acoustic phonetics, it is interesting that this problem is handled at the articulatory level in the theory of Peterson and Shoup [25] by the concept of articulatory state, which is either an articulatory steady state or a controlled articulatory movement. To qualify as a phone, an interval must contain an articulatory state; in the above example the rapid movement of the tongue away from the [s] configuration during voicing onset would disqualify the interval as an articulatory state, while articulatory steady states for the [s] and the [i] would guarantee their status as phones. The intermediate interval would be assigned as a transition. Note that this implies that segmentation is not equivalent to the drawing of boundaries between segments in such a way that the entire time axis is accounted for by contiguous segments; rather, strictly speaking, segmentation is the identification of not-necessarily-contiguous intervals to be associated with phones together with the identification of transition intervals. This is not to say that the transition intervals are subsequently ignored in recognition; it is only to say that not all intervals have to be accounted for by phones, i.e., phonetic segments. It must be pointed out here that the acoustic means for applying the above criterion to the example is not yet developed; however, this will illustrate the kind of thinking that is required if the segmentation problem is ever to be satisfactorily resolved.

The physiological phonetic theory is rather complicated, but is suggested to anyone who wishes to become acquainted with the complex and subtle considerations that enter into a definition of the phone that holds up under all the different conditions of non-simultaneity, overlap, and dynamic change that could be brought forward to test against. The definition of the phone at the acoustic level may be expected to be at least as complex.

The detection of phones can also be difficult when two successive sounds are acoustically similar. In this case, the difficulty is not the selection of a subset of important landmarks, it is the problem of finding any usable landmarks at all. For example, the consonant-vowel combinations in the words ye, woo, and rural have rather similar formant frequencies and the segmentation in these cases evidently depends upon a sufficiently sensitive acoustic analysis. That is, the noise in the formant frequency measurements must not exceed the differences between the sounds. Also, as discussed later, our knowledge of how these sounds are distributed in the acoustic space must be accurate enough to allow the discrimination.

An even more difficult case arises when two identical sounds are adjacent to each other in the speech stream. Very often, when two phones may be expected, they will be found to be merged into a single sound. For example, the phrase thin nails may be realized phonetically as [θIneˈɪz]. In this case, only a single [n] occurs and it would be futile to expect an acoustic phonetic analyzer to extract a sequence of two [n]'s. However, the phrase can also be realized as [θInneˈɪz], for example, to distinguish it unambiguously from the phrase thin ales [θInʔeˈɪz]. What distinguishes the sequence of two identical phones from a single phone in this case? According to the physiological phonetic theory, it is likely to involve a prosodic change, that is, a change in the speech production power and/or a change in the fundamental voice frequency. Thus there is an interaction between phonetic and prosodic concepts. The applicable criterion in this case is that the existence of a phone depends not only on the occurrence of an articulatory state, but it must also contain no more than one prosodic state.

It might be pointed out that duration is frequently suggested as the criterion for distinguishing geminates from single occurrences. This hypothesis, however, has not been found to be reliable in the pilot experiments that we have performed on geminates. Also, for practical use in automatic speech recognizers duration has limited value since a "normal" time measurement for all potential geminates has to be determined for any given discourse. The problem of gemination may perhaps best be handled at a higher level of linguistic analysis until better acoustic determiners are obtained. This will certainly be the case for those instances in which the phonological sequence is realized by a true single phonetic unit.

PHONETIC EQUIVALENCE

Not only must the acoustic-phonetic analyzer convert a continuous function into discrete units, but it must identify the correct phonetic category of each segment. This leads to the second basic problem of acoustic phonetics, namely, the relation of acoustic data to phonetic equivalence classes. Here again we must contend with the fact that we are dealing with units that are not units in the sense that a proton is a unit or a molecule is a unit; the operational procedures that we employ here for defining a unit and for determining when one unit is phonetically equivalent to another depend upon the human perceiver, or perhaps the human speaker. Even when all the desired physical measurements on the speech event have been made, we have not completed the phonetic aspect of the process until we have related those physical observations to the human's world of speech and language. So rather than be reluctant to use the noisy human processes of perception and production, we have to recognize that this is the essence of the problem. In a word, since it is the human that is the user and creator of the language, the human has to be taken as our instrument which defines our phonetic categories.

OPERATIONAL DEFINITIONS

The consequence is that we cannot say externally what the phone is or what the phonetic unit is, without reference to operations that we perform with listeners and speakers, and that we must use certain operational definitions for phonetic equivalence between phones. One might get the impression from linguistics or phonetics texts that these equivalence classes are all very well defined, whereas in reality it is complicated to determine them. Even though it is complicated, considerable methodology in the area of acoustic phonetics has been developed to implement various operational definitions of phonetic equivalence between sounds. As one should expect, when one changes the operational definition, one changes the shape or the structure of the resulting equivalence class. This involves decisions on the form of our phonetic descriptions of speech. Clearly, these decisions affect how the descriptions will look at higher levels.

Now phoneticians do not all write the same symbols for the sounds recorded at the same place on the same tape. Since human agreement on phonetic transcription is so hard to obtain, it is obviously asking for a great deal to expect a machine to perform only the "right" segmentations and identifications.

PHONETIC SPACES

To discuss a concrete case, suppose that our formalized spectrogram uses n-dimensional parameter vectors. The n parameters define a Euclidean n-space and individual occurrences of sounds, or individual 10 ms frames, occupy points in this space. Each point can be tagged with the categories to which it belongs: the phonetic identity of the segment, its phonetic context and the relative time of occurrence for single frames within sounds, the speaker's identity, age, sex, speaking mode, dialect, and physical condition, along with the social context of the speech.

All the points in the phonetic space that belong to a particular category, or combination of categories, or intersection of categories, fill out a certain "cloud" or region in the n-dimensional space. A task of acoustic phonetics is to characterize the regions in the phonetic space defined by the different applicable categories, to state degrees of overlap among these regions, and to determine relations between them.

Unfortunately, our knowledge of how the different relevant categories are distributed inside phonetic spaces is not as complete as we would like to think, and much research still needs to be done. We can nevertheless proceed to illustrate phonetic spaces with available information to show what a complete acoustic phonetic description of speech sounds might look like. Also, the implications of different types of operational definitions for phonetic equivalence will be demonstrated in the process.

Our main illustration of this point is the use of formant space to describe vowel sounds. While the visual representations used will show the plane determined by the frequencies of the first two formants, it should be borne in mind that the concepts discussed can be extended to higher dimensionalities as required, and that this plane is only a small sub-space of the one proposed above. It should also be clear that for different types of sounds different sub-spaces may be most useful for recognition.

Figure 8 shows the results of Peterson and Barney's [23] measurements on the first two formant frequencies for vowels produced by 76 speakers, including men, women, and children. A loop encloses most of the examples for each vowel. This Figure shows

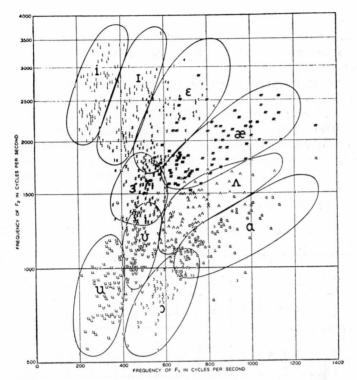

Figure 8. Frequency of the second formant plotted against the frequency of the first formant for vowels read by 76 speakers, including men, women, and children. From Peterson and Barney [23].

considerable separation of the vowel categories, but also demonstrates significant overlap between the categories. This is especially so, since some vowels such as [eᴵ] and [oᵁ] are not included. It is most remarkable that the different vowel categories cluster densely within a set of simply connected regions. This property is fortunate for recognition, and is certainly not a guaranteed property of an arbitrarily selected set of acoustic parameters.

It is important to note that Figure 8 groups vowel symbols according to an operational definition of phonetic equivalence based on the speakers' intentions as they read from a list containing words such as heed, hid, head, etc. Thus the phonetic context was always a preceding [h] and a following [d]. The speakers represented some range of predominantly American English dialect, so that one reason for the large spread in the different categories is that different speakers selected different vowel allophones for given words. For example, some speakers did not distinguish the sounds [ɔ] and [ɑ] in their speech.

What happens if we restrict our view to a single speaker? Figure 9 shows the results that were obtained in the same study for a single subject reading the word list 12 different times on different days. The small inter-repetition variation and the clear separation among the different vowels is remarkable. The specification of the phonetic equivalence between sounds produced by the same speaker under the same conditions is consequently considered to be simpler than the specification of the phonetic equivalence between sounds produced by different speakers.

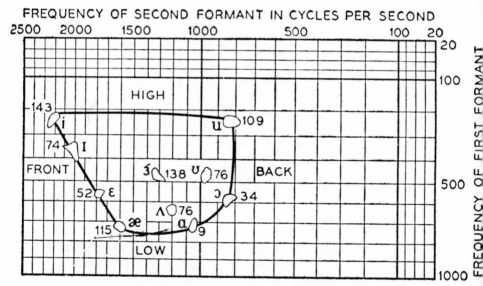

Figure 9. Frequency of the second formant plotted against the frequency of the first formant for vowels produced by a single speaker repeated 12 times on different days. From Peterson and Barney [23].

Peterson and Barney also performed tests in which listeners were asked to identify the words recorded by the 76 speakers. This led to another possible operational definition for phonetic equivalence, namely: unanimous agreement by 70 listeners on the word identity. Figure 10 shows the results obtained for this; some overlap still exists. Neither the definition based on speakers' intentions nor the one based on listeners' perceptions of words permitted direct assessment of the phonetic values of the vowels because some allophonic variation from reader to reader or from listener to listener was permitted and left uncontrolled.

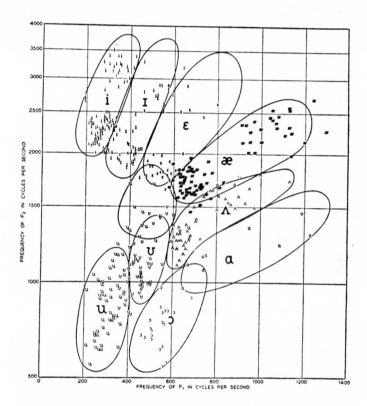

Figure 10. Frequency of the second formant plotted against the frequency of the first formant for the subset of vowels from Figure 8 that were unanimously identified by 70 listeners. From Peterson and Barney [23].

To refine the technique, Peterson [22] then developed yet a third operational definition for phonetic equivalence between vowels. A set of reference vowels was recorded, and played back to subjects who were instructed to imitate the sounds as closely as possible. Figure 11 shows the results for the vowels [I] and [ae]; the effect of this change in definition for phonetic equivalence can be seen more clearly in Figure 12 which has been constructed by superimposing the results of the preceding figure onto the regions defined by speaker intentions about words from Figure 8.

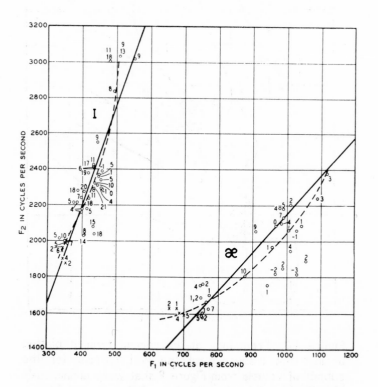

Figure 11. Frequency of the second formant plotted against the frequency of the first formant for various speakers' imitations of recorded reference vowels. From Peterson [22].

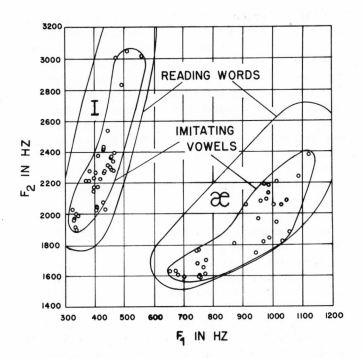

Figure 12. The data for vowel imitation from Figure 11 superimposed on the corresponding regions from Figure 8 for word reading.

It is easy to imagine other operational definitions, any of which could be carried through systematically for every category of interest. One could, for example, use trained phoneticians either as speakers or as listeners. The preceding examples should suffice to show that the concept of phonetic equivalence should be given careful thought, and should not be assumed as given just because agreed-upon phonetic symbols can be used with a sense of comforting familiarity.

Whatever definition one adopts, it is possible to use it to build up a picture of how speech sounds uttered by different speakers under different conditions are distributed in whatever acoustic space one has chosen to use. The term "distribution" here is used in a statistical sense, that is, we are interested not only in the total regions occupied by the different sounds, but also in how densely concentrated they are from point to point. Figure 13 illustrates this point with a plausibly constructed extension of an earlier figure. Here, instead of circumscribing the sounds with some kind of definite boundary, each sound is associated with a concentric series of equal-frequency curves that show the distributions of the vowel samples. For example, the point marked is on the 99% curve for /i/ and the 70% curve for /I/ in the sense that 99% of the /i/ samples are inside the first curve while 70% of the /I/ samples are inside the other curve. A recognizer having access to this information might well regard the recognition of /I/ as almost certain with a reservation that it might be an /i/ if other compelling evidence turns up. Unfortunately, distributions like the ones shown have not yet been determined, though we would expect that only a manageable data base would be required to gain a good idea of what they look like. In particular, a further statistical analysis of the original Peterson and Barney data would be most interesting in this context.

One complication to building up useful descriptions of distributions of sounds in phonetic spaces is the fact that there are variables other than the phonetic value of a sound that determine its position in an acoustic space. We have already seen the dramatic increase in variability when many speakers are studied instead of just one. Another effect is the phonetic context [4,17,29], or coarticulation [20] as it is sometimes called. Figure 14 illustrates the kind of variability that can be expected from speaker identity and phonetic context. The large loop shows the region defined by Peterson and Barney for the vowel /I/ by 76 speakers, all using the /h/-/d/ context. The dot shows the average position for this vowel in the same context as measured by Broad and Fertig [4] in their study of consonantal context effects. The small loop is the 1-standard deviation ellipse for the variation between repetitions for the same vowel in the same context by the same speaker. The medium-sized dashed loop contains all the positions measured for the vowel uttered by the same speaker, but in 576 different consonantal contexts. The inter-speaker variability is seen to be larger than the context variability, while the interrepetition variability is very small. "Inter-speaker variability" here refers to a very wide category of speakers: men, women, and children, and the large loop would therefore shrink considerably if, e.g., only adult male speakers were included. Also note that the comparisons in Figure 14 would be changed somewhat if the 2- or 3-standard deviation ellipses were used instead of the 1-standard deviation ellipse as measures of inter-repetition variability. It is not yet known how similar the context effects for other speakers would be to those for the one speaker shown by the dashed curve. Also, it is not yet known how even that speaker's context effects behave for other vowels.

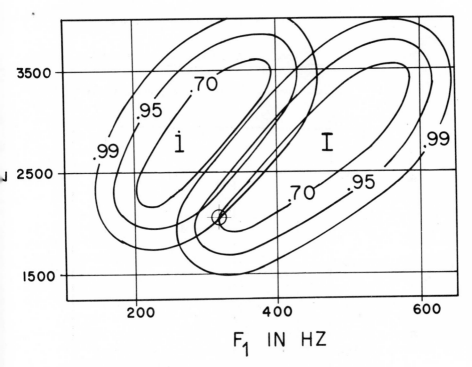

Figure 13. The [i] and [I] regions of the F_1-F_2 plane showing hypothetical statistical distributions based on the data of Figure 8. The point marked represents a possible input from an acoustic analysis.

All the studies mentioned so far used the sound spectrograph for analysis, and it is anticipated that the newer digital methods for speech analysis will make the study of larger bodies of data more attractive.

There is some choice in what variables we select to control versus those we select to vary freely or, for the sake of practicality, choose to treat as if they are randomly varying. By ignoring context effects, for example, one could tag all occurrences of a given sound equivalently and build up some kind of total distribution for the sound. As indicated in Figure 14, the effect would be to enlarge the variances for the sound along the various acoustic dimensions, but the advantage of a smaller data base requirement would be gained. This may well be

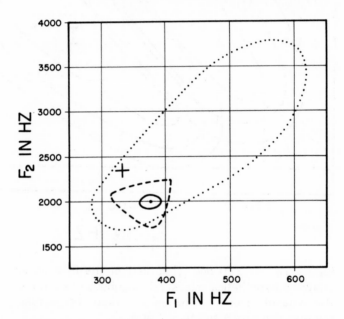

PETERSON-BARNEY REGION FOR /ɪ/ IN CONTEXT /h_d/

BROAD-FERTIG LOCATION FOR /ɪ/ IN CONTEXT /h_d/ INCLUDING 1σ ELLIPSE

BROAD-FERTIG REGION FOR /ɪ/ IN ALL CONTEXTS

Figure 14. Portion of the F_1-F_2 plane showing the distribution of the vowel [I] in the context [h-d] as measured by Peterson and Barney for 76 speakers (large dotted curve); the distribution of the same vowel in the same context as repeated by a single speaker (small solid curve); and the distribution of the same vowel by the same speaker in 576 different consonantal contexts (intermediate dashed curve). The point marked represents a hypothetical input from an acoustic analysis. After Broad [3].

a practical point, especially since at present the first-order effects due to phonetic identity are not yet well enough known for all sounds, for a second-order effect like context to be much help. Results shown on previous figures seem to indicate that some method for normalizing among speakers or for locking in on a single speaker should gain more discrimination than taking context effects into account would. Or, one could say that good handling of context effects requires a prior good handling of inter-speaker variation. It is clear, though, that the context effects are sizable, and therefore tend to be neglected in present-day systems, only because of our temporary ignorance.

What is lost if speaker and context effects are neglected? The answer, in one word, is discrimination. To illustrate how this is so for speaker effects, suppose that our acoustic analysis has given us the point marked with a plus sign (+) on Figure 14. Suppose further that we neglect speaker and context effects. That is, the large loop is taken to define the vowel equivalence class (or to be a measure of the spread of the vowel distribution). In this case the recognition of the vowel as an [I] seems reasonable. But suppose now that the individual speaker's characteristics for all contexts are given by the medium-sized dashed loop. The point marked is far enough away from this region to make the recognition of [I] implausible. The large loop, then, represents the distribution of samples from the population of [I] vowels drawn randomly from different speakers, while the typical situation in speech recognition is more currently modeled as the distribution of samples of sounds quasi-randomly emitted from a single speaker at a time. Analogous examples and arguments apply to the context effects.

This extended example has concerned only the vowel sounds. The extension of the concepts to other kinds of sounds will perhaps involve the use of other subsets of the acoustic parameters, but the basic concepts of operationally defined phonetic equivalence and of distributions with different sources of variability will still apply. There are some sets of sounds which so far have been found to be very difficult to discriminate acoustically. Notably, the distinction between [f] and [θ] and the distinctions among the nasal consonants [m], [n], and [ŋ] have been hard to make. In order to better understand how these distinctions are to be recognized or, indeed, whether they can be made reliably at all, it would be most useful to study their distributions within the space defined by the acoustic parameters proposed for their recognition. The results of such a study could be organized after the fashion of Figure 13 in order to determine the degree of overlap between the sound categories. It is conceivable that appreciable overlap would exist within these classes of sounds, with the result that only limited discrimination would then be even theoretically possible. One would then either have to settle for poor phonetic recognition in these cases or search for other parameters that would yield higher discrimination. An acoustic phonetic study of the distributions of difficult sound pairs would thus address the question of the realizability of a phonetic discriminator; in addition, it would provide a base for designing the best possible discriminator given the available parameters. Such an approach is suggested by the discussion of Figure 13.

The above remarks imply that the applied problem of phonetic recognition might best be approached through the basic study of phonetic distributions. Not only is the design of a recognizer facilitated, but an a priori estimate of its performance can be made relative to a theoretically established optimum performance. For example, suppose that the sounds I and II distribute hypothetically with 30% overlap in some space as shown schematically in Figure 15a and that the sounds III and IV distribute with no overlap as in Figure 15b. For simplicity, the distributions are shown as uniform within their respective regions. In this case, a recognizer that correctly identifies sounds I and II 85% of the time (70% from the regions of certainty, 15% from guessing randomly in the region of overlap) would be considered optimum while a recognizer that discriminated sounds III and IV 90% of the time would be performing poorly.

It is thus obvious that knowledge of the distributions of speech sounds in acoustic spaces is vital to implementing and evaluating automatic phonetic recognition, and one of the great present needs in acoustic phonetics is extensive basic study of these distributions, their sources of variability, their regions of overlap, and their mathematical characterizations.

The above discussion suggests that acoustic phonetic conversion rules might be formulated as statistical decision rules. In order for such rules to work, of course, extensive knowledge of the distributions must be obtained. It should also be noted that the discussion in this section has focused on quasi-static descriptions of speech sounds. In other words, the phonetic value of a sound is described in terms of measurements made on a single frame. From the preceding discussion of segmentation, however, it should be obvious that such a static description will be effective only if the dynamics of the speech parameters are well enough understood to determine appropriate time slices for "steady-state" measurements. Alternately, the statistical description might be generalized to a stochastic description that explicitly includes dynamic changes in the parameter

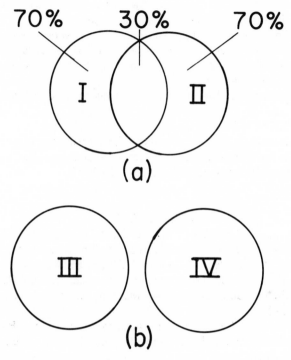

Figure 15. Hypothetical distributions in an acoustic space for two pairs of sounds. (a) 30% overlap; 85% discrimination between sounds I and II would be considered optimum. (b) No overlap; 100% discrimination between sounds III and IV is theoretically possible.

values [4]. At present we do not have enough information to decide whether the quasi-static description suggested here will suffice, and we also do not yet know all the criteria needed for defining the phone acoustically as a discrete segment of the speech stream. It is therefore premature to state the exact nature of acoustic phonetic conversion rules at this time.

To summarize this section, then, we have said that

1. Phonetic recognition requires a definition of phonetic equivalence.

2. Different operational definitions for phonetic equivalence lead to different distributions in phonetic space.
3. It is useful to describe the statistical distributions of the various speech sounds in acoustic space.
4. Phonetic identity, phonetic context, speaker identity, context, and inter-repetition variability are all effects that should ultimately be taken into account in the construction of such statistical descriptions.
5. Knowledge of the distributions provides a basis for recognition.

ACKNOWLEDGEMENT
    The Directorate of Mathematical and Information Sciences of the United States Air Force Office of Scientific Research (AFSC) supported this research under contract F44620-69-C-0078.

REFERENCES

1. Atal, B. S., "Determination of the Vocal Tract Shape Directly from the Speech Wave," The Journal of the Acoustical Society of America, Vol. 47, No. 1, January 1970, p. 65(A).

2. Broad, D. J., "Basic Directions in Automatic Speech Recognition," International Journal of Man-Machine Studies, Vol. 4, 1972, pp. 105-118.

3. Broad, D. J., "Formants in Automatic Speech Recognition," International Journal of Man-Machine Studies, Vol. 4, 1972, pp. 411-424.

4. Broad, D. J. and R. H. Fertig, "Formant-Frequency Trajectories in Selected CVC Syllable Nuclei," The Journal of the Acoustical Society of America, Vol. 47, No. 6, Part 2, June 1970, pp. 1572-1582.

5. Broad, D. J. and G. E. Peterson, "The Acoustics of Speech," Handbook of Speech Pathology and Audiology, edited by L. E. Travis, New York: Appleton-Century-Crofts, 1971, Chapter 6, pp. 141-173.

6. Cooper, F. S., P. C. Delattre, A. M. Liberman, J. M. Borst, and L. J. Gerstman, "Some Experiments on the Perception of Synthetic Speech Sounds," The Journal of the Acoustical Soceity of America, Vol. 24, No. 6, November 1952, pp. 597-606.

7. Cooper, F. S., A. M. Liberman, and J. M. Borst, "The Interconversion of Audible and Visible Patterns as a Basis for Research in the Perception of Speech," Proceedings of the National Academy of Sciences, Vol. 37, 1951, pp. 318-325.

8.   Fant, C. G. M., "On the Predictability of Formant Levels and Spectrum Envelopes from Formant Frequencies," For Roman Jakobson, edited by M. Halle, et al., The Hague: Mouton, 1956, pp. 109-120.

9.   Fant, G., Acoustic Theory of Speech Production, The Hague: Mouton and Company, 1960.

10. Fant, G., "Analysis and Synthesis of Speech Processes," Manual of Phonetics, edited by B. Malmberg, Amsterdam: North-Holland, 1958, pp. 173-277.

11. Flanagan, J. L., Speech Analysis, Synthesis, and Perception, Second Edition, New York: Springer, 1972.

12. Fujisaki, H. and T. Omura, "Characteristics of Durations of Pauses and Speech Segments in Connected Speech," Annual Report of the Engineering Research Institute, Faculty of Engineering, University of Tokyo, Vol. 30, 1971, pp. 69-74.

13. Halle, M. and K. N. Stevens, "On the Mechanism of Glottal Vibration for Vowels and Consonants," Massachusetts Institute of Technology, Research Laboratory of Electronics, Quarterly Progress Report No. 85, April 15, 1967, pp. 267-271.

14. Heinz, J. M., Perturbation Functions for the Determination of Vocal-Tract Area Functions from Vocal-Tract Eigenvalues, Royal Institute of Technology, Speech Transmission Laboratory, Stockholm, Sweden, Quarterly Progress and Status Report, No. 1, April 15, 1967, pp. 1-14.

15. Joos, M., Acoustic Phonetics, Monograph Supplement to Language, Vol. 24, No. 2, April-June, 1948.

16. Koenig, W., H. K. Dunn, and L. Y. Lacy, "The Sound Spectrograph," The Journal of the Acoustical Society of America, Vol. 18, No. 1, July 1946, pp. 19-49.

17. Lindblom, B., "Spectrographic Study of Vowel Reduction," The Journal of the Acoustical Society of America, Vol. 35, No. 11, November 1963, pp. 1773-1781.

18. Markel, J. D., "The SIFT Algorithm for Fundamental Frequency Estimation," IEEE Transactions of Audio and Electroacoustics, Vol. AU-20, No. 5, December 1972, pp. 367-377.

19. Mermelstein, P., "Determination of the Vocal-Tract Shape from Measured Formant Frequencies," The Journal of the Acoustical Society of America, Vol. 41, No. 5, May 1967, pp. 1283-1294.

20. Ohman, S. E. G., "Coarticulation in VCV Utterances, Spectrographic Measurements," The Journal of the Acoustical Society of America, Vol. 39, No. 1, January 1966, pp. 151-168.

21. Oppenheim, A. V., "Speech Spectrograms Using the Fast Fourier Transform," IEEE Spectrum, Vol. 7, No. 8, August 1970, pp. 57-62.

22. Peterson, G. E., "The Information Bearing Elements of Speech," The Journal of the Acoustical Society of America, Vol. 24, No. 6, November 1952, pp. 629-637.

23. Peterson, G. E. and H. L. Barney, "Control Methods Used in a Study of the Vowels," The Journal of the Acoustical Society of America, Vol. 24, No. 2, March 1952, pp. 175-185.

24. Peterson, G. E. and J. E. Shoup, "The Elements of an Acoustic Phonetic Theory," Journal of Speech and Hearing Research, Vol. 9, No. 1, March 1966, pp. 68-99.

25. Peterson, G. E. and J. E. Shoup, "A Physiological Theory of Phonetics," Journal of Speech and Hearing Research, Vol. 9, No. 1, March 1966, pp. 5-67.

26. Potter, R. K. and G. E. Peterson, "The Representation of Vowels and Their Movements," The Journal of the Acoustical Society of America, Vol. 20, No. 4, July 1948, pp. 528-535.

27. Potter, R. K., G. A. Kopp, and H. C. Green, Visible Speech, New York: Van Nostrand, 1947; New York: Dover, 1966.

28. M. R. Schroeder, "Determination of the Geometry of the Human Vocal Tract by Acoustic Measurements," The Journal of the Acoustical Society of America, Vol. 41, No. 4, Part 2, April 1967, pp. 1002-1010.

29. Stevens, K. N., A. S. House, and A. P. Paul, "Acoustical Description of Syllabic Nuclei: An Interpretation in Terms of a Dynamic Model of Articulation," The Journal of the Acoustical Society of America, Vol. 40, No. 1, July 1966, pp. 123-132.

30. Wakita, H., "Direct Estimation of the Vocal Tract Shape by Inverse Filtering of Acoustic Speech Waveforms," IEEE Transactions on Audio and Electroacoustics, Vol. AU-21, No. 5, October 1973, pp. 417-427.

THE PHONOLOGICAL COMPONENT OF AN AUTOMATIC SPEECH-RECOGNITION SYSTEM

Paul S. Cohen
Robert L. Mercer
Computer Sciences Department
IBM Thomas J. Watson Research Center
Yorktown Heights, New York 10598

ABSTRACT *

One of the problems encountered in speech recognition is that of associating with each of the possible phonetic realizations of a particular utterance, the probability of that production as a realization of the utterance. To deal with this problem in the speech-recognition system being constructed at the Thomas J. Watson Research Center of IBM, we have developed a phonological-rule component which employs: (1) A lexicon of American English phonemic base forms; (2) A set of phonological rules to account statistically for phonemic and major allophonic variation resulting from idiolect, dialect, style and pace, and; (3) An algorithm for applying the rules to the base forms for the generation of phonological variants.

We describe in some detail here the generation and format of the base forms, the statistical raison d'etre of the rules, and the logistics of the algorithm for applying the rules.

I. INTRODUCTION

One of the difficulties encountered in automatic speech recognition is that each utterance of a language may be realized phonetically in many ways. Thus, for example the phrase either person may be produced in well over a thousand readily distinguishable ways, a few of which are shown below.†

---

†We have disregarded stress, pitch, and length in order to keep things relatively simple; had we included these, the number of distinguishable productions would, of course, rise tremendously.

1. [|ʔiðɚ | pʰɝsən|]

2. [|ʔiðɚ | pʰɝsɪn|]

3. [|ʔɑˈðɚ |pʰɝsən|]

4. [|ʔɒˈðɚ | pˈɝsən|]

5. [|ʔidðə |pʰɝsɪn|]

6. [|iðə| pʌsn̩|]

7. [|ʔɑˈðə |pˈɜsɨn|]

It is clearly impossible to store all pronunciations for every utterance in the language. Fortunately, the various pronunciations of an utterance are related to one another. For example, 1 and 2 above differ only in the quality of the final vowel. The inspection of a number

---

Our phonetic notation in the body of this paper is basically that of the International Phonetic Alphabet (IPA); those departures we make are generally in keeping with standard American transcriptional practice, with the exception of our notation for boundaries. In the examples given, "|" represents a word boundary. In some of the appendices we use a machine-readable encoding of the phonetic characters; a translation table is found in Appendix 2.

of utterances reveals that the alternation of [e] with [ɪ] is quite common in this phonetic context. In fact, many pronunciations may be accounted for by similar alternations--phonological rules. It would therefore appear that one might represent the multitude of pronunciations of an utterance by positing a single basic pronunciation from which the others may be derived by the application of a set of phonological rules. Indeed, in the majority of cases this works well. The alternation between 1 and 3 above, however, is not suitable for such a treatment. Thus though one might propose a rule to express the alternation between [i] and [ɑ] when followed by [ðə·], such a rule seems to apply only to either and neither, as opposed to, say, lither ('more lithe') or breather. One might conceivably attribute this fact to the presence of a boundary in the latter words which is absent from the former. However, a parallel treatment is clearly impossible for the following example:

till 'until' has [tˑɪl] alternating with [tˑɛl], while till 'cash register', 'cultivate' shows no such alternation.

Even assigning a single representation to each utterance would require an unfeasibly large amount of storage. (Indeed, many linguists would argue that an infinite number of grammatical utterances are producible in any natural language.) The solution to this problem is obvious: utterances can be broken down into subutterances in a number of ways. In English, perhaps the best-defined subutterance is the word. It is especially attractive for our purposes since orthographic output is required from our speech-recognition system at IBM. We have chosen, therefore, to create a lexicon with an inventory of subutterances generally equivalent to individual words, and to maintain for each a small number of basic pronunciations or base forms. From these, in conjunction with the phonological rules mentioned earlier, the entire inventory of utterances and their associated pronunciations may be synthesized.

This process accounts for the different pronunciations of an utterance but not for the frequency with which each is produced. It is necessary for statistical decoding of the speech signal to associate with each utterance, u, and pronunciation, ϕ, a number $P(\phi|u)$, the probability that ϕ is produced as a pronunciation of u. For example:

Version 5 of either person is only to be expected in the casual style of certain speakers from metropolitan New York City. The absence of a glottal stop, as in version 6, is uncommon in utterances beginning with a vowel. The use of [ɑˈ], [ɒˈ] or

[ɑᵋ] in <u>either</u> as in versions 3, 4, and 7 is largely characteristic of cultivated speakers in various areas of the eastern U.S.

We propose to account for these and similar facts by associating speaker-dependent probabilities with both the base forms and the phonological rules. Then, by the combination of the probabilities of all the base forms and rules involved in the creation of a particular pronunciation of an utterance, an overall probability for that pronunciation will be obtained. The base forms and phonological rules together with associated probabilities can be regarded as a speaker model. Note that this is a model of speaker performance rather than competence; we realize, furthermore, that it has certain inadequacies, ignoring as it does semantic influences, for example†.

In the sections which follow, we will deal in greater detail with the issues we have touched on here, and treat other problems as they arise. Sections which give samples of our lexicon and lists of the phonological rules (with explanatory remarks), and an example of an interaction with our rule-applying program are also appended.

II. BASE FORMS AND RULES

In the body of this paper, base forms are represented as strings of phonemes and the output of the phonological rules as gross phonetic strings -- i.e., sequences of phones of approximately phoneme size, but often embodying more phonetic detail††.

---

†Of course, ours is not the first use of phonological rules in a speech-recognition system. (See for example C. C. Tappert, <u>Intermediate Performance of Multistage System for Automatic Recognition of Continuous Speech</u>, RADC-TR-73-16, Rome Air Development Center, Griffis Air Force Base, N.Y., Jan. 1973; and C. C. Tappert and N. R. Dixon, <u>A Procedure for Adaptive Control of the Interaction Between Acoustic Classification and Linguistic Decoding in Automatic Recognition of Continuous Speech</u>, IBM Research Report RC 4249, Yorktown Heights, N.Y., Feb 28, 1973.) Our phonological rule component is a major improvement in at least three ways: 1) the rules are greatly expanded and capable of handling a much wider range of phenomena; 2) they form a module which can be evaluated separately from any acoustic processor; and 3) they allow efficient calculation of statistics.

††We enclose essentially phonetic transcriptions in square brackets, and essentially phonemic transcriptions in diagonals.

Our base forms are gleaned from four sources: Webster's Third New International Dictionary[†], A Pronouncing Dictionary of American English[††], The Pronunciation of English in the Atlantic States[†††], and personal knowledge, with the first of these the major source. Phonological rules are generated, of necessity, less systematically. There is, unfortunately, no unified source of information about American English pronunciational differences, particularly for matters involved with connected speech. Thus rules have largely been formulated on the basis of pronunciations from dictionaries, data from The Pronunciation of English in the Atlantic States, common knowledge of linguists and dialectologists (often very incompletely specified), examination of spectrograms, personal knowledge, introspection, anecdotal experimentation, and just plain listening to speech. We have not yet made a thorough search for the widely scattered rules available from the literature.

When determining the base forms for a word, we are frequently faced with twenty or more phonemically different pronunciations, even if we restrict ourselves to relatively standard American usage. Deciding which of these should be chosen is not always as straightforward as it may have appeared in the Introduction. Normally, any variant pronunciation that can be produced by our phonological rules will not be used as a base form. Where two forms can be produced from each other, the form more nearly characteristic of General American speech is selected as the base form. In some situations (e.g., where a putative rule has exceptions or where data on the occurrence of forms is sparse), it may be difficult to decide whether to express the information in base forms or in rules; in such situations, specific system implementations or the acquisition of new data will often be the deciding factor.

Appendix 6 shows the syntax of the base-form lexicon. A short segment from one of our current base-form lexicons is shown below.

[†] Springfield, Mass., G. & C. Merriam Company, 1966.

[††] John S. Kenyon and Thomas A. Knott, Springfield, Mass., G. & C. Merriam Company, 1953.

[†††] Hans Kurath and Raven I. McDavid, Jr., Ann Arbor, The University of Michigan Press, 1961.

```
1:PROCESS ::       p r ɑ s ɛ s          <12,1>;
2:PROCESS ::       p r o s ɛ s          <12,1>;
3:PROCESS :VRB: (PROCESS 2)             <01>;
1:PROCESSES :NOUP: (PROCESS 1 2) #  ɪ z
                                        <122,102,12>;
2:PROCESSES : : (PROCESS 1 2) #   ɪ z   <12,1>;
3:PROCESSES :VRB: (PROCESS 3)  #  ɪ z   <01>;
```

Each entry consists of optional source and usage markers, an identifying number, the word in its English spelling, an optional part-of-speech restriction[†], a basic phonological representation, and a set of one or more stress patterns.

    In 3:PROCESS the phonological representation given refers to that of 2:PROCESS rather than repeating the phoneme-by-phoneme spelling. This is more than a simple shorthand; it implies that the base forms are statistically related. Thus 1:PROCESSES defines two base forms which are expected to occur with the same relative frequencies as 1:PROCESS and 2:PROCESS. If it were felt that people say / p r ɑ s ɛ s / but / p r o s ɛ s # ɪ z / this device would not be used here.

    We are using a transcription system with three levels of stress: primary (represented by "1"), secondary or reduced (represented by "2"), and unstressed (represented by "0"). Stress is being treated as a characteristic of the vowel nucleus of a syllable[††]. The stress pattern of an entry is represented as a sequence of 1's, 2's, and 0's, with trailing zeroes omitted. Thus, for example, the numbers between angle brackets in the entry of 1:PROCESS above represent two possible stress patterns: primary-secondary and primary-unstressed. It should be noted that the stress patterns given in the entries are (except for some function words) the basic, independent ones. At present we have no rules to handle utterance-dependent stress modification.

    Our present phonological rules, are given in Appendix 5. Each rule comprises four parts: a left-hand side which must be a single

---

[†]VRB stands for <u>verb</u> and NOUP for <u>noun plural</u>.

[††]If it later proves necessary to treat stress as a property of a syllable as a whole, we can do so with the aid of syllable boundaries in our phonological representations.

string of phonemes[†††]; a right-hand side which consists of one or more phoneme strings; a left-hand context which may be empty; and a right-hand context which may also be empty. The rule symbology differs from that of standard transformational phonology in only two ways: (1) Angle brackets are used in place of braces; (2) When the alternatives indicated by angle brackets or parentheses are felt to have a differential influence on the applicability of the rule, the left angle bracket or parenthesis is preceded by an asterisk. Thus to represent the fact that word-final /r/ is more readily deleted in many dialects before consonants than before vowels we could write

$$r \to \emptyset / \_\_ \mid *<\text{vowels,consonants}>;.$$

All our rules are optional.

Though it is common linguistic practice to use cyclic rules (whether ordered or unordered) in the phonological component of a grammar, we have departed from this practice. We feel that with rules of this type, probabilities would be most naturally associated with derivations from the rules, rather than with the individual rules themselves. Therefore we have chosen to use unordered, non-cyclic, left-to-right rules, which greatly simplify both the rule-application machinery and the collection of statistics. Thus although our rules are written in a superficially context-sensitive format they may actually be considered as specifying a probabilistic finite-state machine which, when presented with a base-form string as input, produces a surface-form string as output (with overall probability determined by the probabilities on the various transitions made by the machine). Suppose that one had the rule

$$a \to b / c \_\_ d;.$$

Since our rules are all optional, this is shorthand for the statement that an 'a' in the base-form string becomes a 'b' with some probability p and remains an 'a' with probability 1-p whenever it is immediately preceded in the surface-form string by 'c' and immediately followed in the remaining base-form string by 'd'. Note that left context refers to the already produced surface-form string, while right context refers to the yet unprocessed base-form string.

Figure 1 shows a simple set of rules and their application to a short base-form string. The resulting surface-form strings are displayed as a tree in 1b and, more conveniently, as a graph in 1c.

[†††] Null ('$\emptyset$') and boundaries are permissible in the phoneme strings.

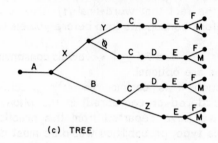

1. $\emptyset \rightarrow Y/X _ $;
2. $CD \rightarrow Z/B\_E$;
3. $B \rightarrow X/A\_C$;
4. $F \rightarrow M/ _ $;

(a) RULES

ABCDEF

(b) BASE-FORM STRING

(c) TREE

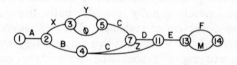

(d) GRAPH

Figure 1. A comparison of Tree and Graph Representation for a Simple Set of Rules and a Short Base-Form String.

The process of rule application is described in greater detail in Section IV.

When we first considered writing phonological rules in this format, we felt that it might be difficult to account for the necessary phonological phenomena without resorting to rules that were unduly intricate at times. Even in the worst cases, however, it has only been necessary to write one or two additional rules. For example, to characterize the two-way articulatory assimilation which gives [sɛb m] from / sɛvən /, we have written the rule

$$ v \partial n \rightarrow bm / \_ \left\{ \begin{matrix} \# \\ | \\ \text{consonants} \end{matrix} \right\} ; . $$

III. SPEAKER MODEL

In this section we discuss the way in which probabilities are associated with the base forms and phonological rules to form our speaker model.

Many of the phonological rules that we have written make use of the asterisk notation described in Section II. The first step in assigning probabilities is to expand these rules so that the asterisks are unnecessary. Thus the rule

$$A \rightarrow *<B,C> \ / \ <D,E> \ \_ \ *(F)G;$$

is rewritten as the four rules

$A \rightarrow B \ / \ <D,E> \ \_ \ FG;$
$A \rightarrow B \ / \ <D,E> \ \_ \ G;$
$A \rightarrow C \ / \ <D,E> \ \_ \ FG;$
$A \rightarrow C \ / \ <D,E> \ \_ \ G;$

This process leads to an expanded set of rules, $R=\{r_1,...,r_n\}$. For any phoneme, A, we denote by R_A the possibly empty subset of R consisting of all rules whose left-hand side begins with A. The set of rules which have empty left-hand sides is denoted by R_o. When a phoneme A appears in a particular context, say, $\alpha A \beta$, not all of the rules in R_A may apply. We denote the set that can apply by $R_{\alpha A \beta}$. Although there are infinitely many possible contexts α_β, since each set $R_{\alpha A \beta}$ is a subset of R_A, there can be only finitely many different sets $R_{\alpha A \beta}$. For each set $R_{\alpha A \beta}$ we define a set $S_{\alpha A \beta}$ which is the union of the right-hand sides of all the rules in $R_{\alpha A \beta}$ with the set $\{A\}$. When R_A consists of the rules:
1. $A \rightarrow \emptyset \ / \ C \ \_;$
2. $A \rightarrow GH \ / \ \_D;$
3. $A \rightarrow E \ / \ \_DF;$,
$R_{\alpha A \beta}$ and $S_{\alpha A \beta}$ are as shown below.

α	β	$R_{\alpha A \beta}$	$S_{\alpha A \beta}$
C	X	{1}	{∅,A}
C	DR	{1,2}	{∅,GH,A}
C	DF	{1,2,3}	{∅,GH,E,A}
Z	DF	{2,3}	{GH,E,A}
Z	DR	{2}	{GH,A}
M	N	{}	{A}

With each string $\gamma \epsilon S_{\alpha A\beta}$, we associate a probability $p\gamma$ such that

$$\sum_{\gamma \epsilon S_{\alpha A\beta}} p\gamma = 1$$

This is the probability that when an A occurs in the context α_β, it will be rewritten as γ. These probabilities then determine for each base-form string, the probability of any surface-form string that can be produced. The probability of a particular base-form string is in turn determined by probabilities associated with the various base forms for the words involved in the underlying text. Each word with its corresponding part of speech makes up a pair that has one or more base forms. To these we assign probabilities which sum to one.

In summary, we model the speaker as follows. Presented with text consisting of a string of word/part-of-speech pairs he chooses independently and at random a base form for each according to the associated probabilities. He then applies the phonological rules to the resulting base-form string. At each point in the string the appropriate set $S_{\alpha A\beta}$ is determined and A is rewritten according to the probabilities associated with the strings $\gamma \epsilon S_{\alpha A\beta}$. Obviously a real speaker is much more complex than our model. We are ignoring among other things, intonation, the influence of semantics beyond simple parts of speech, and dialectal co-occurrence restrictions among the rules and base forms. We hope to refine our model in the future to account for facts of this kind.

IV. THE RULE APPLIER

When rules become as numerous as ours have, it is very difficult to anticipate all of the effects of a proposed modification. To help us in this task, we have written a rule-applying program which accepts base-form strings, applies the rules and produces as output a graph which embodies all of the resulting surface-form strings in a readily comprehended form.

During the application of the rules, that part of the surface form which has already been generated is stored as a directed graph with a number of final nodes each of which points to the next base-form symbol to be processed for that node. This symbol is called the successor of the node. Since some rules have several symbols on the left-hand side, not all of the final nodes need have the same successor at any moment. The rule applier proceeds one symbol at a time through the base-form string. For each base-form symbol, B, the rule applier finds all of the final nodes of the graph for which B is the successor. Each of these nodes is extended in turn, as follows. First, all rules which have an empty left-hand side are applied if the appropriate contexts are satisfied. This produces a set of intermediate nodes, 1. Then, for each node in 1, all rules which have contexts that are satisfied and which have a left-hand side beginning with B are applied. Finally, the graph is reduced by eliminating common subgraphs wherever possible. The rule applier then moves one symbol to the right in the base-form string and repeats the process until the string is exhausted.

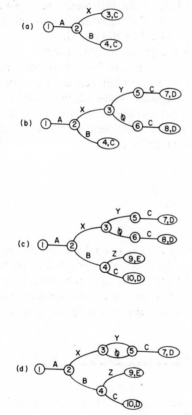

Figure 2. One Step in the Application of Rules to the Base-Form String 'ABCDEF'.

Figure 2 shows a single extension cycle for the example given in Figure 1. In 2a the directed graph is shown just prior to processing 'C' from the base-form string. At this point the final nodes are 3 and 4, each with successor 'C'. Rule 1 applied to node 3 generates intermediate nodes 5 and 6. Since none of the rules applies to either node 5 or node 6, the 'C' is copied directly; this creates two new final nodes 7 and 8, each with successor 'D'. The graph at this point is shown in 2b. After node 4 has been processed, the graph is as shown in 2c. Note that node 9 has 'E' as successor because rule 2, which created it, has two symbols in its left-hand side. Finally, since the subgraph from node 6 to node 8 is identical to the one from node 5 to node 7, it is eliminated, giving 2d as the result.

The complete directed graph for this example is shown in Figure 1. Nodes such as 1, 2, 11, 13 and 14 which must be on any path through the graph are called confluent nodes. Our phonology is such that confluent nodes are usually quite close together and certainly never more than five phonemes apart. When the graph is printed, all strings connecting consecutive confluent nodes are constructed and placed in a column, as shown below.

```
        XYCD
        XCD        F
  * A *        * E *   * G * .
        BCD        M
        BZ
```

The same machinery that is used to apply the rules for testing purposes is used to generate a directed-graph lexicon from the base-form lexicon. The set of base forms for each word may be viewed as a base-form graph which ends with a word-boundary marker "|". Thus for <u>economics</u>, the base-form graph, neglecting stress, would be

To this graph, the phonological rules may be applied to produce a graph accounting for all of the possible pronunciations of <u>economics</u>. Although the phonological rules have bounded context, those which may apply at the ends of words will in general be determined in part by the words which precede and follow them in a particular utterance. For example, the final /s/ may be deleted in front of a word beginning with /s/, /z/ or /s/ but not before a word beginning with /t/. Similarly, although a glide may be present before the initial vowel if the preceding word ends with certain vowels, this will not be the case if the preceding word ends with, say, /m/.

Since much of the phonetic variation in all but the shortest words is independent of the context in which the word is found, it is convenient computationally to have the interior part of the directed graph computed in advance, with boundary conditions specified at the ends. Then, to compute the graph for an utterance consisting of several words, one need only connect the individual word graphs so that the proper conditions obtain at word boundaries.

We will examine in some detail the form that these boundary conditions take. As mentioned earlier, we have a rule which deletes word-final /s/ before /s/, /š/, or /z/. Formally,

$$s \rightarrow \emptyset \; / \; \_\_ \; | \; < s, \check{s}, z > ; .$$

In the base form for economics, we can see the final /s/ and also the /ǀ/ but we cannot guarantee from within economics itself that the rest of the context of this rule will be satisfied. To indicate this, we split the graph for economics after the second /k/.

$$\bigcirc\!\!\!\!i \; \xrightarrow{k \; \ni \; n \; a \; m \; \iota \; k} \overset{\varepsilon}{\underset{s \quad |}{\quad}} | \; [s, \check{s}, z]$$

The path with the deleted /s/ also indicates the part of the rule which remains to be satisfied.

To account for the other rule mentioned above, which we can represent schematically as

$$\emptyset \rightarrow j \; / \; \text{certain vowels} \; | \; \_\_ \; \text{vowels};$$

the graph becomes

$$\overset{[\overset{\text{certain}}{\text{vowels}} \; | \;]j}{\underset{\emptyset}{\quad}} \bigcirc\!\!\!\!i \; \xrightarrow{k \; \ni \; n \; a \; m \; \iota \; k} \overset{\varepsilon}{\underset{s \quad |}{\quad}} | \; [s, \check{s}, z]$$

This procedure cannot be applied when a rule has a left-hand side which contains a word boundary with at least one symbol on each side. Such rules are apparently uncommon but do occur. An example is the following.

$$n \; | \; n \rightarrow | \; \tilde{r} \; / \; \_\_ \; ;$$

Consider the word <u>noon,</u> which has the base-form graph

$$\bullet \overset{n}{\_}\bullet \overset{u}{\_}\bullet \overset{n}{\_}\bullet \overset{|}{\_}\bullet$$

Let R be the label of the rule shown above. Then the directed graph for <u>noon</u> has the following form:

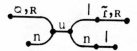

Note that the product of the rule is attached to the end of the word which provides the first part of the match. (This is consistent with our choice for placement of the word boundary.) Branches of this type—— that is, those associated with a rule label——can be connected to other branches only when they carry the same rule label.

To illustrate the connection process, let us consider the synthesis of the utterance <u>brand</u> <u>new</u> from its component words. The directed graphs for these words are

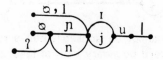

and

These are connected in the following steps. First, all branches labeled with the same rule number are connected. Any remaining branches labeled with a rule number are discarded. Then, those branches of the first word which remain unconnected are compared to the base-form graph of the second word to see which ones have their requisite right context satisfied. Each unconnected branch of the second word is compared with each unconnected branch of the first word to check for the requisite left context. Finally, all allowable connections are made. In our example, the result is

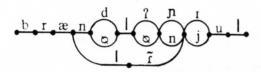

The effort required to make these few connections is considerably less than that required to compute the entire graph from the appropriate base-form string.

ACKNOWLEDGMENTS

We are grateful to the members of the speech recognition project, in particular Lalit Bahl, for helpful comments. We would also like to thank Gretchen Brown for her work on the first version of the rule applier and Denis Croux, who researched many of our base forms and made valuable suggestions about the content of phonological rules.

APPENDIX 1. Notes on the Phonological Rules

Appendix 5 contains all of our phonological rules in detail, in our machine-readable notation. this appendix, we give an overview of those rules in an informal and sometimes abridged notatio along with examples and notes on dialectal and idiolectal occurrence. For the reader's conve ience, we have indicated here the corresponding rules in Appendix 5.

I. / æ / Tensing

$$
æ \rightarrow
\left\{
\begin{matrix}
ɛː \\
\left\{\begin{matrix} ɛ \\ \left\{\begin{matrix} ɪ \\ i \end{matrix}\right\} ʳ \end{matrix}\right\}
\end{matrix}
\right\}
\Big/ \_
\left\{
\begin{matrix}
\text{nasals} \\
\text{fricatives} \\
\text{voiced stops}
\end{matrix}
\right\}
\left\{
\begin{matrix}
\# \\
| \\
\text{obstruents}
\end{matrix}
\right\}
$$

Examples:

camp   /k æmp/ → [k ɛ ʒ mp]

rash   /r æš/ → [r ɛ ʒ š]

rack   /r æk/ → [r æk]

Notes:
    Eastern seaboard (and sporadically elsewhere, esp. before nasals). Details differ widel Often stigmatized. Nucleus lengthening is commonly present. Exceptions include particle (Rules 1.1 and 1.2)

$$
æ \rightarrow æ ɫ \Big/ \_
\left\{
\begin{matrix}
\text{nasals} \\
\left\{\begin{matrix} f \\ g \\ s \\ \theta \\ ð \end{matrix}\right\} \\
š \\ ž \\ ǰ \\ ŋ \\ k
\end{matrix}
\right.
\left.
\begin{matrix}
\text{obstruents} \\
\left\{\begin{matrix} \# \\ | \\ \text{obstruents} \end{matrix}\right\}
\end{matrix}
\right\}
$$

Examples:

camp /k æmp/ → [k æɫ mp]

rack /r æk/ → /r æɫ k/

Notes:
    South, Southern Mountains, Southwest, and New Eng. Not all environments apply to ea(location. (Rule 1.3)

I. *Diphthong-Nucleus Adjustment*

$$a \rightarrow \begin{Bmatrix} \alpha \\ æ \\ \text{ɒ} \\ \text{ə} \end{Bmatrix} / \_\_ \text{ɪ} \qquad\qquad \text{ɔ} \rightarrow \begin{Bmatrix} o \\ \text{ʊ} \\ u \end{Bmatrix} / \_\_ \text{ɪ}$$

$$a \rightarrow \begin{Bmatrix} \alpha \\ æ \\ \text{ə} \end{Bmatrix} / \_\_ \text{ʊ}$$

Examples:

high /h a ɪ / → [h ɒ ɪ]

out   /a ʊ t / → [ə ʊ t]

boy   /b ɔ ɪ / → [b o ɪ]

Notes:

General American usually has [ɑ] or [a] in /aɪ, aʊ/ , [ɔ] in /ɔɪ/.   [ɒ]. common in /aɪ / in the N.Y. City area; [ə] occurs in /aɪ, aʊ/ , e.g., in Va., Md., Martha's Vineyard, and many parts of Canada—esp. when a voiceless consonant follows.   [æ]   common in many areas of the South in /aɪ / ; [æ] usual in /aʊ/ in many areas of the East and South and elsewhere. [ʊ, u] common in the N.Y.City area in [ɔɪ] ; [o]   common in S.C., Del., Md., and E. New Eng.   (Rules 2.1, 2.2, 2.3)

II. *Offglide Adjustment*

$$\text{ɪ} \rightarrow \begin{Bmatrix} \text{ɪ} \\ \text{i} \\ \text{e} \\ \text{ɛ} \\ \text{æ} \\ o \end{Bmatrix} / \begin{Bmatrix} a \\ \alpha \\ æ \\ \text{ɔ} \end{Bmatrix} \_\_ \qquad \text{ɪ} \rightarrow \begin{Bmatrix} \text{ɪ} \\ \text{i} \\ \text{e} \\ \text{ɛ} \\ \text{æ} \end{Bmatrix} / o \_\_$$

$$\text{ɪ} \rightarrow \begin{Bmatrix} \text{ɪ} \\ \text{i} \\ \text{u} \end{Bmatrix} / \begin{Bmatrix} \text{ɒ} \\ \text{ʊ} \\ u \end{Bmatrix} \_\_ \qquad \text{ɪ} \rightarrow \text{i} / \text{ə} \_\_$$

$$\text{ʊ} \rightarrow \begin{Bmatrix} \text{ʊ} \\ \text{o} \\ \text{æ} \\ \text{ɒ} \end{Bmatrix} / \begin{Bmatrix} a \\ \alpha \\ æ \end{Bmatrix} \_\_ \qquad \text{ʊ} \rightarrow \text{ʊ} / \text{ə} \_\_$$

Examples:

high /h a ɪ / → [h æ ɛ]

out   /a ʊ t / → [ɑ·ɒ t]

boy   /b ɔ ɪ / → [b ɔ ɛ]

Notes:

Lower offglides are typical of the South, Southwest, and Southern Mountain area; and are less common everywhere before voiceless consonants. The more upgliding variants tend to occur more in the Northeast and in General American. (Rules 2.4-2.11)

IV. /ɔ/ - /a/ *Mergers*

(1) $a \rightarrow \begin{Bmatrix} ɔ \\ ɒ \end{Bmatrix} / \underline{\quad}$

(2) $a \rightarrow \begin{Bmatrix} ɔ \\ ɒ \end{Bmatrix} / \underline{\quad} \begin{Bmatrix} g \\ ŋ \\ f \\ θ \\ l \end{Bmatrix} \begin{Bmatrix} \# \\ | \\ consonants \end{Bmatrix}$

(3) $ɔ \rightarrow \begin{Bmatrix} a \\ ɒ \\ ɒ̧ \end{Bmatrix} / \underline{\quad} \begin{Bmatrix} \# \\ | \\ consonants \end{Bmatrix}$

Examples:

doll   /d a l / → [d ɔ l] ; but for many doll ar   /d a l ɚ / → [d a l ɚ]

thong   /θ a ŋ / → [θ ɔ ŋ]

stock   /s t a k / → [s t ɔ k]

stalk   /s t ɔ k / → [s t a k]

Notes:
(1) is common in the West. (2) is common in most varieties of General American.
for /ɔ/ occurs in the Northeast, while [ɒ̧] for /ɔ/ is common in the South a
South Midland. The merger of /ɔ/ and /a/ at [ɒ] occurs in Ohio and W.
(Rules 3.1 and 3.2)

V. Intrusive /r/

$ɘ̧ \rightarrow r / \begin{Bmatrix} ɔ \\ ɒ \\ a \\ ə \\ ɚ \end{Bmatrix} \underline{\quad} \begin{Bmatrix} \# \\ | \end{Bmatrix}$ vowels

Examples:

drawing   /d r ɔ # ɪ ŋ / → [d r ɔ r # ɪ ŋ]

Cuba and Africa   /k j u b ə │ æ n d │ æ f r ɪ k ə / → [k j u b ə r │ æ n d │ æ f r ɪ k ə]

Notes:
Common in New Eng. and the N.Y. City area. (Rules 4.1-4.4 and 4.6)

$ɘ̧ \rightarrow r / w \begin{Bmatrix} ɒ \\ ɔ \end{Bmatrix} \underline{\quad} š$

Examples:

Washington   /wɔ š ɪ ŋ t ə n / → [wɔ r š ɪ ŋ t ə n]

squash   /s k wɔ š / → [s k wɔ r š]

Notes:
Occurs at least in Pa. and W.Va. (Rule 4.5)

VI. Alveolar Flapping

(1)   t → ɾ / vowels (r) _ $\begin{Bmatrix} (\#) \text{ unstressed vowels} \\ | \text{ vowels} \end{Bmatrix}$

Examples:

artist   /á r t ɪ s t / → [á r ɾ ɪ s t]

at Albany   /æt |ɔ́ l b ə n i / → [æ ɾ |ɔ́ l b ə n i]

but not

proton   /p r ɔ́ t ɑ̀ n / → [p r ɔ́ ɾ ɑ̀ n]

(2)   d → ɾ / vowels (r) _ $\begin{Bmatrix} (\#) \\ | \end{Bmatrix}$ vowels

Examples:

bidding   /b ɪ d # ɪ ŋ / → [b ɪ ɾ # ɪ ŋ]

and

radon   /r é d ɑ̀ n / → [r é ɾ ɑ̀ n]

(3)   n t → ɾ̃ / vowels (r) _ unstressed vowels

Example:

center   /s ɛ n t ɚ / → [s ɛ ɾ̃ ɚ]

(4)   ɾ → ɾ / θ _

Example:

three   /θ r i / → [θ ɾ i]

Notes:

(1) and (2) are common in virtually all dialects, with some minor differences in context. is common in many varieties of General American. (4) is reported to occur sporadically cultured U.S. speech. (Rules 5.1-5.10)

VII. Glottalization of /t /

$$t \rightarrow (t) \; ? \; / \; \left\{ \begin{matrix} \text{vowels} \\ r \\ l \\ n \end{matrix} \right\} \; - \; \left\{ \begin{matrix} \left\{ \begin{matrix} \# \\ | \end{matrix} \right\} \left\{ \begin{matrix} \text{consonants} \\ \text{silence} \end{matrix} \right\} \\ (\#) \; \partial \left\{ \begin{matrix} l \\ n \end{matrix} \right\} \end{matrix} \right\} \quad \begin{matrix}(1 \\ \\ (2\end{matrix}$$

Examples:

bat /b æt / → [b æt ?]

subtle /s ʌ t ə l / → [s ʌ ? l̩]

$$t \rightarrow (t) \; ? \; / \; \_ \; (\#) \left\{ \begin{matrix} l \\ w \\ j \\ m \\ n \end{matrix} \right\} \qquad (3)$$

Examples:

atmosphere /æt mə s f i ɚ r / → [æ? mə s f i ɚ r]

Etna /ɛ t n ə / → [ɛ t ? n ə]

Notes:

(1) and (3) are common everywhere. (2) is common in the N.Y. City area. (Rules 6.1-6.3

VIII. Aspiration of Stops

$$\partial \rightarrow {}^h \; / \; \text{stops} \; \_$$

Examples:

pin /pɪ n / → [pʰɪ n]

nip /nɪ p / → [nɪ pʰ]

bin /bɪ n / → [bʰɪ n]

spin /s pɪ n / → [s pʰɪ n]

Notes:

Normal in all dialects, with some differences in context. Note that prevocalically,even af /s / ,voiceless stops can be aspirated, though to a lesser degree than elsewhere. Voic stops are also often slightly aspirated. (Rules 7.1 and 7.2)

IX. Affication and Plosion of /θ /, /ð /

$$θ \rightarrow t (θ) \; / \; \_$$

$$ð \rightarrow d (ð) \; / \; \_$$

amples:

this thing   /ðɪ s |θɪ ŋ/ → [dɪ s |t θɪ ŋ]

mother   /mʌ ð ɚ/ → [mʌ d ð ɚ]

ɵtes:

More common initially than finally; more common finally than medially.   Much more frequent in rapid, casual, or uncultured speech.   Part of the "Brooklynese" stereotype but does occur elsewhere. (Rules 8.1-8.6)

Palatalization before /ɾ /.

t → č / _ ɾ

d → ǰ / _ ɾ

camples:

tree   /t r i / → [čr i], [t^{š}r i]

droop   /d r u p/ → [ǰ r u p], [d^{ž}r u p]

ɔtes:

Common in many dialects.   For some speakers, the height or frontness of the following vowel may be significant. (Rules 9.1 and 9.2)

I. /ɪ ŋ / Reduction

$$\eta \rightarrow n \ / \ \text{unstressed vowels} \ \_ \left\{ \begin{array}{c} \# \\ | \\ \text{consonants} \end{array} \right\}$$

camples:

going   /g o #ɪ ŋ / → [g o #ɪ n]

Washington   /wɔ š ɪ ŋt ə n/ → [wɔ š ɪ nt ə n]

something   /s ʌ́ mθ ɪ ŋ/ → [s ʌ́ mθ ɪ n]

but not

everything   /ɛ́ v r i θ ɪ̀ ŋ/ → [ɛ́ v r i θ ɪ̀ n]

otes:

Common everwhere in casual and/or rapid and/or vernacular speech.   Common in cultivated speech in the South, New Eng. and rural areas. (Rule 10)

II. Regressive Nasal Assimilation

$$) \quad n \rightarrow m \ / \ \_ \left\{ \begin{array}{c} \text{labials} \\ \text{labiodentals} \end{array} \right\}$$

(2)   n → ɱ / _ labiodentals

(3)   n → ɲ / _ palatals

(4)   n → ŋ / _ velars

(5)   m → ɱ / _ labiodentals

Examples:

input   /ɪ n # p ʊ t / → [ɪ ɱ # p ʊ t]

infer   /ɪ n f ɚ/ → [ɪ ɱf ɚ]

onion   /ʌ n j ə n/ → [ʌ ɲj ə n]

ingrate   /ɪ n g r e t / → [ɪ ŋg r e t]

triumph   /t r a ɪ̯ ə mf / → [t r a ɪ̯ ə ɱf]

Notes:
Common in many dialects, though (1) and (4) and perhaps (3) are more common than (2) and (5). Operates across morpheme and word boundaries. (Rules 11.1-11.5; cf. rule 44.1-44.5)

XIII. Glottal Stop Insertion

$$\varnothing \rightarrow ʔ \; / \; | \; - \begin{Bmatrix} \text{vowels} \\ \text{nasals} \\ \text{liquids} \\ \text{glides} \end{Bmatrix}$$

Notes:
Normal everywhere before vowels, esp. after silence; many idiolects often insert before liquids and glides and some do so before nasals. (Rule 12)

XIV. Unstressed Vowel Reduction

(1)   unstressed vowel → $\begin{Bmatrix} ə \\ ɪ \\ ɨ \end{Bmatrix}$ / _ consonants

(2)   unstressed i → ɛ / $\begin{Bmatrix} \# \\ | \end{Bmatrix}$ _ consonants

)   unstressed ı → $\left\{{ı \atop ı}\right\}$ / $\_$ $\left\{{\# \atop |}\right\}$

)   unstressed u → əw / $\_$ vowels

Examples:

proceed	/prosid/ → [prəsid]
electric	/ilɛktrık/ → [ɛlɛktrık]
candy	/kændi/ → [kændı]
continuum	/kəntınjuəm/ → [kəntınjəwəm]

but not

lithium	/lıθiəm/ → [lıθəəm] or [lıθəm]

Notes:

Unstressed vowel reduction is normal everywhere, esp. in informal and/or rapid speech. Exact products and significant contexts differ widely in dialectal and idiolectal occurrence. (3) is normal in many parts of the South, Southwest, and New Eng. (Rules 13.1-14.17)

V. /r/ Deletion

)   r → ɚ / vowels $\_$ $\left\{{(\#) \text{ consonants} \atop |}\right\}$

2)   r → ɚ / vowels $\_$ (#) vowels

       Condition: preceding vowel more heavily stressed than following vowel.

Examples:

fork	/fɔɚrk/ → [fɔɚk]
far off	/faɚr |ɔf/ → [faɚr |ɔf], [faɚ |ɔf]
Paris	/pærıs/ → [pærıs]

Notes:

(1) is common in many areas of the South, New Eng. and the N.Y. City area when a consonant follows (whether from the same word or a following word). If a vowel follows, (1) is common only in the South. (2) occurs only in some areas of the South, esp. in casual speech. (Rules 15.1-15.3)

XVI. Glide Insertion

$$\text{ə} \rightarrow \text{j} \ / \ \text{non-low front vowels} \ \left\{ \begin{matrix} (\#) \\ | \end{matrix} \right\} \ \_ \ \text{vowels}$$

$$\text{ə} \rightarrow \text{w} \ / \ \text{non-low back vowels} \ \left\{ \begin{matrix} (\#) \\ | \end{matrix} \right\} \ \_ \ \text{vowels}$$

Examples:

eon   /i ɑ n/ → [i j ɑ n]

go on /g o |ɑ n/ → [g o |w ɑ n]

Notes:
Characteristic of slow or emphatic speech; seems to be more common in the Northeast, New Eng. Presumably, the higher and more peripheral the preceding vowel or offglide more likely the insertion. (Rules 16.1 and 16.2)

XVII. Merger of Front Vowels before Nasals

(1)   ɛ → ɪ / _ nasals

(2)   ɪ → ɛ / _ nasals

(3)   ɪ → æ / _ ŋ

Examples:

any   /ɛ n i / → [ɪ n i]

him   /h ɪ m/ → [h ɛ m]

think /θ ɪ ŋ k/ → [θ æ ŋ k]

Notes:
(1) is common in many varieties of General American and in the South and South Mountain region. Tends to be thoroughgoing except when speaker attempts correction. and (3) occur sporadically in the South and Southern Mountain region. (Rules 17.1-17.3

XVIII. Homorganic Stop Insertion and Deletion

$$\text{ə} \rightarrow \text{t} \ / \ \left\{ \begin{matrix} n \\ l \end{matrix} \right\} \ - \ \left\{ \begin{matrix} s \\ š \\ θ \end{matrix} \right\}$$

$$\text{č} \rightarrow \text{š} \ / \ \left\{ \begin{matrix} k \\ p \end{matrix} \right\} \ -$$

Examples:

wealth   /wɛ l θ / → [wɛ l t θ]

sense   /s ɛ n s / → [s ɛ n t s]

else   /ɛ l s / → [ɛ l t s]

capture   /k æ p č ɚ/ → [k æ p š ɚ]

Notes:
There are several other similar rules. Contexts are dialectally significant. (Rules 18.1-18.8)

XIX. Velar Palatalization

$$\varnothing \to j \; / \; \begin{Bmatrix} g \\ k \end{Bmatrix} \_ \; a_{\chi} r$$

Examples:

garden   /g a_{\chi} r d ə n/ → [g j a_{\chi} d ə n]

car   /k a_{\chi} r / → [k j a_{\chi} r]

Notes:
Occurs in old-fashioned speech here and there in Va. and S.C. (Rule 19)

XX. Palatalization of /l /

$$l \to \begin{Bmatrix} \varnothing \\ j \end{Bmatrix} \; / \; \text{vowels} \_ \begin{Bmatrix} (\#) \\ | \end{Bmatrix} j$$

Examples:

million   /mɪ l j ə n/ → [mɪ j ə n]

will ya   /wɪ l |j ə/ → [wɪ j |j ə]

Notes:
Common in N.J. and some dialects of General American. (Rule 20)

XXI. Unstressed /ɪ / Raising

$$\text{unstressed } ɪ \to i \; / \; \_ \begin{Bmatrix} v \\ \eta \\ k \\ \text{palatals} \end{Bmatrix}$$

Examples:

raking   /r e k #ɪ ŋ/ → [r e k #i ŋ]

vanish   /v æ n ɪ š / → [v æ n i š]

Notes:
Common in some varieties of General American and in the Southwest. (Rule 21)

XXII. Fronting of / o /

$$o \rightarrow \left\{ \begin{matrix} \varepsilon \, \mathrm{y} \\ 3 \, \varrho \end{matrix} \right\} / \, \_\_$$

Example:

go   / g o / → [g ε ɰ]

Notes:
Common in Philadelphia and Pittsburgh, parts of Ohio and N.C. Does not operate befc
/ l /   in some dialects. (Rule 22)

XXIII. [ɚ]   *Insertion*

$$ \vartheta \rightarrow ɚ / \, ɔ \, \_\_$$

Example:

saw   / s ɔ / → [s ɔ ɚ]

Notes:
Common in many dialects, esp. those that drop / r / . (Rule 23.1)

XXIV. / ɑ /   *Shift Before* / r /

$$\alpha \rightarrow \left\{ \begin{matrix} \mathrm{D} \\ \mathrm{a} \end{matrix} \right\} / \, \_\_ \, (ɚ) \, r$$

Example:

card   / k ɑ ɚ r d / → (1) [k ɒ ɚ r d] , (2) [k a ɚ r d]

Notes:
The vowel in (1) is characteristic of the N.Y. City area; the vowel in (2) is normal in r
areas of New Eng. Both are more common with the / r /   deleted. (Rule 23.3)

XXV. / l /   *Deletion*

$$ l \rightarrow \left\{ \begin{matrix} \emptyset \\ ɚ \end{matrix} \right\} / \, \mathrm{vowels} \, \_\_ \, \left\{ \begin{matrix} (\#) \ \ \mathrm{consonants} \\ | \end{matrix} \right\} $$

Examples:

fall   / f ɔ l / → [f ɔ ɚ]

feels   / f i l #z / → [f i ɚ #z]

already   / ɔ l r ε d i / → [ɔ r ε d i]

tes:

Very common before /r/ and /w/ . The offglide is often unrounded even after rounded vowels. Common in Pa. and some varieties of General American. (Rule 24)

XVI. Front Vowel Merger Before Palatals and /š/

)   ɪ → i / _ š

)   i → ɪ / _ g

)   ɛ → e / _ $\left\{ \begin{matrix} g \left\{ \begin{matrix} \# \\ | \end{matrix} \right\} \\ ž ə \end{matrix} \right\}$

xamples:

fish   /fɪš/ → [fiš]

league   /lig/ → [lɪg]

leg   /lɛg/ → [leg]

otes:

(1) is reported from Mo. and elsewhere in the central states. (2) occurs in the South, Southern Mountains, and some varieties of General American. (3) is common in the South, South Midland, and E. New Eng., and occasional in N.Y. and Pa. (Rules 25.1-25.3)

XVII. /t, d/ Deletion in Consonant Clusters

$$\left\{ \begin{matrix} t \\ d \end{matrix} \right\} \rightarrow \emptyset \text{ / obstruents (\#) } \_ \left\{ \begin{matrix} (\#) \\ | \end{matrix} \right\} \left\{ \begin{matrix} \text{obstruents} \\ \text{nasals} \\ \text{silence} \end{matrix} \right\}$$

xamples:

soft   /sɔft/   [sɔf]

softness /sɔft#nɛs/   [sɔf#nɛs]

bandsaw   /bænd#sɔ/   [bæn#sɔ]

Notes: Common everywhere, with contextual differences. (Rules 26.1-26.4)

XVIII. Voicing of /h/

$$h \rightarrow ɦ \text{ / voiced sounds } \left\{ \begin{matrix} (\#) \\ | \end{matrix} \right\} \_ \text{ vowels}$$

Examples:

ahead   /ə h ɛ d / → [ə ɦ ɛ d]

full house   /f ʊ l │h a ɰ s / → [f ʊ l │ɦ a ɰ s]

Notes:

Common; probably an idiolectal matter. (Rule 27)

XXIX. Palatalization of Alveolar Stops

$$ t \begin{Bmatrix} (\#) \\ | \end{Bmatrix} j \rightarrow \check{c} \ / \ \_ $$

$$ d \begin{Bmatrix} (\#) \\ | \end{Bmatrix} j \rightarrow \check{j} \ / \ \_ $$

Examples:

nodule   /n a d j u l / → [n a ǰ u l]

get ya   /g ɛ t │j ə / → [g ɛ │č ə]

Notes:

Common everywhere in casual and/or rapid speech. (Rules 28.1-28.8)

XXX. Phonetic Realizations of / j u /

$$ (1) \quad j u \rightarrow \begin{Bmatrix} u \\ ɪ ɰ \end{Bmatrix} \ / \ \begin{Bmatrix} \# \\ | \\ consonants \end{Bmatrix} \begin{Bmatrix} dentals \\ alveolars \end{Bmatrix} \_ $$

$$ (2) \quad ɪ ɰ \rightarrow u \ / \ \begin{Bmatrix} r \\ palatals \end{Bmatrix} \_ $$

$$ (3) \quad \begin{Bmatrix} u (ə) r \\ ʊ (ə) r \end{Bmatrix} \rightarrow ɝ \ / \ palatals \_ $$

Examples:

new   /n j u / → [n u] , [n ɪ ɰ]

enthusiasm   /ɛ n θ j u z i æ z ə m/ → [ɛ n θ u z i æz ə m] , [ɛ n θ ɪ ɰ z i æz ə m]

rude   /r ɪ ɰ d / → [r u d]

sure   /š u ə r / → [š ɝ]

uranium   /j ʊ r e n i ə m/ → [j ɝ e n i ə m]

Notes:

Loss of /j/ in (1) is normal in many dialects for at least some subset of the context given. (2) is absolute except for a few scattered dialects in the East and South. [ɪ ʊ] (and similar phonetic realizations) has at least three sources: /j u/ , /ʲɪ ʊ/, and /u/. The last of these, e.g., is well-known from the Southern Mountain area. (3) seems to be common in many dialect areas. (Rules 29.1-29.4; cf. rule 30.4)

XI. Phonetic Realization of Tense Vowels

$$ e \rightarrow \left\{ \begin{matrix} \varepsilon \, \iota \\ æ \, ę \end{matrix} \right\} / \_ \qquad\qquad i \rightarrow \left\{ \begin{matrix} \mathrm{I} \, \iota \\ \dot{\iota} \, \iota \end{matrix} \right\} / \_ $$

$$ o \rightarrow \left\{ \begin{matrix} o \, ʊ \\ ɔ \, ǫ \\ ʌ \, ʊ \end{matrix} \right\} / \_ \qquad\qquad u \rightarrow \left\{ \begin{matrix} ʊ \, ʊ \\ ʉ \\ \mathrm{I} \, ʊ \end{matrix} \right\} / \_ $$

Notes:

Many different phonetic realizations in different dialects for all these. Contexts strongly affect amount of diphthongization. For example, [ʉ] or [ʉʉ] for /u/ occurs in the South and South Midland, the Pittsburgh area and sporadically in N.J., and is apparently more common after palatals and less common before /l/ . (Rules 30.1-30.4)

XII. Sibilant Assimilation

$$ s \rightarrow š / \_ \left\{ \begin{matrix} (\#) \\ | \end{matrix} \right\} \text{palatals} $$

$$ z \rightarrow ž / \_ \left\{ \begin{matrix} (\#) \\ | \end{matrix} \right\} \text{palatals} $$

$$ š \rightarrow s / \_ \left\{ \begin{matrix} (\#) \\ | \end{matrix} \right\} \left\{ \begin{matrix} s \\ z \end{matrix} \right\} $$

$$ ž \rightarrow z / \_ \left\{ \begin{matrix} (\#) \\ | \end{matrix} \right\} \left\{ \begin{matrix} s \\ z \end{matrix} \right\} $$

Examples:

fish sandwich   /f ɪ š |s æn d wɪ č/ → [f ɪ s |s æn d wɪ č]

gas shortage   /g æs |š ɔ ṛ t ɪ ʃ/ → [g æš |š ɔ ṛ t ɪ ʃ]

pasture   /p æs č ɚ/ → [p æš č ɚ]

Notes:

Palatalization of /s/ and /z/ seems to be fairly common, at least in rapid and/or casual speech. The modification of /š/ and /ž/ is much less common. (Rules 31.1-31.6)

XIII. Degemination

$$ \text{consonant}_i \rightarrow ø / \_ \left\{ \begin{matrix} (\#) \\ | \end{matrix} \right\} \text{consonant}_i $$

$$ \text{palatal offglide} \rightarrow ø / \_ \left\{ \begin{matrix} \# \\ | \end{matrix} \right\} j $$

rounded offglide → ɒ / _ { # | } w

Examples:

would do   /wu d |d u / → [wʊ |d u]

I yield   /aʟ |j i l d / → [a |j i l d]

now wait   /n a ʏ |we t / → [n a |we t]

Notes:
Common in all but the slowest, most careful speech. (Rules 32.1-32.29)

XXXIV. Desyllabification of High Vowels

unstressed { i | ɪ } → j / { obstruents | nasals | liquids } _ (#) unstressed vowe

unstressed { u | ʊ } → w / palatals _ (#) unstressed vowels

Examples:

germanium   /ǰ ɚ me n i ə m/ → [ǰ ɚ me n j ə m]

casual   /k æ ž u ə l / → [k æ ž wə l]

Notes:
Common, esp. in rapid speech. (Rules 33.1-33.4)

XXXV. Progressive Syllabic-Nasal Assimilation

(1)   ṇ → ŋ̩ / velars _

(2)   ṇ → m̩ / { labials | labiodentals } _

(3)   ṇ → m̩ / labiodentals _

Examples:

bacon   /b e k ə n/ → [b e k ŋ̩]

happen   /h æ p ə n/ → [h æ p m̩]

often   /ɔ f ə n/ → [ɔ f ɱ̩]

(2) seems to be more common than (1), which is much more common than (3). (1) is characteristic of Southern and Southern Mountain speech. All these rules are more common when the point of articulation of the following consonant is appropriate—e.g., as in beck'n'call [b ɛ k | ŋ | k ɔ l]   . (Rules 34.1-34.3; cf. rule 40)

XVI. Obstruent Voicing Assimilation

$$\text{obstruent} \rightarrow \alpha \text{ voice} / \underline{\quad} \begin{Bmatrix} (\#) \\ | \end{Bmatrix} \alpha \text{ voiced obstruent}$$

$$\text{obstruent} \rightarrow \alpha \text{ voice} / \alpha \text{ voiced obstruent} \begin{Bmatrix} (\#) \\ | \end{Bmatrix} \underline{\quad}$$

Example:

obstacle /ɑ b s t ə k ə l / → [ɑ p s t ə k ə l] , [ɑ b z t ə k ə l]

Notes:
Some combinations favor assimilation more strongly than others. Probably an idiolectal matter. (Rules 35.1-35.15)

XVII. Vowel Mergers before Prevocalic /ɾ /

$$\begin{Bmatrix} e \\ æ \end{Bmatrix} \rightarrow \begin{Bmatrix} \varepsilon \\ \varepsilon ɹ \\ ɚ \end{Bmatrix} / \underline{\quad} ɾ \text{ vowels}$$

$$i \rightarrow ɪ / \underline{\quad} ɾ \text{ vowels}$$

Examples:

fairy   /f e r i / → [f ɛ ɹ r i]

carrot   /k æ r ə t / → [k ɛ r ə t]

mysterious /mɪ s t i r i ə s / → [mɪ s t ɪ r i ə s]

Notes:
There are many similar rules. Most are fairly restricted dialectally, though (2), e.g., is normal for most dialects. (Rules 36.1-36.10)

XVIII. Vowel Mergers before Non-Prevocalic /ɾ /

$$\varepsilon \rightarrow \begin{Bmatrix} æ \\ e \\ i \\ ɪ \end{Bmatrix} / \underline{\quad} (\#) ɹ \ ɾ \begin{Bmatrix} \text{consonants} \\ \# \\ | \end{Bmatrix}$$

$$ɝ \rightarrow \begin{Bmatrix} ʌ r \\ ɝ \\ ʌ \end{Bmatrix} / \underline{\quad} \begin{Bmatrix} \# \text{ consonants} \\ | \end{Bmatrix}$$

$$ɝ \rightarrow \begin{Bmatrix} ɝ ɫ \\ ɝ \\ ʌ \end{Bmatrix} / \underline{\quad} \text{consonants}$$

Examples:

fair   /f ɛ ɚ r / → [f ɪ ɚ r]

stir   /s t ɚ/ → [s t ʌ r]

sturdy   /s t ɚd i / → [s t ɜ̧ d i]

but not

stir   /s t ɚ/ → [s t ɛ ̧]

or sturdy   /s t ɚd i / → [s t ʌ r d i]

Notes:
    There are many similar rules. Most are dialect-specific. (Rules 37.1-37.11)

XXXIX. Vowel Mergers before /l /

(1)   i → ɪ / _ l

(2)   ɪ → i / _ l

(3)   ʊ → u / _ l

Examples:

feel   /f i l / → [f ɪ l]

fill   /f ɪ l / → [f i l]

pull   /p ʊ l / → [p u l]

Notes:
    (1) is common in the South and probably in rapid speech elsewhere. (2) and (3) occ
the Southwest, (3) apparently more commonly. (Rules 38.1-38.3)

XL. Offglide Insertion and Deletion before /l /

(1)   ɒ → ɚ / certain vowels _ l

(2)   ɚ → ɒ / certain vowels _ l

xamples:

joule   /ʃ u l / → [ʃ u ɹ l]

jewel   /ʃ u ɹ l / → [ʃ u l]

otes:
(1) is normal for many dialects of General American. (2) is common though stigmatized in some areas. (Rules 38.4-38.5)

LI. / g /   Insertion

$$ ɑ̆ → g \ / \ ŋ \left\{ \begin{matrix} (\#) \\ | \end{matrix} \right\} \_ \ \text{vowels} $$

xamples:

Long Island   /l ɔ ŋ |a ɹ l ə n d / → [l ɔ ŋ |g a ɹ l ə n d]

gingham   /g ɪ ŋ ə m/ → [g ɪ ŋ g ə m]

otes:
Quite common in the Northeast though stigmatized everywhere. (Rule 39)

LII. / ə /   Deletion

unstressed ə → ⊘ / consonants _ consonants (#) vowels

xamples:

(1) toddling   /t ɑ d ə l #ɪ ŋ/ → [t ɑ d l #ɪ ŋ]

(2) samarium   /s ə m æ r i ə m/ → [s m æ r i ə m]

(3) severe   /s ə v i ɹ r/ → [s v i ɹ r]

(4) maniacal   /m ə n a ɹ ə k ə l / → [m n a ɹ ə k ə l]

(5) methodical   /m ə θ ɑ d ɪ k ə l / → [m θ ɑ d ɪ k ə l]

Notes:
We do not understand the context of this rule at all. Obviously however, examples similar to (1) are quite normal; (2), (3) and (4), each less acceptable than its predecessor, do seem possible in rapid speech. We feel that (5) is totally unacceptable. (Rule 41)

XLIII. Phonetic Adjustment of Broad a̲

a → ɑ / _ consonants

Example:

dance   /d a n s / → [d ɑ n s]

Notes:

Merger with   / ɑ / occurs in some New Eng. dialects. (Rule 42)

XLIV. Deletion of /h/ *before Semivowels*

$$h \rightarrow \eth \; / \; \_ \left\{ {w \atop j} \right\}$$

Examples:

(1) <u>when</u>   /h wɛ n/   →   [wɛ n]

(2) <u>huge</u>   /h j u ʃ/   →   [j u ʃ]

Notes: (1) is normal in many dialects. (2) is common in the East and South though stigmatiz
some areas. (Rules 43.1-43.4)

Several rules have been developed through association with and from the writings of W. La
Rule X and details of rules VIII, XIII, and XXVIII were suggested to us by N. R. Dixon and (
Tappert. Some details of rule VII were suggested by G. Kuhn. Rule XXXII is an expansion
rule given in a SUR Note by K. C. Hill and M. H. O'Malley. D. Croux made valuable sugges
about the content of rule XXXVI.

APPENDIX 2. Translation Table for Machine-Readable Phonological Representations

X is a "null character," thus:

PX = **p**	DX = **d**	SX = **s**	NX = **n**
TX = **t**	GX = **g**	ZX = **z**	RX = **r**
KX = **k**	FX = **f**	HX = **h**	LX = **l**
BX = **b**	VX = **v**	MX = **m**	JX = **j** (as in "**y**ap")

WX = **w**

?X = **ʔ** (glottal stop)
QX = **ʰ** (stop aspiration/burst)
XX = silence

TH = **θ**	CH = **č**	N$ = **r̃** (nasalized apical flap;
DH = **ð**	JH = **ǰ**	i.e., flapped [**n**])
SH = **š**	NJ = **ɲ** (palatal nasal)	L$ = **ɾˡ** (i.e., flapped [**l**])
ZH = **ž**	MF = **m̩** (labiodental nasal)	Hə = **ɦ** (voiced **h**)
NG = **ŋ**	R$ = **ɾ** (apical flap)	Wə = **w̥** or **ʍ** (voiceless **w**)
		Jə = **j̥** or **ç** (i.e., voiceless **j̲**)

EE = **i**
IX = **ɪ**
EI = **e**
EH = **ɛ**
AE = **æ**
AX = **a** (New England "broad **a̲**")
AA = **ɑ**
AH = **ɒ** (rounded and/or backed [**ɑ**])
AW = **ɔ**
UH = **ʌ** (when stressed), **ə** (when unstressed)
OX = **o̞ʌ** (i.e., New England "short **o̲**")
OU = **o**
UX = **ʊ**
UU = **u̩**
OE = **ɜ**
ER = **ɝ** (when stressed), **ɚ** (when unstressed)

C, when appended to a vowel, indicates centralization, thus:
IXC = **ɨ**
UUC = **ʉ**
UXC = **ʉ̈**

G, when appended, = offglide, thus:
EEG = **i̯**
UHG = **ə̯**
EHG = **ɛ̯**
IXCG = **ɨ̯**
      etc.

'X =   (i.e., syllabicity of following segment)
= major morpheme boundary
| = word boundary
0 [i.e., zero] = unstressedness
1 = primary stress
2 = secondary or lower (but not 0) stress
(Vowels unmarked for stress are to be operated on with no reference to c
change in their stress)

-> = "may be rewritten as"
/ = "in the environment"
_ = place-holder for what is to be rewritten
( ) = surrounding element(s) which may be omitted
<> = surrounding set of elements of which one must be selected (="{}")
, = separator (i.e., for "ors")
* = indicates that statistics are to be gathered separately
NULL = "null" (i.e., delete what appears to the left of the arrow, or
        insert what appears to the right)

It will be noted that the level of phonetic detail being attended to is fairly broad, and, to s
degree, arbitrary; furthermore, for the present, such things as length and vowel nasalization I
been disregarded, for purposes of simplification.

Appendix 3. Syntax of the Phonological Rules

<PHONOLOGICAL RULE> ::= <RULE ID> <LEFT-HAND SIDE> '→' <RIGHT-HAND SIDE> '/'
      <LEFT-HAND CONTEXT> '_' <RIGHT-HAND CONTEXT> ';';
<RULE ID> ::= '"' string of any characters but '"' followed by '"';
<LEFT-HAND SIDE> ::= string of <PHONEME>'s;
<RIGHT-HAND SIDE> ::= <PHONEME> | '*' followed by a list of <PHONEME>'s
      separated by commas enlcosed in angle brackets;
<LEFT-HAND CONTEXT> ::= <CONTEXT> | empty;
<RIGHT-HAND CONTEXT> ::= <CONTEXT> | empty;
<CONTEXT> ::= list of <CONTEXT ELEMENT>'s;
<CONTEXT ELEMENT> ::= <PHONEME> | <CLASS NAME> | possibly one '*' followed by
      a list of
      <CONTEXT>'s separated by commas enclosed in angle brackets |
      possibly one '*' followed by a <CONTEXT> enclosed in
      parentheses;
<PHONEME> ::= 'NULL' | 'AA' | 'AH' | etc.;
<CLASS NAME> ::= 'VOWELS' | 'CONSONANTS' | etc.;

Appendix 4. Phonological Classes Used in the Rules

```
LIQGLIDES   →  < LX, RX, WX, JX, L$, LL, LL$ >;
NASALS      →  < MX, MF, NX, NJ, NG, N$ >;
STOPS       →  < PX, TX, CH, KX, BX, DX, JH, GX >;
FRICATIVES  →  < FX, TH, SX, SH, VX, DH, ZX, ZH >;
VOWELS0     →  < EE0, IX0, IXC0, EI0, EH0, AE0, AX0, AA0, AH0, AW0,
                 OU0, OX0, UX0, UXC0, UU0, UUC0, ER0, UH0, OE0 >;
VOWELS1     →  < EE1, IX1, IXC1, EI1, EH1, AE1, AX1, AA1, AH1, AW1,
                 OU1, OX1, UX1, UXC1, UU1, UUC1, ER1, UH1, OE1 >;
VOWELS2     →  < EE2, IX2, IXC2, EI2, EH2, AE2, AX2, AA2, AH2, AW2,
                 OU2, OX2, UX2, UXC2, UU2, UUC2, ER2, UH2, OE2 >;
VOWELS01    →  < VOWELS0, VOWELS1 >;
VOWELS02    →  < VOWELS0, VOWELS2 >;
VOWELS12    →  < VOWELS1, VOWELS2 >;
VOWELS      →  < VOWELS0, VOWELS1, VOWELS2 >;
OFFGLIDES   →  < EEG, IXG, IXCG, EIG, EHG, AWG, OUG, UXG, UXCG, UUG, UUCG, UHG >;
CONSONANTS  →  < LIQGLIDES, NASALS, FRICATIVES, STOPS, R$, HX, H@, W@, J@, QX >;
FRONTVOWELS →  < EE, IX, IXC, EI, EH, AE >;
NONFRONTVOWELS →  < AX, AA, AH, AW, OU, OX, UX, UXC, UU, UUC, ER, UH, OE >;
VOICEDSOUNDS →  < VOWELS, OFFGLIDES, LIQGLIDES, NASALS, BX, DX, GX, JH, VX, DH, ZX, ZH >;
```

Appendix 5. Phonological Rules in Machine-Readable Form

```
"1.1"   AE1 → *<EH1,EH1 UHG,EE1 UHG> / _ *<<MX,NX>,NG,<FX,TH,SX,SH>,
        <VX,DH,ZH>,ZX,<DX,BX,GX,JH>,<PX,TX,KX,CH>> *<<STOPS,FRICATIVES,
        NASALS,#,I>,LIQGLIDES,VOWELS>;
"1.2"   AE2 → *<EH2,EH2 UHG,EE2 UHG> / _ *<<MX,NX>,NG,<FX,TH,SX,SH>,
        <VX,DH,ZH>,ZX,<DX,BX,GX,JH>,<PX,TX,KX,CH>> *<<STOPS,FRICATIVES,
        NASALS,#,I>,LIQGLIDES,VOWELS>;
"1.3"   NULL → *<IXG,IXCG,EIG,EHG> / AE _ *<<MX,NX><STOPS,FRICATIVES,NASALS>,
        <FX,GX,SX,TH,DH><STOPS,FRICATIVES,NASALS,#I>,<NG,SH,ZH,JH>,KX>;
"2.1"   AX → <AA,AE,AH,UH> / _ IXG *(<PX,TX,KX,CH,FX,TH,SX,SH>);
"2.2"   AX → <AA,AE,UH> / _ UXG *(<PX,TX,KX,CH,FX,TH,SX,SH>);
"2.3"   AW → *<OU,UX,UU> / _ IXG;
"2.4"   IXG → *<IXCG,EEG,EIG,EHG,UHG,NULL> / *<AX,AA,AE> _
        *(<PX,TX,KX,CH,FX,TH,SX,SH>);
"2.5"   IXG → *<IXCG,EEG> / AH _ *(<PX,TX,KX,CH,FX,TH,SX,SH>);
"2.6"   IXG → EEG / UH _ *(<PX,TX,KX,CH,FX,TH,SX,SH>);
"2.7"   UXG → *<UXCG,UUG,UUCG,OUG,AWG,UHG,NULL> / *<AX,AA,AE> _
        *(*<<PX,TX,KX,CH,FX,TH,SX,SH>,<NASALS>>);
"2.8"   UXG → UUG / UH _ *(*<<PX,TX,KX,CH,FX,TH,SX,SH>,<NASALS>>);
"2.9"   IXG → *<IXCG,EEG,EIG,EHG,UHG,NULL> / AW _ *(<PX,TX,KX,CH,FX,TH,SX,SH>);
"2.10"  IXG → *<IXCG,EEG,EIG,EGH,UGH> / OU _ *(<PX,TX,KX,CH,FX,TH,SX,SH>);
"2.11"  IXG → *<EEG,IXCG> / *<UX,UU> _ *(<PX,TX,KX,CH,FX,TH,SX,SH>);
"3.1"   AA → <AW,AH> / _ *(*(<GH,NG,FX,TH,LX>) <#,I,CONSONANTS>);
"3.2"   AW → *<AA,AH,AH AWG> / _ <#,I,CONSONANTS>;
"4.1"   NULL → RX / <AW,AH,AA,UHO,UHG> _ *<#,I> VOWELS;
"4.2"   UHO → ERO / _ *<#,I> VOWELS;
"4.3"   UUO → ERO / _ *<#,I> VOWELS;
"4.4"   OUO → ERO / _ *<#,I> VOWELS;
"4.5"   NULL → *<UHG RX,RX> / WX <AH,AW,AH AWG> _ SH;
"4.6"   NULL → UHG RX / <AW,AH,AA> _ *<#,I> VOWELS;
"5.1"   TX → R$ / <RX,VOWELS,OFFGLIDES> _ *<(#) VOWELS0,I VOWELS>;
"5.2"   DX → R$ / <RX,VOWELS,OFFGLIDES> _ *<(#)*<VOWELS1,VOWELS02>,I VOWELS>;
"5.3"   NX → N$ / <RX,VOWELS,OFFGLIDES> _ *<(#) VOWELS0,(#) VOWELS12>;
"5.4"   NX TX → N$ / <RX,VOWELS,OFFGLIDES> _ VOWELS0;
"5.5"   RX ↔ R$ / TH _;
"5.6"   DX → R$ / VOWELS0 (OFFGLIDES) *<#,I> _ VOWELS;
"5.7"   DH → R$ / VOWELS0 (OFFGLIDES) *<#,I> _ VOWELS;
"5.8"   LX → L$ / <RX,VOWELS,OFFGLIDES> _ *<(#) VOWELS0,(#) VOWELS12>;
"5.9"   NX I DH → I N$ / _;
"5.10"  NX DX I DH → I N$ / _;
"6.1"   TX → *<?X,TX ?X> / <VOWELS,OFFGLIDES,RX,LX,NX> _ <*,I> <CONSONANTS,XX>;
"6.2"   TX → *<?X,TX ?X> / *<<VOWELS,OFFGLIDES>,RX,LX,NX> _ (#) UHO *<LX,NX>;
"6.3"   TX → *<?X,TX ?X> / _ *(#) *<LX,WX,JX,MX,NX>;
"7.1"   NULL → QX / *<*(<FRICATIVES,PX,KX>) <PX,(#) TX,KX>,<BX,(#) BX,GX>> _
        I *(VOWELS);
"7.2"   NULL → QX / *<<PX,TX,KX>,<BX,DX,GX>> _ *(#) *(LIQGLIDES)
        *<VOWELS12.VOWELS0>;
"8.1"   TH → *<TX,TX TH> / <#,I> _;
"8.2"   TH → *<TX,TX TH> / _ <#,I>;
"8.3"   TH → *<TX,TX TH> / _;
"8.4"   DH → *<DX,DX DH> / <#,I> _;
"8.5"   DH → *<DX,DX DH> / _ <#,I>;
"8.6"   DH → *<DX,DX DH> / _;
"9.1"   TX → CH / _ RX *<NONFRONTVOWELS,FRONTVOWELS>;
```

```
"9.2"    DX → JH / _ RX *<NONFRONTVOWELS,FRONTVOWELS>;
"10"     NG → NX / <VOWELS0,'X> _ *<<#,I>,CONSONANTS>;
"11.1"   NX → MX / _ *((#)#) *<<PX,BX,MX><FX,VX>>;
"11.2"   NX → MF / _ *((#)#) <FX,VX>;
"11.3"   NX → NJ / _ *((#)#) *<<SH,ZH,JH,CH,JX>,RX>;
"11.4"   NX → NG / _ *((#)#) <GX,KX>;
"11.5"   MX → MF / _ *((#)#) <FX,VX>;
"12"     NULL → ?X / *<XX,VOWELS,CONSONANTS,OFFGLIDES> I _
                *<VOWELS,NASALS,LIQGLIDES>;
"13.1"   EE0 → *<IX0,UH0,IXC0> / _ CONSONANTS;
"13.2"   EI0 → *<IX0,UH0,IXC0> / _ CONSONANTS;
"13.3"   EH0 → *<IX0,UH0,IXC0> / _ CONSONANTS;
"13.4"   UU0 → *<UX0,UH0,IXC0> / _ *<<#,I>,CONSONANTS>;
"13.5"   OU0 → *<UX0,UH0,IXC0> / _ *<<#,I>,CONSONANTS>;
"13.6"   AE0 → *<UH0,IXC0F / _ CONSONANTS;
"13.7"   AA0 → *<UH0,IXC0F / _ CONSONANTS;
"13.8"   AW0 → *<UH0,IXC0F / _ CONSONANTS;
"13.9"   UX0 → *<UH0,IXC0F / _ CONSONANTS;
"13.10"  UH0 → *<IX0,IXC0> / _ *(*<#,I>)
                *<<TX,DX,NX,SX,ZX>,<SH,ZH,CH,JH>,<KX,GX,NG>>;
"13.11"  ER0 → *<IX0,IXC0> / _ *(*<#,I>)
                *<<TX,DX,NX,SX,ZX>,<SH,ZH,CH,JH>,<KX,GX,NG>>;
"13.12"  EE0 → EH0 / <#,I> _ CONSONANTS;
"13.13"  EE0 → UH0 / _ CONSONANTS;
"13.14"  UU0 → UH0 WX / _ VOWELS;
"13.15"  IX0 → *<IXC0,UH0> / _ CONSONANTS;
"13.16"  EE0 → *<IX0,IXC0> / _ <#,I>;
"14.1"   EE0 → 'X / *(CONSONANTS (#)) _ *<LX,MX,NX,NG>;
"14.2"   IX0 → 'X / *(CONSONANTS (#)) _ *<LX,MX,NX,NG>;
"14.3"   IXC0 → 'X / *(CONSONANTS (#)) _ *<LX,MX,NX,NG>;
"14.4"   EI0 → 'X / *(CONSONANTS (#)) _ *<LX,MX,NX,NG>;
"14.5"   EH0 → 'X / *(CONSONANTS (#)) _ *<LX,MX,NX,NG>;
"14.6"   AE0 → 'X / *(CONSONANTS (#)) _ *<LX,MX,NX,NG>;
"14.7"   AX0 → 'X / *(CONSONANTS (#)) _ *<LX,MX,NX,NG>;
"14.8"   AA0 → 'X / *(CONSONANTS (#)) _ *<LX,MX,NX,NG>;
"14.9"   AH0 → 'X / *(CONSONANTS (#)) _ *<LX,MX,NX,NG>;
"14.10"  AW0 → 'X / *(CONSONANTS (#)) _ *<LX,MX,NX,NG>;
"14.11"  OU0 → 'X / *(CONSONANTS (#)) _ *<LX,MX,NX,NG>;
"14.12"  UX0 → 'X / *(CONSONANTS (#)) _ *<LX,MX,NX,NG>;
"14.13"  UXC0 → 'X / *(CONSONANTS (#)) _ *<LX,MX,NX,NG>;
"14.14"  UU0 → 'X / *(CONSONANTS (#)) _ *<LX,MX,NX,NG>;
"14.15"  UUC0 → 'X / *(CONSONANTS (#)) _ *<LX,MX,NX,NG>;
"14.16"  ER0 → 'X / *(CONSONANTS (#)) _ *<LX,MX,NX,NG>;
"14.17"  UH0 → 'X / *(CONSONANTS (#)) _ *<LX,MX,NX,NG>;
"15.1"   RX → NULL / *<UH,OU,AW,<AX,AA,AH>> *(UHG) _ <XX,# CONSONANTS>;
"15.2"   RX → NULL / VOWELS12 (OFFGLIDES) _ VOWELS02;
"15.3"   ER0 → UH0 / _ *<(<#,I>) <CONSONANTS,XX>,I VOWELS,*<#,I> RX>;
"16.1"   NULL → JX / *<EEG,IXG,IXCG,EIG,EHG,EE,IX,IXC,EI> *(*<#,I>)
                _ VOWELS;
"16.2"   NULL → WX / *<UUG,UCG,UXG,UXCG,OUG,AWG,UU,UUC,UX,UXC,OU>
                *(*<#,I>) _ VOWELS;
"17.1"   EH → IX / _ *<NX,MX,NG>;
"17.2"   IX1 → EH1 / _ *<NX,MX,NG>;
"17.3"   IX2 → EH2 / _ *<NX,MX,NG>;
"17.4"   IX1 → AE1 / _ NG;
```

```
"17.5"   IX2 → AE2 / _ NG;
"18.1"   NULL → TX / *<NX,LX> _ *(#) *<SX,TH>;
"18.2"   SH → CH / *<NX,NJ,LX,NG KX> _;
"18.3"   NULL → PX / MX _ *(#) <TX,KX,FX,TH,SX,SH,CH>;
"18.4"   PX → NULL / MX _ *(#) <TX,KX,FX,TH,SX,SH,CH>;
"18.5"   NULL → KX / NG _ <SX,SH,TH>;
"18.6"   KX → NULL / NG _ *(#) <SX,SH>;
"18.7"   CH → SH / *<*(NG)KX,PX> _;
"18.8"   JH → ZH / *<NX,NJ,LX> _;
"19"     NULL → JX / *<GX,KX> AA UHG RX;
"20"     LX → *<NULL,JX> / <OFFGLIDES,VOWELS> _ *(<#,|>) JX *<VOWELS0,
         VOWELS12>;
"21"     IX0 → EE0 / _ *<VX,NG,KX,<SH,CH,JH>>;
"22"     OU → *<EH UUG,EH UXG,EH OUG,OE UUG,OE UXG,OE OUG> / _ *(LX);
"23.1"   AW → AW UHG / _ *<XX,*(<#,|>) CONSONANTS,| VOWELS>;
"23.2"   UHG → NULL / <OFFGLIDES,VOWELS> _ *<XX,(<#,|>) CONSONANTS,| VOWELS>;
"23.3"   AA UHG → *<AA,AH,AX> / _;
"24"     LX → *<NULL,OUG> / <VOWELS,OFFGLIDES> _
         *<XX,*(*<#,|>) *<*<RX,WX>,<NASALS,FRICATIVES,STOPS>>,| VOWELS>;
"25.1"   IX → EE / _ SH;
"25.2"   EE → IX / _ GX;
"25.3"   EH → *<EI,EI EEG,EI IXG,EI IXCG,EH IXG,EH IXCG,EH EEG> / _
         *<<GX <#,|,XX>>,<ZH <VOWELS0 RX,ER0>>>;
"26.1"   TX → NULL / <STOPS,FRICATIVES>,LX> *(#) _
         *(<#,|>) *<STOPS,FRICATIVES,NASALS,XX>;
"26.2"   TX → NULL / <STOPS,FRICATIVES>*(#) _ *(<#,|>) LX;
"26.3"   DX → NULL / *<<STOPS,FRICATIVES,NX>,LX> *(#) _
         *(<#,|>) *<STOPS,FRICATIVES,NASALS,XX>;
"26.4"   DX → NULL / <STOPS,FRICATIVES,NX> *(#) _ *(<#,|>) LX;
"27"     HX → H@ / VOICEDSOUNDS (<#,|>) _ VOWELS;
"28.1"   JX → JH / DX | _;
"28.2"   DX | JX → | JH / _;
"28.3"   DX # JX → # JH / _;
"28.4"   DX JX → JH / _;
"28.5"   JX → CH / TX | _;
"28.6"   TX | JX → | CH / _;
"28.7"   TX # JX → # CH / _;
"28.8"   TX JX → CH / _;
"29.1"   JX UU → *<IXC UXCG,UUC,UXC UUCG,UU,IX UUG,IXC UUG,UX UUG> /
         *<CONSONANTS,<#|,>,<VOWELS,OFFGLIDES>>
         *<RX,LX,SH,ZH,NX,TX (QX),DX (QX),TH,SX,ZX,CH,JH,HX> _;
"29.2"   IX UUG → *<IXWC UXCG,UUC,UXC UUCG,UU,UX UUG> /
         *<CONSONANTS,<#|,>,<VOWELS,OFFGLIDES>>
         *<RX,LX,SH,ZH,NX,TX (QX),DX (QX),TH,SX,ZX,CH,JH,HX> _;
"29.3"   IX UUG RX → *<UX RX,UX UHG RX,ER> / _;
"29.4"   UU RX → *<UX RX,UX UHG RX,ER> / JX _;
"30.1"   EI → *<EH IXG,EI IXG,AE IXG,EH EEG,EH EIG,EI EEG,
         AE EEG,AE EIG,AE EHG,EH IXCG> / _;
"30.2"   OU → *<OU UXG,AW UXG,UH UXG,OU UUG,AW UUG,UH UUG,AW OUG,UH OUG,UH AWG>
         / _;
"30.3"   EE → *<IX EEG,IXC EEG> / _;
"30.4"   UU → *<UX UUG,UUC UXC UUCG,IXC UUG,IXC UUCG, IX UUG,IX UUCG> / _;
"31.1"   SX → SH / _ *(*<#,|>) SH;
"31.2"   SX → SH / <OFFGLIDES,VOWELS> _ *(*<#,|>) <CH,JH>;
"31.3"   ZX → ZH / _ *(*<#,|>) SH;
```

```
"31.4"  ZX → ZH / *<<OFFGLIDES,VOWELS>,RX,LX> _ *(*<#,|>) <CH,JH>;
"31.5"  SH → SX / _ *(*<#,|>) *<SX,ZX>;
"31.6"  ZH → ZX / _ *(*<#,|>) *<SX,ZX>;
"32.1"  PX → NULL / _ *<#,|> PX;
"32.2"  TX → NULL / _ *<#,|> *<TX,CH>;
"32.3"  KX → NULL / _ *<#,|> KX;
"32.4"  BX → NULL / _ *<#,|> BX;
"32.5"  DX → NULL / _ *<#,|> *<DX,JH>;
"32.6"  GX → NULL / _ *<#,|> GX;
"32.7"  FX → NULL / _ *<#,|> FX;
"32.8"  TH → NULL / _ *<#,|> TH;
"32.9"  SX → NULL / _ *<#,|> SX;
"32.10" SH → NULL / _ *<#,|> SH;
"32.11" VX → NULL / _ *<#,|> VX;
"32.12" DH → NULL / _ *<#,|> DH;
"32.13" ZX → NULL / _ *<#,|> ZX;
"32.14" MX → NULL / _ *<#,|> MX;
"32.15" NX → NULL / _ *<#,|> NX;
"32.16" RX → NULL / _ *<#,|> RX;
"32.17" LX → NULL / _ *<#,|> LX;
"32.18" CH → TX / _ *<#,|> SH;
"32.19" EEG → NULL / _ *<#,|> JX;
"32.20" IXG → NULL / _ *<#,|> JX;
"32.21" IXCG → NULL / _ *<#,|> JX;
"32.22" EIG → NULL / _ *<#,|> JX;
"32.23" EHG → NULL / _ *<#,|> JX;
"32.24" UUG → NULL / _ *<#,|> WX;
"32.25" UUCG → NULL / _ *<#,|> WX;
"32.26" UXG → NULL / _ *<#,|> WX;
"32.27" UXCG → NULL / _ *<#,|> WX;
"32.28" OUG → NULL / _ *<#,|> WX;
"32.29" AWG → NULL / _ *<#,|> WX;
"33.1"  EE0 → JX / *<<STOPS,FRICATIVES,NASALS>,LX,RX> _ *(#) VOWELS0;
"33.2"  IX0 → JX / *<<STOPS,FRICATIVES,NASALS>,LX,RX> _ *(#) VOWELS0;
"33.3"  UU0 → WX / <JH,SH,ZH,CH> _ *(#) VOWELS0;
"33.4"  UX0 → WX / <JH,SH,ZH,CH> _ *(#) VOWELS0;
"34.1"  NX → NG / <KX,GX> 'X _;
"34.2"  NX → MX / *<<PX,BX>,<FX,VX>> 'X _;
"34.3"  NX → MF / <FX,VX> 'X _;
"35.1"  ZX → SX / _ *(*<#,|>) <PX,TX,KX,FX,TH,SX,SH,CH>;
"35.2"  VX → FX / _ *(*<#,|>) <PX,TX,KX,FX,TH,SX,SH,CH>;
"35.3"  DH → TH / _ *(*<#,|>) <PX,TX,KX,FX,TH,SX,SH,CH>;
"35.4"  SX → ZX / _ *(*<#,|>) <BX,DX,GX,VX,DH,ZX,JH>;
"35.5"  FX → VX / _ *(*<#,|>) <BX,DX,GX,VX,DH,ZX,JH>;
"35.6"  TH → DH / _ *(*<#,|>) <BX,DX,GX,VX,DH,ZX,JH>;
"35.7"  SH → ZH / _ *(*<#,|>) <BX,DX,GX,VX,DH,ZX,JH>;
"35.8"  ZX → SX / <PX,TX,KX,FX,TH,SX,SH,CH> *(*<#,|>) _;
"35.9"  VX → FX / <PX,TX,KX,FX,TH,SX,SH,CH> *(*<#,|>) _;
"35.10" DH → TH / <PX,TX,KX,FX,TH,SX,SH,CH> *(*<#,|>) _;
"35.11" SX → ZX / <BX,DX,GX,VX,DH,ZX,JH> *(*<#,|>) _;
"35.12" FX → VX / <BX,DX,GX,VX,DH,ZX,JH> *(*<#,|>) _;
"35.13" TH → BH / <BX,DX,GX,VX,DH,ZX,JH> *(*<#,|>) _;
"35.14" SH → ZH / <BX,DX,GX,VX,DH,ZX,JH> *(*<#,|>) _;
"35.15" BX → PX / _ *(#) <TX,SX,FX,HX,KX,CH>;
"36.1"  EE → IX / _ RX VOWELS;
```

```
"36.2"   IX → EE / _ RX VOWELS;
"36.3"   EI → *<EH,EH UHG,ER> / _ RX VOWELS;
"36.4"   AE → *<EH,EH UHG,ER> / _ RX VOWELS;
"36.5"   EH → *<EH UHG,ER> / _ RX VOWELS;
"36.6"   ER → UH RX / ¬*(#) VOWELS;
"36.7"   UX → *<UU,ER> / _ RX (#) VOWELS;
"36.8"   OU → *<UU,UX,AW,AH> / _ RX (#) VOWELS;
"36.9"   AW → *<UU,UX,OU,AH> / _ RX (#) VOWELS;
"36.10"  AA → *<AW,AH> / _ RX VOWELS;
"37.1"   EE → *<IX,EI,EH> / _ UHG;
"37.2"   EI → *<EH,EE,IX> / _ *(#) UHG RX <XX,#,I,CONSONANTS>;
"37.3"   EH → *<AE,EI,EE,IX> / _ *(#) UHG RX <XX,#,I,CONSONANTS>;
"37.4"   UU → *<UX,OU,AW> / _ UHG RX <XX,#,I,CONSONANTS>;
"37.5"   OU → *<AW,UU,UX,AH> / _ UHG RX <XX,#,I,CONSONANTS>;
"37.6"   AW → *<AH,OU,UU,UX> / _ UHG RX <XX,#,I,CONSONANTS>;
"37.7"   ER1 → *<UH RX,OE,UH> / _ <# CONSONANTS,I>;
"37.8"   ER2 → *<UH RX,OE,UH> / _ <# CONSONANTS,I>;
"37.9"   ER1 → *<OE IXG,OE IXCG,OE,UH> / _ CONSONANTS;
"37.10"  ER2 → *<OE IXG,OE IXCG,OE,UH> / _ CONSONANTS;
"37.11"  AA → AH / _ UHG RX <XX,I,CONSONANTS>;
"38.1"   EE → IX / _ LX;
"38.2"   IX → EE / _ LX;
"38.3"   UX → UU / _ LX;
"38.4"   NULL → UHG / *<EE,IX,EI,EH,OU,UU,AA,AW,AH,OFFGLIDES> _ LX;
"38.5"   UHG → NULL / *<EI,UU,OU,OFFGLIDES> _ LX;
"39"     NULL → GX / NG _ *<*(<#,I>) VOWELS,I <CONSONANTS,XX>>;
"40"     VX UH0 NX → BX 'X MX / _ <#,I,CONSONANTS>;
"41"     UH0 → NULL / CONSONANTS _ CONSONANTS (#) VOWELS;
"42"     AX → AA / _ CONSONANTS;
"43.1"   HX WX → W@ / _;
"43.2"   HX JX → J@ / _;
"43.3"   HX → NULL / _ WX;
"43.4"   HX → NULL / _ JX UU;
"44.1"   NX I JX → I NJ / _;
"44.2"   NX # JX → # NJ / _;
"44.3"   NX JX → NJ / _;
"44.4"   NX EE0 JX → NJ / _ *(#) VOWELS0;
"44.5"   NX IX0 JX → NJ / _ *(#) VOWELS0;
```

endix 6. Syntax for Base-Form Lexicon

base-form lexicon is a series of entries, each described by the following syntax:

TRY> ::= <COMMENT> <ENTRY NUMBER> ':' <WORD> ':' <POS RESTRICTION> ':' <PRONUNCIATION> ';';
MMENT> ::= '*$' | '*' | '$' | '$*' | empty;
TRY NUMBER> ::= integer;
ORD> ::= string of characters followed by possibly one '_' | any special character;
S RESTRICTION> ::= possibly empty list of <POS>'s separated by commas;
S> ::= 'ADV' | 'ADJ' | 'VRB' | etc.;
ONUNCIATION> ::= list of <ELEMENT>'s followed by a <STRESS PATTERN>;
EMENT> ::= <PHONEME> | '(' <WORD> followed by a possibly empty list of <ENTRY NUMBER>'s
        followed by ')';
ONEME> ::= 'SH' | 'TH' | 'AA' | etc.;
RESS PATTERN> ::= '<' followed by a list of <STRESS NUMBER>'s separated by commas
        followed by '>';
RESS NUMBER> ::= integer;

Appendix 7.   Sample Page from the Laser-Patent Base-Form Lexicon

```
       1:N                  :    : EH NX <1>;
       1:NARROW             :    : NX AE RX OU <12,1>;
       1:NARROWED           :    : (NARROW) # DX <12,1>;
       1:NARROWER           :    : (NARROW) # ER <12,1>;
       1:NARROWEST          :    : (NARROW) # IX SX TX <12,1>;
       1:NATURAL            :    : NX AE CH UH RX UH LX <1>;
    $  2:NATURAL            :    : NX AE CH ER LX <1>;
       1:NATURE             :    : NX EI CH ER <1>;
       1:NEAR               :    : NX EE UHG RX <1>;
       2:NEAR               :    : NX JX EE UHG RX <1>;
       3:NEAR             :PRP : NX EE UHG RX <2>;
       4:NEAR             :PRP : NX JX EE UHG RX <2>;
       5:NEAR             :PRP : NX EE RX <0>;
       6:NEAR             :PRP : NX JX EE RX <0>;
       1:NECESSARILY        :    : NX EH SX IX SX EH RX IX # LX EE <201,102>;
       1:NECESSARY          :    : NX EH SX IX SX EH RX EE <102>;
       1:NECESSITATED       :    : NX UH SX EH SX IX TX EI TX # IX DX <0102>;
       1:NECESSITATING      :    : NX UH SX EH SX XI TX EI TX # IX NG <0102>;
       1:NECESSITY          :    : NX UH SX EH SX IX TX EE <01>;
       1:NEED               :    : NX EE DX <1>;
       1:NEGATIVE           :    : NX EH GX UH TX IX VX <1>;
       1:NEODYMIUM          :    : NX EE OU DX IX MX EE UH MX <201>;
       1:NEON               :    : NX EE AA NX <12,1>;
       1:NET                :    : NX EH TX <1>;
       1:NEW                :    : NX JX UU <1>;
       1:NICKEL             :    : NX IH KX UH LX <1>;
       1:NITROGEN           :    : NX AX IXG TX RX OU JH IX NX <1>;
    ☆  1:NITROTRIACETIC     :    : NX AX IXG TX RX OU TX RX AX IXG AE SX EE
                                   TX IX KX <20201>;
    ☆  2:NITROTRIACETIC     :    : NX AX IXG TX RX OU TX RX AX IXG AE SX EH
                                   TX IX KX <20201>;
       1:NO                 :    : NX OU <1>;
       1:NOBLE              :    : NX OU BX UH LX <1>;
       1:NOISE              :    : NX AW IXG ZX <1>;
       1:NON                :    : NX AA NX <0,1,2>;
       2:NON                :    : NX UH NX <1,2>;
       1:NORMAL             :    : NX AW UHG RX MX UH LX <1>;
       1:NORMALLY           :    : (NORMAL) # EE <1>;
       1:NOT                :    : NX AA TX <1>;
       2:NOT              :ADV : (NOT 1) <2>;
       1:NOTED              :    : NX OU TX # IX DX <1>;
       2:NOTED              :    : NX OX TX # IX DX <1>;
       1:NOW                :    : NX AX UXG <1>;
       2:NOW              :ADV,SUB: NX AX UXG <2,0>;
       1:NUCLEAR            :    : NX JX UU KX LX EE ER <1>;
    $  2:NUCLEAR            :    : NX JX UU KX JX UU LX ER <1>;
       1:NUCLEATION         :    : NX JX UU KX LX EE EI SH UH NX <201>;
       1:NUCLEI             :    : NX JX UU KX LX EE AX IXG <102>;
       1:NUCLEUS            :    : NX JX UU KX LX EE UH SX <1>;
    $☆ 2:NUCLEUS            :    : NX JX UU KX JX UU LX UH SX <1>;
       1:NUMBER           :NOUS,VRB: NX UH MX BX ER <1>;
       2:NUMBER           :ADJ : NX UH MX # ER <1>;
       1:NUMBERS            :    : (NUMBER 1) # ZX <1>;
```

```
1:NUMERAL              :   : NX JX UU MX UH RX UH LX <1>;
1:NUMERALS             :   : (NUMERAL) # ZX <1>;
1:NUMERIC              :   : NX JX UU MX EH RX IX KX <01,12>;
1:NUMERICAL            :   : (NUMERIC) # UH LX <01,12>;
1:NUMEROUS             :   : NX JX UU MX UH RX UH SX <1>;
```

Appendix 8.   Sample Interaction with the Rule Applier (Input: "Robin Hood")

tphon

PLEASE TYPE INPUT STRING. (END WITH ".")
xx I rx aal bx ix0 nx I hx ux2 dx I xx .
. . . .
THE FOLLOWING STRING WAS GIVEN AS INPUT:
XX   NONE
I   NONE
RX   12
AA1   3,1
BX   NONE
IX   14.2 ,13.15 ,7.2
NX   34.2
I   NONE
NX   27
UX2   NONE
DX   NONE
I   7.1
XX   NONE

RESULTING IN THE OUTPUT GRAPH:


```
                                          'X MX

                                          'X NX

                                          IX NX

                        AA1        IXC NX
            NULL                                     HX              NULL
 ☆ XX ☆ I ☆           ☆ RX ☆ AH1 ☆ BX ☆   UH NX   ☆ I ☆   ☆ UX2 ☆ DX ☆       ☆ I ☆ XX ☆
            ?X                                       HO              OX
                        AW1        QX 'X NX

                                   QX IX NX

                                   QX IXC NX

                                   QX UH NX
```

WORD VERIFICATION IN
A SPEECH UNDERSTANDING SYSTEM

Dennis H. Klatt
Department of Electrical Engineering
Massachusetts Institute of Technology
Cambridge, Massachusetts 02139†

1. INTRODUCTION

Automatic speech recognition has long been a seductive topic for engineers and scientists to pursue, but results have been disappointing (Pierce, 1969). The recent shift of emphasis from the construction of a phonetic typewriter to the design of machines that understand spoken commands and requests within a limited task domain shows greater promise of success in that it acknowledges the importance to speech understanding of various non-phonological sources of knowledge (e.g., syntax, semantics, a model of the speaker and a model of the task).

The absence of an acoustic invariance for many of the phonetic segments of a language still makes the initial phonetic analysis process a difficult endeavor. Some researchers have proposed an analysis-by-synthesis strategy for phonetic decoding because of this invariance. Early advocates of analysis by synthesis were concerned with the decoding of stop consonants (Halle and Stevens, 1962; Liberman et.al., 1962) and argued for a motor theory of speech perception. However the arguments to be presented here in support of analysis by synthesis relate to the generative nature of phonological rules and feature-implementation rules of the English language rather than to the complexities of the relations between articulatory states and the acoustic output.

The decoding of a spoken message can be carried out at many different levels including as the clause, the phrase, the word, the syllable, the phonetic segment and the phonetic feature. Human speech perception may involve aspects of an analysis by synthesis strategy at many or all all of these levels. However, for speech understanding by machine, we propose that the best case can be made

---

†The author is also a consultant at Bolt Beranek and Newman, Inc. where most of the research described herein was performed.

for the advantages of an analysis-by-synthesis strategy at the level of the word.

The details of human speech production and perception dictate to a large extent the choices permitted the designer of a reliable word verification component. Pattern generation and pattern matching components of an analysis-by-synthesis strategy must take into account the fact that (1) the acoustic patterns to be expected for a particular word are not related in a simple way to a phonemic lexical representation and (2) the importance of different acoustic cues in the matching paradigm depends on the particular segment being verified. Examples of these problems are included in the description of a proposed verification strategy.

2. SPECTROGRAM READING

One way to study the problems involved in the design of a practical speech understanding system is to hand-simulate the functions of the various components that one hypothesizes as functioning in the recognition process. In a recent paper (Klatt and Stevens, 1973), we described an experiment in which a set of unknown spoken sentences were identified by visual examination of broadband spectrograms and machine-aided scanning of a 200-word lexicon. In that experiment, a phonetic transcription was first made from the information contained on a broadband spectrogram of each utterance. A spectrogram of an unknown utterance is shown in Figure 1. A "correct" phonetic transcription is indicated below the spectrogram along with the transcription choices and subjective probabilities for each alternative considered by the author.

The transcription performance of the investigators was rather poor. Ten percent of the segments went undetected, an additional 17 percent of the segments were mislabeled and 40 percent of the remainder were only partially transcribed in terms of phonetic features.

The lexicon was then scanned by providing a partial feature string to the computer. The computer responded with all lexical items consistent with that feature specification. As might be expected with an input containing errors, the words suggested by the computer were rarely the ones that we sought. There was a median of 5 words in the computer response to each lexical search question, and in only one trial in four was the correct word among those suggested by the computer.

This made the going very tough in the early stages because there were few syntactic and semantic constraints to fall back on. The sentences did not form a connected discourse so global semantic predictions were meaningless. Syntactic and semantic consistency

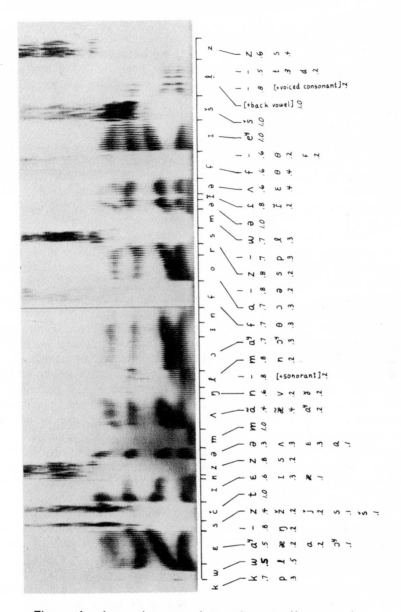

Figure 1. A spectrogram of an unknown utterance. A "correct" phonetic transcription is indicated below the spectrogram along with the transcription choices and subjective probabilities for each alternative considered by the author.

constraints could not be applied with confidence until a nearly complete sentence hypothesis had been worked out because we were uncertain about almost every intermediate decision. However if the syntax had been limited and a motivated discourse were being analyzed, these non-phonological constraints could presumably be applied at earlier stages in sentence processing and used to guide the searching strategy.

The factor that saved the day and ultimately allowed us to identify 97 percent of the words correctly was an ability to return to the spectrographic evidence to accept or reject a word hypothesis. Post-mortem analysis revealed that every time a correct word appeared as one of the lexical hypotheses generated by the computer, it was verified correctly at that time by the experimenter.

2.1 ANALYSIS BY SYNTHESIS

Why should the initial phonetic transcription be so full of errors when, moments later, the investigators could stare at the same spectrographic data with a word hypothesis in mind and be able to say yes or no with surprising reliability? The transcription contained some errors that hopefully we would not make a second time. Other errors may have been due to the fact that five random speakers were used; we were effectively prevented from developing a model of the phonological rules and acoustic-phonetic characteristics employed by a particular speaker. However these caveats are not sufficient to explain the asymmetry between our transcription and word-verification performance. Phonetic transcriptions are difficult for a man or machine to produce because uncertainty as to the identity or presence of one segment leads to uncertainty about its neighbors as well. On the other hand, all of the acoustic cues must be consistent with a particular word hypothesis or the hypothesis can be rejected in a straight-forward way.

Phonetic transcription uncertainty is caused in part by phonological processes such as vowel reduction, assimilation, deletion, alveolar flapping, palatalization, devoicing, etc., and in part by normal coarticulation phenomena which transform the acoustic realization of phonetic segments in certain sentence contexts. Rules that describe these effects are generative in nature and are partially ordered. Inverse analytic rules useful for sentence decoding are not easy to formulate; they require that one assume a specific phonetic, junctural or syntactic environment for rule applicability, when in fact this information is not available at early stages of the analysis.

Some form of analysis-by-synthesis procedure is therefore needed in a speech understanding system to overcome the inherent inaccuracies that will be present in a preliminary phonetic analysis of an unknown utterance, and also to decode the effects of phonological rules. The synthesis rules of the analysis-by-synthesis component must be able to transform an abstract representation for a word or sentence into an acoustic representation suitable for comparison with an acoustic parameterization of the unknown sentence.

3. SPEECH GENERATION BY RULE

A simplified block diagram of human sentence production is shown in Figure 2a. The syntactic component of a grammar of English provides a surface structure description for any well-formed sentence. A set of readjustment rules (not shown) erases certain aspects of the surface structure, preserving only that which is needed to predict the acoustic-phonetic shape of the utterance (Chomsky and Halle, 1968).

Figure 2 incorporates a generative semantics module capable of indicating contrastive stress (Bolinger, 1972), emphasis, contradiction, speaker mood (Williams and Stevens, 1972), speaking rate and any other semantic variables that have an influence on the acoustic realization of a sentence.

The lexicon contains an abstract systematic phonemic representation for each morpheme or word of the sentence. The lexical forms in a speech understanding system need not be as abstract as those postulated to account for the generative competence of a speaker (Chomsky and Halle, 1968). The lexicon need only list or be able to account for normal pronunciation variations encountered in deliberate as well as casual speech.

The surface structure, segmental representation and semantic information serve as input to a set of phonological rules. The output of the phonological rule component is a somewhat less abstract phonetic representation for the sentence. Phonetic features are probably binary at this level of description: thus only segmental substitutions, deletions, insertions and feature changes can be described at the phonological rule level. Examples of phonological rules for English include glottal stop insertion, alveolar flapping and vowel reduction (Zwicky, 1970; Bailey, 1973) and the lexical stress rules and morphological rules described in Chomsky and Halle (1968).

A set of phonetic feature implementation and restructuring rules transforms the string of phonetic segments into sequences of motor commands to the articulators. Interactions between features of adjacent segments (and stress) frequently obscure the presence of a

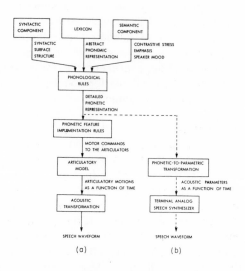

Figure 2. Sentence generation (a) as viewed by a linguist, and (b) as produced by rule in the acoustic domain.

particular feature value for a segment, but the process is incomplete -- some traces of the original feature remain in the acoustic output -- with the result that the process cannot be adequately described in terms of binary features. Examples of phonetic feature recoding rules of English include the spread of palatalization to coronals (e.g., the [S] in "this shirt")[†] partial nasalization of vowels (e.g., the [IY] in "mean"), and voicing assimilation (e.g., the [Z] in "his supper"). Chomsky and Halle (1968) do not describe feature implementation and feature restructuring rules of this kind.

The articulatory model shown in Figure 2 accepts motor command inputs and simulates the neural and muscular dynamics of the speech production apparatus. The output of the articulatory model consists of the shape of the vocal and nasal tracts, the laryngeal configuration and subglottal pressure as a function of time (Henke, 1966). Coarticulation between adjacent segments can often be explained by constraints that apply at this level.

An acoustic model converts this information into a speech

[†]The ARPABET phonemic symbols are used here.

waveform as shown at (a) in Figure 2 by simulating the mechanics and aerodynamics of sound generation and propagation in the articulatory model. Linear system theory can be used to characterize the relationships between vocal tract shapes and the resulting acoustic transfer functions (Fant, 1960). The properties of a turbulence noise source as a function of subglottal pressure and vocal tract/larynx configuration are also fairly well understood (Stevens, 1971), and recent physical models of the larynx are capable of predicting approximate acoustic characteristics of the voicing source volume velocity as a function of subglottal pressure and laryngeal configuration (Ishizaka and Matsudaira, 1972).

Implementation of the model shown in Figure 2a presents serious difficulties due to our lack of detailed knowledge about neural representations of articulatory commands, feedback systems and the detailed anatomy and physiology of the speech-related musculature. An alternative, a terminal analog model of speech production, is proposed in Figure 2b. The output of the phonological rule component is converted directly to a set of acoustic parameters.

The acoustic parameters are selected to form a sufficient set to control a conventional terminal analog speech synthesizer (Klatt, 1972). The output of the synthesizer is the desired speech waveform for the sentence. The synthesizer component is not needed in a word verification application because comparisons are probably best performed between measured spectra and spectra computed theoretically from the parametric representation that is generated by the synthesis rules.

The complexities of feature implementation rules and articulatory modeling do not disappear in the phonetic-to-parametric realization, but the advantage is that relevant data is easily collected. Acoustic parameters can be traced from spectrograms or extracted automatically from digitized recordings of natural speech. Phonetic-to-parametric rules can be discovered and quantified by systematic study of these types of data (assuming the correct phonetic forms can be predicted by the phonological rules).

It may not be possible to state rules as naturally as in a good articulatory model, where many of the coarticulatory effects would be natural consequences of constraints built into the model. However there are advantages to making every detail explicit at an acoustic-phonetic level because it will be necessary to develop related inverse rules for the preliminary analysis component of the analysis-by-synthesis procedure.

There exists a number of speech synthesis by rule programs for

English that embody aspects of several of the components shown in Figure 2. While the speech produced by these programs is generally intelligible, the parameter values generated as a function of time are clearly not a sufficiently accurate model of any speaker to be used as a part of an analysis-by-synthesis procedure. Thus, development of an adequate synthesis component is an essential step in the design of a word verification component. Synthesis strategies whose objective is to model accurately the speech of a single talker are being actively pursued by the author and others.

4. WORD VERIFICATION

Perhaps the best way to introduce the problems involved in the design of a word verification component is to pick a specific design, describe it in detail and point out the advantages and disadvantages of alternative realizations at the relevant points in the discussion. A word verification component is defined here as a device that, for each single word hypothesis that is sent to it, returns a probability that the word is present within a specified time interval of the speech waveform. A clean interface between the word verification component and the remainder of a speech understanding system is preserved by leaving the interpretation of the probability scores to a separate control box.

A partial block diagram of a speech understanding system is shown in Figure 3. The word verification component is identified by enclosing it within dashed lines. It is obviously not a stand-alone item; in order to function properly in a speech understanding system, its inputs and outputs must be matched to the needs and expectations of the control box shown in Figure 3. Thus it is unavoidable that issues relating to total system design and the structure of the control box will be examined. It is convenient to start at the input to the word verifcation component in the following description and trace the flow of information back to the generation of the next word hypothesis.

4.1 LEXICON

The lexical entry for the word "backache" might be

$$/ \ B \ 1 \ AE \ K * 2 \ EY \ K \ / \qquad (1)$$

The slashes indicate a phonemic transcription and will be used here only to refer to the lexical forms for words. The " " signifies a word boundary and "*" indicates a syllable or morpheme boundary. The "1" identifies a vowel carrying primary lexical stress, "2" indicates secondary lexical stress (Chomsky-Halle stress numbers 2 through n), and vowels that are not preceded by a stress mark are unstressed. All of these nonphonemic symbols are needed to ensure that the

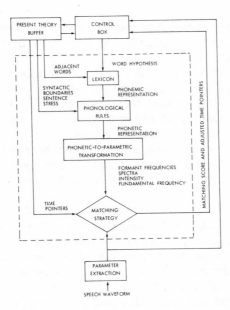

Figure 3. Information flow in a word verification component to be used in a speech understanding system.

correct phonetic forms can be derived from the lexical representations by the application of a set of phonological rules. For example, the morpheme boundary in backache enables a rule to predict that the medial [K] will be weakly aspirated even though [K] is usually strongly aspirated before a stressed vowel.

4.2 PHONOLOGICAL RULES

The systematic-phonemic transcription for a word, plus any surface-structure and semantic information that is available, serves as input to a set of phonological rules whose job it is to predict a more-detailed phonetic form for the word. An example of phonological rule is

DX ===> Q / ...   (syllabic N or L)

===> Q / (+sonorant) ... (+sonorant)   (2)

The first part of the rule states that an alveolar flap may be replaced by a glottal stop if the next segment is a syllabic N or L. The second part of the rule states that a glottal stop may be inserted between two sonorants (sonorant consonants or vowels) if there is a word boundary between them. The rule applies for example to the word "Latin" and to the two word sequence "we eat". The rule is optional, but it is very likely to be applied either by the insertion of a full glottal stop or in the form of laryngeal glottalization in both careful and conversational speaking modes.

Phonological rules that cross a word boundary such as (2) are common. They introduce an obvious problem in the verification of a word because the present theory buffer in Figure 3 usually will not contain information about adjacent words, so it will not be possible to say whether the rule applies or not. This raises a fundamental question about how a word verification component should be organized. There are at least three possible strategies. Whenever rule applicability cannot be determined from the contents of the present theory buffer:

a. The phonological rule could call a subroutine to check the parametric input in the neighborhood of the previous segment for indications of whether the rule applies. Because of the interactions between rules, the added code involved and the messy business of creating additional interfaces between the word verification component and the outside world, it is our opinion that this approach would be of marginal utility.

b. The rule could simply downgrade the importance of finding the word-initial and word-final segments so that if the matching strategy box doesn't find a good match at the ends of a word, the matching score for the total word will not be lowered very much. While this seems like a very practical solution, it is a potential source of difficulties. In the case of an alveolar flapping rule for a word such as "melt", it is important that either a full stop, a flap or a glottal stop be found, if none of these is evident, the word hypothesis should get a low score.

c. The rule could be applied to generate one phonetic form and bypassed to generate a second possibility. This would have to be done in any case for rules that are truly optional. Both phonetic forms would be processed by the remaining phonological rules and sent to the phonetic-to-parametric transformation box.

We favor the third alternative, but realize the explosive possibilities involved. If four optional rules are applied to a lexical entry, as many as 16 different phonetic forms could result. However, if the matching strategy is organized on a segment-by-segment basis, computation time will only increase linearly with the number of applicable rules.

A hypothetical example of the application of phonological rules

to the word "melt" is given below, assuming that the present theory
buffer contains the previous word "will" but not the following word:

Input: / W IH L   M 1 EH L T ... /
Output: -L   M 1 EH -L T   ...
        -L   M 1 EH -L DX   ...
        -L   M 1 EH -L Q   ...
        -L   M 1 EH -L   ...

Rules transform the phoneme /L/ into a velarized postvocalic allophone
[-L], and generate four possible phonetic forms for "melt" ending in a
[T], a flap, a glottal stop and a deleted stop. Each of these forms
requires a particular type of phonetic environent to the right of the
/T/. When the word to the right is tentatively identified, it will be
necessary to reverify the word "melt" to assure that the best-
matching alternative generated by the phonolgical rules was a
legitimate production.

4.3 PRESENT THEORY BUFFER

The present theory buffer contains information concerning the
identity and location of words already verified in the sentence theory
currently being processed. In addition, the present theory buffer
contains information on syntactic boundaries, sentence stress and
semantic information such as the assumed psychological state of the
user if the information is derivable from previous discourse and the
partial word string verified thus far. This information is used primarily
to insert the appropriate stress and syntactic markers in the phonetic
string to aid in the prediction of segmental durations and fundamental
frequency contours.

4.4 PHONETIC-TO-PARAMETRIC TRANSFORMATION

The input phonetic representation for the phonetic-to-
parametric transformation consists of a broad phonetic transcription.
Stress markers, word boundaries, syllable boundaries and syntactic
information are also present. Diphthongs, glides and affricates are
expanded into a sequence of two segments so that each segment in
the transcription represents a single articulatory target.

The output parametric representation consists of a set of time
functions which would ordinarily control a terminal analog speech
synthesizer. Parameters that might be used for word verification
(based on their perceptual importance in synthesis studies) include

a. three formant frequencies
b. a nasal pole-zero pair
c. transfer function zeros and higher poles that are excited during
frication production

d. amplitudes of the sources of voicing, aspiration and frication
e. source spectra shapes
f. fundamental frequency

The first step in the transformation from a discrete phonetic representation to a continuous parametric representation for an utterance is to determine a duration for each segment. Target values for parameters are computed for each segment and a system of rules is employed to modify the parameter targets and time constants of motions between targets in accordance with principles of phonetic feature implementation and segmental coarticulation.

4.4.1 PREDICTION OF SEGMENTAL DURATION

The duration of a phonetic segment spoken in sentence context depends on a number of phonetic, syntactic, and to a limited extent, semantic variables. The primary factors that must be considered in any model (Klatt, in preparation) include

a. differences in inherent segmental durations
b. stressed and unstressed environments
c. influence of the postvocalic consonant on vowel duration
d. articulatory interactions in consonant clusters
e. syllable position within a word
f. syllable position within a phrase
g. use of emphasis or contrastive stress

Aside from differences in inherent durations, by far the largest change in segmental duration in a sentence is governed by the position of the syllable in the phrase. Phrase-final syllables are significantly longer than other syllables. Thus, if in verifying a word, some segments are found to be significantly longer in duration than expected, it is very likely that a syntactic break follows the word and certain predictions can be made as to the syntactic structure of the unknown utterance. For example, a left-to-right parser could use this information to hypothesize the end of a syntactic unit such as a noun phrase and start looking for a new structure to the right. The control box may first attempt to confirm the presence of a syntactic break by examining the fundamental frequency contour and by searching for an optional silent interval following the word.

Word verification calls for more than a prediction of the expected duration for each phonetic segment. The permissible range of durational values is also required because variability is greater in some phonetic environments than in others. For example, stressed segments are less variable in duration than unstressed segments; prepausal lengthening is predictable in the direction of effect, but not as predictable in the amount of lengthening; and some unstressed clusters such as an unstressed nasal-stop sequence have a highly variable duration.

4.4.2 PREDICTION OF FORMANT FREQUENCY MOTIONS

Median formant frequency targets for some stressed allophones in the speech of the author when reading a connected discourse are presented in Table 1. These targets are modified systematically as a function of stress and phonetic environment of the segment (Fant, Stalhammer and Karlsson, 1974). However, changes in midpoint formant frequencies were generally small in this corpus except for vowels adjacent to /R,L/, reduced vowels and /UW/ in the neighborhood of dentals. Longer vowels tended to be more diphthongized, and lax vowels were diphthongized toward schwa in phrase-final positions.

Due to the inertia of individual articulators and the complex organization of motor commands to the various articulators, formants move relatively slowly and continuously toward the underlying target frequencies, but they may never reach the targets. This process can be modeled by specifying (1) a boundary value for each formant frequency, BVFREQ, at the boundary between two adjacent segments, (2) a forward time constant, TCF, for a pseudo-exponential motion from the boundary value toward the next target frequency, and (3) a backward time constant TCB for a pseudo-exponential motion from the boundary value back toward the previously generated formant contour. A quarter of a cylce of a sine wave is used as an approximation to the exponential function. Occasionally the TCF and TCB values differ for the three formants at a particular segment boundary. For example the F1 transition in stops is usually more rapid than other formant motions and the F3 transition in a retroflex consonant is slower than the others.

The procedure is illustrated in Figure 4. The figure shows the steps involved in the generation of formant transitions for the word "beer".

Segment	F1	F2	F3
IY	330	1940	2780
IH	470	1600	2600
EY	490	1730	2500
-EY	410	1850	2550
EH	570	1470	2450
AE	680	1510	2450
AA	670	1260	2630
AO	630	1080	2500
OW	540	990	2300
-O	520	890	2300
UH	480	1050	2250
UW	420	1470	2150
-UW	400	1200	2150
AH	620	1200	2570
ER	450	1300	1600
AY	600	1300	2600
-AY	500	1680	2300
OY	550	950	2450
-OY	460	1630	2150
AW	620	1260	2350
-AW	540	1050	2350
AX	450	1260	2470
IX	420	1680	2520
W	370	830	2100
WH	400	900	2100
Y	370	1830	2360
R	420	1200	1500
-R	430	1250	1550
L	380	950	2700
-L	420	760	2700

Table 1. Target frequencies for the three lowest formants for vowels, liquids and glides in the idiolect of DHK.

The solid curve F'(t) is generated from the dashed curve in each case by successive application of the general formulae:

$$F'(t) = BVFREQ + [[TARGET-BVFREQ]*sin(pi*t/(2*TCF))] \qquad (3)$$
$$0 < t < TCF$$

$$F'(t) = BVFREQ + [[F(t)-BVFREQ]*sin(-pi*t/(2*TCB)) \qquad (4)$$
$$-TCB < t < 0$$

$$F'(t) = TARGET \qquad (5)$$
$$TCF < t$$

In the production of sentences at normal speaking rates, segmental durations are typically comparable to the time constants of articulatory motions. This type of coarticulation results in formant target undershoot. As can be seen in Figure 4, the mechanism described by equations 3 - 5 can model mild coarticulatory undershoot fairly accurately if appropriate time constants TCB and CF are chosen. In some cases, transition time constants are longer than the duration of a phonetic segment. When this happens in the model, coarticulation extends in a natural way over more than a single adjacent segment.

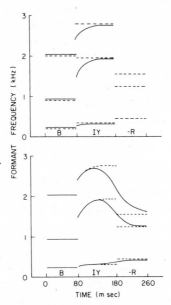

Figure 4. The formant transitions for the syllable [B IY -R] are computed from formant targets by successive iteration of equations 3-5 at the [B IY] boundary (top) and at the [IY -R] boundary (bottom).

4.4.3 PREDICTION OF SPECTRA

The frequency motions of the lowest three formants are the primary cues to the identification of vowels and sonorant consonants. Formant amplitudes also contribute to sonorant identity. For this reason and to avoid the possibility of tracking errors when extracting formant data from the unknown utterance, it is proposed that matching be done at the level of a short-term spectrum whenever possible.

In order to compute a synthetic spectrum, it is necessary to know the acoustic characteristics of the voicing source. There are sufficient individual differences in source characteristics to warrant the use of a speaker normalization procedure at the beginning of a user session. Several vowels can be selected from a test utterance, formants extracted and the average source spectrum determined by inverse filtering. This average spectrum is then used in generating synthetic spectra for vowel and sonorant verifications.

The aspiration in /H/ and the following release of aspirated /P, T, K/ can be synthesized in the same general way. An all pole transfer function is computed by rule and the output spectrum is obtained by multiplying the aspiration source spectrum by this transfer function. Voice onset time relative to plosive release must also be predicted by rule in order to determine the expected duration of the aspiration interval in a voiceless stop.

The verification of nasals is best done by matching at the level of a short-term spectrum because nasal zeros are difficult to extract from natural voicing spectra. Formant locations, especially the presence of a steady low first formant frequency, help to locate a nasal murmur. The zero locations, or equivalently, their effect on the murmur spectrum must be used in conjunction with formant transitions into and out of a nasal to determine place of articulation. The frequency motions of transfer function zeros during nasals and nasalized vowels can be predicted by rules similar in structure to the formant-generating rules described above.

Fricatives and the brief bursts of frication noise at the release of plosive consonants also involve a transfer function with both poles and zeros. The degree of excitation of each formant during frication production contributes information toward the place of articulation of the segment. Since the extraction of zeros from natural frication spectra is not presently feasible, it is again more appropriate to perform the matching at the level of a short-term spectrum. The synthetic spectrum would be derived by first generating pole and zero motions by rule. This pole-zero transfer function, $H(z)$, is then multiplied by the ideal frication source spectrum, $S(z)$, to obtain the expected output spectrum for a particular fricative, P(z). Z-transform notation is used because a digital simulation of the synthesizer program was assumed in designing the parameter synthesis rules.

Speaker differences and differences in recording conditions can influence the general spectral shape of fricatives. In order to handle this variability the source spectrum can be estimated by inverse filtering procedures applied to several fricatives in a normalization utterance at the beginning of a test session.

4.5 MATCHING STRATEGY

The matching strategy concerns time registration, time normalization, computation of a matching score for each segment, and, ultimately the derivation of a matching score for a word. Time registration involves the selection of some time point or points in the hypothesized word corresponding to reliably-detectable acoustic events, and locating the corresponding time point(s) in the unknown utterance. In general the control box will restrict the portion of the unknown utterance over which a match is permitted. Some speech events such as the release of a stop or the onset of voicing are fairly easy to detect reliably. Others such as the boundaries between sequences of sonorants are difficult to define operationally. Thus a good registration strategy would be to pick a distinct acoustic event in the word to be verified and attempt to locate all instances of the same event type within the specified interval in the unknown utterance. Short words with no stops or voiceless consonants such as "are" will be difficult to allign and verify except perhaps in conjunction with a neighboring word hypothesis.

Time normalization involves the nonuniform stretching or compressing of the time scale for the word to be verified in order to fit optimally the acoustic patterns found in the unknown utterance. It is here that efficient mathematical pattern recognition techniques may be required in order to perform the optimization in a practical amount of computation time. If several temporal landmarks occur within the word, time normalization can be facilitated by performing time registration for each event. Time distortions that are too large or too nonuniform should obviously result in a lower matching score.

4.5.1 SEGMENTAL MATCHING SCORES

Segmental scoring and time normalization can be performed separately or simultaneously. The matching score for each segment will depend on pattern differences in all of the parameters that are relevent to that particular segment type, and on the stress assigned to the syllable in which it is embedded. Greater variation is permitted in unstressed syllables.

As an example, consider the computation of a matching score for a fricative. Spectral comparisons can involve differences in total energy and in the details of the energy distributions in the frequency domain. An energy matching score EM would be the difference in dB between the two spectra (properly normalized with respect to adjacent vowel levels) as averaged over the duration of the frication noise. A spectral matching score SM would be a weighted sum of the absolute differences in dB between the smoothed synthetic and measured spectra as a function of frequency. The weighting function, W(f) can be selected to emphasize frequency regions that differentiate between the English fricatives.

Formant transitions into and out of fricatives contribute information concerning place of articulation. A formant transition matching score FT can be defined so as to weight the differences between second and third formant motions into and out of adjacent segments if these motions are detectable.

Segment duration and the low frequency portion of the spectrum contribute to a decision about the voiced-voiceless feature for a fricative. A voicing matching score VO can be defined to weight appropriately differences in these acoustic dimensions.

The composite matching score for a fricative is some combination of the scores EM, SM, FT and VO. In a plosive or affricate, the stop closure duration, presence or absence of a voicebar and voice onset time must also be compared. It is clear that these scores can not be combined linearly to form a total score because a low score on one measure such as the spectral match might be fatal in seeking an [S], but acceptable variation for an [F]. Formulation of effective scoring methods is crucial to the entire word verification concept.

4.5.2 WORD MATCHING SCORES

Each expected segment is subjected to the appropriate matching score algorithm until the word has been processed. If more than one phonetic representation exists for the word, a lattice of segment matching scores is created. The next step is to find the optimum path through the lattice and derive an overall word score. Segment scores cannot be combined by any simple function such as the computation of a mean because a bad mismatch on one critical segment might be obscured. It is difficult to speculate on word-scoring startegies without observing the outputs of a segment scoring algorithm so nothing more will be said on this topic.

4.6 CONTROL BOX

The function of the control box is to build one or more sentence theories, proposing and evaluating new word hypotheses until a complete sentence with a sufficiently high matching score is obtained. The control strategy for obtaining new word hypotheses and evaluating word scores obtained from the verification component depends to a great extent on the task and the nature of syntactic and semantic constraints. However a few general statements can be made concerning how the acoustic characteristics of spoken sentences influence control strategies.

The greatest help in limiting the search space can probably come from prosodic information. Lindblom and Svenson (1972) have shown how prosodic cues can aid in reading spectrograms. We have also indicated in section 4.4.1 how durational cues can be used to identify ends of syntactic units. There are important additonal cues in the fundamental frequency contour.

If the control box cannot be driven in a straight left-to-right fashion by the syntax, then it is necessary to use the most-reliable acoustic cues to hypothesize possible word candidates somewhere in the input utterance. Long words are preferable units upon which to begin a sentence theory because their mid portions are little affected by the phonological and phonetic properties of adjacent words. Hence, a good match is more meaningful.

The control box will have to deal with overlaps and gaps in the time dimension as sequences of words accumulate in a theory. Again simple scoring procedures are dangerous because some gaps and overlaps are of little consequence, while others of the same duration could reflect true incompatibility. It should be possible to send a word candidate pair that overlaps or has a gap between it to the verification component with a request for it to be treated as a single phonological word. The resulting match score would be a reflection of the importance of the gap or overlap. Thus most of the speech-related knowledge could remain in the word verification component.

5. CONCLUSIONS

In the initial phases of the development of a word verification system, it will be necessary to concentrate efforts on synthesis rules for a single speaker. Once the system performs well with this first speaker, it is possible to study the changes that will be needed for the system to handle multiple speakers of the same dialect. Hopefully most synthesis rules, matching strategies and scoring algorithms will not have to change form for a new speaker because the algorithms will have been designed to reflect basic productive-perceptive constraints of language. What is not known is the extent to which target values and synthesis constants must be adjusted in an initialization procedure undertaken by each new speaker. The design and testing of practical speech understanding systems is an exciting scientific endeavor that is closely related to studies of the ways that people produce and understand language. We have argued for the necessity of a word verification component in a speech understanding system and have presented a tentative specification of one. However a complete analysis-by-synthesis system must await the results of research programs whose objectives have been detailed elsewhere (Klatt, 1974). Thus it may not be possible to build a high-performance speech understanding system in the short run, but if this goal is pursued, we may also come closer to understanding the nature of speech perception and the system of rules that govern speech production.

ACKNOWLEDGMENT

This research was supported in part by a grant from the Advanced Research Projects Agency of the Department of Defense.

REFERENCES

Bailey,rC. J., "Variation Resulting from Different Rule Orderings in English Phonology," in New Ways of Analyzing Variation in English, ed. by C. J. Bailey and R. W. Shuy, Georgetown University Press, Washington D.C. (1973).

Bolinger, D., "Accent is Predictable (if you're a Mind-Reader)," Language 48, pp. 633-644 (1972).

Chomsky, N. and M. Halle, The Sound Pattern of English, Harper and Row, N.Y. (1968).

Fant, G., Acoustic Theory of Speech Production, Mouton and Co., the Hague, Netherlands (1960).

Fant, G., U. Stalhammer and I. Karlssson, "Swedish Vowels in Speech Material of Various Complexity," Proc. Speech Communication Seminar, Stockholm, Aug. 1-3, 1974, Almqvist and Wiksell (1974).

Halle M. and K. N. Stevens, "Speech Recognition: A Model and a Program for Research," IRE Transactions on Information Theory IT-8, pp. 155-159 (1962).

Henke, W., "Dynamic Articulatory Model of Speech Processing Using Computer Simulation," Ph.D. Thesis, Mass. Inst. of Tech. (1966).

Ishizaka, K. and M. Matsudaira, "Fluid-Mechanical Considerations of Vocal Cord Vibration," Speech Communications Research Laboratory Monograph No. 8, Santa Barbara, CA. (1972).

Klatt, D. H. and K. N. Stevens, "On the Automatic Recognition of Continuous Speech: Implications of a Spectrogram-Reading Experiment," IEEE Trans. on Audio and Electroacoustics AU-21, pp. 210-216 (1973).

Klatt, D. H., "Acoustic Theory of Terminal Analog Speech Synthesis," in Proc. 1972 International Conference on Speech Communication and Processing, Boston, Ma., IEEE, No. 72 CHO 596-7 AE, pp. 131-135 (1972).

Klatt, D. H., "On the Design of Speech Understanding Systems," Proc. Stockholm Speech Communication Seminar, Aug. 1-3, 1974, Almqvist and Wiksell (1974).

Klatt, D. H., "Vowel Duration is Syntactically Determined in a Connected Discourse," submitted for publications.

Liberman, A. M., F. S. Cooper, K. S. Harris and P. F. MacNeilage, "A Motor Theory of Speech Perception," Proc. Speech Communication Seminar, Royal Institute of Technology, Stockholm (1962).

Lindblom, B. and S. G. Svensson, "Interaction Between Segmental and Non-Segmental Factors in Speech Recognition," Proc. 1972 Boston Speech Conference, IEEE, No. 72 CHO 596-7 AE, pp. 331-333 (1972).

Oshika, B. T., V. W. Zue, R. R. Weeks, H. Nue and J. Aurbach, "The Role of Phonological Rules in Speech Understanding Research," IEEE Speech Symposium, Carnegie-Mellon Univ., (April 1974).

Pierce, J. R., "Whither Speech Recognition," J. Acoust. Soc. Am. 46, pp. 1049-1051 (1969).

Stevens, K. N., "The Quantal Nature of Speech: Evidence from Articulatory-Acoustic Data," in Human Communication: A Unified View, ed. by E. E. David and P. B. Denes, McGraw-Hill, New York (1972).

Stevens, K. N., "Airflow and Turbulence Noise for Fricative and Stop Consonants: Static Considerations," J. Acoust. Soc. Am. 50, pp. 1180-1192 (1971).

Williams, C. and K. N. Stevens, "Emotions and Speech: Some Acoustical Correlates," J. Acoust. Soc. Am. 52, pp. 1238-1250 (1972).

Zwicky, A. M., "Auxiliary Reduction in English," Linguistic Inquiry 1, pp. 323-336 (1970).

Part Four

Syntax and Semantics

SYNTAX, SEMANTICS, AND SPEECH

William A. Woods
Bolt Beranek and Newman Inc.
50 Moulton Street
Cambridge, Massachusetts 02138

INTRODUCTION

Recently, speech understanding research has taken a direction which recognizes the importance of syntactic and semantic constraints as an essential part of the process which deciphers speech signals into sequences of sounds (see Newell et al. 1973). Consequently, it has become important for speech researchers to be acquainted with the work that has been done in the area of computational linguistics, attempting to construct computer programs to model the process of natural language understanding. This paper will attempt to provide an introduction to the techniques and results which have come out of work in computational linguistics which I think have special relevance to the design of speech understanding systems. The paper was written for an audience with some understanding of the nature of speech signals and the difficulties of performing an acoustic and phonetic analysis of such signals but with little familiarity with the techniques for parsing and semantic interpretation of natural language or the ways in which such techniques could be used in a total speech understanding system. However, readers with interests in computational linguistics, linguistics, and artificial intelligence may also find things of interest herein. For the reader with little or no background in the nature of speech production and the characteristics of speech signals, I suggest the papers by Denes and Pinson (1963) and by Jakobson, Fant and Halle (1967) as appropriate introductions. This paper should be readable however without such prior knowledge of speech characteristics.

This paper is not intended to be a survey. Rather, in it I will try to trace the development of what I think are several important ideas and trends in parsing and syntax and in semantic interpretation. I will attempt to convey a feeling for what I think the state of the art is, how it developed conceptually, and some of the new perspectives that the problems of speech understanding place on the processes of parsing and semantic interpretation.

PART I. SYNTACTIC ANALYSIS

There are two parts to the problem of syntactic analysis -- one is a component of judgment or decision (whether a given string of words is a sentence or not) and the other is a component of representation or interpretation (deciding what the pieces of the sentence are and how they relate to each other). In speech understanding we will see that both of these are important.

Let me start with a mini-history describing what I think the current state of the art is, how it developed conceptually, and some of the new perspectives that the problems of speech understanding place on the evaluation of parsing techniques.

PHRASE STRUCTURE GRAMMARS

The field of linguistics was given a great stimulus when the two aspects of syntax (judgmental and structural) were combined in the formalism of phrase structure grammar. Prior to this development, largely due to Chomsky (e.g., Chomsky, 1965), the mechanism whereby a computer program could decide whether a given sequence of words was a grammatical sentence or not would have been difficult to imagine.

The principal component of a phrase structure grammar is a collection of "rewrite rules" such as the following:

S -> NP VP

NP->DET N

VP->V NP

Intuitively, the first rule indicates that a sentence can consist of a noun phrase followed by a verb phrase. Formally, it indicates that in the course of deriving a sentence, one can replace an occurrence of the symbol S in the string derived so far, with the sequence of two symbols NP VP. Similarly, one can replace the NP with the sequence DET N and the VP with the sequence V NP, ultimately deriving the sequence DET N V DET N, which is the sequence of syntactic word categories underlying a sentence such as

"The man bit the dog".

PARSERS AND RECOGNIZERS

The rewrite rules of a phrase structure grammar can be used to characterize the set of possible sequences of words which can be considered grammatical sentences, thereby formally representing the judgmental part of syntax. A formal algorithm for taking a grammar and deciding whether a sequence of words is a sentence with respect to that grammar is called an acceptor or a recognizer.

If in the course of deriving a sentence according to the rules we keep track of which symbols were rewritten into which sequences, one can construct a tree structure such as that represented in figure 1 which gives a very nice representation of what the parts of the sentence are and how they are put together, thus achieving a structural representation of the sentence. An algorithm for constructing such a representation while accepting or recognizing a sentence is called a parser.

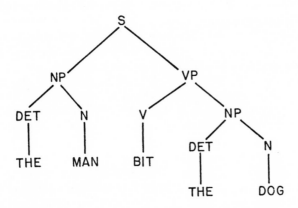

Figure 1. A sample phrase structure tree

LEXICAL CATEGORIES AND DICTIONARIES

Notice that in figure 1 and in the grammar rules there are two different kinds of names of nodes; there are "nonterminal" symbols like S, NP, and VP, which name whole phrase types, and there are other symbols which are essentially lexical word class names, like determiner, noun, and verb. This distinction between terminal and nonterminal symbols is formalized by dividing the vocabulary of special symbols of a phrase structure grammar into a terminal and nonterminal vocabulary.

The initial symbol S, and all of the symbols which later get rewritten by phrase structure rules are in the nonterminal vocabulary. The derivation of a sentence stops when the string consists entirely of terminal symbols. In a simple view of phrase structure grammars, the terminal symbols would be the English words themselves, but this would result in a huge set of "singleton" rules such as

DET -> the

(on the average there would be several such rules for each word in English). Instead, the syntactic word classes usually serve as the terminal vocabulary and the correspondence between syntactic word classes and the words themselves is taken care of by a dictionary.

OTHER GRAMMAR MODELS

All of the above presentation has been a description of what is called context free phrase structure grammars. There are in fact many different types of phrase structure grammars depending on the types of rules permitted and the way that they are applied. For each different type of grammar, there is a corresponding class of languages which can be characterized by grammars of that type; the grammar formalism is said to generate this class of languages. Whenever two formalisms, either grammars or automata, generate the same class of languages, they are said to be generatively equivalent or equivalent in generative power, and if one formalism generates a superset of the class generated by another formalism, then that model is said to be stronger in generative power. There is a well-known hierarchy of successively more powerful phrase structure grammar models, known among formal language theorists as the Chomsky hierarchy. I would like to introduce these here because I want to come back occasionally and refer to the various things which the different models can do.

The grammar models in the Chomsky hierarchy are known as type 0, type 1, type 2, and type 3 grammars. The context free grammar which we have just described is the type 2 grammar and is characterized by the fact that the left hand sides of its rewrite rules consist of a single nonterminal symbol and the right hand sides may be any nonempty string of terminal and nonterminal symbols. The type 3 grammars, also known as finite state grammars, are more restricted than the context free grammars and correspond in generative power to finite state machines. They are characterized by rewrite rules whose left-hand sides are single nonterminals and whose right-hand sides are either a single terminal symbol or a terminal symbol followed by a single nonterminal.

At the other end of the spectrum are the type 0 grammars, also known as general rewriting systems, which correspond in generative power to Turing machines. General rewriting systems are characterized by rewrite rules whose left-hand and right-hand sides can be arbitrary strings of terminal and nonterminal symbols subject only to the constraint that a terminal symbol cannot be rewritten as some different terminal or nonterminal symbol. Type 1 grammars, also known as context sensitive grammars, are strictly less powerful than general rewriting systems and strictly more powerful than context free grammars. They are characterized by rewrite rules in which the left-hand side specifies not only a nonterminal symbol to be rewritten, but also a context of terminal and nonterminal symbols which must be present in order for the rule to be applied.

Figure 2 gives a summary of the types of rules for each class of grammars.

TYPE 0 : GENERAL REWRITING SYSTEM

$$\alpha \longrightarrow \beta \qquad \alpha, \beta \in V^*$$

TYPE 1 : CONTEXT SENSITIVE

$$X \longrightarrow \gamma / \alpha \underline{\quad\quad} \beta \qquad X \in V_N$$
$$\text{OR} \qquad\qquad \alpha, \beta, \gamma \in V^*$$
$$\alpha X \beta \longrightarrow \alpha \gamma \beta \qquad \gamma \neq e$$

TYPE 2 : CONTEXT FREE

$$X \longrightarrow \gamma \qquad X \in V_N, \gamma \in V^* - \{e\}$$

TYPE 3 : FINITE STATE

$$X \longrightarrow a\, Y \qquad X, Y \in V_N$$

$$X \longrightarrow a \qquad a \in V_T$$

Figure 2. Summary of the Chomsky hierarchy of phrase structure grammars

In the figure, the notation V is used to represent the union of the terminal and nonterminal vocabularies of the grammar (VT and VN), and the * operator is used to indicate the set of all possible strings which can be made from a given vocabulary (i.e., VT* indicates the set of all possible terminal strings). The symbol e represents the empty string (i.e., the string with no symbols).

Each of the grammars in the Chomsky hierarchy represents a restriction in generative power (with an attendant ease in parsing or recognition) over the power of grammars with a lower number. Each class with a higher number represents a special case of the classes with lower numbers. The principal difference between the context sensitive grammar and the general rewriting system is that the former is prohibited by the nature of its rules from erasing anything from the working string as it proceeds (i.e., the right-hand sides of rules are always at least as long as the left-hand sides). For the general rewriting systems, this is not the case, and arbitrary amounts of intermediate "scratch work" can be erased out of a derivation without leaving a trace in the resulting string that is generated. This is what gives the general rewriting system its power, and also has the undesirable consequence that a recognition or parsing algorithm cannot be guaranteed to exist for general rewriting systems. For all of the other classes of grammars, it is possible to construct a recognizer which for an arbitrary string will say yes-or-no whether that string is in a given grammar. General rewriting systems are therefore not very desirable as machine models of language due to this inability to guarantee a recognition algorithm.

DERIVATIONS

For each of the type 1, 2, and 3 grammars, formal parsing algorithms can be devised which, given a grammar and a string, can answer the question whether the string is a sentence with respect to the grammar. This is done by attempting to discover a derivation of the string from the initial symbol of the grammar by means of the rewrite rules. A derivation is essentially a sequence of working strings starting with the initial symbol, each of which results from the preceding one by one application of a rewrite rule. A string is said to be generated by the grammar if there is a derivation of the grammar leading to it. An example of a derivation is shown in Figure 3. Notice however that there can be several distinct derivations for a single phrase structure tree corresponding to different orders of applying the rewrite rules. For example, if instead of expanding the subject noun phrase before the verb phrase one were to expand the verb phrase first, one of the derivations of Figure 4 would result. (Figure 4 compactly represents all of the possible derivations of this particular surface string, with the common initial parts of different derivations combined. Alternative choices for expanding a given string are indicated by the arrows, and individual derivations are terminated by underlining.)

SUMMARY OF DERIVATION

S $\xrightarrow{*}$ DET N V DET N

INTERMEDIATE STRINGS

S

NP   VP

DET   N   VP

DET   N   V   NP

DET   N   V   DET   N

Figure 3. A sample derivation

Essentially all of the expansion that appears in the phrase structure tree could be done in any order and each different ordering would give a different derivation which corresponds to effectively the same parse. If we don't want to be swamped with alternative derivations of the same parse, then we need to include in our parsing algorithm some control strategy that will keep it from getting all of them. The typical control strategy that is used in text-based parsers

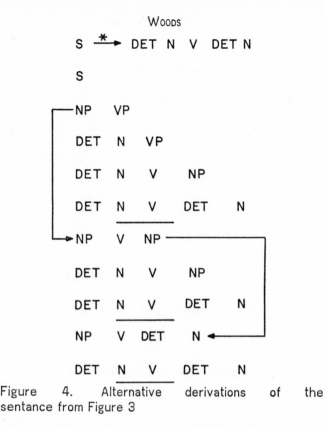

Figure 4. Alternative derivations of the sentence from Figure 3

(as opposed to speech) is to decide arbitrarily that the only derivations which will be considered will be those which expand at each step the leftmost nonterminal in the string. This effectively selects one canonical derivation for each possible parse tree. This makes the derivation shown in Figure 3 the canonical one, and the other two that are shown in Figure 4 are not found.

THE ROOTS OF NONDETERMINISM

The control strategy which we have just described is very simple to state in terms of a generative rule, but if one wants to use it for an analysis algorithm, it seems to suggest the following analysis strategy: as you start scanning along the string, as soon as you find a piece that matches the right-hand side of some rule, then you can collapse that into a single constituent. This is called reduction. However, this strategy will not work in general, as we can illustrate with the grammar of Figure 5. This figure illustrates a very simple grammar for arithmetical expressions. In it, an expression (E) can be a term (T) plus a term or can be just a single term. Likewise a term can be a factor (F) times a factor or just a single factor, and factors can be any of the symbols A, B, or C. Figure 6 shows the structure that we would like to get as a parsing of the string "A+B*C".

E ⟶ T + T

E ⟶ T

T ⟶ F * F

T ⟶ F

F ⟶ A, B, C

Figure 5. A simple grammer for arithmetic expressions

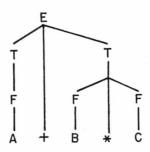

Figure 6. A parse tree for "A+B*C"

The way that we have written the rules of the grammar forces on us the priority that the product comes first and then the sum. (A slightly more expanded grammar would include parentheses to enable one to express the other interpretation if that was what was intended.) Now suppose we took this string of characters and the context free rules of Figure 5 and started doing reductions on the string wherever we could. We could reduce the A to an F and then to a T, then we'd have to go on to the + which can't reduce by itself. We could reduce the B to an F and then to a T and then we could reduce the T + T to a single E. After that we would reduce the C to an F and then to a T and after that we would be stuck because there is no rule which will reduce E * T to anything. The structure that we have built when we come to the impasse is shown in Figure 7. Essentially, in order to obtain the parse tree in Figure 6, it is necessary not to go ahead and reduce the second F to a T. Instead we must postpone that until reducing the C to an F and reducing the F * F to a single F, which can then be reduced to a T and the T + T reduced to a single E.

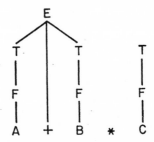

Figure 7. A blocked reverse derivation from "A+B*C"

So one finds that when one is attempting to do an analysis there is a fundamental nondeterminism that must be provided for. One comes to a place where a rule could be applied, but doesn't know whether that's the right place to make the reduction or not. It is necessary to consider both alternatives, follow out the rest of the analysis, and see which one (if any) of the alternative sequences of choices will give a complete parse tree. This is the first of several sources of nondeterminism in both text and speech parsing.

NONDETERMINISTIC ALGORITHMS

There are many applications in computer science, especially in artificial intelligence and language processing, where systematic search in a space of alternative possible choice is required. A conceptual device for devising algorithms for such tasks is the notion of a nondeterministic algorithm or nondeterministic machine. By this, we do not refer to an algorithm whose behavior is unpredictable, but rather to an abstract algorithm in which there is a primitive choice operation which can make one of several choices. This algorithm is then simulated on a real machine by systematically considering all possible sequences of alternative choices of the abstract nondeterministic algorithm. The nondeterministic machine is a conceptual device to enable the writer of a grammar or other such search algorithm to think of the machine as if it were magically making the right choices, freeing him from explicitly keeping track of the alternative choices and cycling through them. One says that a string is accepted by a nondeterministic algorithm, if any of the alternative computation paths leads to a successful analysis.

The first fundamental idea that I would like you to remember is this notion of a nondeterministic algorithm as a device for coping with this type of search in a space of alternative possibilities.

BACKTRACKING VS PARALLEL SEARCH

There are two principal ways of writing simulators for nondeterministic programs. One is called backtracking and its effect is that whenever the program is about to make a choice, it saves somewhere (usually on a pushdown stack) all of the information that is about to be destroyed by the choice so that the simulator can come back later, undo it, and try another choice. The program then parses like a deterministic parser until it encounters a blocked configuration such as the one in Figure 7, at which point it undoes the last choice made and tries the next possible alternative. If there is no other alternate choice, then it undoes the next to last choice, and so on until all possible choice sequences have been considered. Floyd (1967) gives an efficient general technique for implementing backtracking simulators for nondeterministic algorithms. In the case of Figure 7, the result of backtracking would be to undo the last reduction of F to T. Finding nothing else to do, the parser then would undo the reduction of C to F, then undo the reduction of T + T to E, and eventually would back up to the point where the B had been reduced to F, but that F had not been reduced to T. The parser could then go on to reduce the C to an F (a second time -- this was done before on the blocked path) and then reduce the F * F to T, which puts us on the right path for the correct analysis.

A backtracking algorithm does its search by systematically working on one path of the nondeterministic algorithm, saving enough to undo it later. The systematic way in which it walks through the space of possible choices is called "depth first". That is, after making one choice, it proceeds to make a choice that depends on that one, and another that depends on that, and so on, building up a stack of other untried alternatives at different "depths". Only when it encounters a blocked configuration does it undo the most recently made choice, and it tries all possible choices at that "depth" before backing up to the next previous level on the stack of alternatives. If the space of alternative choice sequences were laid out as a tree, the backtracking search would correspond to a left-first tree walk.

Another way of handling nondeterminism is by what I'll call independent alternatives. In such a program, every time that you are about to make a choice, you create an object for each of the possible choices. This object corresponds to a state or configuration of the hypothetical nondeterministic machine which you are simulating. In a real machine, a configuration is basically the contents of the program counter and the register contents; in the simulation of a nondeterministic machine there are many such configurations instead of just one. (This is similar to what goes on in a time sharing system.) For a nondeterministic finite state machine, the configuration is basically the state that you are in and the point in the input string that you have gotten to. In programming a system for handling independent alternatives, every time that you come to a choice point, you make up as many configurations as there are alternative choices, and you are now free to work on those configurations all in parallel (or "breadth first") or you can jump around from one to another (working on the ones that seem most likely of success before working on others for example). With multiple independent alternatives, you can pick up a configuration, determine its state, look at where it is in the input, compute the next configurations which it could get to, and then go to another configuration (which may or may not be one of the ones you just created). Just as in a time-sharing system, you can run a lot of these configurations in pseudo parallel with varying priorities for service.

There is a tremendous advantage for speech understanding and for text parsing in implementing nondeterministic programs in terms of independent alternatives rather than backtracking. With independent alternatives, if you are in a position where it is difficult to decide which of the alternative choices is the best to follow, it is possible for you to follow several parsings in parallel, or to jump from one to another depending on which looks better at any given moment. In the backtracking approach, one has to systematically walk down a long path into barren territory before he can walk back to the place where the next best choice is. The only way to go back and consider one of the alternatives to a choice is to plow on ahead to completely search the space on the current path exhaustively and then back up out of it. Once one has left a given path it is not possible to come back to it and push it further. Even in the simple illustration of backtracking for the example in Figure 7, there were two or three things of an unimaginative nature that had to be undone before getting back to where the right alternative choice had to be made. In more complicated examples, the amount of such "wasted" or uninteresting parts of the space that have to be searched before one can get back to the correct place to make an alternative choice can be astronomical.

I will make a pitch then for a second fundamental idea which you should know about -- namely this difference between systematic backtracking and the following of multiple independent alternatives.

BOTTOM UP, TOP DOWN, PREDICTIVE, AND NONPREDICTIVE PARSING.

The algorithm that we described above for finding a derivation of a given string by reversing the generative rules of the grammar is an algorithm that is referred to as "bottom up". That is, we look into the input string or the current working string until we find something that matches the right-hand side of some grammar rule, and then reduce that matching portion by replacing it with the left-hand side of the rule. (I'm assuming a context free grammar here for simplicity.) We apply this process over and over again until we finally reduce the entire string to a single symbol. (At least the goal we are trying to achieve is such a reduction of the string into a single symbol.) Notice that in the statement we have just made, we have not specifically mentioned the systematic consideration of each of the possible rules that could have applied at each step and the different positions in the working string where rules could have been applied. It is exactly this freedom from consideration of detail that is achieved by thinking of the process as a nondeterministic algorithm. Of course the details need to be considered eventually in order to make the algorithm function on a real machine, but these considerations can be made separately and they can be done once and for all for a parsing system and not have to be redone separately for each grammar or version of a grammar which is written.

There is another kind of parsing algorithm at the other extreme which is called "top down". It gets this name because it starts by expanding the grammar rules "from the top" and only looks for comparison at the input string when a terminal symbol appears in the expansion. A simple version of a top down parser makes use of a pushdown store into which the initial symbol of the grammar is placed before parsing begins. Subsequently the algorithm proceeds as follows: If the topmost symbol on the stack is a nonterminal, then some rule of the grammar with that nonterminal as its left-hand side is selected (another nondeterministic choice) and the topmost symbol of the pushdown stack is replaced with symbols from the right-hand side of the rule (so the leftmost symbol of the right-hand side is now the topmost symbol of the stack). If the topmost symbol of the stack is a terminal symbol, then it is compared with the next unused symbol of the input string. If they are the same then the topmost symbol of the stack is removed and the string is advanced. If they do not match then this configuration is blocked -- i.e., this path of the nondeterministic search is terminated. The string is accepted if the pushdown stack becomes empty at the same time that the last symbol of the input string is used. (Note again our use of the nondeterministic algorithm to simplify the explanation. In an actual parsing algorithm, all possible choices of expanding the topmost nonterminal of the stack are pursued and the string is accepted if any of the alternative computation paths leads to the accepting criterion.) An example of a top-down analysis using a pushdown store is shown in Figure 8. (Here the rectangular enclosure represents the pushdown store, the arrows the steps in the analysis, and the plus sign indicates the consumption of a symbol from the input string by a given stack configuration.)

THE HARVARD PREDICTIVE ANALYZER

The original Harvard Predictive Analyzer (Kuno and Oettinger, 1963) does a slightly more optimized version of the top-down technique just described. It works with a grammar which has been transformed so that all of its rules have a terminal symbol as the first symbol of their right-hand sides. Thus at every step of the pushdown store analysis the algorithm consumes a symbol from the input string, and the number of steps in a given computation path of the nondeterministic machine is at most n, where n is the length of the input string. (Of course the number of steps of the real computer in simulating the nondeterministic algorithm is much greater since it has to follow out all possible alternative computation paths.) An additional advantage of the special form of the context free rules used by the

$$\boxed{S} \longrightarrow \boxed{\begin{matrix} NP \\ VP \end{matrix}} \longrightarrow \boxed{\begin{matrix} DET \\ N \\ VP \end{matrix}} + THE \longrightarrow \boxed{\begin{matrix} N \\ VP \end{matrix}} + MAN \longrightarrow$$

$$\boxed{VP} \longrightarrow \boxed{\begin{matrix} V \\ NP \end{matrix}} + BIT \longrightarrow \boxed{NP} \longrightarrow \boxed{\begin{matrix} DET \\ N \end{matrix}} + THE \longrightarrow$$

$$\boxed{N} + DOG \longrightarrow \boxed{} \quad ACCEPT \quad SENTENCE$$

Figure 8. A sample top-down predictive analysis using a pushdown store.

predictive analyzer (known as Greibach normal form, or standard form) is that it eliminates the possibility of infinite loops due to the symbol on top of the pushdown stack expanding into a string which eventually results in a new instance of the same symbol on top of the stack without advancing the input string. An algorithm due to Greibach (Greibach, 1967) which converts an arbitrary context free grammar into a standard form grammar finds and eliminates the possibility of such "left-recursion".

PREDICTIVE VS. NONPREDICTIVE PARSING

There has been a great deal of discussion in the parsing literature about the differences between top down and bottom up algorithms. An example is a paper by Griffiths and Petrick (1965) which characterizes several varieties of each type. However, in recent years there have been a number of parsing algorithms developed which don't fit into either of these broad categories, and I think that the classical distinction between top down and bottom up is becoming very fuzzy. The distinction which I think is more important -- a distinction which is correlated with the top-down bottom-up distinction for the two simple algorithms presented -- is the distinction between predictive and nonpredictive parsing. A predictive parser is one that will only look at a given point in the input string for things of a sort that it expects to see there, whereas a nonpredictive parser will find a given construction only as a function of the constituents which make it up, irrespective of whether such a constituent is compatible with an analysis of the symbols on either side of it in the input string.

For example, an inherent feature of the top-down pushdown store algorithm which I presented above is that at each point in the analysis there exists on the stack a prediction of the types of phrases which are expected to occur to the right of the current point in the input string. As the algorithm operates, only those constituents will be looked for. Contrast this with the situation in the simple bottom-up algorithm. There, if the terminal symbols could be grouped together to form some constituent, then that alternative would be tried regardless of whether there is an analysis of the symbols to the left with which this constituent could combine.

The predictive parsing technique has an advantage for most parsing applications since it considerably reduces the number of applications of rules that have to be considered and the number of "accidental" constituents that are found (i.e., sequences of words that could make up a constituent in some other context but which are not a constituent of any complete analysis of the current string). For example, in a predictive analysis of "the man bit the dog", using the grammar of Figure 1, the parser looks for a noun phrase at the beginning of the sentence because the grammar says that sentences can begin with noun phrases. However, once it has found the subject noun phrase, it doesn't try to look for a noun phrase at the place that starts with "bit" because there is no grammar rule which would use a noun phrase at that point. In the bottom up approach, all rules are attempted everywhere since there is no prediction. Not only does this result in more rules that have to be tried, but it also results in more spurious matches that do not lead to correct parsings.

For parsing text in the form of sequences of words, there is a great advantage to using the predictive algorithm because it follows fewer blind alleys. On the other hand, there is a problem in continuous speech understanding which reduces its advantage. In continuous speech understanding, there is a fairly high probability that your guess for the word at any given point in the string may be wrong. This is especially true of the first and last word in the sentence due to phonological effects at the beginning and end of utterances. If your guess of the first word is wrong, then all of your predictions later will be influenced by it, and if it induces you to only look for those things that will be consistent with that wrong word, then you may never recover the right parse. The nonpredictive parser that goes up and down the string doing everything it can stands a better chance of recovering from such errors. Specifically, it stands a better chance of finding most of the parse in spite of a wrong or missing word. It can then provide this information as a source for prediction as to what the missing word might be or what kind of word is required in a given region.

Another point that I would like to make concerns this tradeoff between predictive and nonpredictive parsing algorithms for speech understanding. I do not want to make a strong case that one or the other is better; I want to give a feeling for what the tradeoffs are between the two algorithms. The predictive one will do a more selective search, and if one is confident that the things on which it is basing its predictions are right, then it is preferable. On the other hand, if there is a high chance that they are wrong, then the disadvantage is that the prediction may keep you from finding enough of the correct parse to be a useful source of information for error correction.

WELL-FORMED SUBSTRING TABLES

One thing that was found very early in the development of parsing algorithms, especially with the enumerative, top-down, predictive algorithms is that when alternative computation paths are done separately, duplicate work is done on the separate paths. For example, if two possible ways of analyzing the beginning of a sentence cause the analysis to split up into two different computations, the entire remaining analysis will be done twice, even though it may be the same in both cases. A "well-formed substring table" is a mechanism for saving the results of the analysis of a constituent on one path of a nondeterministic computation so that they can be used on other paths without redoing the computation. Whenever in the course of an analysis, a complete constituent is found, it is recorded in a table indexed by the type of constituent and the position where it begins. Whenever the algorithm is about to predict a constituent of a given type at a given position, it consults the well-formed substring table to see if such a constituent has already been found, and if so, then the results are used without recomputation.

TABLE ORIENTED PARSING ALGORITHMS

The use of the well-formed substring table is sufficiently useful that some parsing algorithms have been designed exclusively around that notion. Their central purpose is to fill in this table with entries saying there is a constituent of type x from position y to position z in the input. Their acceptance criterion for a string is finding in the table an entry indicating a constituent of type "sentence" from the beginning to the end of the input sequence. In the design of such an algorithm, one looks for a strategy for filling in the table so that whenever, in applying a grammar rule, one needs the answer to a question "Is there an x from y to z?", the strategy will already have considered all possible ways of filling that entry in the table, and the answer can be determined by simply examining the content of the [x,y,z] entry of the table. The resulting algorithm consists mainly of walking this matrix in an appropriate order and filling in entries on the basis of other entries and the symbols in the input string. For example an algorithm due to Younger (1966) fills in the entries in order of length of the resulting constituent (and forbids grammar rules whose right-hand sides consist of a single nonterminal). Since the lengths of the constituents which match the right-hand side of a rule will be less than the length of the constituent that will result, all the necessary table entries for constituents of a given reduction will already have been made when that reduction is considered. Thus when filling in the table for constituents of length 3 for example, all of the entries for constituents of length 2 and 1 will already have been made and any questions about the existence of such constituents can be answered by merely consulting the table. The constituents of length 1 are found by matching singleton terminal rules against the input string. When such an algorithm terminates, if there is an entry for the initial symbol from the beginning to the end of the input string, then the string is accepted by the parser, otherwise it is rejected.

ELIMINATING REDUNDANCY

In the above type of algorithm, it is critical in order to avoid a lot of excessive computation that a particular order of filling in the table be used. This is so that one can rely on any answer that is needed having been put there at an earlier point in the sequence. This has many efficiency advantages for ordinary text parsing. However, it has a disadvantage for speech understanding applications, since one of the critical elements early in the chain may be misheard or garbled and thereby keep the rest of the analysis from being found (which could be used to help identify the garbled word). This same disadvantage applies to the left-first canonical derivation of a parse which we mentioned earlier, and to any other parsing technique which requires the individual steps in an analysis to be found in a particular canonical order. If one of the critical things that has to be found first in some such ordering is wrong and if all of the subsequent processing is dependent on it, then it will be very difficult to recover from the error. I think, therefore, that it is important for speech understanding to try to relax some of these ordering restrictions. This is a fundamental departure from the way that most text parsing systems operate and it is going to require a different solution to the problem of finding the same parse over and over again in different ways.

In many cases, it may be important to be able to jump over and find the object noun phrase and then the verb phrase when you haven't found the subject yet. For example, in those cases where the subject was not findable because of a garbled word, a well understood verb phrase could be used to predict what kind of subject ought to be there. However, in other cases when you have found the subject first on one path, a computation path which finds the verb phrase and then comes back and works on the subject will find the same parsing over again. The solution that we have been using in the BBN system (Woods, 1974) -- the solution which I think has to be used -- is to put in appropriate checks at various choice points to ask whether the thing that is about to be produced has been found already on some other path and avoid creating a duplicate. When this is done at the level of noun phrases, embedded clauses, etc., it tends to block the redundant generation of larger constituents before the duplication becomes unmanageable. It still carries with it the cost of the additional checking, but I think that this cost is essential in order to cope with the errors that will occur in speech.

LEXICAL AMBIGUITY

I've mentioned a number of things which make the parsing problem for speech understanding more difficult than traditional text parsing. Another difficulty is the ambiguity of word identification in the input sequence of sounds. The major source of lexical ambiguity in text parsing is the possibility of multiple syntactic categories for a given word. In a classical example of sentential ambiguity, "Time flies like an arrow," the word "time" has three possible syntactic categories (noun, verb, or adjective), "flies" can either be a verb or a noun, and "like" can either be a preposition or a verb. If we think of a parser receiving a sequence of these kinds of categories as input, there would be $3 \times 2 \times 2 = 12$ strings of syntactic categories that you could get for this sentence. If you had to put each such sequence through the parser separately (apparently some early parsers did exactly that) you would be doing twelve separate parsings. Imagine what would happen with a sentence of say 20 words with an average ambiguity of 2 categories per word; you would have over 1,000,000 different possible such sequences. In speech understanding, this basic ambiguity is magnified by the inability to unambiguously determine the segmentation of speech sounds into word sequences. Clearly one doesn't want to run a parser on a separate enumeration of each possible sequence of syntactic categories.

WORD LATTICES

A technique that has been very effective for dealing with lexical ambiguity has been the use of a lattice of input symbols rather than a single string. A simple example of such a structure is illustrated in Figure 9. Such a lattice compactly represents all of the possible alternative sequences of input symbols with the common parts of different sequences factored together so that processing on them needs to be done only once. With such an input, grammar rules are matched the same as before, except that as a rule is matched against the input, particular paths are selected through the word lattice which satisfy the match. This technique has a tremendous benefit in terms of the amount of computation required for parsing. When a particular rule is matched at a given point in the word lattice, all of the possible sequences of words in which the matching sequence occurs are effectively factored together so that the result of the reduction is effectively performed just once for an entire equivalence class of word sequences. This technique is very attractive for speech understanding because the possible alternative segmentations of the input signal into words leads to a lattice structure similar to that illustrated in Figure 9 (although of slightly more varied structure). Whereas the structure in Figure 9 is nothing more than a sequence of alternative syntactic categories, the structures for word lattices in speech understanding tend to have much more branching, and the individual branches leaving a given point do not all come together again at the same point. However, the same parsing algorithm runs on this more generalized input lattice and saves a tremendous amount of processing by avoiding the multiplication of combinatorial possibilities.

CHART PARSERS

The concept of a word lattice for the input symbols and the use of a well-formed substring table for representing the intermediate stages of parsing are closely related, and can be combined into a single data structure in a parsing algorithm. The structure of the well-formed substring table is exactly the same as that of the word lattice, and if it is appropriately indexed by position in the input string (or position in the word lattice) then it shares the property of compactly enumerating for a given position all of the constituents which begin at that position and all of the positions where such constituents end. A classical

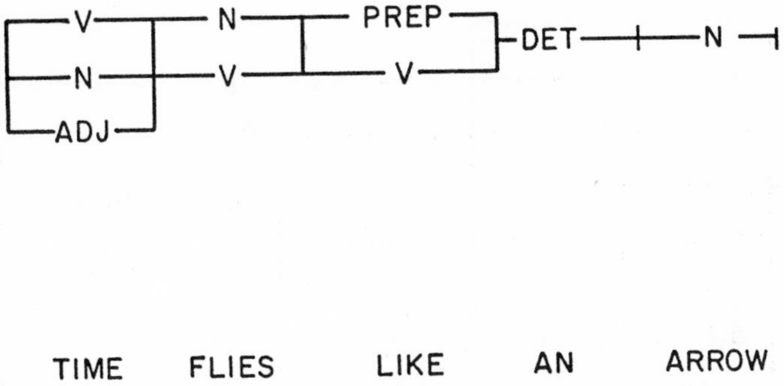

```
 ┌─V───┬──N──┬── PREP ─┐
 │              │           ├─DET──┼──N ─┤
 ├─N──┼──V────┼── V ───┘
 └─ADJ─┘
```

TIME   FLIES   LIKE   AN   ARROW

Figure 9. A sample word lattice

parsing algorithm known as Cocke's algorithm (see Hays, 1962) and a
generalization of that by Martin Kay, which Kay now calls a chart
parser (1967), combine a lattice of input segments with a lattice of
well-formed substrings in a single data structure called a chart. The
goal of such a parser is to expand the initial lattice of input symbols
into a complete lattice (or chart) of all of the constituents that can be
found in any analysis of any path in the initial lattice. An example of
such a lattice for the sentence "Time flies like an arrow" is shown in
Figure 10. Each labeled horizontal line in the figure between vertical
strikes represents a segment added to the chart as a result of the
application of some rule (or one of the initial entries in the word lattice).
Both of these parsing algorithms (Kay's and Cocke's) select a particular
order for walking the chart and adding new segments as a result of
matching rules against the segments already in the chart, and both
produce a very nice recognition algorithm that keeps a great deal of
the common parts of different analyses merged together. The principal
difference between Kay's parser and Cocke's is Kay's generalization of
the method to handle general rewriting systems and an approximation
to transformational grammars. For strictly context free grammars, both
algorithms are effectively the same.

In this paper, I will call all such parsers (both Cocke's and Kay's)
and their derivatives "chart parsers". In particular, the usual
implementation of the classical nonpredictive bottom-up parsing
algorithm is a chart parser.

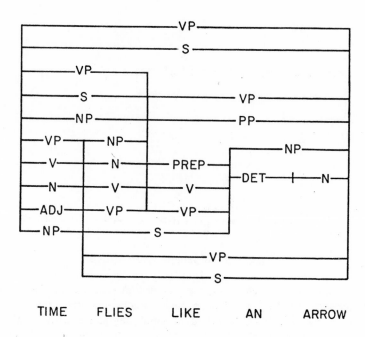

TIME   FLIES   LIKE   AN   ARROW

Figure 10. An example of a well-formed substring lattice or chart

PARSING VERSUS RECOGNITION

In order to be called a parser, an algorithm must not only calculate whether a string is accepted or not, as does a recognizer, but it must also keep a record of the derivation and provide one or more structural analyses of the sentence. In my description of most of the parsing algorithms so far, I have glossed over this distinction and only the recognition aspects have been discussed. In order to be a parser, an algorithm must keep track of and report what constituents were used as pieces of what higher constituents. This can be done conveniently for a chart parser by annotating each of the segments of the chart with a list of the constituents which formed it -- that is, by a list of the segments which were combined by some rule to produce the annotated segment. In general, there can be several ways to form a given segment from different sequences of constituents so the annotation must provide for several such constituent lists in order to represent all possible analyses.

Both Cocke's algorithm and Kay's are bottom up, nonpredictive algorithms and share with other such algorithms the property of finding many accidental constituents that do not form a part of any complete analysis. Such accidental constituents clutter up the chart. Figure 11 shows a chart for our example in which all such accidental segments have been removed. Such a "cleaned up" chart together with its constituent pointers provides a very compact representation of all of the possible alternative analyses of the input with the common parts of the different analyses merged together. Figure 12 shows the chart of Figure 11 with constituent pointers added for one particular parsing of the input, and Figure 13 shows the same chart with all constituent pointers included.

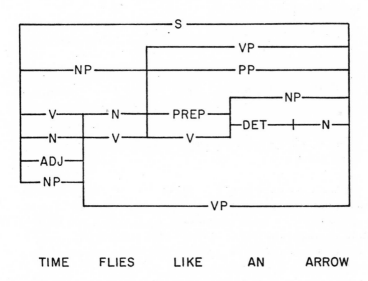

TIME　　FLIES　　LIKE　　AN　　ARROW

Figure 11. A chart with accidental constituents removed

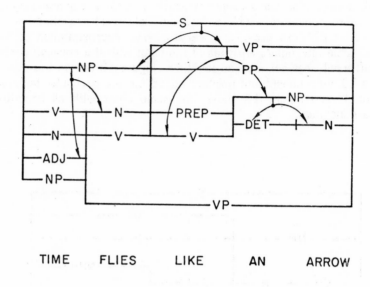

TIME   FLIES   LIKE   AN   ARROW

Figure 12. A chart showing constituent pointers for
one parsing

    In more typical cases, one cannot draw as nice a picture of the
chart as in our example, (in particular it may not be a planar graph), but
inside a computer, a table of positions, each with a set of associated
segments (indicated by the constituent type and the position where the
segment ends) suffices to handle the most general case for a
recognizer. For a parser, the inclusion with each segment of a list of
alternative constituent lists, each of which is a list of segments (where
a segment is named by its left and right end points and the constituent
label) suffices to produce a compact representation of all the possible
parses.

EARLEY'S ALGORITHM
    There is another parsing algorithm for context free grammars
due to Jay Earley (Earley, 1970), which can be thought of as a
predictive chart parser. This algorithm combines the benefits of the
systematic, lattice-oriented parsing of the well-formed substring or

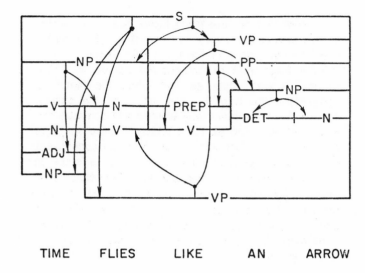

TIME   FLIES   LIKE   AN   ARROW

Figure 13. A chart showing all constituent pointers for two parsings

chart parser with the advantages of predictive analysis. Although the algorithm was developed in the context of parsing for computer programming languages, and is presented as such by Earley, the algorithm has many theoretical advantages for parsing context free grammars in general, and an appreciation of its operation is important for the understanding of context free parsing. Earley's algorithm does not quite fit into either the top down or the bottom up models, or rather it seems to fit equally well into both. Starting from the beginning of the string, it begins to fill in a table (which Earley calls a state table) in which it records, for each position in the input string, each rule of the grammar that has been partially matched up to that point or which might possibly match beginning at that point (i.e., each rule that would be consistent with what has been parsed so far to the left of that point). The table is organized into columns, one for each position in the input string, and the procedure for filling out a given column i+1 is as follows:

1. (transition) Make entries in the column for rules that appear in the preceding column and whose match can be continued by matching the input symbol associated with this column.

2. (prediction or "pushing") Make beginning entries in this column for every constituent which could be used to continue a match for a rule already in this column (each rule remembers the column in which its match was begun so that when the match is completed, the algorithm can return to the column where the constituent was wanted and continue the match of any and all rules which wanted it. This memory of the column in which a subconstituent match was begun replaces the use of a stack in most predictive algorithms, and gains a combinatorial benefit by not having to enumerate all of the different possible stacks which could sit above a given subconstituent computation. A given constituent in a given place will be looked for and found only once.)

3. (completion or "popping") For each rule whose match has just been completed in this column, go back to the column where that match was begun and pick up and continue the match of all rules which can use the constituent just formed.

In Earley's statement of the algorithm the progress of a rule match is recorded by a pair of numbers -- the rule number and the number of symbols in the right-hand side of the rule which have already been matched. An entry in the table consists of these two numbers plus the number indicating the column in which the rule match was begun. A sentence is accepted if, when the last column is filled out, it contains an entry for a rule whose left-hand side is S, whose match has been completed, and whose match was begun in column 0. (The algorithm begins by initializing column 0 to contain all of the rules whose left-hand sides are S.)

Earley's algorithm is frequently thought of as a top-down parsing algorithm because of the way that it starts with the assumption that it is going to build a sentence and successively elaborates its set of rules to be looked for by passing information "down" in step 2. However, once such top down prediction (which incidentally may leap over what will amount to many cycles of left recursion in the final analysis) has determined the set of rules to be used at a given point, the subsequent analysis will do almost the same kind of bottom-up structure building as any other chart parser, the principal difference being that for Earley's algorithm we will get a subset of those entries in the chart that would have been produced by an ordinary chart parser. This is because the prediction technique has eliminated all those entries which are not at least consistent with some analysis of the string to the left. Once again, this prediction is a mixed blessing for speech understanding since if the prediction is made on the basis of unreliable evidence, it may keep us from finding enough of an analysis to benefit error correction.

TRANSITION NETWORK GRAMMARS

The presentation so far has been illustrated by two extremely simple sample grammars. When one begins to write a grammar for any appreciable subset of natural language, one finds that there are some verb phrases which consist of a verb alone, some with a verb plus an object noun phrase, some with a verb, an indirect object and a direct object, any of these three forms with a prepositional phrase added, any of the three forms with two prepositional phrases, etc. If one were to write each of these as a separate context free rule, as illustrated in Figure 14a, we find a very rapid proliferation (possibly infinite) of rules that share a lot of stuff in the right-hand sides.

People who write grammars immediately find themselves falling into notations such as that illustrated in Figure 14b in which optional constituents, alternative constituent sequences, and repeatable constituents are indicated by some notation (usually parentheses for optionality, curly brackets or vertical strokes for alternative sequences, and the Kleene star operator (*) for repeatable constituents). These are usually thought of just as abbreviations for a set of ordinary context free rules, but the actual expansion of such notations into ordinary context free rules is a very bad way to implement them. Instead, one buys an advantage in parsing if he takes advantage of these primitive notions of optionality, alternatives, and repeatability. Transition network grammars provide a mechanism for doing this.

A basic transition network (BTN) is essentially a finite state transition diagram to which recursion has been added by fiat (see Woods, 1969, 1970, 1973a). The result is no longer a finite state device, but rather is formally equivalent to a pushdown store automaton or a context free grammar. The BTN is a labeled, directed graph whose nodes, which we call states, represent states which the grammar can be in in the course of generating (or analyzing) a sentence, and whose arcs represent transitions from state to state. The labels on the arcs indicate the input symbol or type of phrase which must be consumed from the input string in order to make the transition. It is the possibility of arcs (called PUSH arcs) labeled with the names of phrase constituents that provides the recursion which makes this model more than finite state. The grammar contains a start state for each of the types of constituents which can be called for on a PUSH arc, and distinguished states called final states which represent the completion of the analysis of some constituent. A PUSH arc can be taken if some string accepted by the start state associated with the label of that push arc is consumed (or generated). There is a mechanical procedure presented in Woods (1969) for transforming any given context free grammar into an equivalent BTN and performing a number of optimizing transformations on the resulting BTN to produce a grammar which is more compact and more efficient for parsing than the original context free grammar. Essentially the BTN provides a way to factor a context free grammar into a finite state part and a recursive part so that as much of the grammar as possible can be expressed in the finite state part and optimized by the same techniques applicable to finite state grammars.

The set of notations used by linguists for representing alternative sequences and repeatable constituents in their grammar rules correspond to the operations called "union" and "closure" in the theory of finite state automata, which together with the operation of concatenation are known to generate the finite state languages. Thus, the right-hand sides of grammar rules using these notations are merely notational variants of what is in automata theory called a "regular expression", and there exist formal procedures for translating such a representation into an equivalent transition diagram for a finite state machine. These same procedures can be used to translate a context free grammar using these notations into an equivalent BTN, such as the one illustrated in Figure 14c.

Thus, the BTN formalism provides a realization for these notions of alternative sequences and repeatable constituents that is more efficient for a parser, as well as being less redundant as a linguistic specification.

Each of the arcs leaving a given state represents an alternative possible continuation of the string being generated (or of the analysis of a given string).

The transition network grammar effectively provides for the merging of common parts of what would be different context free rules, and this permits parsing operations to be performed only once on such parts instead of separately on each individual copy as would be the case if the expressions were expanded into separate ordinary context free rules. Most of the parsing algorithms for context free

VP⟶V

    V   NP

    V   NP   NP

    V   PP

    V   NP   PP

    V   NP   NP   PP

    ●

    ●

    ●

**a. SEPARATE CONTEXT FREE
GRAMMAR RULES**

VP⟶V (NP (NP)) (PP)*

b. MERGED REPRESENTATION

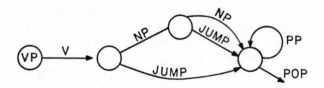

c. REPRESENTATION AS BASIC TRANSITION NETWORK (BTN)

Figure 14. Alternative representations for multiple right-hand sides of grammar rules

grammars have natural generalizations to transition network grammars which take advantage of this merging. In particular, Earley's algorithm is a natural algorithm for BTN grammars and the number of parsing operations required by Earley's algorithm for a parsing of an optimized BTN grammar compared to the parsing of an equivalent context free grammar can easily be less by factors of four or five. A presentation of a version of Earley's algorithm for BTN's is given in Woods (1969).

GRAMMARS FOR NATURAL ENGLISH

In comparing the models of the Chomsky hierarchy with each other, it has been found that whereas the finite state grammars have great computational advantages for parsing (there exist formal, mechanical optimizing procedures of various types for finite state machines), the absence of recursion makes it unsuitable for natural language analysis. On the whole, context free grammars provide the simplest and most natural grammars for natural language but are formally incapable of dealing with certain kinds of coordinate constructions and discontinuous constituents. Context sensitive grammars have sufficient formal power to provide a recognizer for such constructions, but provide no useful structural descriptions. General rewriting systems add no useful power not already present in context sensitive grammars and have the undesirable consequence that it is not possible to have a parsing algorithm for the entire class of such grammars.

TRANSFORMATIONAL GRAMMARS

There are a number of other grammar formalisms that have been proposed for natural language which have been shown to be equivalent to the ordinary context free grammar model. One formalism, however, with considerably more power than context free grammars has stimulated linguistics and served as the vehicle for most of the study of natural language grammar in the last decade.

This is the transformational grammar of Chomsky. A transformational grammar basically consists of a context free "base" grammar plus a set of transformational rules which can permute the order of constituents and in general move, delete, and insert constituents at various positions in the parse tree. Transformational rules can also test conditions such as identity of constituents and the presence of syntactic features associated with the words and sometimes the phrases of the sentence. Perhaps the simplest example of a transformational rule is the passive transformation shown in Figure 15, which produces the "surface structure" for a passive sentence from the "deep structure" that underlies the corresponding active sentence.

PASSIVE

NP	(AUX)	V	NP	
1	2	3	4	$\Rightarrow$
4	2	BE+EN+3	BY+1	

CONDITION: 4 ≠ 1

a. STATEMENT OF THE RULE

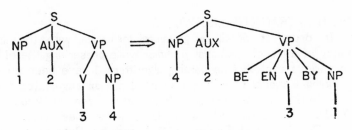

b. EFFECT OF THE RULE ON TREES

Figure 15.   A Sample Transformational Rule: The Passive Transformation

The rule says that if you can analyze an intermediate phrase structure tree into a sequence consisting of a noun phrase, optionally an auxiliary verb, followed by a main verb and an object noun phrase, then you can transform the tree by moving the subject noun phrase (1) to the position of the object noun phrase (4) appending the word "by" on its left, moving the object noun phrase to subject position, and appending the morphemes, "be" and "en", to the left of the main verb. This rule changes the tree structure corresponding to "Mary shot

John" into that corresponding to "John was shot by Mary". (A later rule will move the "en" to the right of the next verb and a "post cyclic" rule will combine the two into a past participal.) The generation of a sentence by a transformational grammar consists of the generation of a deep structure tree by means of the context free base grammar and then transforming this tree through a series of intermediate structures into the surface structure tree by means of the transformational rules, which are usually ordered, marked as optional or obligatory, and applied cyclically to successive embedded clauses in complex sentences.

The transformational grammar appears capable of capturing the major syntactic facts about natural language, and a great deal of our current knowledge about the syntax of English has been discovered and codified in terms of this model. However, it is incredibly inefficient to parse with such a grammar and no parsing algorithm suitable for parsing any significant amount of text has ever been developed for this grammar model, although Stanley Petrick has spent considerable effort in this direction for a number of years and has probably the only working parsing algorithm for transformational grammars in existence (Petrick, 1965).

AUGMENTED TRANSITION NETWORKS

In order to obtain a grammar formalism with the linguistic adequacy of a transformational grammar while preserving the efficiency of the various context free parsing algorithms, I have been developing and refining a model of grammar which I call an augmented transition network (ATN). Presentations of this model appear in Woods (1969, 1970, 1973a). Earlier attempts along similar lines were made by Thorne, Brattley, and Dewar (1968) and by Bobrow and Fraser (1969). An ATN consists of a basic transition network grammar augmented with a set of registers which are carried along with the state and which can hold arbitrary pieces of tree structure, and with arbitrary conditions and actions associated with the arcs of the grammar which can test and set the contents of these registers. As a parsing proceeds with an ATN grammar, the conditions and actions associated with the transitions can put pieces of the input string into registers, use the contents of registers to build larger structures, check whether two registers are equal, etc. It turns out that this model can construct the same kinds of structural descriptions as those of a transformational grammar and can do it in a much more economical way. The merging of common parts of alternative structures, which the network grammar provides, permits a very compact representation of quite large grammars, and this model has served as the basis for several natural language understanding systems such as the LUNAR system (Woods, Kaplan, and Nash-Webber, 1972, Woods, 1973b). For speech understanding, the transition network grammar is one of the few linguistically adequate grammars for natural English that are at all amenable to coping with the combinatorial problems. This model is being used as the basis of the syntactic component of the BBN speech understanding project (Bates, 1974, Woods, 1974). Other types of context free grammars can be augmented by conditions and actions associated with the grammar rules in a similar way, but such grammars lose the benefits of the transition networks (such as merging common parts of different rules) which we discussed previously. Another advantage of the transition network formalism is the ease with which one can follow the arcs backwards and forwards in order to predict the types of constituents or words which could occur to the right or left of a given word or phrase. One of the important roles of a syntactic component in speech understanding is to predict those places where small function words such as "a", "an", "of" should occur since such words are almost always unstressed and difficult to unambiguously find in the input.

In the BBN speech system such words are almost always found as a result of syntactic prediction and are not even looked for during lexical analysis since spurious matches would be found more often than correct ones.

The ATN formalism suggests a way of viewing a grammar as a map with various landmarks and recognizable locations that one encounters in the course of crossing a sentence from left to right. For speech understanding this perspective is beneficial, for example, in attempting to correlate various prosodic characteristics of sentences with such "geographical landmarks" within the structure of a sentence.

Let me conclude this presentation of syntactic techniques with a reiteration that I have not attempted to make a case that any one parsing technique or grammar formalism is uniformly better than others (indeed I do not believe there is a best one for all applications). Rather, I have attempted to give sufficient insight into the relative advantages and disadvantages to enable the reader to make appropriate choices for particular applications.

PART II. SEMANTICS

Turning now to the subject of semantics, I should perhaps first make the point that the word "semantics" means different things to different people. There is a tradition in philosophy and logic that specifies the semantics of formal systems such as the propositional calculus in terms of a set of "truth conditions" for each possible expression in the system. These truth conditions are abstract entities which specify the situations or "possible worlds" in which the statement would be true. In linguistics, on the other hand, concern is usually devoted to finding a notation or representation in which to specify each of the different possible interpretations or "readings" which a natural language sentence can have and to procedures for determining whether a sentence is meaningful or "anomalous" (i.e., not meaningful). The linguist does not usually follow this up by providing a semantics in terms of truth conditions for his notation. In the field of programming languages in computer science, the semantics of a programming language is specified in terms of the computations which the machine is to perform as a result of a given expression. In specifying a formal semantics for such systems however, one usually takes recourse to defining the semantics by reducing it to another notation such as those of elementary arithmetic, whose semantics is presumably understood. In the fields of computational linguistics and artificial intelligence, the term is perhaps most misused. In some cases, it is taken to cover everything that is not syntax -- i.e., everything that is not part of a grammar -- while in others it is asserted to be no different in principle from syntax, and any basis for a distinction between the two is denied.

While I do not have the space here to go into a complete exposition of the different concerns of all of these different perspectives on semantics, I will try to give a brief synopsis of the distinctions.

Let us begin by considering what all of these different things which call themselves semantics have in common. According to my dictionary, semantics is "the scientific study of the relations between signs or symbols and what they denote or mean." This is the traditional use of the term and represents the common thread which links the different concerns discussed above. Notice that the term does not refer to the things denoted or the meanings, but to the relations between these things and the linguistic expressions which denote them. Thus, although it may be difficult to isolate exactly what part of a system is semantics, any system which understands sentences and carries out appropriate actions in response to them is somehow completing this connection, and therefore is applying semantic knowledge to this task. One of the common misuses of the term semantics in the fields of computational linguistics and artificial intelligence is to extend the coverage of the term not only to this relation between linguistic form and meaning, but to all of the retrieval and inference capabilities of the system. This misuse arises since for many tasks in language processing, the use of semantic information to make an evaluation necessarily involves not only the determination of the object denoted, but also some inference about that object. In absence of a good name for this further inference process, terms such as "semantic inferences" have come to be used for the entire process. I regret to say that I have no really good substitute term for such processes and, since the terminology is so well established in some of the literature, I will use the term "semantic inferences" in this paper in referring to inferences that cross the boundary between symbol and referent and then draw conclusions about that referent. (One must be aware, however, that not all writers who use this term mean the same thing by it.)

The concerns of the linguists and the philosophers in the areas of semantics are effectively two halves of the same process, both of which the fields of computational linguistics and speech understanding will have to cope with. In reducing the semantics of natural language sentences to some formal notation, the linguist has only completed half of the job if he does not go on and specify a semantics of the resulting formal system. It is at this point that the concerns of philosophers and logicians in specifying the semantics for formal systems takes over. Notice that specifications of the formal semantics of programming languages in terms of the notations of elementary arithmetic are satisfactory only to the extent that we understand fully what these notations themselves mean. This is also the case for specifying the semantics of natural language.

I hope the above presentation has alerted you to some of the different kinds of things to which the term semantics can refer, and I will attempt to make clear which one I am using in the remainder of this presentation. I should point out that in the field of computational linguistics we don't have nearly as good an understanding of semantics as we do of syntax. I cannot give you the same kind of evolution of ideas through successively more powerful models and techniques, all of which are well understood. Here instead, the mechanisms which we understand thoroughly are known to be inadequate for dealing with many aspects of the problem, and the techniques which hold promise of dealing with some of the more difficult problems are not yet sufficiently understood or tested for anyone to say whether they in fact solve the problem or not. In this area, then, we have many promising approaches, but few definite answers.

What I will attempt to do here is provide an understanding of some basic principles of semantic representation and interpretation that will apply to any system that understands natural language (whether text or speech), and then some specific techniques which I think have direct relevance to speech understanding. In particular, I will describe two techniques which are being applied in the BBN speech understanding system. One is the technique of semantic interpretation into procedural semantics which I have applied effectively to several natural language question-answering applications, and the other is the technique of "semantic intersections" in semantic network representations of knowledge which was developed by Quillian (1968, 1969). For more details on the specific applications of the latter technique to speech understanding, see Nash-Webber (1974 and 1975*). For the most part, the details of many other interesting things that are being done in the area of computational semantics for natural language will have to be left to the references. Articles which may be of interest include: Bruce (1973), Carbonell and Collins (1974), Collins and Quillian (1969), Collins and Warnock (1974), Fillmore (1968), Green and Raphael (1968), Heidorn (1972) Winograd (1972), Woods (1967), and articles by Newell, Simmons, Wilks, Winograd, Schank, Colby, Abelson, Hunt, Lindsay, and Becker in Schank and Colby (1973).

PROCEDURAL SEMANTICS

It appears that the programming language theorists stand on firmer ground than the philosophers or the linguists in specifying the semantics of their systems, since they can define the semantics of their notations in terms of the procedures that the machine is to carry out. Notice that the notion of procedure shares with the notion of meaning that elusive quality of being impossible to present except by means of alternative representations. The procedure itself is something abstract which is instantiated whenever someone carries out the procedure, but otherwise, all one has when it is not being executed is some representation of it.

Although in ordinary natural language not every sentence is overtly dealing with procedures to be executed, it is possible nevertheless to use the notion of procedures as a means of specifying the truth conditions of declarative statements as well as the intended meaning of questions and commands. One thus picks up the semantic chain from the philosophers at the level of truth conditions and completes it to the level of formal specifications of procedures. These can in turn be characterized by their operations on real machines and can be thereby anchored to physics. This notion of characterising the truth conditions of sentences in terms of mechanical procedures is one that I called "procedural semantics" in my 1968 AFIPS paper (Woods,

1968) and the term has since gained wide circulation. The application of this technique in computer systems for natural language understanding has been very effective. Two notable computer systems which make use of this type of semantics are the LUNAR system (Woods, Kaplan, & Nash-Webber, 1972, Woods, 1973b) and the blocks world system of Winograd (1972). The former understands and answers questions such as "What is the average concentration of aluminum in high alkali rocks?", while the latter understands and carries out instructions such as "Put the pyramid on the block in the corner," (including resolving the ambiguity by determining whether there is a pyramid on a block or a block in the corner). Since the semantic techniques used in the LUNAR system are more formalized and rule driven and since I am more familiar with the details of that system, I will use LUNAR as the principal illustration of the technique. I think the rules used there can effectively serve as a formal model for what is going on in a number of other language understanding systems.

SEMANTICS IN LUNAR

The semantic framework of the LUNAR system consists of three parts -- a semantic notation in which to represent the meanings of the sentences, a specification of the semantics or meanings of this notation by means of LISP programs, and a procedure for assigning representations in the notation to input sentences. In LUNAR, the semantic notation (which I have referred to there as a query language) consists of an extended notational variant of the predicate calculus.

The query language contains essentially three kinds of constructions:

1) designators, which name or denote objects or classes of objects in the data base,

2) propositions, which correspond to statements that can be either true or false in the data base, and

3) commands, which initiate and carry out actions.

Designators come in two varieties -- individual specifiers and class specifiers. Individual specifiers correspond to proper nouns and variables. For example, S10046 is a designator for a particular sample, OLIV is a designator for a certain mineral (olivine), and X3 can be a variable denoting any type of object in the data base. Class specifiers are designators used to denote classes of individuals over which quantification can range. They consist of the name of an enumeration function for the class plus arguments. For example, (SEQ TYPECS) is a specification of the class of type C rocks (i.e. breccias) and (DATALINE S10046 OVERALL OLIV) is a specification of the set of lines of a table of chemical analyses which correspond to analyses of sample S10046 for the overall concentration of olivine.

Elementary propositions are formed from predicates with designators as arguments, and complex propositions are formed from these by use of the logical connectives AND, OR, and NOT and by quantification. For example, (CONTAIN S10046 OLIV) is a proposition formed by substituting designators as arguments to the predicate CONTAIN, and (AND (CONTAIN X3 OLIV) (NOT (CONTAIN X3 PLAG))) is a complex proposition corresponding to the assertion that X3 contains olivine but does not contain plagioclase. Elementary commands consist of the name of a command function plus arguments, and like propositions, complex commands can be constructed using logical connectives and quantification. TEST is a command function for testing the truth value of a proposition given as its argument. Thus, (TEST (CONTAIN S10046 OLIV)) will answer yes or no depending on whether sample S10046 contains olivine. Similarly PRINTOUT is a command function which prints out a representation for a designator given as its argument.

The format for a quantified proposition or command is

$$(FOR\ QUANT\ \ X\ /\ CLASS:PX\ ;\ QX\ )$$

where QUANT is a type of quantifier (EACH, EVERY, SOME, THE, numerical quantifiers, etc.), X is a variable of quantification, CLASS is a class specifier for the class of objects over which quantification is to range, PX specifies a restriction on the range, and QX is the proposition or command being quantified. (Both PX and QX may themselves be quantified expressions.) For example (FOR EVERY X1 / (SEQ TYPECS) : (CONTAIN X1 PLAG) ; (CONTAIN X1 OLIV)) is a quantified proposition corresponding to the statement that every type C rock that contains plagioclase also contains olivine. (FOR EVERY X2 / (DATALINE S10046 OVERALL OLIV) : T ; (PRINTOUT X2)) is a quantified command to printout all of the chemical analyses of S10046 for overall olivine concentrations. (For expository reasons, the notation has been slightly simplified here compared to that actually used in the LUNAR system, but the differences are minor.)

SEMANTICS OF THE NOTATION

Having specified our semantic notation for representing the meanings, we must now specify the meanings of our notations. As mentioned before, we do this in LUNAR by relating the notations to procedures which can be executed. For each of the predicate names that can be used in specifying semantic representations, we will specify a procedure or subroutine which will determine the truth of the predicate for given values for the arguments. Similarly for each of the functions which can be used, we will specify a procedure which can compute the value of that function given the values of its arguments. For each of the class specifiers for the FOR function, we will require a subroutine which enumerates the members of the class. The FOR function itself is also defined by a subroutine as are the logical operators AND, OR and NOT and the basic command functions TEST and PRINTOUT. Thus any well formed expression in the query language is a composition of functions which have procedural definitions in the retrieval component and are therefore themselves well defined procedures capable of execution on the data base. In fact in the LUNAR system, the definition of all of these procedures is done in LISP and the notation of the query language is so chosen that its expressions are executable LISP programs. The totality of these function definitions and the data base on which they operate constitute the retrieval component of the system.

It should be pointed out that by virtue of this definition of the primitive functions and predicates as LISP functions, the query language can be viewed simultaneously as a higher-level programming language and as an extension of the predicate calculus. This gives rise to two different possible types of inference for answering questions, corresponding to the philosopher's distinction between intention and extension. First, because of its definition by means of procedures, a question such as "Does every sample contain silicon?" can be answered extensionally (that is by appeal to the individuals denoted by the class name "samples") by enumerating the individual samples and checking whether silicon has been found in each one. On the other hand, this same question could have been answered intentionally (that is by reference to its meanings alone without reference to the objects denoted) by means of the application of inference rules to other (intentional) facts such as the assertion "Every sample contains some amount of each element." Thus the expressions in the query language are capable either of direct execution against the data base (extensional mode) or manipulation by mechanical inference algorithms or theorem provers (intentional mode). Only the former (extensional)

mode of inference is actually used in the LUNAR system. This gives
rise to some limitations (e.g., it is not possible to prove most assertions
about infinite sets in extensional mode), but is very efficient for a
variety of question-answering applications.

SEMANTIC INTERPRETATION

Having specified the notation in which we will represent the
meanings of English sentences in our system and making sure that we
understand the nature of the meanings of the expressions in that
notation, we are left with the specification of the process whereby
meanings are assigned to sentences. This process is referred to as
semantic interpretation, and in LUNAR it is driven by a set of formal
semantic interpretation rules. The semantic interpreter operates on a
syntactic structure or fragment of one which has been constructed by
the parser, assigning semantic expressions in the notation to the nodes
of this structure to indicate the "meanings" of those constructions to
the system. In LUNAR this procedure is such that the interpretation of
nodes can be initiated in any order, but if the interpretation of a node
requires the interpretation of a constituent node, then the
interpretation of that constituent node is performed before the
interpretation of the higher node is completed. Thus, it is possible to
perform the entire semantic interpretation by calling for the
interpretation of the top node (the sentence as a whole), and this is
the normal mode in which the interpreter is operated in the LUNAR
system.

SEMANTIC RULES

In determining the meaning of a construction, two types of
information are used -- syntactic information about sentence
construction and semantic information about constituents. For example,
in interpreting the meaning of the sentence, "S10046 contains silicon,"
it is both the syntactic structure of the sentence (subject = S10046;
verb = "contain"; object = silicon) plus the semantic facts that S10046
is a sample and silicon is a chemical element that determine the
interpretation (CONTAIN S10046 SILICON). (Note that the predicate
CONTAIN here is the name of a procedure in the retrieval component
and it is only by the "accident" of mnemonic design that its name
happens to be the same as the English word "contain" in the sentence
that we have interpreted.)

In LUNAR, this information about the semantic interpretations of
syntactic structures is embodied in semantic rules consisting of patterns
that determine whether a rule can apply and actions that specify how

the semantic interpretation is to be constructed. An example of such a rule is given in Figure 16. The name of the rule is S:SAMPLE-CONTAIN, and the left-hand side, or pattern part of the rule, consists of three templates which match fragments of syntactic structure. The first template requires that the sentence being interpreted have a subject noun phrase which is a member of the semantic class SAMPLE, the second requires that the verb be either "have" or "contain", and the third requires a direct object which is either a chemical element, an oxide or an isotope. The terms S.NP, S.V and S.OBJ name schemata for tree fragments which are used not only to test for the presence of their corresponding syntactic structures in the sentence, but also to associate reference numbers with selected nodes in the structure. These numbers are used for reference by the semantic conditions in the templates and for use in the right-hand side of the semantic rule. For example, the tree fragment S.NP locates the subject noun phrase of the sentence and associates the reference number 1 with that noun phrase.

(S: SAMPLE-CONTAIN

    (S.NP (MEM 1 (SAMPLE)))

    (S.V (OR (EQU 1 HAVE)

           (EQU 1 CONTAIN)))

    (S. OBJ (MEM 1 (ELEMENT OXIDE ISOTOPE)))

    $\longrightarrow$

    (PRED (CONTAIN (#1 1)(#3 1))))

Figure 16. A sample semantic interpretation rule

The right-hand side, or action part, of the rule follows the right arrow and specifies that the interpretation of this node is to be a predicate formed by inserting the interpretations of two constituent nodes into the schema

(CONTAIN (#1 1)(#3 1))

where the expressions (#m n) refer to the interpretation of the node with reference number n for template number m in the match of the left-hand side of the rule.

ORGANIZATION OF RULES

The semantic rules for interpreting sentences are usually governed by the verb of the sentence. That is, out of the entire set of semantic rules, only a relatively small number of them can possibly apply to a given sentence because of the verb mentioned in the rule. Similarly the rules which interpret noun phrases are governed by the head noun of the noun phrase. For this reason, the semantic rules in LUNAR are indexed according to the heads of the constructions to which they could apply and recorded in the dictionary entry for the head words. Each rule then characterizes a syntactic/semantic environment in which a word can occur and specifies its interpretation in that environment. The templates of a verb rule thus describe the necessary and sufficient constituents and semantic restrictions in order for the verb to be meaningful. Nouns in noun phrases behave similarly. That is, the semantic rules not only specify the process of interpretation which assigns semantic representations, but their left-hand sides also specify the conditions under which given words and constructions are meaningful.

SEMANTIC RULES IN GENERAL

The above presentation is oversimplified in a number of respects for the sake of expository brevity. There is in general a greater variety of devices that are used in the semantic rules of the LUNAR system, and there are numerous details of operation that we will not consider here (such as the desired behavior when a template or a rule matches in several different ways). For more details on these issues, the reader is referred to Woods (1967) and to Woods, Kaplan, and Nash-Webber (1972). There are also many other interesting issues in the semantics of natural language which have not been explored in the LUNAR system or any other computer system which are currently more the domain of philosophers than computer scientists but which will eventually have to be handled by computer systems if they are to be facile at understanding human language. The diversity of these issues, however, is beyond the scope of this presentation.

In many question answering systems semantic interpretation rules are paired more directly with the syntactic rules of the grammar so that there is little or no template matching required (and consequently less latitude for producing semantic interpretations that are not in node-for-node correspondence with the syntactic structure). In still other systems, the semantics are not formalized in rules, but are simply embodied in arbitrary computer programs (and consequently totally unconstrained in what could be done theoretically but providing little or no theory or conceptual framework for what is going on.) However, the kind of semantic rules that are used in LUNAR can be used as formal models to explain what is going on in the semantics of these other systems in which the semantics is either more restricted or less formalized.

SEMANTIC JUDGMENTS

As in the case of syntax, semantics has both a judgmental and a structural aspect. That is, semantic information is used both to construct semantic representations of the meanings of the sentences and to reject anomalous or semantically ill-formed sentences. What we have described so far has mostly dealt with the structural aspect -- how to assign a semantic representation to a sentence and what representation to assign. This capability is necessary for any language understanding system whether it is text or speech. In the judgmental component, however, there are a number of things which semantics can do which are particularly important for speech understanding. As we pointed out above, the pattern parts of the semantic interpretation rules can be used to specify what assemblages of syntactic structures and lexical words are meaningful.

In the next few sections, what I would like to do is briefly survey the uses of semantic information which have been made in various question answering systems using the notion of semantic interpretation rules as presented above to unify the discussion. I shall no longer be directly concerned with the use of the rules for the assignment of semantic interpretations to sentences, but with the ancillary use of the information embodied in these rules for other purposes.

Semantic information is used in a number of text oriented language understanding systems to select semantically meaningful parsings from among all of the possible parsings of a sentence. For example, in the context of airline flight schedules in interpreting a sentence such as "Does American have a flight from some east coast city to Chicago" we can tell that the phrase "to Chicago" modifies flight and not city because we have semantic interpretation rules for flights to places while we do not have any rules to interpret cities to places. In speech understanding, this ability to determine whether a given interpretation of a sentence is semantically meaningful is critical not only for choosing between alternative parsings, but also for choosing between alternative segmentations of the input signal into words. In the next few sections I will discuss some of the techniques that have been used in various question answering systems to use semantic information for this judgmental role and discuss their advantages and limitations for speech understanding applications.

SEMANTIC SELECTIONAL RESTRICTIONS

As we mentioned above, the attempt to characterize the difference between semantically well-formed sentences and those which are semantically anomalous has been a major concern of many linguistic semanticists (see e.g. Katz & Fodor, 1964). The device which is used in most such attempts is a notion of semantic selectional restrictions -- restrictions between the verbs of a sentence and semantic features of the arguments which they can sensibly take. For example, the restriction that verbs like "intend" require higher animate subjects is used to explain the oddness of sentences such as "the rock intends to sit there." This account assumes that the nouns of the language can be assigned to semantic classes such as "higher animate" and that there must be "semantic agreement" or at least no semantic disagreement between the verb of a sentence and the subjects, objects and other arguments which it can take. It is in this area of semantics that the misconceptions about the distinction between syntax and semantics arise, since there is usually no difference in principle between the implementation of such semantic restrictions to reject semantically anomalous sentences and implementation of syntactic restrictions such as number agreement to reject syntactically incorrect sentences. For sufficiently restricted and fixed domains of discourse, it is possible to implement such semantic selectional restrictions by subcategorizing the syntactic categories of the grammar with classes like 'animate noun' and 'color adjective' rather than simply noun or adjective. One thereby incorporates the testing of semantic selectional restrictions into the grammar and avoids the need for any special mechanism for testing semantic selectional restrictions.

The technique of semantically subcategorizing the syntactic categories of the grammar has been applied effectively in limited speech understanding applications. It has the advantage of being efficient in execution and easy to implement for sufficiently simple understanding tasks. However, one should understand its limitations. One of the major inadequacies is that the use of semantic selectional restrictions as prerequisites for grammaticality or semantic well-formedness is not quite correct. Rather most such conditions are required only for a sentence to be true. When the sentence is a question or when it asserts a negative possibility, then semantic selectional restrictions may be violated by perfectly reasonable sentences. A speech understanding system which contains such restrictions embedded in its grammar will fail to parse such inputs. (For example, in Terry Winograd's blocks world program the sentence "Can a table like blocks?" fails to parse since the system applies the selectional restriction that "like" requires an animate subject.) A speech understanding system which used such selectional restrictions as a prerequisite for acceptability of an interpretation of a speech signal would be unable to "hear" this sequence of words no matter how well articulated and how successful the acoustic and phonological analysis, but would rather insist on looking for some other interpretation of the signal.

An additional limitation of the semantic selectional restriction approach is that the necessary semantic information associated with a given argument to a verb is not necessarily associated with the lexical items in the noun phrase, but may be associated with the referent of the noun phrase instead. The association of such information with the dictionary entries for the words is really just an approximation (albeit a useful one for many applications) of what one really wants the semantic selectional restrictions to test.

A major practical difficulty with incorporating the semantic selectional restrictions into the syntactic categories of the grammar is the lack of extendibility thus induced. If one wants to apply the system to a different domain of discourse or to extend the domain slightly, he has to redefine the categories of the grammar.

SEMANTIC SCREENING

A somewhat more versatile technique for using semantic information to select an appropriate parsing is to apply semantic rules to the nodes of the syntactic tree structure as the nodes are built by the parser. If the node just constructed fails to have a semantic interpretation, then that computation path of the parser is rejected and the parser looks for other ways to parse the input. This technique of semantic screening applies the semantic selectional restrictions as a filter or a sieve during the parsing operation. In its simplest form, the semantic rules are associated with the rules of a context-free grammar in a one-to-one fashion so that as soon as a syntactic rule is applied, the corresponding semantic rule is tested. Semantic screening is often touted as a mechanism for gaining increased efficiency in parsing since it tends to cause early rejection of parsing paths which otherwise would have been continued further. This argument, however, neglects to count the cost of the semantic interpretation on uncompleted parsings which would not have been completed in any case for syntactic reasons. Whether semantic screening really provides an increase in efficiency depends on the relative costs of the extra or unnecessary semantic processing and the syntactic processing that is thereby eliminated. In many situations, it is more efficient to complete the syntactic analysis and then apply the semantic testing.

Another technique which is related to semantic screening is to apply tests not only of general semantic well-formedness but also tests of factuality in conjunction with the formation of a constituent. This is the case for example in Winograd's system when he makes his decision about "put the pyramid on the block in the corner" on the basis of whether there is a pyramid on a block in the current state of the world and not just on the basis of general information about whether pyramids can be on blocks. This technique can be very useful in some situations, but its exclusive and uncontrolled use would make it impossible to say things that were not already true or to ask about things that were not true.

SEMANTIC SELECTION

A major inadequacy of semantic (and of factual) screening and indeed of any application of semantic selectional restrictions as strict prerequisites for well-formedness is its inability to deal with sentences such as "I saw the man in the park with a telescope" in which there are many possible parsings which are all semantically possible, but are not equally plausible. Although it is possible that I was in a park which contained a telescope when I saw the man somewhere else, this is not the most likely interpretation in absence of specific information that would indicate this interpretation. Rather there is a kind of default interpretation that the telescope was probably used to see the man, and in absence of reason to believe otherwise the man was probably in the park. What is required in general rather than a mere rejection of semantically ill-formed interpretations is a mechanism to select the most plausible interpretation from among a set of syntactically related alternatives. Although the solution of this problem in general is not at hand, a beginning has been made in a mechanism called selective modifier placement in the LUNAR parser (see Woods, 1973a). This mechanism uses information such as the fact that a telescope is an optical instrument and one can see with an optical instrument to prefer the alternative of "with a telescope" modifying "see", while in absence of semantic preference, the modifier "in the park" modifies the syntactically preceding noun phrase "man". The technique has not been systematically developed, however, and except for the placement of prepositional phrase modifiers, the use of semantic judgments in LUNAR to select among alternative parsings is not well developed.

SEMANTIC PREDICTION

All of the preceding techniques for making semantic judgments about completed syntactic constructions are of great importance for speech understanding. There are, however, situations in the course of understanding a speech utterance where one does not have a complete construction to work with and would like to make use of semantic information to guide the speech understander to look for words which might have been slightly garbled or to provide initial preferences among the words that are discovered on the basis of acoustic and lexical analyses alone. Given for example that we have found the words "sample" and "contain" in a speech signal, we would like to make use of our semantic information to predict that there should now occur a word which is a chemical element, an oxide or an isotope. This information is contained in our semantic rules (specifically it is in the left-hand sides of the rules). Similarly upon encountering the words "sample" and "contain" among a large number of other words in the initial word lattice, we would like to use the semantic information to notice that these two words are related and perhaps go together in the interpretation of the utterance. Both of these semantic roles make use, not of the logical or interpretative sense of semantics, but of a kind of associational semantics which studies the semantic relationships among words and concepts. There are a number of psychologists and psycholinguists as well as people in artificial intelligence, sociology and other fields who have been trying to model this aspect of semantics with various kinds of network structures. The initial impetus in this area was created by Ross Quillian (1968, 1969), but other researchers in this area of semantics include Abelson, Carbonell, Collins, Rumelhart and Norman, Schank, Simmons, and others (a sampling of most of these authors is given in Schank & Colby, 1973 and others are cited explicitly in this paper). The work of Fillmore (1968) has also been influential in this area of study, and recently, similar notions have been used at MIT as the basis for programs that analyze visual scenes (Winston, 1970). I will describe here some of the characteristics of semantic networks as Quillian visualized them which have direct application in speech understanding and which have been included in the BBN speech understanding system.

Quillian was not interested in the notions of semantics as

characterizing truth. Indeed he denied (I think erroneously) the psychological relevance of such notions. Rather he viewed the "meaning" of a word as merely a collection of the concepts that are associated with it (without, however, giving any adequate explication of what was meant by a concept). I consider Quillian's original formulation and much of the work that it has stimulated to be inadequate in the respect that it does not give any attention to a specification of the semantics of the network notation itself, but that doesn't lessen the validity of many of the points that he and others of this school have raised.

Quillian was concerned with investigating the structure in which humans store information in their brains. Thus, the so called semantic networks are really attempts at finding structures and organizations for storing knowledge. His concern is not with having a notation in which to write down a list of facts, but rather with an overall memory structure in which the interrelationships among those facts, which humans use for retrieval of information and for construction of inferences, are explicitly and efficiently represented. The important thing for Quillian is not so much the structure of a particular concept, but the network of relations to other concepts that are established. In particular, Quillian sought to devise a mechanism and a structure which could account for the types of semantic associations which people make and the way these associations manifest themselves in human language understanding.

To give a flavor of the kind of network that Quillian had in mind, Figure 17 (taken from Quillian, (1969)), gives an example of the concept associated with the lexical item "client". Each lexical item or word points to one or more "concepts" or nodes in the semantic net (corresponding to different senses of the word) each of which is merely an assemblage of pointers to other concept nodes in the network. In Figure 17 the identifiers PERSON, EMPLOY, and PROFESSIONAL stand for pointers to other concept nodes in the network. In Quillian's view, the meaning of a concept is the sum total of the collection of concept nodes to which it is connected -- no more and no less. While this gives very little leverage on solving any of the problems of semantic interpretation or characterization of truth conditions, it is a superb mechanism for accomplishing the semantic predictions and noticing the coincidences among semantically related words that are required for speech understanding. In particular, Quillian's notion of semantic intersection can play an important role in speech understanding.

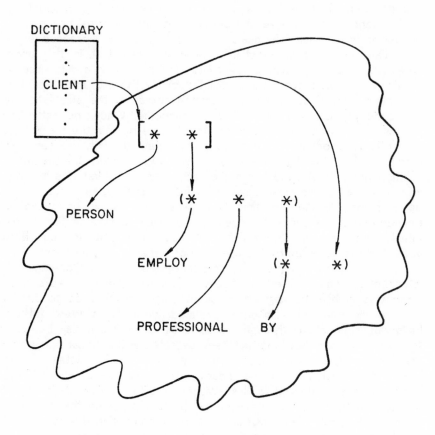

Figure 17. A Fragment of a Quillian Network

SEMANTIC INTERSECTION

Quillian developed the notion of semantic intersection as an attempt to account for the human capability to immediately identify the relationships between diverse things such as between 'plant' and 'alive' or (more subtly) between Madrid and Mexico, and to account for the tendency of people to accept an ambiguous term in a particular sense induced by the appropriateness to the context without noticing the other possible senses (a phenomenon called "foregrounding"). In foregrounding, the appropriate sense is somehow brought forward and made more accessible than the other senses due to the influence of the context. The mechanism which Quillian proposed to account for such phenomena and which he believed was the principal process for accessing information from one's knowledge store was a process which he called semantic intersection. Quillian assumed that in the brain, whenever a concept was brought into consideration in a discourse or whatever, it was somehow stimulated or "activated" and that this activation passed out in waves from the source of the stimulation to the concept nodes to which it was connected. When the activation waves from two different sources met at some node in the memory, a semantic intersection was detected, and a path through the semantic memory was thereby established which represented the semantic relationship between the two source concepts. (e.g., Madrid is in Spain which is like Mexico in language and culture.) Similarly, such activations have some duration in time, and when an ambiguous word is encountered, the sense that people are likely to take is the sense which has semantic connections with concepts that are currently activated (as detected by the presence of semantic intersections).

In speech understanding, this foregrounding effect of semantic intersections can be used to influence the words that one hears in an otherwise ambiguous segment of speech, and can be used to detect the coincidences of semantically related words in a word lattice. Following connections through the semantic network can also be used to predict words that have not been detected in the signal but which are sufficiently likely that they should be looked for. For details on the use of such techniques in the understanding of continuous speech, the reader is again referred to Nash-Webber (1974, 1975*). Notice that the information that we have in the pattern parts of the semantic interpretation rules of LUNAR is one type of information that we would like to have in such a semantic network. Notice also that whereas in LUNAR the information about associated semantic classes is available conveniently if one starts with the head of a construction, similar information in a semantic network format would be equally accessible from any of the concepts involved in the rule. This is one more instance of the importance of breaking a priori orderings of processing in speech understanding in favor of multiple, redundant ways of achieving the same result. In any given utterance, it could be one of the critical head words that is garbled, and one would like to be able nevertheless to find the semantic relationships among the arguments and use them to predict the missing head.

OTHER ASPECTS OF SEMANTIC NETS AND KNOWLEDGE REPRESENTATION

Another notion embedded in Quillian's conception of a semantic network (which also has rudimentary beginnings in Raphael's SIR system (Raphael, 1964)) is that information about a concept can be stored at several different levels up a chain of more and more inclusive concepts (Quillian called them superconcepts). For example, a canary is a bird which is a type of animal which is in turn a physical object. It may thus have certain properties which are stored directly at the level of canary (such as being yellow) but other properties that are common to a great many concepts and which are stored at the most general level of applicability. These would be automatically inherited by subconcepts (in absence of contrary information) without having to be stored over and over again for each of the entities for which they are true.

There is a tremendous amount of interest right now in various semantic network representations, what such structures should look like, how they should be used to do inferences, what kinds of things should be put into a network in response to understanding a sentence, etc. In particular, it is pointed out, notably by Schank and his students, that a great deal of what is understood in response to an input sentence comes from gratuitous assumptions that are made on the basis of knowledge already in memory and not specifically transmitted by the sentence. For example, Schank cites dialog pairs such as "Would you like an ice cream cone?" and "I just ate", in which the second utterance should be interpreted as giving a negative answer to the question. I think it should be apparent that when one attempts to understand spoken discourses and make judgments about the contextual appropriateness of a given interpretation of an utterance, the ability to make such semantic inferences using large amounts of semantic and factual knowledge (as well as pragmatic knowledge about what the speaker is likely to say in a given situation) will be of paramount importance. The inability to account for a given interpretation of an utterance by being able to relate it to what has been said before or to some aspect of the current context should raise the possibility that the utterance has been misheard. The ability to fully use this level of sophisticated inference as part of a speech understanding system, however, will probably have to await further developments in the ongoing studies in knowledge representation and mechanical inference. The techniques which exist today in these areas are either extremely limited or inordinately cumbersome.

CONCLUSION

I have attempted here to provide a perspective on some of the work that has been done in the areas of syntax and semantics for understanding natural language by machines and to call special attention to those techniques which have particular relevance to the problems of speech understanding.

I have tried to cover a range of different parsing algorithms and grammar models with emphasis on the advantages and disadvantages of the various features of these models for the particular types of problems that one will encounter in analyzing continuous speech, and I have tried to give my opinions as to the value of these different features. In particular, I have argued that the use of a predetermined order of finding things (such as left to right across the sentence) is potentially dangerous and perhaps to be avoided. I have pointed out that the ambiguity of syntactic word class, which is one of the major sources of ambiguity in English text, is greatly magnified in speech understanding by the inability to uniquely determine what the word at a given position is. Whereas in text parsing, one at least knows what the word is and therefore has an expectation of two or three possible syntactic categories for it, in speech understanding we may have a half dozen alternative possible words at a given point, each with one or more possible syntactic categories. Hence the combinatorial problems that arise from the multiplication of possible alternative analyses is much worse for speech. This is complicated by the fact that most of the techniques that have been developed in text parsers for minimizing the impact of these combinatorial possibilities require carefully designed sequences of looking for things which conflict with the above observation that such constrained orderings are sensitive to the errors in the lexical analysis of the input that are virtually inevitable in speech.

The use of word lattices as input instead of sequences and the design of parsing algorithms around well-formed substring tables or charts appear to be viable methods for dealing with the combinatorial problem of speech understanding. The merging of common parts of different analyses permitted by transition network grammars is also helpful in this respect. In order to be able to correct errors, it will be essential to be able to come at a given parsing from several directions. Consequently checks will be necessary at appropriate points to avoid duplicating an analysis that has already been found.

Another important role of syntax in a speech understanding system is the prediction of those places where small function words might occur, in order to compensate for the unreliability of their identification by lexical analysis.

Although our understanding of semantics is not as well advanced as that of syntax (which itself is far from complete), there are a number of semantic techniques that language understanding programs have used which can have great benefit in the construction of speech understanding machines. These include the use of procedural semantics for the specification of the operations which are to be carried out in response to the understanding of the sentence, the use of semantic selectional restrictions to rule out unlikely interpretations of the speech signal, and the use of semantic associations as embodied in the Quillian semantic intersection technique to notice coincidences between semantically related words at different points in the input. One should be aware, however, of the limitations of some of these techniques and the need for continued research in the areas both of syntax and semantics in order to increase the range of things which such systems can understand and their abilities to choose correctly between alternative interpretations of a signal.

I think it is clear that in order to cover this scope of material it has been necessary to treat many issues rather shallowly and others not at all. Hopefully the references will provide additional detail for the interested reader. I hope that I have given you some feeling for the issues and some of the things that are going on in computational linguistics, linguistics, psychology, and artificial intelligence relative to syntax and semantics and some of the ramifications of the speech understanding task for these areas. Given the different perspective that the speech understanding task places on the roles of syntax and semantics in language understanding, I believe that the speech understanding problem can have almost as great an impact on research in syntax and semantics as these areas are now having on the problem of automatic speech recognition.

REFERENCES

Bates, M. (1974) "The Use of Syntax in a Speech Understanding System," Proceedings of IEEE Symposium on Speech Recognition, Carnegie-Mellon University, Pittsburgh, Pa. pp. 226-233.

Bobrow, D. G. and Fraser, J. B. (1969) "An Augmented State Transition Network Analysis Procedure," Proceedings International Joint Conference on Artificial Intelligence, Washington, D.C., pp. 557-567.

Bruce, B. (1973) "Case Structure Systems," Proceedings of Third International Joint Conference on Artificial Intelligence, Stanford University, Stanford, Ca., pp. 364-371.

Carbonell, J. R. and Collins, A. M. (1973) "Natural Semantics in Artificial Intelligence," Proceedings of Third International Joint Conference on Artificial Intelligence, Stanford University, Stanford, Ca., pp. 344-351.

Chomsky, N. (1965) Aspects of the Theory of Syntax, MIT Press, Cambridge, Mass.

Collins, A. M. and Quillian, M. R. (1969) "Retrieval Time from Semantic Memory," Journal of Verbal Learning and Verbal Behaviour, 8 (2), pp. 240-247.

Collins, A. M. and Warnock, E. H. (1974) "Semantic Networks," Report 2833, Bolt Beranek and Newman Inc., Cambridge, Mass.

Denes, P. B. and Pinson, E. N. (1963) The Speech Chain, Bell Telephone Laboratories, Inc.

Earley, J. (1970) "An Efficient Context-Free Parsing Algorithm," CACM 13 (2), pp. 94-102.

Fillmore, C. J. (1968) "The Case for Case," in Bach, E. and Harms, R. (eds.) Universals in Linguistic Theory, Holt, Rinehart and Winston, New York.

Floyd, R. W. (1967) "Nondeterministic Algorithms," JACM 14 (4) pp. 636-644.

Green, C. C. and Raphael, B. (1968) "The Use of Theorem-Proving Techniques in Question-Answering Systems," Proc. 1968 ACM National Conference, pp. 169-181.

Greibach, S. A. (1967) "A Simple Proof of the Standard-Form Theorem for Context-Free Grammars," in Mathematical Linguistics and Automatic Translation, Report NSF-18, Harvard University Computation Laboratory, Cambridge, Mass.

Griffiths, T. and Petrick, S. R. (1965) "On the Relative Efficiencies of Context-Free Grammar Recognizers," CACM 5 (8), pp. 289-300.

Hays, D. G. (1962) "Automatic Language-Data Processing," in Harold Borko (ed.), Computer Applications in the Behavioural Sciences, Prentice Hall, Englewood Cliffs, N.J.

Heidorn, G. E. (1972) "Natural Language Inputs to a Simulation Programming System," Ph.D. Thesis, Yale University, New Haven, Conn.

Jakobson, R., Fant, C. G., and Halle M. (1967) Preliminaries to Speech Analysis, MIT Press, Cambridge, Mass.

Katz, J. J. and Fodor, J. A. (1964) "The Structure of a Semantic Theory," in Katz, J. J. and Fodor, J. A. (eds.) The Structure of Language: Readings in the Philosophy of Language, Prentice-Hall, Englewood Cliffs, N.J., pp. 479-518.

Kay, M. (1967) "Experiments with a Powerful Parser," Memorandum, RM-5452-PR, The RAND Corporation, Santa Monica, Ca..

Kuno, S. and Oettinger, A. G. (1963) "Multiple-Path Syntactic Analyzer," Information Processing 62, North-Holland, Amsterdam, pp. 306-312.

Nash-Webber, B. (1974) "Semantic Support for a Speech Understanding System," Proceedings of IEEE Symposium on Speech Recognition, Carnegie-Mellon University, Pittsburgh, Pa., pp. 244-249.

Nash-Webber, B. (1975*) "The Role of Semantics in Automatic Speech Understanding", Representation and Understanding, Bobrow, D. G. and Collins, A. (eds.) Academic Press. (in press)

Newell, A. et al. (1973) Speech Understanding Systems: Final Report of a Study Group, North-Holland/American Elsevier, Amsterdam.

Norman, D. A. and Rumelhart, D. E. (1973) "Active Semantic Networks as a Model of Human Memory," Proc. Third International Joint Conference on Artificial Intelligence, Stanford University, Stanford, Ca., pp. 450-463.

Petrick, S. R. (1965) "A Recognition Procedure for Transformational Grammars," Ph.D. Thesis, Department of Modern Languages, M.I.T., Cambridge, Mass.

Quillian, M. R. (1968) "Semantic Memory," in Minsky, M. L. (ed.) Semantic Information Processing, MIT Press, Cambridge, Mass.

Quillian, M. R. (1969) "The Teachable Language Comprehender: A Simulation Program and Theory of Language," CACM 12 (8), pp. 459-476.

Raphael, B. (1964) "A Computer Program which 'Understands'," AFIPS Conference Proceedings, vol. 26 (1964 FJCC) pp. 577-589.

Sandewall, E. (1971) "A Programming Tool for Management of a Predicate-Calculus-Oriented Data Base," Proc. Second International Joint Conference on Artificial Intelligence, The British Computer Society, London, pp. 159-166.

Schank, R. C. and Colby, K. M. (1973) Computer Models of Thought and Language, W.H. Freeman & Co., San Francisco, Ca..

Thorne, J., Bratley, P. and Dewar, H. (1968) "The Syntactic Analysis of English by Machine," in D. Michie (ed.) Machine Intelligence 3, American Elsevier, New York, N.Y.

Winograd, T. (1972) Understanding Natural Language, Academic Press, New York, N.Y.

Winston, P. H. (1970) "Learning Structural Descriptions from Examples," MAC TR-76, MIT Project MAC, Cambridge, Mass.

Woods, W. A. (1967) Semantics for a Question Answering System, Report NSF-19, The Computation Laboratory, Harvard University, Cambridge, Mass. (NTIS number PB-176-548).

Woods, W. A. (1968) "Procedural Semantics for a Question-Answering Machine," AFIPS Conference Proceedings, vol. 33 (1968 FJCC), pp. 457, 471.

Woods, W. A. (1969) "Augmented Transition Networks for Natural Language Analysis," Report CS-1, Computation Laboratory, Harvard University, Cambridge, Mass.

Woods, W. A. (1970) "Transition Network Grammars for Natural Language Analysis," CACM 13 (10), pp. 591-606.

Woods, W. A. (1973a) "An Experimental Parsing System for Transition Network Grammars," in R. Rustin (ed.), Natural Language Processing, Algorithmics Press, New York, N.Y.

Woods, W. A. (1973b) "Progress in Natural Language Understanding: An Application to Lunar Geology," AFIPS Conference Proceedings, vol. 42, (1973 National Computer Conference) pp. 441-450.

Woods, W. A. (1974) "Motivation and Overview of BBN SPEECHLIS: An Experimental Prototype for Speech Understanding Research," Proc. IEEE Symposium on Speech Recognition, Carnegie-Mellon University, Pittsburgh, Pa., pp. 1-10.

Woods, W. A., Kaplan, R. M. and Nash-Webber, B. (1972) "The Lunar Sciences Natural Language Information System: Final Report," BBN Report No. 2378, Bolt Beranek and Newman, Cambridge, Mass. (NTIS number N72-28984).

Younger, D. H. (1966) "Context-Free Language Processing in Time n^3," Proceedings 1966 Annual Symposium on Switching and Automata Theory, IEEE Conference Record 16 C 40, 1966, pp. 7-20.

PERFORMANCE GRAMMARS[†]

Jane J. Robinson
Stanford Research Institute
333 Ravenswood Avenue
Menlo Park, California 94025

ABSTRACT

Evidence is offered to support the view that linguistic competence cannot in principle be divorced from linguistic performance in order to abstract universal properties of grammars, that rules of grammar inevitably incorporate perceptual strategies and constraints, and that grammaticality and acceptability are related to predictability. A theory of systematic variation affords direction for gathering data on rule-governed language use and for representing the results in formal grammars that predict speech behavior. Some of the strategies and constraints operating in performance and the rule-governed regularities they produce are demonstrated in the analysis of seven tape-recorded task-oriented dialogs.

0. INTRODUCTION

There is a passage in <u>Through</u> <u>the</u> <u>Looking</u> <u>Glass</u> where Alice is being tested by the White Queen and the Red Queen to see if she is worthy to become a queen herself. The White Queen asks her: "What's one and one and one and one and one and one and one and one and one?" Alice says, "I don't know. I lost count." And then the Red Queen says, "She can't do Addition." The Red Queen was obviously wrong to infer from a single performance that Alice was incompetent to 'do Addition.'

It was Chomsky who elevated the distinction between what one is able to do and what one actually does on a given occasion to the

---

[†]The work reported herein was sponsored by the Advanced Research Projects Agency of the Department of Defense under Contract DAHC04-72-C-0009 with the U.S. Army Research Office.

status of a fundamental distinction in linguistic theory. In explicating the notion of 'grammatical rule' (Chomsky 1961), he proposed to use the term _competence_ to refer to a speaker's implicit and intrinsic knowledge of his language and the term _performance_ to refer to the use he makes of that knowledge at particular times. He also proposed to divorce the notion of grammar from all concern with performance; grammar was to be a reflection solely of competence. His stance in this respect goes far beyond the customary acknowledgement of the need to normalize linguistic data before attempting to state the systematic regularities that are discernible in it. His claim is that it is not possible to understand performance without first abstracting the universal properties of the grammars of natural languages from the flux of occasional utterances and thereby gaining insight into the innate structure of the human mind.

A more recent view is that universal linguistic properties are really only manifestations of broader cognitive principles that underlie the observed regularities in behavior (Kuno 1973; Kimball 1973). In this latter view, the internalized rules of our implicit grammars are not innately given but have evolved from the interplay of cognitive processes with our experiences in communicating with each other. As a result of the interplay, the rules incorporate perceptual strategies and constraints; therefore it is impossible to eliminate performance factors from grammars. Some of the evidence for this view is presented in Section 1 (Rules and strategies) in the course of a more detailed examination of Chomsky's initial statements concerning the division between competence and performance. The next section (Rule-governed variation) exhibits an extension of the notion 'rule of grammar,' proposed by Labov, that permits explicit incorporation of data from performance. In Section 3 (Context-sensitive performances) several rule-governed regularities discernible in seven recorded dialogs are analyzed to expose the strategies and constraints operating in actual performances.

1. RULES AND STRATEGIES

Although he is ultimately interested in the human mind and its intuitions about language, the connection Chomsky asserts between grammars and the mind is subtle and indirect. A grammar of a language describes the intrinsic competence of an ideal speaker-hearer in the sense that it generates the sentences he is theoretically capable of producing and comprehending. It is a theory of sentences, not of utterances. Since grammar is timeless and performance takes time, his grammar does not describe even the ideal speaker's performance. The

White Queen asks, "What's one and one and one..." and stops at ten, but her grammar allows her to go on droning "and one and one and...." If she is tireless and immortal, she may never finish. Then all the other sentences she could have uttered will go unperformed.

There is at least one dismaying flaw in the concept of grammar divorced from performance. As long as grammarians are encouraged to sweep awkward phenomena into a dustbin labelled 'performance' and send it off to the psycholinguists, their grammars will generate sentences that no speaker ever utters, no hearer readily understands, and almost every language user rejects as ungrammatical unless coaxed by a linguist. A classic example appears in (1). Given a little time and a little linguistic sophistication, people can comprehend it and paraphrase its content, as in (2). Few would judge (1) to be acceptable, but the claim is that there is no way to exclude it from the grammar of English except on grounds of difficulty of performance, and such grounds are not admissible in grammars that are wholly concerned with competence.

(1)   The house the cheese the rat the cat the dog chased caught ate lay in was built by Jack.

(2)   The house in which lay the cheese that was eaten by the rat that was caught by the cat that the dog chased was built by Jack.

Chomsky argues that this strange state of affairs is "no stranger than the fact that someone who has learned the rules of multiplication perfectly (perhaps without being able to state them) may be unable to calculate 3,872 x 18,694 in his head, although the rules that he has mastered uniquely determine the answer" (Chomsky 1961, pp.7–8). The analogy is not very compelling. One cannot give an example of a product generated by rules of multiplication that is both correct and 'unacceptable.'

Perhaps a better analogy is that of chess. For each piece, a rule in the grammar of chess defines its legitimate moves. But there are also strategies that guide the choices of a competent player, and there is one general requirement that partakes of the nature of rule and strategy. It is the meta-rule that says, "No matter what the other rules say about how this piece can move, they cannot be applied if the result is to put your king in check." An approximate counterpart in the language game is "Don't use rule combinations that create incomprehensible sentences."

Looking again at sentences (1) and (2), we see that their

propositional content is the same; they are close paraphrases. In the difficult sentence, the structure is deeply self-embedded. In the easier one, optional transformations have inverted the relative clauses to produce perceptually simpler right-branching constructions. Some of the surface structure differences between the two are represented in (3a) and (3b), which shows how the embeddings of (2) appear to have been flattened in Figure 3b.

(3a)

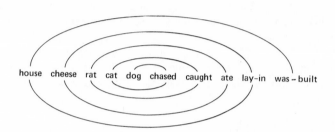

(3b)

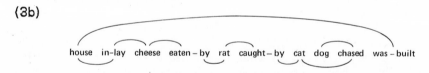

A line drawn above the sentence connects a head noun with the verb it serves as subject; a line beneath the sentence connects it with the verb or preposition for which it is object.

As a result of flattening, sentence (2) is easy to comprehend. It can be parsed on the run without overtaxing one's short-term memory. (In a recent article, Kimball (1973) claims that performance limitations on short-term memory make it impossible to parse the constituents of more than two 'open' S's at the same time. Sentence (1) requires parsing five at once.)

In addition to being flatter, (2) consistently marks the beginnings of constituent boundaries with function words that signal the type of constituent likely to follow. Lacking such cues to the structure of (1), a hearer is in danger of being led down the garden path of a false parse as he processes it, so that he misconstrues the initial series of noun phrases as a single conjoined noun phrase subject. Disillusionment comes when a verb is encountered where a conjunction was anticipated, and he finds that re-parsing is necessary if the sentence is to be properly understood. This consequence, following from the deletion of function words, shows that deletion transformations, like flattening transformations, are related inseparably to performance as well as to competence. To give another example, deletion of the function word that when it introduces an embedded complement clause in subject position is unacceptable and likely to be judged ungrammatical because the result regularly misleads the hearer into processing the embedded clause as if it were the main clause of the sentence. (See the examples in (4) below). On the other hand, it is acceptable and grammatical to delete a that when it introduces an embedded clause in object position, where the class of the preceding predicate predicts the possibility of embedding.

(4) a. *he was angry frightened everyone
     b. everyone was afraid (that) he was angry
     c. that he was angry frightened everyone
     d. it frightened everyone that he was angry

A study of how people process sentences like these has led Bever (1970, p.20) to propose that at least some grammatical rules inevitably obey behavioral constraints because "children will tend not to learn rules which produce speech forms that are hard to understand or hard to say. Thus, whatever aspects of cognition are utilized directly in speech perception will be reflected in certain properties of linguistic grammars."

It is a truism that we tend to see what we are prepared to see and hear what we are prepared to hear. This truism translates into a general linguistic principle that acceptability and grammaticality are related to predictability. The principle shows up in the statistics for texts that have not been 'made up' to illustrate linguistic points. Consider again the preceding example: that he was angry frightened everyone. It is grammatical and the first word signals the possibility of encountering an initial embedded clause. However, the possibility is even more strongly signalled if the embedded clause is extraposed to follow the predicate frightened as in (4d), it frightened everyone that he was angry. It is noticeably rare to find embedded clauses in initial subject position, as if speakers and writers intuitively avoid introducing complex sentences too abruptly with too little advance warning. In examining seven extended dialogs in casual speech (to be described more fully in a following section), I failed to find even one embedded clause in subject position, although there were many embedded object and predicate complement clauses. The examples in (5) are representative; each comes from a different dialog. Places where a that was deleted are marked with a #; retained but deletable thats are enclosed in parentheses. The predicate that precedes and predicts the embedding is underlined.

(5) a. Your first comment was (that) the diagram didn't match ...
b. The purpose for those washers is (that) the motor has to be able to slide ....
c. Before you start, be sure you turn each of those off.
d. Well, that means we'll have to remove ....
e. I don't suppose the consultant knows where ....
f. Make sure the groove in the flywheel lines up with ....
g. Is it correct (that) the strap is attached to the pump?

If the concept of grammar divorced from performance fails us as a theory of sentences, it is completely irrelevant as a theory of sequences of sentences in a discourse. The timeless competence grammar stops at the boundary of each unuttered sentence that it generates and starts over. It can enumerate sentences in some canonical order, but cannot generate them in a functionally appropriate order, even thought the syntactic structure, word choices, use of anaphora, and selection of prosodies of every sentence are affected by past and anticipated utterances. Judgments of the acceptability of sequences of sentences are clearly related to predictability, even though we cannot predict precisely in all cases. For example, if from the sentences in (6), all ordered pairs of (a) followed by (b) are formed, we can predict which pairs will be judged acceptable and which will not. To follow what did John do? with Bill was hit by John is predictably inappropriate. So is the sequence I know Tom hit Harry, but who hit Bill?; John HIT him (with high stress on hit). Some may hesitate to apply the term 'ungrammatical' to sequences of grammatical sentences, and yet it is difficult to say in what respect the reaction to such sequences differs from the reaction to the single sentence: I know Tom hit Harry, but John HIT Bill.

If, in the examples of (6b), the pronoun him is equated with Bill, then the propositional content is the same for all of the examples. Their surface differences arise from options provided by grammar for paraphrasing the propositional content in order to foreground some portions and background others. These options serve a strategic function in the use of language, allowing us to deploy the resources of

(6) a. What happened?
         What happened to Bill?
         What did John do?
         I know Tom hit Harry, but who hit Bill?
         I know Tom hit Harry, but what did John do?

     b. John hit BILL.
         JOHN hit Bill.
         JOHN hit him.
         John HIT him.
         BILL was hit by John.
         Bill was hit by JOHN.

the language so that complex meanings can be delivered gradually and partially, without loss of coherence. We can take into account, as the information is being delivered, what has already been said--what is 'old' information, and link the new information to it. We can do this because the relationship between the old and the new is signalled by the choices among systematic grammatical options available to speakers for organizing their sentences. (Cf., for example, Halliday in press; Sgall et al. 1973.) The reason that Bill <u>was</u> <u>hit</u> <u>by</u> <u>John</u> sounds odd following <u>what</u> <u>did</u> <u>John</u> <u>do?</u> is that the use of the passive in this case puts the item <u>John</u> into the foreground, highlighting it as if it were newly introduced into the discourse, while at the same time placing <u>Bill</u> in the background as if it represented old, and therefore predictable information. When it follows <u>What</u> <u>happened</u> to <u>Bill?</u>, on the other hand, the same sentence is acceptable and the use of the passive enhances the coherence of the two sentences in sequence.

2. RULE-GOVERNED STRATEGIES

We have seen that the passive transformational rule functions in two similar roles, making sentences more comprehensible by flattening the structure of a single complex sentence and by restructuring the content of an independent sentence to relate it coherently to the content of preceding sentences. The passive transformation is optional; the possibility of applying it or not applying it introduces variation into the structure of the same propositional content. Although it is optional, we can predict to some extent when it is likely to be applied.

The notion of systematic rule-governed variation has recently emerged as the central theme of a new paradigm for linguistic research (Bailey 1973; Bailey and Shuy 1973). An important part of the new paradigm is Labov's extension of Chomsky's 'notion rule of grammar' to include the notion of 'systematic variation' (Labov 1969). It is not possible to give an adequate treatment of the theory and methodology of 'variable rule' grammars here. I will instead give one example to illustrate the concept and the conventions for writing variable rules, to show how it is possible to retain the explicitness of generative rules while accommodating the variability of observed performance. (For extended treatments, see Labov, 1972, 1973; G. Sankoff, 1972; Cedergren and D. Sankoff, in press.)

The example is a kind of 'fast speech' rule that asserts that /t/ and /d/ are optionally deleted before a word boundary. The rule is clearly too general. While the final /t/ in the phrase <u>kept going</u>, might be deleted in fairly slow speech the final /t/ of <u>got away</u> is likely to persist at much higher speeds. The contextual features that favor deletion or retention of /t/ and /d/ are given by a variable rule (7).

(7)

$$-t,d \rightarrow \phi / \left\langle \begin{matrix} +cons \\ +cont \end{matrix} \right\rangle \left\langle \begin{matrix} \phi \\ + \end{matrix} \right\rangle \; — \; \#\# \; \left\langle \begin{matrix} +cons \\ -voc \end{matrix} \right\rangle$$

Variability is indicated by angle brackets. Angle brackets enclosing the rewritten element on the right of the arrow means "is variably rewritten as." Combined with 0, this means "is variably deleted." Angle brackets in the contextual part of the rule enclose lists of features or categories whose presence affects the application of the rule, favorably or unfavorably. Elements not enclosed in angle brackets are obligatory.

The rule states that the most favorable environment for deletion of a word-final dental obstruent is in a monomorphemic form in which it is preceded by a continuant and followed by a word beginning with a consonant, as in <u>hold back</u>. The least favorable is the environment in which it functions as a past tense morpheme and precedes a word beginning with a vowel, as in <u>missed it</u>. There are various intermediate likelihoods of deletion, exemplified in (8).

From empirically established frequency counts of /t/, /d/ deletion in various environments, a statistical method derives probability coefficients for each contextual element independently. Given an input string, the values for the contextual elements actually present in the string are inserted into the formula, which combines them and calculates the probability that the dental obstruent will be deleted.

(8) a. hold back --> hol back   hold off --> hol off
     b. last man --> las man   last one ---> las one
     c. kept going --> kep going   kept all of it ---> kep all of it
     d. missed me --> miss me   missed it --->miss it

Cedergren and D. Sankoff (in press) view the probabilities associated
with the rules as "properly part of competence" and claim that
performance is "a statistical reflection of competence."

The example given in (7) for a variable rule contains only
linguistic variables in the contextual part. However, the method
extends to any contextual factors, linguistic or extra-linguistic, assumed
to affect frequency of rule application systematically. Covariation of
application frequency with differences in age, sex, class, and style of
speech have been studied for rules in various languages by various
investigators. (See references previously cited.) It is not necessary for
the contextual factor to appear in the body of the rule as a feature or
category; its probability value can appear in the formula for predicting
application, once the relevant contexts have been identified and
frequencies have been established. In principle we could incorporate
any systematic linguistic behavior into a grammar, even including slips of
the tongue and hesitation pauses, both of which have been shown to
be rule-governed (Fromkin 1971; Goldman-Eisler 1972). More
practically, we now have a theoretical frame to direct the gathering of
data from real performances on the frequency of application of well-
established transformational rules like the passive, so that we can
study the contexts which appear to favor or disfavor their application.
It is a frame that allows us to include the extra-sentential discourse
contexts of what was said before and after.

In the next section we will look at some actual performances,
noting the contexts that appear to shape the utterances, but before
we do, I would like to illustrate more specifically how the passive
transformation, revamped as a variable rule, might operate to produce
the flattening of the kind of self-embedded structures we looked at
earlier. The relevant context for rule application is given in the SD
(structural description) part of (9). SC gives the structural change.
Note that the presence of a V preceding the V affected by the
transformation is a favoring context for applying the rule. The
examples below the rule show some effects of application and non-
application. It is assumed that the rule applies cyclically from deepest
to least embedded sentence.

If we start the cycle with input (9)a.(i) and Passive is not

(9)   Variable Passive Transformation

SD:NP1 X (V1) (V2) ... (Vi) Vj NP2 X

SC:NP2 B E Vj -EN BY NP1 X (V1) (V2) ... (Vi) X

a. (i)   the dog chased(V) some cat
    (ii)   some cat was chased(V) by the dog

b. (i)   the cat the dog chased(V) caught(V) some rat
    (ii)   the cat chased(V) by the dog caught(V) some rat

c. (i)   the rat the cat the dog chased(V) caught(V) ate(V) some
           cheese
    (ii)   the rat the cat chased(V) by the dog caught(V) ate(V)
           some cheese
    (iii) some cheese was eaten(V) by the rat the cat chased(V)
           by the dog caught(V)

applied, we enter the next cycle with input (9)b.(i), which favors application because it has a V immediately before the affected V. If Passive is still not applied, we enter the next cycle with input (9)c.(i), where the presence of two Vs before the affected V makes application still more probable. At some point in very deeply nested structures, the combined effects of preceding Vs should predict application with a probability of one, indicating that no competent speaker has been observed to fail to apply the transformation in that context.

3. CONTEXT-SENSITIVE PERFORMANCES

I propose now to look at some concrete linguistic performances to see what kinds of syntactic constructions occur, what functions they perform, and how they co-vary with features of the context. These are the data needed for generative performance grammars that assign probabilities when given a proposed utterance and the contextual features in which it is embedded. As Halliday has pointed out, if we know the context, it is surprising how many features of the language turn out to be relatable to it. "... not ... that we know what the participants are going to say; [but] ... we can make sensible and informed guesses about certain aspects of what they might say, with a reasonable probability of being right. There is always, in language, the freedom to act untypically but that in itself confirms rather than denies the reality of the concept of what is typical" (Halliday, in press).

The performances to be examined are the seven dialogs previously cited. They belong to the central paradigm for communication: the dialog that occurs when two people are working together at a common task whose nature motivates them to communicate in order to get it done. In each of the seven dialogs there is an expert and an apprentice, and the apprentice is doing some work under the partial guidance of the expert. Conditions differ with respect to vision and channel linkage (see Table 1). In two dialogs the expert can see what the apprentice is doing at any moment; in one he cannot see at all, and the apprentice must describe objects and states of affairs; and in one, vision is limited. In all four of these dialogs, the channel is speech. In another situation, the participants do not communicate directly, but through a monitor, who relays messages between them. The expert uses writing as the channel for communication, while the apprentice uses speech. The monitor accepts messages through either channel and converts them to the other. This interposes a time delay. In this situation the expert cannot see what the apprentice is doing unless he requests that a television camera be turned on and directed to a specific area. Three dialogs were collected under these conditions.

Dialog	Vision	Monitor	Expert	Apprentice
1	yes	no	RF	JT
2	limited	no	RF	FW
3	yes	no	RT	RF
4	no	no	RT	WP
5	on request	yes	JK	DN
6	on request	yes	JK	PB
7	on request	yes	RF	JP

Table 1. Conditions for the Seven Dialogs

The style or 'register' of all the dialogs except the last is that of casual speech. None of the speakers is self-conscious. Once they become task-oriented, there is no discernible awareness that someone is observing their linguistic behavior. The situation appears to solve what Labov calls the Observer's Paradox: "To obtain the data most important for linguistic theory, we have to observe how people speak when they are not being observed" (Labov 1972).

Since the dialogs were not controlled, generalized observations based on them are necessarily impressionistic. We are making some trial runs, to expose the overall problems with a view to designing more controlled experiments later to collect more tractable data. We are interested in seeing the full range of interaction between two participants when the main external structuring is imposed by the nature of the task, and then seeing what changes occur under the distancing effects imposed by lack of shared vision and by the monitoring delays. One of our research goals is the design of a performance grammar for man-machine dialog. We would like the grammar to generate a subset of English that is 'habitable' for the user. That means that we need to consider how the total system hangs together for a given type of discourse and how to excise part of it without severely disrupting the rest.

Our examination of the dialogs will be guided by the model shown schematically in (10). A linguistic performance requires at least two performers, at least one message, in a code, transmitted through a channel, all of them embedded in a context. In the schematic representation for a single message, I have distinguished the two performers as 'sender' and 'receiver,' rather than as 'speaker' and 'hearer,' because the channel may be writing as well as speech. Some models of communication distinguish other elements as well, but this one offers a convenient way of looking at a linguistic performance with a view to getting data for a performance grammar. It is an adaptation of the model of Buhler (1934) as modified by Jakobson (1960). Their schema represents context as if it were an element distinct from the rest. I think it is important to emphasize that the context embeds the other elements. The relationship between sender and receiver is part of the context that affects the shape of the message: the message changes the context even during the course of its delivery, becoming part of the context for messages to come. It also changes the relationship between sender and receiver. This is a dynamic model, and a performance grammar is sensitive to all the features of the changing context.

Although all the elements shown in (10) are 'there' in every single linguistic performance, one or more may be overtly emphasized, and the shape of the message reveals this emphasis in syntax, lexical choice, and prosody. For example, exclamations emphasize the sender. They give more information about his internal state than about his relation to the receiver or to the external context. Interrogatives and imperatives generally emphasize the receiver. Declaratives are the most unmarked form. According to the performative analysis, every underlying structure of a declarative is of the form I tell you (that S), where a highest S embeds the S that becomes the sentence (Ross 1970). Elements of the highest S are deleted transformationally,

(10)

A COMMUNICATION MODEL

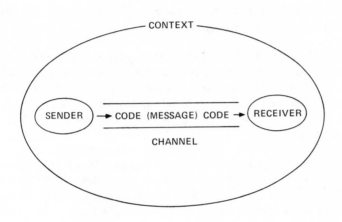

(11)

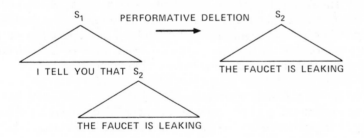

eliminating overt signs of sender and receiver from the utterance, unless the forms I and you show up in the lower S (see (11)). This is a 'deep structure' acknowledgement of the pragmatic fact that sentences are to be uttered and heard.

The forms I and you are not pronouns like it, they, he, she, etc.; they are indexical expressions denoting the sender and receiver of a message during its transmission. When they occur in declarative sentences they are often mixed in varying degrees of emphasis with references to the external context. Compare, for instance, the opening utterances from two different dialogs. ('A' preceding an utterance identifies its sender as an apprentice.)

(12) a. A: I have this faucet here and water seems to be coming out at the wrong place ... water is leaking out from that flat horizontal surface and I don't think it's supposed to .... So can you help me fix that? (Dialog 3).
   b. A: The faucet's leaking around the base of the spout. (Dialog 4).

In (12a) the sender reports his internal state; that is, his reactions to the external context along with information about that part of the context. He ends with an explicit appeal to the receiver coded in an interrogative sentence. In the second example there is no overt I and the appeal to the sender is not explicit. The interpretation of the declarative statement as an appeal is influenced by the apprentice/expert relationship of sender to receiver.

There were a surprising number of exclamations in the dialogs, but expressions of internal states of participants sometimes took the form of an almost impersonal report of relevant data. The range is from the classic example of a four-letter oath to relieve the feelings of an apprentice who brought his hand down hard on some exposed nails through expressions of less painful surprise and on to reports of worry entirely relevant to the task orientation of the context.

(13) a. A: Rats, I made a mistake. (Dialog 2).
   b. A: I found a small screw on the floor which always makes me nervous when I work on machines but I'm almost certain it's not from the compressor.
      E: Show me the screw, please. (Dialog 5)

In the second example we have another case in which a declarative is interpreted as an appeal for advice because of the relationship of the sender to the receiver.

A typical series of messages in the dialogs are exchanges in which the expert directs or advises the apprentice to do something and the apprentice acknowledges receipt of the message. Okay serves the latter function most frequently. The apprentice then initiates a new exchange by indicating that the directive has been fulfilled. Here, again, okay fills this function frequently, but whether with a consistently different intonation from the one accompanying its utterance in the other function is not yet clear. It is a possibility worth investigating. Embedded in these exchanges may be a subordinate exchange in which the apprentice asks a question about a current directive or points to a problem encountered in trying to fulfill it, and the expert replies. Deutsch (1974) analyzes the discourse structure of the dialogs, relating it to the structure of a 'workstation' task model. I shall concern myself mainly with the syntax.

Because of the nature of the task and the relationship between the participants, many messages are oriented towards asking for and giving information, especially the kind of information called 'advice.' When paired messages having request/response functions with this orientation are analyzed, it becomes clear that they are often a single unit syntactically and semantically as well as functionally. For example, the syntactic relationship of each request/response pair in (14) is so regular that it is possible to specify a simple series of transformations that takes the pair as input, outputting a single well-formed declarative that is an answer to the request. The elliptical responses occupy syntactic slots and contain the semantic features defined by the request, with occasional redundant overlap with parts of the request.

(14) a. A: Which side do you call the front?
          E: The side with the Sears label on the tank. (Dialog 7)

      b. A: Which tools should I use to get the bolts that are hard to unscrew?
          E: Use the 1/2" box wrench and the 1/2" combination wrench. (Dialog 6)

      c. A: How tightly should I install this pipe elbow ....
          E: Only snugly. (Dialog 7)

      d. E: What are you doing now?
          A: Using the pliers to get the nuts in underneath the platform. (Dialog 7)

      e. A: Should I take it all the way off?
          E: Take it all the way off. (Dialog 3)

For (14a) the transformations are particularly simple. The request is converted to declarative form by undoing the interrogative inversion and eliminating the auxiliary DO; the you becomes I with the exchange of speakers, and the response replaces the WH-marked NP of the request:

I call WH-side the front →
    I call the side with the Sears label on the tank the front.

In (14a) the word side occurs in both members of the pair: in the WH-marked NP of the request and in its replacement NP in the response. In (14b) the replacement for which tools does not contain an occurrence of the word tools, but does contain nouns referring to objects for which the word tool is a superordinate term. This is a general pattern with respect to replacements involving other parts-of-speech as well. In (14c) the WH-marked phrase is an adverb of degree -- how tightly, which is superordinate to only snugly. In (14d) the pro-verb and the what signal that the request is to be satisfied by specifying an activity. The conversion is I AUX doing what → I am using the pliers. The pro-verb DO is superordinate to the use that that replaces it.

The request in (14e) has no overt WH element. Requests like this are sometimes called Yes/No or 'polar' questions. However, there may be more than two alternatives, so that a more general form underlying the type is the WH-OR or whether interrogative. In the example, a 'yes' would have been appropriate, but a simple 'no' leaves unresolved whether the apprentice should leave it on or take it off or take it part-way off or take some other action. Consequently it is appropriate for the response to repeat the words of the request as it does; it could even have been prefaced with the full you should. In fact, it would not be wrong in any of the examples to spell out the full declarative form of the answer instead of giving the information elliptically, but to do so would be redundant precisely because the request contains the syntactic and semantic specification for everything in the response except for what is different in the response, the new information.

Speaking generally, one concludes from the examples that a performance grammar must include a theory of pairs of sentences that constitute an exchange between participants in a speech event, in order to account on the one hand for the well-formedness of elliptical utterances that when judged by a competence grammar alone are ill-formed and incomplete, and on the other hand for their predictability.

Another grammatical regularity that is discernible in the dialogs is the regular set of relationships holding among certain declaratives, interrogatives, and imperatives, whenever the declaratives and interrogatives contain the indexical words I and you, a performative verb denoting the conveying of information, and the auxiliary should or an equivalent have to. The close relation functionally between interrogatives and imperatives is easily noted. Interrogatives like "would you show me the pressure register so I can identify it?" (Dialog 7) have been cited as 'polite' imperatives. But the dialogs show a relation that both functionally and syntactically goes beyond an adjustment that merely makes an order palatable. Where the function to be performed is satisfaction of a need for information, the request may just as easily take the syntactic form of either an interrogative or an imperative: what are you doing? or tell me what you are doing. Every interrogative can be converted to an imperative with the addition of tell me just as every imperative can be converted to an interrogative with the addition of would you, with appropriate adjustments in word order in each case. By an equally simple transformation, every imperative can be converted to a declarative with the addition of you should, you have to, I would suggest that you, or I would suggest V-ing. See, for example, "I would suggest holding the washer and nut in one hand..." (Dialog 7).

These transformational relationships allow requests and responses to show up in various syntactic guises, depending on optional deletion of variable amounts of material. They are illustrated in (15).

(15)

a. I tell you that you should tell me $\begin{cases} \text{what I should do} \\ \text{whether I should do X} \end{cases}$ (REQUEST)

⟶ you should tell me $\begin{cases} \text{what I should do} \\ \text{whether I should do X} \end{cases}$ (DECLARATIVE)

⟶ tell me $\begin{cases} \text{what I should do} \\ \text{whether I should do X} \end{cases}$ (IMPERATIVE)

⟶ $\begin{cases} \text{what should I do} \\ \phi \text{ should I do X} \end{cases}$? (INTERROGATIVE)

b. I tell you that you should turn it off (RESPONSE)

⟶ you should turn it off (DECLARATIVE)

⟶ turn it off (IMPERATIVE)

Those who have followed the field will recognize, in (16) below, that the transformations involved are independently well motivated. That is, the transformation that produces the imperative from an underlying I tell you for you to go home is like the one producing you should go home from I tell you that you should go home, where the embedded sentence is introduced by the that-complementizer rather than by the for-to-complementizer. In this case, the declarative is generated by deleting the performative elements of the highest S, exactly as proposed by the performative analysis for all declaratives. The imperative involves, in addition, the well-known Equi-NP deletion transformation, which deletes coreferential NPs in structures like that of (16b).

(16)

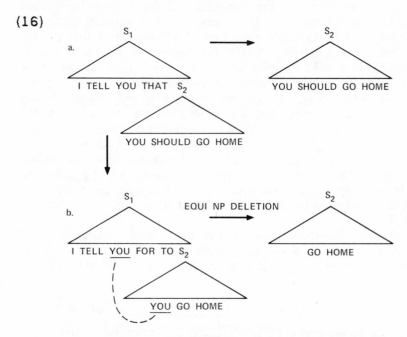

The seemingly more complicated transformation shown in (17) involves the same principles -- deletion of performative and coreferential material. The highest S1 (the performative S) and the S2 embedded in it contain the same predicate, <u>tell</u> and the same indexical <u>I</u> and <u>you</u>; but the roles of the <u>I</u> and <u>you</u> are shifted in S2. I have called the transformation 'Performative Shift' because its effect is to shift the roles of speaker and hearer.

The main point is that the syntactic type of the matrix sentence does not always distinguish between a request, a response to a request, or a neutral statement. If the message is a request, that function may be signalled syntactically by the presence of a WH-marked form in a subordinate clause. However, previous examples have illustrated the influence of extra-linguistic facts, e.g., the apprentice/expert relationship between sender/receiver as a contextual feature that favors the interpretation of a message as a request. A good example of the combination of a request signal in a

(17)

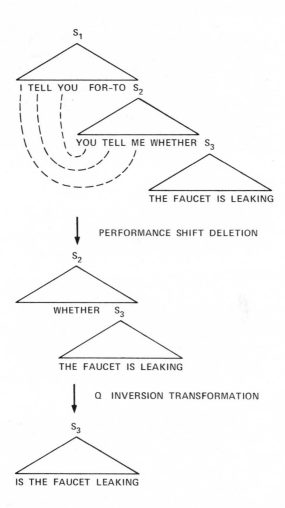

subordinate clause and a covert appeal for assistance shows up in the exchange (18).

(18) A: I don't suppose the consultant [the expert] knows where I put the wrenches.

E: Didn't you put them back on the table?

A: As a matter of fact I did. (Dialog 5)

Notice that the response is in the form of an interrogative. Part of the interpretation of the first utterance as a request depends on other kinds of extra-linguistic knowledge as well: the knowledge of the importance of keeping track of tools when engaged in a task.

    <u>Whether</u>-type questions depend on inversion for marking as interrogative. However, in English as in other language, it is possible in speech to signal this kind of question by intonation: <u>it</u> <u>comes</u> <u>off</u>? rather than <u>does</u> <u>it</u> <u>come</u> <u>off</u>. There are many examples of this kind of marking when apprentice and expert were in voice contact. Usually there were other marks or clues as well, as shown in (19).

(19) E: And these we turn off ... you
        turn to your right.

    A: You mean counterclockwise?

    E: It would be clockwise.

    A: Clockwise. Okay. (Dialog 4)

In this example <u>you</u> <u>mean</u> is a clue, as well as intonation. It is unusual for a sender to tell a receiver what the receiver means; it is usual to ask.

    The exchange in (19) illustrates some other functions toward which messages are oriented markedly. One is <u>code</u> orientation. In (19) the apprentice is checking the meaning of the phrase 'to your right' by offering a recoding. This is corrected and he echoes the correct word. This echoing of parts of the message previously sent was quite common when apprentice and expert spoke directly to each other but were not in eye contact.

    When the expert could not see what the apprentice was doing, the means for code checking were of course affected. Much of our common code for concrete objects is established by pointing or deixis. When this means is withdrawn, verbal description becomes necessary. A striking example shows up in the comparison of two dialogs, one where the expert could see (20 a) and the other where he could not (20 b).

    Another example of the effects of lack of vision appears in (21), where it is combined with effects of lack of a shared coding convention. The crucial phrase is the deictic <u>the</u> <u>front</u>. 'In front' of an object is multiply ambiguous. It may mean 'between the object and

(20) a. E: ... you have a top piece with a knurled section that you can take ahold of ...
      A: What's a knurled section?
      E: You've got your fingers on it. (Dialog 3)

      b. E: Now underneath that is what they call a cap assembly. It has a knurled face around it right above the spout itself.
      A: What does 'knurled' mean?
      E: Little lines running up and down on it so you can take ahold of it. (Dialog 4)

sender or receiver' when either of them is facing it, or it may mean 'forward of the front' of the object itself. The front of an object is established by convention. The front of a car may be behind a sender or receiver; it is still that part of the car that gets there first when the car is travelling normally along its major horizontal axis. The front of a book is what the reader gets to first when he reads it in normal order, and which part of the book _that_ is, in relation to the book's covers, depends on whether the book is written in English or Hebrew. In the exchange of (21), the apprentice cannot interpret the phrase 'in front' because he does not know the expert's convention for orienting the compressor.

(21) E: I assume you positioned the pump so that the longer protrusion, the oil drain, is pointing toward the front.
      A: Which side do you call the front?
      E: The side with the Sears label on the tank. (Dialog 7)

      One of the functions of utterances that was sometimes overtly marked is keeping the channel between sender-receiver open and ready to use, even when information content is low. Such utterances are said to have a phatic function. They include greetings and politeness forms and other social and ritual expressions. They also include the encouraging murmur of the receiver, often overlapping the incoming message, so that the receiver is simultaneously receiving and sending.
      Many of the utterances in the dialogs appear to emphasize this function: for example, "yeah, yeah," "okay," "right," "fine." Lack of vision alone did not affect the incidence or type strongly, but when direct voice contact was lost and there was a delay in response caused by insertion of a monitor, the effects were noticeable. There were expressions of anxiety about the functioning of the channel: e.g., "Can you hear me?" addressed by the apprentice to the monitor, who

was waiting for a long response from the expert to be typed out before relaying it (Dialog 5). It was quite apparent to experts, apprentices, and monitors that the okays and all rights had an important function. As a matter of fact they have at least two distinct functions. One is to signal that the channel is working successfully and the message has been received; the other is to signal readiness to receive a new message.

The utterance most overtly marked for successful reception was "gotcha" (Dialog 3). This function sometimes combined with the previously noted function of checking the decoding by partial repetition of the message just sent. Sometimes the repetition had an intonation and pronunciation that seemed imitative of the previous message and not characteristic of the current sender. This may also have been 'recognition by synthesis,' but it sounded more like checking and reassuring the other sender-receiver.

The second function, signalling readiness to receive a new message, proved unexpectedly important. There have been several studies recently (e.g., Yngve, 1970) of the visual and verbal cues by which people recognize whose turn it is to talk. In those dialogs where direct contact was broken between the two participants, there was considerable confusion when both tried to send messages at the same time. In Dialog 5, the first of the indirect monitored dialogs, some messages put in buffers were delivered out of sequence. On the next session, a strategy of requiring the apprentice to address the monitor and wait for a 'yes' before proceeding proved unworkable. On the last dialog, the monitor simply interrupted the apprentice when a message was underway from the expert, but the problem was not entirely solved and some mixups still occurred.

It appears as if on some occasions the simultaneous sending of messages occurred because both participants got nervous if nothing was coming across the channel, and both were set to go off after an interval of silence that was roughly the same for each. Long silences also made the monitors nervous. Both monitors adopted the strategy of starting to relay the expert's longer messages before they were complete, and to signal by intonation that there was more to come even though the pauses were abnormally long. Unfortunately, we cannot study the acoustic detail of these interestingly deviant intonations for the light they could shed on the function of intonation in signalling suspension or finality. Since these dialogs were trial runs, we had not tried to tape them under good sound conditions. However, the phenomenon is probably reproducible, since different monitors produced it independently.

Dialog 7 records the time of transmission of each utterance. The reader might try the effect of placing a sixteen second delay between the announcement, "The mounting bolts are tight as is all the plumbing," and the reinforcing phatic response, "...................... good." Or a twenty-four second delay between, "How tightly should I install this pipe elbow that fits into the pump?" and the reply "................... only snugly."

5. THE SEVENTH DIALOG

We had expected that the variations in style and syntax among the dialogs would be influenced more by the differences in the conditions under which they were conducted than by the individual differences of the participants. Impressionistically, this is true. The first two dialogs have some common features that set them slightly apart from the others, and this is probably attributable to two factors: The three different participants knew each other well and were all professionally interested in artificial intelligence. Many of their utterances were introspections about what was going through their minds as they solved the problem in front of them. However, it was relatively easy to extract the utterances that were relevant to the immediate task and these were much like the ones in Dialogs 3 and 4 where the apprentices and the expert had never previously met and where the expert was by profession a plumber.

For six of the dialogs, some obvious differences were attributable to the variables of vision and monitoring. When I first saw the transcript of the seventh dialog, the only one at which I had not been present, I was struck by the formality of the style and redundancy of the syntax. The exchanges in (18) exemplify these features.

(22) a. E: Are you now attaching the tubing to the elbow?
      A: The elbow and tubing installation is completed.

      b. A: Is it correct that the strap is attached to the pump by one of the cylinder head bolts?
      E: Yes, that is correct.

Listening to the tape confirmed the impression of formality; the speech was more deliberate, the intonation less varied than that of other dialogs.

I wondered if all the differences were due to the fact that the apprentice was more knowledgeable about compressors than the others and did not know the expert. Finally someone told me of a third variable: This apprentice thought the expert was a computer. When they told him the expert was another human, he responded with an appropriate exclamation. The opening exchanges of Dialog 7 are appended.

APPENDIX

Protocol text of session beginning Wed. 20 Feb. 1974, 10:38

10:39:13 E: GOOD MORNING. I WOULD LIKE FOR YOU TO REASSEMBLE THE COMPRESSOR.

10:39:41 A: ALL RIGHT I'M SUPPOSED TO JUST START DOING THAT AND ASK ANY QUESTIONS?

10:40:01 E: YES, I MAY ASK YOU WHAT YOU ARE DOING AS WE GO ALONG. I SUGGEST YOU BEGIN BY ATTACHING THE PUMP TO THE PLATFORM.

10:40:40 A: SEEMS REASONABLE.

10:41:49 E: WHAT ARE YOU DOING NOW?

10:41:58 A: USING THE PLIERS TO GET THE NUTS IN UNDERNEATH THE PUMP PLATFORM.

10:42:30 E: OK. I ASSUME YOU POSITIONED THE PUMP SO THAT THE LONGEST PROTRUSION, THE OIL DRAIN, IS POINTING TOWARD THE FRONT.

10:43:17 A: WHICH SIDE DO YOU CALL FRONT?

10:43:29 E: THE SIDE WITH THE SEARS LABEL ON THE TANK.

10:43:45 A: ALL RIGHT.

10:43:58 A: DO YOU HAVE AN ALTERNATE BETTER WAY TO GET THE NUTS IN UNDERNEATH THE PLATFORM?

10:44:16 E: I WOULD SUGGEST HOLDING THE WASHER AND NUT IN ONE HAND AND THE SCREW IN THE OTHER HAND. START THE NUT THAT WAY.

10:47:34 E: I REALIZE THIS IS A DIFFICULT STEP. HAVE YOU ANY OF THE NUTS STARTED?

10:48:04 A: I'M TIGHTENING THE BOLTS NOW. THEY ARE ALL IN PLACE.

10:48:20 E: GOOD.

10:49:37 A: HOW TIGHTLY SHOULD I INSTALL THIS PIPE ELBOW THAT FITS INTO THE PUMP?

10:50:00 E: ONLY SNUGLY. THE ELBOW MUST BE CONNECTED TO THE TUBING THAT CONNECTS TO THE TANK. THE END OF THE ELBOW THAT ATTACHES TO THE TUBING MUST BE POINTING TOWARD THE TUBING. THAT DIRECTION SHOULD DETERMINE THE TIGHTNESS.

10:51:20 A: FINE.

10:51:42 E: ARE YOU NOW ATTACHING THE TUBING TO THE ELBOW?

10:51:58 A: THE ELBOW AND TUBING INSTALLATION IS COMPLETED.

10:52:17 E: CHECK THE NUT WHERE THE TUBING IS ATTACHED TO THE TANK. IT MAY NEED TO BE TIGHTENED.

10:52:49 A: YES I TIGHTENED THAT.

10:52:58 E: GOOD.

10:53:36 A: I'M LEFT WITH A SMALL RECTANGULAR PLATE THAT IT ISN'T OBVIOUS WHAT TO DO WITH.

10:53:36 E: THE SMALL METAL STRAP IS A BRACE FOR THE PUMP AND SHOULD BE ATTACHED TO THE BELT HOUSING AND THE TOP OF THE PUMP.

10:53:57 E: THAT'S THE STRAP, OR BRACE.

10:54:20 A: YES.

10:54:51 A: IS IT CORRECT THAT THE STRAP IS ATTACHED TO THE PUMP BY ONE OF THE CYLINDER HEAD BOLTS?

10:55:09 E: YES, THAT IS CORRECT.

10:56:37 E: THIS STEP COMPLETES WORK ON THE FRONT SIDE OF THE COMPRESSOR.

10:56:57 A: YES I'VE FINISHED INSTALLING THE STRAP NOW.

REFERENCES

Bailey, C-J N., Comment on papers presented at the first plenary session. In Sociolinguistics: Current Trends and Prospects. 23rd Annual Georgetown Round Table. Monograph Series on Language and Linguistics, No. 25. Edited by R. Shuy. Georgetown University Press, Washington, D.C., 1973, pp. 89-98.

Bailey, C-J. N., and Shuy, R. (eds.), New Ways of Analyzing Variation in English, Georgetown University Press, Washington, D.C., 1973.

Bever, T. G., "The influence of speech performance on linguistic structure." In Advances in Psycholinguistics. Edited by G. B. Flores d'Arcais and W. J. M. Levelt. North-Holland Publishing Company, Amsterdam-London, 1970, pp. 4-30.

Buhler, K., Sprachtheorie, Jena, 1934.

Cedergren, H. J. and Sankoff, D., Variable rules: performance as a statistical reflection of competence. Language, in press.

Chomsky, N., "On the notion 'rule of grammar.'" In Structure of Language and Its Mathematical Aspects. Proceedings of Symposia in Applied Mathematics, Volume XII. Edited by R. Jakobson. American Mathematical Society, 1961, pp. 6-24.

Chomsky, N., Aspects of the Theory of Syntax. M.I.T. Press, Cambridge, Massachusetts, 1965.

Deutsch, B. G., "The structure of task-oriented dialogs." Proceedings of IEEE Symposium on Speech Recognition, Carnegie-Mellon University, 15-19 April, 1974.

Fromkin, V. A., "The non-anomalous nature of anomalous utterances." Language, 1971, 47, pp. 27-52.

Goldman-Eisler, F., "Pauses, clauses, sentences." Language and Speech, 1972, 15, pp. 103-113.

Halliday, M. A. K., "Language and social man." In Papers of the Programme in Linguistics and English Teaching, Second Series, Longmans, London (in press).

Jakobson, R., "Linguistics and poetics." In Style in Language. Edited by T. Sebeok, M.I.T. Press, Cambridge, Massachusetts, 1960, pp. 350-377.

Kimball, J., "Seven principles of surface structure parsing in natural language." Cognition, 1973, 2(1), pp. 15-47.

Kuno, S., "Functional sentence perspective." Linguistic Inquiry, 1972, 3, pp. 269-320.

Labov, W., "Contraction, deletion, and inherent variability of the English copula." Language, 1969, 45, pp. 715-762.

Labov, W., "Some principles of linguistic methodology." Language and Society, 1972, 1, pp. 97-120.

Labov, W., "Where do grammars stop?" In Sociolinguistics: Current Trends and Prospects. 23rd Annual Georgetown Round Table. Monograph Series on Languages and Linguistics, No. 25. Edited by R. Shuy. Georgetown University Press, Washington, D.C., 1973, pp. 43-88.

Ross, J. R., "On declarative sentences." In Jacobs, R. and Rosenbaum, P. (eds.), Readings in English Transformational Grammar. Waltham, Mass: Blaisdell, 1970, pp. 222-272.

Sankoff, G., "A quantitative paradigm for the study of communicative competence." Preprint from the Conference on the Ethnography of Speaking, Austin, Texas, 1972.

Sgall, P., Hajicova, E., and Benesova, E., Topic, Form, and Generative Semantics. Forschungen Linguistik und Kommunikationswissenschaft 1. Scriptor Verlag, Kronberg Taunus, 1973.

Yngve, V., "On getting a word in edgewise." Papers from the Sixth Regional Meeting, Chicago Linguistic Society, 1970, pp. 567-577.

UNDERSTANDING TASKS STATED IN NATURAL LANGUAGE

John R. Hayes
Herbert A. Simon
Carnegie-Mellon University[†]
Pittsburgh, Pennsylvania 15213

In this paper we describe a system that programs itself to solve problems stated in natural language, and we show, by way of illustration, how the system would handle a particular task, the Tea Ceremony problem.

If a person is to solve a problem, there are several things he must know. First, he must know the set of problem elements -- that is, the materials of the problem. In the Missionaries and Cannibals puzzle (Ernst & Newell, 1969), the set of problem elements includes missionaries, cannibals, a river, and a boat. Second, he must know the initial state of the problem and its goal, e.g., he must know that at the beginning of the problem the missionaries and cannibals are all on the left side of the river, and that at its termination they must all be on the right side. Third, he must know an operator or a set of operators for transforming the initial state into the goal -- in this case, the operator of rowing across the river. Finally, he must know the restrictions under which the operators may be applied, e.g., that cannibals must not outnumber missionaries on either side of the river.

These essential items of information define a basic problem space (Newell and Simon, 1972). A problem space is a subject's representation of the task environment that permits him to consider different problem situations, to characterize these situations in ways that may help him decide what to do, and to apply the operators for

[†]This research has been supported in part by Public Health Service Grant MH-07722 from the National Institute of Mental Health, and in part by the Advanced Research Projects Agency of the Office of the Secretary of Defense (F445620-70-C-0107) which is monitored by the Air Force Office of Scientific Research. A more complete description of the UNDERSTAND program and a discussion of its implications for psychological theory will be found in Hayes and Simon (1974) upon which this paper is largely based.

changing one situation into another. A basic problem space is a minimal space that includes just those things that are essential for defining the problem, the solution, and the operators.

When a person solves a problem of a type with which he is already familiar, he will be able to recall and use elements of the problem space that he constructed while working on previous problems. The naive subject must construct the entire problem space from the beginning by extracting the necessary information (sometimes laboriously) from the problem instructions. Hence, the process of problem space construction is an essential aspect of problem solving which can be an important source of problem solving difficulty. Moreover, the form of the problem instructions may determine which of several alternative problem spaces the subject constructs.

THE TASK

The Tea Ceremony problem (See Figure 1), was constructed as an isomorph of the "Tower of Hanoi" problem (Rouse-Ball 1962), the familiar puzzle in which disks of various sizes must be transferred among three pegs subject to restrictions on the set of legal moves. When we say that the Tea Ceremony is an isomorph of the Tower of Hanoi, we mean that it is the same problem as the Tower of Hanoi but disguised in different words. Any solution of the Tower of Hanoi puzzle may be translated, step by step, into a solution of the Tea Ceremony and vice versa by using the following correspondences:

Tea Ceremony	Tower of Hanoi
three participants	three pegs
five tasks	five disks
nobility of tasks	size of disks

The problem space information that the program had to identify from the problem description included: (1) problem elements, such as the set of three participants in the Tea Ceremony and the list of five tasks, (2) the initial state in which the host was performing all the tasks, and the goal state in which the senior guest performed them all, (3) the operator for requesting and effecting the transfer of tasks, and (4) the complex restrictions contained in sentences 6 and 7 under which a task could be transferred.

THE MODEL

In our model (Figure 2), we will view problem interpretation by the naive solver as employing two complex and interacting processes: an UNDERSTANDING process that generates a problem space from the text of the problem instructions, and a SOLVING process that uses the

1. IN THE INNS OF CERTAIN HIMALAYAN VILLAGES IS PRACTICED A MOST CIVILIZED AND REFINED TEA CEREMONY.
2. THE CEREMONY INVOLVES A HOST AND EXACTLY TWO GUESTS, NEITHER MORE NOR LESS.
3. WHEN HIS GUESTS HAVE ARRIVED AND HAVE SEATED THEMSELVES AT HIS TABLE, THE HOST PERFORMS FIVE SERVICES FOR THEM.
4. THESE SERVICES ARE LISTED BELOW IN THE ORDER OF THE NOBLITY WHICH THE HIMALAYANS ATTRIBUTE TO THEM;
   STOKING THE FIRE,
   FANNING THE FLAMES,
   PASSING RICE CAKES,
   POURING TEA,
   RECITING POETRY.
5. DURING THE CERAMONY, ANY OF THOSE PRESENT MAY ASK ANOTHER, "HONORED SIR, MAY I PERFORM THIS ONEROUS TASK FOR YOU?".
6. HOWEVER, A PERSON MAY REQUEST OF ANOTHER ONLY THE LEAST NOBLE OF THE TASKS WHICH THE OTHER IS PERFORMING.
7. FURTHER, IF A PERSON IS PERFORMING ANY TASKS, THEN HE MAY NOT REQUEST A TASK WHICH IS NOBLER THAN THE LEAST NOBLE TASK HE IS ALREADY PERFORMING.
8. CUSTOM REQUIRES THAT BY THE TIME THE TEA CEREMONY IS OVER, ALL OF THE TASKS WIL HAVE BEEN TRANSFERRED FROM THE HOST TO MOST SENIOR OF THE QUESTS.
9. HOW CAN THIS BE ACCOMPLISHED?

Figure 1. The Tea Ceremony Problem.

problem space to explore steps toward solving the problem. The text of the instructions is interpreted only to the extent that is necessary in order for the SOLVING process to arrive at a problem solution. Any parts of the text that are irrelevant to that goal may remain uninterpreted or only partly interpreted.

The UNDERSTANDING process consists of two subprocesses (Figure 2): a LANGUAGE interpreting process and a problem space CONSTRUCTION process. The process for interpreting LANGUAGE reads the problem text sentences and extracts information from them, guided by a set of information extraction rules. These rules identify the moods of the text sentences, identify noun groups that refer to physical objects and activities, and assign such relations to them as "agent," "instrument," "property," "location," and so on, much in the manner of a case grammar (see Fillmore, 1968). In the Tea Ceremony problem, the LANGUAGE process must recognize "the inns" and "a most civilized and refined tea ceremony" as noun groups, "in the inns" as a locative phrase, and so on.

UNDERSTANDING PROCESS
    LANGUAGE PROCESS
        SYNTAX
        SEMANTICS1
        SEMANTICS2
        CROSS-REFERENCE
    CONSTRUCTION PROCESS
        DESCRIBE-SITUATION
        DESCRIBE-OPERATOR
        INTEGRATION
        DESCRIBE-CONDITIONS
    SOLVING PROCESS

Figure 2. Organization of a Problem Solving Program

The CONSTRUCTION process accepts information, sentence by sentence, from the LANGUAGE interpreting process and builds a representation of the problem space, consisting of two parts: a SITUATION description and a set of OPERATORS. The description of the SITUATION, based on information extracted from sentences in the indicative mood, represents the problem elements (e.g., inns, villages, host, and so on), relations among problem elements (e.g., the inns are located in the villages), and the initial and goal states of the problem.

The set of OPERATORS, identified from information extracted from conditional statements and sentences in the subjunctive mood, may be represented as a production system, in which the conditions are represented as states (or aspects of states) of the SITUATION, and the actions are represented as processes for making changes in the SITUATION. As we shall see, a major responsibility of the CONSTRUCTION process is to make certain that the representation of the SITUATION is compatible with the representation of the OPERATORS, so that the OPERATOR processes will perform correctly in changing the SITUATION.

The problem SOLVING process works by running the OPERATORS generated by the CONSTRUCTION process under the control of a problem solving strategy of some kind. If the SOLVING process fails to achieve a solution, either because it runs out of things to do, or because it encounters a contradiction, it calls back the UNDERSTANDING process to elaborate or alter the problem space in order to resolve the conflict.

PREVIOUS LANGUAGE UNDERSTANDING PROGRAMS

The broad outlines of the understanding program we shall describe here derive from the HEURISTIC COMPILER (1963, 1972), an early exploration of the possibilities of constructing a problem-solving program capable of writing computer programs from English-language instructions. The problem-solving component of the HEURISTIC COMPILER was modelled on the GENERAL PROBLEM SOLVER; that is, it accepted as input a formalized description of the program to be written, and used means-ends analysis to produce code corresponding to the description. The "front end" of the HEURISTIC COMPILER, a rather primitive interpreter of natural language, accepted an English-language description of the programming problem, and produced from it the formalized description that the problem-solving component required as its input.

The HEURISTIC COMPILER's capabilities for interpreting natural language instructions were primarily semantic rather than syntactic in character. It was not capable of handling a wide range of English constructions, but only relatively simple descriptive prose; hence, needed only relatively simple processes to discover the underlying phrase structure and convert the input sentences into internal list structures. Of more interest is the fact that it was capable of expanding these input sentences, supplying various omissions and ellipses, by matching them to information already stored in semantic memory. Thus if the input sentences referred to a "state description," the HEURISTIC COMPILER would find in semantic memory a full and rather elaborate characterization of a state description, and could use the information contained in that characterization to supply missing information about state descriptions that was needed to formulate the programming problem for the problem-solving component of the system. Since we will be using the same techniques in the present system (but with rather more elaborate syntactic capabilities), there is no need to describe here just how the HEURISTIC COMPILER accomplished this semantic analysis. The interested reader is referred to the published descriptions (see Simon, 1972).

Bobrow (1964; in Minsky, 1969) constructed an early program for understanding natural language in algebra story problems in order to set up the equations for solving the problems. His program demonstrated that only relatively simple syntactic analysis was required when the task itself supplied a sufficiently rich semantic environment. In addition, there are, of course, a considerable number of question-answering schemes that accept natural-language input.

The state of the art of natural language processing, as of about

1972, is captured very well by Winograd's (1972) SHRDLU program. SHRDLU interprets statements and questions in English, using a case grammar that facilitates matching syntactic with semantic information. On the basis of the input questions or commands, SHRDLU then provides answers or carries out the commands, using for this purpose a reasoning program, PLANNER. Thus the language-processing component and the problem-solving component of SHRDLU stand in the same relation as the language-processing component and the problem-solving component of the HEURISTIC COMPILER, or of the system to be described here.

THE "UNDERSTAND" PROGRAM

As we stated earlier, the process of understanding a task begins with the presentation of the task instructions to the task performer, and ends when the performer has acquired a program that enables him to undertake to perform the task. If the task involves solving a problem, then the product of the understanding process is a problem-solving program appropriate to the task in question.

The problem-solving program that the performer acquires through the understanding process defines for him: (1) a basic problem space in which he can carry on a search for the problem solution, (2) one or more operators for moving through the problem space, and (3) one or more tests for determining the presence or absence of particular features at any node in the problem space. The problem solving program that is developed under these circumstances need not be manufactured out of whole cloth. The performer may come to the situation already provided with more or less general problem-solving capabilities. Under these circumstances, understanding means representing the new task in such a way that some of these general problem-solving capabilities can now be used for tackling it. We can imagine the SOLVING processes mentioned earlier as having two components: a more or less general program for solving problems, and a set of specific inputs to that program which define a particular problem for it in such terms that it can go to work on the problem. If such a factorization is possible, then the task of the UNDERSTANDING processes is to provide this second component, in proper format, to the problem-solving program.

In the present instance, we will assume that the problem-solving program which is the target of the understanding process resembles the General Problem Solver (GPS) in its general shape (Ernst & Newell, 1969). The principal inputs that GPS requires, before it can go to work on a problem, are: (1) a representation of the successive states of the problem-solving situation (i.e., of the nodes in the problem space), (2) one or more processes or actions for changing one of these states into another (for making legal, and possibly illegal, moves), (3) a set of differences for describing states and comparing pairs of states, and (4) a table of connections between differences and actions, which prescribes the possible actions that may be taken when each kind of difference is encountered. Providing GPS with these four kinds of information about a task environment enables it to undertake problem-solving activity in that environment.

Not all of this information needs to be supplied to GPS from external sources. Equipped with appropriate learning programs, GPS might be expected to develop the third and fourth classes of information by itself -- that is, to induce from the description of the problem space a list of differences, and to induce from these and from the operator or operators for changing states a table of connections between differences and actions. Several investigators have discussed learning programs for GPS-like problem solvers that are capable of carrying out these learning tasks -- of inducing differences and the table of connections. (A number of such learning programs are described and discussed in Newell, Shaw & Simon, 1960; Newell, 1963; Ernst & Newell, 1969; and Eavarone & Ernst, 1970.)

To strip our problem to its barest essentials, we will assume that GPS is equipped with such a learning program. Hence, what remains for the understanding process is to generate from the problem instructions the representation of problem states, one or more processes for changing states, and one or more tests for the presence or absence of particular features in a state.

In the problem before us, the Tea Ceremony, the task for the understanding program is to find a way to represent the successive situations during the ceremony -- specifically, to represent the distribution of tasks among the participants -- and to construct a program for transferring a task from one participant to another. Moreover, the transfer program must operate properly upon whatever representation has been constructed. The latter is a non-trivial requirement, for we shall see that it is probably most expedient to generate the two main outputs of the understanding program -- the representation of situations and the transfer process -- more or less independently of each other. Hence, the transfer process must be sufficiently flexible to adapt itself to the particular representation that has been chosen, whatever that may be.

PROCESSING STAGES

The understanding program carries out its work in two discrete stages which correspond to two of the components of the model described earlier (Figure 2).

1. The task instructions are read and re-read. They are analysed syntactically and semantically to extract from them their "deep structure," as linguists use that term. As before, we will refer to the processes that do this as the LANGUAGE processes.

2. The deep structures of the sentences describing the task are analysed further by matching them against a set of requirements that specify the form of an acceptable input to GPS. We can think of these requirements as a set of templates in long-term memory that provide a model for a well-formed problem, in the sense of GPS. We will call this second set of processes the CONSTRUCTION processes.

The input to the first stage is the text of the task instructions (Figure 1); the output is the deep structure of the text (Appendix III). The input to the second stage is the deep structure, the output is a task specification in a form suitable as inputs to GPS (Figures 3 and 5). Since the problem-solving process can now go to work on this task specification, the latter represents the solver's understanding of the problem.

LANGUAGE: EXTRACTING DEEP STRUCTURE FROM TEXT

That portion of the simulation which is concerned with extracting the deep structure from the text has been realized mostly in PAS-II (Waterman & Newell, 1972). PAS-II is a flexible interactive computer program designed as an aid to the process of protocol analysis. In particular, it was designed to take as input a problem-solving protocol and a description of the problem space that the subject used to solve the problem, and from these to trace the sequence of operators that the subject applied in solving the problem. For example, PAS-II will provide an analysis of a cryptarithmetic protocol if it is given a description of the subject's problem space, including both the knowledge elements that the subject identifies in the problem (e.g., letters, digits, parity, and so on), and a list of the operators that are available to the subject (e.g., operators that assign a value to a digit or that process a column.

In the present context, we have made use of PAS-II in a manner parallel to, but different from, its originally intended use. We have used it to accept as input the problem text and a set of text-reading rules, and to generate as output a set of syntactically and semantically interpreted elements from which the second part of the

UNDERSTAND program can derive the problem space that is implied in the problem description.

Since PAS-II has convenient facilities for defining sets of processing rules (e.g., segmentation rules, grammar rules, etc.) that can be applied in an arbitrary order designated by the user, it is well adapted to this new task. PAS-II also provides compact notations for expressing grammatical and semantic relations, a number of editing, storage, and other utility functions, and interactive capabilities.

GENERAL ORGANIZATION

We have divided the task of extracting the deep structure (see Figure 2) into three phases, accomplished in sequence: (1) a syntactic phase that parses sentences, (2) a semantic phase that identifies significant relations and assembles structures that have special meaning (e.g., lists and quotes), and (3) a cross-reference phase that handles inter-sentence relations such as anaphoric reference. The first two of these phases operate on the text one sentence at a time. In the third, or cross-reference, phase, the text is considered as a whole.

THE SYNTACTIC PHASE

The syntactic analysis is accomplished by applying three types of rules to the input sentences. These are segmentation rules, grammar rules, and integration rules. The function of the segmentation rules is to break complex sentences into smaller, more easily handled, segments. For example, the segmentation rules separate the subject from the predicate of a sentence by breaking after a noun that is followed by a verb. This separation simplifies the identification of the object of the sentence by preventing confusion between the subject and the object. The segmentation rules also break after commas, colons, semicolons, and relatives such as "which" and "that."

For example, Sentence 2 of "The Tea Ceremony" (See Figure 1) is broken into three parts by the segmentation rules:

"the ceremony"
"involves a host and exactly two guests,"
"neither more nor less."

The grammar rules assign grammatical classes to words and to groups of words. First, single words are classified as nouns, verbs, adjectives, determiners, and so on. Then more complex units are identified by the ordering and grammatical classes of the words that comprise them. For example, in parsing the segment of Sentence 1, " ... a most civilized and refined tea ceremony.", the words were classified respectively as determiner, adjective, adjective, conjunction, adjective, noun, noun.

The string adjective-conjunction-adjective was classed as a conjoined adjective, and the two nouns were classed as a noun string. Then the whole structure, because it consisted of a noun string preceded by an optional adjective string preceded, in turn, by an optional determiner, was classed as a noun-group with "ceremony" as its head. Finally, the structure was reclassified -- as are all noun-groups, and pronouns that are not possessive pronouns -- as an object. The output of the grammar rules for this segment was the element (OBJ CEREMONY).

The output of the grammar rule for the segment " ... is practiced ... " is the element (VG IS PRACTICED), indicating a verb group, with "practiced" as the main verb and "is" as the auxiliary. When there is no auxiliary, the marker "aux" appears in the auxiliary position.

In addition to noun-groups and verb-groups, the grammar identifies prepositional phrases ("... to them ..." = (PHR TO THEM)), time marks ("When ..." = (TMARK)), modal auxiliaries ("... may ..." = (MODAL)), groups defined as a digit followed by a plural noun ("... two guests ..." = (GR TWO GUESTS)), and about twenty others. Appendix I shows the output of the grammar rules for each of the sentences of the problem text.

The integration rules are applied to the output of the grammar rules. These rules serve the function of assembling correctly parsed sentences from the grammatically classified elements. Included among the integration rules are rules that identify sets of objects (defined as a group or an object joined to another group or object by "and"), subsets of sets, and lists (defined as ordered sets). Other integration rules assemble predicates from verb-groups, objects, phrases, and time markers, and then construct sentences by adding subjects to these predicates. The output of the integration rules for Sentence 2 is:

    (sen ceremony involves (host (two guests)) d t)
    (set host (two guests))(subset (two guests))
    (negadj more)(negadj less)

In the first line of the output above, "d" is a placeholder for an indirect object and "t" is a placeholder for a time mark such as "INITIAL" or "FINAL." The negative adjectives will be ignored by the program hereafter, since they have failed to find a place in any structure of interest to the UNDERSTAND processes. Execution of the integration rules marks the end of the syntactic phase of the LANGUAGE program.

SEMANTIC PHASE

Processing in the semantic phase is accomplished by two sets of rules which we will call the Semantic1 rules and the Semantic2 rules. The Semantic1 rules search for sentences that have verbs denoting important relations, such as ASK, DO, and PARTICIPATE, and transform them into the corresponding relations. For example, the segment of sentence 7, "... if a person is performing any tasks, ...", which the syntactic phase has coded as

(if)(sen person performing tasks) d t)

is transformed into:

(if)(rel do person tasks) d t).

Appendix II shows the output of the Semantic1 rules for each of the sentences in the problem text.

The Semantic2 rules carry out the final stage of semantic processing. These rules use the special marks left in the text by the earlier processing stages, e.g., (QUOTE), (QUEST), (STRING X), and so on, to assemble complex structures (quotes, questions, and lists -- ordered sets). For example, sentence 5 in Appendix II is transformed to:

(rel ask (group (those present)) lit (of another) t)

(rel (ask do) i (memb this onerous task) (for you) t)

In the first line, the marker "LIT" indicates that the object of the relation "ASK" is a quote, the interpretation of which follows in the next line. The relation (ASK DO) stands for the complex relation of "asking to do" constructed from the "ASK" relation and the action of doing involved in the quote that the relation contained. Sentence 4 in Appendix II is transformed into

(list tasks nobility ((act stoking fire)

(act fanning flames) (act passing cakes)

(act pouring tea)(act reciting poetry))

CROSS REFERENCING

Currently, cross-referencing is handled by an auxiliary SNOBOL program called "JTEA." This program performs two functions:

1. It traces anaphoric references and replaces pronouns with the referenced nouns.

2. It handles words such as "further" and "however" that link sentences together. It does this by (a) matching elements in the two sentences to be sure that the subscripts are assigned in a consistent way across sentences (e.g., that "PARTICIPANT.1" in Sentence 5 refers to the same object as "PARTICIPANT.1" in Sentence 6). The matching is accomplished by searching for an identical verb in the two

sentences and establishing that the matched objects bear identical relations to it. (b) It then assembles the two sentences into a single sentence and deletes the linking word.

CONSTRUCTION: REPRESENTATION AND TRANSFER PROCESSES

In Appendix III, we show the interpreted text as it emerges from the parsing process -- that is, in the form of the "deep structure" of the original problem instructions. In the present section, we describe the portions of the understanding program that take this interpreted text as input, and produce a representation for the various states of the problem situation, and a process for transfering tasks from one of the participants to another. The latter process will also incorporate tests for guaranteeing that the conditions stated in the problem for a "legal" transfer are satisfied: that is, that the task being transferred is the least noble of the tasks being performed by the person from whom it is taken, and is less noble than any of the tasks of the person who takes it.

REPRESENTING THE SITUATION

In preparation for subsequent processing steps, the program examines the text to find the whole set of participants, and the whole list of tasks, and converts this set and this list into an appropriate internal representation, assigning to the set and list their types, to the list its ordering relation (ORDER), and to the members of each their respective types. The resulting structures, obtained by processing Sentences 2 and 3, respectively, are shown in Figure 3.

The program searches the text for a sentence in the declarative mood that is labelled with a time tag, on the assumption that such a sentence will be descriptive of the situation at some stage in the problem. The first such sentence it discovers in the processed text is Sentence 2, which describes the problem situation at the outset of the Tea Ceremony. The program takes this as the information from which it will undertake to construct a representation of the situation. The sentence asserts a relation between one of the participants, the host, and the tasks.

Now the program is ready to create a description of the initial situation. Sentence 2 asserts a relation, DO, between an object of the class, PARTICIPANT, and a list of objects of the class, TASK. The attribute, PARTICIPANT, is associated with the structure, SITUATION; and the list of participants is associated with this attribute as its value. The participant on this list that is synonymous with "HOST" is assigned the attribute, TASK, and the list of tasks that, according to Sentence 2, the host is performing is assigned as the value of this attribute. The resulting description of the situation is shown in Figure 3.

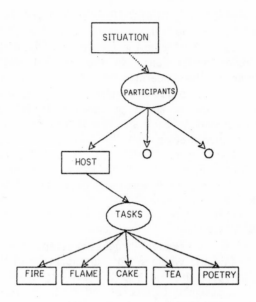

SITUATION = ' :,PARTICIPANT L1,'
L1 = ' HOST GUEST.1 GUEST.2 :,TYPE SET,'
HOST = ' :,TYPE PARTICIPANT,TASK L2,'
L2 = ' FIRE FLAME CAKE TEA POETRY :,TYPE LIST,
        ORDER NOBILITY,'

Figure 3. Program Description of Initial Situation.

THE TRANSFER PROCESS

The program next seeks information about the operators for the Tea Ceremony. Employing as its cue the use of the subjunctive mood, it discovers that Sentences 5 through 7 of Appendix III have been tagged as a production -- that is, as describing an action. In Sentence 5 it discovers the relation ASK:DO having three arguments: the task, the participant making the request, and the participant currently performing the task. That is, ASK:DO is of the form:

rel(task,participant.1,participant.2).

The next step is to search semantic memory for the meaning of this relation -- that is for a known process, having the same formal structure as ASK:DO, and having associated with it a procedure for actually executing the process. In the present version of the system, the proper formal structure is identified by MATCH, a process that compares the given relation with a relational structure in semantic memory, and determines whether the former is isomorphic with the latter. Here "isomorphic" means that the given relation has the same number of arguments as the relation in semantic memory, and that these arguments are distributed in the same way among arguments of different types. To accomplish its task, MATCH makes us of a subroutine, CLASS, which identifies the types of the arguments in each relation, and counts the number of arguments of each type.

In the instance before us, the given relation has three arguments, one of one type (TASK), and two of another type (PARTICIPANT). In semantic memory, we find the relation, TRANSFER, which also has three arguments, one of the type OBJECT, and two of the type ACTOR. The MATCH process therefore succeeds in mapping REL upon TRANSFER, with TASK corresponding with OBJECT, and PARTICIPANT.1 and PARTICIPANT.2 corresponding with ACTOR.F and ACTOR.T, respectively. (See Figure 4.)

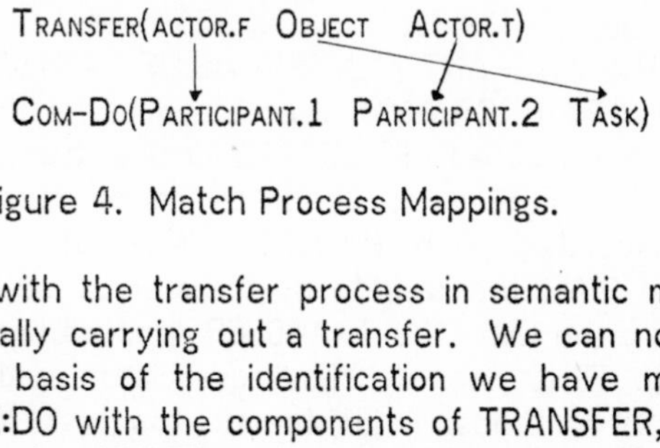

Transfer(actor.f Object Actor.t)

Com-Do(Participant.1 Participant.2 Task)

Figure 4. Match Process Mappings.

Associated with the transfer process in semantic memory is a procedure for actually carrying out a transfer. We can now use that procedure, on the basis of the identification we have made of the components of ASK:DO with the components of TRANSFER, to execute the action called for by ASK:DO -- that is to transfer a task from one participant to another. However, two things remain to be done: to add to ASK:DO the specific conditions for a legal move in the Tea Ceremony, and to adapt the code for the transfer operation to the particular representation we have chosen for the problem space. We will take up these two points in reverse order.

FITTING PROCESS TO REPRESENTATION

The coded procedure associated in semantic memory with TRANSFER is very general and flexible. If it is provided with information about the representation that has been selected, the procedure will perform a transfer operation appropriate to that representation. In the case before us, a task is a member of the value list of the attribute TASK of the participant who is performing it. To transfer that task from one participant to another, we must delete it from the list on which it appears, and add it to the list of tasks that is the value of the attribute TASK of the participant who receives it.

The information that TRANSFER needs about the representation is provided by the process called DESCRIBE. DESCRIBE examines the representation of the situation, and produces a description of the way in which the relation between a task and the participant who is performing it is represented (Figure 5).

VSIT = ' :, WHICH PARTICIPANTS, PARTICIPANTS MEMBER,
TASKS MEMBER VALUE TASKS, '

Figure 5. Results of Describe Process.

In the case before us, the description would read: TASKS, MEMBER VALUE TASKS, which may be translated, "TASKS are stored as MEMBERS of the list of VALUES of the attribute TASK of the structure PARTICIPANT.X." The description produced by DESCRIBE also indicates where information about the participants is stored in relation to the structure, SITUATION. In the present case, the description would read: PARTICIPANT MEMBER VALUE PARTICIPANT, which may be translated, "PARTICIPANTS are stored as MEMBERS of the list of VALUES of the attribute PARTICIPANT of the structure SITUATION."

The TRANSFER process uses the latter description to FIND the structure associated with PARTICIPANT.1, then uses the former description to FIND the task to be transferred on this structure, and deletes it from the list. The TRANSFER process next uses the second description to FIND the structure associated with PARTICIPANT.2, then uses the first description to add the task to the list of tasks associated with this structure.

The TRANSFER process will use the same method to carry out the transfer for other representations of the data -- it will FIND the first participant, delete the task to be transfered, FIND the second participant, and add the task to the tasks associated with him. The transfer will also be performed correctly if participants are associated with tasks instead of tasks with participants. In this case (which will be disclosed by the description provided by DESCRIBE) TRANSFER will FIND the task to be transfered, FIND the participant associated with it, and change the latter to the participant who is to receive the task.

CONDITIONS FOR A LEGAL TRANSFER

To define a complete process for a legal move (i.e., a legal transfer of a task) in the Tea Ceremony, the program must be able to test whether a particular task is the least noble of the tasks being performed by one of the participants (the donor); and whether this task is less noble than all the tasks being performed by another participant (the one requesting the task). The process LIST('TASK','PARTICIPANT.X') will produce a list, in order of nobility, of all the tasks that are being performed by PARTICIPANT.X. The LIST process, like TRANSFER, is independent of the particular representation that has been selected to describe the situation. It acquires this independence by making use of the description of the situation produced by DESCRIBE to find PARTICIPANT.X in the structure that describes the situation, and then to find all of the tasks assigned to PARTICIPANT.X. From the list, TASK, it obtains the tasks, ordered by the relation of NOBILITY.

LIST will operate equally well if the situation is described in terms of tasks and the participants responsible for them, as if it is described, inversely, in terms of participants and the tasks they are performing. In either case it produces an ordered list of those tasks that are being performed by the participant in question. With the output of LIST in hand, it becomes an easy matter to determine whether a particular task is the least of an ordered list (i.e., its last member), and whether the task is less than all members of such a list. The former test is performed by the function LEAST, the latter by the function LESSA (for "less than all"). Thus to test whether the conditions are satisfied for transfering TASK.4 from PARTICIPANT.2 to PARTICIPANT.3, we first execute the test

least('task.4',list('task','participant.2'))

and then, if that test succeeds, the test:

lessa('task.4',list('task','participant.3')).

ACCOMMODATING THE TRANSFER AND FIND PROCESSES

Making the TRANSFER process, and the FIND process that it employs, independent of the representation exacts a heavy price in terms of processing time and complexity. Each time these processes are executed, the description of the representation must be re-examined, and a multitude of tests must be carried out to choose the correct path through the routines. The inefficiency is twofold: (1) only a small part of the total routine, TRANSFER, or FIND, is relevant to any particular problem representation; and (2) tests on the description of the representation to determine which path to follow make up a considerable part of the processing. The processing could be carried out much more rapidly if these inefficiencies could be removed.

The phenomenon we are describing has a clear human counterpart. When a human subject learns a new procedure that is necessary for carrying out a task, he executes the procedure haltingly, stopping along the way to ask himself: "What do I do next?", or "Where am I?" As he executes the procedure repeatedly, he begins to transfer more and more of the steps to long-term memory, so that he can retrace the path "automatically," without these halts, hesitations, and tests. It is our hypothesis that his increasing speed and sureness of performance results specifically from replacing a "general purpose" program, replete with tests for selecting his path in a given situation, by a special program, tailored to the current representation he is employing, and omitting the tests as inessential.

To simulate this hypothesized human assimilation process, we assume a gradual transfer to long-term memory of the steps in TRANSFER and FIND that are actually executed, omitting those steps that are information-gathering tests on the description of the representation. Thus, there are gradually created in long-term memory, streamlined versions of TRANSFER and FIND -- call them STRANSFER and SFIND, respectively -- that permit automatization of these operations.

LESSONS FOR UNDERSTANDING

In a recent paper, Moore and Newell (1974) provide a general discussion of what it means for a system to "understand." Their viewpoint is that a system understands knowledge to the extent that it uses the knowledge whenever it is appropriate. How well does the UNDERSTAND system meet this criterion?

DOES THIS TASK REQUIRE UNDERSTANDING?

Clearly learning about a task from written instructions is a test of understanding of those instructions. The instructions contain knowledge about the task embedded in English prose, and the evidence that the program has used the knowledge appropriately is that, after a time, it is able to try to perform the task. We say "try to perform," because the issue is not whether it can solve the Tea Ceremony problem, but whether it comes to know what the problem is. The nature of the understanding so achieved is most evident from an examination of the UNDERSTAND program. "Using the knowledge when appropriate" means, in this context, using it to construct a problem representation that will serve as input to a problem-solving program.

Understanding is not an all-or-none affair. One can speak of degree, range, and depth of understanding. Newell and Moore take up eight dimensions of understanding in their analysis: representation (completeness, "grain," multiplicity of representations), ability to convert knowledge to action, assimilation of the external environment, accommodation to the external environment, directionality, efficiency, tolerance of error, and depth of understanding. Let us see how UNDERSTAND fares with respect to each of these.

REPRESENTATION

UNDERSTAND does not encode information into specialized formats, but holds it internally in the form of list structures -- that is, lists and descriptions (alias semantic nets, association networks, colored graphs). It is well known that these are quite general structures: anything that can be symbolized can be symbolized with their help.

But to encode something is one matter, to encode it in such a way that it is usable is another. UNDERSTAND has no particular capabilities for selecting a problem representation that will facilitate solving the problem. It is, in fact, closely bound to the stimulus in the representation it constructs. Change in the wording of the text of the instructions will cause UNDERSTAND to change its representation of the problem.

CONVERTING KNOWLEDGE TO ACTION

The UNDERSTAND program has a number of important capabilities for translating knowledge into action. These capabilities exist at two levels. In the first place, the central objective of the program is to translate static knowledge, in the form of English language prose, into an input suitable to a general problem solving program like GPS. We can view the problem solving program itself as an interpreter, and the input that defines a particular task domain and problem for it as a program to be interpreted. Thus, the translation process dynamicizes the knowledge contained in the static instructions -- makes it interpretable.

The second way in which the UNDERSTAND program translates knowledge into action is by assimilating information in the task instructions that refers to task actions or moves (e.g., the transfer of a task from one participant to another in the Tea Ceremony). Stored in the program's long-term memory is information about how to execute certain quite general processes, like the TRANSFER process. Assimilating an action mentioned in the task instructions to such a general process stored in memory gives the UNDERSTAND program the ability actually to execute that action in the context of the problem representation.

ASSIMILATION

The generality of the UNDERSTAND program's assimilative powers depends on the generality of its capabilities for processing the English language, and the repertoire of actions that is stored in its long-term memory. The actual program as it now stands is quite limited in these respects. But the limits are mainly limits of education and not limits of educability. The machinery of PAS-II makes it quite easy to supplement the syntactical and semantic rules with new or modified ones.

Similarly, while UNDERSTAND now possesses knowledge of only a few active processes (TRANSFER, LEAST, LESSA), there is no in-principle reason why this repertoire cannot be expanded. Moreover, examination of the TRANSFER process, and the matching procedure that underlies its application, suggests that the number of different processes that commonly arise in representing problem situations may not be large. The TRANSFER process as it now stands, for example, can be interpreted to handle all the kinds of processes that are defined as "moves" in common games.

ACCOMMODATION

The UNDERSTAND program does relatively little that can be interpreted as accommodation. It does not store the results of its understanding in long-term memory in such a way as to facilitate the solution of new problems that may be posed to it. The one process we have described that might be considered to be accommodation is the process for streamlining the TRANSFER process once it has been adapted to a particular problem representation.

DIRECTIONALITY

The UNDERSTAND program's strong sense of directionality derives from its single-purpose nature. It is designed to do just one kind of task: to translate problem instructions into a form that makes them compatible as inputs to a problem solver. It can do whatever the situation calls for, provided that is what it does call for. This does not mean that the general principle underlying the UNDERSTAND program could not be used in programs with other goals. Indeed, the HEURISTIC COMPILER is an example of an earlier program that used the same idea to another end. The HEURISTIC COMPILER also derived its directionality from templates stored in long-term memory of the kind of object it was seeking to construct. In that case, the desired object was a computer program in a certain format.

Hence, we can say of directionality, as we said of assimilation, that the underlying principle of the UNDERSTAND program is quite general, while its present implementation is quite limited and specific.

EFFICIENCY

There is little we can say about the efficiency of the UNDERSTAND program, beyond what has already been said in the discussion of representation and accommodation.

ERROR

The UNDERSTAND program has little or no capability for recovering from error. Its chief protection against erroneous interpretation of information is to leave it uninterpreted unless the interpretation is clear. This is an important technique that has not been much exploited in artificial intelligence programs (however, see Simon and Siklossy, 1972).

DEPTH OF UNDERSTANDING

Does a human "understand" arithmetic if he can add two numbers and get the correct sum? Or does he understand only if he can state Peano's postulates for the integers and derive the sums table from them? Or do we have to test his understanding in some other way?

We would probably be inclined to say that the second test implies deeper understanding than the first. It implies that the performer cannot merely do something, but that he knows what makes it work.

We could ask a whole host of comparable questions about the UNDERSTAND program. It understands the text of instructions well enough to construct a problem representation, but it doesn't understand why it wants such a representation. It can "understand" the structure of a representation well enough to write a description of it, for use by the FIND and TRANSFER processes, but not well enough to manipulate the representation into a more useful form. Understanding in complex environments of this kind is not a unitary thing; it can be tested in many ways, and passing one test offers no guarantee of passing others.

CONCLUSION

The UNDERSTAND program may be viewed as an organization of processes that extracts task information from natural-language text to provide input to a problem solving program like GPS. Many real-world tasks can be put in this form -- the task of automatic program generation is an example. The experiment described in this paper with the Tea Ceremony problem shows that the UNDERSTAND program does indeed possess the basic capabilities required for the understanding, in this specific sense, of non-trivial natural language text.

REFERENCES

Bobrow, D. G. "Natural language input for a computer problem-solving system." In M. Minsky (ed.) Semantic Information Processing. Cambridge, Mass.: M.I.T. Press, 1968.

Eavarone, D. G. and G. W. Ernst. "A program that discovers good difference orderings and tables of connections for GPS." Proceedings of 1970 IEEE Systems Science and Cybernetics Conference. New York: IEEE, 1970, 226-233.

Ernst, G. W. and A. Newell. GPS: A case study in generality and problem solving. New York: Academic Press, 1969.

Fillmore, C. J. "The case for case." In E. Bach and R. T. Harms (eds.) Universals in Linguistic Theory. New York: Holt, Rinehart and Winston, 1968.

Hayes, J. R. and H. A. Simon. "Understanding written problem instructions." In L. W. Gregg (ed.) Knowledge and Cognition. Potomac, Maryland: Lawrence Erlbaum Associates, 1974.

Moore, J. and A. Newell. "How can Merlin understand?" In L. W. Gregg (ed.) Knowledge and Cognition. Potomac, Maryland: Lawrence Erlbaum Associates, 1974.

Newell, A. "Learning, generality, and problem solving." Proceedings of the IFIP Congress 62: 1963, 407-412.

Newell, A., J. C. Shaw and H. A. Simon. "A variety of intelligent learning in a general problem solver." In M. C. Yovits and S. Cameron (eds.) Self-organizing Systems: Proceedings of an Interdisciplinary Conference. New York: Pergamon Press, 1960.

Newell, A. and H. A. Simon. Human Problem Solving. Englewood Cliffs, N. J.: Prentice-Hall, 1972.

Rouse Ball, W. W. Mathematical Recreations and Essays. New York: Macmillan, 1962.

Simon, H. A. "The heuristic compiler." In H. A. Simon and L. Siklossyi (eds.) Representation and Meaning. Englewood Cliffs, N. J.: Prentice-Hall, 1972.

Simon, H. A. and L. Siklossy. (eds.) Representation and Meaning. Englewood Cliffs, N. J.: Prentice-Hall, 1972.

Waterman, D. A. and A. Newell. "PAS-II: An interactive task-free version of an automatic protocol analysis system." Pittsburgh: Department of Computer Science, Carnegie-Mellon University, 1972.

Winograd, T. "Understanding natural language." Cognitive Psychology 3: 1-191, 1972.

APPENDIX I. OUTPUT OF SYNTACTIC PROCESSING.

LINGUISTIC2 MODE
:: SENTENCE 1
(PHR IN INNS) (PHR OF VILLAGES)
(VG IS PRACTICED) (OBJ CEREMONY)
:: SENTENCE 2
(OBJ CEREMONY)
(GR TWO GUESTS) (VG <AUX> INVOLVES) (OBJ HOST) (AND)
(ADJNEG MORE) (ADJNEG LESS) (COMMA)
:: SENTENCE 3
(OBJ GUESTS) (TMARK)
(PHR AT TABLE) (CONJVG (VG HAVE ARRIVED) (VG HAVE SEATED))
(OBJ THEMSELVES)
(OBJ HOST) (COMMA)
(GR FIVE SERVICES) (PHR FOR THEM) (VG <VAUX> PERFORMS)
:: SENTENCE 4
(OBJ SERVICES)
(LIST) (EXTD NOBILITY)
(OBJ HIMALAYANS)
(PHR TO THEM) (VG <AUX> ATTRIBUTE) (COLON)
(ACT STOKING FIRE)
(ACT FANNING FLAMES) (COMMA)
(ACT PASSING CAKES) (COMMA)
(ACT POURING TEA) (COMMA)
(ACT RECITING POETRY) (COMMA)
:: SENTENCE 5
(COTEMP CEREMONY)
(GROUP THOSE-PRESENT) (COMMA)
(VG <VAUX> ASK) (OBJ ANOTHER) (MODAL)
(OBJ SIR) (QUOTE) (COMMA)
(OBJ I) (MODAL) (COMMA)
(MEMB THIS ONEROUS TASK) (PHR FOR YOU)
(VG <VAUX> PERFORM) (QUOTE) (QUEST)
:: SENTENCE 6
(HOWEVER)
(OBJ PERSON) (COMMA)
(PHR OF ANOTHER) (VG <AUX> REQUEST) (MODAL)
(EXTM LEAST NOBLE TASKS) (ONLY)
(OBJ OTHER)
(VG IS PERFORMING)
:: SENTENCE 7
(FURTHER)

(OBJ PERSON) (IF) (COMMA)
(GROUP TASKS) (VG IS PERFORMING)
(OBJ HE) (COMMA) (THEN)
(EXTO TASK) (VGNEG <AUX> REQUEST) (MODAL)
(MEMB NOBLEST <ADJ> TASK) (VG <AUX> IS)
(OBJ HE) (COMP NOBLER <ADJ>)
(VG IS PERFORMING)
  :: SENTENCE 8
(OBJ CUSTOM)
(VG <AUX> REQUIRES) (REL)
(OBJ CEREMONY) (TMARK)
(VG <AUX> IS) (FINAL)
(GROUP TASKS) (COMMA)
(MEMB MOST SENIOR GUESTS) (PHR FROM HOST)
(VG WILL TRANSFERRED) (PREP TO)
  :: SENTENCE 9
(OBJ THIS) (QWORD HOW) (MODAL)
(VG BE ACCOMPLISHED) (QUEST)

APPENDIX II. OUTPUT OF SEMANTIC PROCESSING.

SEMANTIC2 MODE
:: SENTENCE 1
(REL LOC INNS VILLAGES) (REL LOC CEREMONY INNS)
(PRED (IS PRACTICED) CEREMONY D T)
:: SENTENCE 2
(REL PART CEREMONY (HOST (TWO GUESTS)) D T)
(SET HOST (TWO GUESTS)) (SUBSET (TWO GUESTS))
(ADJNEG MORE) (ADJNEG LESS)
:: SENTENCE 3
(TMARK Q) (REL LOC GUESTS TABLE)
(SEN GUESTS (VG HAVE SEATED) GUESTS D Q) ←
    (sen guests (vg have arrived) nil d q)
(rel do host (five tasks) (for guests) q)
(set (five tasks))
:: SENTENCE 4
(list tasks (nobility a) l)
(sen himalayans (<aux> attribute)
  (nobility a) (to them) t)
(string ((act stoking fire) (act fanning flames)
(act passing cakes) (act pouring tea) (act reciting poetry)))
:: SENTENCE 5
(cotemp ceremony) (modal)
(rel ask (group those-present) ob (of another) t)
(quote) (ndir sir)
(quest) (rel do i (memb this onerous task)
  (for you) t)
(quote)
:: SENTENCE 6
(however) (modal)
(rel ask person (memb only (least noble)
  (tasks a)) (of another) t)
(rel do other (tasks a) d t)
:: SENTENCE 7
(further)
(if) (modal) (rel do person (group tasks) d t)
(then) (rel (no ask) he (task a) d t)
(sen (task a) (is (comp nobler <adj>))
  (memb noblest <adj> task) d t)
(rel do he ob d t)
:: SENTENCE 8
(sen custom (<aux> requires) rel d final)

(tmark final) (sen ceremony (<aux> is) ob d final)
(rel trans (group tasks) host
  (memb most senior guests) final)
      :: SENTENCE 9
(qword how) (quest) (rel do this ob d t)

Appendix III.　Results of Processing Sentence 2 and Sentence 3.

```
( REL LOC INNS VILLAGES D T )
( REL LOC ( ANY CEREMONY.1 ) INNS D T )
( REL PART CEREMONY.1 ( SET ( HOST ( TWO GUESTS ) ) ) D T )
( SET  GUESTS.N1 GUESTS.N2 HOST )
( SUBSET  GUESTS.N1 GUESTS.N2 )
( REL LOC GUESTS TABLE D Q )
( REL DO HOST ( SET ( FIVE TASKS.1 ) ) ( FOR GUESTS ) T )
( SET  TASKS.N1 TASKS.N2 TASKS.N3 TASKS.N4 TASKS.N5 )
( LIST TASKS ( NOBILITY ( SEN HIMALAYANS
  ( <AUX> ATTRIBUTE ) OB ( TO TASKS.1 ) T )
 ( ( STOKING FIRE ) ( FANNING FLAMES )
   ( PASSING CAKES ) ( POURING TEA) ( RECITING POETRY )
( MODAL )
( REL ASK ( ANY PARTICIPANT.1 )
  LIT ( OF PARTICIPANT.2 ) ( COTEMP CEREMONY.1 ) )
( REL ( ASK DO ) PARTICIPANT.1
  ( THIS ONEROUS TASK.1 )  (FOR PARTICIPANT.2 ) T )
( MODAL )
( HOWEVER )
( REL ( ASK DO ) ( ANY PARTICIPANT.1 )
   ( ONLY ( ( LEAST NOBLE TASK.1 )
    ( REL DO PARTICIPANT.2 OB D T ) ) )
     ( OF PARTICIPANT.2 ) T )
( MODAL )
( FURTHER )
( IF )
( REL DO ( ANY PARTICIPANT.1 ) ( ANY TASK.1 ) D T )
( REL ( NO ( ASK DO ) ) PARTICIPANT.1
   ( ANY ( TASK.1 ( REL ( COMP NOBLER <ADJ> )
    TASK ( ( LEAST NOBLE TASK )
     ( REL DO PARTICIPANT.1 OB D T ) ) D T ) ) ) D T )
( REL EQ CEREMONY.1 D FINAL )
( REL TRANS ( ANY TASK.1 )
   HOST ( MOST SENIOR GUEST ) FINAL )
( REL ( QUEST ( HOW DO ) ) THIS OB D T )
```

Part Five

Systems Organizations
and
Analysis Systems

TUTORIAL ON
SYSTEM ORGANIZATION FOR SPEECH UNDERSTANDING

D. Raj Reddy
Lee D. Erman
Computer Science Department
Carnegie-Mellon University
Pittsburgh, Pennsylvania 15213

ABSTRACT

Speech Understanding Systems tend to require more complex program organization than conventional programming tasks. Part of this complexity is necessitated by the need to explore, discover, and modify solutions as we better understand various phenomena associated with speech. The aspects of system organization that require careful attention are models of speech understanding, representation of data and control in errorful situations, real-time system design, reconfiguration of systems, interactive debugging, and performance analysis. In this paper we will present the problems that arise in each of these areas, examine solutions that have been found to be useful in present systems, and discuss their limitations.

INTRODUCTION

This tutorial is on system organization for speech understanding. What is system organization? Briefly stated, it is a catch-all term that describes the art of transforming ideas into working programs. In the case of speech understanding, this term assumes an added dimension in that many of the problems of speech understanding are not well defined, let alone have known solutions. We know that somehow all the available sources of knowledge, including semantics and pragmatics, must be brought to bear on the solution. But we do not know how to do it effectively or efficiently. In many cases knowledge is incomplete and imprecise. We do not know how to add knowledge conveniently to already existing knowledge while retaining coherence and integrity. The purpose of this tutorial is to present the problems that arise in transforming potential solutions for speech understanding into working programs and to discuss possible tradeoffs and limitations. Since we do not yet have an integrated theory of such system organization, many of the ideas will be presented in the form of examples.

Many of the examples used here are drawn from the Hearsay-I system (Reddy, Erman, & Neely, 1973; Erman, 1974). This system is chosen because a) it is one of the few that was designed with these aspects prominently in mind, b) it is working, stable (being about three years old), and at least somewhat analyzed, and c) it is the one best-known to us.[†] Figure 1 gives the initial conceptualization of the Hearsay system (Reddy, 1971). In this figure, the knowledge to be used in the system is identified and potential interactions between knowledge sources are indicated. But many other aspects of the system are left unspecified: how is knowledge represented, how is the flow of control and communication accomplished, how are the errors at each level detected and/resolved, what facilities are needed for the validation and evaluation of system performance, and so on. These are essentially the problems that fall into the domain of system organization. The specific solutions eventually adopted in the case of Hearsay-I are presented in detail by Erman (1974).

The problems that arise can be divided into several subtopics: model of speech understanding systems, representation of data and control in errorful situations, real-time system design, dynamic reconfiguration of systems, interactive debugging, and performance analysis. In this paper we introduce and discuss these problems in the context of present research in speech understanding. Additional discussions of one or more of these topics can be found in Erman (1974), Rovner (1975), Tappert(1975), and Lowerre (1975). The papers of Newell, Baker, Barnett, and Lesser appearing in this volume add to and compliment the material presented in this paper.

MODELS OF SPEECH UNDERSTANDING SYSTEMS

A principal component of system organization is the formulation of a general framework within which knowledge sources can cooperate in the decoding of an utterance. The two main problems that arise are

---

[†]The Hearsay-II system (Lesser et al, 1975) is the logical successor to Hearsay-I and as such carries the implementation of some of these design concepts even further. In most cases, however, the concepts remain very much the same from the one generation to the next; if Hearsay-II were used, the examples would be similar.

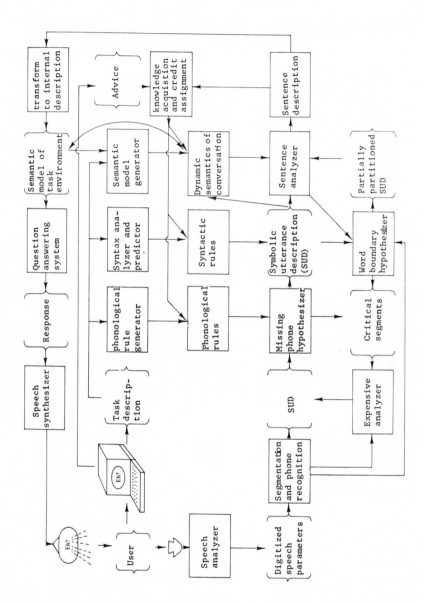

Figure 1: Initial Conceptualization of Hearsay-I (after Reddy (1971)).

1) the representation of knowledge and 2) control structures for converting knowledge into action.

REPRESENTATION OF KNOWLEDGE

In speech understanding systems, knowledge is usually grouped in terms of linguistic levels, e.g., acoustic, phonetic, phonemic, syllabic, lexical, syntactic, semantic, and pragmatic. An interesting aspect of this decomposition is that the levels generally cover increasingly larger units of speech. As a result, knowledge can be usually viewed as a set of rewriting rules which transforms an utterance represented at one level into a corresponding representation at the next higher level. However, there is often knowledge that transcends levels, as, for example, in the case of prosodics, where the stress on a particular phone may affect the semantic interpretation of the utterance.

The second aspect that affects the representation of knowledge is the non-deterministic (and errorful) nature of decisions at each level. If a given set of events (or features) give credence to several different phonemes, all these phonemes must be treated as competing hypotheses which have to be verified and further refined through the use of other sources of knowledge. In addition, the evaluation of an individual hypothesis may be dependent on other hypotheses. The multiplicity of hypotheses and their contextual interaction requires some form of network representation at each level which can be pruned by various sources of knowledge.

Figure 2 gives an example of a network representation of various hypotheses that arise in the analysis of an utterance. At the bottom of the figure, we see the speech waveform for part of an utterance: '. . . all about . . .'. The "true" locations of phone and word boundaries are given below the waveform as marked by a phonetician after hearing what was spoken and looking at the waveform. In a recognition system, the choices of segment boundaries and labels to be associated with each of the segments are not as clear cut. A segmentation and labeling program might produce segment boundaries as indicated by the dotted lines connecting the waveform to the segment level. Given the segmental features, the phone represented by the first segment might be /aw/, /ah/, or /ow/. Similarly, several different labels can be given to each of the other segments. Given the necessary acoustic-phonetic rules, it is possible to combine, regroup, and delete segments, forming larger phone-size units, as shown in the figure. Note, for example, that /ah/ and /l/ have been combined to form a longer /ah/ arc at the phone level. This is because the spectral characteristics of /ah/ and /l/ are very similar, and it is not impossible

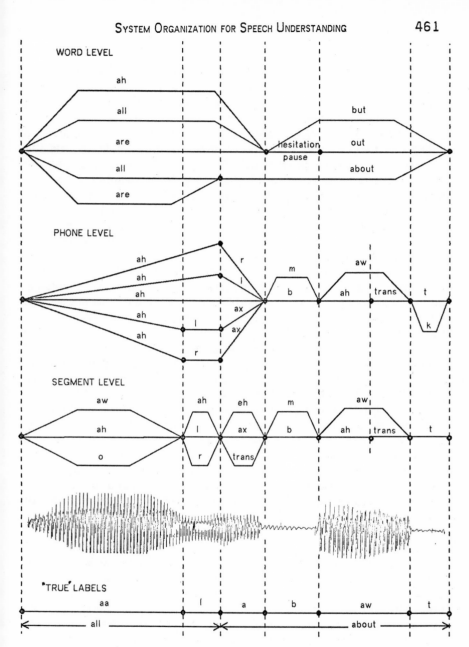

Figure 2: Example of Network Representation of Alternatives.

that the minor parametric variability that caused the segment boundary at the lower level is just free variation. These phone hypotheses give rise to a multiplicity of word hypotheses such as 'ah but', 'all out', 'all about', 'all but', 'are about', and so on.

When knowledge is applied to produce a new hypothesis, a rating can also be generated which represents the confidence that the new hypothesis reflects what actually occurred. The goal is that the correct phone or word have a higher rating than the other, incorrect, choices. Though not shown in the figure, these ratings are usually part of the internal representation of the multi-level analysis network.

Looking at Figure 2, it is clear that a system must be provided with different types of knowledge, in the form of analytical rules (or programs), to transform a network of hypotheses at one level to a corresponding set of hypotheses at another level. Most of the work in developing a speech understanding system is associated with isolating and identifying knowledge that is relevant, representing this knowledge within the machine in an easily extendable form, and validating its usefulness in the analysis of speech.

The literature of artificial intelligence contains several different proposals for representation and use of knowledge. Semantic nets (Quillian, 1968), transition nets (Woods, 1970), production systems (Newell, 1973), and procedural embedding of knowledge (Winograd, 1972) are some of the currently popular schemes for representation of knowledge. Of these, production systems and network representations are easily modifiable and extendable, while production systems and procedural embedding provide for representation of control to be associated with the knowledge. All of these techniques for representation of knowledge are currently being used by different speech understanding systems, and we can expect to hear more about their utility in the future.

REPRESENTATION OF CONTROL

Speech understanding systems use many diverse sources of knowledge. Each of these knowledge sources (KS's) "speaks a different language", yet they must communicate and cooperate with each other in the decoding of an utterance. While it is possible to build systems with minimal communication among knowledge sources, cooperation is often desirable (and sometimes essential) in resolving ambiguity and pruning the number of choices to be considered at each level. The flow of control from knowledge source to knowledge source, i.e., the sequence in which knowledge sources should be activated so as to minimize the combinational explosion, is not well understood. Several global models that have been proposed are given in Figure 3. These are hierarchical, generative, heterarchical, and blackboard models.

In the hierarchical model (Figure 3a), knowledge-source activation proceeds bottom-up, so to speak, from environmental processes (noise subtraction, transducer normalization, amplitude normalization, etc.) to semantic and pragmatic sources. The assumption here is that each KS accepts as input the output from a lower level, transforms the data into larger-sized units, and provides it as input to the next higher level. The main problem with this model is that errors propagate from level to level. A large number of unacceptable choices has to be considered at each level; without some goal direction, all the possible combinations of these are propagated to the next higher level, thus providing evidence for almost anything that one seeks to find in the utterance.

The generative model (Figure 3b) proposes activation of KS's in a top-down manner. All the legal sentences are generated and passed on to the lower levels with the instructions to look for evidence that would support various hypotheses. The main problem here is that it is usually impossible to formulate generators that account for all the non-grammaticality and non-wellformedness of spoken language. Even if the task domain and the vocabulary are substantially restrictive, it is still difficult to provide for free variation on the part of the speaker. The analysis-by-synthesis model (Stevens and Halle, 1962) is a special case of generative models and suffers from many of the same limitations.

The heterarchical model (Figure 3c) permits any knowledge source to activate any other KS. Each can generate questions, request specific processing to be done, receive answers, and so on. This assumes that each KS knows how to formulate meaningful questions in a form answerable by some other KS and also knows which KS that is. Each inter-KS communication path may be specialized to the two communicators; also, the control flow is explicit. The system shown in Figure 1 was envisioned to be of this kind but was modified, partly because of the difficulties of generating each of the separate interfaces and, more importantly, because of the necessity of specifying the explicit control scheme. Woods and Makhoul (1973) describe a method, called incremental simulation, in which the control and interaction scheme is developed by a) having humans simulate the individual KS's, b) inducing a control regime by observing the kinds of actions that occur, and c) progressively replacing the humans by programs.

The blackboard model (Figure 3d) conceives of each knowledge

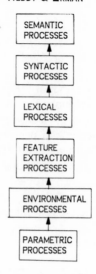

Figure 3a: Hierarchical Model.

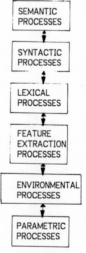

Figure 3b: Generative Model.

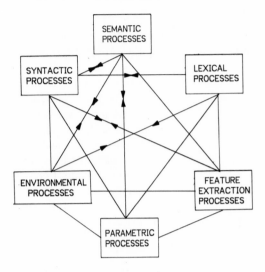

Figure 3c: Heterarchical Model.

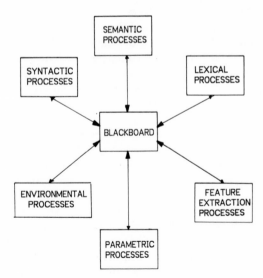

Figure 3d: Blackboard Model.

source as an information gathering and dispensing process. When it discovers information that might be useful for others, it broadcasts it by writing it on the "blackboard" -- a structurally uniform global data base. It is up to each KS to decide if there is any information on the blackboard that would help it to further constrain the number of choices. In this type of system the KS's are activated when conditions relevant to them occur on the blackboard, can work independently of each other, can work even when some of the knowledge sources are absent (i.e., the system is highly modular), and are amenable to multi-processor implementations. The critical issue here is in "correctly" specifying the structure of the blackboard so that any things the KS's may wish to communicate may be represented. Another important issue is keeping down the overhead costs of the data-directed activation of the KS's.

REPRESENTATION OF CONTROL IN ERRORFUL SITUATIONS

There are many sources of error in speech analysis. Knowledge sources are incomplete and often inaccurate (in terms of the theories and models on which they are built and in terms of their implementations). The speech signal a) often does not contain all the information necessary to decipher the meaning of the utterance, b) contains a huge amount of variation (both inter- and intra-speaker) which does not contribute to the meaning of the utterance, c) and is contaminated by different types of noise (including speech-like noises such as coughs and hesitation pauses). Signal conditioning and sampling lead to quantization errors. Thus every system organization must cater to the inevitability of errors and handle them in a graceful and natural manner.

Given this errorful nature of speech processing, a hypothesis which appears to be most probable may not always be the correct one. Thus one may have to consider (many) alternatives at every decision point. In the case of connected speech, this leads to a combinatorial explosion.

Let us propose a simple model of this explosion: Given an utterance with n words and M alternatives for each word, the number of alternative sequences to be considered is M^n. The problem of connected speech recognition can thus be seen as the problem of searching through a space of M^n word sequences to find the most acceptable sequence (i.e., the highest rated sequence) consistent with all the sources of knowledge.[†]

[†]If this simple model is expanded to include other levels of processing

Once the problem is formulated as one of search through a space, many of the search techniques developed in artificial intelligence literature (Nilsson, 1971) become potentially useful. There are many variants of search: depth-first, breadth-first, best-first, branch-and-bound, and so on. We will consider two of these here, two that represent those most commonly used in speech systems and which are also quite different from each other.

One technique is to search all possible paths in parallel but constrain the search only through those sequences which are valid paths in a specific network (Baker, 1975). This network is constructed to be an integrated representation of all the available sources of knowledge. Exponential growth is constrained through the use of a Markov assumption which limits the relevant context and collapses many alternative sequences to a single state. With this technique, search time is linear in the number of states in the network and in the length of the utterance. The paper by Baker in this volume describes this technique in greater detail.

The second strategy is to use best-first probabilistic tree searching. This technique is used in Hearsay-I and in Caspers (Klovstad and Mondshein, 1975). It is best explained by an example. In Figure 4 we see a tree of possible alternatives that had arisen in the analysis of the utterance 'Are your headaches severe?'. We find that there are nine alternatives for the first word: 'have', 'are', 'where', and six others. The ratings indicating the likelihood are given under each word. Given that the word 'have' has the highest rating of 470, we begin to explore that path. 'Have' is followed by a single alternative 'you'. The combined rating for the sequence 'have you' is given under 'you'. The rating of 455 makes the sequence 'have you' better than the other alternative paths. Proceeding along this path we have three alternative words that can follow 'have you'. The sequence 'have you had' receives the highest rating of 447 but is no longer the highest rated path. Search is suspended along this path and we begin exploring the alternatives that can follow 'are'. Of the three alternatives, the path 'are you' has the highest rating of 453. Proceeding along this path, we get a rating of 445 for the sequence 'are your headaches'. Since this is lower than 447, we now suspend this search and resume search along the path 'have you had'. The

---

(e.g., phonetic and syntactic) and is also relaxed so that the alternatives at each level are not required to line up in the time domain (e.g., overlapping and imbedded alternatives), the combinatoric possibilities grow even much larger.

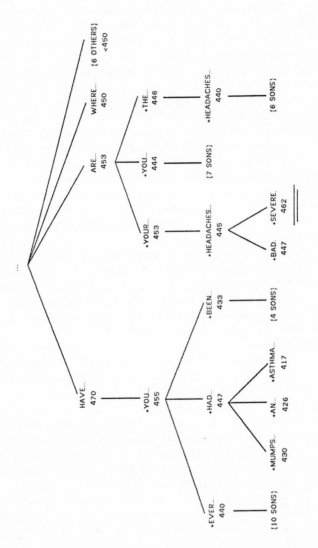

Figure 4: Example of Probabilistic Tree Searching.

highest rated sequence 'have you had mumps' is lower than 445, so we resume the path of are your headaches' again. Now we find that 'are your headaches severe' has the highest rating of 462 and, being the end of a sentence, cannot proceed any further. We accept this as the most probable sentence and return it as the answer to the search.

There are several other search techniques, such as sequential decoding (Tappert, 1975), prosodically guided search (Lea et al, 1975), anchor points and focus of attention (Lesser et al, 1975), a few alternative paths in parallel (Lowerre, 1975), and so on. The relative advantages and disadvantages of these techniques are not clearly understood.

RESEARCH FACILITIES AND SYSTEM ORGANIZATION

If we were solving a problem whose solution is known and well understood, the system organization would be affected only by the aspects of problem solution. In speech understanding research, however, we do not have a single widely acceptable solution. Indeed, the space of possible solutions appears to be very large. It is therefore necessary to use the computer as a research tool for rapid exploration of the solution space. To be useful as such, it must provide real-time input, reconfiguration of systems, and interactive debugging. In Hearsay-I, for example, the code associated with these aspects of the system accounts for more than 60% of the total space requirement. Thus, not only do these aspects require careful attention in system organization, but they also seriously affect the total resources (both human and machine) required to accomplish such a project.

REAL-TIME INPUT

Unlike most other forms of computer input, speech is critically data directed. That is, initiation and termination of the input depends on the incomming data itself rather than program control. Thus a system must be prepared to continuously monitor the speech input device (analog-to-digital converter, filter bank, or what have you) to determine if the signal is speech or noise.

The high data rates associated with speech input (100 to 300 kbps) imply that a system cannot afford to have resident in primary memory more than a few seconds of speech (usually no more than a single utterance). Thus the data must be either immediately processed, stored on disk (or tape), or played back. Keeping two high data rate devices serviced is not a major problem if the system is dedicated. However, if the system has a general purpose operating system, special care must be taken to see that the device service overhead is low, to avoid loss of data. This often becomes difficult to achieve with two active devices because of the costs associated with process synchronization, buffer service routines, and signal detection (Erman, 1974). Other system primitives available within the system for performing these operations tend to be too slow and need to be reprogrammed.

RECONFIGURATION OF SYSTEMS

In an experimental research system there are literally hundreds of options and alternatives available to the user: what task, which speaker, which data set, which knowledge sources, do we use live data or prerecoded data, which parametric representation, which output devices (e.g., graphics, line printer, or teletype), which debugging options, which performance analysis options, and so on. In addition, there are many thresholds associated with heuristics that the user might want to modify. Given the myriad of alternatives, it becomes necessary to provide a flexible, fast, and convenient system for specifying the desired alternatives. This is done in Hearsay-I by the use of "cliche" files (Erman, 1974) -- these are text files which contain the various commands to the system for selecting the desired configuration. A more general purpose facility for dynamically linking different modules has been developed by Barnett (see the paper in this volume).

INTERACTIVE DEBUGGING AND EXPLORATION

Traditional low-level debugging tools (i.e., at the machine instruction or programming language levels) are not sufficient for complex systems. The interaction between the user and the system should, as much as possible, be at the functional level of the system. Thus it becomes necessary to incorporate a flexible and powerful debugging facility specially tailored for speech understanding research.

It is often necessary to display different types of structured data in formats which would be impossible or cumbersome to specify in general-purpose low-level debugging systems. For example, facilities should be provided for examining and modifying the complex data structures used, in addition to the simple scaler variables. By associating specific formatting and display information with important data structures, the system permits convenient and rapid examination and debugging.

Figure 5 illustrates a typical display that is used routinely in the Hearsay-I system. The six parameters extracted from the speech signal are graphically displayed. The dotted vertical lines indicate the

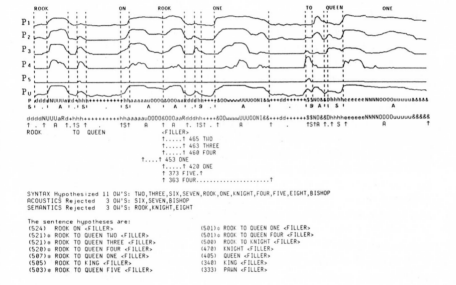

Figure 5: Example of Debugging Output.

results of segmentation. Other information under the graphics indicates present location of analysis, hypotheses being considered and rejected, and the alternative sentence hypotheses under consideration (See Chapter IV, Erman (1974), for a more detailed explanation).

Besides examining the functioning of the system, one wants to be able to dynamically modify its execution path, i.e., to change the control flow manually in midstream during execution. This is often necessary, e.g., if you want to see if you can correct an error by a different sequence of knowledge-source activations. Hearsay-I accomplishes this easily because of its framework of globally controlled independent knowledge sources. A process does not care whether it receives an activation message from another process or a human.

A seemingly small but, in practice, important feature is the ability to accept interrupt requests from the user. This ability to make unplanned asynchronous interrupts permits the user to react quickly to an unanticipated need without having to restart the system with special breakpoints and reanalyze the utterance. This facility is easily implemented in Hearsay-I, for example, via a polling technique between knowledge-source activations and at other convenient points.

PERFORMANCE ANALYSIS

Newell (in this volume) has a general discussion of the need for systematic performance analysis and a list of methods that may be applicable in speech understanding research. In this section we will give specific examples of performance analysis that have been found to be useful in our research at Carnegie-Mellon University. These can be grouped under three broad categories: analysis of systems, analysis of knowledge sources, and analysis of algorithms.

ANALYSIS OF SYSTEMS

Several different facilities are needed within a system to continuously monitor its performance as it goes through a series of iterations. The most commonly used measures of performance are accuracy, time, and space required for the analysis of a standard set of test sentences. Figure 6 gives the results of a typical run using the Hearsay-I system for some sentences in the chess task. Note that even though 88% of the words were recognized correctly, only 46% sentences had all the words within the sentence correctly identified. Since the time for analysis is usually a function of the length of the utterance, it is convenient to provide times normalized by the duration. In this case it took, on the average, six seconds to process a second of speech, i.e., the system was running at six times real-time on a

PDP10/KA10. The space required varies depending on a number of factors: the length of the utterance, the number of alternatives kept around for use in the search, and the number of knowledge sources. For Hearsay-I, it varies around 120K to 140K of 36-bit words.

Task: Chess

Speaker: JB2

No. of Sentences: 21

No. of Word tokens: 105

Sentences correct: 46%

Words correct: 88%
Ave. computation time on PDP10-KA10
    (Time/second of speech): 6.0

Space required (36-bit words): 120K - 140K

Figure 6: Hearsay-I Performance on the Chess-Task Data Set.

Ablation experiments permit evaluation of knowledge sources within a total system context. Figure 7 illustrates some results obtained from the Hearsay-I system using ablation techniques. The three knowledge-source (KS) processes in the system, i.e., Semantics, Syntax, and Acoustic-phonetics, can be run on the system in different configurations. For the task given in Figure 6, when all the knowledge sources are used, the accuracy at the word level is 88%. If the Semantic KS is disabled the accuracy decreases to 65%. It decreases further to 45% when both Syntax and Semantics are disabled, i.e., when using the Acoustic-phonetic KS only.

Accuracy using all KS's: 88%

Accuracy without semantics: 65%

Accuracy without syntax and semantics: 45%

Figure 7: Example of Results of Ablation Experiments on Hearsay-I.

"Certify mode" is a technique used in Hearsay-I to prevent error compounding. Each time the system makes an error, it is detected (by referring to a human-provided script of nominally "correct" results) and recorded by a performance analysis sub-module. This module then corrects the error and puts the system back onto the correct path to see if any further errors might have resulted had this original error not occurred.

ANALYSIS OF KNOWLEDGE SOURCES

Each time a change is made to a knowledge source it is important to be able to determine whether the most recent changes have helped or hindered the performance of the system. This is done in Hearsay-I by a technique known as incremental improvement analysis. To analyze the effectiveness of a KS change, it is not adequate to merely indicate the increase or decrease in accuracy. It is important to know when it helped and when it hindered and by how much. This requires the availability of the "correct" solution and the most recent results produced by the system prior to the change.

N -	K	B	3	*	P -	Q	4			Correct move.
1 3	2	4	2	8	1 1	1	1			Rank order of the correct word in the run before modifying the KS.
1 1	1	1	2	1	1 1	3	4			Rank order of the correct word.
+ + +		+			-	-				Affect on performance.

Figure 8: Example of Incremental Improvement Analysis in Hearsay-I.

An example of such an analysis is given in Figure 8. The sentence being analyzed is 'Knight on king's bishop three takes pawn on queen four'. In the run, five out of the ten words were recognized correctly. The second row of Figure 8 shows the rank order of the correct word when compared with the word that received the highest rating from the acoustic-phonetic KS. Row 3 shows the rank order after some modifications were made to the Acoustic-phonetic KS. The most dramatic improvement is seen in the recognition and rating of the word 'takes', which was only the 8th best choice preceding the change. Words 'on king's bishop' are also now recognized correctly. However, the words 'queen' and 'four' are now recognized incorrectly. This illustrates a major problem with adding new knowledge to a KS, that of knowledge-source interaction. In general, a careful and systematic analysis of errors is required to arrive at a consistant set of "facts" within the KS's.

Incremental improvement analysis can be done on any KS or sets of KS's. However, the formats of the result files and the type of statistical analysis performed varies from KS to KS. At present we have a number of special-purpose programs for determining the accuracy of segmentation and labeling, the effect of different types of acoustic-phonetic rules, and so on. Figure 9 illustrates the type of display used for segmentation and labeling error analysis. The top three rows, above the oscillogram, show the partial sentence, the words ('. . . were all away . . .') with the "correct" boundaries, and the phones with their "correct" boundaries (as defined by a phonetician). The bottom rows indicate syllabic segmentation and phonetic segmentation and labeling, as performed by a program.

Note that misalignment of boundaries, multiple labels, and missing and extra segments make any simple-minded error analysis program impossible in this case. There are several alternative ways of evaluating segmentation and labeling systems, no one of which seems to satisfy all the needs. One of the major problems is establishing the "truth". Even phoneticians using no higher order linguistic knowledge seem to only agree among themselves about 53% of the time (Shockey and Reddy, 1974). A more detailed discussion and several performance analysis techniques useful in segmentation and labeling evaluation is given by Goldberg (1975).

The third example of KS analysis can be illustrated by considering heuristic evaluation. Every knowledge source contains many specific heuristics, each of which is applicable under some special conditions. Suppose we have a heuristic that looks at features of a segment to determine if it (the segment) is a vowel. One wants to know how often it is applied correctly. Figure 10 illustrates the different cases that arise. The segment might be a vowel and be recognized as non-vowel, or it might be a non-vowel and be recognized as a vowel.[†] Of the 31 cases to which this rule was applied, in 81% of the cases the segment was a vowel and detected as one, in 13% of the cases it was not a vowel but was classified as being a vowel, and in 6% of the cases it was correctly rejected as not being a vowel.

[†]In statistics literature these are called Type I error and Type II error. Further, the goodness of the rule can be parameterized in terms of a single number, d' (Green and Swets, 1966).

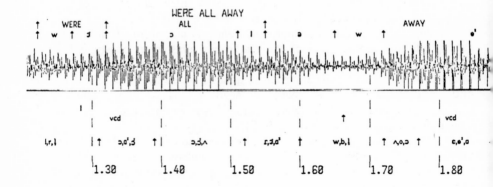

Figure 9: Segmentation and Labeling Analysis Display.

Rule Number 780

#Found	#Not Found		%Found	%Not Found
25	0	Is a Vowel	81	0
4	2	Is not a Vowel	13	6

Figure 10: Heuristic Evaluation: Vowel Detector Heuristic.

Algorithm Analysis

Algorithm analysis is perhaps the most common type of performance analysis that appears in computer science literature. The purpose is to understand the algorithm well enough to make further refinements of it. These might include reformulation of the algorithm, reformulation of the data structures, and, most commonly, reprogramming of the algorithm. Figure 11 gives the computation times for the autocorrelation LPC technique (See Makhoul's paper in this volume). As can be seen, the calculation of the autocorrelation coefficients is much more expensive than the solution of the Toeplitz matrix. This type of analysis provides for potential sources for algorithm improvement. For example, it indicates that if one can use reflection coefficients (or partial correlation coefficients) in speech recognition instead of the LPC spectrum, one can expect to save about 40% of the signal analysis time.

Operation	Time in msec. on a PDP-10
Difference	6.04
Window	6.75
Autocorrelation	153.06
Solve Toeplitz	25.30
Pruned FFT	141.79

Figure 11: Execution Times for LPC Operations.

CONCLUSION

In this paper we have attempted to present the problems that arise in transforming ideas about speech understanding systems into working programs. The topics that are included under the label of "system organization" can be grouped under models, representation of control in errorful situations, research facilities, and facilities for performance analysis. Careful attention to each of these aspects is essential if we are to gain deep insights into the speech understanding process and build systems which can perform the task.

REFERENCES

Baker, J. K. (1975), "The DRAGON system -- an overview," IEEE Trans. ASSP, 23, 24-29.

Erman, L. D. (1974), "An environment and system for machine understanding of connected speech," (Ph.D. Thesis, Stanford University), Tech. Report, Computer Science Dept., Carnegie-Mellon University, Pittsburgh.

Goldberg, H. G. (1975), Ph. D. Thesis, Computer Science Dept., Carnegie-Mellon University, Pittsburgh (in preparation).

Green, D. M. & J. A. Swets (1966), Signal Detection Theory and Psychophysics, John Wiley and Sons, NY.

Klovstad, J. N. and L. F. Mondshein (1975), "The CASPERS linguistic analysis system," IEEE Trans. ASSP, Vol. 23, pp. 118-123.

Lea, W. A., M. F. Medress, T. E. Skinner (1975), "A prosodically guided speech understanding strategy," IEEE Trans. ASSP, Vol. 23, pp. 30-37.

Lesser, V. R., R. D. Fennell, L. D. Erman, and D. R. Reddy (1975), "Organization of the Hearsay II speech understanding system," IEEE Trans. ASSP, Vol. 23, pp. 11-23.

Lowerre, B. (1975), Ph. D. Thesis, Computer Science Dept., Carnegie-Mellon University, Pittsburgh (in preparation).

Nilsson, N. J. (1971), Problem Solving Methods in Artificial Intelligence, McGraw-Hill, N. Y.

Newell, A. (1973), "Production Systems: Models of control structures," Tech. Report, Computer Science Dept., Carnegie-Mellon University, Pittsburgh.

Quillian, M. R. (1968), "Semantic Memory," in M. Minsky (ed.) Semantic Information Processing, MIT Press, Cambridge.

Reddy, D. R. (1971), "Speech recognition: Prospects for the seventies," Proc. IFIP 1971, Ljubljana, Yugoslavia, Invited papers, I5-I13.

Reddy, D. R., L. D. Erman, R. B. Neely (1973), "A model and a system for machine recognition of speech," IEEE Trans. ASSP, Vol. 21, pp. 229-238.

Rovner, P., B. Nash-Webber, & W. A. Woods (1975), "Control concepts in a speech understanding system," IEEE Trans. ASSP, Vol. 23, pp. 136-139.

Shockey, L. & D. R. Reddy (1974), "Quantitative analysis of speech perception: Results from transcription of connected speech from unfamiliar languages," Speech Communication Seminar, Stockholm, Sweden.

Stevens, K. N. & M. Halle (1962), "Speech recognition: A model and a program for research," IRE Trans. PGIT, IT-8, pp. 155-159.

Tappert, C. C. (1975), "Experiments with tree search method for converting noisy phonetic representation into standard orthography," IEEE Trans. ASSP, Vol. 23, pp. 129-135.

Winograd, T. (1972), Understanding Natural Language, Academic Press, N.Y.

Woods, W. A. (1970), "Transition network grammars for natural language analysis," Comm. ACM, Vol. 13, pp. 591-606.

Woods, W. A & J. Makhoul (1973), "Mechanical inference problems in continuous speech understanding," Proc. 3rd Int. Joint Conf. Artificial Intelligence, pp. 200-207.

PARALLEL PROCESSING IN SPEECH UNDERSTANDING SYSTEMS:
A Survey of Design Problems

Victor R. Lesser
Department of Computer Science
Carnegie-Mellon University
Pittsburgh, Pennsylvania 15213

INTRODUCTION

Speech understanding systems (SUS), by their very nature, appear to be computer intensive. A substantially unrestricted system capable of reliably understanding connected speech in "real time" consisting of a large vocabulary and spoken by multiple speakers is likely to require a system of 10 to 100 million instructions per second (mips).[†] As these systems are developed and become "smarter" and faster, the requirements on them are likely to be extended; i.e., large vocabularies, more complex syntax and semantics etc. The resulting computing requirements are thus not likely to diminish dramatically. If speech understanding systems are to become commercially viable, some economical ways of effecting this tremendous amount of computer power must be found.

Recent trends in technology indicate that this computing power can be obtained economically through a closely-coupled, asynchronous[††] network of "simple" processors (10-100). These processors can be interconnected to communicate in a variety of ways (e.g., directly with each other through a highly multiplexed, centralized switch connected to a large memory (C.mmp, Bell et al., 1971) or through a regular or irregular distributed network of buses (Bell et al., 1973, and Heart et al., 1973). The major problem with this network approach to generating computer power is finding algorithms which have the appropriate structure for exploiting this type of parallelism.

The potential for parallelism in a speech understanding system

---

[†]Hearsay-I (Reddy, 1973) and Dragon (Baker, 1974) require approximately 10-40 mips of computing when handling small vocabularies (30-250 words).

[††]The asynchronous distinction is meant to exclude from the discussion synchronous networks such as ILLIAC-IV (Slotnick, 1967).

exists in two very different ways. The first way comes out of the need to preprocess a large volume of raw input data (i.e., acoustic parameters) in order to begin meaningful recognition. This preprocessing task involves the repetition of a sequence of transformations on the acoustic data, e.g., detection of the beginning and end of speech, amplitude normalization, a simple phonetic-like labeling, segmentation, formant tracking, smoothing. The type of parallelism resulting from these tasks does not generate the potential for significant amounts of parallel activity (>10) for an asynchronous network.[†] The small grain of computation in each tranformation makes it difficult to further decompose the task for more parallelism and causes communication and synchronization costs to overwhelm any gain achieved by a more parallel decomposition.

The second way of exploiting parallelism in a speech understanding system, which is the major focus of this paper, occurs because connected speech processing must contain problem-solving techniques that resolve ambiguities resulting from the ambiguity in the acoustic data and the imprecise and errorful nature of knowledge sources. These problem-solving techniques are implemented through sophisticated control structures which 1) permit the selective searching (usually heuristic) of a large part of the state-space of possibilities and 2) allow the combining of multiple, diverse sources of knowledge (e.g., acoustics, syntax, semantics, prosodics) so as to cooperate in resolving ambiguity (Reddy, 1973, Barnett, 1973, Woods,2 1974 and Lesser et al., 1975). The state-space searching in existing systems is implemented through backtracking control structures; these are basically sequential implementations of non-deterministic control structures. Thus, a big potential for parallelism in speech systems arises from implementing these non-deterministic control structures in a parallel manner, i.e., searching different parts of the state space in parallel. In addition, if these diverse knowledge sources (KS) can be made independent, there exists the potential for a proportional speed-up in the recognition process by executing them in parallel. Finally, there is the possibility of decomposing each KS into separate parallel processes.

The central thesis of this paper is that the control structures necessary in performing the speech understanding task allow efficient implementation on an asynchronous multiprocessor network. If this is

---

[†]There is the possibility that there could be a high degree of parallelism if implemented on a synchronous or special purpose network, such as a pipeline processor or ILLIAC-IV.

correct, the next generation of SUS's should be designed with a parallel implementation in mind; otherwise, these systems' structures may have to be completely redesigned when it comes time to develop a parallel, real-time implementation.[†] It is felt that speech understanding systems have already reached a degree of sophistication such that the next-generation of systems will be the prototypes for commercial systems. If this is true, these next-generation systems must be adapted to future hardware technologies (i.e., multiprocessor networks) that will make them economically feasible.

The focus of the remainder of this paper is on providing the speech system designer with an intuitive feel for the different types of parallel representational frameworks that can be used to exploit the parallelism of a speech system and for the associated problems, both in terms of hardware and software, that are likely to be encountered.

ISSUES IN PARALLEL PROCESS DECOMPOSITION

There are two important aspects to any decomposition of an algorithm into a collection of processes[††] that can execute in parallel: 1) the mechanisms for communication (sharing data) among processes, and 2) the mechanisms for sequencing (sharing control structure) among processes. These two aspects of process cooperation are often closely intertwined, making it sometimes difficult to clearly differentiate between them. For example, a parallel schema that combines both aspects is a "data flow model" (Adams, 1968) in which the receipt by a process of a specified number and types of messages is the basis of its activation. This intertwined relationship between data sharing and control always exists to some degree because, as will be discussed later, an important aspect of any control structure is the "control data base", and likewise, any sharing relationship presupposes (imposes) certain sequencing relationships among processes that access a shared data base. Thus, the designer of a process decomposition will usually use in a mutually simplifying manner a combination of communication and sequencing mechanisms to achieve the desired dynamic and static cooperation relationships among processes.

[†]This is similar to the problem with some numerical algorithms which are optimal in a sequential environment but when transfered to a parallel environment perform extremely poorly (Stone, 1973).

[††]A process is considered to be a program together with enough of its state information (e.g., program status words, instruction counter, stack) so that it can be executed independently of and potentially concurrently with other similarly constituted processes.

DATA COOPERATION AMONG PROCESSES

In designing any sharing mechanism among processes, there are two properties that are generally desired: "functional determinism" and "deadlock free." The property of "functional determinism" is said to exist when changes in the time to execute a process or in the order of execution of processes which are ready to run do not produce incorrect (inconsistent) results (see example 1). In order to prevent the generation of this type of incorrect results when two or more processes are sharing a common data structure, locking primitives, such as the Dijkstra Semaphore (Dijkstra, 1965) and the Wakeup-Waiting Switch (Saltzer, 1966), have been developed. These locking primitives, when appropriately added to the code that updates or accesses a shared base, are used to guarantee that the data base will remain consistent. This guarantee is accomplished by allowing only one process at a time (i.e., sequential order) to execute the critical sections of the code that each process executes when it wants to update or examine the shared data base.

Example 1

An Example of Non-Determinism

Consider two identical processes P_1, P_2 which increment a cell in memory if it is non-zero. The following timing diagram indicates how inconsistent results can be produced if these processes are executed in a certain order.

	time	R_1	R
	t_0		1
P_1:			
$R_1 \leftarrow R$	t_{10}	1	1
if $R_1 > 0$ then	t_{20}	1	1
store $R_1 + 1$ into R	t_{30}	1	2

	time	R_2	R
P_2:			
$R_2 \leftarrow R$	t_{15}	1	1
if $R_2 > 0$ then	t_{25}	1	1
store $R_2 + 1$ into R	t_{35}	1	2

After both processes increment R, the value of R is 2 rather than 3.

An alternative mechanism for producing the same effect is to have only one process that is allowed to access the shared data base; access and modification to this shared data base is then accomplished by sending messages, which request a particular type of access or modification of the data base, to this special process. This latter approach does have some drawbacks in that it generally requires more processing time to access the data base because of communication overhead, but it does have the virtue of allowing the process requesting the access to continue processing if it does not immediately need the results of the request. A more serious drawback of this latter approach occurs when there are a large number of shared data bases that can be accessed concurrently. In this case, the cost in terms of operating system overhead (time and memory) to create and hold a description of a large number of these special data base accessing processes may make this scheme impractical.

This property of "functional determinism" is weaker than the more general property of "determinism" which requires that the same results are always produced. In AI problem solving, where the solution space is only partially searched and criterion for a final solution is often based on the first solution that is above a certain threshold, it is very difficult to design sharing and control mechanisms which exploit the maximum amount of parallelisms and still guarantee the same answer independent of the order to execution of processes. Thus, the emphasis should be put on creating consistent results rather than always creating the same results.

The property of "deadlock free" is closely related to that of "functional determinism" in that it is caused by the inappropriate use of locking primitives which results in two or more processes waiting on the completion of another before each can resume its processing (see example 2). If this condition occurs, then the processes are said to be "deadlocked." There are a variety of strategies to guarantee that the processing never stops prematurely because of this type of deadly embrace: 1) detection and recovery, 2) a priori prevention, and 3) a hybrid of 1 and 2. The detection and recovery strategies involve first being able to detect that an actual deadlock has occurred, rather than a case of processes that are waiting on locks which will eventually be unlocked. In order to recover from an actual deadlock, one of the processes must release its control of the shared data base so that another can continue. This recovery strategy is often difficult to implement because it may require a process to undo parts of its modifications to the shared data base so as to leave the data base in a consistent state before it releases control.

The second strategy for prevention of deadlocks, which is based on an a priori guarantee that there will never be a deadlock is the most preferable. A sufficient condition for this guarantee to be

Example 2
An Example of Deadly Embrace

Consider two processes P_1, P_2 which both need to access and modify memory cells R_1, R_2. In order to avoid non-determinism they both lock the memory cells before performing the modification. P_1 first locks R_1 then R_2 while P_2 performs te locks in the reverse order. The following timing diagram indicates how a deadly embrace can occur. Each process waiting on the termination of the other.

	time	R_1	R_2
	to	1	1

P_1:

lock R_1	t_{10}	
if $R_1>0$ then		
lock R_2	t_{20}	
$R_2 \leftarrow R_2 + 1$		
unlock R_2		
unlock R_1		

P_2:

lock R_2	t_{15}	1
if $R_2>0$ ten		
lock R_1	t_{25}	
$R_1 \leftarrow R_1 + 1$		
unlock R_1		
unlock R_2		

A deadly embrace occurs at t_{20}, P_1 becomes blocked because P_2 locked R_2 at t_{15}, while at t_{25} P_2 becomes blocked because R_1 was locked at t_{10}.

implemented occurs when it is possible to define an explicit linear ordering[†] for access and modification to the shared data bases. For example, assume there are three shared data bases, S1, S2 and S3, if process 1 needs S1 and S3 it will lock S1 first, then S3, while if process 2 needs S2 and S3 it will lock S2 first then S3. This approach is feasible if it is possible to anticipate for each process in the decomposition what shared data bases it will need to access. However, this constraint is difficult to achieve in an experimental SUS in which knowledge sources are being constantly added or modified and in

---

[†] Recent work by Campbell and Habermann (1974) on path expressions relaxes the linear constraint on the ordering relationship.

which knowledge sources can search in some arbitary way a directed graph structure where each node of the graph is considered a separate shared data base. The third strategy for deadlock prevention, which combines the strategies of deadlock prevention and recovery with that of defining an explicit ordering of locks, has been developed for Hearsay-II(HS-II). This hybrid strategy is based on performing shared data base modifications in three distinct steps. The first step is for the process to determine the (shared) data bases that will define the context (environment) for its processing; the key idea is that rather than locking these data bases as they are sequentially or arbitrarily acquired, they are "tagged". The "tag" on a shared data base represents a reminder to the data base handler to send a message to the particular process which created the tag if this shared data base is changed by some other process. The second step occurs after the context for the proposed modification is completetely constructed: at this point, this context is locked. An explicit ordering relationship is now used to sequentially lock each element of this context without creating a deadlock. The third step occurs after the locking is complete: A check is made for whether any tag messages have been received. If there are no messages, the desired processing can immediately take place; if there were changes, however, the changes must be examined to see whether the assumptions necessary for the proposed modification are still valid (e.g., context revalidation). If not, the proposed modification is aborted, the context unlocked and the process terminated; otherwise, the processing continues as normal.

The one caveat on this discussion of deadlock prevention is that the justification of the overhead for these complicated schemes to avoid deadlock is based on the idea of permitting maximum concurrency in accessing shared data bases; however, by carefully selecting which parts of the shared data base can be accessed concurrently (i.e., making larger units of sharing), the overhead of these complicated deadlock avoidance schemes can be sharply reduced without significantly reducing potential parallelism.[†] This represents a conjecture of the author which is currently being explored in simulation studies of HS-II executing in a simulated multiprocessor environment (Fennell and Lesser, 1975).

[†]For example, Hearsay-II has a two dimensional data structure index by level and time. It is possible to lock a region which consists of all nodes at particular level and time interval. This region locking operation is used in place of tagging and then locking a specific set of nodes in a region.

PARALLEL CONTROL STRUCTURES

Before discussing the different characteristics of parallel control structures (see table-1), it is worthwhile to consider an abstract model of a control structure. The control structure of a language consists of 1) a control data base (i.e., program status word, processor state, etc.), 2) a built-in control algorithm, and 3) control statements that are primitives of the language being controlled (e.g.,"go-to," "if-then," "create process," "suspend process"). The control algorithm consists of a fixed set of rules that operate on the control data base to determine, at each meaningful unit of activity, which statement or statements of the language will next be executed. For example, if the control data base of a simplified computer consists of a program counter and an interrupt register, the control algorithm of this simplified computer might be the following paradigm: if there are no interrupts pending, execute the instruction at the location specified by the program counter and increment the program counter by one so that it points to the next instruction to execute, otherwise, store the program counter at a fixed location in the program memory, reset the interrupt flip-flop, place the address of the interrupt handling routine in the program counter, and execute the first instruction of the interrupt handling routine.

TABLE 1

Taxonomy of Parallel Control Structures

deterministic	vs.	non-deterministic
implicit	vs.	explicit
synchronous	vs.	asynchronous
homogenous	vs.	hetrogeneous
distributed	vs.	centralized
loosely-coupled	vs.	closely-coupled
fixed	vs.	variable

This definition of a control structure makes a clear distinction between the implicit control specified by the control alogrithm, and the explicit control specified through execution of control statements of a language. For example, consider the results of executing the control statement "BRANCH TO LOCATION X" in terms of the control structure of the simplified computer discussed previously. The branch statement, when executed, places the address X in the program counter; however, the next instruction to be executed may not be at address X, since during the time the branch instruction was executed an interrupt could have occurred.

This distinction between implicit and explicit control is important because it represents one of the major ways of categorizing different types of parallel control structures. It is also the author's conjecture that as the techniques for parallel decomposition are better understood, this understanding will be reflected in more sophisticated implicit control mechanisms, i.e., more complex control data bases and their associated control algorithms. The next sections will discuss each of the dimensions listed in Table 2 for characterizing parallel control structures.

IMPLICIT VS EXPLICIT CONTROL

Implicit parallel control structures are generally based on a data-flow (message transaction network) model (Baer, 1973). Each process in the network has a set of input data requirements and generates a set of output data; the satisfaction of the appropriate input data requirements is the basis of the activation of the process, which in turn, upon its execution, generates outputs. These outputs in turn trigger the satisfaction of the input requirements of other processes in the network. In these network models, an output of a process is explicitly linked with an input of another process. This explicit linking (i.e., only one process can access the output), combined with some restrictions on input activation conditions, allows these data flow models to have the property of being determinate and deadlock-free. However, the restrictions on the nature of communication imposed by the explicit linking of output to input make it difficult to program complex parallel decompositions.†

The HS-II parallel control structure which is used for determining whether a knowledge source (KS) process should be activated is based on a variant of the data-flow model in which there are not explicit connections between the inputs and the outputs of KS's. In HS-II, there is a centralized blackboard (global data base)

---

†It should be mentioned that Kaplan (1973) has used a modified data-flow model with explicit input/output connections to design a parallel processing version of a complicated syntax parser.

shared by all knowledge sources which holds the current dynamic state of the speech recognition. All the input requirements and outputs produced by a KS are stored in the blackboard in terms of hypotheses about the current state of the recognition. A KS is executed if its input requirements are satisfied in the blackboard; if there are multiple satisfactions of the input requirements then there can be multiple executions of the KS working on different parts of the blackboard. Because there is the possibility in this scheme of several KS's modifying a particular hypothesis simultaneously, explicit techniques need to be used to guarantee the properties of functional-determinism and deadlock-free as developed in the previous sections. The drawbacks of the HS-II control structure over the simpler data flow models is that 1) it is more difficult to monitor for the input conditions necessary for the invocation of KS processes and 2) the input context of a KS process can be modified between the time it is decided to execute the KS process (i.e., invocation) and the time it executes. This latter problem can also be handled through the tagging mechanism discussed in the previous section (see HS-II for more details). The advantages of the HS-II control schema over the simpler data flow model are 1) it is easier to incorporate new KS's with diverse input requirements, 2) it permits complex data sharing relationships among KS's to be easily specified, 3) it allows the detection of KS input requirements to be seperated from its execution; this separation permits the implementation of complex focus-of-attention mechanisms, and 4) it avoids (through use of the centralized blackboard) repeated recomputation of the same hypothesis, and allows for quick refocusing when constraints fail.

   An alternative and more explicit control structure for a parallel processing SUS is represented by the SDC system (Barnett, 1973). In SDC's parallel control structure, the activation of and synchronization among processes is explicitly specified through control statements such as "FORK" and "JOIN" (Barnett, 1974). A FORK control statement explicitly initiates the execution of a list of KS's processes while the JOIN statement provides a synchronizing primitive which temporarily suspends execution of a particular control path until the completion of a list of currently executing KS's. In addition to these control statements, explicit input/output relationships are established among KS's over "software buses", or through shared data bases. The passage of information over the software buses is, however, not asynchronous because information put on the bus is not immediately available but must wait the completion of the current bus cycle. Likewise, a KS can not wait for the arrival of data over a bus but just retrieves the data output on a bus in the last cycle; the cycling of each bus is again explicitly controlled. An interesting aspect of this parallel control structure is that these explicit control statements are not executed from the KS processes but rather from the supervisory process. Thus, from the viewpoint of a KS process this supervisory process can be thought of as a sophisticated control structure tailored to the particular KS's and their input/output connections that currently define the SUS.

It is difficult to compare explicit versus implicit parallel control structures in any absolute way except to say that implicit schemes are generally more expensive in systems overhead and more complicated to code from the systems viewpoint but simpler from KS's writer viewpoint. In addition, it is easier in an implicit control structure to decompose, debug, understand, and change large process networks and usually generate more potential parallelism.

SYNCHRONOUS VS. ASYNCHRONOUS CONTROL

Another important aspect of parallel control structures relates to the use of time as means of synchronizing the activity of processes (i.e., does the control data structure contain time as a parameter). A parallel control structure that is asynchronous does not use time for synchronization and makes no assumption about the time it takes to complete the execution of any process, whereas synchronous control structures use the concept of time explicitly, often to guarantee that data sharing leads to determinate results. Examples of such use of pseudo-time for synchronization is the concept of a bus cycle in the SDC system, and the HS-I SUS which executes KS's in lockstep sequence consisting of three phases: "poll," "hypothesize" and "test." For each HS-I phase, all KS's are invoked for that phase, and the next phase does not commence until all KS's have completed the current one. A use of real time for synchronization is the ILLIAC-IV computer which executes 64 identical instruction streams in a lockstep fashion. These synchronous control structures are in contrast to HS-II which uses a completely asynchronous control structure in which as soon as the appropriate input requirements for a KS are generated, the KS may be executed, and its execution is not tied to the completion of any other KS.

The relative merits of synchronous versus asynchronous control structure are again difficult to discuss in any absolute sense. Communication protocols in synchronous systems are easier to implement and guarantee correct and are more efficient because more assumptions about the state of execution of a process can be made. Asynchronous control structures allow more parallelism to be exploited, are easier to modify in terms of adding or changing the process structure, and allow the system to refocus its attention quicker when new information is generated.

HOMOGENEOUS VS. HETEROGENOUS CONTROL

A homogeneous parallel control structure refers to one where all processes are treated identically, whereas a heterogeneous control structure is one where there are different classes of processes, each class being controlled in a different way. The HS-II system is an example of homogeneous control structure while the SDC system, with its explicit sequencing of processes, is a heterogeneous control structure.

DISTRIBUTED VS CENTRALIZED CONTROL

The aspect of distributed versus centralized control relates to the parallelism in the execution of the control algorithm of the control structure. A centralized control structure allows only one process at a time to execute the control rules while in a distributed control structure many processes may be simultaneously executing the control rules. For example, HS-II has a distributed control structure, each KS process makes its changes to the blackboard by calling system routines that, in addition to performing the modification, also look at these changes to see whether they cause the satisfaction of input requirements of other KS's; if so, these KS's are activated. The HS-II control structure is distributed, since there can be many KS's simultaneously accessing the blackboard. The SDC system, with its supervisory process, is a more centralized control structure. There is also the secondary issue of being able to partition the data base for control into separate data modules rather than being contained in one centralized data structure. The advantages of distributed data base for control is that it leads to less potential memory interference caused by simultaneous multiple accesses to the same storage module. In addition it is a more natural structure for large processor networks where communication is through a network of buses to the local memories of processors rather than through a large shared memory directly accessible by all processors.

LOOSELY-COUPLED VS CLOSELY-COUPLED COMMUNICATION

The characterization of parallel decomposition in terms of loosely-coupled versus closely-coupled refers to the frequency of communication among processes. This frequency is measured relative to the amount of computation between occurrences of communication.

A closely-coupled system having more communication than a loosely-coupled; the looser the coupling of processes the better the system operates because of lower communication overhead.[†] However, it is often necessary to break processes into smaller units of computation in order to get more parallelism; this in turn, makes the system more closely-coupled. In any decomposition, the designer must balance the gains in concurrency achieved by a closer coupling with increased system overhead caused by message communication and process context swapping. In addition, the more closely-coupled the system, the greater the need for a distributed control structure (scheduler) because of the higher potential for bottlenecks to occur in the scheduler.

FIXED VS. VARIABLE CONTROL

The final characterization of a parallel control structure is <u>fixed</u> versus <u>variable</u>. A control structure is considered fixed if its control algorithm and data base for control do not change in structure during the execution of a process system. Both HS-II and SDC systems are examples of a variable control structure in which multiple instantiations of a particular KS can be dynamically generated if appropriate input requirements are satisfied. Thus, the number of active processes, together with their associated activation records held in the control data base, varies during the execution of the system; this is in contrast to a more fixed control structure where the number of processes in the system is predefined. The fixed control structure is more effecient to implement but may lead to less exploitation of available parallelism.

These discussions on the taxonomy of parallel control structures together with those on communication schemes have presented a wide number of choices that need to be made in designing a parallel process decomposition. The next section discusses the problems in implementing the chosen process decomposition on an actual multiprocessor.

BINDING OF A PROCESS NETWORK TO A PROCESSOR NETWORK

Once a process decomposition is specified, the next design problem faced is how to effeciently map the potential parallelism, as specified in the process network, into actual parallelism in the processor network. This mapping problem in turn centers on three design issues, each of which relates to how processes interact: 1) the

---

[†]The communication overhead cost can vary greatly depending upon the particular type of processor network (centralized vs. distributed) and the type of built-in primitives for communication

design of the interlock structure for a shared data base, 2) the choice of the smallest computational grain at which the system exhibits parallel activity, and 3) the techniques for scheduling a large number of closely-coupled processes.

The first design issue is important because in a closely-coupled process structure many processes may attempt to access a shared data base at the same time. In a uniprocessor system, the sequentialization of access to this shared data base does not significantly affect performance because there is only one process running at a time. However, in a multiprocessor system, if the interlock structure for a shared data base is not properly designed so as to permit as many non-interfering accesses as possible, then access to the shared data base becomes a significant bottleneck in the system's performance (McCredie, 1972). The severity of this bottleneck depends on how long it takes to make the access and the mean time between processes making an access.

The second issue relates to how closely-coupled processes can interact. If the grain of decomposition is such that the overhead involved in process communication is significant in relation to the amount of computation done by the process, then the added virtual parallelism achieved by a finer decompositon can decrease, rather than increase, the performance of the system. Thus, understanding the relationship between the grain of decomposition and the overhead of communication is an important design parameter.

The third issue relates to a phenomenon called the "control working set" (Lesser, 1972). This phenomenon predicts that the execution of a closely-coupled process structure on a multiprocessor may result in a significant amount of supervisory overhead caused by a large number of process context switches. The reason for this high number of process context switches is analogous to the reason for "thrashing" within a data working set (Denning, 1968). For example, in a uniprocessor system if two parallel processes closely interact with each other, each time one process suspends to wait for a communication from the other, the processor must perform a context switch inorder to allow the other process to execute and generate the message. If these two processes suspend to wait for communication often, then a large number of context switches takes place. However, if there were two processors, each containing one of the processes, no context switching would be necessary.

The possible implications of this working set phenomenon on construction of process structures are the following:

1. Processes should be formed into clusters in which communication among cluster members is closely-coupled whereas communication among clusters is loosely-coupled. This process structuring paradigm has also been suggested as a model for the operation of complex human and natural systems (Simon, 1962).

2. The size of a process cluster cannot be chosen independent of the particular hardware configuration that will be used to execute it. For example, a cluster size of eight may be appropriate for a hardware system containing sixteen processors while being inappropriate for a system containing six processors.

3. The scheduler of a multiprocessor system should use a strategy that schedules process clusters rather than single processes. This is analogous to the advantage of preloading the data working set rather than dynamically constructing the working set at each context swap. For example, it may not be worthwhile to context swap a process that is waiting for a message from another process in its own process cluster. The time to context swap the waiting process may be longer that the time to busy wait until the receipt of the message.

ISSUES IN IMPLEMENTING A MULTIPROCESSOR VERSION OF HS-II

A preliminary, synchronous version of HS-II has been operating on CMU's PDP-10 since January, 1974. A fully asynchronous, multiprocess version of HS-II is also now operating on the PDP-10, using the process capabilities of SAIL (Feldman et al., 1972), and consists of approximately 10 independent knowledge sources. This multiprocess version of HS-II contains the capability of simulating the effect of operating in a multiprocessor environment. Experience with this multiprocess version of HS-II, together with simulation data on the effects of operating in a multiprocessor environment, will form the basis for a multiprocessor version of HS-II on C.mmp. It is hoped that following types of questions can be examined:

1) Test modularity of control structures (process structuring) -- how easy is it to add (delete) KS processes or change their interactions with other KS's.

2) Determine amount of potential parallelism -- how many processors can be exploited effectively.

3) Measure process interference -- how much inteference is caused by data base locking.

4) Measure amount of context invalidation -- how often will KS's interfere with each others data environment so as to invalidate the proposed data base modification.

5) Measure effect of locking/examining parts of GDB (global data base) -- how will process interference and system overhead be effected by locking larger regions of the data base.

6) Measure time spent accessing GDB vs. local data bases -- how will a centralized versus decentralized processor network effect performance i.e., what is a good balance between the time to access local memory versus global memory.

7) Measure system overhead (process invocation/cleanup, overhead to access GDB) -- how does the grain of decomposition relate to the overhead of communicaiton.

8) Try various scheduling strategies -- how do different scheduling strategies such as one based on process clusters effect performance.

An initial implementation of HS-II on C.mmp using the L* language system (Newell et al., 1970) and the HYDRA operating system (Wulf et al., 1974) has just begun (Dec. 1974). Another interesting software problem that has to be faced in this implementation occurs because of the small address space (32K words) that each basic processing element of C.mmp can directly access (via the current contents of a set of processor relocation registers) in the large global memory. Thus, in addition to worrying about process partitioning, the problem of partitioning the global data base and its auxiliary structure must be dealt with. This is especially serious because dynamic modification of the relocation register contents in a protected operating system such as HYDRA is expensive in terms of time.

It is felt that this implementation of HS-II on C.mmp will provide much information on how to do parallel process decomposition in a complex AI task environment, and the associated costs of using a sophisticated multiprocess operating system as the underlying software support.

ACKNOWLEDGMENTS

I would like to thank my colleagues Lee Erman and Rick Fennell for their thoughtful reading of the paper, and their help in the design and implementation of the Hearsay-II SUS which is the basis for much of the discussions in the paper.

REFERENCES

Adams, D. A., (1968). "A Computational Model with Data Flow Sequencing," Ph.D. Thesis, Report No. CS117, Computer Science Dept., Stanford University

Baer, J. L., (1973). "A Survey of Some Theoretical Aspects of Multiprocessing," ACM Computing Surveys, Vol. 5, No. 1.

Baker, James, (1974). "The DRAGON System -- An Overview," Proc. IEEE Symp. on Speech Recognition, Pittsburgh, pp. 22-26.

Barnett, J., (1973). "A Vocal Data Management System," IEEE Trans. Audio and Electroacoustics, AU-21, 3.

Barnett, J., (1974). "Module Linkage and Communication in Large Systems," Proc. IEEE Symp. on Speech Recognition, Pittsburgh, Pa.

Bell, C. G., W. Broadley, W. Wulf, A. Newell, et al., (1971). "C.mmp: The CMU Multi-mini-processor Computer," Tech. Rep., Comp. Sci. Dept., Carnegie-Mellon University, Pittsburgh, Pa.

Bell, C. G., R. C. Chen, S. H. Fuller, J. Grason, S. Rege, and D. P. Siewiorek, (1973). "The Architecture and Application of Computer Modules: A Set of Components for Digital Stystems Design," COMCON 73, San Francisco, Ca.

Campbell, R. H. and N. Habermann, (1974). "The Specification of Process Synchronization by Path Expressions," University of Newcastle Upon Tyne, Technical Report Series No. 55.

Denning, P. J. (1968). "The Working Set Model for Program Behavior," Comm. ACM, 11; 5, 323-333.

Dijkstra, E. W., (1965). "Solution of a Problem in Concurrent Programming Control," Comm. ACM, Vol. 8, pp. 569-570.

Erman, L. D. (1974). "An Environment and System for Machine Understanding of Connected Speech," Ph.D. Thesis, Computer Science Dept., Stanford University

Erman, L. D., R. D. Fennell, V. R. Lesser, and D. R. Reddy, (1973). "System Organizations for Speech Understanding: Implications of Network and Multiprocessor Computer Architectures for AI," Proc. 3rd. Inter. Joint Conf. on Artificial Intelligence, Stanford, Ca., pp. 194-199.

Feldman, J. A. et al., (1972). "Recent Developments in SAIL -- An Algol-based Language for Artificial Intelligence," Fall Joint Computer Conference.

Fennell, R. and V. Lesser, (1975). "Parallelism in A. I. Problem Solving: A Case Study of Hearsay II," Computer Science Dept., Carnegie-Mellon University

Heart, F. E., S. M. Ornstein, W. R. Crowther, and W. B. Barker, (1973). "A New Minicomputer/multiprocessor for the ARPA Network," Proc. AFIPS, NDD42, pp. 529-537.

Kaplan, R. M., (1973). "A Multi-processing Approach to Natural Language", National Computer Conference.

Lesser, V. R., (1972) "Dynamic Control Structures and Their Use in Emulation," Ph.D. Thesis, Tech. Rep. CS-309, Computer Science Dept, Stanford University

Lesser, V. R., R. D. Fennell, L. D. Erman, and D. R. Reddy, (1975). "Organization of the Hearsay-II Speech Understanding System," IEEE Trans. on Acoustic Speech and Signal Processing, Vol. ASSP-23, pp. 11-24.

McCredie, J. W., (1972). "Analytic Models of Time-Shared Computing Systems: New Results, Validations and Uses," Ph.D. Thesis, Computer Science Dept., Carnegie-Mellon University, Chapter 5.

Newell, A., P. Freeman, D. McCracken, and G. Robertson, (1970). "The Kernel Approach to Building Software Systems," Computer Science Research Review, Carnegie-Mellon University

Reddy, D. R., L. D. Erman, R. D. Fennell, and R. B. Neely, (1973). "The Hearsay Speech Understanding System: An example of the Recognition Process," Proc. 3rd Inter. Joint Conf. on Artificial Intelligence, Stanford, Ca., pp. 185-193.

Saltzer, J. H., (July 1966). "Traffic Control in a Multiplexed Computer System," MAC-TR-30, Ph.D. Thesis, Project MAC, Mass. Inst. of Tech.

Simon, H. A., (1962). "The Architecture of Complexity," Proc. Am. Phil. Soc., 106.

Slotnick, D. L., (1967). "Achieving Large Computing Capabilities Through an Array Computer," Spring Joint Comput. Conf., AFIPS Conf. Proc., Vol. 30. Wash., D.C., Thompson Books, pp. 477-482.

Stone, H., (1973). "Problems of Parallel Computation," Complexity of Sequential and Parallel Numerical Algorithms, Academic Press, p. 1-16.

Wulf, W., et al., (1974) "HYDRA: The Kernel of a Multiprocessor Operating System," Comm. ACM, Vol. 17, No. 6, pp. 337-345.

Woods, W. A., (1974). "Motivation and Overview of BBN SPEECHLIS: An Experimental Prototype for Speech Understanding Research," Proc. IEEE Symp. on Speech Recognition, Pittsburgh, Pa., pp. 1-10.

MODULE LINKAGE AND COMMUNICATION IN LARGE SYSTEMS

Jeffrey A. Barnett
System Development Corporation
Santa Monica, California 90202

ABSTRACT

This paper was originally intended to address only the problems associated with implementing Artificial Intelligence programs. However, an examination of the trends in AI shows that project teams are growing in size and becoming multi-disciplinary, as they are in other program development projects. Even though the object of AI research may be the discovery of an appropriate system organization, the presence of a large implementation staff strongly suggests the use of highly modular techniques, the minimization of the number of dependencies among system components, and the development of techniques for ensuring that the remaining dependencies are visible.

This paper advocates the use of a formal, executable language to specify and make visible the dependencies among the modules of a system. Such a language has been developed to organize the control monitor for a speech understanding system. In the course of developing this language, which is called Control Structure Language (CSL), several techniques that aid in organizing systems were explored: "Parnas" modules for representing permanent and semi-permanent data, software bus structures for dynamic data communication among modules, and non-guaranteed parallelism. These techniques are reviewed, and the properties and the use of the language are discussed.

TRENDS IN AI SYSTEMS

The field of Artificial Intelligence encompasses a wide variety of activities: natural language processing, game playing, speech understanding, theorem proving, visual scene evaluation, symbolic integration, etc. These activities share the characteristic that they are normally considered to require some thought or intelligence. However, determining whether a particular activity is truly AI is not easy; in fact, an old bromide says that if a particular activity has been well modeled by a computer or if the solution space is well understood, then the activity is no longer considered a part of AI.

Many early AI efforts were conducted by individual investigators or small groups concentrating on very specific problems such as game playing. The major tools developed were heuristic searching and tree-pruning algorithms. Also, many of the problematic issues were highly computer intensive; for example, some of the key problems with constructing a chess-playing machine were such things as how the board is stored internally or how a trial move sequence or strategy is represented. Such issues led to the development of many programming languages and systems in which it was easy to represent a variety of structures: IPL, LISP, COMIT, etc.

Recently, research and development activities undertaken by the AI "community" have changed. Perhaps the most important difference is in the mode of operation. Large groups and organizations are working on joint projects. The Speech Understanding Research (SUR) project, organized and sponsored by ARPA, is becoming a model (see [9]). Also, the kind of problem drawing attention is more general. The goal is no longer to automate a class B chess player, but to construct a speech understanding system or a functioning robot. In these cases, the initial objective for the system is not final; the ultimate objective may be defined as a system with large bases of diverse knowledge, having learning (adaptive) capabilities rivaling a human's. Along with this open-endedness of goal is a change in primary task to modeling of human functions: speech, vision, motion, communication (language), general problem solving, and combinations of these. In many of these areas, because so much is known outside the computer and AI community, research teams have become more interdisciplinary, and techniques other than heuristic search have been brought to bear. In speech and vision systems, for example, the body of results from signal processing are being incorporated. Work in computational linguistics is drawing on machine-readable versions of Webster's 7th Collegiate Dictionary and Roget's Thesaurus, etc. These developments, taken together, suggest a trend in AI systems work toward highly interdisciplinary endeavors that involve many people cooperating on the same project.

COMMUNICATIONS IN AI SYSTEMS

A system that models human intelligence can be said to comprise a set of Knowledge Sources (KSs). In a computer, a KS is represented as a combination of data and procedure. Further, the allowable communication paths to and from a KS must be adequately defined to allow an implementation. For example, a KS in a chess-playing program may be a module that maintains the board position; the board itself is represented as some data structure. The communications with this module are the control actions necessary to interrogate the present position, update the present position, and save (restore) the present position.

In general, the set of allowable communications with a KS will be more complicated than this and should also be more precise. (For instance, does this module legality check proposed position updates? Are positions named by squares or pieces? etc.) In normal system building, a lack of precision is unforgivable; in an AI system, however, it may be unavoidable because the discovery of an adequate system organization, and hence communication network, may be the whole essence of the research. Such questions as "what should be the interaction between syntax and pragmatics?" or "what is the contribution of a position evaluator to the total system?" become critical. In fact, the problem of necessary and sufficient communications, and the problems of instrumentation and measurement of the contributions of each KS to total system performance, are becoming the main issues in AI. If one can accurately specify answers to the above types of questions, then the activity is no longer considered AI. (New bromide.)

WHAT IS A SYSTEM?

A system (or program) is a collection of procedure and data specifications, called modules, written in some formal language(s) plus a control structure for performing an interpretation. In [1], Fisher defines a control structure as follows:

> By control structure we mean programming environments or operations which specify the sequencing and interpretation rules for programs and parts of programs.

Fisher goes on to say that any control structure can be described by the use and amalgamation of six types of control primitives:

> 1) There must be means to specify a necessary chronological ordering among processes and 2) a means to specify that processes can be processed concurrently. There must be 3) a conditional for selecting alternatives, 4) a means to monitor (i.e. nonbusy wait) for given conditions, 5) a means for making a

process indivisible relative to other processes, and 6) a means for making the execution of a process continuous relative to other processes.

The terms module, process, and data are used to describe systems. A module is a collection of forms written in some programming language and is therefore a lexical representation. Included in the collection may be constant data and specifications for storing dynamic data structures that are either computed or obtained from the external environment. A module may comprise, besides its data storage, a set of entry points in the traditional sense of functions, subroutines, coroutines, etc. Access may also be provided through a macro facility. Thus, procedural knowledge such as algorithms and heuristics is embedded into a system as modules.

The term process, on the other hand, refers to a thing in execution; or, stated differently, a program counter operating an interpretation upon a module with an associated state is a process. Thus, if our computer has more than one CPU (program counter), we may have parallel processes. Note that, if more than one program counter is simultaneously acting on the same module, then each program counter is associated with a separate process. Many systems, for example time sharing and multiprogramming systems, partially achieve the effect of multiple program counters by time slicing a single processor.

(The distinction between data and procedure in a system is not always sharp. It may depend upon which level of system description is viewed. For example, consider the structure of two different recognizers for the same grammar: One system represents each grammar equation as a tree (a data structure) that is operated upon by a generalized interpreter. In the other, each grammar equation is represented as a procedure. In detail, there is a definite distinction between these two recognizers: the difference between data and procedure. But viewed as processes in execution, the two are not distinguishable. And so it is for most procedures; the module may at some level of interpretation be viewed as data. However, this observation should not inhibit us from noting that there are many instances in which data is not conveniently or adequately described as procedure. Examples of such data would be the parameter values passed to an ordinary subroutine, the results of a computation not conveniently described by a table lookup, or dynamically derived control parameters such as the value of a program counter. It may be concluded that, even though the distinction between procedure and data could almost be erased, it is desirable at some levels of system interpretation.)

DEPENDENCIES AMONG SYSTEM COMPONENTS

A system is built from two kinds of components, data and modules. We do not distinguish "private" data from the module that owns it. Therefore, only data (or data paths) visible to more than one module are considered as system components. A dependency is defined as an order relationship in time. To say that y depends on x is to say that if the state of x reaches one of a specified set of configurations, then there will be some effect on y. There are four general categories of dependencies: (1) process p2 depends on process p1, (2) data structure d depends on process p, (3) process p depends on data structures d, and (4) data structure d2 depends on data structure d1.

Dependency category (1), process p2 depends on process p1, is the best-understood category of system dependency. The most important examples of this relationship are

.p1 decides whether p2 should execute,

.p2 needs results (data) produced by p1,

.p3 needs result computed by p1 before result computed by p2,

.p1 is more "urgent" than p2,

.both p1 and p2 need a common resource whose
   access methods cannot tolerate simultaneous use.
In the last case, it may not matter whether p1 or p2 operates first, only that some ordering be imposed.

Dependency category (2), data structure d depends on process p, normally occurs when p calculates an update for d. Category (3), process p depends on data structure d, has the popular names "demon" and "monitor." In many ways it resembles an interrupt; that is, if d achieves some unusual shape or value, then a process is initiated.

Dependency category (4), data structure d2 depends on data structure d1, is interesting because it describes a time relationship between data without an explicit, intervening calculation. There are two slightly different cases of category (4) dependencies. First, the same information is kept in multiple copies; thus, if the information is updated at one location, then it may need to be updated at its other locations. Second, some information may be stored as a common substructure of several data structures, and any update to the common portion will be simultaneously reflected in all the parent structures.

MANAGEMENT OF DEPENDENCY

In the above discussions, we have talked about dependencies involving processes and dependencies involving modules without making a distinction. Strictly speaking, we should have mentioned only dependencies involving processes, because the ordering was on execution, a property of processes. However, this misses an important problem with system construction. It is that people code modules not processes. And, if a group is working on a program together, they will make assumptions about and use each others' work. In [2], Parnas says,

The connections between modules are the assumptions which the modules make about each other.

These assumptions may cover many types of dependencies not included in the four categories outlined above. Some examples are
.Subroutine s in module m performs a specific task.
.Data structure d has a certain format.
.The name of an entity is n.
.Subroutine s may be used recursively.
.Module m has an unfixed bug. (!)
There are two opposing viewpoints on the desirable amount of inter-module dependencies (or connections). The first, attributed to Minsky is called verticality and has special significance to AI systems. It assumes that to model a complex process on a computer, it is necessary to have as much flexibility as possible in interconnecting sources of Knowledge (KSs) at whatever level of detail is necessary. (This kind of organization is sometimes called a heterarchy.) The other viewpoint states that a system with too many interconnections is hard to change and impossible to debug. Therefore, it is important to compartmentalize knowledge in a system, thus minimizing interdependencies. This approach is often called modularity. The argument for verticality is based upon modeling of complex processes, while the argument for modularity is based upon practical considerations of system development.

In recent years, several programming language systems have been created to better support vertically integrated systems; PLANNER, MICRO PLANNER, Q-LISP, and CONNIVER are a few. So there are some definite feelings that verticality is important. However, most reported uses of the above systems or concepts have involved a single investigator or a small implementation team. (See [3] and [4] for some examples.) The advantages of verticality are that knowledge is not hidden and that real-world activities can be modeled within a natural structure. The problem is that the degree of dependency is large, and therefore the resulting system is hard to instrument or change. Further, the control structure may be quite complex, making it very difficult to follow program flow.

There are several arguments for modularity: the initial design task is relatively straightforward; it is easy to change the details of implementation; the control structure, on the level at which the system is modularized, can be fairly simple; and, as a side effect of the latter, it should be possible to document the system easily. The disadvantges of the modular approach are that the system architecture may be or may become rigid and therefore mask essential knowledge and communication. This happens when too much attention is given to the modularization and not enough to the problem at hand. Also, subcomponents may be duplicated.

The choice between the use of a modular or vertical strategy can be most difficult. The difficulty is that the virtues of each are desirable and complementary. Verticality is a more flexible structure, and modularity is a better organization for working. However, if a system is to be implemented by a large group of people, the modular approach is a clear winner. The ability to divide the work effort and specify the available interfaces is essential when the efforts of more than two or three people are involved. With the trend in AI systems towards larger groups working on the same project, we will see growing use of modularity. Verticality will be reserved for use by individuals or small groups searching for appropriate representation strategies, and it will probably be their efforts that point out some new directions for the development of larger systems.

In [2] and [5], Parnas suggests criteria for decomposing systems into modules. The basic idea is that a module should comprise the total knowledge of the system about some closely related set of design decisions. In the first section of this paper, a module for maintaining the status of a chess game was briefly mentioned. The external interfaces were functional, but using them made no assumptions about the actual representation of the board. Thus, the design decision hidden by this module was the selection of the board's representation. The merit of the Parnas criterion is that it reduces the amount of global knowledge necessary to program parts of a system because communications, and hence interdependencies, are well defined.

The idea of hiding a design decision is useful when applied to data but not so useful when applied to a procedural module. If the hidden design decision is the module's algorithm, then we have not really hidden very much. (How often can the user of a fast Fourier transformation routine make use of the fact that the computation is radix 4 instead of radix 2?)

Maintenance of data, on the other hand, is the prime candidate for the use of the Parnas approach. Examples of some good decisions to hide away are

.Is data kept in core or on disk?
.Is data tabular or computed?
.What is the format of the data?
.Is structure shared?
.Is the representation unique?

If communication with data is through functionals, the above kinds of design decisions do not have to become public, and we avoid global trouble when one of the decisions is changed.

The kinds of functionals necessary to communicate with a data store are update functionals to change, add, and delete items, and interrogation functionals to retrieve items or relationships about the data. These functionals can be implemented as functions, as macros, or even parametrically, as long as their exact inner workings do not need to be known. Two additional functionals should be provided for completeness: an initializer and a closer, both of which may perform no operation for many data stores. Since the possibility of storing data outside main memory is allowed, and since many operating systems require open and close catalogue calls for each file used, the initializer and closer can be used for these purposes. Even for data kept in main memory, the initializer can be used to lay out storage or compute initial values. The programming system in which the data is embedded calls the initializers for all stores at the start of program execution and the closers at the end.

FEATURES OF DATA

In this section, some features of data will be examined. In particular, we will look at the usage, longevity, ownership, and visibility of data. (The structuring and formatting problems covered by Standish in [6] are not discussed.) The particular features selected for examination were chosen because they may have a major impact on the organization and modularization of a system.

In a system, a collection of data is usually known by name. Many times, the name of the collection is the same as the name of the module that provides the access paths to the members of the collection. We will assume that knowing the name of a collection is equivalent to begin able to access members of the collection. A distinction is to be made between a data name (or collection) and a structure. A structure is a single, static entity. A name may refer to different sets of structures at different times, e.g., the name, PRESENT.WEATHER.CONDITIONS, will refer to different weather conditions at different times. Thus, the access function, TEMPERATURE, does not refer to a particular datum, but is more correctly a data path into the collection.

Data structures and collections are used for many purposes. A partial list of usage categories is

control information,

argument passing,

result passing,

accumulation of state of computation,

representation of procedure,

information pooling (data bases).

Data longevity refers to the amount of time a collection holds data structures. Thus, longevity is a property of a collection, not a structure. There are three useful categories of longevity: dynamic, permanent, and semi-permanent. Examples of dynamic data are control information and argument and result passing. In most system organizations, dynamic data does not receive a name (except through bound variables local to a particular module). It is created and passed to its ultimate destination then disappears from the system. Permanent data usually appears in the form of lexicons or data bases that are not ordinarily updated by operating the system. Semi-permanent data collections have the property that updates may occur, but entrance of a new member does not automatically delete old members. An example of a semi-permanent data collection in a speech system would be a memory of each word that has been successfully recognized in an utterance. As new words are found, they are added to the collection and remain there for the duration of the processing of the utterance. Before work is started on the next utterance, the collection is cleared.

Data ownership and data visibility are discussed together. To say that data collection d is visible to system component c (c knows d's name) can mean either that d depends on c or that c depends on d. If we use the modularity approach for maintaining data in a system, then the owner of the data is the module that allocates storage and provides the access paths. We can now say that a collection is private (or local) if it is visible only to its owner, and a collection is public (or global) if it is visible to at least one module that is not its owner. Being public does not necessarily grant access privileges to all system components. In fact, it is a basic part of the modularity philosophy that the system design should severely restrict the visibility (hence dependencies) of any components to those that have a "need to know." As defined here, ownership and visibility are properties of modules.

In general, permanent and semi-permanent data are global and are appropriately implemented as modules. A problem arises when one attempts to define ownership and visibility of dynamic data, because it is not natural to implement it as a module. (For example, the control and state parameters of a process belong to the process, not to a particular module.) Moreover, the unit of interest is a data structure, not a collection. (This is the case for subroutine arguments and values.) Further, because knowing the name of data is equated with its visibility, we can conclude that most dynamic data is invisible in the system, and private to its sender and receiver (or its single user).

DYNAMIC DATA VISIBILITY

There are times when it is appropriate to make dynamic data globally visible. A particular case is broadcasting information and requests among Knowledge Sources (KSs). Above, an example was given of a semi-permanent data collection in a speech system that remembers recognized words in an utterance. As various modules locate words in the utterance, they ship the words along the LOCATED.WORD data path to the storage module. In normal use, the KSs could interrogate the store to see if a particular word has already been located. It is also appropriate to broadcast the information placed on the LOCATED.WORD data path to various KSs. For instance, this would be a reasonable way to wake up (or create) a bottom-up parsing process. As another example, a top-down parsing process could broadcast a request for a particular word without consideration of who should respond. If the word had not been previously located, a word recognizer would examine the acoustic data and report results along the LOCATED.WORD data path.

The broadcasting technique described above closely resembles an important control structure capability provided by some program language systems for implementing vertically integrated systems. In particular, request broadcasting is the major linkage method, e.g., goal specification in PLANNER. The request receiver (as opposed to the request) is named. Thus, the catalogue of data paths is the set of routine names. Changes to the system at almost any level of detail change this catalogue. Such changes represent a major type of design decision. Obviously, this should not be allowed to happen on a day-to-day basis when the implementation staff is large.

An alternative can be used to preserve some of the flexibility inherent in the broadcast invocation strategy: name a few major data paths; for each path, specify the KSs that should operate whenever an item traverses that path; augment the control to create a process for each specified KS whenever the path is used. There are two important differences between this and the goal-invocation approach. First, the data paths as well as the receiving KSs are named, making them global. Second, a "process depends on a process" dependency has become a "process depends on data" dependency. If the path name is made global, hence visible, the inter-KS communication can become a specified and integral part of the system design and a candidate for instrumentation and measurement studies. Also, the "process depends on data" dependency seems more natural.

An analogue to this strategy for making dynamic data visible is implemented in computer hardware as buses. A bus is a data path to which modules are connected. It is usually the case that the modules do not have to know each other's names. Requests and information are broadcast on the bus. Each module examines the data and can do something with it or disregard it. Therefore, we may call the above system technique for broadcasting dynamic data "software busing."

PARALLELISM

Intuitively, parallelism means that two or more processes are operating simultaneously. Figure 1 shows a single process splitting into two parallel processes, a and b, which then rejoin to make a single process. Process a comprises the four sequential steps "a1", "fa=1", "wait until fb eq 1", and "a2". Process b comprises the four sequential steps "b1", "fb=1", "wait until fa eq 1", and "b2". The numbered steps are assumed to be total; that is, a1, a2, b1, and b2 are all finite calculations for any set of external conditions. Clearly, the processing scheme shown in Figure 1 will not itself be total unless there is some guarantee of parallelism. If a sequential interpreter attempts to operate one process to completion (run a to end, then b, or vice versa), then a block will occur on the wait operation because the other process has not been able to unlock the control flag, either fa or fb.

The facade of guaranteed parallelism may be achieved by a variety of techniques. If multiple program counters exist, they may be organized in a network or as a multiprocessor where each CPU shares a memory and other resources. The method of performing parallel processing on a sequential computer with a single program counter is called interleaving. The concept of parallelism in such an arrangement is guaranteed at only some levels of interpretation. Thus, in Figure 1, a

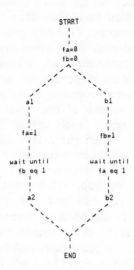

Figure 1. Example Flow

single processor could switch back and forth from process a to b after completing one of the four steps in either process. In fact, process switching is necessary only when an unsatisfied wait operation is encountered. Thus, at the level shown in Figure 1, we must guarantee parallelism. However, there need not be a guarantee that a1 and b1 will be operated simultaneously. The control structure need to guarantee only the facade of parallelism, and then only at particular levels of interpretation. The levels are only those in which synchronization operations (such as the wait) are present.

Two issues raise the question of whether parallel processing is worth thinking about in system design. First, almost no one has actual equipment available that is capable of doing real multiprocessing. Second, even if the equipment were available, the use of a parallel control structure introduces extra dependencies into a system in the form of synchronization operations. These extra dependencies are of an implementation variety and may have little to do with the problem-level intercommunications of the KSs. Since our general conclusion is that the number of dependencies (communications paths) in a system should be kept to a reasonable minimum, it may be inferred that parallelism is inappropriate in systems developed by large groups.

Non-guaranteed parallelism is a technique that has advantages in a control structure and does not run into the above objections. As the name implies, non-guaranteed parallelism does not promise to operate active processes simultaneously. The only guarantee is that, when an unsatisfied wait is encountered, some other process(es) not at an as yet unsatisfied wait will continue, start, or resume processing. The only legal inter-process order dependencies are those that occur in conjunction with explicit synchronization operations. Thus, guaranteed parallelism in the control regime of one level of system description cannot be hereditary to lower levels unless these levels also have synchronization primitives. When guaranteed parallelism is confined to higher levels of description, many inter-dependencies are "bubbled" outward and become visible or disappear.

The advantages of this approach are numerous. The number of explicit dependencies is reduced and the implicit, undocumentable dependencies are forced to disappear or become explicit at a higher level. Unexpected, implicit dependencies will eventually show themselves as software "race" conditions when parallelism is used in a system. The manifestation is usually that the same initial state produces different results. Even though this is not desired, it has a good effect. It forces the implementors and designers of a system to look for a cause, and this may lead to the discovery of a necessary but overlooked relationship among the KSs. If parallelism of some sort had not been used, the implementors would have selected some arbitrary sequential ordering and the problem may or may not have appeared. If it had not, then a discovery experience would have been missed. If the problem had occurred, it would have been solved by switching the order of a few statements rather than by analyzing the problem in sufficient depth. Thus, the use of parallelism is a motivator to understanding a system. Non-guaranteed parallelism preserves this characteristic and has the advantage of reducing the number of implicit and explicit dependencies. It allows efficient simulation on single CPU computers. (The use of a randomizing technique for selecting among the eligible execution paths ensures that implicit dependencies, if present, have an opportunity to appear.)

LEVELS OF SYSTEM DESCRIPTION

Throughout this paper, reference has been made to levels of system description, levels of representation, and levels of interpretation. The relationship between these three concepts and the concepts themselves are vague because they have many different intuitive connotations. My personal preference defines level of description in terms of representation and interpretation as follows:

A level of system description is a representation of the system which allows an accurate simulation of the system to some level of detail. The simulator or interpreter for a level of description is the realization of the control structure for the representation.

Thus, a level of description implies that the system can be simulated, which in turn implies the existence of a language for the representation and a control structure for that language.

The concept of level implies a hierarchy. For something as complex as a large program, there exist a variety of choices for the set of description levels. Some choices are more natural than others because they arise as steps in the evolution of the system design. Normally, the first level of system description is a diagram of the major components and dependencies. The control structure for interpreting the diagram is usually prose and informal.

The next iteration of the system design identifies the KSs that the system comprises. Data and process dependencies are also identified. At this level, a KS receives a name that reflects a problem-level label such as pragmatics, parser, eye, etc. Following this, the most crucial system description is attempted: the definition of modules. The importance is obvious because each defined module becomes a work assignment for one or perhaps two people. It is also at this level that all global dependencies must be defined and external module specifications created.

The bottom-most set of levels comprise program language forms organized into layers of subroutines and functions. These are the only levels for which there generally exist a formal representation and a control structure. The KS and module level are not formalized. Probably the best representation of the KSs and their interdependencies is a diagram with adequate explanation. However, this lack of accurate representation should not exist at the module level. In [2], Parnas argues strongly that all global dependency decisions be documented at this level and form the basis for individual work assignments. However, this is not enough. For a variety of reasons, the module level should be described in a formal, executable language that acts as the system control monitor. The most important reasons for formalizing the module level are the enhancements of the abilities to instrument and measure the system's performance, debug the system, change the system in a way that affects the least number of people, and test the system for compliance with the design specifications. All of these benefits accrue because a control monitor can create and order executable processes and can supervise the global data paths. It is at this level that the system description can best be augmented with test facilities.

A MODULE-LEVEL DESCRIPTION LANGUAGE

Ritea in [7] and Barnett in [8] describe a speech understanding system implemented at System Development Corporation in Santa Monica, California. The system accepts spoken utterances in a formal data management language that has a vocabulary of approximately 150 words. Users' questions are interactively answered, reports may be formatted, and the user may request help in understanding the system or the data base.

The system operates on an IBM 370/145 computer with the acoustic preprocessor operating on a Raytheon 704 computer. The organization of the system at the module level was accomplished using a control monitor language. The language is named Control Structure Language, CSL. CSL facilitated the use of the techniques mentioned above such as software buses, parallelism (guaranteed in CSL, non-guaranteed in the modules), visible declaration of dependencies, and "Parnas" modules for data storage. Three kinds of system components may be declared: buses, common (global) storage modules, and processing modules. The functional data paths to a common storage module are also specified and include: initializer, closer, updater, and interrogators.

A processing module has a single entry point, receives no arguments, and returns no value. All external communication must be over the buses or through the common storage modules. A processing module declaration includes the names of the buses and common storage modules it reads, and the names of the buses and common storage modules it writes. This is sufficient information to construct a data-dependency graph of the system. Alias names may also be declared for processing modules to allow a variety of usages in the system.

Besides passive declaration of major components, CSL provides for a description of program flow and order dependencies. The set of invocation primitives are; conditional, sequential, parallel, and fork. "FORK L" creates a process starting each place the label L, appears. Additional flow synchronization is accomplished using AFTER forms, BEFORE forms, and labels. AFTER waits for a specified set of processing modules to complete execution. BEFORE causes a specified sequence of preceding events to happen each time a specified module is activated or before a fork to a specified label is completed. BEFORE is normally used for debugging and instrumentation. Labels may be placed singly or in groups. Processing does not start at a label until a fork to each label in the group has occurred.

Two data-synchronizing operations are present in CSL. First, CYCLE clears visible data structures from the specified buses and places new items, accumulated by operating processing modules, on the buses. Second, UPDATE passes the data structures accumulated since the last update for this common storage module to the update functional given in the common declaration.

Debugging facilities include trace and breakpoint capabilities. Also, a system monitor written in CSL may bind variables and operate expressions written in LISP. CSL was implemented as a language extension of the SDC LISP Infix Language and operates in three phases; compile, graph linking, and run-time control monitor execution. The appendix to this paper contains a brief description of CSL.

Experience with the use of CSL for organizing a speech system has confirmed the desirability of having a formal description level for modules and their interdependencies. Several experiments have been performed where one or more modules were deleted from the system and performance measured to determine their contribution. This was accomplished without disturbing the interior of any module; only the CSL system description was modified. It has been possible to debug each module in isolation by using CSL to configure a test facility specifically suited to testing that module. Another benefit has been the ability to borrow modules from the system in order to manufacture other programs quickly. Also, as the system has been used, the dependencies and flow have been altered to improve performance. In no case was a module reprogrammed; the changes were reflected only at the CSL description level.

ACKNOWLEDGMENTS

I wish to thank Douglas Pintar who worked on the implementation of CSL and who made many valuable contributions to the design of the language. I also wish to thank John Like for his help in organizing and improving this paper.

This research was supported by the Advanced Research Projects Agency of the Department of Defense under Contract Number DAHC15-73-C-0080.

REFERENCES

1. Fisher, D. A. "Control Structures for Programming Languages," Doctoral Dissertation, Carnegie-Mellon University, May, 1970.
2. Parnas, D. L. "Information Distribution Aspects of Design Methodology," Information Processing 71, North-Holland Publishing Company, 1972, pp. 339-344.
3. Miller, P. L. "A Locally-Organized Parser for Spoken Input," Doctoral Dissertation, Massachusetts Institute of Technology, March, 1973.
4. Winograd, T. "Procedures as a Representation for Data in a Computer Program for Understanding Natural Languages," Doctoral Dissertation, Massachusetts Institute of Technology, February, 1971.
5. Parnas, D. L. "On the Criteria to be Used in Decomposing Systems into Modules," Communications of the ACM, December, 1972, Volume Vol. 15, No. 12, pp. 1053-1058.
6. Standish, T. A. "A Data Definition Facility for Programming Languages," Doctoral Dissertation, Carnegie-Mellon University, May, 1967.
7. Ritea, H. B. "A Voice-Controlled Data Management System," Contributed Papers of IEEE Symposium on Speech Recognition, April, 1974, Carnegie-Mellon University, Pittsburgh, Pa., pp. 28-32.
8. Barnett, J. A. "A Vocal Data Management System," IEEE Transactions on Audio and Electroacoustics, Volume AU-21, Number 3, June, 1973, pp. 185-188.
9. Newell, A. et al. "Speech Understanding Systems: Final Report of a Study Group," Published for Artificial Intelligence by North-Holland/American Elsevier, 1973.

APPENDIX: CSL LANGUAGE DESCRIPTION

By example, several kinds of CSL statements and language forms are introduced. Declaration statements are presented first, followed by the flow and synchronization primitives. DECLARATION STATEMENTS

Buses, common storage modules, and processing modules can be declared in CSL. Bus Declarations

Bus declarations are introduced by the word, BUS, followed by a sequence of bus names. To declare B1, B2, and B3 buses, write:

BUS B1,B2,B3;

Common Storage Module Declarations

Common storage module declarations are introduced by the word, COMMON, followed by a declaration for each common storage module:

COMMON X(XI,XU,XC,XA1,XA2),
    Y(YI,YU,UC,UA1,YA2,YA3);

In this example, X and Y are declared as common storage modules. XI,XU, and XC are the names of the initalizer, updater, and closer functions, respectively, for X. XA1 and XA2 are the name of the interrogators. YI, YU, and YC are the names of the initalizer, updater, and closer functions, respectively, for Y. YA1, YA2, and YA3 are the interrogators. All access functions are specified by function or macro names. Processing Module Declarations

Processing module declarations are introduced by the word, MODULE, followed optionally by the specification of alias names, data input names, and data output names:

MODULE M ALIAS(M1,M2) READ(B1)(X,Y) WRITE(B2,B3)(X);

The module, M, may also be referenced as M1 or M2. M reads from bus B1 and writes on buses B2 and B3. M reads and writes common storage module X and reads common storage Y. FLOW AND SYNCHRONIZATION FORMS

Flow and synchronization control forms are built up from the names of buses, common storage modules, processing modules, labels, and expressions written in LISP Infix language. The interpretation of a processing module name is an execution of that module. Label definitions may be made either singly or in groups. The label name(s) is surrounded by asterisks. Thus, to place the group of labels L1, L2, and L3 at some spot, you write

L1,L2,L3

In order for a process to be initiated at or continue through a label group, a fork to each label must be executed.

The AFTER primitive forces a wait until a specified group of processing modules have been executed. To wait on modules M1 and M2, write:

AFTER(M1,M2)

FORK

A fork to label L is written

FORK L

FAKE

A FAKE form tells the control monitor to initiate all activity dependent on a processing module without first executing the module. To "fake" the execution of M, write

FAKE M

Conditional

A conditional form is written in standard if-them-else format with the else-clause optional. The predicate is any expression written in LISP Infix language. The conditional,

IF P EQ Q THEN M1 ELSE M2

executes M1 if the value of P equals the value of Q. Otherwise, M2 is executed. The then-clause and the else-clause may be any flow or synchronization form except a BEFORE statement. Parallel and Sequential

To operate a set of forms in sequential order, write the forms enclosed in parentheses. To operate a set of forms in parallel, write the forms enclosed in square brackets.

[(A,B),(C,D,E)]

The above will initiate two parallel processes. One process consists of the sequential execution of the processing modules A and B in that order. The other process is the sequential execution of the processing modules C, D, and E in that order.

Top-level CSL statements are assumed to specify a sequential ordering within the statements so that the outer parentheses may be dropped. No ordering among statements is implied by their lexical order of appearance; therefore, each control flow statement must begin with a label definition or an AFTER form. The control monitor always begins execution by forcing a "FORK START". BEFORE STATEMENT

A BEFORE statement specifies a sequence of events that should happen before a processing module is executed or before a fork to a label is completed.

$$BEFORE \ M \ X,[Y,Z];$$

When M would normally be executed, the sequence of events is: execute X, operate Y and Z in parallel, and then execute M. CYCLE

Execution of a CYCLE form discards data items presently on the named buses and makes new data items visible. To cycle buses B1 and B2, write

$$CYCLE(B1,B2)$$

UPDATE

Execution of an UPDATE form passes their accumulated updates to the named common storage modules. To update data collections X and Y, write

$$UPDATE(X,Y)$$

BREAK

A debugging breakpoint may be specified using the BREAK form. The body of the BREAK is an expression written in LISP Infix language. When executed, all processes are immediately suspended, the expression is evaluated and its value is printed on the interactive terminal, identification of the suspended processes is printed, and a debugging supervisor is entered for interaction with the user. To create a breakpoint which outputs the message hello, write:

$$BREAK \ "HELLO$$

STOP

Execution of a STOP form immediately terminates all processing and return to the LISP supervisor. A STOP form is just the word, "STOP". DATA FUNCTIONS

The CSL run-time package provides modules with three functions for accessing the data paths: GETBUS, PUTBUS, and PUTCOM. Other accesses are made through the interrogators declared with the common storage modules.

GETBUS(bus-name)

The argument to GETBUS is the name of a bus. The value is a list of the data structures on the bus.

PUTBUS(bus-name,data-structure)

The arguments to PUTBUS are the name of a bus and a data structure to put on that bus. The new value becomes visible the next time the bus is cycled.

PUTCOM(common-storage-module-name,update)

The arguments to PUTCOM are the name of a common storage module and an update (data structure) for the named module. The accumulated updates are passed to the update function specified in the module declaration the next time an UPDATE form addresses the module.

STOCHASTIC MODELING FOR AUTOMATIC SPEECH UNDERSTANDING

James K. Baker
IBM T.J. Watson Research Center
Yorktown Heights, New York 10598

There are many situations in automatic speech recognition/understanding in which decisions have to be made based on incomplete or uncertain information. Stochastic modeling is a flexible general method for handling such situations. Stochastic modeling consists of employing a specific probabilistic model for the uncertainty or incompleteness of the information. The uncertainty in automatic speech recognition arises for many reasons. The acoustic signal is ambiguous because the acoustic cues for the individual speech sounds become reduced or are deleted in normal continuous speech. Automatic segmentation and labeling procedures make insertion, deletion and substitution errors in addition to the fundamental ambiguity of the signal. Other sources of knowledge, such as syntax and semantics, seldom limit the possible word candidates to a single word, so although their information may be precise, it is incomplete in terms of making a decision on a unique word for a given place in the utterance.

An abstract model for these situations of uncertainty is that there are two sequences of random variables: Y(1), Y(2), Y(3),..., Y(T) and X(1), X(2), X(3),...,X(T). The X's represent some sequence which we wish to know, but which we are not able to observe directly (for example, the words in an utterance). The Y's represent some sequence which are related to the X's and which we can observe or which we have already deduced by other means (for example, the sequence of acoustic parameter values). Stochastic modeling consists of formulating a probabilistic model for generating sequences of X's and for producing a sequence of Y's based on the sequence of X's. These models can then be used to make inferences in a speech recognition system. When a sequence of Y's is observed, techniques are used for finding the sequence of X's which best fits the observed sequence of Y's -- that is, the sequence of X's which, according to the model, is the sequence which is the most likely to produce the observed sequence of Y's.

In this paper a specific class of stochastic models is discussed -- models based on the theory of a probabilistic function of a Markov process. First the properties of the general model are discussed and then some examples are considered of situations in automatic speech analysis in which such models can be applied.

Let Y(1), Y(2), Y(3),..., Y(T) be a sequence of random variables representing the external (acoustic) observations. Let X(1), X(2), X(3),..., X(T) be a sequence of random variables representing the internal states of a stochastic process such that the probability distributions of the Y's depend on the values of the X's, but the X's are not directly observed. As a convenient abbreviation we use a bracket and colon notation to represent sequences. Thus, Y[1:T] represents Y(1), Y(2), Y(3),..., Y(T) and X[1:T] represents X(1), X(2), X(3),..., X(T). Let y[1:T] be the observed sequence of values for the random variables Y[1:T].

We wish to make inferences about the sequence X[1:T] in light of the knowledge of y[1:T]. For example, we would like to know the conditional probability PROB(X(t)=j | Y[1:T]=y[1;T]) for each t and j (the conditional probability of a specific internal state at a specific time, given the entire sequence of external observations). Assuming we have a model for speech production, we can evaluate the a priori probability PROB(X[1:T]). Assuming a model for the generation of acoustic events associated with a specific sequence of internal states, we can evaluate the conditional probability PROB(Y[1:t] =y[1:T] | X[1:T]=x[1:T]) (That is, the model yields conditional probabilities of external observations, given the sequence of internal states). Thus we know the conditional probabilities in the generative or synthetic form.

We can compute the desired conditional probabilities using Bayes' formula

(1) PROB(X(t)=j | Y[1:T]=y[1:T])

=PROB(X(t)=j, Y[1:T]=y[1:T]/PROB(Y[1:T]=y[1:T])

if we can evaluate the factors on the right hand side. The numerator is given by

(2) $PROB(X(t)=j, Y[1:T]=y[1:T])$

$$=\Sigma_{x[1:T],x(t)=j}\ PROB(X[1:T]=x[1:T]Y[1:T]=y[1:T])$$

$$=\Sigma_{x[1:T],x(t)=j}\ PROB(Y[1:T]=y[1:T]\ |\ X[1:T]=x[1:T])PROB(X[1:T]=x[1:T])$$

where the sum is taken over all possible sequences x[1:T] subject to the restriction x(t)=j. (The joint probability of an internal sequence and an external sequence is the product of the a priori probability of the internal sequence and conditional probability of the external sequence given by the model. The probability for the event X(t)=j is obtained by summing over all internal sequences which meet that restriction.) We can evaluate the a priori probability that Y[1:T] would be y[1:T] as

(3) $PROB(Y[1:T]=y[1:T])$

$$=\Sigma_{x[1:T]}\ PROB(Y[1:T]=y[1:T]\ |\ X[1:T]=x[1:T])PROB(X[1:T]=x[1:T])$$

where the sum is taken over all possible sequences x[1:T]. (The total probability of an external sequence is the sum of its joint probability with all possible internal sequences.)

Therefore

(4) PROB(X(t)=j | Y[1:T]=y[1:T])

=PROB(X(t)=j, Y[1:T]=y[1:T])/PROB(Y[1:T]=y[1:T])

$$= \frac{\Sigma_{x[1:T],x(t)=j} \ \text{PROB}(Y[1:T]=y[1:T] | X[1:T]=x[1:T])\text{PROB}(X[1:T]=x[1:T])}{\Sigma_{x[1:T]} \ \text{PROB}(Y[1:T]=y[1:T] | X[1:T]=x[1:T])\text{PROB}(X[1:T]=x[1:T])}$$

where the sum in the denominator is taken over all sequences x[1:T] and the sum in the numerator is taken over all such sequences subject to the restriction x(t)=j. (This is the probability of the internal event X(t)=j conditional on the observed external sequence, as desired.)

The derivation of equation (4) is just a standard application of Bayes' theorem. It represents a formal inversion of the conditional probabilities from the generative form to the analytic form. (Note: The word "analytic" is used here in a special sense. "Analytic" means "taking apart" as opposed to "synthetic," "generative," or "putting together." In terms of speech, the generative form predicts the observations (Y's) in terms of the internal sequence (X's). The analytic form computes the a posteriori probability of the X's conditional on the observed Y's.) The speech-recognition knowledge sources provide the conditional probabilities in a generative form. They must be converted into an analytic form to make inferences about a particular utterance from the observed acoustics. However, the formal inversion formula given in equation (4) is not computationally practical since in general the set of all possible sequences x[1:T] is prohibitively large. It is necessary to apply the restrictions of a more specific model to obtain a computationally efficient formula.

The model used in this paper is that the sequences represent a probabilistic function of a Markov process. Specifically, it is assumed that the conditional probability that X(t)=j given X(t-1) is independent of t and of the values of X[1:t-2] and that the conditional probability that Y(t)=k given X(t) and X(t-1) is independent of t and of the values of any of the other X's and Y's. Let $B=\{b_{i,j,k}\}$ and $A=\{a_{i,j}\}$ be arrays such that

(5) PROB(Y(t)=y(t) | X[1:t]=x[1:t], Y[1:t-1]=y[1:t-1])

$\qquad$ =PROB(Y(t)=y(t) | X(t-1)=x(t-1),X(t)=x(t))

$\qquad$ =$b_{x(t-1),x(t),y(t)}$

and

(6) PROB(X(t)=x(t) | X[1:t-1]=x[1:t-1])

$\qquad$ =PROB(X(t)=x(t) | X(t-1)=x(t-1))

$\qquad$ =$a_{x(t-1),x(t)}$

This restriction to a Markov model is the fundamental assumption which allows the computations to be practical. In the Markov model the conditional probabilities depend only on X(t) and X(t-1) and not on the entire sequence X[1:T] as in equations (1) to (4). This specialization makes it possible to evaluate the desired conditional probabilities by an indirect but computationally efficient procedure.

The Markov assumption might be parapharased by saying that the conditional probabilities are independent of context, but such a simple statement would be misleading. Since the state speace of the Markov process for our speech recognition application has not yet been formulated, the assumption of the Markov properties should be regarded as a prescription to be followed in the formulation of the state space. Specifically, two situations which differ in "relevant" context must be assigned two separate states in the state space of the random variables X[1:T]. Then all "relevant" context is included in the state space description, and the conditional probabilities are indeed independent of further context. The fundamental assumption that we are making is that it is possible to meet this prescription and still have a state space of manageable size.

Under the assumptions of equations (5) and (6) we have

$$(7)\ PROB(X[1{:}s]{=}x[1{:}s]){=}PROB(X(1){=}x(1)(\Pi_{t=2,s}\ a_{x(t-1),x(t)})$$

(The a priori probability of a given internal state sequence is the product of the transition probabilities for all the transitions in the sequence.) To simplify, add a special extra state to the Markov process; let $x(0)$ be this special state and define $a_{x(0),j}$ =PROB(X(1)=j). Similar conventions are assumed throughout this paper, unless specifically mentioned otherwise. Then

$$(8)\ PROB(X[1{:}s]{=}x[1{:}s]){=}\Pi_{t=1,s}\ a_{x(t-1),x(t)}$$

also

$$(9)\ PROB(Y[1{:}s]{=}y[1{:}s]\ |\ X[1{:}s]{=}x[1{:}s]){=}\Pi_{t=1,s}\ b_{x(t-1),x(t),y(t)}$$

(the model-defined probability of an external sequence, conditional on the internal sequence) where $b_{x(0),j,k}$ is defined appropriately. Combining (8) and (9) yields

$$(10)\ PROB(X[1{:}s]{=}x[1{:}s],\ Y[1{:}s]{=}y[1{:}s]){=}\Pi_{t=1,s}\ a_{x(t-1),x(t)}\ b_{x(t-1),x(t),y(t)}$$

(the joint probability of an internal sequence and an external sequence as given by the Markov model).

To make possible the efficient computation of the sums in equations (3) and (4), we introduce the probabilities of partial sequences of states and observations (Baum). Using (2) with t=T=s and using (10), we can set

(11) $\alpha(s,x(s)) = \text{PROB}(X(s)=x(s), Y[1{:}s]=y[1{:}s])$

$$= \Sigma_{x[1:s-1]} \Pi_{t=1,s} a_{x(t-1),x(t)} b_{x(t-1),x(t),y(t)}$$

where the sum is over all possible sequences $x[1{:}s-1]$. (This is the joint probability of the partial external sequence, up to time s, and the event that the process is in state x(s) at time s.) Let

(12) $\beta(s,x(s)) = \text{PROB}(X(s)=x(s)\ Y[s+1{:}T]=y[s+1{:}T])$

$$= \Sigma_{x[s+1:T]} \Pi_{t=s+1,T} a_{x(t-1),x(t)} b_{x(t-1),x(t),y(t)}$$

where the sum is over all possible sequences $x[s+1{:}T]$. (This is the joint probability of the partial external sequence from time s+1 to the end, and the event that process is in state x(s) at time s.) The benefit of introducing the functions α and β is that the values of $\alpha(s,j)$ for a given s can be computed from the values of $\alpha(s-1,j)$. Similarly, β for a given s can be computed from the values of β for s+1.

In fact

(13) $\alpha(s,j) = \Sigma_i \alpha(s-1,i) a_{i,j} b_{i,j,y(s)}$

(because every sequence $x[1{:}s]$ must have $x(s-1)=i$ for some i) and

(14) $\beta(s,j) = \Sigma_i \beta(s+1,i) a_{j,i} b_{j,i,y(s+1)}$

But $\alpha(T,j)=PROB(X(T)=j,Y[1:T]=y[1:T])$ hence

(15) $PROB(Y[1:T]=y[1:T])=\Sigma_j\alpha(T,j)$

We can compute the conditional probability distribution for X(t)

(16) $PROB(X(t)=j \mid Y[1:T]=y[1:T])$

$=PROB(X(t)=j, Y[1:T])/PROB(Y[1:T]=y[1:T])$

$=\alpha(t,j)\beta(t,j)/\Sigma_i\alpha(T,i)$

In speech recognition problems, we usually want to know the particular sequence x[1:T] which maximizes the joint probability $PROB(X[1:T]=x[1:T],Y[1:T]=y[1:T])$. Again, the problem can be solved by induction from partial sequences (Bellman). Let

(17) $\gamma(t,j)=Max_{x[1:t-1]}PROB(X[1:t-1]=x[1:t-1], X(t)=j, Y[1:t]=y[1:t])$

Then γ may be computed by

(18) $\gamma(t,j)=Max_i\gamma(t-1,i)a_{i,j}b_{i,j,y(t)}$

Notice that equation (18) is just like equation (13) except that Max has been substituted for Σ. It is convenient to save "back-pointers" while computing γ. Therefore, let I(t,j) be any value of i for which the maximum is achieved in equation (18). Then a sequence x[1:T] for which PROB(X[1:T]=x[1:T],Y[1:T]=y[1:T]) is maximized is obtained by

(19) x(T)=j, where j is any index such that $\gamma(T,j)=Max_i\gamma(T,i)$

and

(20) x(t)=I(t+1,x(t+1)), t= T-1,T-2, ... ,2,1

So far the analysis has assumed that the matrices A and B are fixed and known. However, if A and B are not known but must be estimated, than the α and β computed above may be used to obtain a Bayesian a posteriori re-estimation of A and B. The matrix A is re-estimated by

$$(21)\ \hat{a}_{i,j} = \frac{\Sigma_{t=1,T-1}\ PROB(X(t)=i,X(t+1)=j\ |\ Y[1:T]=y[1:T], \{a_{i,j}\},\{b_{i,j,k}\})}{\Sigma_{t=1,T-1}PROB(X(t)=i\ |\ Y[1:T]=y[1:T], \{a_{i,j}\},\{b_{i,j,k}\})}$$

$$= \frac{\Sigma_{t=1,T-1}\alpha(t,i)a_{i,j}b_{i,j,y(t+1)}\beta(t+1,j)}{\Sigma_{t=1,T-1}\alpha(t,i)\beta(t,i)}$$

The matrix B is re-estimated by

$$(22)\ \hat{b}_{i,j,k} = \frac{\Sigma_{t=1,T-1,y(t+1)=k}\ PROB(X(t)=i,X(t+1)=j\ |\ Y[1:T]=y[1:T],\ \{a_{i,j}\},\{b_{i,j,k}\})}{\Sigma_{t=1,T-1}PROB(X(t)=i,\ X(t+1)=j\ |\ Y[1:T]=y[1:T],\ \{a_{i,j}\},\{b_{i,j,k}\})}$$

$$= \frac{\Sigma_{t=1,T-1,y(t+1)=k}\alpha(t,i)a_{i,j}b_{i,j,k}\beta(t+1,j)}{\Sigma_{t=1,T-1}\alpha(t,i)a_{i,j}b_{i,j,y(t+1)}\beta(t+1,j)}$$

In fact it can be shown (Baum) that

$$(23)\ PROB(Y[1:T]=y[1:T]\ |\ \{\hat{a}_{i,j}\},\{\hat{b}_{i,j,k}\}) \geq PROB(Y[1:T]=y[1:T]\ |\ \{a_{i,j}\},\{b_{i,j,k}\})$$

Hence the re-estimation given by equations (21) and (22) may be used iteratively in an attempt to obtain $\{a_{i,j}\}$ and $\{b_{i,j,k}\}$ which maximize $PROB(Y[1:T]=y[1:T]\ |\ \{a_{i,j}\},\{b_{i,j,k}\})$. Thus we can obtain an approximation to maximum likelihood estimates for $\{a_{i,j}\}$ and $\{b_{i,j,k}\}$.

In re-estimating the matrices A and B, the special structure of the speech recognition problem can be used to good advantage. Although it is convenient to use a single integrated model for the actual analysis and recognition of utterances, the re-estimation of the structural matrices can be performed separately for each of the levels in the hierarchy. Also note that any entry in A or B which is zero remains zero in the re-estimations of equations (21) and (22). Therefore we are able to maintain and utilize the sparseness of these matrices in the re-estimation process.

The general model of a probabilistic function of a Markov process can be applied to some degree to almost any situation in which there is an observed sequence (Y's) which depends probabilistically on an unobserved sequence (X's). Let's consider several examples of such situations in automatic speech analysis.

ISOLATED WORD RECOGNITION (ITAKURA, WHITE)

One method of isolated word recognition involves matching the sequence of acoustic parameters in the word to be recognized against a set of prototypes, where each prototype is the sequence of acoustic parameters for an instance of a word in the lexicon. Assuming that we have a method for measuring the match between the acoustic parameter values for an elementary segment in the prototype and an elementary segment in the word to be recognized, we still must take account of the fact that protions of the word to be recognized may be spoken faster or more slowly than the corresponding protions of the prototype. In matching a given word and a given prototype, we have a hidden stochastic process in which the observed sequence (Y's) consists of the sequence of acoustic parameters for the word to be recognized, and the internal sequence represents the information as to how the times in the word to be recognized correspond to the times in the prototype.

Specifically, we let Y(t) be the acoustic parameter values observed for the elementary segment at time t in the word to be recognized, and we let X(t)=s if the elementary segment at time t in the word to be recognized corresponds to the elementary segment at time s in the prototype. The possibility of a portion of the word being faster or slower than the prototype is represented by conditional probabilities such as those given in equation (24)

$$(24)\begin{cases} \text{PROB}(X(t)=s \mid X(t-1)=s)=a \\ \text{PROB}(X(t)=s \mid X(t-1=s-1)=1-a-b \\ \text{PROB}(X(t)=s \mid X(t-1)=s-2)=b \end{cases}$$

where a and b are parameters which can be estimated by experiment. Thus the matrix $A=\{a_{i,j}\}$ of equation (6) is determined by equation (24). Note that $a_{i,j}=0$ unless j is equal to i or i+1 or i+2. The conditional probability in equation (5) is estimated by the procedure which matches an elementary segment of the word with an elementary segment of the prototype. Thus, we have modeled the situation as a probabilistic function of a Markov process and can find the best internal sequence by using equations (18) and (20). The problem can also be viewed as one of finding the best path through the following network.

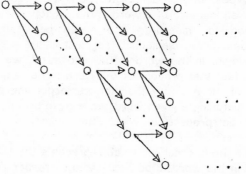

Figure 1. Dynamic Time Warping Network

The node in row s and column t of this network corresponds to the event X(t)=s. The state space network is a simple linear network, as shown in Figure 2.

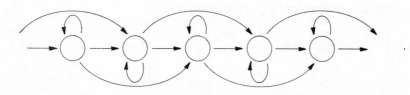

Figure 2. Isolated Word Recognition

A model similar to this one has been used successfully for automatic recognition of isolated words (Itakura).

WORD SPOTTING (BAKIS, BRIDLE)
        Suppose we wish to find all instances of a particular word in a long recording of continuous speech. If we have a prototype for the word then we can formulate a model which is similar to the one we used for isolated word recognition, except there is an extra state in the network to represent all acoustic segments which occur between instances of the word, and the network loops back to allow repeated instances of the word. The schematic network is shown in Figure 3.

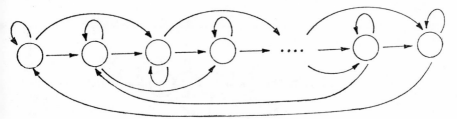

Figure 3. Word Spotting

If either in the isolated word recognition or in the word spotting we desire to construct prototypes not just from a single instance of a lexical item but rather from a collection of instances, then we must find which elementary segments in each instance corresponds with each elementary segment in the combined prototype. This correspondence can be found by equations (13) and (14) and we can automatically train for a generalization of the parameters a and b in equation (24) by the re-estimation procedure of equations (22) and (23). A word spotting procedure based on a model similar to the one described here, with a training procedure, has proven to be very successful (Bakis).

MACHINE AIDED SEGMENTATION (BAKER)

Automatic segmentation of continuous speech into acoustic segments corresponding to a broad phonetic transcription is a component of many speech recognition systems, but it is difficult to achieve high accuracy. A much simpler segmentation problem results if we assume that we have available a phonetic transcription of the utterance and merely want to know the times at which the given phones occur. Abstractly, this problem is just like that of comparing an isolated word to a prototype. The Markov model is again a simple linear network. In this case, however, the match and dynamic time warping is performed on an entire sentence. The prototype is constructed by concatenating prototypes for each of the phones in the given transcription.

MACHINE-AIDED PHONETIC TRANSCRIPTION (BAHL)

Suppose we are given an orthographic transcription of a sentence and wish to estimate the phonetic transcription. Given any sequence of words and a list of phonological rules, there exist automatic procedures (Cohen and Mercer) for applying the phonological rules to baseforms obtained from a phonemic dictionary to yield a network representation of all possible surface forms, that is, all possible proununciations of the sentence. A simple example of such a network is shown in Figure 4.

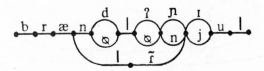

Figure 4. Phonetic Transcription

Each arc in this network corresponds to a particular phone. For each arc in the network we substitute a small network which represents a prototype for the phone corresponding to the arc. We can now use equations (18) and (20) to find the best path through this expanded network. The transition probabilities in this model are determined from the probabilities associated with the frequency of application of each of the phonological rules (conditional on the context of the rule being satisfied). These statistics can be estimated by an automatic procedure similar to the one represented by equations (22) and (23). Such a machine-aided phonetic transcriber has recently been successfully trained (Bahl).

PITCH TRACKING
        Let the state space for the Markov process be a set of quantized values for the pitch frequency, plus a special state representing unvoiced speech. The transition probabilities are estimated from the frequencies of occurence of corresponding pitch changes in a set of training utterances. The random variable Y(t) is a vector of elementary pitch estimates. The conditional probability distribution for a typical component of Y(t) would have most of the probability clustered around the true pitch frequency, but also might have modes at half the true frequency or twice the true frequency, and so forth. The Bayesian estimate of X(t) given by equation (16) is then the best estimate of the pitch frequency at time t taking into account the whole sequence of elementary estimates Y[1:T] and the known (statistical) constraints on the rate of change of X. Thus the stochastic model allows us to combine estimates from an arbitrary number of elementary estimators and to use past, present and future pitch estimates to compute X(t).

FORMANT TRACKING

The state space for formant tracking is a vector of quantized frequencies, one element for each formant. The random variable Y(t) would be a list of frequencies that are candidates for formant frequencies (for example, they could be the peaks in a smoothed spectrum). In addition to the Markov process with time index t, there is a little Markov process whose index is the formant number. The little Markov process is run repeatedly, once for each time t. This little Markov process determines which formant corresponds to which candidate frequency and which formants correspond to no candidate frequencies at all. The state space variable for the little Markov process is a vector (C,M) where C is the number of candidate frequencies that are less than or equal to the current formant frequency, and M is a boolean variable indicating whether the current formant corresponds to any of the candidate frequencies. The transition network restricts C to be non-decreasing and the transition probabilities reflect the probabilities of missing peaks, two formants with a single peak, and so forth. The transition probabilities can be estimated by training on speech samples for which the formants have been tracked by hand.

DETERMINING SYNTACTIC-SEMANTIC CATEGORIES (RICH)

The grammatical categories of the words in a sentence are constrained by the syntax and can be used for prediction in a probabilistic sense. For example, a noun is frequently preceded by an adjective, but is less frequently followed by an adjective. Using a probabilistic function of a Markov process, we can generalize this notion, associating the words with arbitrary categories whether grammatically determined or otherwise. The random variable Y(t) in this model is the word which occurs at position t in a long sequence of words. The random variable X(t) is the category at position t. The words do not need to be assigned to disjoint categories. Category membership is represented by the conditional probability distributions PROB(Y(t)=w | X(t)=c), which includes word frequency information. It is possible to re-estimate the parameters of the Markov process by equations (22) and (23). The result would correspond to associating the words with categories in such a way as to maximize the predictive power of the categories. Such categories could reflect syntax, semantics, and word frequencies. These categories could then be used as a simplified representation of the syntax and semantics in a speech understanding system.

LINGUSTIC SEQUENTIAL DECODING
(TAPPERT ET AL., PAUL ET AL., JELINEK ET AL.)

Speech recognition may be viewed as a sequential decoding problem. That is, we may view the sequence of labels produced by an automatic segmentation and labeling program as the true sequence of phones transmitted over a noisy channel. Sequential decoding algorithms developed for decoding convolution codes have been adapted to speech recognition/understanding problems. If we represent the true sequence of phones as a Markov process, then the output of the noisy channel is a probablistic function of a Markov process. Equations (18) and (20) correspond to an algorithm known in communications theory as the Viterbi algorithm (Viterbi). There are other algorithms for sequential decoding, which are also based on maximizing the a posteriori probability according to such a stochastic model, and several of them have been successfully applied to speech recognition (Tappert et al., Jelinek et al.).

INTEGRATED SPEECH RECOGNITION NETWORK (BAKER)

The DRAGON speech recognition system extends the Markov model to include not only the linguistic decoder but also the lexical, phonological, and acoustic-phonetic knowledge. In addition semantics, both intra-sentence and inter-sentence, could be introduced. By formulating the entire speech recognition system in terms of a single abstract model, a great conceptual simplicity is achieved. Each knowledge source is represented as a probabilistic function of a Markov process, in a manner similar to that used in the examples above. The individual processes are organized into a hierarchy and the integrated system is also a probabilistic function of a Markov process. This integrated system could be treated by any of the sequential decoding techniques used in the linguistic sequential decoders, but in the DRAGON system an optimal search strategy has been adopted which performs the recognition by applying equations (18) and (20).

These equations correspond to searching all possible paths through the network to find the optimum path. In the application to an integrated speech recognition system, this search represents a search of all possible sentences of the language (constrained only by the length of the observed sequence of acoustic parameters), of all possible pronunciations of each sentence, and of all possible time warpings to match each such pronunciation to the observed acoustic sequence. It might seem that such an exhaustive search is impossible, but the essential feature of the Markov model is that it permits such a search to be performed with the number of computations being a linear function of the length of the utterance, as shown in equations (18) and (20).

The number of computations in each application of equation (18) is related to the number of pairs i,j for which $a_{i,j}$ is non-zero. If the integrated speech recognition network is too large and too complex, then optimal search would be impractical even though the time of computation is linear in the length of the utterance. To demonstrate that it is possible to satisfy the prescription to include all "relevant" context in the representation of the Markov state space and still obtain a network of manageable size, the DRAGON system has been implemented for several speech recognition tasks. Each task is based on a specialized language for a specific interactive computer task. The most complex task implemented so far is an interactive formant tracking task. The language has an infinite number of possible sentences, with about 16^n sentences of length n words. The lexicon and grammar are designed to fit the task: no restriction was placed on either the lexicon or the grammar to prevent acoustical confusions (for example, "Hamming" and "Hanning" are both used as possible window types and are syntactically equivalent).

The current implementation of the DRAGON system has been tested on a total of 61 sentences from three speech understanding tasks. An earlier test on 17 sentences including a fourth task gave comparable results. Detailed statistics of the performance on the 61 sentences are given in Tables 1-3. Since the number of words in the sentence output by the system is not necessarily the same as the number of words in the actual input sentence, there is no unique way to calculate the percentage of words correctly recognized. The statistic (words corrct)/(words in) ranges from 85.2% to 94.6%; the statistic (words correct)/(words out) ranges from 89% to 93.9%. The statistic (utterances correct)/(number of utterances) is 68.1%, 80.9% and 44.4%, respectively for the three tasks.

These statistics demonstrate that the concepts of stochastic modeling of knowledge sources and optimal search are viable. Note that this level of performance is achieved by a simplified system with no semantic knowledge, no explicit phonological rules, only one pronunciation modeled for each word, and a very simple set of acoustic parameters. Each of these limitations is a feature merely of the current implementation, in each case a more sophisticated model can easily be substituted. An experiment is being done to compare the performance of the HEARSAY system and the DRAGON system on the same set of sentences (Lowerre).

TASK: VOICE CHESS

PHRASE#	#IN	#OUT	#CORRECT	#SEMCOR	LENGTH	MAIN	ACO
1	5	5	5	5	2450	21.2	16.2
2	6	6	6	6	2740	21.8	16.0
3	5	5	5	5	2590	21.1	15.5
4	9	9	8	8	3990	21.9	16.6
5	3	3	3	3	2130	22.1	15.8
6	11	11	11	11	5800	21.0	15.6
7	5	5	5	5	2430	21.4	16.0
8	5	6	5	5	2300	22.9	15.6
9	6	6	4	4	2970	22.1	15.5
10	4	4	4	4	2120	22.0	15.8
11	3	3	3	3	1800	22.2	16.1
12	7	7	6	6	3410	22.6	15.9
13	5	5	5	5	2370	21.7	16.1
14	8	8	8	8	3920	21.2	15.6
15	6	6	6	6	3260	21.2	15.3
16	6	6	6	6	3160	20.6	15.3
17	7	7	6	6	3800	22.1	15.3
18	6	6	5	5	2870	21.1	15.3
19	6	6	6	6	2930	22.0	15.3
20	5	5	5	5	2210	21.6	15.3
21	6	6	5	5	3050	21.0	16.1
22	6	6	6	6	2630	20.0	16.0

(WORDS CORRECT)/(WORDS IN) = .946
(WORDS CORRECT)/(WORDS OUT) = .939
(WORDS SEMANTICALLY CORRECT)/(WORDS OUT) = .939

#IN = NUMBER OF WORDS IN ACTUAL (INPUT) PHRASE
#OUT = NUMBER OF WORDS IN OUTPUT PHRASE
#CORRECT = NUMBER WORDS CORRECTLY RECOGNIZED
#SEMCOR = NUMBER WORDS SEMANTICALLY CORRECT
            (ERROR IRRELEVANT TO TASK)
LENGTH = DURATION OF PHRASE IN MILLISECONDS
MAIN = (COMPUTATION TIME OF MAIN RECOGNITION ROUTINE)/LENGTH
ACO = (COMPUTATION TIME OF ACOUSTICS MODULE)/LENGTH
APPROXIMATE AMOUNT OF CORE NEEDED = 60K

Table 1

In evaluating the computation time and storage requirements, note that these figures are given only as a rough guide to what is possible. No attempt has been made to optimize the programs in terms of either computation time or storage requirements. The indicated computation time is the amount of central processor time used in running time used in running the program on a PDP-10 computer. The most important fact about the computation time is that for a given task the computation time is essentially proportional to the length of the utterance.

TASK: MEDICAL QUESTIONNAIRE

PHRASE#	#IN	#OUT	#CORRECT	#SEMCOR	LENGTH	MAIN	ACO
1	3	3	3	3	1340	37.2	20.8
2	3	3	3	3	1240	38.4	19.6
3	4	3	1	1	1740	37.2	21.0
4	4	4	4	4	1720	38.1	19.6
5	4	3	0	0	1740	37.1	21.1
6	4	4	4	4	2120	36.4	19.6
7	4	4	4	4	1580	38.3	19.6
8	4	4	4	4	2120	37.8	19.6
9	4	4	4	4	2370	38.0	19.7
10	4	4	4	4	1880	36.0	19.6
11	4	4	4	4	2050	36.7	19.7
12	5	5	5	5	2600	35.9	19.6
13	5	5	5	5	1990	38.2	19.6
14	6	6	6	6	2400	36.0	19.7
15	6	7	3	6	2510	36.0	20.8
16	6	6	6	6	2640	35.7	19.7
17	4	4	4	4	2730	35.1	19.6
18	5	5	5	5	2170	37.5	19.7
19	5	5	4	4	1820	37.4	19.6
20	4	4	4	4	2090	37.0	19.7
21	4	4	4	4	2180	37.9	19.7

(WORDS CORRECT)/(WORDS IN) = .880
(WORDS CORRECT)/(WORDS OUT) = .890
(WORDS SEMANTICALLY CORRECT)/(WORDS OUT) = .923

#IN = NUMBER OF WORDS IN ACTUAL (INPUT) PHRASE
#OUT = NUMBER OF WORDS IN OUTPUT PHRASE
#CORRECT = NUMBEER WORDS CORRECTLY RECOGNIZED
#SEMCOR = NUMBER WORDS SEMANTICALLY CORRECT
           (ERROR IRRELEVANT TO TASK)
LENGTH = DURATION OF PHRASE IN MILLISECONDS
MAIN = (COMPUTATION TIME OF MAIN RECOGNITION ROUTINE)/LENGTH
ACO = (COMPUTATION TIME OF ACOUSTICS MODULE)/LENGTH
APPROXIMATE AMOUNT OF CORE NEEDED = 80K

Table 2

A point of major significance is that the computation time does not depend on how well the recognition proceeds. On the Voice Chess task the HEARSAY system takes, on the average, about 10 to 12 times real time for the complete recognition process, which is nearly 4 times as fast as the DRAGON system. However, the HEARSAY system uses a best-first search technique, so its computation time can vary greatly depending on how many errors are made in intermediate recognition decisions. With most search techniques, decisions in the recognition process control the direction of search and errors in early decisions can greatly increase the computation time. In fact, programs based on such techniques sometimes have to be terminated because they

TASK: INTERACTIVE FORMANT TRACKING

PHRASE#	#IN	#OUT	#CORRECT	#SEMCOR	LENGTH	MAIN	ACO
1	6	6	6	6	2170	126.9	18.7
2	9	8	8	8	4270	119.4	18.7
3	8	8	8	8	3730	119.4	18.3
4	9	8	7	7	3690	118.5	18.6
5	7	7	5	5	3490	123.7	18.6
6	9	9	9	9	5670	115.9	18.5
7	10	10	10	10	4510	121.2	18.4
8	7	7	7	7	3200	124.5	18.3
9	11	11	10	11	5120	118.1	17.6
10	7	6	6	6	3300	120.0	17.5
11	4	4	4	4	3070	119.6	18.5
12	10	9	8	8	4480	118.0	18.7
13	4	4	4	4	2760	124.0	18.8
14	4	3	0	0	2300	131.2	18.5
15	10	9	8	9	4260	126.3	19.2
16	11	11	7	8	5160	119.7	18.7
17	10	10	8	9	4060	121.9	17.9
18	6	6	6	6	3110	123.4	17.9

(WORDS CORRECT)/(WORDS IN) = .852
(WORDS CORRECT)/(WORDS OUT) = .890
(WORDS SEMANTICALLY CORRECT)/(WORDS OUT) = .919

#IN = NUMBER OF WORDS IN ACTUAL (INPUT) PHRASE
#OUT = NUMBER OF WORDS IN OUTPUT PHRASE
#CORRECT = NUMBER WORDS CORRECTLY RECOGNIZED
#SEMCOR = NUMBER WORDS SEMANTICALLY CORRECT
              (ERROR IRRELEVANT TO TASK)
LENGTH = DURATION OF PHRASE IN MILLISECONDS
MAIN = (COMPUTATION TIME OF MAIN RECOGNITION ROUTINE)/LENGTH
ACO = (COMPUTATION TIME OF ACOUSTICS MODULE)/LENGTH
APPROXIMATE AMOUNT OF CORE NEEDED = 120K

Table 3

exhaust the available time or storage before they complete the analysis of an utterance. The DRAGON system uses a complete optimal search which takes the same length of time no matter how much noise there is in the data or how many errors there are in the recognition process.

The amount of computation time required does depend on the size and complexity of the task. As a rough measure of complexity, the vocabulary sizes for the Voice Chess, Medical Questionaire, and Formant Tracking tasks are, respectively, 24 words, 76 words, and 195 words. In terms of the number of possible sentences, the Formant Tracking task is by far the most complex. It has a recursive grammar and the language has approximately 16^n sentences of length n. Notice that, although the computation time is greater for the more complex task, the level of performance remains high.

CONCLUSIONS

This collection of examples demonstrates that stochastic modeling is a versatile and valuable procedure for automatic speech analysis. Many situations in speech analysis can be represented as a hidden stochastic process. Stochastic modeling allows us to make inferences about the internal or hidden process from its influence on an external process which we observe. The possible applications of these techniques are as many as we have the ingenuity to model. Their success in any application is dependent on our care in constructing the model.

REFERENCES

Bahl, Lalit R., personal communication.

Baker, James K., "Machine-Aided Labeling of Connected Speech," in "Working Papers in Speech Recognition -- II," Computer Science Department, Carnegie-Mellon University, 1972.

Baker, James K., "The DRAGON System -- an Overview," Proc. IEEE Symposium on Speech Recognition, Pittsburgh, Pa., 1974, pp. 22-26.

Bakis, Raimo, personal communication.

Baum, Leonard E., "An Inequality and Associated Maximization Technique in Statistical Estimation for Probabilistic Functions of a Markov Process," Inequalities, Vol. III, 1972, pp. 1-8.

Bellman, Richard E., Dynamic Programming, Princeton University Press, 1957.

Bridle, John, personal communication.

Cohen, P. S. and R. L. Mercer, "The Phonological Component of an Automatic Speech-Recognition System," Proc. IEEE Symposium on Speech Recognition, Pittsburgh, Pa., 1974, pp. 177-187.

Itakura, F., "Minimum Prediction Residual Principle Applied to Speech Recognition," Proc. IEEE Symposium on Speech Recognition, Pittsburgh, Pa., 1974, pp. 101-105.

Jelinek, Fredrick, Lalit Bahl, and Robert L. Mercer, "Design of a Linguistic Statistical Decoder for the Recognition of Continuous Speech," Proc. IEEE Symposium on Speech Recognition, Pittsburgh, Pa., pp. 255-260.

Lowerre, Bruce T., "Comparison of Two Speech Understanding Systems," JASA, Vol. 56, Supplement, Fall 1974, p. 527.

Paul, J. E., A. S. Rabinowitz, J. P. Raganati, V. A. Vitols, and M. L. Griffith, "Automatic Recognition of Continuous Speech: Further Development of a Hierarchial Strategy," RADC-TR-73-319, 1973.

Rich, Elaine, personal communication.

Tappert, C. C., N. R. Dixon, A. S. Rabinowitz, and W. D. Chapman, "Automatic Recognition of Continuous Speech Utilizing Dynamic Segmentation, Dual Classification, Sequential Decoding, and Error Recovery," IBM, RADC-TR-71-146, 1971.

Viterbi, A. J., "Error Bounds for Convolutional Codes and an Asymtotically Optimum Decoding Algorithm," IEEE Transactions on Information Theory, Vol. IT-13, April, 1967.

White, George, personal communication.

JC